Fiscal Policies and Growth in the World Economy

Fiscal Policies and Growth in the World Economy

Third Edition

Jacob A. Frenkel and Assaf Razin
with the collaboration of Chi-Wa Yuen

The MIT Press
Cambridge, Massachusetts
London, England

© 1996 Massachusetts Institute of Technology
First and second editions published in 1987 and 1992 as *Fiscal Policies and the World Economy*.

This book was set in Palatino by Asco Trade Typesetting Ltd., Hong Kong and printed and bound in the United States of America.

Library of Congress Cataloging-in-Publication Data

Frenkel, Jacob A.
  Fiscal policies and growth in the world economy / Jacob A. Frenkel, Assaf Razin, Chi-Wa Yuen—3rd ed.
     p. cm.
  Includes bibliographical references and index.
  ISBN 0-262-56149-2.—(pb : alk. paper)
  1. Fiscal policy. 2. International economic relations.
I. Razin, Assaf. II. Yuen, Chi-Wa, 1960–   III. Title.
HJ141.F74   1996
339.5'2—dc20   96-4076
                                                                    CIP

Contents

VI Epilogue   483

Preface to the Third Edition

A few major episodes that occurred since the publication of the two previous editions of our book have brought to a sharp focus key issues of open economy macroeconomics: the European currency crisis of 1992 ("Black Wednesday"), the problem of sustainability of current-account deficits (in the wake of the "Mexican peso crisis"), and the devolution of states after the end of the cold war (the "new map" of Central and Eastern Europe). These developments pose a new challenge to existing theories of international economics.

The traditional Mundell-Fleming approach was found useful in explaining the ERM crisis, which followed the big fiscal expansion in the aftermath of the German unification. This traditional model requires, however, an extension in the stochastic dimension to be able to be seriously confronted with the rich time-series data. In this vein we develop the extended stochastic Mundell-Fleming model in this edition.

The intertemporal approach, in turn, was also found useful in explaining the recent current-account crises in countries persistently plagued by deficits. To study these problems in the presence of sizable shocks, however, a stochastic extension of the intertemporal model that can be matched with real world data is called for. Accordingly, an extended stochastic trade-balance model and a stochastic-growth model (in the real business cycle tradition) are developed and incorporated into this edition. In addition a policy overview chapter on current-account substainability is included in this edition.

The emergence of economies in transition from central planning to market economy, and the breakup of countries into states and regions, in Central and Eastern Europe bring out again a real possibility of significant barriers to international capital mobility due to risk or capital controls and country deviations from tax harmonization across the different economic entities that used to be under the control of a single sovereignty. For the economies in transition, in particular, the reinstated barriers to capital mobility can undermine the process of growth. At the same time, the single market in Europe brings out the issue of cross-country convergence within the European Union.

Through the 1992 "single market" initiative, Western Europe has reached almost complete integration in capital markets. Risk-adjusted and currency-adjusted rates of return on capital are, to a large extent, equalized. However, labor markets are still very much segmented across these countries mainly because the safety net systems are still confined within national borders. Compared with the United States as a benchmark, a key difference for the European single market lies in the degree of labor mobility and the speed of adjustment of the labor markets to regional disturbances. It remains as a challenge for the European Union to design policies to facilitate the movement of labor across different regions. Per-capita income levels are significantly different between North and South Europe. Labor mobility may act as a channel through which convergence in income levels can be achieved faster than through mobility in capital and goods and services alone. A new feature that we introduce in this edition is concerned with the interaction among factor mobility, convergence in levels and rates of growth of income across countries, and international taxation. The new part of this edition, devoted to growth in the world economy, provides an analysis of the role of capital and labor mobility and tax harmonization in the international convergence process. This new feature justifies the addition of "growth" to the title of this third edition.

Stochastic dynamic (rational expectations) equilibrium models have become a workhorse of quantitative macroeconomic analysis, thanks to the development and adoption of new theories and new computational methods. These methods enable us to study the complex interplay between exogenous stochastic processes and the endogenous macro variables that are driven by them. They are now also becoming an important tool of analysis in open economy macroeconomics. Given the spectacular advances in computer technology, computational costs are no longer an obstacle to numerical analysis. In this vein we introduce in this new edition a brief guide to the numerical solution of a typical dynamic macro problem in a user-friendly way, with the objective of allowing the reader to learn and apply them quickly to his/her own research agenda. A printout of the main solution routines and some sample programs in GAUSS are included at the end of the book.

Our objective remains the same as in the previous editions: to provide a unified treatment of major topics in open economy macroeconomics and open-economy public economics by presenting traditional and modern approaches. Part I overviews recent developments in the world economy, with special emphasis on fiscal restructuring among industrial countries in the 1980s and the 1990s. Part II provides a comprehensive exposition of the traditional approach, in ascending order of complexity ranging from the simple income-expenditure model to the more advanced stochastic Mundell-Fleming model. A treatise of the intertemporal approach, covering the simple deterministic two-period models for both single and multiple goods, and stochastic infinite horizon models, is presented in part III. Part IV then analyzes fiscal policies in the global economy. Topics of analysis include government spending, budget deficits, and similarities and differences among various instruments of international taxation. Economic growth in the world economy is the subject matter of part V. We distinguish between exogenous growth and endogenous growth models, and analyze the interactions among international convergence (in levels and growth rates of income), capital and labor mobility, and taxation. Part VI provides a theoretical overview, a policy overview, and a summary of the evolution of economic thought in the areas of fiscal policies and growth in the world economy.

Some of the new materials in this edition draw on our previous work. Section 1.4 draws on Bartolini, Razin, and Symansky (1995); chapter 7 on Razin (1995); chapter 13 on Razin and Yuen (1995c); chapter 14 on Razin and Sadka (1995); chapter 15 on Razin and Yuen (1995b, 1996); and chapter 17 on Milesi-Ferretti and Razin (1996a,b). We are indebted to Leonardo Bartolini, Gian-Maria Milesi-Ferretti, Efraim Sadka, and Steve Symansky for agreeing to include in the book sections drawing on our joint work. We would also like to thank Sergio Rebelo for allowing us to use the KPR (King, Plosser, and Rebelo (1988)) code as subroutines in some of our computer programs.

By covering a full line of topics in open-economy macro and open-economy public economics, the book has been used success-fully in graduate and senior undergraduate courses in international economics and public finance. It has been translated to Japanese and Spanish, and is presently being translated to Chinese. As in the previous edition we include at the end of each part a set of old and new problems and exercises. An updated and extended companion manual, *Problems and Solutions in Intertemporal Open-Economy Macro-economics: Third Edition*, by Thomas H. Krueger, Jonathan D. Ostry, and Chi-Wa Yuen, contains a detailed analysis and solutions to the exercises, and a user guide for the computer programs. We thank Michael Burda, Ida Liu, and Michael Sarel for useful comments and Yoram Hamo for exceptional research assistance.

Finally, while the previous editions reflected the effort of the first two authors alone, this new edition is the result of collaboration among the three of us.

J. A. F. and A. R., with C-W. Y.
February 1996

Preface to the Second Edition

Since our book came out in 1987, there has been a continuing process of increased economic integration among the industrialised economies, which culminated in the unification of the European market in 1992. The globalization process has resulted in growing interest in fiscal policies in the integrated world economy.

Concurrently scientific progress has been made in three important directions:

1. The ongoing interaction between international economics and public economics has resulted in deepening and refinement of the overlapping area of research, international taxation. This progress in research can shed light on key policy issues, such as international tax competition and tax harmonization, effects of taxes on the location and destination of production, investment and saving, and the like.

2. Calibration and dynamic simulation methods have been applied to tax and budget issues to assess the policy-relevant dimensions of the more analytical treatment based on the traditional as well as the intertemporal approaches.

3. The incorporation of stochastic elements into international macroeconomics has become more widespread. The new developments in theory have proven to be especially useful for a more rigorous interpretation of international time series data.

These recent developments are incorporated into the Second Edition of *Fiscal Policies and the World Economy*.

Our original objective remains the same, to provide a comprehensive and coherent treatment of the intertemporal approach to international macroeconomics. Part I provides an overview of the facts and developments in the world economy in the last decade. To offer a self-contained treatment we devote part II to the traditional approach to fiscal policies in the open economy and part III to a systematic analysis of the key elements of the intertemporal approach. Part IV applies the intertemporal approach to key issues of spending and debt-tax policies. Extensions of the analysis to incorporate the effects of distortionary taxation on labor-leisure, saving-consumption, and investment choices are developed in part V. In part VI we extend the intertemporal framework to incorporate into the analysis risk-sharing behavior. The implications of the intertemporal model are illustrated by means of dynamic simulations in part VII. The simulations highlight the role of international considerations in the design of tax policies. Theoretical overview, extensions, and bibliographical notes are provided in part VIII.

Some of the new material in the second edition draws on our previous work: Chapters 3 and 16 draw on Jacob A. Frenkel and Assaf Razin, "Fiscal Policy in the Open Economy," in *The New Pelgrave Dictionary of Money and Finance*, Macmillan, 1992; chapter 9 draws on Alan Auerbach, Jacob A. Frenkel, and Assaf Razin, "Notes on International Taxation," mimeo, February 1987; chapter 11 draws on Jacob A. Frenkel and Assaf Razin, "Spending, Taxes, and Deficits: International-Intertemporal Approach," International Finance Section, Princeton University, 1988; chapter 12 draws on Assaf Razin and Efraim Sadka, "Vanishing Tax on Capital Income in the Open Economy," NBER, Working Paper 3796, 1991; chapter 13 draws on Assaf Razin, "Fiscal Policies and the Integrated World Stock Market," *Journal of International Economics*, 1990; and chapter 14 draws on Jacob A. Frenkel, Assaf Razin, and Steve Symansky, "International VAT Harmonization: Macroeconomic Effects," *IMF Staff Papers*, 1991. We are indebted to Alan Auerbach, Efraim Sadka, and Steve Symansky for agreeing to include in the book chapters drawing on our joint work.

By covering a full line of topics in international economics, the book has been used successfully in graduate courses in international economics, and recently has been translated to Japanese and Spanish.

To increase its classroom usefulness, we include at the end of each analytical chapter a set of problems and exercises prepared by Tom Krueger and Jonathan Ostry. A companion manual, *Exercises in Intertemporal Open-Economy Macroeconomics*, by Thomas H. Krueger and Jonathan D. Ostry, contains a detailed analysis and solutions to the exercises.

We are indebted to numerous students and colleagues for useful comments on the revision. We wish to thank especially Alan Auerbach, Efraim Sadka, Tom Krueger, Jonathan Ostry, Steve Symansky, Steve Turnovsky, Alberto Giovannini, Torsten Persson, and Enrique Mendoza.

J. A. F.
A. R.
February 1991

Preface to the First Edition

Recent theoretical developments in closed-economy macroeconomics have not yet been fully incorporated into the main corpus of international macroeconomics. This book aims at filling this void. We develop a unified conceptual framework suitable for the analysis of the effects of government expenditure and tax policies on key macroeconomic aggregates in the interdependent world economy.

The analysis is motivated by stylized facts characterizing recent major developments. These include unsynchronized changes in national fiscal policies resulting in large budgetary imbalances, volatile real rates of interest, sharp changes in real exchange rates, and significant imbalances in national current account positions. Associated with these developments were drastic changes in public-sector debt and in the international allocation of external debt. Although these real-world developments provide the impetus for the analysis, the orientation of the book is theoretical. Its purpose is to identify and clarify the main channels and the pertinent economic mechanisms through which government-spending and tax policies influence the world economic system. We develop a unified coherent theory capable of interpreting the stylized facts and at the same time, provide a framework for the analysis of the normative issues related to the welfare implications of fiscal policies in the world economy.

The main characteristic of the analysis is the detailed attention given to dynamic and intertemporal considerations. In contrast with the more traditional analyses, the modern approach is based on solid microeconomic foundations. These foundations "discipline" the analysis and impose constraints on the modeling of macroeconomic behavior. Specifically, an explicit account of temporal and intertemporal budget constraints and of the forward-looking behavior consistent with these constraints restrict the permissible behavior of households and governments and thereby sharpen the predictive content of the economic theory. Furthermore, by deriving the economic behavior from utility maximization, the modern analytical framework allows for meaningful treatment of issues in welfare economics.

The resulting macroeconomic model is capable of dealing with new issues in consistent manner. Among these issues are the effects of various time patterns of government spending and taxes. We can thus distinguish between temporary and permanent, as well as between current and expected future policies. Likewise, the model is capable of analyzing the macroeconomic consequences of alternative specifications of the tax structure, including the effects of different types of taxes (income tax, value-added tax, etc.).

By being grounded on solid microeconomic foundations, this approach to open-economy macroeconomics narrows the gap between the modes of analysis typical to the branch of international economics dealing with the pure theory of international trade and the branch dealing with open-economy macroeconomics.

To provide a self-contained treatment of the subject matter and to motivate the logical progression of the analysis, we devote a part of the book to a review and a synthesis of traditional approaches to open-economy macroeconomics. This part yields the rationale for the developments of the modern treatment which is the key contribution of the book. In addition it also provides the analytical continuity and completeness necessary for the use of this book as a text. Readers familiar with the traditional approach to international macroeconomics may skip part II (chapters 2 through 3).

The focus of this inquiry is the international dimensions of fiscal policies. This instrument of macroeconomic policy is placed at the center stage for two reasons. First, budget deficits in major industrial countries have played a leading role in the world economic scene in recent years. The prominance of, and the complex interactions among, budget policies and key macroeconomic variables in the world economy provide a justification for a book-length study that focuses on various aspects of this policy instrument. Second, even though we touch in various chapters on some issues of monetary policy, we believe that in contrast with fiscal policies, the state of the art of monetary economics is not yet ripe for an analogous unified comprehensive treatment of the international dimensions of monetary policies based on solid microeconomic foundations.

This book was written while J. A. Frenkel was the David Rockefeller Professor of International Economics at the University of Chicago and A. Razin was the Daniel and Grace Ross Professor of International Economics at Tel-Aviv University. Our joint work on the international dimensions of fiscal policies started at Tel-Aviv University in the fall of 1983. During this period, as well as during the summer of 1985, J. A. Frenkel was a fellow at the Sackler Institute of Advanced Studies and a Visiting Professor in the Department of Economics. Our collaboration continued during the winter of 1984 while A. Razin held a visiting professorship at Princeton University. The main work on the book was carried out at the University of Chicago during the spring, summer, and fall of 1986 while A. Razin was a visiting professor in the Department of Economics and the Graduate School of Business. Further work was done in Cambridge, Massachusetts, during our participation in the summer institute sessions of the National Bureau of Economic Research (1984 to 1986), as well as in Washington, DC, during our visit to the World Bank in the summer of 1986. We wish to thank these institutions for providing a comfortable and stimulating environment which made this research and the preparation of the book possible.

Some of the chapters in this book draw on material contained in our joint articles. Chapter 4 is based on "The Mundell-Fleming Model: A Quarter Century Later" (*IMF Staff Papers*, forthcoming). Chapters 5, 7, and 8 draw on "Spending, Taxes and Deficits: International-Intertemporal Approach" (*Princeton Studies in International Finance*, forthcoming) and on "Deficits with Distortionary Taxes: International Dimensions" (NBER, Working Paper 2080, November 1986). Chapter 9 draws on "Fiscal Policies and Real Exchange Rates in the World Economy" (NBER, Working Paper 2065, November

1986). Chapters 10 through 13 draw on our articles, "Government Spending, Debt and International Economic Interdependence" (*Economic Journal* 95, September 1985:619–36); "Fiscal Expenditures and International Economic Interdependence" (in W. H. Buiter and R. C. Marston, eds., *International Economic Policy Coordination*, Cambridge: Cambridge University Press, 1985:37–73); "The International Transmission and Effects of Fiscal Policies" (*American Economic Review* 76, May 1986:330–35); "Fiscal Policies in the World Economy" (*Journal of Political Economy* 94, June 1986:564–94); "Real Exchange Rates, Interest Rates and Fiscal Policies" (*The Economic Studies Quarterly* 37, June 1986:99–113); and "The International Transmission of Fiscal Expenditures and budget Deficits in the World Economy" (in A. Razin and E. Sadka, eds., *Economic Policy in Theory and Practice*, London: Macmillan, 198751–96). Finally, some of the arguments in chapter 15 draw on "The Limited Viability of Dual Exchange-Rate Regimes" (NBER, Working Paper 1902, April 1986) and "Exchange-Rate Management Viewed as Tax Policies" (unpublished manuscript, 1987).

During the course of this research we have benefited from useful coments and suggestions by Joshua Aizenman, Alan Auerbach, Olivier Blanchard, William Branson, Willem Buiter, Guillermo Calvo, Avinash Dixit, Rudiger Dornbusch, Martin Feldstein, Stanley Fischer, Robert Flood, John Geweke, Itzhak Gilboa, Jeremy Greenwood, Vittorio Grilli, Koichi Hamada, Elhanan Helpman, Peter Howitt, John Huizinga, Kent Kimbrough, Robert Lucas, Franco Modigliani, Michael Mussa, Maurice Obstfeld, Torsten Persson, Thomas Sargent, Don Schlagenhauf, Alan Stockman, Larry Summers, and Lars Svensson. During the past three years we have also received numerous suggestions in seminars and workshops at the Brookings Institution, the University of Chicago, CEPR (London), CEPREMAP (Paris), Columbia University, Duke University, Harvard University, Hebrew University, International House in Tokyo, the University of Michigan, MIT, NBER (Cambridge), New York University, Princeton University, Stanford University, Tel-Aviv University, University of Washington, University of Western Ontario, the World Bank, and the Latin-American Econometric Society meeting held in Cordoba.

In preparing the book we benefited from comments and efficient research assistance by our graduate students at the University of Chicago, including Ken Kasa, Thomas Krueger, Jonathan Ostry, and Kei-Mu Yi. We owe special thanks to Thomas Krueger who thoroughly read the entire manuscript and provided us with numerous comments and suggestions that improved the presentation and sharpened the arguments.

We wish to thank June Nason of the University of Chicago for her tireless efforts and high efficiency in cheerfully typing successive drafts of the manuscript. Her willingness to work long hours is deeply appreciated. Thanks are also due to Terry Vaughn, the economics editor at the MIT Press, for his remarkable professionalism and dedication in the various stages of this enterprise.

The writing of a jointly authored book under a very tight time schedule always entails complicated arrangements, coordination, and discipline. In our case the need for transatlantic communications added logistical difficulties that could not have been surmounted without the understanding, selflessness, and unfailing support of our wives, Niza Frenkel and Shula Razin. It is only appropriate that we dedicate this book to them.

J. A. F.
A. R.
February 1987

I

Prologue

1

Stylized Facts on Fiscal Policies and International Economic Interdependence

This book deals with the international dimensions of fiscal policies. The opening chapter surveys key facts relevant for the analysis of the effects of government spending and tax policies in the world economy. The empirical regularities exhibited by the stylized facts serve to identify the issues and the macroeconomic variables that play central roles in the interdependent world economy. The main purpose of the discussion in this chapter is to motivate the theoretical analysis that follows.

We devote the first section of this chapter to a brief review of major developments related to the effects of public-sector spending policies and budget deficits during the 1980s and the first half of the 1990s. Relative to other recent periods, this decade and a half stands out in terms of the major changes taking place in the fiscal policies of the major countries. To identify empirical relations among the key economic variables that are likely to be related to, and influenced by fiscal policies, we present in section 1.2 summary statistics pertaining to comovements among these variables. The summary statistics describe various combinations of temporal, intertemporal, and international correlations among the key variables. These correlations, together with the stylized facts outlined in section 1.1, can be useful in the construction of theoretical models. Section 1.3 surveys recent and anticipated major fiscal restructuring in the seven largest industrial countries. The final section of this chapter summarizes key characteristics emerging from the data. These characteristics provide a guide to the choice of variables incorporated into the analytical framework, and they highlight issues that need to be addressed by the theory.

1.1   Selected Facts

During the 1980s the world economy was subject to large and unsynchronized changes in fiscal policies, high and volatile real rates
of interest, large fluctuations in real exchange rates and significant
variations in private-sector spending. During this period national
fiscal policies have exhibited large divergencies. The United States
adopted an expansionary course while the other major countries
taken together followed a relatively contractionary course. These
policies undertaken by the major economies affected the rest of the
world through the integrated goods and capital markets, and resulted in increased concern in each country over policy measures
under-taken in the rest of the world.

Since the beginning of 1980 short- and long-term real rates of
interest exhibited different patterns. As illustrated in figure 1.1, a
weighted average of the annual short-term real interest rates in
the five major industrial countries (the United States, Japan, France,
West Germany, and the United Kingdom) rose from about 2.0 percent at the beginning of 1980 to about 5.0 percent in 1986; the
short-term rate then fell to about 4.0 percent at the end of the
decade. The corresponding long-term rates rose from about 0.5 percent in early 1980 to about 8.0 percent in 1984, to about 3–4
percent in 1989–90. Both rates peaked and surpassed 8 percent in
mid-1982. Thus, during 1980 to 1985, real rates of interest were
high (in comparison with early 1980) and the slope of the real yield
curve, which was negative until the third quarter of 1981, turned
positive starting from mid-1982; while real interest rates fell further
in 1986, they rose again in 1987. Toward the end of the decade the
slope of the real yield curve became negative.

The decade also witnessed sharp changes in real exchange rates.
In the first quarter of 1985 the real effective value of the U.S. dollar
(calculated on the basis of unit labor cost) was about 43 percent
above its average value for the decade 1974 to 1983 and 57 percent
above its low point of the third quarter of 1980. By the end of the
decade the real effective value of the U.S. dollar was about 35
percent below the 1985 peak. Likewise, in the last quarter of 1985

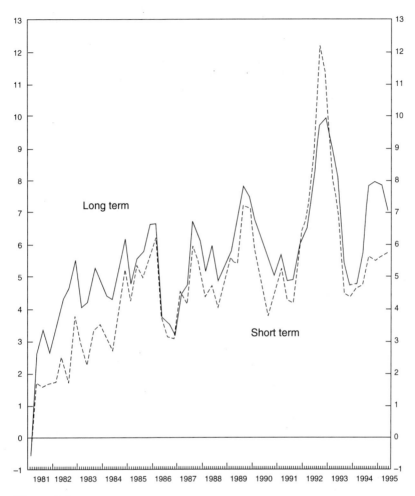

Figure 1.1
Five major industrial countries: Short- and long-term real interest rates, first quarter 1981 to second quarter 1995. Real interest rates are defined as nominal interest rates minus the four-quarter percentage change in GDP deflators, weighted by the U.S. dollar value of GDPs over the preceding three years. Source: IMF, *Current Economic Indicators database.*

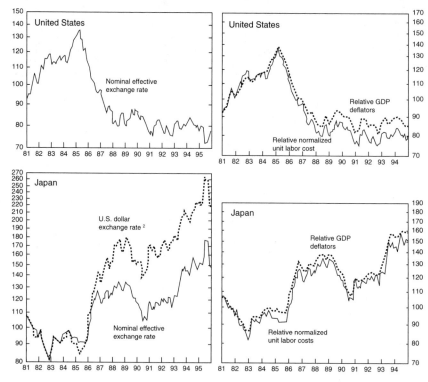

Figure 1.2
Major industrial countries: Exchange rate vis-à-vis U.S. dollar and indexes of nominal effective exchange rates, January 1981 to October 1995. (1) Index, 1980 = 100, based on relative normalized unit labor costs in manufacturing. (2) U.S. dollar exchange rate measured as U.S. dollar value of the domestic currency. Source: IMF, *International Financial Statistics.*

the real effective value of the Japanese yen was about 50 percent above its low point in the first quarter of 1980. By 1989 the real effective value of the Japanese yen was about 35 percent higher than its mid-1980s level. The other major currencies (especially the British pound, the French franc, and the Italian lira) have also exhibited very large fluctuations. Figure 1.2 illustrates the extent of the changes in the effective nominal exchange rates of the U.S. dollar, Japanese yen, British pound, German mark, French franc, Canadian dollar, and Italian lira. The sharp changes in the real exchange rates (as measured by the relative GDP deflators and by the relative unit labor costs) are shown in figure 1.3. As shown by these figures, the U.S. dollar, after several years of consecutive appreciation, depreciated significantly beginning in March 1985. Its depreciation continued throughout 1988. Correspondingly, the currencies of other major industrial countries, especially Japan and West Germany, appreciated in nominal and real terms throughout the decade.

Another key fact characterizing this period is the large and divergent pattern of the current-account positions of the major industrial countries. These divergencies are especially pronounced in the comparison between the developments of the current-account positions of the United States with that of Japan and Germany. For example, the U.S. current-account position switched from a surplus of about 0.25 percent of GNP in 1980 to a deficit of about 3 percent of GNP in 1985. The deficit in the U.S. current account remained throughout the 1980s, but declined to about 1.8 percent of GNP in 1990. During 1980–1986 the current-account position of Japan switched from a deficit of about 1 percent of GNP in 1980 to a surplus of about 4.4 percent of GNP in 1986. The Japanese surplus declined toward the end of the decade and reached the level of 1.7 percent of GNP in 1990. Likewise the current-account position of Germany also switched from a deficit of about 1.7 percent of GNP in 1980 to a surplus of about 4.4 percent of GNP in 1986 and then declined to 3.3 percent in 1990. These developments in the current accounts of the balance of payments reflected themselves in correspondingly large changes in the external debt position of these countries. (The source of the data used in this section is International Monetary Fund: *World Economic Outlook.*)

These developments in real interest rates, real exchange rates, and current-account positions were associated with large and divergent changes in world fiscal policies. The budget deficit of the general U.S. government as a fraction of GNP rose from about 1 percent in 1980 to about 3.5 percent in 1985 (after reaching a peak of 3.8 percent in 1983). The deficit stabilized at about 1.7 percent of GNP in 1986–90. At the same time the budget deficit as a fraction of GNP declined in Japan until 1986 and became a surplus of about 3

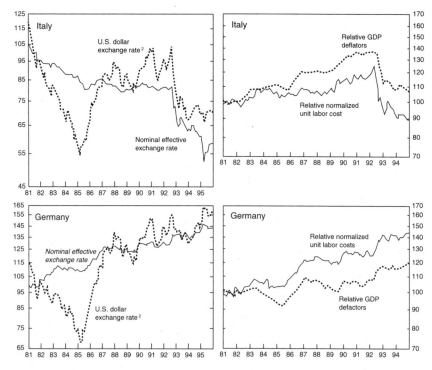

Figure 1.3
Major industrial countries: Indexes of real effective exchange rates, first quarter 1981 to fourth quarter 1994. Index, 1981 = 100. Source: IMF, *International Financial Statistics and Surveillance* database.

percent of GNP toward the end of the decade. Similarly the 1977–86 average budget deficit of about 3.7 percent of GNP in the United Kingdom turned into a surplus in 1987–90 of about 1 percent, on average. In Germany the 1977–88 deficit of about 2.4 percent, on average, turned to surplus in 1989 and then switched to a deficit of about 3–4 percent in 1990–91, following the unification of Germany. Similarly, since 1982, according to IMF measures, the fiscal impulse (which is a more exogenous measure of fiscal policy) has been expansionary for Canada, France, and the United States and contractionary for the other industrial countries taken together. This pattern is shown in figure 1.4, in which a positive fiscal impulse

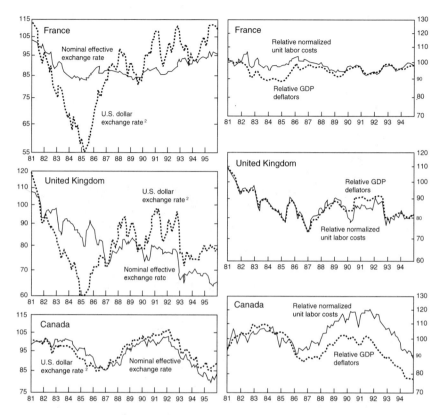

Figure 1.3 (continued)

indicates injection of stimulus while a negative impulse indicates withdrawal of stimulus.

The reunification of East and West Germany in 1990 was a major economic disturbance that the EMS was poorly designed to handle. Germany's trade partners very quickly felt the effects of Germany's decision to ease its fiscal policy, in the form of huge transfers to East Germany, and at the same time to tighten its monetary policy sharply in order to reduce inflationary pressures. This event placed France, Italy, the United Kingdom, and other EMS partners in a dilemma: Should they tighten their own monetary policies in order to maintain EMS exchange rates, or should they devalue their currencies against the DM, to stimulate demand for their products. The

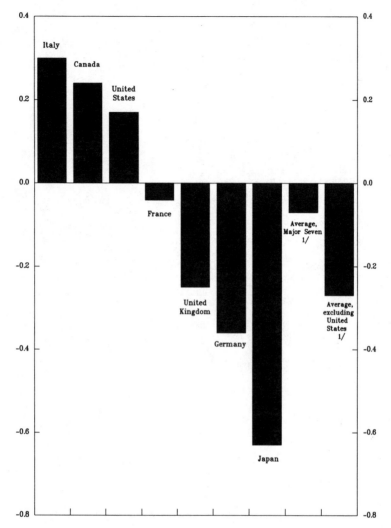

Figure 1.4
Fiscal impulses for the major industrial countries, 1980 to 1990 (in percent of GDP
annual rates). (1) Averages weighted by U.S. dollar GNPs in the preceding three
years.

uncertainty about the ratification of the Maastricht Treaty (with an upcoming referendum in France) encouraged foreign exchange market participants to gamble on a devaluation of the weak currencies, and an all-out speculative attacks first on the Finnish markka and the Swedish Krona. Both countries did not belong to the EMS but desired to become members of the EC (the EU, by now). These speculative attacks spread to the currencies of the EMS members, such as Italy, the United Kingdom; even the French franc came under attack. On September 16, 1992, a day now known as "Black Wednesday," the British pound was allowed to float, and Italy took its currency out of the EMS exchange rate mechanism.

For the U.S. dollar the real effective exchange rate across trading partners has declined by about 8 percent from 1990 to 1995; notably, vis-à-vis the German and the Japanese currencies. However, since mid-1995 the U.S. dollar has rebounded.

Bond yields have posted relatively large movements over 1994 and 1995. During 1994 long-term interest rates rose between 175 and 500 basis points across the industrial countries. They then fell in 1995, largely reversing the 1994 increases in many cases. But with current low rates of inflation, real rates of interest in the industrial countries are still high relative to the historical record.

The cumulative implications of the budgetary imbalances are reflected in the size of public debt. The rapid rise in net public debt as a ratio of GNP in Germany and Japan leveled off toward the end of the first half decade of the 1980s (at around one-quarter of GNP). In the United Kingdom the same quantity remained relatively stable at around one-half of GNP. On the other hand, and in contrast with these countries, the ratio of net government debt to GNP in the United States rose sharply during the same period from about one-fifth of GNP to close to one-third of GNP. These developments are reflected in a relative rise of the debt-service burden imposed on the U.S. government budget.

Another indicator of the levels and divergencies among national fiscal policies is provided by a comparison among annual percentage changes in public-sector consumption. As seen in table 1.1, the percentage annual growth of U.S. public-sector consumption accelerated

Table 1.1
Differences in private and public consumption: United States, Japan, and Europe, 1977–1990 (in percent per annum)

	United States		United States minus Japan		United States minus Europe	
	Private	Public	Private	Public	Private	Public
1977	4.4	1.5	0.3	−2.6	1.4	0.2
1978	4.1	2.6	−1.3	−2.5	0.1	−1.3
1979	2.2	0.8	−4.3	−3.5	−1.9	−2.2
1980	−0.2	1.9	−1.3	−1.4	−2.0	−0.4
1981	1.2	1.5	−0.4	−3.3	0.6	−0.4
1982	1.3	1.9	−3.1	−0.1	0.4	0.6
1983	4.7	1.1	1.2	−1.9	2.8	−0.6
1984	4.8	4.4	2.1	1.7	3.3	2.7
1985	4.7	7.9	1.3	6.2	2.2	6.0
1986	3.9	4.2	0.5	−0.3	−0.4	2.0
1987	2.8	2.3	−1.4	1.9	−0.9	0.1
1988	3.6	0.2	−1.6	−2.0	−0.5	−2.0
1989	1.9	2.3	−2.4	0.1	−0.9	2.4
1990	0.9	2.8	−3.1	1.4	−2.0	0.4

Source: Computed from data in IMF, *World Economic Outlook*, May 1991; and IMF, *International Financial Statistics*.

in the second part of the period, exceeding 7 percent in 1985, and then decelerating to 3.1 percent in 1989. During the late 1970s and early 1980s, public-sector consumption in Japan and Europe grew faster than in the United States (the difference for Japan reaching 3.3 percent in 1981, and for Europe 2.2 percent in 1979), and during 1984–85, public-sector consumption in Japan and Europe grew more slowly (the difference in "favor" of the United States reaching in 1985 6.2 percent in comparison with Japan and 5.9 percent in comparison with Europe). In the second half of the decade, public consumption in the United States and Japan exhibited roughly the same growth rates, but growth rate of the United States exceeded that of Europe.

Table 1.2
Differences in real GNP and gross fixed investment: United States, Japan, and Europe, 1977–1990 (in percent per annum)

	United States		United States minus Japan		United States minus Europe	
	GNP	Investment	GNP	Investment	GNP	Investment
1977	4.7	14.1	−0.1	11.3	1.8	13.6
1978	5.3	9.8	0.3	2.0	1.8	7.1
1979	2.5	3.7	−3.2	−2.5	−1.5	−1.2
1980	−0.2	−7.9	−3.6	−7.9	−1.3	−10.0
1981	1.9	1.1	−1.5	−1.3	1.7	5.6
1982	−2.5	−9.6	−6.0	−9.4	−3.3	−7.8
1983	3.6	8.2	0.8	9.1	1.8	7.0
1984	6.8	16.8	2.5	12.1	4.5	14.7
1985	3.4	5.3	−1.8	0.0	1.0	3.5
1986	2.7	1.0	0.1	−3.8	−0.0	−2.2
1987	3.4	1.9	−0.9	−7.7	0.7	−3.2
1988	4.5	5.6	−1.8	−6.3	0.4	−2.6
1989	2.5	1.6	−2.2	−7.3	−0.7	−4.4
1990	1.0	−0.1	−4.7	−11.0	−1.7	−4.1

Source: Computed from data in IMF, *World Economic Outlook*, May 1991; and IMF, *International Financial Statistics*.

Concomitantly, the anual percentage changes in real private-sector consumption also displayed large fluctuations that differed across countries. In the United States these changes ranged from −0.2 percent in 1980 to 4.8 percent in 1984, and, as seen in table 1.1, the growth of private-sector consumption in Japan exceeded that in the United States during 1979–82, fell short of it during 1983–86, and exceeded it during 1987–89. The growth of private-sector consumption in Europe exceeded that in the United States during 1978–81, fell short of it during 1982–85, and then exceeded the rate in the United States in 1986–89. As illustrated in table 1.2, the international differentials among growth rates of GNP and of fixed investment also displayed a similar pattern.

1.2   Comovements of Key Economic Variables in the World Economy: Summary Statistics

In this section we present stylized facts concerning the comovements of selected economic variables. These facts are based on data pertaining to the thirty-year period from 1955 to 1989 (obtained from IMF, *International Financial Statistics*). In so doing, we gain insight into some of the empirical regularities characterizing the international transmission mechanism of economic policies and exogenous shocks. We start by presenting figures showing the international comovements of some key variables and proceed with the presentation of summary statistics concerning the temporal, intertemporal, and international correlations among these variables. Throughout, we focus on the seven major industrial countries: Canada, United States, Japan, France, Germany, Italy, and the United Kingdom. We divide these countries into two blocks: the United States and the "rest-of-the-world" (comprised of the other six countries taken together as an aggregate). Our analysis of the stylized fact is based on this "two-country" world economy.

Figures 1.5 and 1.6 show, respectively, the international comovements of the rates of growth of government consumption and of (gross) tax revenue. The main features exhibited by these figures are the large amplitude of these series, the low contemporaneous international correlation between growth rates of government consumption, and the somewhat higher correlation between the growth rates of tax revenue (as reported in table 1.3, the correlation between growth rates of public consumption is 0.14, while we found that the tax-revenue correlation is 0.26 for the period 1955–85). As shown in figure 1.5, the largest changes in the growth rate of U.S. government consumption occurred in the second half of the 1960s in conjunction with the Vietnam War. It is relevant to note, however, that significant variations also took place in other years.

The pattern of tax revenue shown in figure 1.6 reflects in large measure the growth rates of GNP shown in figure 1.7. Indeed, for 1955–85 the contemporaneous correlation between the growth rates of GNP and of tax revenue is 0.64 in the United States and

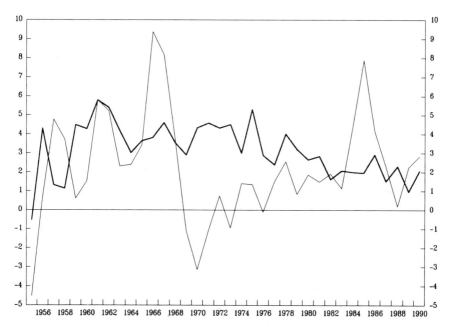

Figure 1.5
Growth rates of government consumption: United States (thin line) versus rest of the world (thick line)

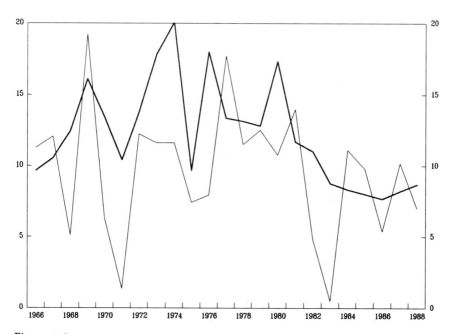

Figure 1.6
Growth rates of tax revenue: United States (thin line) versus rest of the world (thick line)

Table 1.3
National and international contemporaneous correlations of growth rates, 1955–90 (in percent per annum)

	Y	I	C	G	Y*	I*	C*	G*	C + C*
Y	1.00								
I	0.92	1.00							
C	0.84	0.81	1.00						
G	0.10	−0.12	−0.01	1.00					
Y*	0.52	0.45	0.51	−0.10	1.00				
I*	0.43	0.34	0.34	−0.07	0.86	1.00			
C*	0.42	0.36	0.50	−0.21	0.89	0.77	1.00		
G*	0.09	−0.01	0.05	0.14	0.26	0.04	0.35	1.00	
C + C*	0.74	0.69	0.88	−0.12	0.80	0.63	0.85	0.22	1.00

Note: $Y = $ GNP, $I = $ private-sector investment, $C = $ private-sector consumption, $G = $ government consumption, and an asterisk (*) denotes "rest-of-the-world" variables, which are constructed as weighted averages of real growth rates. Each country's weight corresponds to the average over the previous three years of the U.S. dollar value of its GNP as a fraction of the six-country sum of the U.S. dollar values of GNP.

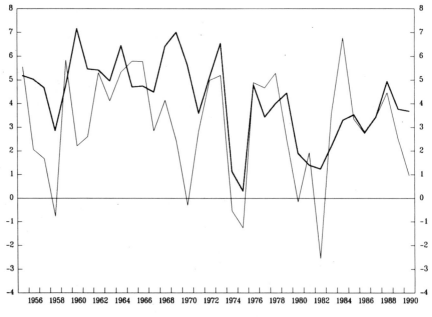

Figure 1.7
Growth rates of GNP: United States (thin line) versus rest of the world (thick line)

0.44 in the rest-of-the-world. The comovements of GNP growth rates reflect the outcomes of macroeconomic policies, as well as external and internal shocks. All these manifest themselves in the characteristics of the international transmission of business cycles. For example, the high correlation exhibited during the period 1973 to I976 reflects the common external shock associated with the first oil crisis. On the other hand, the low correlation exhibited during the early part of the 1980s reflects the divergencies of internal policies (discussed in section 1.1). On the whole, as indicated in table 1.3, the international correlation between the growth rates over the entire period is 0.55.

Changes in the fiscal stance (government spending and tax revenue) and the induced changes in GNP are associated with corresponding adjustments of private-sector spending (consumption and investment). Figure 1.8 shows the international comovements of the

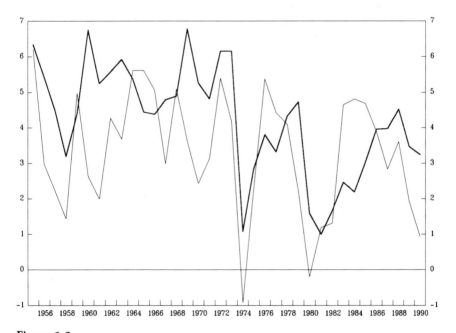

Figure 1.8
Growth rates of private-sector consumption: United States (thin line) versus rest of the world (thick line)

rates of growth of private-sector consumption. As revealed by this figure, in some years (especially during the first half of the period) the growth rates of private-sector consumption were negatively correlated internationally, whereas in other years (especially during the second half of the period) these growth rates were positively correlated. On the whole, as indicated by table 1.3, the international correlation over the entire period was 0.50. We also note that during the second half of the period, the amplitude of this series for the United States exceeds that of the rest of the world.

Finally, figure 1.9 shows the comovements of the rates of growth of investment. Typically, the amplitude of these series is very high (exceeding those of the other series), and the United States exhibits higher volatility than the rest-of-the-world. As for the international correlations, table 1.3 indicates that overall there is a (weak) positive

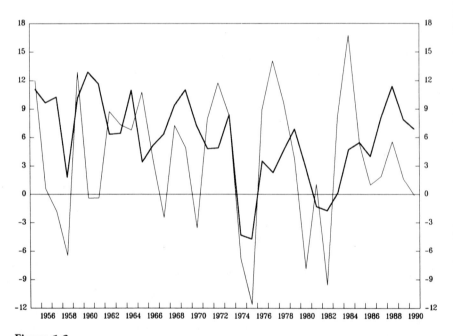

Figure 1.9
Growth rates of private-sector investment: United States (thin line) versus rest of the world (thick line)

correlation between the United States and the rest-of-the-world series. In general (as with tax revenue), the rates of growth of investment in both the United States and the rest-of-the world are highly correlated with the corresponding growth rates of GNP. As indicated in table 1.3, these correlations are 0.92 for the United States, and 0.86 for the rest-of-the-world.

The bilateral pairwise relations exhibited by figures 1.5 through 1.9 is supplemented by the national and international time-series correlations reported in tables 1.3 and 1.4. Noteworthy among these correlations is the persistence of growth rates of domestic and foreign government consumption as reflected by the magnitudes of the autocorrelation coefficients (0.55 for the United States and 0.37 for the rest-of-the-world). The other feature revealed by the correlations is the relatively high positive association between the growth rates of current (and lagged) government spending of the rest-of-the-world and the corresponding growth rates of foreign output, consumption, and investment. The association between the growth rate of current U.S. government spending and the corresponding growth rates of U.S. GNP and private-sector consumption is posi-

Table 1.4
International and intertemporal correlations of growth rates: autocorrelations with one-year lag, 1955–1990 (in percent per annum)

	Y	I	C	G	Y^*	I^*	C^*	G^*	$C + C^*$
Y_{-1}	0.18	0.06	0.05	0.35	0.36	0.31	0.32	0.02	0.21
I_{-1}	0.18	0.13	0.08	0.19	0.32	0.28	0.32	0.03	0.23
C_{-1}	0.40	0.32	0.30	0.19	0.51	0.41	0.45	0.02	0.44
G_{-1}	0.18	0.02	0.23	0.55	0.10	0.09	0.07	−0.03	0.18
Y^*_{-1}	−0.01	−0.05	−0.15	0.03	0.49	0.41	0.48	0.31	0.18
I^*_{-1}	−0.09	−0.13	−0.25	0.06	0.46	0.52	0.42	0.10	0.08
C^*_{-1}	0.10	0.03	−0.05	−0.11	0.61	0.52	0.59	0.35	0.30
G^*_{-1}	0.16	0.09	0.11	0.04	0.32	0.05	0.34	0.37	0.26
$C_{-1} + C^*_{-1}$	0.30	0.21	0.16	0.06	0.64	0.54	0.59	0.21	0.43

Note: For identification of variables and explanation of weighting scheme, see table 1.3; the subscript −1 indicates one-year lag.

tive, but relatively weak. However, the (positive) correlation between the growth rates, one-period lagged, of U.S. government
spending and the growth rates of U.S. GNP and private-sector consumption are more sizable. Finally, it is relevant to note that the
contemporaneous correlation between U.S. government spending
and U.S. investment is negative (-0.12).

1.3   Fiscal Restructuring in the G-7 Countries

The massive effort of the seven largest industrialized countries (G-7)
in the 1990s to restructure and rationalize their expenditure and tax
policies is part of a general reaction to the growth of public debt and
deficits during the 1980s. Each country, however, has responded
to particular motivations, ranging from the need to mobilize domestic resources toward reconstruction in Germany, to an attempt at
reducing the burden of public deficits in the United States, Italy,
and Canada, and to the desire to stimulate the economy during the
rescession and change the tax structure in a more revenue-neutral
fashion over the medium term, in Japan, France, and the United
Kingdom.

Many of these changes have had effects beyond domestic borders.
For instance, the impact of German unification has been profoundly
felt on international capital markets, and is often believed to have
contributed to the persistence of high interest rates in Europe, to
have provided impetus for fiscal restructuring elsewhere in Europe,
and ultimately to have catalyzed the exchange rate mechanism
(ERM) crisis of 1992. The ongoing U.S. debt reduction plan and the
harmonization of indirect taxes spurred by European unification also
represent policy shocks with potentially far-reaching implications for
all industrial countries.

Table 1.5 shows that all the G-7 countries except Japan entered
the 1990s with large structural (cyclically-adjusted) overall deficits,
and four of them (the United States, Germany, the United Kingdom,
and Italy) with structural primary deficits.

In response to domestic and external pressures to reduce these
imbalances, several policy changes have already occurred in the G-7

Table 1.5
Government debt and structural budget deficits in the 1980s (general government, in percent of GDP)

	Gross debt 1980 (net debt)	Gross debt 1985 (net debt)	Gross debt 1990 (net debt)	Overall structural balance 1990	Primary structural balance[1] 1990
United States	39.6 (26.1)	51.3 (36.9)	59.6 (45.8)	−3.2	−1.1
Japan	51.9 (17.3)	68.7 (26.5)	69.8 (9.5)	2.3	3.2
Germany	31.8 (11.3)	41.7 (20.7)	39.6 (18.4)	−3.2	−1.1
France	37.2 (na)	45.4 (22.9)	46.9 (25.1)	−2.3	0.1
United Kingdom	41.8 (22.0)	51.2 (28.1)	34.6 (27.8)	−2.9	−0.5
Italy	58.9 (na)	84.0 (71.6)	104.8 (93.2)	−11.9	−1.8
Canada	44.6 (13.5)	64.9 (34.9)	72.3 (43.4)	−5.2	0.2

Sources: IMF, *World Economic Outlook*, various issues, and World Economic Outlook data-base. OECD, *Economic Outlook*, various issues. OECD, *Economic Surveys*, various issues. U.S. Office of Management and Budget, *Mid-session Review of the 1994 Budget*, September 1993. Kato, H., Chairman of the Tax Commission, Remarks at the press conference held after the session of the Commission on May 20, 1994. Press and Information Office of the Federal Government, *Aktuelle Beiträge zur Wirtschafts und Finanzpolitik*, No.25/1991. *Wirtschaft und Statistik*, Statistiches Bundesbereit, various issues. Bundesministerium der Finanzen, *Finanzbericht*, 1994. *Projet de Loi de Finances Rectificative pour 1993*, Assemblee Nationale, May 1993. HM Treasury, *Treasury Bulletin, Summer 1992*. HM Treasury, *Financial Statement and Budget Reports, 1993–1994 and 1994–1995*. Banca d'Italia, *Bollettino Economico*, various issues. Consiglio dei Ministri, *Documento di Programmazione Economico-Finanziaria per gli Anni 1994–1996*, various issues. *The Budget, 1993*, Department of Finance, Canada.
1. Estimated from overall balance and interest payment data.

countries since 1990, but much of the restructuring effort is still
planned to take place in the next few years. The United States and
Italy, for instance, started in earnest only in 1993. Having implemented the tax changes since the late 1980s, France, the United
Kingdom, and Canada are now expected to tackle the spending side
of the budget in the next few years, while Japan is expected to
increase its reliance on indirect taxes starting in 1997. Large tax
increases are anticipated in Germany in the next few years, despite
the sharp rise in the tax burden recorded since 1990.

Bartolini, Razin, and Symansky (1995) overview the key fiscal
initiatives undertaken in the G-7 countries since 1990, focusing on
developments in four fiscal instruments: indirect, labor, and capital
taxes, and government spending (inclusive of transfers). Table 1.6
summarizes these developments by reporting annual changes in average effective tax rates and cyclically adjusted expenditure in the
G-7 countries since 1990. They assess the macroeconomic effects of
such measures. The general picture is one where fiscal restructuring
initially leads to output losses followed by a recovery. In the longer
run the choice of fiscal instruments makes a significant difference.
Those countries which rely primarily on expenditure cuts or indirect
tax increases in their fiscal restructuring (the United Kingdom, France,
and Japan) are projected to enjoy output gains from the adjustment over the long run, while those countries relying mainly on
labor and capital taxes (Italy, Germany, and the United States) are
projected to suffer output losses.

1.4   Facts and Theory

The selected facts from the 1980s and the first half of the 1990s,
along with the correlations obtained from the more extended time
period, serve as a guide for the selection of variables and for the
identification of channels through which the effects of fiscal policy
are transmitted throughout the world economy. Accordingly, the
discussion in section 1.1 suggests that in modeling the international
effects of fiscal policies, allowance should be made for the special
role that real exchange rates, short- and long-term interest rates,

current-account adjustment, and the size of foreign debt play in the international transmission mechanism. A proper theory of the effects of fiscal policy on the inter-dependent world economy should be capable of clarifying the mechanisms underlying the varying patterns of responses of these macroeconomic variables to such policies. Furthermore the theory should also illuminate and uncover the economic forces responsible for the large fluctuations and for the varying cross-country correlations of private-sector consumption, investment, and output growth rates.

The comovements of the key economic variables discussed in section 1.2 also indicate the significance of an additional consideration that should be incorporated into theoretical modeling of interdependencies. The correlations imply that the timing of the various fiscal measures plays a critical role. In this context the degree of persistence exhibited by the series measuring growth rates of government spending, and the lack of such a persistence in the growth rates of tax revenues suggest that the theory should distinguish between permanent and transitory policies.

The stylized facts reported in this chapter motivate the choice of topics and issues examined in this book. Although the various real-world developments provide the impetus for the analysis, the orientation of the book is theoretical. Its purpose is to identify and clarify the main channels and the pertinent mechanisms through which government-spending and tax policies influence the world economic system. The models that are developed are aimed at providing a coherent theory capable of interpreting the stylized facts, and at the same time, they provide a framework for the analysis of the normative issues related to the desirability of fiscal policies in the interdependent world economy.

In part II of this book we introduce the key issues and concepts within the traditional income-expenditure models of interdependent economies. These models attempt to clarify the factors underlying the patterns of comovements of national outputs, consumption, investment, and fiscal policies observed in the data. Following the presentation of the traditional income-expenditure models, we review their limitations and proceed in parts III through V to develop

Table 1.6
Summary of fiscal developments in the G-7 countries (General Government, in percent of GDP)

	Period	Indirect taxes	Labor income taxes	Capital income taxes	(Decline in) transfers and direct expenditure	Change in the primary structural balance
United States	1991	0.2	0.1	—	−0.2	0.1
	1992	—	−0.2*	—	−0.6	−0.8
	1993	—	0.2** + 0.1	0.1	−0.3	—
	1994–1998	0.2	0.2	0.3	0.6	1.3
Japan	1991	—	—	—	—	—
	1992	—	—	—	−0.7*	−0.7
	1993	—	—	—	−0.5* − 0.7*	−1.2
	1994	—	−0.9	−0.3	1.2** − 0.7* − 0.8*	−1.5
	1995–1997	1.3	—	—	1.4** + 0.8**	3.5
Germany	1991	0.4	1.1 + 0.6*	0.2 + 0.3*	−4.6	−2.0
	1992	0.1	1.3 − 0.6**	0.1 − 0.3**	1.5	2.1
	1993	0.4	0.1	—	0.9	1.4
	1994–1996	0.3	0.7	0.3	1.1	3.4
France	1991	−0.4	0.4	0.2	—	0.2
	1992	−0.1	−0.1	−0.2	−0.6	−1.0
	1993	0.1	0.1	−0.2	0.1	0.1
	1994–1997	—	−0.1	0.1	1.8	1.8

United Kingdom	1991	0.5	−0.2	−0.5	−0.2	−0.4
	1992	1.0	−0.2	−0.6	−0.7	−0.5
	1993	—		−0.1	−0.9	−1.0
	1994–1996	1.1	0.8	0.1	1.0	3.0
Italy	1991	$0.3 + 0.2^*$	$0.2 + 0.2^*$	0.1	$0.4 + 0.3^*$	1.7
	1992	$-0.2^{**} + 0.1^*$	$0.5 - 0.2^{**} + 0.3^*$	$0.2 + 1.4^*$	$0.4 - 0.3^{**} + 0.3^*$	2.5
	1993	$-0.1^{**} + 0.1$	$-0.3^{**} + 1.1$	$-0.7^{**} + 0.9$	$-0.3^{**} + 0.4$	1.1
	1994–1996	0.1	−0.2	$-0.7^{**} + 0.3$	0.7	0.2
Canada	1991	0.6	0.2	−0.1	0.1	0.8
	1992	0.2	0.1	0.1	0.3	0.7
	1993	—	0.1	−0.1	0.1	0.1
	1994–1998	−0.2	−0.1	−0.1	0.7	0.3

Sources: IMF, *World Economic Outlook*, various issues, and World Economic Outlook data-base. OECD, *Economic Outlook*, various issues. OECD, *Economic Surveys*, various issues. U.S. Office of Management and Budget, *Mid-session Review of the 1994 Budget*, September 1993. Kato, H., Chairman of the Tax Commission, Remarks at the press conference held after the session of the Commission on May 20, 1994. Press and Information Office of the Federal Government, *Aktuelle Beiträge zur Wirtschafts und Finanzpolitik*, No.25/1991. *Wirtschaft und Statistik*, Statistiches Bundesbereit, various issues. Bundesministerium der Finanzen, *Finanz-bericht*, 1994. *Projet de Loi de Finances Rectificative pour 1993*, Assemblee Nationale, May 1993. HM Treasury, *Treasury Bulletin, Summer 1992*. HM Treasury, *Financial Statement and Budget Reports, 1993–1994 and 1994–1995*. Banca d'Italia, *Bollettino Economico*, various issues. Consiglio dei Ministri, *Documento di Programmazione Economico-Finanziaria per gli Anni 1994–1996*, various issues. *The Budget, 1993*, Department of Finance, Canada.

Note: The ∗ indicates one-off measure; the ∗∗ indicates the corresponding offsetting measure.

an approach that highlights important intertemporal considerations. Factors playing a critical role in this approach include forward-looking behavior, private and public-sectors' intertemporal solvency, and the specification of the time pattern and credibility of policies. This approach, which rests on microeconomic foundations, permits a meaningful analysis of the welfare implications of government-spending and tax policies.

II

Traditional Approaches

2

The Income-Expenditure Model: Fiscal Policies and the Determination of Output

This chapter, along with chapters 3, and 4, is devoted to the presentation of the traditional income-expenditure approach to open-economy macroeconomics. Its focus on factors underlying the determination of output reflects a Keynesian heritage. The great depression of the 1930s, and the "beggar thy neighbor" policies adopted during that period by many countries, stimulated the development of this approach. Interest in this type of modeling is also stimulated by the observation (reported in tables 1.3 and 1.4 of chapter 1) on the cross-country correlations between private-sector absorption, government spending, and, in particular, national outputs.

In this chapter we outline the analytical framework of the income-expenditure model of the world economy. This framework is employed in the subsequent analysis of fiscal policies and income determination. Here we present a "Keynesian" two-country model in which prices are given while the levels of output and employment adjust in response to changes in aggregate demand. A similar framework could present a "classical" model in which the assumptions concerning the fixity of prices and the flexibility of output and employment are replaced by the assumption that prices are flexible while output is given at the full employment level. The analytical framework outlined in section 2.1 serves both of these analyses.

2.1 The Analytical Framework of the Income-Expenditure Model

Consider a two-country model of the world economy. The two countries are referred to as the home (domestic) country and the foreign country. Each country produces a distinct commodity: the domestic economy produces good x, and the foreign economy produces good m. The domestic level of output is denoted by Y_t, and the foreign level of output by Y_m^*. Throughout the analysis foreign variables are denoted by an asterisk. We assume that there is one noninterest-bearing asset—money, whose domestic and foreign quantities are denoted by M and M^*, respectively. The budget constraint requires that during each period, t, the value of the resources at the disposal of individuals equal the value of the uses of these resources. Accordingly, the domestic and foreign budget constraints are

$$Z_t^* + M_t = P_t(Y_{xt} - T_t) + M_{t-1}, \tag{2.1}$$

$$Z_t^* + M_t^* = P_t^*(Y_{mt}^* - T_t^*) + M_{t-1}^*, \tag{2.2}$$

where Z_t and P_t denote, respectively, nominal spending and the GDP deflator, and where Y_{xt} and T_t denote, respectively, real GDP and real taxes—both measured in terms of the domestic good. Equation (2.1) states that the individuals who allocate their resources between spending (Z_t) and asset holding (M_t) are constrained by the total available resources. These resources are the value of disposable income $[P_t(Y_{xt} - T_t)]$ and assets carried over from the previous period (M_{t-1}). As revealed by this formulation, money serves as a store of value facilitating the transfer of purchasing power from one period to the next. Similar notations (with an asterisk) and a similar interpretation apply to the foreign country budget constraint in equation (2.2).

In characterizing the behavior of domestic and foreign individuals, suppose that the desired levels of spending and asset holding depend only on the values of currently available resources. Thus, making use of the budget constraints, the *spending functions* are

$$Z_t = Z(P_t y_{xt}, M_{t-1}), \tag{2.3}$$

$$Z_t^* = Z^*(P_t^* y_{mt}^*, M_{t-1}^*), \tag{2.4}$$

where y_{xt} and y_{mt}^* denote, respectively, the values of domestic and foreign real disposable incomes $(Y_x - T$ and $Y_m^* - T^*)$. Analogously, the implied money-demand functions are

$$M_t = M(P_t y_{xt}, M_{t-1}),$$ (2.5)

$$M_t^* = M^*(P_t^* y_{mt}^*, M_{t-1}^*).$$ (2.6)

In this formulation we have specified the spending and the money-demand functions in nominal terms. Naturally the choice of units of measurement should not affect individuals' behavior with respect to real spending and real money demand. It follows that the *nominal* spending and money-demand functions are homogeneous of degree one in their arguments. Accordingly, we can define the *real spending functions* by

$$E_t = E\left(y_{xt}, \frac{M_{t-1}}{P_t}\right),$$ (2.7)

$$E_t^* = E^*\left(y_{mt}^*, \frac{M_{t-1}^*}{P_t^*}\right),$$ (2.8)

where $E_t = Z_t/P_t$ denotes the real value of domestic spending measured in terms of the domestic good, and where $E_t^* = Z_t^*/P_t^*$ denotes the real value of foreign spending, measured in terms of the foreign good.

The marginal propensity to save out of income, s, is assumed to be positive but less than unity, and thus the marginal propensity to spend, $1 - s$, is a positive fraction. Likewise, the marginal propensity to spend out of assets is positive. Similar properties characterize the foreign-spending function.

The domestic private sector is assumed to allocate its spending between domestic goods, C_{xt}, and foreign goods, C_{mt}. Analogously, the foreign private sector also allocates its spending between these two goods, C_{xt}^* and C_{mt}^*. Thus the real values of domestic and foreign spending (each measured in terms of own GDP) are

$$E_t = C_{xt} + p_{mt} C_m,$$ (2.9)

$$E_t^* = \frac{1}{p_{mt}} C_{xt}^* + C_{mt}^*,$$ (2.10)

where p_{mt} denotes the *relative* price of good m in terms of good x. This relative price is assumed to be equalized across countries through international trade. The relative share of domestic spending on good m (the foreign good) is denoted by $\beta_m = p_{mt} C_{mt}/E_t$. Likewise, the relative share of foreign spending on good x (the good produced by the home country) is denoted by $\beta_x^* = C_{xt}^*/p_{mt} E_t^*$. Thus β_m and β_x^* are the relative shares of domestic and foreign spending on their corresponding importable good. These expenditure shares are assumed to be constant.

The levels of real government spending in period t in each country (measured in terms of own GDP) are denoted by G_t and G_t^*, respectively. Analogously to the private sectors, the governments also allocate their spending between the two goods. Domestic government spending on importables (good m) is $\beta_m^g G_t/p_{mt}$, and foreign government spending on their importables (good x) is $\beta_x^{g*} p_{mt} G_t^*$, where β_m^g and β_x^{g*} denote, respectively, the domestic and foreign relative shares of government spending on importables.

The surplus in the domestic economy's *trade account* in period t, $(TA)_t$, is defined as the difference between its exports and imports. The economy's export equals the difference between domestic production and national consumption of exportables, where the latter consists of private-sector and government purchases. Here exports are $Y_{xt} - [(1 - \beta_m)E_t + (1 - \beta_m^g)G_t]$. Analogously, the economy's imports equal the difference between national consumption and production of importables. Here, since in the present formulation the importable good is not produced domestically, imports are $\beta_m E_t + \beta_m^g G_t$. It follows that the trade-balance surplus can be expressed as the difference between GDP and national spending (absorption):

$$(TA)_t = Y_{xt} - (E_t + G_t). \tag{2.11}$$

Equation (2.11) can be used together with the budget constraint (2.1) to yield

$$M_t - M_{t-1} = P_t[(TA)_t - (T_t - G_t)]. \tag{2.12}$$

Equation (2.12) expresses private savings (the accumulation of assets by the private sector) as the difference between national savings (indicated by the trade-balance surplus) and government savings (indicated by the surplus in the government budget).

We assume that the economy operates under a fixed exchange-rate regime and that the exchange rate is pegged by the monetary authority. The absence of interest-bearing debt implies that discrepancies between government spending and taxes are met by corresponding changes in the money supply. Thus, abstracting from the commercial-banking system, changes in the money supply reflect two activities of the monetary authorities: those associated with pegging the exchange rate, and those associated with financing government budget deficits. The two terms on the right-hand side of equation (2.12) correspond to these two sources of changes in the money supply. The first is the surplus in the official settlements account of the balance of payments, indicating the official accumulation of international reserves induced by the exchange-rate-pegging operation of the monetary authorities. Since in the present stage of the analysis we do not allow for international borrowing and lending, the official settlements balance equals the trade-balance surplus, $P_t(TA)_t$. The second term on the right-hand side of equation (2.12) is the monetary change induced by the surplus in the government budget, $-P_t(T_t - G_t)$.

Similar considerations apply to the foreign economy. Therefore the foreign-country analogue to the trade-balance and the monetary-flow equations (2.11) and (2.12) is

$$(TA)_t^* = Y_{mt}^* - (E_t^* + G_t^*) \tag{2.13}$$

and

$$M_t^* - M_{t-1}^* = P_t^*[(TA)_t^* - (T_t^* - G_t^*)], \tag{2.14}$$

where the real magnitudes are measured in terms of the foreign good, m.

Equilibrium in the world economy requires that world demand for each good equals the corresponding supply. Accordingly,

$$(1 - \beta_m)E_t + (1 - \beta_m^g)G_t + p_{mt}(\beta_x^* E_t^* + \beta_x^{g^*} G_t^*) = Y_{xt}, \tag{2.15}$$

$$\frac{1}{p_{mt}}(\beta_m E_t + \beta_m^g G_t) + (1 - \beta_x^*)E_t^* + (1 - \beta_x^{g^*})G_t^* = Y_{mt}^*. \tag{2.16}$$

The two equilibrium conditions (2.15) and (2.16), together with the definitions of the trade balance in equations (2.11) and (2.13), imply that in equilibrium the surplus in the home country's trade account is equal to the foreign country's deficit so that $(TA)_t = -p_{mt}(TA)_t^*$, where $(TA)_t$ is

$$(TA)_t = p_{mt}(\beta_x^* E_t^* + \beta_x^{g^*} G_t^*) - (\beta_m E_t + \beta_m^g G_t). \tag{2.17}$$

The relative price of good m in terms of good x, p_{mt}, which is assumed to be equal across countries, can be written as

$$p_{mt} = \frac{e P_t^*}{P_t}, \tag{2.18}$$

where e is the nominal exchange rate expressing the price of the foreign currency in terms of the domestic currency. With this expression the equality between the surplus in the domestic trade balance and the deficit in the foreign trade balance (expressed in common units) states that $(TA)_t = -(e P_t^*/P_t)(TA)_t^*$. This equality together with equations (2.12) and (2.14) implies that

$$(M_t - M_{t-1}) + e(M_t^* - M_{t-1}^*) = P_t(G_t - T_t) + e P_t^*(G_t^* - T_t^*). \tag{2.19}$$

Equation (2.19) indicates that the change in the world money supply is the sum of the deficits in the domestic and the foreign governments' budget (all measured in terms of domestic currency units). This equality reflects the assumed fixity of the world stock of international reserves. As a result of this fixity changes in the foreign-exchange component of the monetary base in any given economy are fully offset by opposite changes in the rest of the world, and changes in the world money supply arise only from public-sector deficit finance.

It should be obvious that the automatic monetization of budget deficits reflects the absence of credit markets. If credit markets existed, then the governments could also finance their budget through borrowing. In chapter 3 we allow for both domestic and international credit markets. For the present analysis, in order to focus only on pure fiscal policies (rather than on monetary policies), we consider only balanced-budget changes in government spending. The analysis of the effects of budget deficits is relegated to chapter 3.

The analytical framework of the income-expenditure model outlined earlier is general in that it encompasses the Keynesian and the classical versions of the model. To simplify the exposition and to highlight the symmetry between the two versions, we conclude this section by presenting a simplified specification of the model. Accordingly, we assume that the marginal propensities to spend and save out of disposable income are the same as the corresponding propensities to spend and save out of assets. With this assumption, the spending and money-demand functions of equations (2.3) through (2.6) become

$$Z_t = Z(P_t Y_t - P_t T_t + M_{t-1}), \qquad Z_t^* = Z^*(P_t^* Y_t^* - P_t^* T_t^* + M_{t-1}^*),$$

$$M_t = M(P_t Y_t - P_t T_t + M_{t-1}), \qquad M_t^* = M^*(P_t^* Y_t^* - P_t^* T_t^* + M_{t-1}^*),$$

$$(2.20)$$

where we have suppressed the commodity subscripts x and m. With this specification the equilibrium conditions (2.15) and (2.16) become

$$\frac{1 - s - a}{1 - s} Z(P_t Y_t - P_t T_t + M_{t-1}) + (1 - a^g) P_t G_t$$

$$+ \frac{a^*}{1 - s^*} e Z^*(P_t^* Y_t^* - P_t^* T_t^* + M_{t-1}^*) + a^{g^*} e P_t^* G_t^* = P_t Y_t \quad (2.15a)$$

$$\frac{a}{1 - s} Z(P_t Y_t - P_t T_t + M_{t-1}) + a^g P_t G_t$$

$$+ \frac{1 - s^* - a^*}{1 - s^*} e Z^*(P_t^* Y_t^* - P_t^* T_t^* + M_{t-1}^*) + (1 - a^{g^*}) e P_t^* G_t^*$$

$$= e P_t^* Y_t^*, \qquad (2.16a)$$

where s and a denote, respectively, the domestic marginal propensities to save and import out of income (or assets), a^g denotes the government marginal propensity to import out of government spending, and where similar notations (with an added asterisk) apply to the foreign country. The relations between the propensities to save and spend out of income and the corresponding propensities to save and spend out of expenditures are stated in section 2.3. In the specification of the equilibrium conditions we have used the law-of-one-price according to which $p_{mt} = eP_t^*/P_t$.

The specification of equations (2.15a) and (2.16a) reveals the symmetry between the Keynesian and the classical versions of the income-expenditure model. Specifically, in the absence of government spending and taxes and for given levels of money holdings, the system determines the values of domestic and foreign *nominal* incomes, $P_t Y_t$ and $P_t^* Y_t^*$. In this system the specific values of output and prices generating the equilibrium values of nominal incomes are immaterial. The Keynesian version of the model postulates fixed prices. Thereby the equilibrium changes in nominal incomes are brought about through output adjustments. The classical version postulates fixed outputs and employment. Thereby the equilibrium changes in nominal incomes are brought about through price adjustments. Since both versions of the income-expenditure model generate the same paths of nominal incomes, they also generate the *same* paths of spending and balance-of-payments adjustments. Inspection of equations (2.15a) and (2.16a) also reveals that in the presence of government spending and taxes the relation between the two versions of the model depends on the specification of the paths of government spending and taxes.

2.2   The Keynesian Version

For the remainder of this chapter we analyze the Keynesian version of the income-expenditure model. Under this specification prices are given while the levels of output are determined by aggregate demand. For expository purposes we normalize units so that $e = P_t = P_t^* = p_{mt} = 1$, and accordingly, we suppress the commodity subscripts x and m. In this specification of the model the spending and money-demand functions of equation (2.20) become

$$E_t = E(Y_t - T_t + M_{t-1}), \quad E_t^* = E^*(Y_t^* - T_t^* + M_{t-1}^*),$$

$$M_t = M(Y_t - T_t + M_{t-1}), \quad M_t^* = M^*(Y_t^* - T_t^* + M_{t-1}^*).$$

(2.20a)

In the appendix to this chapter we analyze the more general system that corresponds to equations (2.5) through (2.8).

In the next three sections we analyze the equilibrium levels of output and the balance of payments for the short run, the long run, and the adjustment period characterizing the transition between the short and the long runs.

2.3 Short-Run Equilibrium Levels of Output

In order to characterize the short-run equilibrium of the system, we differentiate the equilibrium conditions (2.15a) and (2.16a) and obtain

$$\begin{pmatrix} -(s+a) & a^* \\ a & -(s^*+a^*) \end{pmatrix} \begin{pmatrix} dY_t \\ dY_t^* \end{pmatrix}$$

$$= \begin{pmatrix} a^g - a - s \\ -(a^g - a) \end{pmatrix} dG + \begin{pmatrix} s - (1 - a - a^*) \\ -s^* + (1 - a - a^*) \end{pmatrix} dM_{t-1}, \qquad (2.21)$$

where we recall that in this specification $s = 1 - E_y = 1 - E_M$ and $a = \beta_m E_y = \beta_m E_M$ denote, respectively, the domestic marginal propensities to save and to import, $a^g = \beta_m^g$ denotes the government marginal propensity to import out of government spending (E_y and E_M denote the partial derivatives of private real spending, E, with respect to income and assets). In the derivation of the system (2.21) we have assumed that governments run balanced budgets, that the paths of government spending and taxes are stationary (i.e., $G_t = T_t = G = T$ and $G_t^* = T_t^* = G^* = T^*$), and that foreign policies are given. We have also made use of the implication of the balanced-budget assumption, according to which $dM_{t-1} = -dM_{t-1}^*$ (from equation 2.19).

The system shown in (2.21) indicates that changes in the levels of domestic and foreign GDP are induced by two distinct factors. The first corresponds to changes in the level and commodity composition of aggregate demand induced by fiscal policy; the second corresponds to dynamic changes in the distribution of the world money supply. As is evident, the (balanced-budget) changes in the level of government spending induce immediate changes in the levels of domestic and foreign outputs. On the other hand, the effects of redistributions of the world money supply only occur through time.

In what follows, we analyze the effects of balanced-budget changes in government spending on the equilibrium of the system. In the short run the international distribution of the world money supply is given. This distribution may change over time through surpluses or deficits in the official-settlements account of the balance of payments. Long-run equilibrium obtains when the dynamic process of the redistribution of world money reaches a halt.

The short-run equilibrium of the system is depicted in figure 2.1. The YY and the Y^*Y^* schedules are, respectively, the domestic and the foreign goods-market equilibrium schedules. Along the YY

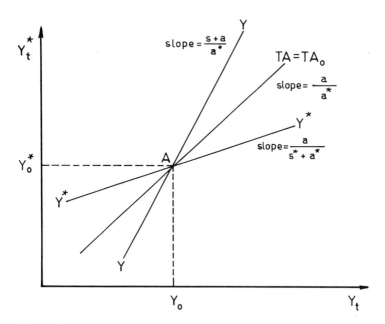

Figure 2.1
Short-run equilibrium outputs

schedule world demand for domestic output equals domestic GDP, and along the Y^*Y^* schedule world demand for foreign output equals foreign GDP. The domestic schedule YY is positively sloped since a unit rise in domestic GDP raises domestic demand for the domestic good by $1 - s - a$, and thereby creates an excess supply of $1 - (1 - s - a) = s + a$ units. To restore equilibrium, foreign output must rise. A unit rise in foreign output raises foreign demand for the domestic good by a^* units, and therefore, to eliminate the excess supply of $s + a$ units, foreign output must rise by $(s + a)/a^*$. Thus, along the YY schedule, the slope is

$$\frac{dY^*}{dY} = \frac{s + a}{a^*}. \tag{2.22}$$

Analogously, the foreign schedule Y^*Y^* is also positively sloped, and by similar reasoning, along the Y^*Y^* schedule, the slope is

$$\frac{dY^*}{dY} = \frac{a}{s^* + a^*}. \tag{2.23}$$

As is evident, the YY schedule is steeper than the Y^*Y^* schedule. Both of these schedules are drawn for a given level of government spending and for a given distribution of the world money supply.

The equilibrium of the system obtains at point A at which domestic GDP is Y_0 and foreign GDP is Y_0^*; the trade balance associated with these levels of outputs can be inferred from equation (2.17). To complete the characterization of the equilibrium and to set the stage for the analysis of the dynamic effects of government spending, we differentiate the trade-balance equation (2.17) and obtain

$$d(TA)_t = (a^* dY_t^* - a dY_t) - (a^g - a) dG - (a + a^*) dM_{t-1}. \tag{2.24}$$

The three terms on the right-hand side of equation (2.24) correspond to the three factors governing trade-balance adjustments. The first reflects adjustments induced by (endogenous) changes in the levels of output, the second reflects the trade-balance implications of (balanced-budget) changes in government spending, and the third reflects the trade-balance implications of the dynamic process effecting the international distribution of the world money supply.

As seen from equation (2.24), for given values of government spending and the money supply, maintenance of a given level of the trade balance requires that domestic and foreign outputs move in the same direction. These considerations are embodied in the $TA = TA_0$ locus exhibited in figure 2.1. This schedule shows combinations of domestic and foreign outputs along which the balance of trade (which in our case is the official settlements balance) is constant. The TA locus is positively sloped since a unit rise in domestic GDP worsens the balance of trade by a units, and this worsening can be offset by a rise in foreign output. Since a unit rise in foreign output improves the domestic trade balance by a^* units, it follows that foreign output must rise by a/a^* units. Thus, along the $TA = TA_0$ schedule, the slope is

$$\frac{dY^*}{dY} = \frac{a}{a^*}. \tag{2.25}$$

As is evident, by comparison with equations (2.22) and (2.23), this slope falls in between those of the YY and the Y^*Y^* schedules. To the right of the $TA = TA_0$ locus the domestic economy's balance of trade worsens, and to the left of this locus the domestic trade balance improves.

The foregoing analysis implies that for a given level of government spending and for a given distribution of the world money supply, the *short-run* equilibrium is fully characterized by the intersection between the YY and the Y^*Y^* schedules as at point A in figure 2.1. The trade balance, TA_0, associated with this short-run equilibrium, determines the direction of the international redistribution of the world money supply. If TA_0 is negative, the home country's money supply is falling over time while the foreign country's money supply is rising. In the long run, as seen from equations (2.12) and (2.14), with balanced budgets the trade account is balanced (so that $TA = 0$), and as a result the international distribution of the world money supply does not tend to change.

2.4   Long-Run Equilibrium Levels of Output

In this section we analyze the determinants of the long-run equilibrium. As was already indicated, in the long run, the endogenously determined distribution of the world money supply is such that international monetary flows cease and $TA = 0$. Thus in the long run, $M_t = M_{t-1} = M$ and $M_t^* = M_{t-1}^* = M^* = \overline{M} - M$, where $\overline{M}$ is the world money supply which is assumed to be given. Accordingly, using the money-demand equations from (2.20)—omitting the time subscripts of domestic and foreign GDPs and replacing the taxes, T and T^*, by the corresponding levels of government spending, G and G^* (due to the balanced-budget assumption which is necessary for the maintenance of the fixed world money supply)—yield equation (2.26) as the condition for world monetary equilibrium

$$M(Y - G + M) + M^*(Y^* - G^* + \overline{M} - M) = \overline{M}. \qquad (2.26)$$

Similar considerations indicate that in the long run (in which the stocks of assets do not vary over time) the budget constraints (2.1) and (2.2) imply that private spending in each country equals the corresponding level of disposable income; in addition the balanced-budget assumption implies that in each country disposable income equals the level of GDP net of government spending. Hence, using (2.20), the long-run budget constraints are

$$E(Y - G + M) = Y - G, \qquad (2.27)$$

$$E^*(Y^* - G^* + \overline{M} - M) = Y^* - G^*. \qquad (2.28)$$

The system (2.26) through (2.28) yields the combinations of long-run Y and Y^* that are consistent with money-market equilibrium in the world economy. These combinations are depicted by the negatively sloped $\overline{MM}$ schedule in figure 2.2. The schedule is drawn for given levels of government spending and world money supply. The slope of the $\overline{MM}$ schedule is negative since a rise in domestic resources ($dY + dM$) raises spending by $(1 - s)$ times this quantity, and since in the long run the rise in spending equals the rise

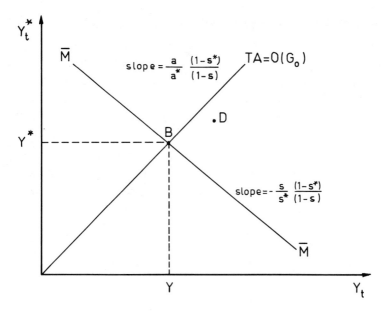

Figure 2.2
Long-run equilibrium outputs

in GDP, it follows that $(1 - s)(dY + dM) = dY$. Thus the rise in domestic GDP raises the domestic long-run demand for money by $[s/(1 - s)]dY$. Similarly, a fall in foreign output by dY^* induces a decline in foreign money demand by $[s^*/(1 - s^*)]dY^*$. With a given world money supply the maintenance of world monetary equilibrium necessitates that the rise in the domestic money demand equals the fall in the foreign demand. Hence, along the $\overline{MM}$ schedule,

$$\frac{dY^*}{dY} = -\frac{s}{s^*}\frac{(1 - s^*)}{(1 - s)}. \tag{2.29}$$

In addition to the requirement of world monetary equilibrium, the conditions for long-run equilibrium also require that the goods market clear. In the long run this requirement implies trade-balance equilibrium. Accordingly, since in the absence of monetary flows $M_t = M_{t-1} = M$ and $M_t^* = M_{t-1}^* = M^* = \overline{M} - M$, it follows that

$$\bar{a}^*E^*(Y^* - G^* + \overline{M} - M) + a^{g^*}G^* - [\bar{a}E(Y - G + M) + a^gG]$$

$$= 0, \tag{2.30}$$

where $\bar{a} = a/(1 - s)$ and $\bar{a}^* = a^*/(1 - s^*)$ are, respectively, the domestic and foreign marginal propensities to import out of *spending* (these propensities should be distinguished from a and a^* which are the corresponding propensities to import out of *income*). Equation (2.30) is the goods-market analogue to the monetary-equilibrium condition (2.26). The system (2.27), (2.28), and (2.30) yield the combinations of long-run values of domestic and foreign outputs that are consistent with goods-market equilibrium in the world economy. Formally, substituting (2.27) and (2.28) into (2.30) yields

$$\bar{a}^*Y^* - \bar{a}Y = (a^g - \bar{a})G - (a^{g^*} - \bar{a}^*)G^*. \tag{2.30a}$$

Equation (2.30a) is shown in figure 2.2 by the positively sloped $TA = 0$ schedule. This schedule is drawn for given levels of government spending and world money supply. Its slope is positive since a rise in domestic output worsens the trade balance, whereas a rise in foreign output improves it. Thus, along the $TA = 0$ schedule, analogously to equation (2.25), the slope is

$$\frac{dY^*}{dY} = \frac{\bar{a}}{\bar{a}^*}. \tag{2.31}$$

Along the $\overline{MM}$ schedule the stationary distributions of the world money supply, M and $M^* = \overline{M} - M$, and world outputs, Y and Y^* (determined from the system 2.26 through 2.28), generate world demand for money that equals the existing stock, $\overline{M}$. However, the levels of output and the distribution of world money necessary to bring about such a monetary equilibrium may not be consistent with goods-market equilibrium. Analogously, along the $TA = 0$ schedule, the stationary distributions of world money supply and outputs (determined from the system 2.27, 2.28, and 2.30) generate world demand for each output that equals the corresponding supply. However, the levels of output and the distribution of world money necessary to bring about such an equilibrium in the goods market may not generate world money demand that is equal to the existing stock.

The long-run equilibrium obtains at the intersection of the $\overline{MM}$ and the $TA = 0$ schedules. At such an intersection both goods and money markets clear, and the levels of output and money holdings do not change over time. Point B in figure 2.2 depicts the long-run equilibrium. In the next section we complete the characterization of the equilibrium by analyzing the dynamic process that underlies the transition between short- and long-run equilibria.

2.5   Dynamics of Adjustment and the Balance of Payments

The short-run equilibrium depicted by point A in figure 2.1 is associated with an imbalance in the balance of payments equal to TA_0. The international monetary flows induced by this imbalance disturb the initial short-run equilibrium. As indicated by the goods-market equilibrium conditions (2.21), changes in the international distribution of the world money supply (as measured by dM_{t-1}) alter the positions of the YY and the Y^*Y^* schedules and result in a new short-run equilibrium associated with the prevailing new distribution of the world money supply. In this section we analyze the transition period characterized by a sequence of such short-run equilibria and show that this dynamic process converges to the long-run equilibrium. The impact of a given change in domestic money holdings, dM_{t-1}, on the goods-market equilibrium schedules is shown on the right-hand side of (2.21). Accordingly, a unit rise in the domestic money holdings, accompanied by a unit fall in the foreign money holdings, raises the domestic demand for home output by c units (where c denotes the domestic marginal propensity to spend on domestic goods, $c = 1 - s - a$) and lowers the foreign demand for home output by a^*. Hence, whether at the initial levels of output this change in the distribution of money holdings creates an excess demand or an excess supply of domestic output depends on whether $c - a^*$ is positive or negative. If it is positive, then the rise in domestic money holdings shifts the YY schedule to the right, and vice versa. Similarly, the fall in the foreign money holdings creates an excess supply of foreign output if $c^* - a$ is positive, and it creates an excess demand if $c^* - a$ is negative (where c^* denotes the foreign marginal propensity to spend on foreign goods, $c^* = 1 - s^* - a^*$). If it is positive, then the fall in foreign money holdings shifts the Y^*Y^* schedule downward, and vice versa.

The effects of a redistribution of the world money supply on the short-run equilibrium levels of domestic and foreign outputs are obtained by solving (2.21). Hence

$$\frac{dY_t}{dM_{t-1}} = \frac{s^*c - sa^*}{ss^* + sa^* + s^*a}, \quad (2.32)$$

$$\frac{dY_t^*}{dM_{t-1}} = \frac{s^*a - sc^*}{ss^* + sa^* + s^*a}. \quad (2.33)$$

As seen, the direction of the change in domestic output depends on whether the ratio of the domestic to the foreign saving propensities, s/s^*, exceeds or falls short of the ratio of the domestic to the foreign propensities to spend on *domestic* goods, c/a^*. Analogously, the direction of the change in foreign output depends on whether the ratio of the saving propensities, s/s^* exceeds or falls short of the ratio of the domestic to foreign propensities to spend on *foreign* goods, a/c^*. Thus the direction of the long-run changes in output depends on the saving propensities and on the commodity composition of spending. The role of the saving propensities is clarified by noting that if the domestic saving propensity, s, is small, then a redistribution of the world money supply toward the domestic economy raises the levels of output in both countries. On the other hand, if the foreign saving propensity, s^*, is small, then the same redistribution lowers the levels of output in both countries. The opposite pattern of output changes arises in the other extreme cases in which the corresponding saving propensities are large. The role of the commodity composition of spending is clarified by noting that if the import propensities, a and a^*, are relatively small (i.e., if c and c^* are relatively large so that expenditures in each country are biased toward locally produced goods), then the redistribution of world money toward the domestic economy diverts world demand toward the domestically produced good and away from the foreign-produced goods. This change in the pattern of world demand raises the equilibrium level of domestic output. The opposite holds if each country's demand is biased toward imported goods.

Thus far we have determined the changes in the international *distribution* of world output induced by the dynamic redistribution of world money. The dynamic process is also associated with changes in the *level* of world GDP, $Y_t + Y_t^*$. Accordingly, adding the results in (2.32) and (2.33) yields

$$\frac{d(Y_t + Y_t^*)}{dM_{t-1}} = \frac{s^* - s}{ss^* + sa^* + s^*a}. \tag{2.34}$$

The interpretation of equation (2.34) can be stated in terms of the "transfer-problem" criterion familiar from the theory of international transfers. Accordingly, at the prevailing levels of output the redistribution of the world money supply raises domestic spending by $(1 - s)$ times the rise in the domestic money supply and lowers foreign spending by $(1 - s^*)$ times the same quantity. Hence *world* spending rises if s^* exceeds s, and world spending falls if s^* falls short of s. In the former case the rise in world spending creates an excess demand for world output which, in order to restore equilibrium between world spending and output, necessitates a corresponding rise in world GDP. The opposite holds in the latter case for which s^* falls short of s.

The redistribution of the world money supply and the induced changes in the short-run equilibrium levels of output also alter the initial trade-balance position and bring about additional changes in the money supply. Specifically, substituting equations (2.32) and (2.33) into (2.24) yields

$$\frac{d(TA)_t}{dM_{t-1}} = -\frac{sa^* + s^*a}{ss^* + sa^* + s^*a},$$

and noting that $M_t = M_{t-1} + (TA)_t$, it follows that dM_t/dM_{t-1} is a positive fraction, where

$$\frac{dM_t}{dM_{t-1}} = \frac{ss^*}{ss^* + sa^* + s^*a} < 1. \tag{2.35}$$

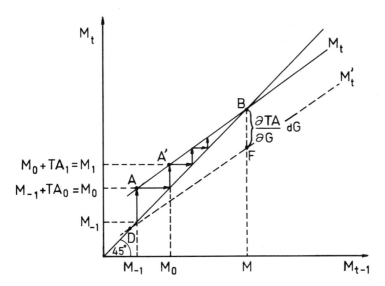

Figure 2.3
Balance-of-payments dynamics

Equation (2.35) shows that the additions to the domestic quantity of money induced by the sequence of balance-of-payments surpluses diminish over time. It follows that the dynamic process of the redistribution of the world money supply that is effected through balance-of-payment adjustments converges to the long-run equilibrium.

Figure 2.3 shows the path of adjustment and demonstrates the stability of the dynamic process. In this figure the initial equilibrium is indicated by point A along the M_t schedule at which the level of domestic money holding is M_{-1} and the associated surplus in the balance of payments is TA_0. This initial short-run equilibrium corresponds to the one depicted in figure 2.1, and as before, the M_t schedule in figure 2.3 is drawn for a given level of government spending. The surplus in the balance of payments raises the domestic money supply from M_{-1} to M_0 and results in a new short-run equilibrium at point A' along the M_t schedule. In this equilibrium the trade surplus diminishes to TA_1. The sequence of short-run equilibria is associated with a path along which the positive increments to the money supply (associated with trade surpluses) diminish over time.

This path converges to the long-run equilibrium at point B at which the long-run money holding by the home country is M. The long-run equilibrium shown in this figure corresponds to the one in figure 2.2.

Before concluding, we note that even though the direction of monetary flows during the adjustment process is clear cut, the directions of changes in domestic and foreign outputs depend on the relations between the marginal saving ratio, s/s^*, and the marginal consumption ratios of domestic goods, c/a^*, and of foreign goods, a/c^*. Independent, however, of the precise pattern of output adjustments, the system characterizing the world economy as a whole (including the level and the international distribution of world output) is dynamically stable.

2.6 Fiscal Policies and Outputs

In this section we use the results of the previous analysis to determine the short- and long-run effects of balanced-budget changes in the domestic government spending. For this purpose suppose that the world economy is initially in a long-run equilibrium, corresponding to point B in figures 2.2 and 2.3. At the prevailing levels of output, a unit rise in government spending raises the demand for domestically produced goods by $1 - a^g$, and the rise in taxes necessary to balance the budget lowers private demand for domestic output by $1 - a - s$. Thus the excess demand for domestic goods induced by this balanced-budget rise in government spending is $s + a - a^g$. By similar reasoning the excess demand for foreign goods induced by the unit rise in government spending is $a^g - a$ (these changes are represented by the coefficients of dG in the system of equations 2.21).

As is evident, the patterns of excess demands generated by the balanced-budget rise in government spending depend critically on the magnitude of the government propensity to import, a^g. For example, in the extreme case for which all government spending falls on domestic goods (so that $a^g = 0$), the excess demand for domestic goods is $(s + a)$, and the excess supply of foreign goods is a. In the other extreme case for which all government spending falls on importables (so that $a^g = 1$), the excess supply of domestic goods is $1 - (s + a)$, whereas the excess demand for foreign goods is $1 - a$.

The relative magnitudes of the government and the private sector marginal propensities to import also determine whether at the prevailing levels of output the trade balance improves or deteriorates. The unit rise in government spending raises imports by a^g, and the corresponding unit rise in taxes lowers private imports by a. Hence (as indicated by equation 2.24) at the prevailing levels of output the trade balance improves if a, the private import propensity, exceeds the government import propensity, a^g, and it deteriorates if a falls short of a^g. If the two import propensities are the same, then at the prevailing levels of output the redistribution of income between the private and the public sectors does not impact on the balance of trade.

In the diagrammatic analysis that follows, we consider the intermediate bench-mark case for which the private and the public sectors have the same marginal propensities to import (so that $a = a^g$). Consider figure 2.4, and let the initial long-run equilibrium be at point B. The equilibrium schedules YY and Y^*Y^* are drawn for the given initial level of government spending and for the initial distribution of the world money supply. The levels of output associated with this equilibrium are Y_0 and Y_0^*, and since the initial position is that of a long-run equilibrium, point B lies on the $TA = 0$ schedule along which the balance of payments is balanced.

A unit balanced-budget rise in the domestic government spending induces an excess demand for domestic goods by s units (in the bench-mark case for which $a = a^g$) and necessitates an equilibrating rise in domestic output by $s/(s + a)$ units (for a given level of foreign output). In terms of figure 2.4 the balanced-budget rise in government spending shifts the YY schedule rightward by $s/(s + a)$ units times the rise in government spending. This horizontal shift corresponds to the conventional balanced-budget foreign trade

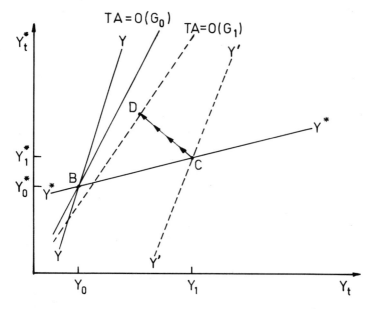

Figure 2.4
The short- and long-run effects of a balanced-budget rise in government spending

multiplier for a small open economy. The new equilibrium schedule is indicated by $Y'Y'$. Since with $a = a^g$ the balanced-budget rise in the domestic government spending does not generate an excess demand or an excess supply of foreign output, the Y^*Y^* schedule remains intact, and the new short-run equilibrium obtains at point C.

In the short-run equilibrium at point C, domestic and foreign outputs are higher than their initial levels. Thus, measured in terms of comovements of domestic and foreign outputs, the domestic fiscal expansion is transmitted positively to the rest of the world. It is also relevant to note that the magnitude of the equilibrium rise in domestic output exceeds the rise implied by the small-country foreign trade multiplier (a rise that is indicated by the rightward shift of the YY schedule).

In the more general case the private and public sectors' marginal propensities to import may differ from each other. In that case the short-run effects of the balanced-budget rise in government spending are obtained from the system in (2.21). Accordingly,

$$\frac{dY_0}{dG} = 1 - \frac{s^* a^g}{ss^* + sa^* + s^* a},$$

(2.36)

$$\frac{dY_0^*}{dG} = \frac{sa^g}{ss^* + sa^* + s^* a}.$$

(2.37)

Equation (2.36) illustrates the negative dependence of the short-run equilibrium change in domestic output on the magnitude of the government import propensity. If the government import propensity, a^g, does not exceed the corresponding private-sector propensity, a, then the balanced-budget rise in government spending must raise domestic output. On the other hand, if a^g is relatively large, then domestic output may fall in the short run. This fall stems from the fact that the redistribution of income between the private and the public sectors diverts spending away from domestic output.

Equation (2.37) shows that in general foreign output rises. It also shows that this rise is proportional to the magnitude of the domestic government import propensity, a^g. In the extreme case for which all government spending falls on domestic goods (so that $a^g = 0$), foreign output does not change. In that case the rise in domestic output is maximized, and the balanced-budget multiplier is unity. The comparison between the directions of domestic and foreign output changes reveals that (in contrast with the bench-mark case) *the short-run international transmission of the effects of domestic balanced-budget fiscal policies may be positive or negative.*

Thus far we have characterized the nature of the international transmission mechanism in terms of the sign of the correlation between changes in domestic and foreign *outputs*. The focus on the levels of output reflects concern with respect to resource utilization and employment. An alternative measure characterizes the transmission mechanism in terms of the correlation between domestic and foreign *private-sector spending*. The latter is governed by changes in private disposable incomes. As is evident from equations (2.36) and (2.37), domestic disposable income falls, and foreign disposable income rises (in the limiting case in which $a^g = 0$ both disposable incomes remain unchanged). Thus, measured in terms of comovements of the domestic and the foreign private-sector spending, *the short-run international transmission of the effects of domestic balanced-budget fiscal policies is negative.*

The preceeding analysis examined the short-run effects of fiscal policies on the international *distribution* of world output and spending. The change in the *level* of world output is obtained by adding equations (2.36) and (2.37). Similarly, the change in the level of world private-sector spending reflects changes in each country's disposable income multiplied by the corresponding propensity to spend. Thus using equations (2.36) and (2.37) yields

$$\frac{d(Y_0 + Y_0^*)}{dG} = 1 + \frac{(s - s^*)a^g}{ss^* + sa^* + s^*a}, \tag{2.38}$$

$$\frac{d(E_0 + E_0^*)}{dG} = \frac{(s - s^*)a^g}{ss^* + sa^* + s^*a}. \tag{2.39}$$

Equation (2.38) shows that, in general, the direction of the change in world output depends on the relative magnitudes of the saving and import propensities. If, however, the government propensity to import, a^g, does not exceed the corresponding private-sector propensity, a, then world output must rise. The bench-mark case shown in figure 2.4 illustrates this result. Equation (2.39) shows that the direction of the change in world private-sector spending depends on whether the domestic economy's saving propensity exceeds or falls short of the foreign saving propensity. In the former case world spending rises, and in the latter case world spending falls.

The short-run effects of a balanced-budget rise in government spending are also reflected in the balance of payments. Using equation (2.24) along with the expressions for the equilibrium changes in outputs from equations (2.36) and (2.37) yields

$$\frac{d(TA)_0}{dG} = \frac{ss^*a^g}{ss^* + sa^* + s^*a}. \tag{2.40}$$

Thus, unless all government spending falls on the domestic goods, the rise in government spending induces a deficit in the home country's balance of payments. This deficit initiates the dynamic process by which the world money supply is redistributed over time from the domestic economy to the rest of the world.

In the benchmark case shown in figure 2.4 the short-run equilibrium at point C is associated with a deficit in the balance of payments since it lies to the right of the $TA = 0$ schedule. (As seen from equation 2.24, this schedule is invariant with respect to government spending as long as $a = a^g$.) The fall in the domestic money supply, and the corresponding rise in the foreign money supply consequent on the payments imbalances lower domestic spending and raises foreign spending. As a result the $Y'Y'$ schedule shifts leftward, and the Y^*Y^* schedule shifts upward. Their new intersection yields a new short-run equilibrium. This process continues as long as the payments imbalances prevail. The location of this new short-run equilibrium relative to point C depends on whether the ratio of the domestic to the foreign-saving propensities, s/s^*, exceeds or falls short of the ratios of the domestic to the foreign propensities to consume domestic goods, c/a^*, and foreign goods, a/c^*.

Diagrammatically, the slope of the adjustment path characterizing the sequence of short-run equilibria is obtained by dividing equation (2.33) by equation (2.32). Accordingly, along the path of adjustment,

$$\frac{dY_t^*}{dY_t} = \left(\frac{(a/c^*) - (s/s^*)}{(c/a^*) - (s/s^*)} \right) \frac{c^*}{a^*}. \tag{2.41}$$

As is evident, depending on the relative magnitudes of the parameters, this slope may be positive or negative. In figure 2.4 the path of adjustment is drawn with a negative slope corresponding to the case in which the spending patterns are such that the saving ratio, s/s^*, is bounded by the ratios of the two countries' propensities to spend on the domestic good, c/a^*, and on the foreign good, a/c^*. Accordingly, the sequence of short-run equilibria is described in figure 2.4 by the path connecting the initial short-run equilibrium point C with the long-run equilibrium point D. In general, as seen from equation 2.34, along the path of adjustment world output (and spending) rises or falls depending on whether the domestic saving propensity, s, exceeds or falls short of the foreign saving propensity, s^*.

The dynamics of adjustment can also be illustrated in terms of figure 2.3. In that figure the M_t schedule is drawn for a given level of government spending. The rise in government spending (at the initial distribution of the world money supply) worsens the trade account by $[\partial(TA)/\partial G]\,dG$ and shifts the M_t schedule downward to the position indicated by M'_t (since $M_t = TA_t + M_{t-1}$). This shift sets off the dynamic process (not drawn) that converges to the new long-run equilibrium point D (at which $M_t = M_{t-1}$ along the M'_t schedule). The new equilibrium point corresponds to the new international distribution of the world money supply.

The characteristics of the new long-run equilibrium can be examined with the aid of figure 2.2. The position of the new long-run equilibrium point depends on the effects of the balanced-budget rise in government spending on the world monetary-equilibrium schedule, $\overline{MM}$ and on the balance-of-payments equilibrium schedule, $TA = 0$. It is evident by inspection of equations (2.26) through (2.28) that the $\overline{MM}$ schedule shifts rightward and that the extent of the horizontal shift equals the rise in government spending. The reason for the rightward shift of the $\overline{MM}$ schedule is that given the initial distribution of world money, the rise in domestic output is necessary in order to keep domestic disposable income unchanged for any given level of foreign output (and disposable income). Such a rise ensures the maintenance of world monetary equilibrium since, as long as the initial distribution of world money and the initial levels of disposable incomes do not change, the world demand for money remains intact.

By similar reasoning equation (2.30a) indicates that a unit balanced-budget rise in government spending induces a rightward shift of the $TA = 0$ schedule by $(\bar{a} - a^g)/a$ units. Given the initial distribution of world money, this change in domestic output ensures that the home country's total (private sector plus government) imports are unchanged. With unchanged imports the trade balance is also unchanged since, for a given level of foreign output, domestic exports are given. As is evident, the direction to which the $TA = 0$ schedule shifts depends on whether, at the prevailing situation, the redistribution of income between the domestic private sector and the government (consequent on the balanced-budget rise in government spending) raises or lowers long-run imports. If the private sector's marginal propensity to import out of spending, $\bar{a}$, exceeds the government propensity to import, a^g, then the balanced-budget rise in government spending improves the trade balance. Therefore, ceteris paribus, domestic output must rise in order to restore balanced trade. In this case the $TA = 0$ schedule shifts to the right. The opposite holds if a falls short of a^g.

The long-run equilibrium point D shown in figure 2.2 (as well as in figure 2.4) corresponds to the bench-mark case (used in the short-run analysis) in which the private sector's marginal propensity to import out of *income* equals that of the public sector (so that $a = a^g$). Under such circumstances the private sector's marginal propensity to import out of *spending*, $\bar{a}$, exceeds a^g, and therefore the balanced-budget rise in government spending shifts the $TA = 0$ schedule to the right.

In characterizing the long-run effects of fiscal policies, it is convenient to consider the case in which the initial $TA = 0$ schedule in figure 2.2 goes through the origin. As seen from equation (2.30a), this arises if the initial levels of domestic and foreign government spending are such that $(a^g - \bar{a})G = (a^{g^*} - \bar{a}^*)G^*$. This initial configuration is indicated in figure 2.2 by the parameteric value of G_0 which is held constant along the $TA = 0$ schedule. In that case a balanced-budget rise in domestic government spending is *neutral* in its long-run effects on the distribution of world outputs if $\bar{a} = a^g$ since it raises both domestic and foreign outputs equiproportionally. On the other hand, if $\bar{a}$ exceeds a^g, then the long-run output effects of the domestic fiscal expansion are *home-output biased*. In that case (indicated by point D in figure 2.2) the percentage long-run rise in domestic output exceeds the corresponding foreign rise. In the opposite case in which $\bar{a}$ falls short of a^g, the long-run output effects of the domestic fiscal expansion are *foreign-output biased*.

An additional factor determining whether the long-run effects are neutral or biased is the initial level of domestic and foreign government spending. For example, if initially foreign government spending is zero while the level of spending by the domestic government is positive, and if $\bar{a} = a^g$, then the $TA = 0$ schedule intersects the horizontal axis to the right of the origin. In that case a balanced-budget rise in domestic government spending biases the long-run distribution of outputs in favor of the foreign country.

The formal solutions for the long-run effects of the balanced-budget rise in government spending on outputs and on the distribution of the world money supply (as implied by equations A.14 through A.16 of the appendix) are

$$\frac{dY}{dG} = 1 - \frac{s^*(1-s)a^g}{sa^* + s^*a}, \tag{2.42}$$

$$\frac{dY^*}{dG} = \frac{s(1-s^*)a^g}{sa^* + s^*a}, \tag{2.43}$$

$$\frac{dM}{dG} = -\frac{ss^*a^g}{sa^* + s^*a}, \tag{2.44}$$

Equation (2.42) indicates that the direction of the long-run effects of the fiscal expansion on domestic output depends on the magnitude of the government import propensity. As is evident, if the government import propensity, a^g, does not exceed the private-sector propensity, a, then domestic output must rise in the long run. Equations (2.43) and (2.44) show that in the long run foreign output rises, and the world money supply is redistributed toward the foreign country (unless government spending falls only on domestic goods).

Finally, we note that in the long run world output changes according to

$$\frac{d(Y + Y^*)}{dG} = 1 + \frac{(s - s^*)a^g}{sa^* + s^*a}. \tag{2.45}$$

Thus the balanced-budget multiplier of world output exceeds or falls short of unity according to whether the domestic saving propensity exceeds or falls short of the foreign saving propensity.

A comparison between the short-run responses (equations 2.36 through 2.38) and the corresponding long-run responses (equations 2.42, 2.43, and 2.45) reflects the dynamic path of outputs during the adjustment periods. As seen from equations (2.32) and (2.33), the characteristics of the path depend on whether the ratio of the two saving propensities exceeds or falls short of the ratios of the domestic to the foreign propensities to spend on a given good. Accordingly, the long-run level of domestic output falls short of the level obtained in the short run if $s/s^* < c/a^*$, and vice versa. Likewise, the long-run level of foreign output exceeds the level obtained in the short run if $s/s^* > a/c^*$, and vice versa.

So far we have focused mainly on the output effects of fiscal policies. These effects are of interest especially as indicators of employment levels. In order to obtain indicators for private-sector spending, we need to determine the long-run effects of fiscal policies on disposable incomes. Equation (2.42) implies that the balanced-budget rise in the domestic government spending lowers the long-run level of domestic disposable income. Since in the long run private-sector spending equals disposable income, it follows that the domestic private-sector spending also falls in the long run. On the other hand, the foreign private sector, whose taxes have not changed, enjoys (as indicated by equation 2.43) a rise in its long-run disposable income and spending. Finally, using equations (2.42) and (2.43), the effect of the balanced-budget rise in government spending on the long-run level of world spending:

$$\frac{d(E + E^*)}{dG} = \frac{(s - s^*)a^g}{sa^* + s^*a}.$$ (2.46)

As seen, in the long run world private spending rises if the domestic saving propensity, s, exceeds the foreign propensity, s^*, and vice versa. A comparison between equations (2.46) and (2.39) shows that the short-run changes in world private spending (which may be positive or negative) are magnified in the long run.

2.7 Summary

In this chapter we developed the analytical framework underlying the income-expenditure model of the interdependent world economy. Throughout the analysis it was assumed that there is a single noninterest-bearing asset (money) that is held by both countries. The international monetary system was assumed to operate under a fixed exchange-rate regime, and the international distribution of the world money supply was shown to be effected through international payments imbalances.

Following the outline of the analytical framework, we have adapted the extreme version of the Keynesian assumptions by which prices were assumed to be given while output was assumed to be demand determined. To focus on the pure effects of fiscal policies, we have assumed that the government (which in the absence of interesting-bearing debt instruments can not finance its spending through debt issue) finances its spending through taxes rather than through monetary creation. Thus we have analyzed the effects of balanced-budget changes in government spending.

Throughout, we focused on the effects of fiscal policies on domestic output and private-sector spending as well as on foreign output and foreign spending. We drew a distinction between the short-run and long-run effects. In the short run the international distribution of the world money supply is given, whereas in the long run this distribution is endogenously determined so as to yield equality between income and spending in each country. Short-run discrepancies between income and spending yield international payments imbalances and generate a dynamic process by which the world money supply is redistributed internationally. We have demonstrated that the system of the world economy is dynamically stable. Thus the sequence of short-run equilibria converges to the long-run equilibrium.

The short-run and long-run effects of a unit balanced-budget rise in domestic government spending are summarized in table 2.1. It is seen that in the short run foreign output and spending rise while the level of the domestic private-sector spending falls. In the short run the balance of payments (which also equals the trade balance) deteriorates. This deterioration sets off the dynamic process of the redistribution of the world money supply toward the rest of the world. As is also shown in table 2.1, the short-run effects on the level of domestic output depend critically on the spending patterns of the government. If the import propensity of the government does not

Table 2.1
The effect of a unit balanced-budget rise in domestic government spending

	Y	Y^*	E	E^*	TA	M
Short run	$1 - \dfrac{s^* a^g}{\Delta}$	$\dfrac{s a^a}{\Delta}$	$-\dfrac{(1-s)s^* a^g}{\Delta}$	$\dfrac{(1-s^*)s a^g}{\Delta}$	$\dfrac{ss^* a^g}{\Delta}$	—
Long run	$1 - \dfrac{(1-s)s^* a^g}{\Delta - ss^*}$	$\dfrac{(1-s^*)s a^g}{\Delta - ss^*}$	$-\dfrac{(1-s)s^* a^g}{\Delta - ss^*}$	$\dfrac{(1-s^*)s a^g}{\Delta - ss^*}$	—	$-\dfrac{ss^* a^g}{\Delta - ss^*}$

Note: $\Delta = ss^* + sa^* + s^*a > 0$, where s, s^*, a, and a^* are, respectively, the domestic and foreign marginal propensities to save and import out of income and a^g is the domestic government import propensity.

exceed that of the private sector, domestic output rises in the short run. If, on the other hand, government spending falls heavily on foreign goods, then domestic output may fall.

The second line in table 2.1 shows the long-run effects. A comparison between the two lines reveals that the long-run changes in domestic and foreign output may exceed or fall short of the short-run changes. The key factors determining whether the long-run changes magnify or dampen the corresponding short-run changes are the relations between the ratio of the two countries' saving propensities and the ratios of the two countries' spending propensities on domestic and foreign goods.

The comparison between the long- and the short-run changes in the levels of domestic and foreign private-sector spending shows that the short-run changes are always magnified in the long run. The mechanism responsible for this magnification is the redistribution of the world money supply occurring throughout the adjustment process. This dynamic process of the monetary flows is effected through payments imbalances. The cumulative imbalances characterizing the sequence of short-run equilibria are reflected in the long-run change in each country's money holding. The factor of magnification linking short-run and long-run changes in spending manifests itself in the link between the short-run payments imbalance and the ultimate long-run change in money holdings.

2.8   Appendix

In this appendix we derive the short-run and the long-run solutions for the income-expenditure model of output determination. The equilibrium conditions (2.15) and (2.16) (for fixed $p_{mt} = P_t = P_t^* = e = 1$) are

$$(1 - \beta_m)E(Y_t - G, M_{t-1}) + (1 - \beta_m^g)G$$

$$+ \beta_x^* E^*(Y_t^* - G^*, \overline{M} - M_{t-1}) + \beta_x^{g^*}G^* = Y_t, \tag{A.1}$$

$$\beta_m E(Y_t - G, M_{t-1}) + \beta_m^g G + (1 - \beta_x^*)E^*(Y_t^* - G^*, \overline{M} - M_{t-1})$$

$$+ (1 - \beta_x^{g^*})G^* = Y_t^*. \tag{A.2}$$

Differentiating this system yields

$$\begin{pmatrix} -(s+a) & a^* \\ a & -(s^*+a^*) \end{pmatrix}\begin{pmatrix} dY_t \\ dY_t^* \end{pmatrix} = \begin{pmatrix} a^g - a - s \\ a - a^g \end{pmatrix} dG$$

$$+ \begin{bmatrix} \dfrac{a^*}{1-s^*}\gamma_z^* - \left(\dfrac{1-s-a}{1-s}\right)\gamma_z \\[2ex] \left(\dfrac{1-s^*-a^*}{1-s^*}\right)\gamma_z^* - \dfrac{a}{(1-s)}\gamma_z \end{bmatrix} dM_{t-1}, \qquad (A.3)$$

where γ_z and γ_z^* denote, respectively, the domestic and foreign marginal propensities to spend out of assets and where $\beta_m = a/(1-s)$ and $\beta_x^* = a^*/(1-s^*)$. In the case analyzed in the text, we have assumed that the marginal propensities to spend out of income and assets are equal to each other so that $\gamma_z = 1 - s$ and $\gamma_z^* = 1 - s^*$.

The Short Run

The *short-run* equilibrium changes in the values of domestic and foreign outputs in response to a balanced-budget change in domestic government spending are

$$\frac{dY_t}{dG} = 1 - \frac{s^* a^g}{\Delta_s}, \qquad (A.4)$$

$$\frac{dY_t^*}{dG} = \frac{s a^g}{\Delta_s} > 0, \qquad (A.5)$$

where $\Delta_s = ss^* + sa^* + s^*a > 0$.

The short-run equilibrium responses of domestic and foreign outputs to a redistribution of the world money supply are

$$\frac{dY_t}{dM_{t-1}} = \frac{1}{\Delta_s}\left[a^*(\gamma_z - \gamma_z^*) + s^*\left(\frac{1-s-a}{1-s}\gamma_z - \frac{a^*}{1-s^*}\gamma_z^*\right)\right], \qquad (A.6)$$

$$\frac{dY_t^*}{dM_{t-1}} = \frac{1}{\Delta_s}\left[a(\gamma_z - \gamma_z^*) + s\left(\frac{a}{1-s}\gamma_z - \frac{1-s^*-a^*}{1-s^*}\gamma_z^*\right)\right]. \qquad (A.7)$$

The balance-of-trade equation in a differentiated form (corresponding to equation 2.24) is

$$d(TA)_t = (a^* dY_t^* - a dY_t) - (a^g - a) dG$$

$$- \left(\frac{a^*}{1 - s^*} \gamma_z^* + \frac{a}{1 - s} \gamma_z \right) dM_{t-1}. \tag{A.8}$$

Substituting equations (A.4) and (A.5) into (A.8) yields

$$\frac{d(TA)_t}{dG} = -\frac{ss^* a^g}{\Delta_s} < 0. \tag{A.9}$$

Similarly, substituting equations (A.6) and (A.7) into (A.8) yields

$$\frac{d(TA)_t}{dM_{t-1}} = - \left(\frac{a}{1 - s} s^* \gamma_z + \frac{a^*}{1 - s^*} s \gamma_z^* \right). \tag{A.10}$$

Finally, using equation (A.10) along with the definition $M_t - M_{t-1} = (TA)_t$ yields

$$\frac{dM_t}{dM_{t-1}} = \frac{ss^* + sa^*[1 - \gamma_z^*/(1 - s^*)] + s^* a[1 - \gamma_z/(1 - s)]}{ss^* + sa^* + s^* a}. \tag{A.11}$$

Equation (A.9) implies that the impact effect of a (balanced-budget) rise in government spending is to worsen the trade account (as long as $a^g > 0$). Equation (A.11) is the stability condition of the system. As is evident for the case analyzed in the text ($\gamma_z = 1 - s$ and $\gamma_z^* = 1 - s^*$), dM_t/dM_{t-1} must be a positive fraction, and stability is ensured. In the general case of equation (A.11) a convergence to long-run stationary equilibrium requires that

$$2ss^* > sa^* \left(\frac{\gamma_z^*}{1 - s^*} - 1 \right) + s^* a \left(\frac{\gamma_z}{1 - s} - 1 \right). \tag{A.12}$$

Hence, if the spending propensities out of income do not fall short of the spending propensity out of assets, the sequence of short-run equilibria converges to the long-run equilibrium.

The Long Run

Long-run equilibrium requires that in addition to market clearing of domestic and foreign goods, the balance of payments is balanced so that $M_{t-1} = M_t = M$, $M_{t-1}^* = M_t^* = \overline{M} - M$ (where $\overline{M}$ denotes the given world money supply), and the levels of output are stationary so that $Y_t = Y$ and $Y_t^* = Y^*$. Imposing the requirement of trade-balance equilibrium into equation (A.8), and supplementing the system (A.3) with this additional condition, we obtain the differentiated form of the long-run equilibrium conditions. This system is

$$
\begin{bmatrix}
-(s+a) & a^* & \dfrac{1-s-a}{1-s}\gamma_z - \dfrac{a^*}{1-s^*}\gamma_z^* \\[2ex]
a & -(s^*+a^*) & \dfrac{a}{1-s}\gamma_z - \dfrac{1-s^*-a^*}{1-s^*}\gamma_z^* \\[2ex]
-a & a^* & -\left(\dfrac{a}{1-s}\gamma_z + \dfrac{a^*}{1-s^*}\gamma_z^*\right)
\end{bmatrix}
\begin{bmatrix}
dY \\[2ex]
dY^* \\[2ex]
dM
\end{bmatrix}
$$

$$
=
\begin{bmatrix}
a^g - a - s \\[1ex]
-(a^g - a) \\[1ex]
a^g - a
\end{bmatrix}
dG.
\tag{A.13}
$$

The *long-run* changes in the values of domestic and foreign outputs and in the domestic money holdings (induced by the cummulative redistribution of the given world money supply) are

$$
\frac{dY}{dG} = 1 - \frac{\gamma_z s^* a^g}{\Delta_L},
\tag{A.14}
$$

$$
\frac{dY^*}{dG} = \frac{\gamma_z^* s a^g}{\Delta_L} > 0,
\tag{A.15}
$$

$$
\frac{dM}{dG} = -\frac{s s^* a^g}{\Delta_L} < 0,
\tag{A.16}
$$

where

$$
\Delta_L = \frac{\gamma_z s^*}{1-s} a + \frac{\gamma_z^* s}{1-s^*} a^* > 0.
$$

3

The Mundell-Fleming Model: Deterministic Dynamics

For the past three decades, the "workhorse" model of international macroeconomics has been the Mundell-Fleming model. The foundations of this model of international macroeconomics were laid during the 1960s by Mundell (1960, 1963), and Fleming (1962). It provides a systematic analysis of the role played by international capital mobility in determining the effectiveness of fiscal and monetary policies under alternative exchange rate regimes (for an exposition and evaluation, see Frenkel and Razin 1987a). The model extends the simple Keynesian approach to output determination by incorporating considerations of asset-market equilibrium.

To provide an overview consider the extreme case of capital market integration and suppose that arbitrage among identical assets denominated in domestic and foreign currencies ensures complete interest parity. Accordingly, $(1 + r) - (e^f/e)(1 + r_f)$, where r and r_f denote, respectively, the rates of interest on domestic and foreign securities identical in all respects except for the currency of denomination; and e and e^f denote, respectively, the current and the expected future exchange rates (the price of foreign exchange in terms of domestic currency).

Consider first the flexible exchange rate regime. Panel I of figure 3.1 shows the relation between the current exchange rate, e, and the domestic rate of interest, r, implied by interest arbitrage, for given values of the expected future exchange rate, e^f, and the foreign rate of interest, r_f. The positively sloped schedule, LM, in panel II, is the conventional money market equilibrium schedule, and the negatively sloped schedule, IS, is the goods market equilibrium schedule,

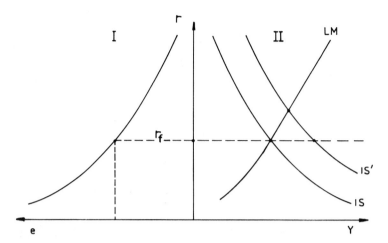

Figure 3.1
The Mundell-Fleming model

adopted to the open economy and adjusted to incorporate the interest parity relation. A current transitory fiscal expansion that does
not alter expectations concerning the future value of the exchange
rate induces a rightward shift of the IS schedule, raises the level of
output (under the Keynesian assumptions of price rigidity) and induces a rise in the domestic rate of interest. In order to maintain
interest parity, the rise in the rate of interest results in an appreciation of the domestic currency (a fall in e). As is evident, the rise in
the rate of interest (and the associated appreciation of the domestic
currency) crowds out some domestic absorption, worsens the current account position, and mitigates the expansion of output. In
contrast, if the fiscal expansion is permanent and expectations
accordingly adjust, then the expected future exchange rate, e^f, falls
to conform with the fall in e. Consequently, the IS schedule which
has shifted rightward as a result of the fiscal expansion, is shifted
back leftward due to the deterioration of the balance of trade caused
by the appreciation of the future value of the currency. It follows
that a fiscal expansion that is reflected in a current and future appreciation of the currency loses its effectiveness in altering the level of
output. If both current and future exchange rates change in the same

proportion, then the domestic rate of interest cannot deviate from the foreign rate and fiscal policy becomes completely ineffective. In the absence of debt revaluation effects the flexible exchange rate permits almost full insulation of the foreign economy from the consequences of the domestic tax-financed fiscal policies (see Frankel and Razin 1987b).

Under a fixed exchange rate interest arbitrage ensures equality between domestic and foreign rates of interest (because $e = e^f$). Consequently, a fiscal expansion that induces a rightward shift of the IS schedule gains full potency in raising the level of output, because the offsetting force induced by currency appreciation is absent. The commitment to the maintenance of the fixed exchange rate ensures that the rise in the demand for money, caused by the rise in economic activity, is fully satisfied through a complete monetization of the capital inflows induced by the upward pressure on the domestic rate of interest. If the home country is relatively large in the world economy, then the rise in the demand for money would necessitate a rise in the world rate of interest which would mitigate the fiscally led expansion of domestic economic activity. The rise in the rate of interest under a fixed exchange rate regime is sharper than under a flexible exchange rate regime because in the former the deterioration of the home country's competitive position (caused by its currency appreciation) reduces the expansionary effect of the fiscal policy and thereby diminishes the growth of money demand. It is also evident that a shift from a flexible to a fixed exchange rate regime amplifies the factors responsible for a negative transmission of domestic fiscal expansion to the output in the rest of the world.

The foregoing exposition of fiscal policies in open economies has aimed at highlighting key channels of international transmission under alternative exchange rate regimes. Other considerations relevant for the international effects of fiscal policies include debt versus tax-finance of government budgets, domestic and international debt-revaluation effects induced by the exchange rate changes, distinctions between short- and long-term multipliers, formulation of exchange rate expectations, the role of wage and price flexibility, risk and international capital mobility, and portfolio choice (for an incorporation of these elements, see Frenkel and Razin 1987b).

In this chapter we extend the analytical framework used in chapter 2 in two dimensions. First, we expand the menu of assets by adding interest-bearing bonds to the portfolio of assets. Second, we assume that the world capital markets are highly integrated and that all bonds are internationally tradable. The inclusion of interest-bearing bonds permits an analysis of the consequences of debt-financed changes in government spending. These consequences can then be compared with those of tax-financed changes in government spending. In conformity with the analysis in chapter 2 we continue to assume that the prices (GDP deflators) are fixed and that the levels of output are demand determined. In this context we analyze the short- and long-run effects of fiscal policies under fixed and flexible exchange-rate regimes.

As in chapter 2 the fixity of the GDP deflators implies that exchange-rate changes alter the relative prices of the domestically produced goods in terms of the foreign-produced goods (i.e., the terms of trade). Here, due to the expanded menu of assets traded in the integrated world capital market, exchange-rate changes impact on the economic system through two additional channels. First, they alter the real value of existing debts. Second, they influence expectations and thereby impact on the desired composition of the portfolio of assets. Thus the inclusion of interest-bearing assets and international capital mobility introduces new mechanisms governing the effects of fiscal policies and their international transmission.

3.1 The Analytical Framework

In specifying the behavioral functions, it is convenient to focus on the domestic economy. Accordingly, the budget constraint is

$$Z_t + M_t - B_t^p = P_t(Y_t - T_t) + M_{t-1} - R_{t-1}B_{t-1}^p, \tag{3.1}$$

where B_{t-1}^p denotes the domestic-currency value of private-sector's one-period debt issued in period t, and R_t denotes one plus the rate of interest. Analogously to equation (2.1) of chapter 2, the right-hand side of equation (3.1) states that in each period, t, the resources available to individuals are composed of disposable income, $P_t(Y_t - T_t)$—where for notational convenience we denote domestic output, Y_{xt}, by Y_t—and the net value of assets carried over from period $t - 1$. The latter consist of money, M_{t-1}, net of debt commitment $R_{t-1}B^p_{t-1}$ (including principal plus interest payments). For subsequent use we denote these assets by A_{t-1}, where

$$A_{t-1} = M_{t-1} - R_{t-1}B^p_{t-1}. \tag{3.2}$$

The left-hand side of equation (3.1) indicates the uses of these resources including nominal spending, Z_t, money holding, M_t, and bond holding, $-B^p_t$.

Throughout this chapter we assume that the GDP deflator, P_t, is fixed and normalized to unity. In that case nominal spending also equals real spending, E_t. Due to the absence of changes in prices we identify the real rate of interest, $r_t = R_t - 1$, with the corresponding nominal rate of interest (we return to this issue later in the chapter where we analyze the implications of exchange-rate changes).

Assuming that the various demand functions depend on the available resources and on the rate of interest, we express the spending and the money-demand function as

$$E_t = E(Y_t - T_t + A_{t-1}, r_t), \tag{3.3}$$

$$M_t = M(Y_t - T_t + A_{t-1}, r_t). \tag{3.4}$$

In specifying these functions, we have used a simplification similar to the one underlying equation (2.20) in chapter 2; we assume that the marginal propensities to spend and to hoard out of disposable income are the same as the corresponding propensities to spend and hoard out of assets. A similar specification underlines the demand for bonds which is omitted due to the budget constraint. We assume that desired spending and money holdings depend positively on available resources and negatively on the rate of interest.

A similar set of demand functions characterizes the foreign economy, where, as before, its variables are denoted by an asterisk and where its fixed GDP deflator, P^*, is normalized to unity. The specification of the equilibrium in the world economy depends on the exchange-rate regime. We start with the analysis of equilibrium under a fixed exchange-rate regime.

3.2   Capital Mobility with Fixed Exchange Rates

Equilibrium in the world economy necessitates that the markets for goods, money, and bonds clear. Under a fixed exchange rate, domestic and foreign money (in their role as assets) are perfect substitutes. Therefore money-market equilibrium can be specified by a single equilibrium relation stating that the world demand for money equals the world supply. Likewise, the assumptions that bonds are internationally tradable assets and that the current and future exchange rates are equal imply that in equilibrium these bonds command the same real return, $r_t = r_{ft}$, and that bond-market equilibrium can also be specified by a single equation pertaining to the unified world bond market. These considerations imply that the world economy is characterized by four markets: the markets for domestic output, foreign output, world money, and world bonds. By Walras's law we omit the bond market from the equilibrium specification of the two-country model of the world economy. Accordingly, the equilibrium conditions are

$$(1 - \beta_m)E(Y_t - T_t + A_{t-1}, r_t) + (1 - \beta_m^g)G + \beta_x^* \bar{e}E^*(Y_t^* + A_{t-1}^*, r_t)$$

$$= Y_t, \tag{3.5}$$

$$\beta_m E(Y_t - T_t + A_{t-1}, r_t) + \beta_m^g G + (1 - \beta_x^*)\bar{e}E^*(Y_t^* + A_{t-1}^*, r_t)$$

$$= \bar{e}Y_t^*, \tag{3.6}$$

$$M(Y_t - T_t + A_{t-1}, r_t) + \bar{e}M^*(Y_t^* + A_{t-1}^*, r_t) = \overline{M}, \tag{3.7}$$

where we continue to assume that foreign government spending and taxes are zero and where $\bar{e}$ denotes the fixed exchange rate expressing the price of foreign currency in terms of domestic currency. The (predetermined) value of foreign assets is measured in foreign-currency units so that $A_{t-1}^* = M_{t-1}^* + R_{t-1}B_{t-1}^p/\bar{e}$. Due to the assumed fixity of the GDP deflators, $\bar{e}$ also measures the relative price of importables in terms of exportables (defined in equation 2.18). As before, $\overline{M}$ denotes the world supply of money, measured in terms of domestic goods (whose domestic-currency price is unity); we continue to assume that the government does not finance its spending through money creation. Here it is relevant to note that in contrast with the analysis in chapter 2, the presence of capital markets permits discrepancies between spending and taxes which is made up for by debt issue.

The specification of the equilibrium system (3.5) through (3.7) embodies the arbitrage condition by which the yields on domestic and foreign bonds are equal. This equality justifies the use of the same rate of interest in the behavioral functions of the domestic and the foreign economies. The system (3.5) through (3.7) determines the short-run equilibrium values of domestic output, Y_t, foreign output, Y_t^*, and the world rate of interest, r_t, for given (predetermined) values of domestic and foreign net assets, A_{t-1} and A_{t-1}^*, and for given levels of government spending, G_t, and taxes, T_t.

The international distribution of the given world money supply associated with the short-run equilibrium is determined *endogenously* according to the demands. Thus

$$M_t = M(Y_t - T_t + A_{t-1}, r_t), \tag{3.8}$$

$$M_t^* = M^*(Y_t^* + A_{t-1}^*, r_t). \tag{3.9}$$

This equilibrium distribution obtains through international asset swaps.

A comparison between this short-run equilibrium system and the one used in chapter 2 reveals the significant role played by international capital mobility. In the absence of such mobility the short-run equilibrium determines the levels of domestic and foreign output from the goods-market equilibrium conditions (2.15) and (2.16) of chapter 2. Associated with these levels of outputs are equilibrium monetary *flows*, as shown by equations (2.12) through (2.14) and (2.19). These flows cease in the long run in which a stationary equilibrium distribution of the world money supply obtains, as indicated by the long-run equilibrium condition (2.26). In contrast, the equilibrium system (3.5) through (3.7) shows that with perfect capital mobility equilibrium in the world money market obtains through instantaneous asset swaps involving exchanges of money for bonds. This instantaneous *stock* adjustments is reflected in equation (3.7).

Fiscal Policies in a Small Country

To illustrate the effects of fiscal policies under a regime of fixed exchange rates with perfect capital mobility, it is convenient to begin with an analysis of a small country facing a given world rate of interest, $\bar{r}_f$, and a given world demand for its goods, $\bar{D}^* = \beta_x^* E^*$. Under these circumstances the equilibrium condition for the small economy reduces to

$$(1 - \beta_m)(E(Y_t - T_t + A_{t-1}, \bar{r}_f) + (1 - \beta_m^g)G + \bar{e}\bar{D}^* = Y_t. \qquad (3.5a)$$

This equilibrium condition determines the short-run value of output for the given (predetermined) value of assets and for given levels of government spending and taxes. As before, the money supply, M_t, associated with this equilibrium is obtained from the money-market equilibrium condition (3.8a):

$$M(Y_t - T_t + A_{t-1}, \bar{r}_f) = M_t. \qquad (3.8a)$$

This quantity of money is endogenously determined through instantaneous asset swaps at the prevailing world rate of interest.

To analyze the effects of fiscal policies, we differentiate equation (3.5a). Thus

$$\frac{dY_t}{dG} = \frac{1 - a^g}{s + a} \qquad \text{for } dT_t = 0, \qquad (3.10)$$

and

$$\frac{dY_t}{dG} = 1 - \frac{a^g}{s + a} \qquad \text{for } dT_t = dG, \qquad (3.11)$$

where, as before, $a^g = \beta_m^g$ is the government marginal propensity to import, and $1/(s + a)$ is the small-country foreign-trade multiplier. Equations (3.10) and (3.11) correspond, respectively, to a bond-financed and a tax-financed rise in government spending. As is evident, if all of government spending falls on domestic goods (so that $a^g = 0$), then the fiscal expansion that is financed by government borrowing raises output by the full extent of the foreign trade multiplier, while the balanced-budget fiscal expansion yields the closed-economy balanced-budget multiplier of unity. If, on the other hand, all of government spending falls on imported goods (so that $a^g = 1$), then the bond-financed multiplier is zero, whereas the balanced-budget multiplier is negative and equal to $(s + a - 1)/(s + a)$.

The changes in output induce changes in the demand for money. The induced changes in money holding can be found by differentiating equation (3.8a) and using (3.10) and (3.11). Accordingly, the debt-financed unit rise in government spending raises money holdings by $(1 - a^g)M_y/(s + a)$ units, and the balanced-budget rise in government spending lowers money holdings by $a^g M_y/(s + a)$.

This analysis is summarized by figure 3.2 in which the IS schedule portrays the goods-market equilibrium condition (3.5a). It is negatively sloped since both a rise in the rate of interest and a rise in output create an excess supply of goods. The initial equilibrium obtains at point A at which the rate of interest equals the exogenously given world rate, $\bar{r}_f$, and the level of output is Y_0. As indicated, the schedule IS is drawn for given levels of government spending and taxes, G_0 and T_0. The LM schedule passing through point A portrays the money-market equilibrium condition (3.8a). It is positively sloped since a rise in income raises the demand for money, whereas a rise in the rate of interest lowers the money demand. As indicated, the LM schedule is drawn for a given level of (the endogenously determined) money stock, M_0.

A unit rise in government spending creates an excess demand for domestic product (at the prevailing level of output). If it is bond financed, then the excess demand is $1 - a^g$ units, and if it is tax financed, then the excess demand is of $s + a - a^g$ units (which, depending on the relative magnitudes of the parameters, may be

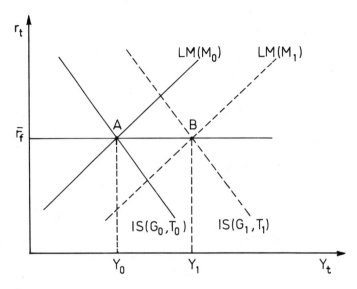

Figure 3.2
The short-run effects of fiscal policy under fixed exchange rates: The small-country case

negative). The excess demand is reflected by a horizontal shift of the IS schedule from $IS(G_0)$ to $IS(G_1)$. As drawn, the IS schedule shifts to the right, reflecting the positive excess demand at the prevailing level of output. The new equilibrium obtains at point B, at which the level of output rises to Y_1. This higher level of output raises the demand for money, which is met instantaneously through an international swap of bonds for money that is effected through the world capital markets. The endogenous rise in the quantity of money from M_0 to M_1 is reflected in the corresponding rightward displacement of the LM schedule from $LM(M_0)$ to $LM(M_1)$.

The foregoing analysis determined the *short-run* consequences of an expansionary fiscal policy. The instantaneous asset swaps induced by the requirement of asset-market equilibrium alter the size of the economy's external debt. Specifically, if initially the economy was in a long-run equilibrium (so that $B_t^p = B_{t-1}^p = B^p$, $M_t = M_{t-1} = M$, $A_t = A_{t-1} = A$, and $Y_t = Y_{t-1} = Y$), then the fiscal expansion, which raises short-run money holdings as well as the size of the external debt, raises the debt-service requirement and (in view of the positive rate of interest) lowers the value of net assets $M_t - (1 + \bar{r}_f)B_t^p$ carried over to the subsequent period. This change sets in motion a dynamic process that is completed only when the economy reaches its new long-run equilibrium. We turn next to determine the long-run consequences of government spending.

The long-run equilibrium conditions can be summarized by the system (3.12) through (3.14):

$$E[Y - T + M - (1 + \bar{r})B^p, \bar{r}_f] = Y - \bar{r}_f B^p - T, \tag{3.12}$$

$$(1 - \beta_m)E[Y - T + M - (1 + \bar{r}_f)B^p, \bar{r}_f] + (1 - \beta_m^g)G + \bar{e}\bar{D}^*$$
$$= Y, \tag{3.13}$$

$$M[Y - T + M - (1 + \bar{r}_f)B^p, \bar{r}_f] = M, \tag{3.14}$$

where the omission of the time subscripts indicates that in the long run the various variables do not vary over time. Equation (3.12) is obtained from the budget constraint (3.1) by using the spending function from equation (3.3) and by imposing the requirement that in the long run $M_t = M_{t-1}$ and $B_t^p = B_{t-1}^p$. This equation states that in the long run, private-sector spending equals disposable income, so that private-sector savings are zero. Equation (3.13) is obtained from (3.5a) and (3.8a) together with the long-run stationary requirement. This equation is the long-run market-clearing condition for domestic output. Finally, equation (3.14), which is the long-run counterpart to equation (3.8a), is the condition for long-run money-market equilibrium.

Up to this point we have not incorporated explicitly the government budget constraint. In the absence of money creation the long-run government budget constraint states that government outlays on purchases, G, and debt service, $\bar{r}_f B^g$ (where B^g denotes government debt), must equal taxes, T. Accordingly,

$$G + \bar{r}_f B^g = T. \tag{3.15}$$

Substituting this constraint into equation (4.12) yields

$$E[Y - G + M - B^p - \bar{r}_f(B^p + B^g), \bar{r}_f] + G$$

$$= Y - \bar{r}_f(B^p + B^g). \qquad (3.12a)$$

Equation (3.12a) states that in the long run the sum of private-sector and government spending equals GNP. This equality implies that in the long run the current account of the balance of payments is balanced.

Using equations (3.12), (3.14), and (3.15), we obtain the combinations of output and debt that satisfy the long-run requirement of current-account balance as well as money-market equilibrium. These combinations are portrayed along the $CA = 0$ schedule in figure 3.2. Likewise, using equations (3.13) through (3.15), we obtain the combinations of output and debt that incorporate the requirements of goods- and money-market equilibrium. These combinations are portrayed along the YY schedule in figure 3.2. The slopes of these schedules are

$$\frac{dB^p}{dY} = -\frac{(s - M_y)}{(1 - s) - \bar{r}_f(s - M_y)} \qquad \text{along the } CA = 0 \text{ schedule,}$$

$$(3.16)$$

$$\frac{dB^p}{dY} = -\frac{(s - M_y) + a}{(1 + \bar{r}_f)(1 - s - a)} \qquad \text{along the } YY \text{ schedule.} \qquad (3.17)$$

The term M_y is the marginal propensity to hoard (the inverse of the marginal income velocity) and $s - M_y$ represents the marginal propensity to save in the form of bonds. As is evident, the numerators in equations (3.16) and (3.17) are positive. The denominator of equation (3.17) is positive since $1 - s - a > 0$, and the denominator of equation (3.16) is positive on the assumption that $(1 - s) > \bar{r}_f(s - M_y)$. The latter assumption is a (partial) stability condition, ensuring that the perpetual rise in consumption $(1 - s)$ made possible by a unit rise in debt exceeds the perpetual return on the saving in bonds $\bar{r}_f(s - M_y)$ made possible by the initial unit rise in debt. (The condition for full stability is not explored). If this inequality does not hold, then consumption and debt rise overtime and do not converge to a long-run stationary equilibrium. The foregoing discus-

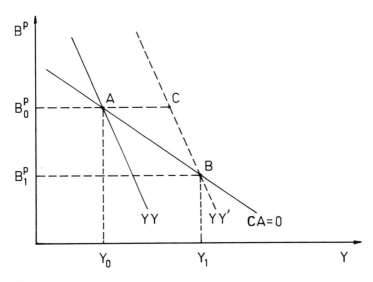

Figure 3.3
The long-run effects of a unit debt-financed rise in government spending under fixed exchange rates: The small-country case

sion implies that the slopes of both the $CA = 0$ and the YY schedules are negative. Further, since the numerator of (3.17) exceeds the one in (3.16) and the denominator of (3.17) is smaller than the one is (3.16), the YY schedule in figure 3.3 is steeper than the $CA = 0$ schedule. The initial long-run equilibrium is indicated by point A in figure 3.2 in which the levels of output and private-sector debt are Y_0 and B_0^p.

Consider the long-run effects of a *debt-financed* rise in government spending. As is evident by inspection of the system (3.12) through (3.14), as long as taxes remain unchanged, the $CA = 0$, which is derived from equations (3.12) and (3.14), remains intact. On the other hand, the rise in government spending influences the YY schedule, which is derived from equations (3.13) and (3.14). Specifically, to maintain goods-market equilibrium (for any given value of private-sector debt, B^p), a unit rise in government spending must be offset by $(1 - a^g)/(s + a)$ units rise in output. Thus, as long as some portion of government spending falls on domestic goods so that

$a^g < 1$, the YY schedule in figure 3.3 shifts to the right. The new equilibrium is indicated by point B at which the level of output rises from Y_0 to Y_1 and private-sector debt falls to B_1^p. The new equilibrium is associated with a rise in money holdings, representing the cumulative surpluses in the balance of payments during the transition period.

A comparison between the short-run multiplier shown in equation (3.10) and the corresponding long-run multiplier (shown in equation A.7 of appendix A) reveals that the latter exceeds the former. In terms of figure 3.3, in the short run the output effect of the debt-financed rise in government spending is indicated by the point C, whereas the corresponding long-run equilibrium is indicated by point B.

Consider next the effects of a *tax-financed* rise in government spending. Such a balanced-budget rise in spending alters the positions of both the $CA = 0$ and the YY schedules. Using equations (3.12) and (3.14) together with the balanced-budget assumption that $dG = dT$, it can be shown that a unit rise in government spending induces a unit rightward shift of the $CA = 0$ schedule. By keeping the value of $Y - T$ intact and holding B^p constant, such a shift maintains the equality between private-sector spending and disposable income, and it also satisfies the money-market equilibrium condition. Likewise, using equations (3.13) and (3.14) together with the balanced-budget assumption, it is shown in appendix A that as long as the government import propensity, a^g, is positive, the YY schedule shifts to the right by less than one unit. The resulting new long-run equilibrium is indicated by point B in figure 3.4. For the case drawn, the long-run level of output falls from Y_0 to Y_1, and private-sector debt rises from B_0^p to B_1^p. Since government debt remains unchanged, the rise in private-sector debt corresponds to an equal rise in the economy's external-debt position. In general, however, depending on the parameters, domestic output may either rise or fall in the long run.

The size of the long-run multiplier of the balanced-budget rise in government spending depends on the government import propensity. At the limit, if all government spending falls on domestic

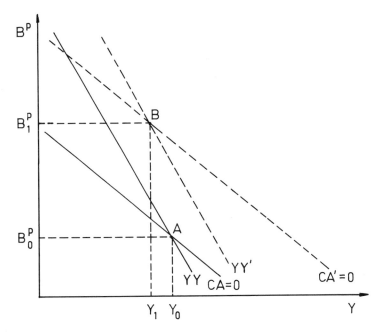

Figure 3.4
The long-run effect of a unit balanced-budget rise 1n government spending under fixed exchange rates: The small-country case

output so that $a^g = 0$, the long-run balanced-budget multiplier is unity. In this case the YY schedule in figure 3.4 shifts to the right by one unit, the long-run level of output rises by one unit, and private-sector debt (and the economy's external debt) remains unchanged. At the other limit, if all government spending falls on foreign goods so that $a^g = 1$, the long-run balanced-budget multiplier is negative. In that case the rise in the economy's external debt is maximized.

The comparison between the short-run balanced-budget multiplier shown in equation (3.11) with the corresponding long-run multiplier (shown in equation A.10 of appendix A) highlights the contrasts between the two. If the government propensity to spend on domestic goods $(1 - a^g)$ equals the corresponding private-sector propensity $(1 - s - a)$, then the short-run multiplier is zero while the long-run multiplier is negative. On the other hand, if the government propensity $(1 - a^g)$ exceeds the private sector propensity

$(1 - s - a)$, the short-run balanced-budget multiplier is positive, while the long-run balanced-budget multiplier is positive or negative. If both are positive, the short-run multiplier exceeds the long-run multiplier. Finally, if government spending falls entirely on domestically produced goods (so that $a^g = 0$), then the short-run and the long-run multipliers are equal to each other, and both are unity.

Fiscal Policies in a Two-Country World

In this section we return to the two-country model outlined in equations (3.5) through (3.7) and analyze the short-run effects of a debt and tax-financed rise in government spending on the equilibrium levels of domestic and foreign outputs as well as on the equilibrium world rate of interest. The endogeneity of the last two variables distinguishes this analysis from the one conducted for the small-country case. To conserve space, we do not analyze here the long-run effects; the formal system applicable to the long-run equilibrium of the two-country world is presented in appendix A.

The analysis is carried out diagrammatically with the aid of figures 3.4 and 3.5. In these figures the YY schedule portrays combinations of domestic and foreign levels of output that yield equality between the levels of production of domestic output and the world demand for it. Likewise, the Y^*Y^* schedule portrays combinations of output that yield equality between the level of production of foreign output and the world demand for it. The two schedules incorporate the requirement of equilibrium in the world money market. It is shown in appendix A that the slopes of these schedules are

$$\frac{dY_t^*}{dY_t} = \frac{1}{\bar{e}} \frac{(s + a)(M_r + \bar{e}M_r^*) + M_y H_r}{a^*(M_r + \bar{e}M_r^*) - M_{y^*}^* H_r} \quad \text{along the } YY \text{ schedule,}$$

$$(3.18)$$

$$\frac{dY_t^*}{dY_t} = \frac{1}{\bar{e}} \frac{a(M_r + \bar{e}M_r^*) - M_y F_r}{(s^* + a^*)(M_r + \bar{e}M_r^*) + M_{y^*}^* F_r} \quad \text{along the } Y^*Y^* \text{ schedule,}$$

$$(3.19)$$

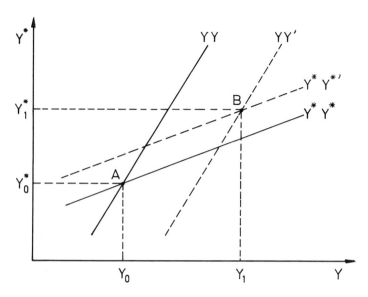

Figure 3.5
A unit debt-financed rise in government spending under fixed exchange rates: The two-country case

where H_r and F_r denote the partial (negative) effect of the rate of interest on the world demand for domestic and foreign outputs, respectively, and where E_r, M_r, E_r, and M_r^* denote the partial (negative) effects of the world rate of interest on domestic and foreign spending and money demand. As may be seen, the slopes of the two schedules may be positive or negative. To gain intuition, we note that the new element introduced in this chapter, which was absent from the analysis in chapter 2, is the role played by the market clearing world rate of interest in influencing spending. Indeed, in the special case for which spending does not depend on the rate of interest (so that $H_r = F_r = 0$), the slopes of the schedules indicated in equations (3.18) and (3.19) coincide with the slopes indicated in equations (2.22) and (2.23). Thus in that case both schedules must be positively sloped. If, on the other hand, the rate of interest exerts a strong negative effect on world spending, then the excess supply induced by a rise in one country's output may have to be eliminated by a fall in the other country's output. Even though this fall in foreign output lowers directly the foreign demand for the first country's exports, it also induces a decline in the world rate of interest which indirectly stimulates spending and may more than offset the direct reduction in demand. In that case market clearance for each country's output implies that domestic and foreign outputs are negatively related.

Even though the two schedules may be positively or negatively sloped, it may be verified (and is shown in appendix A) that if the two schedules have the same sign, then the YY schedule must be steeper than the Y^*Y^* schedule in absolute value. This restriction leaves four possible configurations of the schedules. The common characteristic of these configurations is that starting from an initial equilibrium, if there is a rightward shift of the YY schedule that exceeds the rightward shift of the Y^*Y^* schedule, then the new equilibrium must be associated with a higher level of domestic output.

Two cases capturing the general pattern of world-output allocations are shown in figures 3.5 and 3.6. The other possible configurations do not yield different qualitative results concerning the effects of fiscal policies. In both figures the initial equilibrium is indicated by point A at which the domestic level of output is Y_0 and the foreign level is Y_0^*.

A debt-financed rise in government spending raises the demand for domestic output and induces a rightward shift of the YY schedule from YY to YY'. On the other hand, the direction of the change in the position of the Y^*Y^* schedule depends on the relative magnitudes of the two conflicting effects influencing world demand for foreign output. On the one hand, the rise in the domestic government spending raises the demand for foreign goods, but on the other hand, the induced rise in the world rate of interest lowers the demand. If the Y^*Y^* schedule is positively sloped, as in figure 3.5, then the rise in the domestic government spending induces a leftward (upward) shift of the Y^*Y^* schedule. The opposite holds if the Y^*Y^* schedule is negatively sloped as in figure 3.6. The formal expressions indicating the magnitudes of the displacements of the schedules are provided in appendix A.

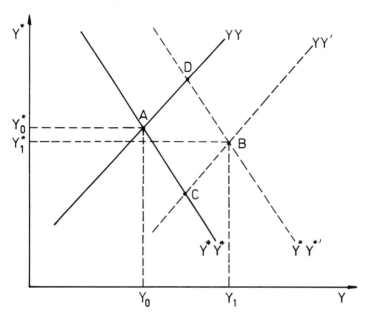

Figure 3.6
A unit debt-financed rise in government spending under fixed exchange rates: The two-country case

The new equilibrium obtains at point B at which domestic output rises from Y_0 to Y_1. In the case shown in figure 3.5 (for which the interest-rate effect on the world demand for foreign output is relatively weak) foreign output rises. On the other hand, in the case shown in figure 3.6 (for which the interest-rate effect on the world demand for foreign output is relatively strong) foreign output may rise or fall depending on the magnitudes of the parameters, especially the composition of government spending. For example, if government spending falls entirely on domestic output (so that $a^g = 0$), the Y^*Y^* schedule does not shift, and the new equilibrium obtains at a point like point C in figure 3.6 at which foreign output falls. In the other extreme, if government spending falls entirely on foreign goods (so that $a^g = 1$), then the YY schedule does not shift, and the new equilibrium obtains at a point like point D at which foreign output rises.

It is shown in appendix A that independent of the direction of output changes, the debt-financed rise in government spending must raise the world rate of interest. The expressions reported in the appendix also reveal that if the (negative) interest-rate effect on the world demand for domestic output is relatively strong, then domestic output might fall. The balance-of-payments effects of the debt-financed rise in government spending are not clear cut, reflecting transfer-problem criteria. But, if the behavioral parameters of the domestic and foreign private sectors are equal to each other, and the government spending falls chiefly, on domestic output, then the balance of payments must improve, and the domestic money holdings are raised.

A tax-financed rise in government spending also alters the positions of the various schedules, as shown in the appendix A where we also provide the formal expressions for the various multipliers. In general, in addition to the considerations highlighted in the debt-financed case, the effect of a tax-financed fiscal spending also reflects the effects of the reduction in domestic disposable income on aggregate demand. This effect may more than offset the influence of government spending on domestic output. The effect on foreign output is also modified. If the interest-rate effect on world demand for foreign output is relatively weak (the case underlying figure 3.5), then the shift from a debt to a tax finance mitigates the expansion in foreign output. If, on the other hand, the interest-rate effect on the demand for foreign output is relatively strong (the case underlying figure 3.6), then the shift from debt to tax finance exerts expansionary effects on foreign output.

It is shown in appendix A that the direction of the change in the rate of interest induced by the tax-financed rise in government spending depends on a transfer-problem criterion, indicating whether the redistribution of world disposable income consequent on the fiscal policy raises or lowers the world demand for money. Accordingly, the rate of interest rises if the domestic-country ratio, s/M_y, exceeds the corresponding foreign-country ratio, $s^*/M_{y^*}^*$, and vice versa. Independent, however, of the change in the rate of interest, the tax-financed rise in government spending must deteriorate the domestic-country balance of payments and reduce its money holdings.

3.3 Capital Mobility with Flexible Exchange Rates

In this section we assume that the world economy operates under a flexible exchange-rate regime. With this assumption national monies become nontradable assets whose relative price (the exchange rate, e) is assumed to be determined freely in the world market for foreign exchange. We continue to assume that in each country, the GDP deflators, P and P^*, are fixed and equal to unity. Under such circumstances the nominal exchange rates represent the terms of trade, and the nominal rates of interest in each country equal the corresponding (GDP-based) real rates. Further, as was traditionally postulated in the early literature on modeling macroeconomic policies in the world economy, we open the analysis by assuming that exchange-rate expectations are static. Under such circumstances the international mobility of capital brings about equality among national (GDP-based) real rates of interest. We return to the issue of exchange-rate expectations in a subsequent section.

Equilibrium in the world economy requires that world demand for each country's output equal the corresponding supply and that in each country the demand for cash balances equal the supply. Accordingly, the system characterizing the equilibrium in the two-country world economy is

$$(1 - \beta_m)E(Y_t - T_t + A_{t-1}, r_t) + (1 - \beta_m^g)G + e_t\beta_x^*E^*(Y_t^* + A_{t-1}^*, r_t)$$

$$= Y_t, \tag{3.20}$$

$$\beta_m E(Y_t - T_t + A_{t-1}, r_t) + \beta_m^g G + e_t(1 - \beta_x^*)E^*(Y_t^* + A_{t-1}^*, r_t)$$

$$= e_t Y_t^*, \tag{3.21}$$

$$M(Y_t - T_t + A_{t-1}, r_t) = M, \tag{3.22}$$

$$M^*(Y_t^* + A_{t-1}^*, r_t) = M^*. \tag{3.23}$$

Equations (3.20) and (3.21) are the goods-market equilibrium conditions (analogous to equations 3.5 and 3.6), and equations (3.22) and (3.23) are the domestic and foreign money-market equilibrium conditions, where M and M^* denote the supplies of domestic and foreign money. In contrast with the fixed exchange-rate system in which each country's money supply was determined endogenously, here it is determined *exogenously* by the monetary authorities. We also note that by Walras's law the world market equilibrium condition for bonds has been left out.

Finally, it is noteworthy that the value of securities may be expressed in terms of domestic or foreign currency units. Accordingly, the domestic-currency value of private-sector debt, B_t^p, can be expressed in units of foreign currency to yield $B_{ft}^p = B_t^p/e_t$. Arbitrage ensures that the expected rates of return on securities of different currency denomination are equalized. Accordingly, if r_t and r_{ft} are, respectively, the rates of interest on domestic- and foreign-currency-denominated bonds, then $1 + r_t = (\tilde{e}_{t+1}/e_t)(1 + r_{ft})$, where $\tilde{e}_{t+1}$ denotes the expected future exchange rate. By equating r_t to r_{ft}, the system (3.20) through (3.22) embodies the assumption of static exchange-rate expectations and perfect capital mobility. In appendix B we return to the issue of exchange-rate expectations.

Fiscal Policies in a Small Country

Analogously with our procedure in the analysis of fiscal policies under fixed exchange rates, we start the analysis of flexible exchange rates with an examination of the effects of fiscal policies in a small country facing a given world rate of interest, $\bar{r}_f$, and a given foreign demand for its goods, $\bar{D}^*$. The equilibrium conditions for the small country state that world demand for its output equals domestic GDP and that the domestic demand for money equals the supply. In contrast with the situation prevailing under a fixed exchange-rate regime where the monetary authorities, committed to peg the exchange rate, do not control the domestic money supply, under a flexible exchange-rate regime the supply of money is a policy instrument controlled by the monetary authorities.

The goods- and money-market equilibrium conditions are

$$(1 - \beta_m)E(Y_t - T_t + A_{t-1}, \bar{r}_f) + (1 - \beta_m^g)G + e_t\bar{D}^* = Y_t, \quad (3.20a)$$

$$M(Y_t - T_t + A_{t-1}, \bar{r}_f) = M, \quad (3.22a)$$

where

$$A_{t-1} = M_{t-1} - (1 + \bar{r}_f)e_t B_{f,t-1}^p.$$

As indicated, the valuation of the foreign-currency-denominated debt commitment, $(1 + \bar{r}_f)B_{f,t-1}^p$, employs the current exchange rate, e_t. These equilibrium conditions determine the short-run values of output and the exchange rate, and for comparison we recall that under the fixed exchange-rate regime the money supply rather than the exchange-rate was endogenously determined.

The equilibrium of the system is exhibited in figure 3.7. The downward-sloping IS schedule shows the goods-market equilibrium condition (3.20a). It is drawn for given values of government spending, taxes, and the exchange rate (representing the terms of trade). The upward-sloping LM schedule portrays the money-market equilibrium condition (3.22a). It is drawn for given values of the money supply, the exchange rate, and taxes. The initial equilibrium obtains at point A at which the rate of interest equals the world rate, $\bar{r}_f$, and the level of output is Y_0. The endogenously determined exchange rate associated with this equilibrium is e_0. It is relevant to note that in this system if the initial debt $B_{f,t-1}^p$ is zero, the LM schedule does not depend on the exchange rate and the level of output is determined exclusively by the money-market equilibrium condition, whereas (given the equilibrium level of output) the equilibrium exchange rate is determined by the goods-market equilibrium condition. This case underlies figure 3.7. Again a comparison with the fixed exchange-rate system is relevant. There, the equilibrium money stock is determined by the money-market equilibrium condition, whereas the equilibrium level of output is determined by the goods-market equilibrium condition.

Consider the effects of a debt-financed unit rise in government spending from G_0 to G_1, and suppose that the initial debt commitment

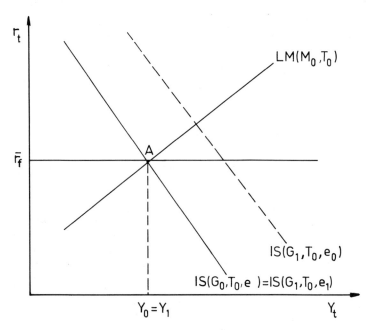

Figure 3.7
The short-run effects of a unit debt-financed rise in government spending under
flexible exchange rates: The small-country case

is zero. At the prevailing levels of output and the exchange rate, this
rise in spending creates an excess demand for domestic output and
induces a rightward shift of the IS schedule by $(1 - a^g)/(s + a)$
units. This shift is shown in figure 3.7 by the displacement of the
IS schedule from the initial position indicated by $IS(G_0, T_0, e_0)$ to
the position indicated by $IS(G_1, T_0, e_0)$. Since with zero initial debt
the LM schedule is unaffected by the rise in government spending, it
is clear that given the world rate of interest, the level of output that
clears the money market must remain at Y_0, corresponding to the
initial equilibrium indicated by point A. To restore the initial equilibrium in the goods market, the exchange rate must fall (i.e., the
domestic currency must appreciate). The induced improvement in
the terms of trade lowers the world demand for domestic output and
induces a leftward shift of the IS schedule. The goods market clears
when the exchange rate falls to e_1 so that the IS schedule indicated

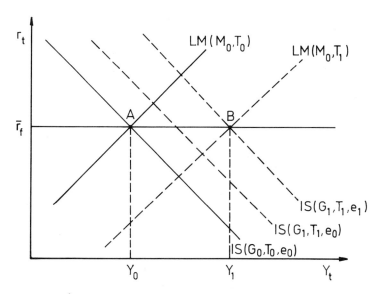

Figure 3.8
The short-run effects of a unit debt-financed rise in government spending under flexible exchange rates: The small-country case

by $IS(G_1, T_0, e_1)$ also goes through point A. We conclude that under flexible exchange rates with zero initial debt, a debt-financed fiscal policy loses its potency to alter the level of economic activity; its full effects are absorbed by changes in the exchange rate (the terms of trade).

Consider next the effects of a tax-financed unit rise in government spending from G_0 to G_1, shown in figure 3.8. In that case, at the prevailing levels of output and the exchange rate, the excess demand for domestic output induces a rightward displacement of the IS schedule by $1 - a^g/(s + a)$ units to the position indicated by $IS(G_1, T_1, e_0)$. In addition the unit rise in taxes lowers disposable income by one unit and reduces the demand for money. To maintain money-market equilibrium at the given world rate of interest, the level of output must rise by one unit so as to restore the initial level of disposable income. Thus the LM schedule shifts to the right from its initial position indicated by $LM(M_0, T_0)$ to the position indicated by $LM(M_0, T_1)$. With a zero level of initial debt (the case assumed in the figure), the LM schedule does not depend on the value of the exchange rate, and the new equilibrium obtains at point B, where the level of output rises by one unit from Y_0 to Y_1. Since at the initial exchange rate the horizontal displacement of the IS schedule is less than unity (as long as government spending falls in part on imported goods), it follows that at the level of output that clears the money market there is an excess supply of goods. This excess supply is eliminated through a rise in the exchange rate (i.e., a depreciation of the domestic currency) from e_0 to e_1. This deterioration in the terms of trade raises the world demand for domestic output and induces a rightward shift of the IS schedule to the position indicated by $IS(G_1, T_1, e_1)$. We conclude that under flexible exchange rates with zero initial debt, the tax-financed rise in government spending regains its full potency in effecting the level of economic activity.

Up to this point we have assumed that the initial debt position was zero. As a result the only channel through which the exchange rate influenced the system was through altering the domestic-currency value of the exogenously given foreign demand, $\overline{D}^*$. In general, however, with a nonzero level of initial debt, $B^p_{f,t-1}$ (denominated in units of foreign currency), the change in the exchange rate also alters the domestic currency value of the initial debt, and thereby of the initial assets, A_{t-1}. The revaluation of the debt commitment constitutes an additional channel through which the exchange rate influences the economic system. As a result the demand for money, and thereby the LM schedule, also depend on the exchange rate.

To appreciate the role played by debt-revaluation effects, we examine in figure 3.9 the implications of a nonzero level of initial debt. The various IS and LM schedules shown in the figure correspond to alternative assumptions concerning the level of initial debt $B^p_{f,-1}$; the rest of the arguments governing the position of the schedules are suppressed for simplicity. The initial equilibrium is shown by point A, and the solid schedules along which $B^p_{f,-1} = 0$ correspond to the cases analyzed in figures 3.7 and 3.8. With a positive value of initial debt, a rise in the exchange rate lowers the value of assets and lowers the demand for money. Restoration of

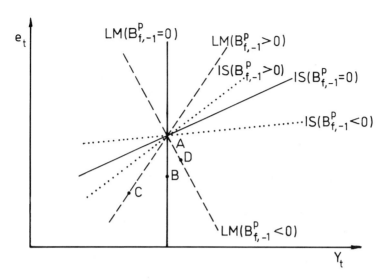

Figure 3.9
The short-run effect of a unit debt-financed rise in government spending under flexible exchange rates: The debt-revaluation effect

money-market equilibrium requires a compensating rise in output. As a result in that case the LM schedule is positively sloped. By a similar reasoning, a negative value of initial debt corresponds to a negatively sloped LM schedule. The level of initial debt also influences the slope of the IS schedule. As shown in the figure, using similar considerations, the IS schedule is steeper than the benchmark schedule (around point A) if $B^p_{f,-1} > 0$, and vice versa.

We can now use this figure to illustrate the possible implications of the initial debt position for the effects of fiscal policy in the figure we assume that the initial debt commitment falls short of foreign demand for the domestic output. A debt-financed fiscal expansion induces a rightward shift of the IS schedule and leaves the LM schedule intact. The short-run equilibrium of the system is changed from point A to point B if the level of initial debt is zero, to point C if the level of initial debt is positive, and to point D if this level is negative. Thus the debt revaluation effects critically determine whether a debt-financed rise in government spending is contractionary or expansionary.

Using the system (3.20a) and (3.22a), the changes in the level of output are

$$\frac{dY_t}{dG} = \frac{(1 - a^g)(1 + \bar{r}_f)B^p_{f,t-1}}{(1 + \bar{r}_f)B^p_{f,t-1} - \bar{D}^*} \qquad \text{for } dT_t = 0, \qquad (3.24)$$

$$\frac{dY_t}{dG} = 1 - \frac{a^g(1 + \bar{r}_f)B^p_{f,t-1}}{(1 + \bar{r}_f)B^p_{f,t-1} - \bar{D}^*} \qquad \text{for } dT_t = dG. \qquad (3.25)$$

Likewise the induced changes in the exchange rates are

$$\frac{de_t}{dG} = \frac{1 - a^g}{(1 + \bar{r}_f)B^p_{f,t-1} - \bar{D}^*} \qquad \text{for } dT_t = 0, \qquad (3.26)$$

and

$$\frac{de_t}{dG} = \frac{-a^g}{(1 + \bar{r}_f)B^p_{f,t-1} - \bar{D}^*} \qquad \text{for } dT_t = dG. \qquad (3.27)$$

These results highlight the role played by the debt-revaluation effect of exchange-rate changes. Specifically, as is evident from equations (3.24) and (3.25), a rise in government spending may be contractionary if the initial debt commitment is positive. If, however, the private sector is initially a net creditor, then, independent of its means of finance, government spending must be expansionary. In the benchmark case shown in figures 3.7 and 3.8, the initial debt position is zero, a tax finance is expansionary (yielding the conventional balanced-budget multiplier of unity), and a debt finance is not. The key mechanism responsible for this result is the high degree of capital mobility underlying the fixity of the rate of interest faced by the small country. With the given rate of interest and with a given money supply, there is in the short run a unique value of disposable income that clears the money market as long as the initial debt commitment is zero. Hence in this case a rise in taxes is expansionary, and a rise in government spending is neutral.

A comparison between the exchange-rate effects of government spending also reveals the critical importance of the means of finance and of the debt-revaluation effect. In general, for the given money supply the direction of the change in the exchange rate induced by a rise in government spending depends on whether the government finances its spending through taxes or through debt issue. If the initial debt commitment falls short of the (exogenously given) foreign demand for domestic output, then a debt-financed rise in government spending appreciates the currency, whereas a tax-financed rise in government spending depreciates the currency. The opposite holds if the initial debt commitment exceeds exports.

The foregoing analysis determined the short-run effects of government spending. We proceed to analyze the long-run effects of these policies. The long-run equilibrium conditions are shown in equations (3.28) through (3.30). These equations are the counterpart to the long-run fixed exchange-rate system (3.12) through (3.14). Accordingly,

$$E[Y - T + M - (1 + \bar{r}_f)eB_f^p, \bar{r}_f] = Y - \bar{r}_f eB_f^p - T, \qquad (3.28)$$

$$(1 - \beta_m)E[Y - T + M - (1 + \bar{r}_f)eB_f^p, \bar{r}_f] + (1 - \beta_m^g)G + e\bar{D}^*$$
$$= Y, \qquad (3.29)$$

$$M[Y - T + M - (1 + \bar{r}_f)eB_f^p, \bar{r}_f] = M. \qquad (3.30)$$

To set the stage for the analysis, consider first the benchmark case for which the initial equilibrium was associated with a zero private-sector debt. For this case the long run is analyzed in figure 3.10. The $CA = 0$ schedule portrays combinations of private-sector debt and output that yield equality between spending and income, and thereby satisfy equation (3.28). In view of the government budget constraint shown in equation (3.15), this equality between private-sector income and spending also implies current-account balance. The MM schedule portrays combinations of debt and output that yield money-market equilibrium, and thereby satisfy equation (3.30). Around zero private-sector debt, both of these schedules are independent of the exchange rate. The slope of the $CA = 0$ schedule is $-s/e[1 - s(1 + \bar{r}_f)]$. Analogously to the previous discussion of the long-run equilibrium under fixed exchange rates, this slope is assumed negative for stability. The slope of the MM schedule is

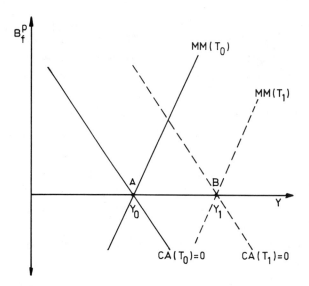

Figure 3.10
The long-run effects of a unit rise in government spending under flexible exchange rates: The small-country case

$1/(1 + \bar{r}_f)e$. It indicates that a unit rise in long-run private-sector debt raises debt commitment (principal plus debt service) by $(1 + \bar{r}_f)e$ and lowers the demand for money. To offset the reduction in disposable resources and restore the demand for money to its initial level, output must be raised by $(1 + \bar{r}_f)e$ units.

The initial long-run equilibrium is shown by point A, at which the level of private-sector debt is assumed to be zero and the level of output is Y_0. As is evident from equations (3.28) and (3.30), changes in the levels of government spending and government debt do not alter the $CA = 0$ schedule and the MM schedule. It follows that with zero private-sector debt a debt-financed rise in government spending does not alter the long-run equilibrium value of private sector debt indicated by point A in figure 3.10. In this long-run equilibrium the level of output remains unchanged, and the currency appreciates to the level shown in the short-run analysis of figure 3.7.

A rise in taxes alters both the $CA = 0$ and the MM schedules. As is evident from equations (3.28) and (3.30), a rise in output that keeps disposable income unchanged (at the given zero level of private-sector debt) maintains the initial current-account balance as well as money-market equilibrium intact. Thus a tax-financed unit rise in government spending induces a unit rightward displacement of both the $CA = 0$ and the MM schedules and yields a new long-run equilibrium at point B. At this point private-sector debt remains at its initial zero level. Also the level of output rises to Y_1, and the currency depreciates to e_1, as shown in the short-run analysis of figure 3.8.

The preceding discussion shows that under flexible exchange rates with zero initial private-sector debt, the long-run and the short-run effects of fiscal policies coincide. This characteristic is in contrast to the one obtained for fixed exchange rates, where the long-run effects of fiscal policies differ from the corresponding short-run effects. In interpreting these results, we note that due to the nontradability of national monies under a flexible exchange-rate regime, the mechanism of adjustment to fiscal policies does not permit instantaneous changes in the composition of assets through swaps of interest-bearing assets for national money in the world capital markets. As a result the only mechanism by which private-sector debt can change is through savings. Since with zero initial private-sector debt both debt-financed and tax-financed government spending do not alter disposable income (as seen from equations 3.24 and 3.25), it follows that these policies do not affect private-sector saving. Hence, if the initial position was that of a long-run equilibrium with zero savings and zero debt, the instantaneous short-run equilibrium following the rise in government spending is also characterized by zero savings. This implies that the economy converges immediately to its new long-run equilibrium.

The foregoing analysis of the long-run consequences of government spending abstracted from the debt-revaluation effect arising from exchange-rate changes. In general, if in the initial equilibrium the level of private-sector debt differs from zero, then the debt-revaluation effect breaks the coincidence between the short- and the long-run fiscal policy multipliers. Using the system (3.28) through (3.30), the long-run effects of a debt-financed rise in government spending are

$$\frac{dY}{dG} = 0 \qquad \text{for } dT = 0, \tag{3.31}$$

$$\frac{dB_f^p}{dG} = \frac{(1 - a^g)B_f^p}{e\overline{D}^*} \qquad \text{for } dT = 0, \tag{3.32}$$

$$\frac{de}{dG} = -\frac{(1 - a^g)}{\overline{D}^*} \qquad \text{for } dT = 0. \tag{3.33}$$

Likewise the long-run effects of a balanced-budget rise in government spending are

$$\frac{dY}{dG} = 1 \qquad \text{for } dT = dG, \tag{3.34}$$

$$\frac{dB_f^p}{dG} = -\frac{a^g B_f^p}{e\overline{D}^*} \qquad \text{for } dT = dG, \tag{3.35}$$

$$\frac{de}{dG} = \frac{a^g}{\overline{D}^*} \qquad \text{for } dT = dG. \tag{3.36}$$

These results show that independent of the debt-revaluation effects, a rise in government spending does not alter the long-run level of output if it is debt financed, but the same rise in government spending raises the long-run level of output by a unit multiplier if it is tax financed. Thus, in both cases the long-run level of disposable income, $Y - T$, is independent of government spending. The results also show that if government spending is debt financed, and if the initial private-sector debt was positive, then in the long run it rises while the currency appreciates. The opposite holds for the case in which government spending is tax financed.

In comparing the extent of the long-run changes in private-sector debt with the corresponding changes in the exchange rate, we note that the *value* of debt, eB_f^p (measured in units of domestic output) remains unchanged. This invariance facilitates the interpretation of the long-run multipliers. Accordingly, consider the long-run equilibrium system (3.28) through (3.30), and suppose that government spending is debt financed. In that case as is evident from the money-market equilibrium condition (3.30), the equilibrium level of output does not change as long as the money supply, taxes, and the value of the debt commitment are given. Since, however, the rise in government spending creates an excess demand for domestic output, it is seen from equation (3.29) that the currency must appreciate (i.e., e must fall) so as to lower the value of foreign demand, $e\bar{D}^*$, and thereby maintain the same equilibrium output. Obviously, since e falls, (the absolute value of) private sector debt, B_f^p, must rise by the same proportion so as to maintain the product eB_f^p unchanged. Finally, these changes ensure that the zero-saving condition (3.28) is also satisfied. A similar interpretation can be given to the effects of a tax-financed rise in government spending, except that in this case the level of output rises in line with the rise in taxes so as to keep disposable income unchanged.

A comparison between these long-run effects and the corresponding short-run effects shown in equations (3.24) and (3.25) reveals that the relative magnitudes of these multipliers depend on the initial debt position. For example, if the initial debt commitment is positive but smaller than export earnings, then the short-run multiplier of tax finance is positive and larger than unity. In this case the long-run multipliers are more moderate than the corresponding short-run multipliers. If, however, the initial debt commitment exceeds export earnings, then the short-run debt-finance multiplier is positive (in contrast with the long-run multiplier), and the short-run tax-finance multiplier is smaller than unity, and could even be negative (in contrast with the unitary long-run balanced-budget multiplier).

Fiscal Policies in a Two-Country World

In this section we extend the analysis of the small-country case to the two-country model outlined in equations (3.20) through (3.23). To develop a diagrammatic apparatus useful for the analysis of fiscal policies, we proceed in three steps. First, we trace the combinations of domestic and foreign output levels that clear each country's goods market, incorporating the conditions of market clearing in the two national money markets (which under flexible exchange rates are the two nontradable assets). Second, we trace the combinations of domestic and foreign output levels that bring about a money-market equilibrium in each country and, at the same time, yield equality between the domestic and the foreign rates of interest, thereby conforming with the assumptions of perfect capital mobility and static expectations. Finally, in the third step, we find the unique combination of domestic and foreign levels of output that satisfy simultaneously the considerations underlying the first two steps.

Using the domestic money-market equilibrium condition (3.22), we can express the domestic money-market-clearing rate of interest, r_t, as a positive function of disposable resources, $Y_t - T_t + A_{t-1}$, and as a negative function of the domestic money stock, M; that is, $r_t = r(Y_t - T_t + A_{t-1}, M)$. Applying a similar procedure to the foreign country, we can express the foreign money-market-clearing rate of interest, r_t^*, as a function of foreign disposable resources and money stock; that is, $r_t^* = r^*(Y_t^* + A_{t-1}^*, M^*)$, where $A_{t-1}^* = M_{t-1}^* + R_{t-1}B_{t-1}^p/e_t$. By substituting these money-market-clearing rates of interest into the goods-market equilibrium conditions (3.20) and (3.21), we obtain the reduced-form equilibrium conditions (3.37) and (3.38):

$$(1 - \beta_m)\tilde{E}(Y_t - T_t + A_{t-1}, M) + (1 - \beta_m^g)G$$

$$+ e_t\beta_x^*\tilde{E}^*(Y_t^* + A_{t-1}^*, M^*) = Y_t, \tag{3.37}$$

$$\beta_m\tilde{E}(Y_t - T_t + A_{t-1}, M) + \beta_m^g G$$

$$+ e_t(1 - \beta_x^*)\tilde{E}^*(Y_t^* + A_{t-1}^*, M^*) = e_t Y_t^*, \tag{3.38}$$

where a tilde ($\tilde{\ }$) indicates a reduced-form function incorporating the money-market equilibrium conditions. For each and every value of the exchange rate, e_t, equations (3.37) and (3.38) yield the equilibrium combination of domestic and foreign output that clears the world market for both goods. The schedule ee in figure 3.11 traces these equilibrium output levels for alternative values of the exchange rate. The detailed derivation of this schedule is provided in

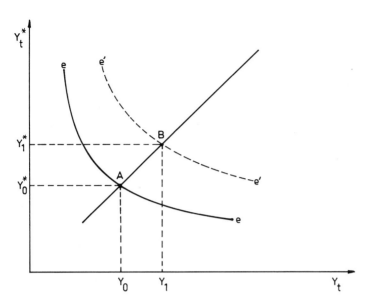

Figure 3.11
A debt-financed unit rise in government spending under flexible exchange rates:
The two-country case

appendix B, where it is shown that around balanced-trade equilibria
with a zero initial private-sector debt (so that exchange-rate changes
do not exert revaluation effects), this schedule is negatively sloped.
In general, the ee schedule is negatively sloped if a rise in the exchange rate (a deterioration in the terms of trade) raises the world
demand for domestic output and lowers the world demand for foreign output, allowing for the proper adjustments in each country's
rate of interest so as to clear the national money market.

So far we have not yet incorporated the constraints imposed by
the perfect international mobility of capital. To incorporate this constraint, the national money-market-clearing rates of interest, r_t and
r_t^*, must be equal. This equally implies that

$$r(Y_t - T_t + A_{t-1}, M) = r^*(Y_t^* + A_{t-1}^*, M^*). \tag{3.39}$$

The combinations of domestic and foreign output levels conforming
with the perfect capital-mobility requirement are portrayed by the

rr^* schedule in figure 3.11. With a zero level of initial debt (so that the debt revaluation effects induced by exchange-rate changes are absent) this schedule is positively sloped since a rise in domestic output raises the demand for domestic money and the domestic rate of interest; international interest-rate equalization is restored through a rise in foreign output that raises the foreign demand for money and the foreign rate of interest.

The short-run equilibrium is indicated by point A in figure 3.11. At this point both goods markets clear, both national money markets clear, and the rates of interest are equalized internationally. The levels of output corresponding to this equilibrium are Y_0 and Y_0^*.

A debt-financed unit rise in government spending alters the position of the goods-market equilibrium schedule ee but does not impact on the capital-market equilibrium schedule, rr^*. It is shown in appendix B that for an initial trade-balance equilibrium with zero debt, the ee schedule shifts to the right by $1/\tilde{s}$ units. The new equilibrium is indicated by point B in figure 3.11. Thus (in the absence of revaluation effects) in the new short-run equilibrium both the domestic and the foreign levels of output rise from Y_0 and Y_0^* to Y_1 and Y_1^*, respectively.

For the given supply of money and for the higher level of output (which raises the demand for money), money-market equilibrium obtains at a higher rate of interest (which restores money demand to its initial level). Finally, it is shown in appendix B that the exchange-rate effects of the debt-financed rise in government spending are not clear cut, reflecting transfer-problem criteria. These criteria reflect the relative pressures on the rates of interest in the domestic and foreign money markets induced by the changes in world demands for domestic and foreign outputs. If these pressures tend to raise the domestic rate of interest above the foreign rate, then the domestic currency must appreciate so as to lower the demand for domestic output and reduce the upward pressure on the domestic rate of interest. The opposite follows in the converse circumstances. But, if the behavioral parameters of the two private sectors are equal to each other, and the government spending falls chiefly on domestic output, then the domestic currency must appreciate.

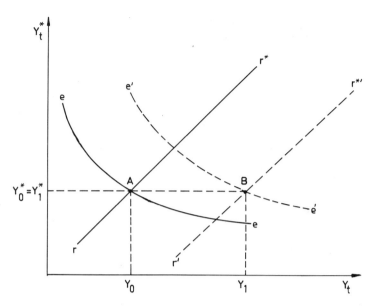

Figure 3.12
A tax-financed unit rise in government spending under flexible exchange rates:
The two-country case

A tax-financed unit rise in government spending alters the positions of both the *ee* and the *rr** schedules. As is evident by inspection of equations (3.37) through (3.39), both schedules shift to the right by one unit. This case is illustrated in figure 3.12 where the initial equilibrium is indicated by point *A* and the new short-run equilibrium by point *B*. At the new equilibrium the domestic level of output rises by one unit so that disposable income remains unchanged. With unchanged levels of disposable income the demand for money is not altered, and the initial equilibrium rate of interest remains intact. As a result the initial equilibrium in the foreign economy is not disturbed, and the foreign level of output remains unchanged. Finally, in order to eliminate the excess supply in the domestic-goods market arising from the rise in domestic output and the unchanged level of disposable income, the currency must depreciate so as to raise the domestic-currency value of the given foreign demand. It follows that in the absence of revaluation effects, the flexible exchange-rate regime permits a full insulation of the foreign economy from the consequences of the domestic tax-financed fiscal policies. The more general results allowing for revaluation effects are provided in the appendix B. Analogously to the procedure adopted in the fixed exchange-rate case, we do not analyze explicitly the long-run equilibrium of the two-country world under the flexible exchange-rate regime. The formal equilibrium system applicable for such an analysis is presented in appendix B.

3.4   Summary and Overview

In this chapter we analyzed the effects of government spending under fixed and flexible exchange-rate regimes. Throughout we have assumed that the world capital markets are highly integrated so that capital is perfectly mobile internationally. To focus on the pure effects of fiscal policies, we assumed that there is no active monetary policy. In particular, we abstracted from money-financed government spending. Accordingly, we analyzed the short- and long-run consequences of debt-financed and of tax-financed changes in government spending. In this context we focused on the effects of fiscal policies on the levels of output, debt, and the rate of interest under the two alternative exchange-rate regimes. In addition, for the fixed exchange-rate regime, we examined the induced changes in the money supply, and for the flexible exchange-rate regime, we determined the induced change in the exchange rate.

The short- and long-run effects of a unit debt and tax-financed rise in government spending for a small country facing a fixed world rate of interest are summarized in table 3.1. In this table we show the various multipliers applicable to the fixed as well as to the flexible exchange-rate regimes. The output multipliers under the fixed exchange-rate regime are the typical simple foreign-trade multipliers. These results are of course expected since the rate of interest is exogenously given to the small country. The fixity of the rate of interest implies that the typical crowding-out mechanism induced by changes in the rate of interest are not present.

Table 3.1
The short- and long-run effects of a unit rise in government spending under fixed and flexible exchange rates: The small-country case

	Debt financed		Tax financed	
	Short run	Long run	Short run	Long run
Fixed exchange rates:				
Y	$\dfrac{1-a^g}{s+a}$	$\dfrac{1-a^g}{\Delta}[1-s-\bar{r}_f(s-M_y)]$	$1-\dfrac{a^g}{s+a}$	$1-\dfrac{a^g}{\Delta}[1-s-\bar{r}_f(s-M_y)]$
$B^p_{f,t-1}$	0	$-\dfrac{1-a^g}{\Delta}(s-M_y)$	0	$\dfrac{a^g}{\Delta}(s-M_y)$
M	$\dfrac{(1-a^g)M_y}{s+a}$	$\dfrac{1-a^g}{\Delta}M_y$	$-\dfrac{a^g}{s+a}M_y$	$-\dfrac{a^g}{\Delta}M_y$
Flexible exchange rates:				
Y	$\dfrac{(1-a^g)R_f B^p_{f,t-1}}{R_f B^p_{f,t-1}-\bar{D}^*}$	0	$1-\dfrac{a^g R_f B^p_{f,t-1}}{R_f B^p_{f,t-1}-\bar{D}^*}$	1
$B^p_{f,t-1}$	0	$\dfrac{(1-a^g)B^p_f}{e\bar{D}^*}$	0	$-\dfrac{a^g B^p_f}{e\bar{D}^*}$
e	$\dfrac{(1-a^g)}{R_f B^p_{f,t-1}-\bar{D}^*}$	$-\dfrac{(1-a^g)}{\bar{D}^*}$	$\dfrac{-a^g}{R_f B^p_{f,t-1}-\bar{D}^*}$	$\dfrac{a^g}{\bar{D}^*}$

Note: $\bar{D}^*$ denotes export earnings measured in units of foreign currency, $R_f = 1+\bar{r}_f$ and $\Delta = a-\bar{r}_f(s-M_y)$. $\Delta > 0$ under the assumption that a rise in income worsens the current account of the balance of payments. The term $1-s-\bar{r}_f(s-M_y) > 0$ for stability.

Under flexible exchange rates the short-run output multipliers of fiscal policies depend crucially on the debt-revaluation effect induced by exchange-rate changes. Indeed, in the absence of such an effect (as would be the case if the initial debt position is zero) fiscal policies lose their capacity to alter disposable income. Accordingly, with debt finance the output multiplier is zero, and with tax finance the corresponding multiplier is unity. In general, however, the signs and magnitudes of the *short-run* output multipliers depend on the size of the initial debt. In contrast, these considerations do not influence the *long-run* output multipliers. As seen in the table, with perfect capital mobility and flexible exchange rates, the long-run value of disposable income cannot be affected by fiscal policies.

One of the important points underscored by the results reported in table 3.1 is the critical dependence of the direction of change in the key variables on the means of fiscal finance. Specifically, a shift from a debt finance to a tax finance reverses the signs of the multipliers of B_f^p, M, and e.

For example, a tax-financed rise in government spending under a fixed exchange-rate regime induces a balance-of-payments deficit and reduces both the short- and the long-run money holdings. On the other hand, a similar rise in government spending that is debt-financed induces a surplus in the balance of payments and raises money holdings in the short run as well as in the long run. Likewise, under a flexible exchange-rate regime the tax-financed rise in government spending depreciates the long-run value of the currency, whereas the debt-financed rise in government spending appreciates the long-run value of the currency. As indicated earlier, a similar reversal in the direction of the change in the exchange rate also pertains to the short-run, but whether the currency depreciates or appreciates in the short run depends on the size of the debt which in turn governs the debt-revaluation effect.

To study the characteristics of the international transmission mechanism, we extended the analysis of the small-country case to a two-country model of the world economy. The new channel of transmission is the world rate of interest which is determined in the unified world capital market. Table 3.2 summarizes the short-run

Table 3.2
The direction of the short-run effects of a rise in government spending under fixed
and flexible exchange rates: The two-country world

	Debt financed	Tax financed
Fixed exchange rates:		
Y	+ (for small H_r)	+ (for small $a^g \leq a$)
Y^*	+ (for small F_r)	+
r	+	+ (for $A > 0$)
n	+ (for $B + C < 0$)	−
	− (for $B + C > 0$)	− (for $A < 0$)
Flexible exchange rates:		
Y	+	+
Y^*	+	0
r	+	0
e	+ (for $\tilde{B} > 0$)	+
	− (for $\tilde{B} < 0$)	

Note: The signs indicated in flexible exchange-rate part of the table are
applicable to the case of an initial equilibrium with balanced trade and zero
initial debt. H^r and F_r denote, respectively, the negative effect of the rate of
interest on the world demand for domestic and foreign goods, $A = s - M_y$
$- s^* - M_{y^*}^*$, $B = \bar{e}(M_y/M_r)[a^* + s^*(1 - a^g)] - (M_{y^*}^*/M_r^*)(a + sa^g)$, and $\tilde{B} =$
$e_t(M_y/M_r)[\tilde{a}^* + \tilde{s}^*(1 - a^g)] - (M_{y^*}^*/M_r^*)(\tilde{a} + \tilde{s}a^g)$, correspond, respectively, to
the fixed and flexible exchange-rate regimes and $C = M_y M_{y^*}^* \cdot M_r M_r^*[F_r(1 - a^g)$
$- H_r a^g]$.

effects of fiscal policies under the two alternative exchange-rate
regimes. To avoid a tedious taxonomy, the summary results for the
flexible exchange rates reported in the table are confined to the case
in which the twin revaluation effects—debt revaluation and trade-
balance revaluation—induced by exchange-rate changes are absent;
accordingly, it is assumed that the initial debt is zero and that the
initial equilibrium obtains with a balanced trade.

As shown, independent of the exchange-rate regime, a debt-
financed rise in government spending raises the world rate of interest. Under the flexible exchange-rate regime the debt-financed rise
in government spending stimulates demand for both domestic and

foreign goods and results in an expansion of both outputs. Thus in this case the international transmission of the rise in government spending, measured by comovements of domestic and foreign outputs, is positive. On the other hand, under a fixed exchange-rate regime the rise in the world rate of interest may offset the direct effect of government spending on aggregate demand and may result in lower levels of output. But, if the (negative) interest-rate effect on aggregate demand is relatively weak, then both domestic and foreign outputs rise, thereby resulting in a positive international transmission. Finally, we note that there is no presumption about the direction of change in money holdings (under fixed exchange rates) and in the exchange rate (under flexible exchange rates) in response to the debt-financed fiscal expansion. As indicated, depending on the relative magnitudes of the domestic and foreign saving and import propensities, and the domestic and foreign sensitivities of money demand with respect to changes in the rate of interest and income, the balance of payments may be in a deficit or in a surplus, and the currency may depreciate or appreciate.

The results in table 3.2 also highlight the significant implication of alternative means of budgetary finance. Indeed, in contrast with debt finance, a tax-financed rise in government spending under a flexible exchange-rate regime leaves the world rate of interest unchanged, raises domestic output, and depreciates the currency. The reduction in the domestic private-sector demand for foreign output, induced by the depreciation of the currency, precisely offsets the increased demand induced by the rise in government spending. As a result, foreign output remains intact, and the flexible exchange rate regime fully insulates the foreign economy from the domestic tax-financed fiscal policy. In this case the analysis of the two-country world economy reduces to the one carried out for the small-country case. Therefore the long-run multipliers for the two countries operating under flexible exchange rates coincide with the short-run multipliers, the domestic short- and long-run output multipliers are unity, and the corresponding foreign output multipliers are zero.

In contrast with the flexible exchange-rate regime in which the currency depreciates to the extent needed to maintain world demand for (and thereby the equilibrium level of) foreign output, the fixed exchange-rate regime does not contain this insulating mechanism. As a result the tax-financed rise in the domestic government spending raises the world demand for (and thereby the equilibrium level of) foreign output. On the other hand, depending on the relative magnitude of the domestic-government import propensity, the domestic level of output may rise or fall. If, however, the government import propensity does not exceed the corresponding private-sector propensity, then domestic output rises, and the international transmission, measured by comovements of domestic and foreign outputs, is positive. Finally, since at the prevailing rate of interest domestic disposable income falls and foreign disposable income rises (as shown in chapter 2), these changes in disposable incomes alter the world demand for money and necessitate equilibrating changes in the world rate of interest. As shown in table 3.2, the change in the world demand for money (at the prevailing rate of interest) reflects a transfer-problem criterion. If the ratio of the domestic saving to hoarding propensities, s/M_y, exceeds the corresponding foreign ratio, $s^*/M_{y^*}^*$, then the international redistribution of disposable income raises the world demand for money and necessitates a rise in the world rate of interest. The opposite holds if s/M_y falls short of $s^*/M_{y^*}^*$. Independent, however, of the direction of the change in the interest rate, the tax-financed rise in government spending must worsen the balance of payments and lower the short-run equilibrium money holdings.

Throughout this chapter (except in the initial overview) we assume that expectations are static. Since under a flexible exchange-rate regime the actual exchange rates do change, the assumption that exchange-rate expectations are static results in expectation errors during the period of transition toward the long-run equilibrium. The incorporation of a consistent expectations scheme introduces an additional mechanism governing the short-run behavior. Aspects of this mechanism are examined in appendix B.

We conclude this summary with an overview of the income-expenditure model analyzed in chapters 2 and 3. The issues on which we focus are chosen so as to provide the motivation for, and the link to, the formulations and analyses carried out in the subsequent parts of the book.

A key characteristic of the formulation of the income-expenditure model used in this part of the book is the lack of solid micro-economic foundations underlying the behavior of the private and the public sectors, and the absence of an explicit rationale for the holdings of zero interest-bearing money in the presence of safe interest-bearing bonds. The latter issue is of relevance in view of the central role played by monetary flows in the international adjustment mechanism. Furthermore no attention was given to the intertemporal budget constraints, and the behavior of both the private and the public sectors was not forward-looking in a consistent manner. As a result there was no mechanism ensuring that the patterns of spending, debt accumulation, and money hoarding (which are the key elements governing the equilibrium dynamics of the economic system) are consistent with the relevant economic constraints. The implication of this shortcoming is that in determining the level and composition of spending, saving, and asset holdings, the private sector does not incorporate explicitly the intertemporal consequences of government policies.

To illustrate the significance of this issue, consider a debt-financed rise in current government spending. A proper formulation of the government's intertemporal budget constraint must recognize that to service the debt and maintain its solvency, the government must accompany this current fiscal expansion by either cutting down future spending or raising future (ordinary or inflationary) taxes. Furthermore a proper specification of the private sector's behavior must allow for the fact that the forward-looking individuals may recognize the future consequences of current government policies and incorporate these expected consequences into their current as well as planned future spending, saving, and asset holdings.

The neglect of the intertemporal budget constraints and of the consequences of forward-looking behavior consistent with these constraints are among the main deficiencies of the income-expenditure model as formulated in this part of the book. In the subsequent parts of the book we rectify these shortcomings. In doing so, we develop a unified model that is derived from optimizing behavior consistent with the relevant temporal and intertemporal economic constraints. The resulting macroeconomic model, which is grounded upon microeconomic foundations, is capable of dealing with new issues in a consistent manner. Among these issues are the effects of various time patterns of government spending and taxes. We can thus distinguish between temporary and permanent as well as between current and future policies. Likewise, the model is capable of analyzing the macroeconomic consequences of alternative specifications of the tax structure. We can thus distinguish between the effects of different types of taxes (e.g., income taxes, value-added taxes, and international capital flow taxes) used to finance the budget.

In this chapter as in chapter 2 we assumed that producer prices were given and that outputs were demand determined. In this framework nominal exchange-rate changes amounted to changes in the terms of trade. As a result the characteristics of the economic system were drastically different across alternative exchange-rate regimes. Throughout the subsequent parts of the book we relax the fixed-price assumption and allow for complete price flexibility. With this flexibility prices are always at their market-clearing equilibrium levels. Accordingly, changes in the terms of trade induced by equilibrium changes in prices trigger an adjustment mechanism that is analogous to the one triggered by nominal exchange-rate changes in the income-expenditure model. Therefore, we do not consider issues arising from nominal exchange-rate changes, yet we allow for the effects of terms of trade and real exchange-rate changes on the international adjustment mechanism.

Finally, it is noteworthy that an important feature of the intertemporal approach adopted in the rest of this book is its capability of dealing explicitly with the welfare consequences of economic policies and events. This feature reflects the basic attribute of the macroeconomic model: the economic behavior underlying this model is derived from, and is consistent with, the principles of individual utility maximization. Therefore, in contrast with the traditional approach underlying the discussion in this part of the book, the intertemporal optimizing approach to which we turn next provides a framework suitable for the normative evaluation of international macroeconomic policies.

3.5   Appendix A: Fixed Exchange Rates

Long-Run Equilibrium: The Small-Country Case

The long-run equilibrium conditions are specified by equations (3.12) through (3.15) of the text. Substituting the government budget constraint (3.15) into equations (3.12) through (3.14) yields

$$E[Y - G + M - B^p - \bar{r}_f(B^p + B^g), \bar{r}_f] + G = Y - \bar{r}_f(B^p + B^g),$$
$$\text{(A.1)}$$

$$(1 - \beta_m)E[Y - G + M - B^{p'} - \bar{r}_f(B^p + B^g), \bar{r}_f]$$
$$+ (1 - \beta_m^g)G + \bar{e}\bar{D}^* = Y, \tag{A.2}$$

$$M[Y - G + M - B^p - \bar{r}_f(B^p + B^g), \bar{r}_f] = M. \tag{A.3}$$

Equations (A.1) and (A.3) yield the combinations of output and private-sector debt underlying the $CA = 0$ schedule, and equations (A.2) and (A.3) yield the combinations of these variables underlying the YY schedule. To obtain the slope of the $CA = 0$ schedule, we differentiate equations (A.1) and (A.3) and obtain

$$\begin{pmatrix} -s & s(1 + \bar{r}_f) - 1 \\ M_y & -(1 + \bar{r}_f)M_y \end{pmatrix} \begin{pmatrix} dY \\ dB^p \end{pmatrix} = \begin{pmatrix} -(1 - s) \\ 1 - M_y \end{pmatrix} dM, \tag{A.4}$$

where $s = 1 - E_y$ and $a = \beta_m E_y$. Solving (A.4) for dY/dM and dividing the resultant solutions by each other yields the expression for dB^p/dY along the $CA = 0$ schedule. This expression is reported in equation (3.16) of the text.

Likewise differentiating equations (A.2) and (A.3) yields

$$\begin{pmatrix} -(s + a) & -(1 + \bar{r}_f)(1 - s - a) \\ M_y & -(1 + \bar{r}_f)M_y \end{pmatrix} \begin{pmatrix} dY \\ dB^p \end{pmatrix}$$
$$= \begin{pmatrix} -(1 - s - a) \\ 1 - M_y \end{pmatrix} dM. \tag{A.5}$$

Following a similar procedure, we obtain the expression for dB^p/dY along the YY schedule. This expression is reported in equation (3.17) of the text.

To obtain the horizontal displacements of the $CA = 0$ schedule following a balanced-budget rise in government spending, we differentiate equations (A.1) and (A.3), holding B^g and B^p constant. Accordingly, equation (A.1) implies that $(1 - s)(dY - dG + dM) = dY - dG$, and equation (A.3) implies that $dM = M_y(dY - dG)/(1 - M_y)$. Substituting the latter expression into the former reveals that $dY/dG = 1$. Thus a unit balanced-budget rise in government spending induces a unit rightward shift of the $CA = 0$ schedule.

Analogously, to obtain the horizontal shift of the YY schedule, we differentiate equations (A.2) and (A.3), holding B^g and B^p constant. Equation (A.2) implies that $(1 - s - a)(dY - dG + dM) + (1 - a^g)dG = dY$, where $a^g = \beta_m^g$, and equation (A.3) implies that $dM = M_y(dY - dG)/(1 - M_y)$. Substituting the latter into the former shows that the horizontal shift of the YY schedule is

$$1 - \frac{(1 - M_y)a^g}{s + a - M_y}.$$

Thus, in contrast with the unit rightward displacement of the $CA = 0$ schedule, the unit balanced-budget rise in government spending shifts the YY schedule to the right by less than one unit. These results underly the diagrammatic analysis in figures 3.3 and 3.4.

The long-run effects of fiscal policies are obtained by differentiating the system (3.12) through (3.14) of the text and solving for the endogenous variables. Accordingly,

$$\begin{bmatrix} -s & s(1 + \bar{r}_f) - 1 & 1 - s \\ -(s + a) & -(1 + \bar{r}_f)(1 - s - a) & 1 - s - a \\ M_y & -(1 + \bar{r}_f)M_y & -(1 - M_y) \end{bmatrix} \begin{bmatrix} dY \\ dB^p \\ dM \end{bmatrix}$$

$$= \begin{bmatrix} 0 \\ -(1 - a^g) \\ 0 \end{bmatrix} dG + \begin{bmatrix} -s \\ 1 - s - a \\ M_y \end{bmatrix} dT. \tag{A.6}$$

Using this system, the long-run effects of a debt-financed rise in government spending (i.e., $dT = 0$) are

$$\frac{dY}{dG} = \frac{1 - a^g}{\Delta}[1 - s - \bar{r}_f(s - M_y)] \geqslant 0 \qquad \text{for } dT_t = 0, \qquad \text{(A.7)}$$

$$\frac{dB^p}{dG} = -\frac{1 - a^g}{\Delta}(s - M_y) \leqslant 0 \qquad \text{for } dT_t = 0, \qquad \text{(A.8)}$$

$$\frac{dM}{dG} = \frac{1 - a^g}{\Delta} M_y \geqslant 0 \qquad \text{for } dT_t = 0, \qquad \text{(A.9)}$$

where $\Delta = a - \bar{r}_f(s - M_y) > 0$ under the assumption that a rise in income worsens the current account of the balance of payments. Correspondingly, the long-run effects of a balanced-budget rise in government spending (i.e., $dG = dT$) are

$$\frac{dY}{dG} = \frac{1}{\Delta}[a - \bar{r}_f(s - M_y) - a^g\{1 - s - \bar{r}_f(s - M_y)\}]$$

$$\qquad \gtrless 0 \qquad \text{for } dG = dT_t, \qquad \text{(A.10)}$$

$$\frac{dB^p}{dG} = \frac{a^g}{\Delta}(s - M_y) \geqslant 0 \qquad \text{for } dG = dT_t, \qquad \text{(A.11)}$$

$$\frac{dM}{dG} = -\frac{a^g}{\Delta} M_y \leqslant 0 \qquad \text{for } dG = dT_t. \qquad \text{(A.12)}$$

Short-Run Equilibrium: The Two-Country World

In this part of the appendix we analyze the short-run equilibrium of the system (3.5) through (3.7). This system determines the short-run equilibrium values of Y_t, Y_t^*, and r_t. The YY and Y^*Y^* schedules in figure 3.5 show combinations of Y_t and Y_t^* that clear the markets for domestic and foreign output, respectively. Both of these schedules incorporate the world money-market equilibrium condition (3.7) of the text. To derive the slope of the YY schedule, we differentiate equations (3.5) and (3.7). This yields

$$\begin{pmatrix} -(s + a) & \bar{e}a^* \\ M_y & \bar{e}M_{y^*}^* \end{pmatrix} \begin{pmatrix} dY_t \\ dY_t^* \end{pmatrix} = -\begin{pmatrix} H_r \\ (M_r + \bar{e}M_r^*) \end{pmatrix} dr_t, \tag{A.13}$$

where H_r denotes the partial (negative) effect a change in the rate of interest on the world demand for domestic output; that is, $H_r = (1 - \beta_m)E_r + \bar{e}\beta_x^* E_r^*$, where E_r, M_r, E_r^*, and M_r^* denote the partial (negative) effects of the rate of interest on domestic and foreign spending and money demand. To eliminate r_t from the goods-market equilibrium schedule, we solve (A.13) for dY_t/dr_t and for dY_t^*/dr_t, and divide the solutions by each other. Along the YY schedule, this yields

$$\frac{dY_t^*}{dY_t} = \frac{1}{\bar{e}} \frac{(s + a)(M_r + \bar{e}M_r^*) + M_y H_r}{a^*(M_r + \bar{e}M_r^*) - M_{y^*}^* H_r}. \tag{A.14}$$

Analogously, differentiating equations (3.13) and (3.14) yields

$$\begin{pmatrix} a & \bar{e}(s^* + a^*) \\ M_y & \bar{e}M_{y^*}^* \end{pmatrix} \begin{pmatrix} dY_t \\ dY_t^* \end{pmatrix} = -\begin{pmatrix} F_r \\ M_r + \bar{e}M_r^* \end{pmatrix} dr_t, \tag{A.15}$$

where $F_r = \beta_m E_r + \bar{e}(1 - \beta_x^*)E_r^*$ denotes the partial (negative) effect of the rate of interest on the world demand for foreign output. Applying a similar procedure as before, along the Y^*Y^* schedule, the slope is

$$\frac{dY_t^*}{dY_t} = \frac{1}{\bar{e}} \frac{a(M_r + \bar{e}M_r^*) - M_y F_r}{(s^* + a^*)(M_r + \bar{e}M_r^*) + M_{y^*}^* F_r}. \tag{A.16}$$

A comparison of the slopes in (A.14) and (A.16) shows that there are various possible configurations of the relative slopes of the YY and Y^*Y^* schedules. However, two configurations are ruled out: if both schedules are positively sloped, then the slope of the Y^*Y^* cannot exceed the slope of the YY schedule. This can be verified by noting that in the numerator of (A.7) the negative quantity $a(M_r + \bar{e}M_r^*)$ is augmented by additional negative quantities, whereas the same negative quantity in the numerator of (A.16) is augmented by an additional positive quantity. A similar comparison of the denominators of (A.14) and (A.16) shows that the negative quantity $a^*(M_r + \bar{e}M_r^*)$

is augmented by additional negative quantities in (A.16) and by a positive quantity in (A.14). Likewise, if both schedules are negatively sloped, then, by substracting one slope from the other, it can be verified that the Y^*Y^* schedule cannot be steeper than the YY schedule. These considerations imply that for all situations in which there is a rightward shift of the YY schedule exceeding the rightward shift of the Y^*Y^* schedule, the new equilibrium must be associated with a higher level of domestic output.

A rise in the domestic government spending alters the position of both schedules. To determine the horizontal shift of the YY schedule, we use equations (3.5) and (3.7), holding Y^* constant and solving for dY/dG after eliminating the expression for dr/dG. A similar procedure is applied to determine the horizontal shift of the Y^*Y^* schedule from equations (3.6) and (3.7). Accordingly, the horizontal shifts of the schedules induced by a debt-financed rise in government spending are

$$\frac{dY}{dG} = \frac{1 - a^g}{s + a + [M_y H_r / (M_r + \bar{e} M_r^*)]} \geq 0 \qquad \text{for the } YY \text{ schedule,}$$

(A.17)

$$\frac{dY}{dG} = \frac{-a^g}{a - [M_y F_r / (M_r + \bar{e} M_r^*)]} \geq 0 \qquad \text{for the } Y^*Y^* \text{ schedule.}$$

(A.18)

The corresponding shifts for the tax-financed rise in government spending are

$$\frac{dY}{dG} = 1 - \frac{a^g}{s + a + [M_y H_r / (M_r + \bar{e} M_r^*)]} \qquad \text{for the } YY \text{ schedule,}$$

(A.19)

$$\frac{dY}{dG} = 1 - \frac{a^g}{a - [M_y F_r / (M_r + \bar{e} M_r^*)]} \qquad \text{for the } Y^*Y^* \text{ schedule.}$$

(A.20)

In equations (A.19) and (A.20), we assume that the government spending falls chiefly on domestic output. Comparisons of (A.17) with (A.18) and of (A.19) with (A.20) reveal the difference between the shifts of the YY and the Y^*Y^* schedules.

To compute the short-run multipliers of fiscal policies, we differentiate the system (3.5) through (3.7). Thus

$$
\begin{bmatrix}
-(s + a) & \bar{e}a^* & H_r \\
a & -\bar{e}(s^* + a^*) & F_r \\
M_y & \bar{e}M_{y^*}^* & M_r + \bar{e}M_r^*
\end{bmatrix}
\begin{bmatrix}
dY_t \\
dY_t^* \\
dr_t
\end{bmatrix}
$$

$$
= -
\begin{bmatrix}
1 - a^g \\
a^g \\
0
\end{bmatrix}
dG +
\begin{bmatrix}
1 - s - a \\
a \\
M_y
\end{bmatrix}
dT_t. \tag{A.21}
$$

With a debt-financed rise in government spending $dT_t = 0$ and thus the short-run effects are

$$
\frac{dY_t}{dG} = \frac{1}{\Delta}\{[s^*(1 - a^g) + a^*](M_r + \bar{e}M_r^*) + M_{y^*}^*[F_r(1 - a^g) - a^g H_r]\}
$$

$$
\text{for } dT_t = 0, \tag{A.22}
$$

$$
\frac{dY_t^*}{dG} = \frac{1}{\bar{e}\Delta}\{(sa^g + a)(M_r + \bar{e}M_r^*) - M_y[F_r(1 - a^g) - a^g H_r]\}
$$

$$
\text{for } dT_t = 0, \tag{A.23}
$$

$$
\frac{dr_t}{dG} = -\frac{1}{\Delta}\{[s^*(1 - a^g) + a^*]M_y + (sa^g + a)M_{y^*}^*\} > 0
$$

$$
\text{for } dT_t = 0, \tag{A.24}
$$

where

$$
\Delta = s[(s^* + a^*)(M_r + \bar{e}M_r^*) + M_{y^*}^* F_r] + a[s^*(M_r + \bar{e}M_r^*)
$$

$$
+ M_{y^*}^*(F_r + H_r)] + M_y[s^* H_r + a^*(F_r + H_r)] < 0.
$$

Differentiating the domestic demand for money function (equation 3.8) and using (A.22) and (A.24) yields the short-run change in the domestic money holdings, that is, the balance of payments:

$$\frac{dM_t}{dG} = \frac{1}{M_r M_r^* \Delta} \left\{ \frac{\bar{e} M_y}{M_r} [a^* + s^*(a - a^g)] - \frac{M_y^*}{M_r^*}(a + sa^g) \right.$$

$$\left. + M_y M_y^* \cdot M_r M_r^* [F_r(1 - a^g) - H_r a^g] \right\} \qquad \text{for } dT_t = 0.$$

$$(A.25)$$

With a balanced-budget rise in government spending $dG = dT_t = dT$. Accordingly, the solutions of (A.21) are

$$\frac{dY_t}{dG} = \frac{1}{\Delta} \{ s[(s^* + a^*)(M_r + \bar{e} M_r^*) + M_y^* F_r]$$

$$+ (a - a^g)[s^*(M_r + \bar{e} M_r^*) + M_y^* \cdot (F_r + H_r)]$$

$$+ M_y[s^* H_r + a^*(F_r + H_r)] \} \qquad \text{for } dG = dT_t, \qquad (A.26)$$

$$\frac{dY_t^*}{dG} = \frac{a^g}{\bar{e}\Delta} [M_y(F_r + H_r) + s(M_r + \bar{e} M_r^*)] > 0 \qquad \text{for } dG = dT_t,$$

$$(A.27)$$

$$\frac{dr_t}{dG} = \frac{a^g}{\Delta} (s^* M_y - s M_y^*) \qquad \text{for } dG = dT_t. \qquad (A.28)$$

Differentiating the domestic money demand function and using (A.26) and (A.28) yields

$$\frac{dM_t}{dG} = -\frac{a^g}{\Delta} [(s M_r M_y^* + s^* \bar{e} M_r^* M_y) + M_y M_y^* \cdot (F_r + H_r)] < 0$$

$$\text{for } dG = dT_t. \qquad (A.29)$$

Long-Run Equilibrium: The Two-Country World

The long-run equilibrium of the system is specified by equations (A.30) through (A.36), where the first five equations are the long-run counterpart to the short-run conditions (3.5) through (3.9) and the last two equations are the zero-savings requirements for each country implying (once the government budget constraint is incorporated) current account balances. By employing a common rate of interest, this long-run system embodies the assumption of perfect capital mobility.

$$(1 - \beta_m)E[Y - T + M - (1 + r)B^p, r] + (1 - \beta_m^g)G$$

$$+ \beta_x^* \bar{e}E^*\left[Y^* + M^* + (1 + r)\frac{B^p}{\bar{e}}, r\right] = Y, \tag{A.30}$$

$$\beta_m E[Y - T + M - (1 + r)B^p, r] + \beta_m^g G$$

$$+ (1 - \beta_x^*)\bar{e}E^*\left[Y^* + M^* + (1 + r)\frac{B^p}{\bar{e}}, r\right] = Y^*, \tag{A.31}$$

$$M[Y - T + M - (1 + r)B^p, r] + \bar{e}M^*\left[Y^* + M^* + (1 + r)\frac{B^p}{\bar{e}}, r\right]$$

$$= \overline{M}, \tag{A.32}$$

$$M[Y - T + M - (1 + r)B^p, r] = M, \tag{A.33}$$

$$M^*\left[Y^* + M^* + (1 + r)\frac{B^p}{\bar{e}}, r\right] = M^*, \tag{A.34}$$

$$E[Y - T + M - (1 + r)B^p, r] = Y - rB^p - T, \tag{A.35}$$

$$E^*\left[Y^* + M^* + (1 + r)\frac{B^p}{\bar{e}}, r\right] = Y^* + \frac{rB^p}{\bar{e}}. \tag{A.36}$$

By Walras's law one of the seven equations can be omitted, and the remaining six equations can be used to solve for the long-run equilibrium values of Y, Y^*, B^p, M, M^*, and r as functions of the policy variables.

3.6 Appendix B: Flexible Exchange Rates

Short-Run Equilibrium: The Two-Country World

In this appendix we analyze the short-run equilibrium of the two-country model under flexible exchange rates. Using the domestic money-market equilibrium condition (3.22), the domestic market-clearing rate of interest is

$$r_t = r(Y_t - T_t + A_{t-1}, M), \tag{A.37}$$

where a rise in disposable resources raises the equilibrium rate of interest while a rise in the money supply lowers the rate of interest. Similarly, using the foreign money-market-clearing condition (3.23) but not imposing yet an equality between the foreign rate of interest, r_t^*, and the domestic rate r_t, yields

$$r_t^* = r^*(Y_t^* + A_{t-1}^*, M^*). \tag{A.38}$$

Substituting (A.37) into the domestic expenditure future (3.3) and substituting (A.38) into the corresponding foreign expenditure function yields

$$E_t = \tilde{E}(Y_t - T_t + A_{t-1}, M), \tag{A.39}$$

$$E_t^* = \tilde{E}^*(Y_t^* + A_{t-1}^*, M^*). \tag{A.40}$$

Equations (A.39) and (A.40) are the reduced-form expenditure functions that incorporate the conditions of money-market equilibrium. A rise in disposable resources exerts two conflicting influences on the reduced-form expenditure function. On the one hand, it stimulates spending directly; on the other hand, by raising the equilibrium rate of interest, it discourages spending. Formally, $\tilde{E}_y = E_y - (E_r/M_r)M_y$. In what follows we assume that the direct effect dominates so that $\tilde{E}_y > 0$. For subsequent use we note that the reduced-form saving propensity $\tilde{s} = 1 - \tilde{E}_y$ exceeds $M_y[1 + (E_r/M_r)]$. This follows from the assumption that bonds are normal goods (so that $1 - E_y - M_y > 0$) together with the former expression linking $\tilde{E}_y$ with E_y.

Substituting the reduced-form expenditure functions (A.39) and (A.40) into the goods-market-clearing conditiohs yields

$$(1 - \beta_m)\tilde{E}(Y_t - A_{t-1}, M) + (1 - \beta_m^g)G + e_t\beta_x^*\tilde{E}(Y_t^* + A_{t-1}^*, M^*)$$

$$= Y_t, \tag{A.41}$$

$$\beta_m \tilde{E}(Y_t - T_t + A_{t-1}, M) + \beta_m^g G + e_t(1 - \beta_x^*)\tilde{E}^*(Y_t^* + A_{t-1}^*, M^*)$$

$$= e_t Y_t^*, \tag{A.42}$$

where we recall that $A_{t-1} = M_{t-1} - (1 + r_{t-1})B_{t-1}^p$ and $A_{t-1}^* = M_{t-1}^* + (1 + r_{t-1})B_{t-1}^p/e_t$. Thus, though A_{t-1} is predetermined, the value of A_{t-1}^* depends on the prevailing exchange rate. Equations (A.41) and (A.42) are the reduced-form goods-market-clearing conditions. These conditions link the equilibrium values of domestic output, foreign output, and the exchange rate. In the first step of the analysis we derive the ee schedule of the text which portrays alternative combinations of Y and Y^* satisfying equations (A.41) and (A.42) for alternative values of the exchange rate (which is treated as a parameter). The slope of this schedule is obtained by differentiating equations (A.41) and (A.42) and solving for dY_t^*/dY_t. Accordingly,

$$\begin{pmatrix} -(\tilde{s} + \tilde{a}) & e_t\tilde{a}^* \\ \tilde{a} & -e_t(\tilde{s}^* + \tilde{a}^*) \end{pmatrix}\begin{pmatrix} dY_t \\ dY_t^* \end{pmatrix}$$

$$= \begin{pmatrix} -IM_t^* + \tilde{a}^*H \\ IM_t + (1 - \tilde{s}^* - \tilde{a}^*)H \end{pmatrix}de_t - \begin{pmatrix} 1 - a^g \\ a^g \end{pmatrix}dG$$

$$+ \begin{pmatrix} 1 - \tilde{s} - \tilde{a} \\ \tilde{a} \end{pmatrix}dT_t, \tag{A.43}$$

where $H = (1 + r_{t-1})B_{t-1}^p/e_t$ denotes the debt commitment of the home country, the reduced-form saving and import propensities are designated by a tilde (˜), and where $IM_t^* = \beta_x^*\tilde{E}^*$ and $IM_t = Y^* - (1 - \beta_x^*)\tilde{E}^*$ are, respectively, the foreign and the domestic values of imports expressed in units of foreign goods. The coefficient matrix in (A.43) is the counterpart of the system (2.21) shown in chapter 2. For given fiscal policies we obtain

$$\frac{dY_t}{de_t} = \frac{\tilde{s}^*IM_t^* + \tilde{a}^*(IM_t^* - IM_t) - \tilde{a}^*H}{\Delta}, \tag{A.44}$$

$$\frac{dY_t^*}{de_t} = -\frac{\tilde{s}IM_t - \tilde{a}(IM_t - IM_t) + [\tilde{s}(1 - \tilde{s}^* - \tilde{a}^*) + \tilde{a}(1 - s^*)]H}{e_t\Delta}, \tag{A.45}$$

where

$$\Delta = \tilde{s}\tilde{s}^* + \tilde{s}\tilde{a}^* + \tilde{s}\tilde{a} > 0.$$

To obtain the slope of the *ee* schedule, we divide (A.45) by (A.44), yielding along the *ee* schedule

$$\frac{dY_t^*}{dY_t} = -\frac{\tilde{s}IM_t - \tilde{a}(IM_t^* - IM_t) + [\tilde{s}(1 - \tilde{s}^* - \tilde{a}^*) + \tilde{a}(1 - \tilde{s}^*)]H}{e_t[\tilde{s}^*IM_t^* + \tilde{a}^*(IM_t^* - IM_t) - \tilde{a}^*H]}.$$

(A.46)

Around a trade-balance equilibrium with zero initial debt (i.e., $IM_t = IM_t^*$ and $H = 0$) this slope is negative and is equal to $-\tilde{s}/e_t\tilde{s}^*$. With the negatively sloped *ee* schedule a downward movement along the schedule (i.e., a rise in Y_t and a fall in Y_t^*) is associated with higher values of e_t.

To determine the effects of changes in government spending, we compute the horizontal shift of the *ee* schedule by setting $dY_t^* = dT_t = 0$ in the system (A.43) and solving for dY_t/dG. For the *ee* schedule this yields

$$\frac{dY_t}{dG} = \frac{IM_t + a^g(IM_t^* - IM_t) + [(1 - \tilde{s}^*)(1 - a^g) - \tilde{a}^*]H}{\tilde{s}IM_t - \tilde{a}(IM_t^* - IM_t) + [\tilde{s}(1 - \tilde{s}^* - \tilde{a}^*) + \tilde{a}(1 - \tilde{s}^*)]H}.$$

(A.47)

Thus around trade-balance equilibrium and zero initial debt, the schedule shifts to the right by $1/\tilde{s}$.

By setting $dY_t^* = dG = 0$ and following a similar procedure, the horizontal shift of the *ee* schedule induced by a unit rise in taxes is

$$\frac{dY_t}{dT_t} = -\frac{\tilde{a}(IM_t^* - IM_t) + (1 - \tilde{s})IM_t + \{(1 - \tilde{s})[1 - \tilde{s}^* - \tilde{a}^*(1 - \tilde{s}^*)]\}H}{-\tilde{a}(IM_t^* - IM_t) + \tilde{s}IM_t + [\tilde{s}(1 - \tilde{s}^* - \tilde{a}^*) + \tilde{a}(1 - \tilde{s}^*)]H}.$$

(A.48)

Thus around trade-balance equilibrium and zero initial debt, the schedule shifts to the left by $(1 - \tilde{s})/\tilde{s}$ units.

By combining the results in (A.47) and (A.48), we obtain the effect of a balanced-budget unit rise in government spending. Accordingly, for the *ee* schedule with $dG = dT_t$,

$$\frac{dY_t}{dG} = \frac{\bar{s}IM_t + (a^g - \tilde{a})(IM_t^* - IM_t) + [\bar{s}(1 - \bar{s}^* - \tilde{a}^*) + (1 - \bar{s}^*)(\tilde{a} - a^g)]H}{\bar{s}IM_t - \tilde{a}(IM_t^* - IM_t) + [\bar{s}(1 - \bar{s}^* - \tilde{a}^*) + \tilde{a}(1 - \bar{s}^*)]H}.$$

(A.49)

Thus around trade-balance equilibrium with zero initial debt, a balanced-budget unit rise in government spending shifts the ee schedule to the right by one unit.

In the second step of the diagrammatic analysis we assume that $H = 0$, and we derive the rr^* schedule portraying combinations of Y and Y^* along which the money-market-clearing rates of interest (under the assumption of static exchange-rate expectations) are equal across countries so that

$$r(Y_t - T_t + A_{t-1}, M) = r^*(Y^* + A_{t-1}^*, M^*).$$ (A.50)

Along the rr^* schedule the slope of this schedule is $r_y/r_{y^*}^*$, which can also be expressed in terms of the characteristics of the demands for money according to

$$\frac{dY_t^*}{dY_t} = \frac{M_y}{M_{y^*}^*} \frac{M_{r^*}^*}{M_r} > 0.$$ (A.51)

Obviously, around $r = r^*$, $M_{r^*}^* = M_r^*$. As is evident, the level of government spending does not influence the rr^* schedule, whereas a unit rise in taxes shifts the schedule to the right by one unit.

Formally, the effects of fiscal policies can be obtained by differentiating the system (A.41), (A.42), and (A.50). Thus

$$\begin{bmatrix} -(\bar{s} + \tilde{a}) & e_t \tilde{a}^* & IM_t^* - \tilde{a}^* H \\ \tilde{a} & -e_t(\bar{s}^* + \tilde{a}^*) & -IM_t - (1 - \bar{s}^* - \tilde{a}^*)H \\ \dfrac{M_y}{M_r} & -\dfrac{M_{y^*}^*}{M_r^*} & \dfrac{HM_{y^*}^*}{e_t M_{r^*}^*} \end{bmatrix} \begin{bmatrix} dY_t \\ dY_t^* \\ de_t \end{bmatrix}$$

$$= -\begin{bmatrix} 1 - a^g \\ a^g \\ 0 \end{bmatrix} dT_t, dG + \begin{bmatrix} 1 - \bar{s} - \tilde{a} \\ \tilde{a} \\ \dfrac{M_y}{M_r} \end{bmatrix} dT_t.$$ (A.52)

Solving (A.52), the short-run effects of a debt-financed rise in government spending are

$$\frac{dY_t}{dG} = \frac{M^*_{y^*}}{\Delta M^*_r}[IM_t(1 - a^g) + IM^*_t a^g + (1 - a^g)H] \qquad \text{for } dT_t = 0,$$

(A.53)

$$\frac{dY^*_t}{dG} = \frac{M_y}{\Delta M_r}[IM_t + a^g(IM^*_t - IM_t)]$$

$$+ \frac{1}{\Delta}\left\{\frac{M^*_{y^*}}{M^*_r}(\tilde{a} + \tilde{s}a^g) + \frac{M_y}{M_r}[(1 - a^g)(1 - \tilde{s}^*) - \tilde{a}^*]\right\}H$$

for $dT_t = 0,$ (A.54)

$$\frac{de_t}{dG} = \frac{1}{\Delta}\left\{\frac{M^*_{y^*}}{M^*_r}(\tilde{a} + \tilde{s}a^g) - \frac{e_t M_y}{M_r}[\tilde{a}^* + \tilde{s}^*(1 - a^g)]\right\} \qquad \text{for } dT_t = 0,$$

(A.55)

where

$$\Delta = \frac{M^*_{y^*}}{M^*_r}[(\tilde{s} + \tilde{a})IM_t - \tilde{a}IM^*_t] + \frac{e_t M_y}{M_r}[(\tilde{s}^* + \tilde{a}^*)IM^*_t - \tilde{a}^* IM_t]$$

$$+ \left[(\tilde{s} + \tilde{a})\frac{M^*_{y^*}}{M^*_r} - e_t \tilde{a}^* \frac{M_y}{M_r}\right]H.$$

Thus with an initial balanced trade and with zero initial debt, $\Delta < 0$. Differentiating the money-market equilibrium condition (equation 3.8) and using (A.53), we obtain the equilibrium change in the rate of interest:

$$\frac{dr_t}{dG} = -\frac{M_y M^*_{y^*}}{M_r M^*_{r^*}\Delta}[IM_t + a^g(IM^*_t - IM_t) + (1 - a^g)H]$$

for $dT_t = 0.$ (A.56)

Likewise the short-run effects of a tax-financed rise in government spending are

$$\frac{dY_t}{dG} = \frac{1}{\Delta}\left\{\frac{M_{y^*}^*}{M_r^*}[\bar{s}IM_t^* + (\tilde{a} - g^g)(IM_t - IM_t^*)]\right.$$

$$+ \frac{e_tM_y}{M_r}[\bar{s}^*IM_t^* + \tilde{a}^*(IM_t^* - IM_t)]$$

$$\left. + \left[\frac{M_{y^*}^*}{M_r^*}(\bar{s} + \tilde{a} - a^g) - \frac{e_tM_y}{M_r}\tilde{a}^*\right]H\right\} \qquad \text{for } dG = dT_t,$$

$$\text{(A.57)}$$

$$\frac{dY_t^*}{dG} = \frac{a^g}{\Delta}\left\{\frac{M_y}{M_r}(IM_t^* - IM_t) - \left[\frac{M_y}{M_r}(1 - \bar{s}^*) - \frac{M_{y^*}^*}{M_r^*}\bar{s}\right]H\right\}$$

$$\text{for } dG = dT_t, \qquad \text{(A.58)}$$

$$\frac{de_t}{dG} = \frac{a^g}{\Delta}\left(\frac{e_tM_y}{M_r}\bar{s}^* + \frac{M_{y^*}^*}{M_r^*}\bar{s}\right) \qquad \text{for } dG = dT_t. \qquad \text{(A.59)}$$

Using the money-market equilibrium condition together with (A.57) yields

$$\frac{dr_t}{dG} = -\frac{M_y}{M_r\Delta}\left\{a^g(IM_t^* - IM_t) + \left[\frac{M_{y^*}^*}{M_r^*}(\bar{s} + \tilde{a} - a^g) + \frac{e_tM_y}{M_r}\tilde{a}^*\right]H\right\}$$

$$\text{for } dG = dT_t. \qquad \text{(A.60)}$$

Long-Run Equilibrium: The Two-Country World

The long-run equilibrium of the system is characterized by equations (A.61) through (A.65), where the first three equations are the long-run counterparts to equations (A.41), (A.42), and (A.50) and the last two equations are the requirements of zero savings in both countries implying (once the government budget constraint is incorporated) current-account balances. Embodied in the system are the requirements of money-market equilibria and perfect capital mobility.

$$(1 - \beta_m)\tilde{E}[Y - T + M - (1 + r)B^p, M] + (1 - \beta_m^g)G$$

$$+ e\beta_x^*\tilde{E}^*\left[Y^* + M^* + \left(\frac{1 + r}{e}\right)B^p, M^*\right] = Y. \qquad \text{(A.61)}$$

$$\beta_m \tilde{E}[Y - T + M - (1 + r)B^p, M] + \beta_m^g G$$

$$+ e(1 - \beta_x^*)\tilde{E}^* \left[Y^* + M^* + \left(\frac{1 + r}{e}\right) B^p, M^* \right] = eY^*, \qquad (A.62)$$

$$r[Y - T + M - (1 + r)B^p, M]$$

$$= r^* \left[Y^* + M^* + \left(\frac{1 + r}{e}\right) B^p, M^* \right], \qquad (A.63)$$

$$\tilde{E}[Y - T + M - (1 + r)B^p, M] = Y - rB^p - T, \qquad (A.64)$$

$$\tilde{E}^* \left[Y^* + M^* + \left(\frac{1 + r}{e}\right) B^p, M^* \right] = Y^* + \frac{rB^p}{e}. \qquad (A.65)$$

This system, which determines the long-run equilibrium values of Y, Y^*, e, B^p, and r, can be used to analyze the effects of government spending and taxes on these endogenous variables.

Exchange-Rate Expectations

Up to this point we have assumed that the expectations concerning the evolution of the exchange rate are static. This assumption implied that the rates of interest on securities denominated in different currencies are equalized. Since, however, the actual exchange rate does change over time, it is useful to extend the analysis and allow for exchange-rate expectations that are not static. Specifically, in this part of the appendix we assume that expectations are rational in the sense of being self-fulfilling. We continue to assume that the GDP deflators are fixed. To illustrate the main implication of exchange-rate expectations, we consider a stripped-down version of the small-country flexible exchange-rate model, and for expository convenience, we present the analysis using a continuous-time version of the model.

The budget constraint can be written as

$$E_t + \dot{M}_t - e_t \dot{B}_{ft}^p = Y_t - T_t - \bar{r}_f e_t B_{ft}^p, \qquad (A.66)$$

where a dot over a variable represents a time derivative. The spending and money-demand functions (the counterparts to equations 3.3 and 3.4) are

$$E_t = E(Y_t - T_t - \bar{r}_f e_t B_{ft}^p, M_t - e_t B_{ft}^p, \bar{r}_f), \tag{A.67}$$

$$M_t = M\left(Y_t - T_t - \bar{r}_f e_t B_{ft}^p, M_t - e_t B_{ft}^p, \bar{r}_f + \frac{\dot{e}_t}{e_t}\right), \tag{A.68}$$

where the demand for money is expressed as a negative function of the expected depreciation of the currency, $\dot{e}_t/e_t$. In what follows we simplify the exposition by assuming that the world rate of interest, $\bar{r}_f$, is very low (zero), and that the effect of assets $(M_t - e_t B_{ft}^p)$ on spending is negligible. With these simplifications the goods and money-market equilibrium conditions (the counterparts to equations 3.20a and 3.22a) are

$$(1 - \beta_m)E(Y_t - T_t) + (1 - \beta_m^g)G + e_t \bar{D}^* = Y_t, \tag{A.69}$$

$$M\left(Y_t - T_t, M - e_t B_{ft}^p, \frac{\dot{e}_t}{e_t}\right) = M. \tag{A.70}$$

Equation (A.69) implies that the level of output that clears the goods market depends positively on the level of the exchange rate and on government spending, and negatively on taxes. This dependence can be expressed as

$$Y_t = Y(e_t, G, T_t), \tag{A.71}$$

where $\partial Y_t/\partial e_t = \bar{D}^*/(s + a)$, $\partial Y_t/\partial G = (1 - a^g)/(s + a)$, and $\partial Y_t/\partial T_t = -(1 - s - a)/(s + a)$ are the conventional foreign-trade multipliers. Substituting the functional relation (A.71) into the money-market equilibrium condition and solving for the (actual and expected) percentage change in the exchange rate yields

$$\frac{\dot{e}_t}{e_t} = f(e_t, B_{ft}^p, G, T_t, M), \tag{A.72}$$

where

$$\frac{\partial f}{\partial e} = \frac{-M_y \overline{D}^* / (s + a) + M_A B^p_{ft}}{M_r},$$

$$\frac{\partial f}{\partial B^p_{ft}} = \frac{e_t M_A}{M_r},$$

$$\frac{\partial f}{\partial G} = -\frac{1 - a^g}{(s + a) M_r},$$

$$\frac{\partial f}{\partial T_t} = \frac{1 - s - a}{(s + a) M_t},$$

and where M_A and M_r denote, respectively, the derivatives of the demand for money with respect to assets $(M - e_t B^p_{ft})$ and the rate of interest. The former is positive, and the latter negative. The interpretation of the dependence of the percentage change in the exchange rate, representing the money-market-clearing interest rate, on the various variables follows. A rise in the exchange rate raises the goods-market-clearing level of output and raises the demand for money. To restore money-market equilibrium, the rate of interest must rise; that is, $\dot{e}_t / e_t$ must rise. On the other hand, the rise in e raises the domestic-currency value of the debt B^p_{ft}. If the private sector is a net creditor, the depreciation of the currency raises the domestic-currency value of assets and raises the demand for money. This in turn also contributes to the rise in the rate of interest. If, however, the private sector is a net debtor, then the value of assets falls, and the demand for money is reduced, thereby contributing to a downward pressure on the rate of interest. The net effect on the rate of interest depends therefore on the net debtor position of the private sector; if, however, B^p_{ft} is zero, then the rate of interest must rise so that $\partial f / \partial e_t > 0$. Analogous interpretations apply to the other derivatives where it is evident that $\partial f / \partial B^p_{ft} < 0$, $\partial f / \partial G \geqslant 0$ and $\partial f / \partial T_t < 0$.

Equation (A.72) constitutes the first differential equation of the model governing the evolution of the exchange rate over time. The second variable whose evolution over time characterizes the dynamics of the system is the stock of private-sector debt. Substituting the goods-market equilibrium condition (A.71) into the budget constraint (A.66), and using the fact that in the absence of monetary policy $\dot{M}_t = 0$, we can solve for the dynamics of private-sector debt. Accordingly,

$$\dot{B}^p_{ft} = \frac{1}{e_t} h(e_t, G, T_t)$$

$$= \frac{1}{e_t} \{E_t[Y(e_t, G, T_t) - T_t] - Y(e_t, G, T_t) + T_t\}. \tag{A.73}$$

Equation (A.73) expresses the rate of change of private-sector debt as the difference between private-sector spending and disposable income. The previous discussion implies that $\partial h/\partial e_t = -\bar{D}^*s/(s + a) < 0$, $\partial h/\partial G = -(1 - a^g)s/(s + a) \leqslant 0$, and $\partial h/\partial T_t = s/(s + a) > 0$.

In interpreting these expressions, we note that the function h represents the negative savings of the private sector. Accordingly, a unit rise in e_t or G raises savings by the saving propensity times the corresponding multiplier. Analogously, a unit rise in taxes that lowers disposable income lowers savings by the saving propensity times the corresponding disposable-income multiplier.

The equilibrium of the system is exhibited in figure 3A.1. The positively sloped $\dot{e}_t = 0$ schedule shows combinations of the exchange rate and private-sector debt that maintain an unchanged exchange rate. The schedule represents equation (A.72) for $\dot{e}_t = 0$. Its slope is positive around a zero level of private-sector debt, and its position depends on the policy variables G, T_t, and M. Likewise, the $\dot{B}^p_{ft} = 0$ locus represents equation (A.73) for $\dot{B}^p_{ft} = 0$. It is horizontal since, as specified, the rate of change of private-sector debt does not depend on the value of debt. The arrows around the schedules indicate the directions in which the variables tend to move, and the solid curve shows the unique saddle path converging toward a stationary state. As is customary in this type of analysis, we associate this saddle path with the equilibrium path. The long-run equilibrium of the system is shown by point A in figure 3A.1, where for convenience we show a case in which the long-run value of private-sector debt is zero.

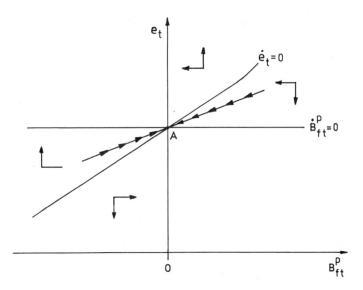

Figure 3A.1
The equilibrium exchange-rate dynamics and debt accumulation

The effects of a unit debt-financed rise in government spending from G_0 to G_1 are shown in figure 3A.2. Starting from an initial long-run equilibrium at point A, the rise in G shifts the $\dot{B}^p_{ft} = 0$ schedule from point A downward by $-(1 - a^g)/\bar{D}^*$, and it also shifts the $\dot{e} = 0$ schedule from point A downward by $-(1 - a^g)/M_y\bar{D}^*$. For $M_y < 1$, the vertical displacement of the $\dot{e} = 0$ schedule exceeds the corresponding displacement of the $\dot{B}^p_{ft} = 0$ schedule, and the new long-run equilibrium obtains at point C, at which the domestic currency has appreciated and private-sector debt has risen. The short-run equilibrium obtains at point B along the new saddle path, and transition toward the long run follows along the path connecting point B and C. As is evident, the initial appreciation of the currency overshoots the long-run appreciation.

The effects of a unit tax-financed rise in government spending are shown in figure 3A.3. With $dG = dT$, the $\dot{B}^p_{ft} = 0$ schedule shifts upward by $a^g/\bar{D}^*$ while the $\dot{e} = 0$ schedule shifts vertically by $(s + a - a^g)/M_y\bar{D}^*$. The benchmark case shown in figure 3A.3 corresponds to the situation in which the private sector and the govern-

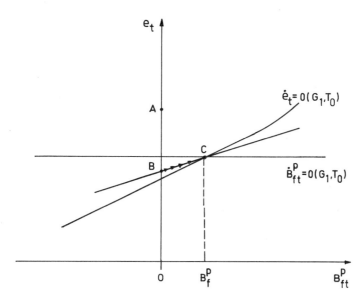

Figure 3A.2
The effects of a debt-financed rise in government spending on the paths of the exchange rate and private-sector debt

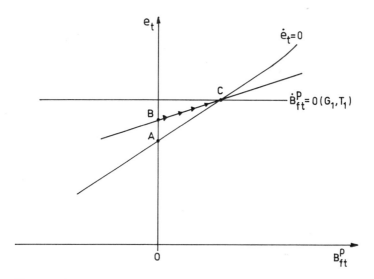

Figure 3A.3
The effect of a tax-financed rise in government spending on the paths of the exchange rate and private-sector debt

ment have the same marginal propensities to spend on domestic goods (i.e., $s + a = a^g$). In that case the $\dot{e} = 0$ remains intact, the short-run equilibrium is at point B, and the long-run equilibrium is at point C. As seen in this case the domestic currency depreciates, and the short-run depreciation undershoots the long-run depreciation. These results are sensitive to alternative assumptions concerning the relative magnitudes of $(s + a)$ and a^g.

4

The Mundell-Fleming Model: Stochastic Dynamics

The Mundell-Fleming model, which has been a "workhorse model" of international macroeconomics, can now be usefully cast in a stochastic framework. Such a framework assumes a set of exogenous stochastic processes (e.g., money supply) that drives the dynamics of the equilibrium system. Since economic agents are forward-looking, each short-term equilibrium is based on expectations about future shocks and the resulting future short-term equilibria.

4.1   The Stochastic Framework

Let us begin with a description of the stochastic version of the Mundell-Fleming model. For simplicity, we express all variables in logarithmic forms (except for the interest rates) and assume all behavioral relations are linear in these log variables. This linear system (similar to the one in Clarida and Gali 1994) can be viewed as an approximation from an original nonlinear system.

Aggregate demand in period t, y_t^d, specified as a function of an exogenous demand component d_t, the real exchange rate q_t, and the domestic real rate of interest r_t, is given by

$$y_t^d = d_t + \eta q_t - \sigma r_t, \tag{4.1}$$

where η and σ are positive elasticities. This equation is an analogue of equation (3.5) of the previous chapter. As is usual, the real variables are derived from the following nominal variables: s_t, the spot exchange rate (the domestic value of foreign currency); p^*, the foreign price level; p_t, the domestic price level; and i_t, the domestic nominal rate of interest. More specifically, $q_t = s_t + p^* - p_t$ and $r_t = i_t - E_t(p_{t+1} - p_t)$. For simplicity, we assume the foreign price level p^* to be constant over time.

Aggregate demand is positively related to the exogenous demand shock, capturing external, fiscal, and other internal shocks. The real exchange rate affects positively aggregate demand by stimulating the traded sector (exportables and domestic production of importables). The real interest rate affects negatively aggregate demand by discouraging investment and consumption.

Money market equilibrium is specified as

$$m_t^s - p_t = y_t - \lambda i_t, \tag{4.2}$$

where m_t^s is the money supply at time t, and λ (> 0) the interest semielasticity of the demand for money. This equation is an analogue of equation (3.7) of the previous chapter. As usual the domestic nominal rate of interest (i_t) has a negative effect on the demand for money, while domestic output (y_t) has a positive effect. To simplify matters, the output demand elasticity is assumed to be unity.

Price setting is based on a mix of auction markets and long-term contract markets. The market-clearing price in the auction market is p_t^e. The price in the long-term contract market is set one period in advance according to expectations of the future market clearing price in that market, $E_{t-1}p_t^e$. Accordingly, the general price level in the domestic economy p_t is given by a weighted average of these two prices:

$$p_t = (1 - \theta)E_{t-1}p_t^e + \theta p_t^e, \tag{4.3}$$

where $0 < \theta < 1$ is the share of the auction market in domestic output. The long-term contract element is akin to Taylor (1981) and Fischer (1981). This introduces an element of price rigidity into the system.

Due to free capital mobility, interest parity prevails. Assuming risk neutrality, uncovered interest parity should hold:

$$i_t = i^* + E_t(s_{t+1} - s_t), \tag{4.4}$$

where i^* is the world rate of interest, assumed for simplicity to be constant over time. Through costless arbitrage, the return on investing one unit of domestic currency in domestic security i_t, is made equal to the expected value of the domestic currency return on investing the same amount in foreign security, which yields a foreign currency return i^* plus an expected depreciation of domestic currency $E_t(s_{t+1} - s_t)$.

The equilibrium system consists of the four equations (4.1)–(4.4) at each point in time. Observe that domestic output is demand determined, as in all models with price rigidity.

The shock (or forcing stochastic) processes that drive the dynamics of the equilibrium system are

$$y_t^s = g_y + y_{t-1}^s - \varepsilon_{yt}, \tag{4.5a}$$

$$d_t = g_y + d_{t-1} + \varepsilon_{dt}, \tag{4.5b}$$

$$m_t^s = g_m + m_{t-1}^s + \varepsilon_{mt}, \tag{4.5c}$$

where g_y and g_m are the deterministic growth rates of output and money, and ε_{yt}, ε_{dt}, ε_{mt} are independently and identically distributed (i.i.d.) *supply*, *demand*, and *money* shocks with zero means and constant variances.[1] Accordingly, our specification assumes that the system is bombarded by permanent shocks (in a random walk fashion).[2]

4.2 Flex-Price Equilibrium

Since our stochastic framework is both forward- and backward-looking, a systematic procedure is required to obtain a solution. We apply a two-stage procedure for solving the equilibrium system (4.1)–(4.5). In the first stage we solve for a flexible price equilibrium that corresponds to this system. In the second stage we use the flex-price equilibrium to arrive at a full-fledged solution for the mixed fix–flex-price system.

Using superscript e to denote flex-price equilibrium values, we can express the first-stage solution in the following form:

$$y_t^e = y_t^s, \tag{4.6}$$

$$q_t^e = \frac{1}{\eta}(y_t^s - d_t + \sigma i^*), \tag{4.7}$$

$$p_t^e = m_t^s - y_t^s + \lambda(i^* + g_m - g_y), \tag{4.8}$$

$$\pi_t^e \ (\equiv E_t p_{t+1}^e - p_t^e) = g_m - g_y, \tag{4.9}$$

$$r_t^e = i^*, \tag{4.10}$$

$$i_t^e = i^* + g_m - g_y, \tag{4.11}$$

$$s_t^e = m_t^s + \left(\frac{1}{\eta} - 1\right)y_t^s - \frac{1}{\eta}d_t + \left(\frac{\sigma}{\eta} + \lambda\right)i^* - p^*$$

$$+ \lambda(g_m - g_y). \tag{4.12}$$

The flex-price equilibrium is economically intuitive. When prices are flexible and the supply of output is exogenous, output must be supply determined; hence (4.6). With constant money demand elasticities, the expected rate of inflation (which turns out also to be the actual inflation rate) must be equal to the difference between money growth and output growth; hence (4.9). Since world prices are constant in the foreign country (hence zero world inflation), the world real and nominal rates of interest must be equal to i^*. Under the assumption of free capital mobility, the domestic real rate of interest must be equal to i^* as well; hence (4.10). From (4.9) and the Fisher equation linking the nominal rate of interest to the real rate and the expected rate of inflation, we can obtain the corresponding domestic nominal interest rate as (4.11). Using the domestic real interest rate expression in (4.10), the real exchange rate that equates output demand to the exogenous supply of output can be solved from the aggregate demand equation (4.1) to yield (4.7). Given the domestic nominal rate of interest (4.11) and output (4.6), the domestic price level that is consistent with money market equilibrium (4.2) can be expressed as in (4.8). Finally, we can derive the nominal exchange rate from (4.7) and (4.8) together with the definition of real exchange rate in terms the nominal exchange rate and domestic and foreign price levels; hence (4.12).

As an application, consider an expansionary fiscal policy indicated by a positive $\Delta(d_t)$, where $\Delta(\cdot)$ is a difference operator. From (4.7) and (4.12) we can verify that the real and nominal exchange rates will appreciate, without any effects on output, prices, and interest rates. This should be familiar to the reader from the result established in the previous chapter that, under a flexible exchange rate system with perfect capital mobility, fiscal policies are neutral.

Consider next an expansionary monetary policy indicated by a positive $\Delta(m_t^s)$. From (4.8) the domestic price level will go up. From (4.12) the domestic nominal exchange rate will depreciate. Output, interest rates, and the domestic real exchange rate will not be affected. This is obviously consistent with the classical dichotomy between real and nominal magnitudes associated with monetary policy under flexible prices, in addition to the familiar Mundell-Fleming effects of monetary policy on the nominal exchange rate discussed in the previous chapter.

4.3 Full-fledged Equilibrium

Following our two-stage solution procedure, we can now use the flex-price equilibrium values obtained in the first stage to solve for the full-fledged equilibrium in this second stage. The equilibrium, derived in appendix A, is as follows:

$$y_t = y_t^e + \left(\frac{\sigma + \eta}{\lambda + \sigma + \eta} \right)(1 + \lambda)(1 - \theta)(\varepsilon_{mt} - \varepsilon_{yt}). \tag{4.13}$$

$$q_t = q_t^e + \left(\frac{1}{\lambda + \sigma + \eta} \right)(1 + \lambda)(1 - \theta)(\varepsilon_{mt} - \varepsilon_{yt}). \tag{4.14}$$

$$p_t = p_t^e - (1 - \theta)(\varepsilon_{mt} - \varepsilon_{yt}). \tag{4.15}$$

$$\pi_t = \pi_t^e + (1 - \theta)(\varepsilon_{mt} - \varepsilon_{yt}). \tag{4.16}$$

$$r_t = r_t^e - \left(\frac{1}{\lambda + \sigma + \eta} \right)(1 + \lambda)(1 - \theta)(\varepsilon_{mt} - \varepsilon_{yt}). \tag{4.17}$$

$$i_t = i_t^e + \left(\frac{\sigma + \eta - 1}{\lambda + \sigma + \eta}\right)(1 - \theta)(\varepsilon_{mt} - \varepsilon_{yt}). \tag{4.18}$$

$$s_t = s_t^e - \left(\frac{\sigma + \eta - 1}{\lambda + \sigma + \eta}\right)(1 - \theta)(\varepsilon_{mt} - \varepsilon_{yt}). \tag{4.19}$$

The full-fledged equilibrium values in equations (4.13)–(4.19) reveal interesting features:

1. *Price rigidity and the classical dichotomy.* Price rigidity is reflected in (4.15), since a positive excess money shock generates a price increase which falls short of the market-clearing price. With preset prices, the classical dichotomy no longer holds. Accordingly, in (4.13) one can observe that output responds to the innovation in the money supply in excess of the innovation in domestic output supply. The real exchange rate is positively affected and the domestic real rate of interest negatively affected by the difference in innovations. The magnitudes of these effects depend on the degree of price flexibility, indicated by θ. Indeed, in the extreme case of complete price flexibility ($\theta = 1$), these real effects of monetary policy will vanish (as shown also in the previous chapter).

2. *The Phillips curve.* Define excess output capacity $y_t^e - y_t$ (which is directly related to the rate of cyclical unemployment) by u_t. Then we can obtain an expectations-augmented Phillips curve relation between inflation (π_t) and excess capacity (u_t) as follows:

$$\pi_t = \pi_t^e - \left(\frac{1}{1 + \lambda}\right)\left(\frac{\lambda}{\sigma + \eta} + 1\right)u_t. \tag{4.20}$$

Equation (4.20) shows that the Phillips curve is flatter when the aggregate demand elasticities η (with respect to the real exchange rate) and σ (with respect to the domestic real rate of interest) are larger. The effect of the interest semielasticity of money demand (λ) on the slope of the Phillips curve is, however, ambiguous, depending on whether $\sigma + \eta$ exceeds or falls short of unity. The source of this ambiguity is derived from the more fundamental ambiguous effects of excess innovations on the domestic nominal interest rate (4.18) and spot exchange rates (4.19).

3. *Real exchange rate and real rate of interest.* Substituting (4.17) into (4.14) yields a contemporaneous negative relation between the real exchange rate and the domestic real interest rate as follows:

$$q_t = q_t^e - (r_t - r_t^e). \qquad (4.21)$$

This unambigous prediction has been subject to a large body of empirical studies (see Campbell and Clarida 1987; Meese and Rogoff 1988; Edison and Pauls 1993), with mixed results. It thus seems that the Mundell-Fleming model should account for this inconsistency with data before it can be used with confidence for policy advice.

4. *Expected long-run values.* Applying the expectation operator as of period t to the system of equations (4.13)–(4.19) in periods $t + 1$ and on reveals that the expected long-run equilibrium values are equal to the flex-price solution. Equation (4.19) then shows that an excess money innovation will lead to exchange rate overshooting *à la* Dornbusch (1976) if the sum of demand elasticities $(\sigma + \eta)$ falls short of unity.

4.4   Capital Immobility

The hallmark of the Mundell-Fleming model is the distinct role played by international capital movements on the effectiveness of policies. Thus restricting capital flows should have a significant effect on the working of the international macro system.

Consider the extreme case where capital flows are completely restricted. In this case the interest parity (4.4) will no longer hold, and trade balance will be equilibrated fully by the market-clearing exchange rate.

The final form of the aggregate demand equation (4.1), derived from the structural equation, will have to be modified. We can write the original structural equation as

$$y_t^d = (\tilde{d}_t^A + A_y y_t^d + A_r r_t) + (d_t^X + X_y y_t^d + X_q q_t),$$

where the first parenthetical expression refers to domestic absorption A, and the second to net trade balance X. The autonomous component of absorption is denoted by $\tilde{d}_t^A$, the income elasticity of absorption by A_y (>0), and the interest elasticity of absorption by A_r (<0). Similarly, d_t^X denotes the autonomous component of trade balance, X_y (<0) the income elasticity of trade balance, and X_q (>0) the real exchange rate elasticity of trade balance. To arrive at the final form (4.1), we simply solve for y_t^d as a function of r_t and q_t. Define the sum of marginal propensities to save and import, $1 - A_y - X_y$, as α. Notice that $d_t = (\tilde{d}_t^A + d_t^X)/\alpha$, $\eta = X_q/\alpha > 0$, and $\sigma = -A_r/\alpha > 0$.

In the presence of full capital controls, the net trade balance X is zero. Hence $d_t^X + X_y y_t^d + X_q q_t = 0$, which can be rewritten as

$$d_t^X - \mu y_t^d + \alpha\eta q_t = 0, \tag{4.1}'$$

where $\mu = -X_y$ and $\alpha\eta = X_q$. Substituting this into the structural equation for aggregate demand, we can modify the final form as

$$y_t^d = d_t^A - \sigma\gamma r_t, \tag{4.1}''$$

where $d_t^A = \tilde{d}_t^A/(1 - A_y)$ and $\gamma = (1 - A_y - X_y)/(1 - A_y) > 1$. As an analogue to (4.5b), we specify the stochastic process for d_t^A as

$$d_t^A = g_y + d_{t-1}^A + \varepsilon_{dt}^A, \tag{4.5b}'$$

where ε_{dt}^A is assumed to have similar properties as ε_{dt}.

We lay out the solutions for the flex-price and full-fledged equilibria in appendix B. Here we focus on the effect of capital controls on output y_t, the real exchange rate q_t, and the inflation rate π_t. The full-fledged equilibrium output, real exchange rate, and inflation rate are given respectively by

$$y_t = y_t^e + \left(\frac{\sigma\gamma}{\lambda + \sigma\gamma}\right)(1+\lambda)(1-\theta)\left[\varepsilon_{mt} - \left(\frac{\lambda + \sigma\gamma}{\sigma\gamma}\right)\varepsilon_{yt} + \left(\frac{\lambda}{\sigma\gamma}\right)\varepsilon_{dt}^A\right],$$
$$\tag{4.13}'$$

where $y_t^e = y_t^s$.

$$q_t = q_t^e + \left(\frac{\mu}{\alpha\eta}\right)\left(\frac{\sigma\gamma}{\lambda + \sigma\gamma}\right)(1+\lambda)(1-\theta)\left[\varepsilon_{mt} - \left(\frac{\lambda + \sigma\gamma}{\sigma\gamma}\right)\varepsilon_{yt} + \left(\frac{\lambda}{\sigma\gamma}\right)\varepsilon_{dt}^A\right],$$
$$\tag{4.14}'$$

where $q_t^e = (\mu y_t^s - d_t^X)/\alpha\eta$.

$$\pi_t = \pi_t^e + (1 - \theta)\left[\varepsilon_{mt} - \left(\frac{\lambda + \sigma\gamma}{\sigma\gamma}\right)\right]\varepsilon_{yt} + \left(\frac{\lambda}{\sigma\gamma}\right)\varepsilon_{dt}^A, \qquad (4.16)'$$

where $\pi_t^e = g_m - g_y$.

Comparing these equilibrium values with those under free capital flows (4.13) and (4.14), we can highlight four main hypotheses:

1. *Demand shocks.* Under capital controls, the absorption shock ε_{dt}^A has a positive effect on $y_t - y_t^e$, $q_t - q_t^e$, and $\pi_t - \pi_t^e$, through its negative effect on the domestic real rate of interest r_t. In contrast, it has no effect in the case of free capital flows, since the real rate of interest there is nailed down by the world rate of interest.

2. *Monetary shocks.* The monetary shock ε_{mt} will have a smaller effect on $y_t - y_t^e$ (through a stronger negative effect on r_t) under capital controls if $\sigma\gamma < \sigma + \eta$, and the opposite is true if $\sigma\gamma > \sigma + \eta$. The relative sensitivity of $q_t - q_t^e$ to the shock under the two capital mobility regimes is also ambiguous in general, depending on the relative magnitudes of $\mu(\sigma\gamma)/\alpha\eta(\lambda + \sigma\gamma)$ and $1/(\lambda + \sigma + \eta)$. Finally, the shock has the same effect on $\pi_t - \pi_t^e$ as in the free capital mobility case.

3. *Supply shocks.* Since $(\sigma + \eta)/(\lambda + \sigma + \eta) < 1$, the productivity shock ε_{yt} has a bigger negative effect on aggregate demand $y_t - y_t^e$ (through a stronger positive effect on r_t) under capital controls. The relative sensitivity of $q_t - q_t^e$ to the shock under the two capital mobility regimes is again ambiguous. The shock will nonetheless produce a more pronounced effect on $\pi_t - \pi_t^e$ under capital controls.

4. *The Phillips curve.* Substituting equation (4.13)' into equation (4.16)' and defining $u_t = -(y_t - y_t^e)$ as before, we can express the Phillips curve under capital controls as follows:

$$\pi_t = \pi_t^e - \left(\frac{1}{1 + \lambda}\right)\left(\frac{\lambda}{\sigma\gamma} + 1\right)u_t. \qquad (4.20)'$$

The steepest (flattest) line in figure 4.1, portrays the open-economy Phillips curve under capital controls when $\sigma\gamma < (>)\sigma + \eta$, while

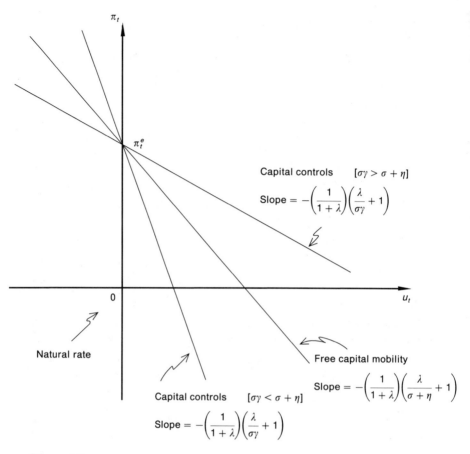

Figure 4.1
The open-economy Phillips curves

the line with intermediate slope depicts the Phillips curve under perfect capital mobility. In other words, fluctuations in inflation rates will be associated with smaller or bigger variations in unemployment depending on whether $\sigma\gamma <$ or $> \sigma + \eta$.

The intuition behind the changing slopes of the Phillips curve has to do with the impact effect of capital controls on aggregate demand. Comparing the aggregate demand functions under capital controls (4.1)″ and under free capital mobility (4.1), we observe that in the former case the interest semielasticity becomes bigger ($\sigma\gamma > \sigma$, since

$\gamma > 1$) and the real exchange rate effect disappears ($0 < \eta$) from the reduced form equation for aggregate demand. This is because under capital controls the interest rate parity need not hold, leaving more room for adjustment in the domestic interest rate to shocks (the "r-effect"), while the zero net trade balance restriction (given that the capital account is closed) limits the flexibility of the real exchange rate (the "q-effect"). On the other hand, capital controls do not alter the mechanisms underlying the determination of prices (i.e., the price-setting equation (4.3) and the money market equation (4.2)).

Indeed, a comparison between equations (4.20) and (4.20)′ reveals that the difference in the slopes of the Phillips curve under free capital mobility and capital controls depends solely on the aggregate demand parameters $\sigma + \eta$ versus $\sigma\gamma$, and not on the money market parameter λ and the price-setting parameter θ. In particular, when the q-effect dominates the r-effect ($\sigma\gamma < \sigma + \eta$), the overall output effect due to, say, any policy change that moves the economy along its Phillips curve will be smaller with than without capital controls, while the price (or inflation) effect remains unchanged. In other words, restrictions on capital flows will generate less variations in unemployment rates (excess output capacity) at the expense of more variations in inflation rates. The reverse is true when the r-effect dominates the q-effect (i.e., then $\sigma\gamma > \sigma + \eta$).

Presumably, the natural rate of unemployment ($= 0$ in our case) and the expected rate of inflation (π^e) are unaffected by capital controls. This is reflected by the intersection of the two Phillips curves at the point $(0, \pi^e)$. While the various shocks will move economy away from this point along the respective Phillips curve (depending on the capital mobility regime), changes in the expected rate of inflation due to permanent changes in the relative money-output growth rates ($g_m - g_y$) will shift the Phillips curve around.

4.5 Some Policy Implications

There exist three types of gains from trade: trade of goods/services for goods/services; trade of goods/services for assets (intertemporal trade), and trade of assets for assets (for diversification of risk).

Evidently capital controls limit the potential gains of the last two types. However, there are second-best and other suboptimal (e.g., due to non-market-clearing) situations where capital controls can improve efficiency.

When, for example, taxation of foreign-source income from capital is not enforceable, it proves efficient to "trap" capital within national borders so as to broaden the tax base and to alleviate other tax distortions (see Razin and Sadka 1991 and chapter 14).

This chapter introduces another argument in favor of constraints on capital mobility. We show that capital controls alter the inflation-unemployment trade-offs. In particular, output/employment variations may be reduced or magnified at the expense of variations in inflation rates (depending on whether $\sigma\gamma <$ or $> \sigma + \eta$). With estimates of the relative magnitude of the aggregate demand parameters, policymakers who put asymmetric weights on stable employment and stable inflation can have their objective more easily attained by appropriate choice of the degree of capital mobility. For instance, they can impose capital controls to achieve less variability in output by accepting more variability in inflation when $\sigma\gamma < \sigma + \eta$.

4.6   Appendix A: Derivation of the Full-fledged Equilibrium Solution

This appendix derives the solution for the full-fledged equilibrium (4.13)–(4.19), taking as given the flex-price equilibrium.

1. *Derivation of p_t (4.15).* To get the solution for the domestic price level (4.15), we simply substitute (4.5c) and (4.8) into (4.3).

2. *Derivation of q_t (4.14).* Substituting (4.4) and (4.7) into (4.1), using the definitions of real exchange rate $q_t = s_t + p^* - p_t$ and real interest rate $r_t = i_t - E_t(p_{t+1} - p_t)$, and subtracting $(\lambda + \sigma)E_t q^e_{t+1}$ and adding $(\lambda + \sigma)q^e_t$, we get

$$\eta(q_t - q^e_t) = (\lambda + \sigma)[E_t(q_{t+1} - q^e_{t+1}) - (q_t - q^e_t)]$$

$$+ (1 + \lambda)(1 - \theta)(\varepsilon_{mt} - \varepsilon_{yt}). \tag{A.1}$$

Observe, from (4.5a), (4.5b), and (4.7) and the properties of ε_{yt+1} and ε_{dt+1}, that $E_t q_{t+1}^e = q_t^e$. We guess a solution of the form $q_t = q_t^e + \kappa(\varepsilon_{mt} - \varepsilon_{yt})$ and apply it to (A.1).

$$\eta\kappa(\varepsilon_{mt} - \varepsilon_{yt}) = (\lambda + \sigma)E_t[\kappa(\varepsilon_{mt+1} - \varepsilon_{yt+1}) - \kappa(\varepsilon_{mt} - \varepsilon_{yt})]$$

$$+ (1 + \lambda)(1 - \theta)(\varepsilon_{mt} - \varepsilon_{yt}).$$

Since $E_t(\varepsilon_{mt+1} - \varepsilon_{yt+1}) = 0$, we can obtain $\kappa = (1 + \lambda)(1 - \theta)/(\lambda + \sigma + \eta)$ from the above equation. This value of κ in our guess solution yields the solution for the real exchange rate (4.14).

3. *Derivation of y_t (4.13) and i_t (4.18).* Substituting the solutions for p_t and q_t from (4.15) and (4.14) just derived above into the aggregate demand equation (4.1) while using the interest parity (4.4) yields the solutions for y_t (4.13) and i_t (4.18).

4. *Derivation of π_t (4.16).* Applying the definition of the expected rate of inflation, $\pi_t = E_t(p_{t+1} - p_t)$, to (4.15) derived in step 1 and (4.9) yields the solution for the inflation rate (4.16).

5. *Derivation of r_t (4.17).* Using i_t derived in step 3 and π_t in step 4 and the Fisher equation yields the solution for the domestic real rate of interest r_t.

6. *Derivation of s_t (4.19).* Using the solutions for p_t derived in step 1 and q_t in step 2 and applying them to the definition of the real exchange rate $q_t = s_t + p^* - p_t$ yields a solution for the nominal exchange rate s_t.

4.7 Appendix B: Solutions for the Capital Controls Model

This appendix provides the solution to (4.1)', (4.1)", (4.2), and (4.3), subject to the stochastic processes (4.5) and (4.5b)'. The flex-price equilibrium conditions are

$$y_t^e = y_t^s, \tag{A.2}$$

$$q_t^e = \frac{1}{\alpha\eta}(\mu y_t^s - d_t^X), \tag{A.3}$$

$$p_t^e = \lambda\left[\frac{1}{\sigma\gamma}(d_t^A - y_t^s) + g_m - g_y\right] + m_t^s - y_t^s, \tag{A.4}$$

$$\pi_t^e = g_m - g_y, \tag{A.5}$$

$$r_t^e = \frac{1}{\sigma\gamma}(d_t^A - y_t^s), \tag{A.6}$$

$$i_t^e = \frac{1}{\sigma\gamma}(d_t^A - y_t^s) + g_m - g_y, \tag{A.7}$$

$$s_t^e = m_t^s + \left(\frac{\mu}{\alpha\eta} - \frac{\lambda + \sigma\gamma}{\sigma\gamma}\right)y_t^s - \left(\frac{1}{\alpha\eta}d_t^X - \frac{\lambda}{\sigma\gamma}d_t^A\right)$$

$$\quad - p^* + \lambda(g_m - g_y). \tag{A.8}$$

To solve the full-fledged equilibrium, we use the flex-price solution to obtain the equilibrium price p_t and inflation rate π_t. We then use the Fisher equation along with the aggregate demand and money market equilibrium equations (4.1)″ and (4.2) to get the solutions for the real interest rate r_t and output y_t simultaneously. From the trade balance equation (4.1)′, we can calculate the real exchange rate q_t. The nominal interest rate i_t and the nominal exchange rate s_t are then derived from the Fisher equation and the definition of the real exchange rate respectively. Below we lay out the solution for the full-fledged equilibrium:

$$y_t = y_t^e + \left(\frac{\sigma\gamma}{\lambda + \sigma\gamma}\right)(1 + \lambda)(1 - \theta)\left[\varepsilon_{mt} - \left(\frac{\lambda + \sigma\gamma}{\sigma\gamma}\right)\varepsilon_{yt}\right.$$

$$\left. + \left(\frac{\lambda}{\sigma\gamma}\right)\varepsilon_{dt}^A\right]. \tag{A.9}$$

$$q_t = q_t^e + \left(\frac{\mu}{\alpha\eta}\right)\left(\frac{\sigma\gamma}{\lambda + \sigma\gamma}\right)(1 + \lambda)(1 - \theta)\left[\varepsilon_{mt} - \left(\frac{\lambda + \sigma\gamma}{\sigma\gamma}\right)\varepsilon_{yt}\right.$$

$$\left. + \left(\frac{\lambda}{\sigma\gamma}\right)\varepsilon_{dt}^A\right]. \tag{A.10}$$

$$p_t = p_t^e - (1 - \theta)\left[\varepsilon_{mt} - \left(\frac{\lambda + \sigma\gamma}{\sigma\gamma}\right)\varepsilon_{yt} + \left(\frac{\lambda}{\sigma\gamma}\right)\varepsilon_{dt}^A \right]. \tag{A.11}$$

$$\pi_t = \pi_t^e + (1 - \theta)\left[\varepsilon_{mt} - \left(\frac{\lambda + \sigma\gamma}{\sigma\gamma}\right)\varepsilon_{yt} + \left(\frac{\lambda}{\sigma\gamma}\right)\varepsilon_{dt}^A \right]. \tag{A.12}$$

$$r_t = r_t^e - \left(\frac{1}{\lambda + \sigma\gamma}\right)(1 + \lambda)(1 - \theta)\left[\varepsilon_{mt} - \left(\frac{\lambda + \sigma\gamma}{\sigma\gamma}\right)\varepsilon_{yt} \right.$$
$$\left. + \left(\frac{\lambda}{\sigma\gamma}\right)\varepsilon_{dt}^A \right]. \tag{A.13}$$

$$i_t = i_t^e + \left(\frac{\lambda(1 - \sigma\gamma)}{\lambda + \sigma\gamma}\right)(1 - \theta)\left[\varepsilon_{mt} - \left(\frac{\lambda + \sigma\gamma}{\sigma\gamma}\right)\varepsilon_{yt} \right.$$
$$\left. + \left(\frac{\lambda}{\sigma\gamma}\right)\varepsilon_{dt}^A \right]. \tag{A.14}$$

$$s_t = s_t^e + \left[\left(\frac{\mu}{\alpha\eta}\right)\left(\frac{\sigma\gamma}{\lambda + \sigma\gamma}\right)(1 + \lambda) - 1 \right](1 - \theta)$$
$$\times \left[\varepsilon_{mt} - \left(\frac{\lambda + \sigma\gamma}{\sigma\gamma}\right)\varepsilon_{yt} + \left(\frac{\lambda}{\sigma\gamma}\right)\varepsilon_{dt}^A \right]. \tag{A.15}$$

Comparing the full-fledged equilibrium under capital controls (A.9)–(A.15) with the corresponding equilibrium under free capital flows (4.13)–(4.19), we can assess the significant role that capital mobility plays in the Mundell-Fleming model.

Problems

1. Consider the fixed-price, fixed-exchange rate, flexible-output model of chapter 2. Assume that all demand functions are such that the propensities to spend and save out of assets are the same as the propensities to spend and save out of disposable income. Assume that government spending is constant and, without loss of generality, equal to zero in all periods.

a. What is the effect on domestic and foreign output in period zero, Y_0 and Y_0^*, of a unit increase in the domestic money supply M_0 brought about by a unit decrease in domestic taxes in period zero, T_0, holding T_t constant and equal to 0 for all $t > 0$? What is the effect of this policy on the period zero trade balance TA_0 and on the domestic money supply M_0?

b. With taxes returning to their previous value of zero and all quantities stationary over time, what is the effect on the value of domestic and foreign output in the long run? Also how is the distribution of the world money supply affected by this policy? In answering this part of the question, you may assume that expenditure and money demand functions are linear.

2. Consider the "dual" to the fixed-price Keynesian model of chapter 2, in which prices were fixed and output variable. Assume that output is fixed at its full employment level, which is normalized to unity in both countries, and that the prices of all goods are perfectly flexible. As in chapter 2 let the exchange rate be fixed and set equal to unity. Finally, assume as in exercise 1b that all behavioral functions are linear, that the domestic and foreign

governments run balanced budgets in all periods, and that government spending in the foreign country is equal to zero in all periods.

a. Write down the conditions that must be satisfied in the short-run equilibrium. Also write down an expression for the nominal trade balance.

b. Solve explicitly for the (short-run) equilibrium domestic and foreign price level in terms of the level of *nominal* government spending and the world money stock. Substitute these solutions into your expression for the nominal trade balance, and obtain an expression for the latter in terms of these exogenous variables. Using the expression for the trade balance and the relation $M_t = M_{t-1} + TA_t$, show that the coefficient multiplying M_{t-1} in the equation for M_t is positive and less than unity and hence that the changes in the domestic money supply that occur during the process of adjustment eventually come to a halt (i.e., the system converges to its long-run equilibrium).

c. Show that if the initial level of government spending is equal to zero, then a rise in M_{t-1} (consequent on a trade balance surplus) worsens the home country's terms of trade (i.e., raises P_t^*/P_t) if the sign of the parameter b is positive, where $b = a^*(s^*a - sc^*) - a(1 - s^*)(s^*c - sa^*)$.

d. Solve explicitly for the domestic and foreign price levels in the long run.

e. Show that the effect of a balanced-budget increase in government spending by the home country results in a negative comovement of domestic and foreign levels of nominal private sector spending in both the short run and the long run. Are short-run changes in nominal spending smaller or larger than the corresponding long-run changes? Why?

3. Consider the model with fixed output and flexible prices outlined in exercise 2.

a. Prove that a balanced budget increase in government spending improves the home country's long-run terms of trade if and only if the domestic private sector's propensity to import out of spending $(\bar{a} = a/(1 - s))$ exceeds the government import propensity a^g.

b. Define the domestic consumer price index P_c as a geometric weighted average of the domestic and foreign GDP deflators P and P^*, with weights equal to the domestic expenditure shares. Thus the weight of domestic goods in P_c would be $\bar{c} = (1 - s - a)/(1 - s)$, and the weight of foreign goods would be $\bar{a} = a/(1 - s)$, and clearly $\bar{c} + \bar{a} = 1$. Define the level of domestic and foreign real spending as nominal spending in the particular country divided by the corresponding consumer price index, namely $E = Z/P_c$, and $E^* = Z^*/P_c^*$, where E and E^* denote real spending levels at home and abroad, respectively. Show that, from an initial position in which $G = G^* = 0$, the long-run proportional change in E^* from a balanced budget rise in government spending originating in the domestic economy is positive if and only if $a^g < \bar{a}$. Also show that the long-run proportional change in E caused by a balanced budget increase in G is always negative, independent of differences in the import propensities between the government and the private sector. In this last part, you will need to recall the restriction that $1 - s - a > 0$ (i.e., that the marginal propensity to consume domestic goods is positive).

4. Consider the fixed exchange rate, perfect capital mobility model of chapter 3. Consider the case of a small country that takes foreign demand for its output (assumed for convenience to be zero) as given, and faces a given exogenous world rate of interest. Suppose that initial government spending, taxes, and debt are all zero, and that in the initial stationary equilibrium, this economy is neither a net borrower nor a net lender in world capital markets. Consider the effect of an exogenous increase in the world rate of interest.

a. What is the effect on output and the equilibrium money stock in the short run?

b. How does output behave In the long run? In signing your answer, you may assume, as in the chapter, that a rise in income worsens the current account of the balance of payments (i.e., $a > r(s - M_y)$).

c. Compare your answers to a and b. Does output move in the same direction in the short run as in the long run? If so, does it move by more or less on impact than in the long run? If not, what accounts for the different behavior of output in the short run and long run?

d. Show that although the long-run effect on money holdings is ambiguous, a rise in the world rate of interest necessarily increases the private sector's holdings of financial assets, $M - B$, in the steady state.

5. Consider the small-country model of chapter 3 with flexible exchange rates and capital mobility. Assume that there is no government spending or taxes, nor government debt. Assume that initially the private sector is a net debtor (i.e., $B_{t-1} > 0$).

a. Compute the effects on output and the exchange rate in the short run of debt forgiveness in the amount of one unit (i.e., $dB_{t-1} = -1$).

b. Compute the effects on output in the case where the small country operates with a fixed exchange rate.

c. Suppose that export earnings D are approximately equal to the amount of initial debt, B (in 1990 external debt for all developing countries amounted to about $1\frac{1}{4}$ times annual export earnings, so this isn't too bad an approximation). Would you expect debt forgiveness of the type analyzed in parts a and b of this question to have a larger effect on output under fixed or flexible exchange rates?

6. Consider the Mundell-Fleming model of chapter 3. Compare the long-run effects of changes in the nominal supply of money for a small country with a flexible exchange rate regime to those of a change in the nominal exchange rate in the fixed exchange rate regime version of the model. Does the flexible exchange rate model exhibit long-run neutrality in the sense that a doubling of the money stock leads to a doubling of the exchange rate, with no change in real variables? In the case of the model with fixed exchange rates, does a doubling of the exchange rate lead to a doubling of the nominal quantity of money? Explain.

7. An important simplifying assumption in the model presented in chapter 3 was the assumption that the actual current and expected future values of the exchange rate would always be equal to one another (static expectations). Suppose, in contrast to chapter 3, that people do not necessarily expect the exchange rate to remain con-

stant at its current level. If we denote by e_t^a the anticipated or expected future value of the exchange rate, then the assumption that domestic and foreign assets are identical in all respects except for currency denomination implies that the following arbitrage condition holds at all times:

$$(1 + i_t) = \left(\frac{e_t^a}{e_t}\right)(1 + i_t^*),$$

where i_t and i_t^* are the domestic and foreign nominal interest rates at time t. Under the fixed-price assumption of chapter 3, the same arbitrage condition also holds with respect to real interest rates so that

$$(1 + r_t) = \left(\frac{e_t^a}{e_t}\right)(1 + r_t^*).$$

a. Consider the effects of a debt-financed increase in government spending on domestic goods under the assumption of fixed exchange rates, so that anticipated and actual exchange rates are always equal to one another (and may be assumed equal to unity). Assume that the country undertaking the fiscal expansion is small in world markets, that in the initial steady state the country is neither a net lender nor a net borrower in world capital markets, and that the effects of interest rate changes on domestic absorption are negligible so that the partial derivative E_r the expenditure function with respect to the domestic interest rate is zero. Consider only the short-run effects.

b. Now consider the same policy experiment under flexible exchange rates, under the flexible exchange rates, under the assumption that the expected future exchange rate is constant. Is the effect on output larger or smaller than under fixed exchange rates?

c. Suppose now that the increase in government spending lasts for some time and that the expected exchange rate moves in the same direction as the actual exchange rate moved in part b. Is the rise in output larger or smaller than in b? If the expected exchange rate moves by the same proportion as the actual exchange rate, by how much does output change in response to the fiscal expansion?

8. Consider the stochastic dynamic version of the Mundell-Fleming model with perfect capital mobility. Introduce transitory shocks to the money supply process by adding an extra term $-\phi\varepsilon_{mt-1}$ ($\phi > 0$) to the right-hand side of (4.5c). Decompose the variance of the real exchange rate q_t into transitory and permanent components of the monetary shock.

9. Consider the stochastic dynamic version of the Mundell-Fleming model with perfect capital mobility. Introduce a correlation between the money supply process m_t^s and aggregate demand process d_{t-1} by adding ρd_{t-1} to the right-hand side of (4.5c). One can view this as a feedback rule whereby current monetary policy is conditioned on fiscal impulse in the previous period. What value of ρ will minimize output variance? Inflation variance?

10. Consider the stochastic dynamic version of the Mundell-Fleming model with and without capital controls.
a. Compare the sensitivity of the following economic indicators to the various shocks between the two capital mobility regimes: p_t, π_t, r_t, i_t, s_t.
b. Compare the slopes of the Phillips curves under the two regimes.
c. Check whether the negative relation between the real exchange rate and the domestic real rate of interest under perfect capital mobility holds also under capital controls.

III

The Intertemporal Approach

5

The Two-Period Composite-Commodity World

The main characteristic of the modern analysis of fiscal policies is the detailed attention given to dynamic and intertemporal considerations. In contrast with earlier analyses, the modern approach is based on more solid microeconomic foundations. These foundations "discipline" the analysis and impose constraints on the modeling of macroeconomic behavior. Specifically, an explicit account of temporal and intertemporal budget constraints restricts the permissible behavior of households and governments and sharpens the predictive content of the economic model. Furthermore, by deriving the private sector's *aggregate* behavior from the utility maximization behavior of *individuals,* the modern analytical framework allows for a meaningful treatment of normative issues. Hence within this framework a macroeconomic analysis is applicable for both positive economic issues as well as issues in welfare economics.

In this chapter we review basic elements of intertemporal open-economy macroeconomics. To motivate the discussion, we start in section 5.1 with a specification of a simple stylized two-period model of a small open economy that has free access to world capital markets and that produces and consumes a single aggregate tradable good. In this context we characterize the maximizing behavior of firms and households and determine the general equilibrium levels of investment, consumption, savings, and the various accounts of the balance of payments.

The intertemporal disparities between the paths of consumption and income are reflected in debt accumulation and decumulation. To highlight the central motives underlying the determination of intertemporal allocations of debt, we introduce in section 5.2 three basic concepts: consumption smoothing, consumption tilting, and consumption augmenting. These concepts are useful for interpreting the role that capital markets play in facilitating the adjustments of consumption paths over time.

In section 5.3 we illustrate the usefulness of the three concepts by applying the stylized model to the analysis of supply shocks. In this context we analyze the effects of temporary (current or anticipated future) and permanent supply shocks on the levels of consumption, investment, and the trade balance.

In section 5.4 we extend the analysis of the small open economy to the familiar home-country-foreign-country model of the world economy. The analysis identifies the factors that determine the equilibrium level of the world rate of interest and the associated international and intertemporal distribution of trade imbalances. The key factors governing the equilibrium are the relation between the home and the foreign marginal saving propensities (reflecting differences between marginal rates of time preference), the relation between the home and the foreign percentage rates of growth of GDP, the percentage rate of growth of world GDP, and the initial distribution of world debt. The impact of the initial distribution is illustrated through an analysis of the effects of international transfers on the equilibrium level of the world rate of interest.

In section 5.5 we extend the analysis of the small open economy to the analysis of stochastic supply shocks. In this context we demonstrate the effect of consumption smoothing on the variability of consumption compared to the variability of GDP.

5.1   A Stylized Model

Let us consider a small open economy producing and consuming one aggregate tradable good and facing a given world rate of interest. The aggregation of goods into a single aggregate commodity is done to focus attention on intertemporal trade, that is, on international borrowing and lending. Obviously, in designing a model that is suitable for intertemporal analysis, we need to extend the single-period perspective into a multi-period setting. In the context of the stylized model we adopt the minimal framework of a two-period model.

We start by specifying the supply side of the model. The economy is endowed with an initial stock of capital, K_0, and a production function that depends on capital, $F_0(K_0)$. We assume that the production function exhibits positive and diminishing marginal returns.

The investment technology is assumed to exhibit increasing average as well as marginal costs of investment due to adjustment costs. The latter, indicated by the coefficient $g \geqslant 0$, reflect installation, job reassignment, or training. To simplify we assume quadratic costs:

$$Z_0 = I_0 \left(1 + \frac{\frac{1}{2}g I_0}{K_0} \right), \tag{5.1}$$

where I_0 is the level of investment, and Z_0 is the cost of investment. Average costs of investment, $1 + \frac{1}{2}g I_0 / K_0$, fall short of the marginal costs of investment, $1 + g I_0 / K_0$, implying increasing average costs. Putting it differently, there are diminishing returns to capital formation.

The capital stock in period one, K_1, is augmented by the investment that takes place in period zero, according to

$$K_1 = I_0 + K_0, \tag{5.2}$$

where for simplicity we ignore depreciation.

The investment process modifies the intertemporal pattern of available outputs (GDP). Formally, output in period one, Y_1, is linked to the initial stock of capital, K_0, and the level of investment, I_0, through the production function

$$Y_1 = F_1(K_1) = F_1(I_0 + K_0). \tag{5.3}$$

Naturally, in the absence of investment the capital stock cannot be augmented, and future output is $Y_1 = F_1(K_0)$.

Firms are assumed to maximize the present value of profits. Formally, the firm's investment policy is determined by solving the maximization problem

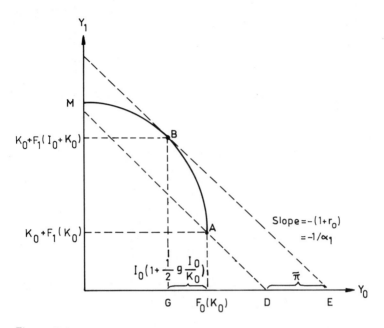

Figure 5.1
The determination of investment and profits

$$\tilde{\pi} = \max_{I_0} \left\{ \alpha_1[F_1(I_0 + K_0) + (I_0 + K_0)] - I_0\left(1 + \frac{\frac{1}{2}gI_0}{K_0}\right)\right\}, \qquad (5.4)$$

where $\alpha_1 = 1/(1 + r_0)$ denotes the present value or discount factor, and r_0 is the world rate of interest between periods one and zero. The formulation in (5.4) indicates that a unit of current investment, I_0, bears fruits, $F_1(I_0 + K_0)$, only in the subsequent period; this is reflected by the discounting in the profit function. Figure 5.1 illustrates the maximization problem and the firm's investment policy. In the absence of investment the output sequence is $(F_0(K_0), K_0 + F_1(K_0))$. This pair of outputs is denoted by point A, and the present value of this sequence of outputs is denoted by point D. The (absolute value of the) slope of the dashed line connecting points A and D is the intertemporal price $(1/\alpha_1) = 1 + r_0$. Point M represents the maximum level of investment, so that the domestic production that is allocated for present consumption is zero (i.e., $Z_0 = F_0(K_0)$). The schedule originating from point A and passing through point B specifies the transformation schedule linking current period production that is allocated for consumption with future period production that is allocated for consumption.

Diagrammatically, investment spending is measured in a leftward direction from $F_0(K_0)$. In the absence of investment, future profits are zero. Thus, the dashed line AD is a zero-profit locus. The profit-maximizing firm seeks to reach the highest isoprofit locus subject to its technological constraints. Point B in figure 5.1 represents the outcome of the firm's profit-maximizing investment policy. With such policy the present value of future profits, $\tilde{\pi}$, is measured by the distance DE, and the level of investment spending, Z_0, is measured by the distance from G to $F_0(K_0)$.

As is evident from figure 5.1, the firm will carry out positive investment only if the transformation function emerging at the initial endowment point, A, is steeper at that point than $1 + r_0$. At point B the present value of future profits is maximized, and the (absolute value of the) slope of the transformation function equals $1 + r_0$. Formally we note from equation (5.4) that the first-order condition for profit maximization requires that

$$\frac{F_1'(I_0 + K_0) - gI_0/K_0}{q_0} = r_0, \tag{5.5}$$

where $q_0 = 1 + gI_0/K_0$ is the marginal adjustment cost. Diminishing returns, that is, $F_1''(I_0 + K_0) < 0$, and increasing marginal costs of adjustment, that is, $g > 0$, imply that a higher rate of interest lowers the profit-maximizing level of investment. In terms of figure 5.1, a higher rate of interest steepens the isoprofit loci and slides point B rightward along the transformation schedule toward point A. The new profit-maximization point is associated with a smaller level of investment.

We turn next to an analysis of the demand side of the model. Consider a representative consumer maximizing lifetime utility subject to budget constraints. The individual's resources are composed of the initial endowments, $F_0(K_0)$ and $K_0 + F_1(K_0)$, and profits,

$F_1(I_0 + K_0) + (I_0 + K_0) - [F_1(K_0) + K_0]$, that firms distribute as dividends to share holders. These resources are used in the first period for consumption and saving. During the second (and last) period, total income is fully consumed. Hence, the first-period budget constraint is

$$C_0 = F_0(K_0) - Z_0 + B_0 - (1 + r_{-1})B_{-1}, \tag{5.6}$$

and the second-period budget constraint is

$$C_1 = F_1(K_0 + I_0) + (K_0 + I_0) - (1 + r_0)B_0. \tag{5.7}$$

In equations (5.6) and (5.7), C_0 and C_1 denote first- and second-period consumption; B_0 denotes first-period borrowing, which can be positive or negative; Z_0 denotes the initial investment spending corresponding to the losses of firms (negative dividends); and $(1 + r_{-1})B_{-1}$ is the historically given initial debt commitment of the representative individual corresponding to the economy's external debt. Finally, the term $-(1 + r_0)B_0$ in equation (5.7) indicates that in the second period individuals must repay debts incurred in the previous period. Obviously, in this two-period model the solvency requirement ensures that in the second period the individual does not incur new debt. Thus, in the final period all debt commitments are settled.

From national income accounting, the sum of consumption, investment, and the surplus in the current account of the balance of payments equals GNP. In terms of equation (5.6), GDP is $F_0(K_0)$, external debt payments are $r_{-1}B_{-1}$, GNP is $F_0(K_0) - r_{-1}B_{-1}$, and the current-account surplus (equal to the capital-account deficit) is $-(B_0 - B_{-1})$. Alternatively, the current-account surplus also equals savings $(F_0(K_0) - r_{-1}B_{-1} - C_0)$ minus investment (Z_0). Hence, the specification in equation (4.6) conforms with national income accounting. Similar considerations apply to the second-period budget constraint in equation (5.7).

Because the representative individual has free access to world capital markets, he or she can lend and borrow freely subject to the world rate of interest, r_0. This access to capital markets implies that the individual's choices are constrained by a consolidated present-value budget constraint rather than two separate periodic budget constraints. To derive the consolidated constraint, we divide equation (5.7) by $(1 + r_0)$, add the resulting equation to equation (5.6), and obtain

$$C_0 + \alpha_1 C_1 = F_0(K_0) + \alpha_1 [F_1(I_0 + K_0) + (I_0 + K_0)]$$

$$- Z_0 - (1 + r_{-1})B_{-1}$$

$$\equiv W_0. \tag{5.8}$$

The right-hand side of equation (5.8) defines the value of wealth in period zero, W_0. The consolidated budget constraint highlights the fact that the key decisions that individuals make concern the choices of C_0 and C_1. Implicit in these decisions is the magnitude of new borrowing, B_0, which appears explicitly in the temporal budget constraints (5.6) and (5.7).

It is relevant to note that intertemporal solvency implies that the discounted sum of the periodic surpluses in the trade account must equal the sum of the principal plus interest payments on the historically given initial debt. The trade-balance surplus in each period equals GDP minus domestic absorption (consumption plus investment). Formally, using equations (5.6) and (5.7)—or equivalently using the consolidated equation (5.8)—we note that

$$(TA)_0 + \alpha_1 (TA)_1 = (1 + r_{-1})B_{-1}, \tag{5.9}$$

where $(TA)_i$ denotes the surplus in the trade balance in period $i = 0, 1$. Formally $(TA)_0 = F_0(K_0) - C_0 - Z_0$, and $(TA)_1 = F_1(K_0 + I_0) + (K_0 + I_0) - C_1$. It follows therefore that the discounted sum of the periodic surpluses in the current account must equal the discounted sum of the trade balance surplus plus the discounted sum of the surplus in the debt-service account. Formally,

$$(CA)_0 + \alpha_1 (CA)_1 = (1 + r_{-1})B_{-1} + (DA)_0 + \alpha_1 (DA)_1, \tag{5.9a}$$

where $(CA)_i$ denotes the surplus in the current account (equal to GNP minus domestic absorption), and DA_i denotes the surplus in

the debt-service account (equal to minus interest payments on previous period debt) in period $i = 0, 1$. Hence, in our two-period model
$(DA)_0 = -r_{-1}B_{-1}$ and $(DA)_1 = -r_0 B_0$. Equation (5.9) reveals that
in the absence of initial debt, a trade-balance surplus in a given
period must equal (in present-value terms) the trade-balance deficits
in all other periods taken as a whole. As illustrated by equation
(5.9a), a similar property does not apply to the intertemporal pattern
of the current account.

Let the representative individual's utility depend on the levels of
consumption, and let his or her lifetime utility function be denoted
by $U(C_0, C_1)$. As usual, we assume that the marginal utilities of
consumption in each period are positive and that the marginal rate
of substitution of consumption between two consecutive periods is
diminishing along any given indifference curve (a quasi-concave U).
The individual seeks to maximize lifetime utility subject to the
consolidated lifetime budget constraint. Formally, the individual's
maximization problem is

$$\tilde{U} = \max_{\{C_0, C_1\}} U(C_0, C_1), \tag{5.10}$$

subject to

$$C_0 + \alpha_1 C_1 = W_0.$$

The solution to this maximization problem is shown in figure
5.2, which incorporates the relevant information from the firm's
profit maximization problem of figure 5.1. In this figure point E
measures the discounted sum of current and future GDPs, minus
investment (Z_0), and W_0 measures the value of wealth in period
zero. That is, E measures $F_0(K_0) + \alpha_1[F_1(K_0 + I_0) + (K_0 + I_0)] - Z_0$,
whereas W_0 measures $F_0(K_0) + \alpha_1[F_1(K_0 + I_0) + (K_0 + I_0)] -
Z_0 - (1 + r_{-1})B_{-1}$. The horizontal distance between E and W_0
corresponds therefore to the initial external debt commitment
$(1 + r_{-1})B_{-1}$. The maximized level of utility obtains at point C at
the tangency of indifference curve $\bar{U} = U(C_0, C_1)$ with the budget
line. The budget line in turn emerges from point W_0—correspond-

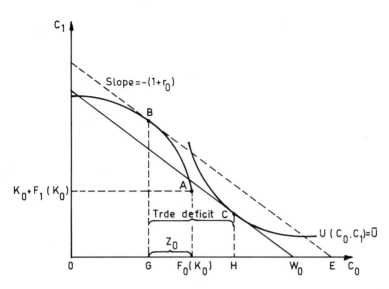

Figure 5.2
The general equilibrium of consumption, investment, and the trade balance

ing to the value of wealth in period zero—and its slope (in absolute terms) equals $1/\alpha_1 = 1 + r_0$.

The equilibrium portrayed in figure 5.2 represents the general equilibrium of the small open economy incorporating both the profit maximization by firms and the utility maximization by households. The case shown in the figure corresponds to a situation in which period zero's absorption (consumption, OH, plus investment, $GF_0(K_0)$) exceeds that period's GDP, $F_0(K_0)$. As a result, the economy runs in period zero a trade-balance deficit that is equal to GH. Obviously, the corresponding current-account deficit is obtained by adding the debt service, $r_{-1}B_{-1}$, to the trade-balance deficit.

5.2 Three Determinants of Borrowing and Lending

The equilibrium pattern of consumption portrayed in figure 5.2 is associated with discrepancies between the periodic levels of consumption and incomes. The lack of a complete synchronization between the time series of consumption and income is reconciled by a reliance on the world capital markets. Accordingly, in obtaining the optimal time profile of consumption, individuals find it beneficial to incur debt during some periods of their life. In determining the extent of the optimal departure of the path of consumption from that of income, and thereby the optimal reliance on capital markets and debt accumulation, it is useful to identify three separate motives: the consumption-smoothing motive, the consumption-tilting motive, and the consumption-augmenting motive. These three motives govern the desired volume of borrowing and lending.

In introducing the three concepts we need to define the concept of the subjective discount factor, which plays a critical role in determining the intertemporal allocations. The subjective discount factor, δ, measures the marginal rate of substitution between consumption in two consecutive periods evaluated at the point of a flat time profile of consumption ($C_0 = C_1 = C$). Thus

$$\delta = \frac{\partial U(C, C)/\partial C_1}{\partial U(C, C)/\partial C_0}. \tag{5.11}$$

The subjective discount factor, δ, is related to the subjective marginal rate of time preference, ρ, according to $\delta = 1/(1 + \rho)$.

To facilitate the exposition, we suppose that the subjective discount factor is fixed and that the utility function is

$$U(C_0, C_1) = U(C_0) + \delta U(C_1), \tag{5.12}$$

where U exhibits diminishing marginal utilities (i.e., U is concave): As is evident from the first-order condition of the consumer's maximization problem of equation (5.10), utility maximization implies an equality between the intertemporal marginal rate of substitution and the discount factor. Hence,

$$\frac{U'(C_0)}{\delta U'(C_1)} = \frac{1}{\alpha_1}. \tag{5.13}$$

Armed with these preliminaries, we turn now to illustrate the basic concepts. To sharpen the exposition of each concept, we focus on special cases designed to isolate each factor separately. In all

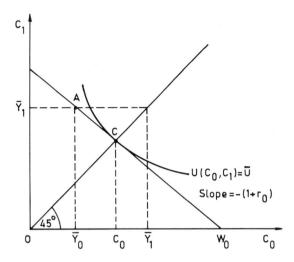

Figure 5.3
The consumption-smoothing effect

cases we assume that there is no initial debt. We consider first the consumption-smoothing motive. In figure 5.3 we assume that the subjective and the market discount factors are equal to each other (i.e., $\delta = \alpha_1$), that there is no investment, but that the periodic levels of income (endowments) differ from each other ($\overline{Y}_0 \equiv F_0(K_0) \neq K_0 + F_1(K_0) \equiv \overline{Y}_1$). In that case equilibrium consumption is described by point C along the 45° ray. As is evident, because of the equality between the subjective and the market discount factors, δ and α_1 (or equivalently, between the subjective rate of time preference, ρ, and the market rate of interest, r_0), individuals wish to smooth the time profile of consumption relative to the fluctuating levels of current income, and as seen in the figure, consumption (which is equal across periods) falls between $\overline{Y}_0$ and $\overline{Y}_1$. This consumption-smoothing motive is effected through borrowing in period zero and repaying the loan plus interest in the subsequent period.

We consider next the consumption-tilting motive. In figure 5.4 we assume that the subjective and the market discount factors differ from each other (i.e., $\alpha_1 \neq \delta$), that there is no investment, and that

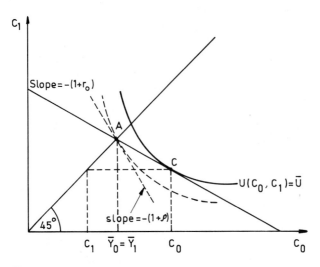

Figure 5.4
The consumption-tilting effect

the periodic levels of income (endowments) are equal (i.e., $\overline{Y}_0 = \overline{Y}_1$). In that case the equilibrium consumption point C does not lie along the $45°$ ray. In the case drawn, $\delta < \alpha_1$, so that the subjective rate of time preference (ρ) exceeds the world rate of interest (r_0). As a result, individuals facing a flat time profile of income wish to tilt the time profile of consumption toward period zero. This consumption-tilting motive is also effected through the world capital markets in which the individuals borrow in period zero and settle their debts in period one.

Finally, we consider the consumption-augmenting motive. In figure 5.5 we assume equality between the subjective and the market discount factors (i.e., $\delta = \alpha_1$) and between the periodic levels of income (endowments) so that $\overline{Y}_0 = \overline{Y}_1$; we also assume that there is positive investment, because $F_1(K_0) > 1 + r_0$. In that case equilibrium consumption is at point C. As seen, the investment opportunities, which tilt the time profile of income, augment the levels of consumption in each period without introducing variability to its time profile. As with the other cases, this consumption-augmenting motive is also effected through the world capital markets in which

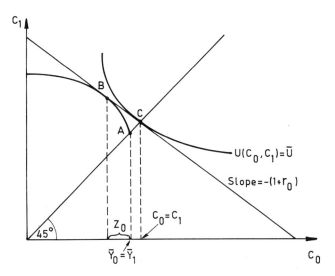

Figure 5.5
The consumption-augmenting effect

Table 5.1
Assumptions generating pure consumption-smoothing, consumption-tilting, and consumption-augmenting effects

	Smoothing	Tilting	Augmenting
Discount	$\delta = x_1$	$\delta \neq \alpha_1$	$\delta = \alpha_1$
Endowments	$\bar{Y}_0 \neq \bar{Y}_1$	$\bar{Y}_0 = \bar{Y}_1$	$\bar{Y}_0 = \bar{Y}_1$
Investment profitability	$F_1'(K_0) \leq r_0$	$F_1'(K_0) \leq r_0$	$F_1'(K_0) > r_0$

individuals borrow in period zero and repay debt commitment in period one. As is evident, in the absence of international capital markets the investment carried out in period zero would have crowded out private-sector consumption in that period. Access to the world capital markets facilitates the augmentation of consumption at a rate that is uniform over time.

The assumptions needed to generate the pure consumption-smoothing, consumption-tilting, and consumption-augmenting effects are summarized in table 5.1. In all cases these motives are expressed through borrowing and lending in the capital market.

Although we have isolated each of the three effects, in general, it is likely that the three motives coexist and interact in generating the equilibrium patterns of consumption, investment, and debt accumulation.

5.3 The Intertemporal Adjustment to Supply Shocks

In this section we illustrate the operation of the three factors in the context of adjustment to supply shocks. To analyze the equilibrium response to supply shocks and to highlight the intertemporal considerations involved in such an adjustment, we distinguish between temporary and permanent shocks and between current and anticipated future shocks. The supply shocks are reflected in either a change in the endowment, $(\overline{Y}_0, \overline{Y}_1)$, or a change in the technological coefficient governing investment, g. Throughout we consider positive supply shocks that increase the endowment bundle or improve the technology of investment. To facilitate the exposition in this discussion, we assume that the utility function $U(C_0, C_1)$ is homothetic. This assumption implies that for a given rate of interest the ratio of consumption in different periods is independent of the level of wealth.

Figure 5.6 illustrates the effects of supply shocks. To focus on the essentials, we assume that the historically given debt, B_{-1}, is zero; that the subjective rate of time preference, ρ, equals the rate of interest, r_0; that initially the endowments are uniformly distributed over time (so that $\overline{Y}_0 = \overline{Y}_1$, and that initially there is no profitable investment. In that case the initial equilibrium is described by point A along the 45° ray, and thus consumption in each period equals the corresponding level of the endowment. Hence, in the initial equilibrium the trade-balance deficit is zero. Furthermore, because there is no initial debt, the current account of the balance of payments is also balanced.

Consider first a permanent supply shock that raises the endowment in each period by the same proportion. In terms of figure 5.6 the new endowment is represented by point H. Because we have assumed that the utility function is homothetic, the consumption-

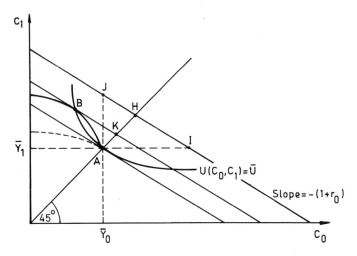

Figure 5.6
Supply shocks

expansion locus is the ray from the origin going through the initial
equilibrium point. Hence, the new pattern of consumption coincides
with the new endowment point H on the new higher budget line. In
this case the permanent supply shock results in neither a surplus nor
a deficit in the balance of trade. The supply shock yielding this
outcome is referred to as a *neutral supply shock*.

Obviously, if the utility function is not homothetic, then the
consumption-expansion locus would not be characterized by the 45°
ray in figure 5.6; in that case a permanent supply shock is not neutral
with respect to its effect on the current account of the balance of
payments. For example, if the rate of time preference is high at low
levels of wealth and falls as wealth rises, then the consumption-
expansion locus is steeper than the 45° ray (it intersects point A in
figure 5.6 from below), and a permanent positive supply shock induces a trade-account surplus in the early period.

We consider next a temporary supply shock that raises the endowment only in period zero to point I in figure 5.6. In the figure
we have assumed that this temporary supply shock yields the same
budget line as the one obtained in the previous case of a permanent
shock. Because we are interested only in the qualitative effects of the

various shocks, we make this assumption to simplify the diagrammatic exposition. With this shock, equilibrium consumption is described by point H. To bring about this pattern of consumption, the economy runs a surplus in its balance of trade equal to the difference between the new endowment in period zero (corresponding to point I) and the new consumption in period zero (corresponding to point H). Obviously the counterpart to this trade surplus is a trade deficit in the subsequent period in which consumption exceeds the endowment level.

Analogously, an expected future supply shock that raises the endowment in period one is illustrated by point J in figure 5.6 (which is again designed to yield the same budget as in the previous cases). As before, the consumption point is described by point H, and the economy runs a trade-balance deficit in period zero and a corresponding surplus in period one.

The key factor underlying the consumption response to the various supply shocks is the consumption-smoothing motive. Accordingly, the utility-maximizing consumers smooth the time profile of consumption and disregard the variability in the time profile of GDP. The mechanism that facilitates such consumption smoothing operates through the world capital market, and the variability of the stream of GDP is reflected in the time profile of the trade balance. If the (positive) supply shock is temporary, it leads to a trade-balance surplus in the period in which the shock occurs and to trade-balance deficits in all other periods. By analogy with our definition of a neutral (permanent) supply shock, we define a prolending supply shock as the situation in which the positive temporary shock occurs in the present, and we define a proborrowing supply shock as the situation in which the positive temporary shock is expected to occur in the future. Obviously the description of the shocks as being prolending or proborrowing is valid from the perspective of the current period.

The foregoing analysis examined the response of the economy to supply shocks that take the form of exogenous changes in the levels of GDP. Another possible (positive) supply shock may stem from a technological improvement in the process of investment. In terms of figure 5.6 suppose that under the initial technology the investment opportunities schedule is the dashed schedule emerging from point A. Because the marginal product of investment falls short of the rate of interest, no investment takes place at the initial equilibrium. The technological improvement is represented in figure 5.6 by the higher investment opportunities schedule emerging from point A and passing through point B. In that case, as shown earlier, the level of production is characterized by point B, and the level of consumption by point K. Thus, the current level of consumption rises even before the process of investment bears fruit. This represents both the consumption-smoothing and the consumption-augmenting effects. Following our previous definitions, this type of supply shock may be classified as a proborrowing shock.

5.4 The Determination of the World Interest Rate

In the previous sections the analysis of the stylized model treated the world rate of interest as given to the small open economy. In this section we analyze the determination of the equilibrium rate of interest in the world economy. For this purpose we consider the familiar home-country–foreign-country model. As usual, we designate all variables pertaining to the foreign economy by an asterisk.

In determining the world equilibrium intertemporal terms of trade (the rate of interest) and the associated patterns of intertemporal trade (trade-account surplus or deficit), it is convenient to separate the effects of three distinct factors: international differences in subjective rates of time preference, international differences in GDP growth rates, and the growth rate of world output. In the exposition of these three factors we abstract from initial debt and from endogenous investment.

We consider first the role of the subjective rates of time preference. To isolate this factor, let us suppose that home and foreign endowments are stationary and equal to each other; that is, let $\bar{Y}_0 = \bar{Y}_1 = \bar{Y}_0^* = \bar{Y}_1^*$. Also, suppose that the home subjective rate of time preference exceeds the foreign rate, so that $\rho > \rho^*$. The equilibrium of the world economy is portrayed by the Edgeworth

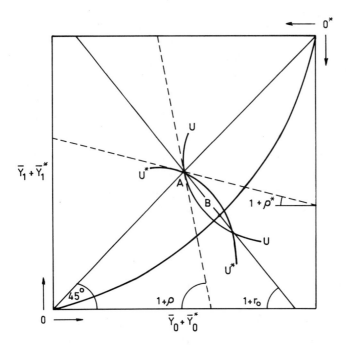

Figure 5.7
International differences in time preferences

box in figure 5.7. In that figure the horizontal axis measures world
GDP in period zero, $\overline{Y}_0 + \overline{Y}_0^*$, and the vertical axis measures the
corresponding quantity for period one $\overline{Y}_1 + \overline{Y}_1^*$. By construction the
box is squared, and the international and intertemporal distribution
of world outputs is specified by point A, the midpoint along the
diagonal OO^*. As usual, quantities pertaining to the home country
are measured from point O as an origin, and quantities pertaining to
the foreign country are measured from point O^* as an origin. At the
initial endowment point A the slope of the domestic indifference
curve, UU, equals one plus the domestic subjective rate of time
preference $(1 + \rho)$, whereas the slope of the foreign indifference
curve, U^*U^*, equals one plus the foreign subjective rate of time
preference $(1 + \rho^*)$.

Because $\rho > \rho^*$, it follows that the equilibrium patterns of international and intertemporal consumption must be located to the

southeast of point A, at a point like point B on the contract curve (the locus of tangencies between home and foreign indifference curves). At the equilibrium point B the rate of interest, r_0, is equalized across countries, and its magnitude must be bounded between the domestic and the foreign subjective rates of time preference; that is, $\rho > r_0 > \rho^*$. As is evident from a comparison of the patterns of consumption at point B with the patterns of GDPs at point A, in period zero the home country runs a deficit in its trade account while the foreign country runs a corresponding surplus of an equal magnitude. In the subsequent period this pattern of trade is reversed to ensure that the discounted sum of each country's trade balance is zero. This intertemporal pattern of international trade reflects the consumption-tilting effect operating in each country. Hence the less patient country (the country with the higher rate of time preference) runs a trade deficit in the early period.

We consider next the role of international differences in GDP growth rates. To isolate this factor, let us suppose that the home and the foreign subjective rates of time preference are equal to each other, so that $\rho = \rho^*$. Our previous analysis implies that in equilibrium the rate of interest equals the common value of the subjective rates of time preference; that is, $\rho = r_0 = \rho^*$. Let us suppose further that world output is stationary, so that $\overline{Y}_0 + \overline{Y}_0^* = \overline{Y}_1 + \overline{Y}_1^*$, but let the growth rate of the home country GDP exceed the foreign growth rate. We denote the percentage growth of GDP by θ, where $\theta = (\overline{Y}_1/\overline{Y}_0) - 1$, and a similar definition applies to the foreign growth rate, θ^*.

The equilibrium of the world economy is portrayed in figure 5.8, where the international and the intertemporal distributions of GDP are specified by point A. This point lies to the left of the diagonal OO^*, thereby reflecting the assumption that $\theta > \theta^*$. (Notice that because, by assumption, world output is stationary, it follows that $\theta > 0$, whereas $\theta^* < 0$). The international and intertemporal distribution of world output equilibrium consumption is specified by point B. This point lies on the diagonal OO^*, thereby reflecting the assumptions that the world output is stationary and that $\rho = \rho^*$. As is evident, in this case the home country runs a trade deficit in the

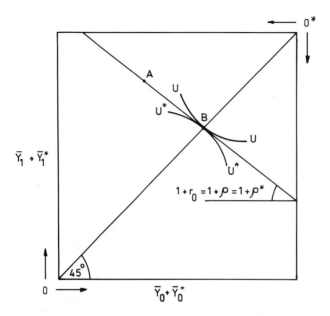

Figure 5.8
International differences in GDP growth rates

early period while the foreign country runs a corresponding surplus. Obviously this pattern of trade imbalances is reversed in the subsequent period. This intertemporal pattern of international trade reflects the consumption-smoothing effect operating in each country. Hence, the faster-growing country runs a trade deficit in the early period.

Finally, we consider the role of the rate of growth of world output. To isolate this factor we continue to assume that the domestic and the foreign subjective rates of time preference are equal, so that $\rho = \rho^*$. We also assume that world output is growing at the percentage rate, θ, that is common to the percentage growth rate of each country's GDP. Thus let $\overline{Y}_1/\overline{Y}_0 = \overline{Y}_1^*/\overline{Y}_0^* = 1 + \theta$. The equalities between the home and the foreign marginal rates of time preference and between the home and the foreign growth rates imply that in this case the two factors analyzed here do not play a role in determining the rate of interest, nor do they determine the patterns of trade. If we assume that the home and the foreign utility functions

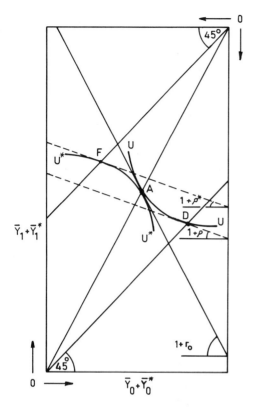

Figure 5.9
Growth of world output

are identical and homothetic, then we can specify the equilibrium without taking account of international differences in the levels of GDP.

The equilibrium of the world economy is shown in figure 5.9, in which point A describes the international and the intertemporal distributions of both GDP and consumption. Obviously, in that case, because of the equality between the patterns of production and consumption in each country, there are no trade imbalances. The main point that is demonstrated by the figure concerns the equilibrium value of the world rate of interest. As shown, the equilibrium rate of interest (corresponding to the common slope of the home and the foreign indifference curves at point A) exceeds the home and foreign common subjective rates of time preference (corresponding to the slopes of the domestic and the foreign indifference curves at points D and F on the 45° lines). The difference between the equilibrium rate of interest and the rates of time preference rises with the growth rate of world GDP. Hence the higher the growth rate of the world economy, the higher is the equilibrium world rate of interest.

To derive the precise relation between the equilibrium rate of interest and the rate of growth of the world economy, we denote the consumption ratio C_1/C_0 by c and the intertemporal elasticity of substitution by σ, where

$$\sigma = \frac{\partial \log c}{\partial \log[(\partial U/\partial C_0)/(\partial U/\partial C_1)]} > 0. \tag{5.14}$$

Assuming that the elasticity of substitution is constant and using these notations, we observe from figure 5.9 that

$$\log c(A) = \log c(D) + \sigma[\log(1 + r_0) - \log(1 + \rho)], \tag{5.15}$$

where $c(A)$ and $c(D)$ are the consumption ratios in figure 5.9 at points A and D, respectively. Because point D lies on the 45° line, $c(D) = 1$. Further, since point A lies on the diagonal OO^*, it is evident that $c(A) = 1 + \theta$. It follows that $\log(1 + \theta) = \sigma \log[(1 + r_0)/(1 + \rho)]$; therefore

$$(1 + r_0) = (1 + \rho)(1 + \theta)^{1/\sigma}. \tag{5.16}$$

This means that $1/\sigma$ is the equilibrium elasticity of the rate of interest with respect to the percentage rate of growth of world GDP. Hence, the positive association between the equilibrium rate of interest and the percentage rate of growth of world GDP decreases with the elasticity of substitution between the levels of consumption in two consecutive periods.

The foregoing analysis presumed that the growth of world output stemmed from an exogenous rise in the levels of the endowments. A similar analysis also applies to the case in which the growth of world output (evenly distributed across countries) arises from an improved availability of investment opportunities. In that case, figure 5.9 applies, except that the dimensions of the box are endogenous. Specifically, although in the previous case the dimensions of the box reflected the exogenously given growth rate of world GDP, $1 + \theta = \overline{Y}_1/\overline{Y}_0 = \overline{Y}_1^*/\overline{Y}_0^*$, in the present case they reflect the endogenously determined growth rate of GDP net of investment

$$
\begin{aligned}
1 + \theta &= \frac{F_1(I_0(r_0) + K_0) + I_0(r_0) + K_0}{F_0(K_0) - I_0(r_0)(1 + (\frac{1}{2})gI_0(r_0)/K_0)} \\[2ex]
&= \frac{F_1^*(I_0^*(r_0) + K_0^*) + I_0^*(r_0) + K_0^*}{F_0^*(K_0^*) - I_0^*(r_0)(1 + (\frac{1}{2})g^*I_0^*(r_0)/K_0^*)},
\end{aligned}
\tag{5.17}
$$

where $I_0(r_0)$ and $I_0^*(r_0)$ denote desired investment as a function of the rate of interest. The equilibrium rate of interest is determined as the solution to equations (5.16) and (5.17), and as before, in equilibrium there are no trade imbalances.

If investment opportunities are not distributed evenly between the two countries, then the two (endogenous) growth rates of GDP also differ from each other. In that case the total effect exerted by the investment opportunities on the rate of interest and on the patterns of trade reflects the considerations underlying the cases analyzed in figures 5.8 and 5.9. Specifically, suppose that the home country faces a more profitable set of investment opportunities than the foreign country. Then the (endogenously determined) growth rate of the home country's GDP, net of investment, exceeds the corresponding growth rate of the foreign economy, and the world rate of interest exceeds the subjective rate of time preference according to equation (5.16) in which the growth rate, θ, is now interpreted as the weighted average of the two countries' growth rates. The resulting patterns of trade are similar to those portrayed by figure 5.8, reflecting the general principle that the faster-growing country runs a trade deficit in the early period.

Up to now we have abstracted from the role that the historically given initial debt position plays in determining the equilibrium world rate of interest and the patterns of trade. To examine the consequences of the initial debt position, it is useful to compare an

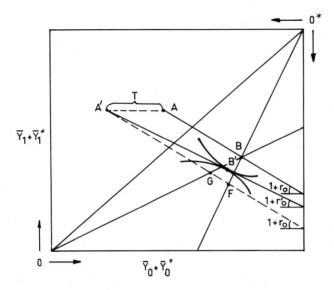

Figure 5.10
The effect of a redistribution of world debt

equilibrium without an initial debt commitment with another equilibrium in which the initial debt commitment of the home country is
positive. Hence, we consider an initial zero-debt equilibrium that is
disturbed by a transfer of $T = (1 + r_{-1})B_{-1}$ units of current output
from the home to the foreign country. The effects of such a transfer
are examined with the aid of figure 5.10, which is familiar from the
famous transfer-problem analysis.

 Suppose that at the initial equilibrium the international and intertemporal distributions of GDP are specified by point A and the corresponding distributions of consumption by point B. Analogously to
our discussion of figure 5.7, this pattern of consumption reflects the
assumption that the home marginal propensity to save falls short of
the foreign marginal propensity. This difference between the two
marginal saving propensities is reflected in the relative slopes of the
home and foreign consumption-expansion loci, OGB and O^*BF, respectively. As shown in figure 5.10, at the initial equilibrium the rate
of interest is r_0, and the two expansion loci are drawn for this rate of
interest.

As a brief digression, we compute now the slopes of the expansion loci. Using the representative individual's maximization problem of equation (5.8), we obtain the implied demand functions for current and future consumption:

$$C_0 = C_0(\alpha_1, W_0), \tag{5.18}$$

$$C_1 = C_1(\alpha_1, W_0). \tag{5.19}$$

If we assume normality, we can invert equation (5.18) to read

$$W_0 = h(\alpha_1, C_0). \tag{5.20}$$

Substituting (5.20) into (5.19) yields

$$C_1 = C_1[\alpha_1, h(\alpha_1, C_0)]. \tag{5.21}$$

The slope of the consumption-expansion locus is obtained by differentiating equation (5.21) and noting that from (5.20) $\partial h/\partial C_0 = 1/(\partial C_0/\partial W_0)$. Thus,

$$\frac{dC_1}{dC_0} = \frac{\partial C_1/\partial W_0}{\partial C_0/\partial W_0} = \frac{1 - (\partial C_0/\partial W_0)}{\alpha_1(\partial C_0/\partial W_0)}, \tag{5.22}$$

where the second quality follows from the budget constraint in equation (5.10).

It follows that if the foreign and the home residents face the same rate of interest, then the differences between the slopes of their consumption-expansion loci depend only on the relations between their marginal propensities to consume (or save) out of wealth. Our previous analysis of figure 5.7 indicates that in the absence of world output growth there is also a unique relation between the equilibrium pattern of the two countries' consumption ratios (C_1/C_0 and C_1^*/C_0^*) and the difference between their subjective rates of time preference. Specifically, as illustrated by point B in figure 5.7, if $\rho > \rho^*$, then $(C_1/C_0) < (C_1^*/C_0^*)$, and vice versa. Hence, in the absence of growth the pattern of consumptions exhibited in figure 5.10, and the analysis of the effects of a redistribution of world debt that is carried out with the aid of the same figure, can also be characterized in terms of differences between the subjective rates of time preference rather than differences between the marginal propensities to save. Finally, we note that if the utility functions are homothetic, then the difference between the home and foreign marginal propensities to save depends only on the difference between their subjective rates of time preference. In that case, the general-equilibrium configuration exhibited by figure 5.7 is also applicable to a situation in which there is growth.

We consider now the effects of a transfer from the home to the foreign country. Following the transfer, the net endowments of the two countries are specified in figure 5.10 by point A', where the horizontal distance between A and A' equals the size of the transfer, T. The new endowment alters the patterns of demand in both countries, and since the two subjective rates of time preference differ from each other, the new pattern of demand alters the rate of interest. Specifically, following the transfer at the initial rate of interest, the home demand for current and future goods is described by point G, and the corresponding foreign demand is described by point F, where points G and F lie on the consumption-expansion loci associated with the initial interest rate. Obviously this pattern of world demand creates an excess supply of current-period goods and an excess demand for future-period goods. To eliminate this disequilibrium, the relative price of current goods in terms of future goods (i.e., the rate of interest) must fall. Put differently, world savings rise because the transfer redistributes wealth from the home country (with the low saving propensity) to the foreign country (with the high saving propensity). The fall in the rate of interest is necessary to eliminate excess savings in the world economy. Diagrammatically, the fall in the rate of interest from r_0 to r_0' raises the desired consumption ratios C_0/C_1 and C_0^*/C_1^* and alters accordingly the slopes of both the home and the foreign consumption-expansion loci. The new equilibrium obtains at point B', at which the slopes of the two countries' indifference curves are equal to $1 + r_0'$, where $r_0' < r_0$. As is evident, point B' must be located inside the triangle BGF. It follows that if the foreign rate of time preference exceeds the home rate, the contract curve in figure 5.10 would be located above the diagonal OO^*, and the transfer from the home to the foreign country would necessitate a rise rather than a fall in the world rate of interest.

It is relevant to note that as is typical in transfer-problem analyses, the relevant criterion determining the effect of a redistribution of world debt on the rate of interest involves a comparison between the home and the foreign marginal propensities to save rather than the average saving propensities. In fact, the initial endowment in figure 5.10 could have been placed to the southeast of point B along the extension of the line segment AB. The analysis of the effect of the transfer on the rate of interest remains intact as long as the home marginal propensity to save is smaller than the foreign marginal propensity, even though in that case the (positive) home average propensity to save exceeds the (negative) foreign average propensity to save.

5.5 Extension: Infinite Horizon and Random Shocks

To shed more light on the basic motives underlying saving decisions we now incorporate random shocks into the analysis. Consider a small open economy with perfect access to the world capital market. Output (net of investment) is subject to random shocks. If they reverse themselves, they can be viewed as *transitory shocks*. Alternatively, if they behave like a random walk, they can be viewed as *permanent shocks*. To simplify the exposition, we assume that time is continuous and the horizon is infinite. (See, for example, Faig 1991 and Pitchford and Turnovsky 1977.)

As usual, the household chooses a consumption path so as to maximize the expected utility over the infinite horizon:

$$U_t = E_t \int_t^\infty e^{-\delta(\tau-t)} u(c_\tau)\, d\tau, \tag{5.23}$$

subject to the flow-budget constraint

$$dA_t = (rA_t + c_t)\, dt + Y_t, \tag{5.24}$$

where E, δ, c, A, r, and Y denote the expectation operator, the discount rate, consumption level, asset position, the rate of interest, and the output level, respectively. Naturally, the initial value of assets is predetermined.

Transitory Shocks

The representative household does not know exactly when a transitory shock will occur, nor how long it will last. To fix ideas, assume that output shocks follow a Poisson process, so that each state of nature has a random duration which is distributed exponentially. To simplify, we consider a two-state distribution so that the high-output event lasts b_H units of time, on average, and the corresponding low-output event lasts b_L units of time. To obtain closed-form solutions, we assume that the Arrow-Pratt measure of absolute risk aversion is constant. Thus the von Neumann-Morgenstern utility function is specified as

$$u(c_t) = -\frac{1}{\eta} e^{-\eta c_t}, \tag{5.25}$$

where η denotes the measure of absolute risk aversion.

Denoting the value function (that is, the maximized utility as a function of the predetermined variables) in the low-output state by V^L, and the corresponding value function in the high-output state by V^H, the Bellman's equation must hold for each state. Accordingly (see appendix A), the maximization problem must satisfy

$$(\delta + b^L) V^L(A_t) - b^L V^H(A_t) = \max_{c_t} [u(c_t) + V_A^L(A_t)(rA_t - c_t)] \tag{5.26}$$

and

$$(\delta + b^H) V^H(A_t) - b^H V^L(A_t) = \max_{c_t} [u(c_t) + V_A^H(A_t)(rA_t - c_t)]. \tag{5.27}$$

A solution can be found by the method of undetermined co-efficients, using the Bellman's equations and an initial guess for the high-output and low-output value functions. Our initial guess is

$$V^L(A) = -\frac{p^L}{q^L}e^{-q^L A}, \quad V^H(A) = -\frac{p^H}{q^H}e^{-q^H A}. \tag{5.28}$$

Solving the maximization problem in (5.26) and (5.27) yields

$$q^H = q^L = r\eta, \quad c^L = \frac{1}{\eta}(-1np^L + r\eta A), \quad c^H = \frac{1}{\eta}(-1np^H + r\eta A). \tag{5.29}$$

Finally, upon substituting (5.28) and (5.29) into (5.26) and (5.27), it can be shown that $p^L = p^H$ and the implied consumption function is

$$c_t = \frac{\delta - r}{r\eta} + rA_t. \tag{5.30}$$

The implication is that in a small open economy with perfect access to the world capital market, transitory output shocks do not affect current consumption. Thus, consumption is *perfectly* smoothed. In contrast, if the domestic capital market is completely closed, consumption must equal income (net of investment). By the general-equilibrium considerations in this case the output variance must be equal to the consumption variance, and consumption smoothing cannot be achieved.

Permanent Output Shocks

To analyze the effects of permanent shock (as in a random walk) we assume that the output process follows a Brownian motion:

$$dY_t = \mu\,dt + \sigma\,dz, \tag{5.31}$$

where μ is a drift and z is a standard Weiner process with zero mean and unitary standard deviation. Asset accumulation is specified as $dA_t = (rA_t - c_t)\,dt + Y_t$. The Bellman's equation is

$$\delta V(A_t) - \mu V_A(A_t) - \tfrac{1}{2}\sigma^2 V_{AA}(A_t) = \max_{c_t} [u(c_t) + V_A(A_t)(rA_t - c_t)],$$

$$(5.32)$$

where use has been made of Ito's lemma to evaluate the expected rate of change in the value function (see Ingersoll 1987).

Following the same solution procedure as in the previous section, the implied consumption function is now given by

$$c_t = \left(\frac{\delta - r}{r\eta} + \mu - \frac{r\eta\sigma^2}{2}\right) + rA_t + Y_t. \tag{5.33}$$

The implication is that under permanent output shocks the conditional output variance (net of investment) is equal to the consumption variance.[1]

Stock Markets and Fiscal Policy

Consider a small open economy in which the representative household solves an infinite-horizon problem. As in section 5.6, we assume that time is a continuous variable and we consider *permanent* productivity and fiscal shocks (see also Merton 1971). Accordingly, the consumer chooses the consumption stream and portfolio composition so as to maximize the expected intertemporal utility (5.23). Starting with time intervals of size Δt our approximate specification for the flow budget constraint is given by

$$A_{t+\Delta t} = (A_t - c_t\Delta t)(\theta(1 + r\Delta t) + (1 - \theta)(1 + \rho_t\Delta_t)) + Y\Delta t - g_t. \tag{5.34}$$

Thus, at time t, an amount of consumption, $c_t\Delta t$, is taken from assets, A_t. The remaining assets, $A_t - c_t\Delta t$, are invested in a portfolio in which a share θ is invested in the safe asset with a fixed rate of return, r, and a risky asset with a stochastic rate of return, ρ_t, which follows a Brownian motion with mean ρ ($> r$) and standard deviation σ_p. In addition, asset accumulation between period t and period $t + \Delta t$ is augmented by the assumed fixed labor income, $Y\Delta t$, and is reduced by taxes, g, assumed to be equal to government spending, state by state. Government spending is assumed to follow a Brownian motion. At the limit Δg approaches dg such that

$$dg = \mu \, dt + \sigma_g \, dz, \tag{5.35}$$

where μ represents the drift in government spending and z is a standard Wiener process so that dz has a zero mean and a unitary standard deviation.

The moments of the stochastic return, ρ_t, are given by

$$E(\rho_t) = \rho \, dt,$$

$$\text{var}(\rho_t) = \sigma_\rho^2 \, dt, \tag{5.36}$$

$$\text{cov}(\rho_t, g_t) = \rho_{g\rho} \, dt.$$

Appendix B demonstrates that at the limit the Bellman's equation for the consumption-portfolio choice problem is

$$0 = \max_{\{\theta, c\}} [u(c_t) - \delta V(A_t) + V_A(A_t)(A_t(\theta r + (1 - \theta)\rho) - c_t + Y - \mu)$$

$$+ \tfrac{1}{2} V_{AA}(A_t)(A_t^2(1 - \theta)^2 \sigma_\rho^2 + \sigma_g^2 - 2(1 - \theta)A_t \sigma_{g\rho})]. \tag{5.37}$$

The first-order conditions are

$$0 = u_c(c_t) - V_A(A_t), \tag{5.38}$$

$$0 = V_A(A_t)(r - \rho) + \tfrac{1}{2} V_{AA}(A_t)(-2(1 - \theta)\sigma_\rho^2 + 2A_t \sigma_{g\rho}). \tag{5.39}$$

Equation (5.39) can be used to solve for the portfolio share, $1 - \theta$:

$$(1 - \theta) = \left(-\frac{V_A(A_t)}{A_t V_{AA}(A_t)} \right) \frac{1}{\sigma_\rho^2} (\rho - r) + \frac{1}{A_t} \frac{\sigma_{g\rho}}{\sigma_\rho^2}. \tag{5.40}$$

Assume that the measure of absolute risk aversion is constant, which implies that the utility function is exponential as in (5.25).

A solution to equations (5.38)–(5.39) can then be found by the method of undetermined coefficients and a guess for the value function $V(A_t)$ (see appendix B).

The solution for the consumption function and the portfolio shares yields

$$c_t = Y - \mu + rA_t + \frac{\delta - r}{r\eta} + (\rho - r)\frac{(r - \rho) + r\eta\sigma_{g\rho}}{r\eta\sigma_\rho^2}, \tag{5.41}$$

$$(1 - \theta)A_t = \frac{\rho - r}{\sigma_\rho^2 r\eta} + \frac{\sigma_{g\rho}}{\sigma_\rho^2}. \tag{5.42}$$

Thus the resulting linear consumption function depends negatively on government spending through the fiscal drift parameter, μ, and positively on the correlation between government spending and the risky rate of return, $\sigma_{g\rho}/\sigma_\rho^2$. The amount invested in the risky asset, $(1 - \theta)A_t$, depends positively on the correlation between the fiscal and the productivity shocks, reflecting the fact that the risky asset provides an hedge against tax change risks.

5.6   Appendix A: An Application of the Bellman Equation

In an approximate and discrete model, with time intervals of size Δt, the Bellman's equation for the low output state is given by

$$V^L(A_t) = \max_{c_t} u(c_t)\Delta t + [e^{-(\delta + b^L)\Delta t}]V^L(A_{t+\Delta t})$$

$$+ (e^{-\delta\Delta t} - e^{-(\delta + b^L)\Delta t})V^H(A_{t+\Delta t}), \tag{A.1}$$

where the evolution of assets is given by

$$A_{t+\Delta t} = A_t + (rA_t - c_t)\Delta t + Y_t. \tag{A.2}$$

In the limit as Δt goes to zero (as usual for a time derivative), the term $(1/\Delta t)[e^{-(\delta + b^L)\Delta t}V^L(A_{t+\Delta t}) - V(A_t)]$ approaches $(\delta + b^L)V^L(A_t) + V_A(A_t)(rA_t - c_t)$, while the term $(1/\Delta t)[e^{-\delta\Delta t} - e^{-(\delta + b^L)\Delta t}]V^H(A_{t+\Delta t})$ approaches $b^L V^H(A_t)$. The Bellman's equation for the high-output state is derived in a similar fashion. This limiting process underlies the Bellman's equations, (5.26)–(5.27), in the text.

5.7 Appendix B: Consumption and Portfolio Selection for the Infinite Horizon Case

The discrete-time version of the Bellman's equation, with time intervals of size Δt, is

$$V(A_t) = \max E_t \left[\int_t^{t+\Delta t} e^{-\delta(t-s)} u(c_s)\, ds + e^{-\delta \Delta t} V(A_{t+\Delta t}) \right], \qquad (A.3)$$

where the asset-accumulation equation is given by

$$A_{t+\Delta t} = (A_t - c\Delta t)(\theta(1 + r\Delta t) + (1 - \theta)(1 + \rho_t \Delta t) + Y\Delta t - g_t, \qquad (A.4)$$

where ρ follows a Brownian motion, $d\rho_t = \rho \delta_t + \sigma_p\, dz$, and z is a Wiener process. A second-order expansion of $V(\cdot)$ by Taylor's theorem yields

$$e^{-\delta \Delta t} V(A_{t+\Delta t}) = V(A_t) - \delta V(A_t)\Delta t + V_A(A_t)\Delta A_t + \tfrac{1}{2} V_{AA}(A_t)(\Delta A_t)^2$$

$$+ \tfrac{1}{2}\delta^2 V(A_t)(\Delta t)^2 - \delta V_A(A_t)\Delta t\Delta A_t. \qquad (A.5)$$

Taking the expectations of (A.5) and eliminating terms of small order of magnitude (such as $\Delta t \Delta A_t$) yields

$$E_t[e^{-\delta \Delta t} V(A_{t+\Delta t})] = V(A_t) - \delta V(A_t)\Delta t + V_A(A_t) E_t(\Delta A_t)$$

$$+ \tfrac{1}{2} V_{AA}(A_t) E_t(\Delta A_t)^2. \qquad (A.6)$$

With g_t following a Brownian motion, the asset-accumulation equation, (A.4), has the following stochastic properties:

$$E_t(\Delta A_t) = -c\Delta t + A_t[\theta r + (1 - \theta)\rho]\Delta t + (Y - \mu)\Delta t,$$

$$\text{var}(\Delta A_t) = [A_t^2(1 - \theta)^2\sigma_\rho^2 + \sigma_g^2 - 2(1 - \theta)A_t\sigma_{g\rho}]\Delta t. \qquad (A.7)$$

Substituting (A.7) into (A.6), and the resulting expression into equation (A.3) while ignoring small order terms, yields the Bellman's equation, (5.37), in the text.

To solve the consumption-portfolio problem, our initial guesses are

$$V(A_t) = -\frac{p}{q}e^{-qA_t}t,$$

$$c_t = h + rA_t, \tag{A.8}$$

$$q = \eta r.$$

Substituting (A.8) into the first-order condition $u_c(c)V_A(A)$ yields $\log p = -r\eta$. Substituting (A.8) into (5.39), we get

$$0 = \max\left\{-\frac{1}{\eta}e^{-\eta c} + \frac{\delta p}{q}e^{-qA}\right.$$

$$+ pe^{-qA}(A(\theta r + (1-\theta)\rho) + Y - c - \mu)$$

$$\left. -\frac{1}{2}pqe^{-qA}[A^2(1-\theta)^2\sigma_\rho^2 + \sigma_g^2 - 2(1-\theta)A\sigma_{g\rho}]\right\}. \tag{A.9}$$

Setting the partial derivative of (A.9) with respect to θ equal to zero yields

$$\theta A = A - \frac{(\rho - r)/q + \sigma_{g\rho}}{\sigma_\rho^2}. \tag{A.10}$$

Substituting (A.10) into (A.11) yields

$$c_t = Y - \mu + rA_t + \frac{\delta - r}{r\eta} + (\rho - r)\frac{(r - \rho) + r\eta\sigma_{g\rho}}{r\eta\sigma_\rho^2}. \tag{A.11}$$

Equations (A.10) and (A.11) represent the solution for the portfolio selection and consumption determination problem.

6

The Two-Period Multiple-Good World

The formulation of the stylized model discussed in the previous chapter adopted a high degree of commodity aggregation; it assumed a single composite-commodity world. With this level of aggregation the only price relevant for individual decision making was the relative price of consumption in different periods. This formulation enabled us to focus on the role played by the intertemporal terms of trade—the rate of interest. In this chapter we extend the stylized model to include multiple goods. This extension introduces the temporal terms of trade (the relative price of different goods in a given period) and facilitates the analysis of the interactions between *temporal* and *intertemporal* relative prices in influencing private-sector behavior and in determining the equilibrium of the system. In extending the model, we introduce the concepts of *consumption-based* real rate of interest and real wealth. We use the extended model to determine the effects of shocks to the commodity terms of trade on saving behavior, and thereby on current account adjustments. These results will prove useful in the subsequent analysis of the intertemporal effects of fiscal policies operating through the induced changes in temporal and intertemporal terms of trade.

6.1 The Analytical Framework

Consider a two-good, two-period model, and suppose that good X is exportable and good M is importable. For simplicity assume that there is no investment. Analogously to equations (5.6) and (5.7), the budget constraints of the representative individual (measured in terms of exportables) are

$$c_{x0} + p_0 c_{m0} = \bar{Y}_{x0} + p_0 \bar{Y}_{m0} + B_0 - (1 + r_{x,-1})B_{-1}, \qquad (6.1)$$

$$c_{x1} + p_1 c_{m1} = \bar{Y}_{x1} + p_1 \bar{Y}_{m1} - (1 + r_{x0})B_0, \qquad (6.2)$$

where c_{xt} and $\bar{Y}_{xt}$ denote, respectively, the levels of consumption and production of exportables in period t, c_{mt} and $\bar{Y}_{mt}$ denote, respectively, the levels of consumption and production of importables in period t, p_t denotes the relative price in period t of importables in terms of exportables, and $t = 0, 1$. The rate of interest, r_{xt}, and the levels of new borrowing, $B_t(t = -1, 0)$ are measured in units of exportables that serve as the numeraire throughout this section.

Before proceeding with the analysis, two points are worth noting. First, using the conventions of national income accounting, the budget constraints can also be expressed by the equality between the current-account surplus, $(CA)_t$, and the capital account deficit $-(KA)_t$. The trade-account surplus, $(TA)_t$, equals the difference between exports (the excess of production over consumption of exportables; i.e., $\bar{Y}_{xt} - c_{xt}$) and imports (the excess of the values of consumption over production of importables; i.e., $p_t[c_{mt} - \bar{Y}_{mt}]$); the current-account surplus is the difference between the surplus in the balance of trade and the deficit in the debt-service account; thus $(CA)_t = (TA)_t - (DA)_t$, where the debt-service account, $(DA)_t = r_{xt-1}B_{t-1}$, and finally, $(KA)_t = B_t - B_{t-1}$. Using these definitions, it can be verified that $(CA)_t + (KA)_t = 0$.

Second, our assumption that the debt commitment is denominated in units of good X may be material when there are unanticipated changes in the terms of trade yielding unanticipated capital gains or losses. Obviously, if all changes in the terms of trade are anticipated, interest-rate parity (across debt instruments denominated in units of different commodities) requires that $1 + r_{xt} = (p_{t+1}/p_t)(1 + r_{mt})$, where r_{mt} denotes the rate of interest in period t on debt denominated in units of importables. In that case the fully anticipated terms of trade changes do not alter the individuals' wealth position. It follows that an unexpected change in p_0 exerts different wealth effects depending on whether the initial debt commitment was

$(1 + r_{x,-1})B_{-1}$ (as in equation 6.1) or $p_0/p_{-1}(1 + r_{m,-1})B_{-1}$. We will return to this issue in the subsequent analysis of terms of trade shocks.

The representative individual maximizes lifetime utility subject to the consolidated budget constraint (obtained by dividing equation 6.2 by $(1 + r_{x0})$ and adding the resultant expression to equation 6.1). The utility function is defined over the four goods $(c_{x0}, c_{m0}, c_{x1}, c_{m1})$. We assume that utility can be expressed as a function of two components, C_0 and C_1, which are in turn linearly homogeneous subutility functions of the consumption of goods in period zero (c_{x0}, c_{m0}) and in period one (c_{x1}, c_{m1}), respectively. Formally, the maximization problem is

$$\tilde{U} = \max_{\left\{ \substack{c_{x1}, c_{m1} \\ c_{x0}} \right\}} U[C_0(c_{x0}, c_{m0}), C_1(c_{x1}, c_{m1})], \tag{6.3}$$

subject to

$$c_{x0} + p_0 c_{m0} + \alpha_{x1}(c_{x1} + p_1 c_{m1})$$
$$= \overline{Y}_{x0} + p_0 \overline{Y}_{m0} + \alpha_{x1}(\overline{Y}_{x1} + p_1 \overline{Y}_{x1}) - (1 + r_{x-1})B_{-1}$$
$$= W_0, \tag{6.4}$$

where $\alpha_{x1} = 1/(1 + r_{x0})$ is the discount factor applicable to consumption in period one.

The solution to the maximization problem can be decomposed into two parts. The first involves the *temporal* allocation of spending, $z_t = c_{xt} + p_t c_{mt}$, between the two goods so as to maximize the subutility $C_t(c_{xt}, c_{mt})$, and the second involves the *intertemporal* allocation of lifetime spending $(z_0 + \alpha_{x1}z_1 = W_0)$ so as to maximize the lifetime utility $U(C_0, C_1)$. In the first stage of the temporal maximization the consumer may be viewed as minimizing the cost, z_t, of obtaining a given level of subutility, C_t. The assumption that the subutility functions are linear homogeneous imply that the "cost" function is $z_t = P_t(p_t)C_t$, where $P_t(p_t)$ is the "marginal cost" of obtaining a unit of C_t (and the marginal cost depends on the relative price, p_t). In what follows we refer to P_t as the *consumption-based price index*. This price index exhibits the familiar properties of similar price indexes; in each period the elasticity of the price index, P, with respect to the price of importables, p, equals the expenditure share of this commodity in total spending.[1]

In the second stage the consumer, who has already optimized the temporal allocation of spending, attempts to optimize the intertemporal allocation. Formally, this maximization problem is

$$\tilde{U} = \max_{\{C_0, C_1\}} U(C_0, C_1), \tag{6.5}$$

subject to

$$P_0(p_0)C_0 + \alpha_{x1} P_1(p_1)C_1 = W_0. \tag{6.6}$$

For subsequent use it is convenient to normalize the budget constraint (6.6) and express it in *real* terms. For this purpose we divide both sides by the price index P_0 and obtain

$$C_0 + \alpha_{c1} C_1 = W_{c0}, \tag{6.6a}$$

where

$$\alpha_{c1} = \frac{P_1}{P_0} \alpha_{x1},$$

$$W_{c0} = \frac{W_0}{P_0}.$$

We refer to α_{c1} as the (consumption-based) real *discount factor* and to W_{c0} as the (consumption-based) *real wealth*. As seen, the real discount factor equals the discount factor expressed in terms of the numeraire (α_{x1}) adjusted by the "rate of inflation," that is, by the percentage change in the consumption-based price index.

The maximization of the utility function (6.5) subject to the normalized budget constraint (6.6a) yields conventional demand functions for the "goods" C_0 and C_1. As usual, these functions depend on the relevant relative price α_{c1}, and on the relevant concept of "income," which in our case is real wealth, W_{c0}. Thus the periodic demand functions (for $t = 0, 1$) are $C_t = C_t(\alpha_{c1}, W_{c0})$. These demand functions are the conventional consumption-based *real spending* functions. Obviously, we could also have used the previous analysis to define and characterize spending in terms of other baskets of goods, such as exportables, importables, or GDP; in these cases spending would have been measured by $P_t(p_t)C_t$, $P_t(p_t)C_t/p_{m,t}$, and $P_t(p_t)C_t/(\overline{Y}_{xt} + p_{m,t}\overline{Y}_{m,t})$, respectively. The choice of units is, of course, of prime importance in circumstances where relative prices change. In the subsequent analysis of the effects of terms of trade changes, we choose to express spending and the current account in terms of the consumption basket. This choice is made in order to obtain indicators useful for welfare evaluations. But first we digress briefly to define the consumption-based real rate of interest.

6.2   The Real Rate of Interest

Corresponding to the concept of the real discount factor, we can define the concept of the (consumption-based) *real rate of interest*. Accordingly, the real interest rate, r_{c0}, is

$$r_{c0} = \frac{1 + r_{x0}}{P_1/P_0} - 1. \tag{6.7}$$

As is evident, this consumption-based real rate of interest, r_{c0}, depends positively on the rate of interest in terms of the numeraire, r_{x0}, and negatively on the rate of "inflation," P_1/P_0, which in turn reflects the path of the relative price of importables, p_0 and p_1. In order to characterize the dependence of the real rate of interest on the path of the temporal terms of trade, p_0 and p_1, we differentiate equation (6.7) and obtain

$$\left(\frac{1}{1 + r_{c0}}\right)dr_{c0} = \left(\frac{1}{1 + r_{x0}}\right)dr_{x0} + \beta_{m0}\frac{dp_0}{p_0} - \beta_{m1}\frac{dp_1}{p_1}, \tag{6.8}$$

where β_{m1} denotes the expenditure share of importables in total spending in period t. Equation (6.8) reveals that, ceteris paribus, a temporary current deterioration in the commodity terms of trade (a rise in p_0) raises the real rate of interest while an expected future deterioration in the commodity terms of trade (a rise in p_1) lowers the real rate of interest. The effect of a permanent deterioration of the commodity terms of trade (so that p_0 and p_1 rise in the same proportion) depends on the intertemporal changes in the expenditure shares. If these shares do not vary over time, a permanent change in the commodity terms of trade is neutral in its effect on the real rate of interest.

6.3   The Terms of Trade and Real Spending

In this section we analyze the effects of transitory and permanent shocks to the commodity terms of trade on real spending, C, measured in terms of the consumption basket. This analysis will aid the subsequent discussion of current-account adjustments. As was shown previously, the periodic spending functions depend on the consumption-based real discount factor and on real wealth. Accordingly, the current-period-spending function is

$$C_0 = C_0(\alpha_{c1}, W_{c0}). \tag{6.9}$$

We use this function in order to analyze the effects of changes in the terms of trade.

Consider a temporary change in the *current*-period terms of trade. Differentiating the spending function with respect to p_0 and expressing the results in terms of elasticities, it can be shown that

$$\frac{\partial \log C_0}{\partial \log p_0} = \beta_{m0}\{-\eta_{c\alpha} + [(1 - \gamma_s)\mu_{m0} - 1]\eta_{cw}\}, \tag{6.10}$$

where β_{m0} denotes the relative share of consumption of importables in current-period spending ($p_0 c_{m0}/z_0 = p_0 c_{m0}/P_0 C_0$), $\eta_{c\alpha}$ and η_{cw} denote the elasticities of C_0 with respect to α_{c1} and W_{c0}, respectively, $\gamma_s = \alpha_{c1} C_1 / W_{c0}$ is the share of saving in wealth, and $\mu_{m0} = \overline{Y}_{m0}/c_{m0}$ is the ratio of production to consumption of importables, which ranges between zero and one. The two terms on the right-hand side of equation (6.10) reflect the effects of changes in the two variables appearing on the right-hand side of equation (6.9), α_{c1} and W_{c0}, induced by the current change in the commodity terms of trade, p_0. Equation (6.10) can be manipulated further by using the Slutsky decomposition (according to which $\eta_{c\alpha} = \overline{\eta}_{c\alpha} - \gamma_s\eta_{cw}$, where $\overline{\eta}_{c\alpha}$ denotes the compensated demand elasticity) and noting that $\overline{\eta}_{c\alpha} = \gamma_s\sigma$ (where σ, the intertemporal elasticity of substitution, is defined by equation 5.12). Hence

$$\frac{\partial \log C_0}{\partial \log p_0} = \beta_{m0}[-\eta_{cw} + \gamma_s(\eta_{cw} - \sigma) + (1 - \gamma_s)\mu_{m0}\eta_{cw}]. \qquad (6.11)$$

In interpreting the bracketed term on the right-hand side of equation (6.11), we note three channels through which changes in current-period terms of trade alter current-period spending. The first term represents the *deflator effect*, which operates through the change in the price index used to deflate wealth; the second term represents the *intertemporal-price effect*, which operates through the change in the real discount factor; and the third term represents the *wealth effect*, which operates through the change in real wealth induced by the change in the valuation of the output of importables.

The deterioration in the terms of trade raises the price index by β_{m0}; this lowers the real value of wealth equiproportionally and (assuming normality) lowers spending according to the elasticity η_{cw}—hence the negative term—η_{cw} on the right-hand side of equation (6.11). The intertemporal-price effect depends on the sign of $\eta_{cw} - \sigma$. Finally, the wealth effect is the product of η_{cw} and the percentage rise in wealth due to the appreciation of the output of importables. This can be verified by noting that $\partial \log W_0 / \partial \log p_0 = p_0 \bar{Y}_{m0}/W_0$ and that this can also be written as $(1 - \gamma_s)\beta_{m0}\mu_{m0}$. In interpreting this expression, we note that a given percentage rise in the price of importables appreciates the value of output of importables, but since their consumption exceeds production, the potential rise in the former is only a fraction μ_{m0} of the rise in price. To express the potential rise in consumption of importables in terms of lifetime spending, we need to multiply μ_{m0} by the share of consumption of importables in current spending, β_{m0}, times the share of current spending in lifetime spending $(1 - \gamma_s)$. Hence the last expression on the right-hand side of equation (6.11) is the wealth effect which, by normality, is positive.

The foregoing discussion indicated the signs of the deflator effects, the intertemporal-price effects, and the wealth effect. Combining these effects, we can rewrite equation (6.11):

$$\frac{\partial \log C_0}{\partial \log p_0} = -\beta_{m0}[(1 - \gamma_s)(1 - \mu_{m0})\eta_{cw} + \gamma_s\sigma]. \qquad (6.11a)$$

As is evident, since γ_s and μ_{m0} are bounded between zero and unity, the deterioration in the current terms of trade must lower current real spending.

To gain further insight into the factors governing the effects of changes in the terms of trade on spending, consider the extreme case in which $\mu_{m0} = 1$, so that in the current-period production and consumption of importables are equal to each other and imports are zero. In that case, as is evident from equation (6.11a), the negative change in spending arises only from the pure intertemporal substitution effect $(-\beta_{m0}\gamma_s\sigma)$. This case is of special interest since it highlights the importance of intertemporal considerations. It demonstrates that even though real income does not change (since net imports are zero), the utility-maximizing individual responds to the rise in the domestic consumption-based real rate of interest (induced by the temporary deterioration in the terms of trade) by substituting away from current spending toward future spending.

Consider next the effect of an expected *future* deterioration in the terms of trade (i.e., a rise in p_1) on current-period spending. Formally, differentiating equation (6.9) with respect to p_1, expressing in terms of elasticities and manipulating as before, yields

$$\frac{\partial \log C_0}{\partial \log p_1} = \beta_{m1}\gamma_s[(\sigma - \eta_{cw}) + \mu_{m1}\eta_{cw}]. \tag{6.12}$$

A comparison between the expressions showing the effects of current and future deteriorations in the terms of trade reveals that the deflator effect, $-\beta_{m0}\eta_{cw}$, which appears in equation (6.11), does not appear in equation (6.12). The other important difference concerns the direction of the intertemporal-price effect. As seen in equation (6.8), a rise in p_0 raises the real rate of interest, whereas a rise in p_1 lowers the real rate of interest. Because of these differences the effect of an anticipated future deterioration on spending is ambiguous. This should be contrasted with the unambiguous response of current spending to a current terms of trade change. The ambiguous effect depends, in part, on whether current consumption, C_0, and future consumption, C_1, are gross substitutes (i.e., $\eta_{c\alpha} > 0$) or gross complements (i.e., $\eta_{c\alpha} < 0$). This is indicated by the term $(\sigma - \eta_{cw})$ in equation (6.12).

The ambiguity of the effects of the expected future deterioration in the terms of trade can be clarified by considering a simple case in which the utility function is homothetic and the level of production of importables in the future is zero. Thus consider the case in which $\eta_{cw} = 1$ and $\mu_{m1} = 0$. Under these circumstances equation (6.12) becomes

$$\frac{\partial \log C_0}{\partial \log p_0} = \beta_{m1} \gamma_s (\sigma - 1), \qquad \qquad (6.12a)$$

and as is evident, the response of current spending to an anticipated future deterioration in the terms of trade depends only on whether the intertemporal elasticity of substitution, σ, exceeds or falls short of unity.

The foregoing analysis of the effects of temporary (current or future) deteriorations in the terms of trade on current spending provides the ingredients necessary for determining the effects of a *permanent* deterioration. Formally, assuming that the percentage rise in p_0 equals the corresponding rise in p_1 so that $d \log p_0 = d \log p_1 = d \log p$, the effect of the permanent deterioration in the terms of trade on current spending is obtained by adding the expressions in equations (6.11) and (6.12). Hence

$$\frac{\partial \log C_0}{\partial \log p} = -\beta_{m0} \eta_{cw} + \gamma_s (\beta_{m0} - \beta_{m1})(\eta_{cw} - \sigma)$$

$$+ [(1 - \gamma_s)\beta_{m0}\mu_{m0} + \gamma_s \beta_{m1}\mu_{m1}]\eta_{cw}. \qquad (6.13)$$

The three terms on the right-hand side of equation (6.13) correspond to the three channels through which a deterioration in the terms of trade affects spending. The first term—the *deflator effect*—represents exclusively the effects of the *current* deterioration in the terms of trade as it operates through the deflation of wealth; the second term —the *intertemporal-price effect*—operates through changes in the real rate of interest that occur only if the shares of expenditure on importables vary through time (as seen in equation 6.8); the third term—the *wealth effect*—operates through changes in the value of output occurring in both periods and stemming from the permanent rise in the price of importables. In general, these three effects exert conflicting influences on current spending.

The relation between the terms of trade and spending can be clarified, however, by considering the special case in which the utility function is homothetic and in which the expenditure shares, the output-consumption ratio of importables, and real spending (in present value) are all constant over time (i.e., let $\eta_{cw} = 1$, $\beta_{m0} = \beta_{m1} = \beta_m$, $\mu_{m0} = \mu_{m1} = \mu_m$, and $\gamma_s = 1 - \gamma_s$). In that case equation (6.13) becomes

$$\frac{\partial \log C_0}{\partial \log p} = -\beta_m(1 - \mu_m). \tag{6.13a}$$

Under these conditions (as long as $\mu_m < 1$) the permanent deterioration in the terms of trade lowers current spending. The fall in current spending arises exclusively from the reduction in real income (by the proportion $\beta_m[1 - \mu_m]$) consequent on the deterioration in the terms of trade. Since this deterioration applies equally to both the current and the future periods, it does not alter the real rate of interest (as seen from equation 6.8), and therefore it does not induce intertemporal substitution. Finally, we note that in the limiting case for which production and consumption of importables are equal to each other (so that $\mu_m = 1$), real income is constant, and the permanent deterioration in the terms of trade does not alter spending.

6.4   The Terms of Trade and the Balance of Trade

The foregoing analysis determined the effects of temporary and permanent shocks to the commodity terms of trade on spending. In this section we use these results to determine the effects of such changes in the terms of trade on the balance of trade. This analysis highlights the principal mechanisms underlying the famous Laursen-Metzler-Harberger effect. Further the results provide the main ingredients necessary to determine the dynamics of the current account and of debt accumulation.

By definition, the balance of trade equals the difference between the value of production and spending. In what follows we express the balance of trade in terms of the consumption basket. Accordingly, we denote the consumption-based real balance of trade in period t by $(TA_c)_t$. Hence $(TA_c)_t = (TA)_t / P_t$, where, as before, $(TA)_t$ denotes the balance of trade in terms of exportables. Using the previous definitions, the consumption-based real balance of trade in the current period is

$$(TA_c)_0 = (GDP)_{c0} - C_0(\alpha_{c1}, W_{c0}), \tag{6.14}$$

where

$$(GDP)_{c0} = \frac{(GDP)_0}{P_0(p_0)} = \frac{\bar{Y}_{x0} + p_0 \bar{Y}_{m0}}{P_0(p_0)}.$$

A given percentage deterioration in the terms of trade influences the balance of trade through its effects on the real value of output and on real spending. The proportional change in $(GDP)_{c0}$ is

$$\frac{\partial \log (GDP)_{c0}}{\partial \log p_0} = \frac{\beta_{m0}}{\mu_{c0}} (\mu_{m0} - \mu_{c0}), \tag{6.15}$$

where $\mu_{c0} = (GDP)_{c0}/C_0$. Thus μ_{c0} exceeds or falls short of unity as the trade balance is in surplus or deficit, respectively; if the balance of trade is balanced, $\mu_{c0} = 1$.

The effects of temporary (current or future) and permanent changes in the terms of trade on the balance of trade can be obtained by differentiating equation (6.14). Substituting equations (6.11), (6.12), and (6.13), respectively, for the change in spending, and substituting equation (6.15) for the change in $(GDP)_{c0}$ yields

$$\frac{\partial (TA_c)_0}{\partial \log p_0} = \beta_{m0}[(\mu_{m0} - \mu_{c0}) + (1 - \gamma_s)(1 - \mu_{m0})\eta_{cw} + \gamma_s \sigma] C_0, \tag{6.16}$$

$$\frac{\partial (TA_c)_0}{\partial \log p_1} = -\beta_{m1} \gamma_s [(\sigma - \eta_{cw}) + \mu_{m1} \eta_{cw}] C_0, \tag{6.17}$$

$$\frac{\partial (TA_c)_0}{\partial \log p} = \{ \beta_{m0}(\mu_{m0} - \mu_{c0}) + \beta_{m0} \eta_{cw} - (\beta_{m0} - \beta_{m1})\gamma_s(\eta_{cw} - \sigma)$$

$$- [(1 - \gamma_s)\beta_{m0}\mu_{m0} + \gamma_s \beta_{m1} \mu_{m1}]\eta_{cw} \} C_0. \tag{6.18}$$

Equations (6.16) through (6.18) reveal that the response of the balance of trade to current, future, and permanent deteriorations in the terms of trade depends on the key parameters of the economic system. These parameters are the expenditure share of importables (β_m), the ratio of production to consumption of importables (μ_m), the ratio of GDP to spending (μ_c), the average saving propensity (γ_s), the wealth elasticity of spending (η_{cw}), and the intertemporal elasticity of substitution (σ). The ratio of production to consumption of importables determines the changes in the real values of GDP and real income consequent on a given percentage deterioration in the terms of trade. The ratio of GDP to spending reflects the imbalance in the balance of trade; if this ratio exceeds unity, then the initial position is that of a trade-balance surplus, and vice versa. The average saving propensity influences both the extent of the intertemporal-price effect as well as the wealth effect consequent on the change in the terms of trade. The wealth elasticity of spending translates direct and indirect changes in wealth into spending. Finally, the intertemporal elasticity of substitution determines the pure substitution effect induced by changes in the real rate of interest consequent on the terms of trade change.

In order to clarify the precise role played by these parameters, consider the case of a permanent rise in the price of importables. As shown by the four terms on the right-hand side of equation (6.18), there are four effects that operate. The first is the real GDP effect— $\beta_{m0}(\mu_{m0} - \mu_{c0})$. The direction of this effect depends on the difference between two measures of imbalances: the import sector imbalance (μ_{m0}) and the trade-account imbalance (μ_{c0}); this real GDP effect is negative if the trade account is in surplus. The second effect is the deflator effect— $\beta_{m0}\eta_{cw}$. This effect improves the trade balance due to the reduction in spending induced by the β_{m0} percent rise in the price index used to deflate wealth. This change in real wealth is translated into the reduction in spending through the spending elasticity. The third effect is the intertemporal-price effect— $(\beta_{m0} - \beta_{m1})\gamma_s(\eta_{cw} - \sigma)$. The direction of this effect depends on whether the rate of interest rises or falls as well as the response of spending to the change in the rate of interest. As is evident from equation (6.8), the permanent rise in the price of importables raises the rate of interest if β_{m0} exceeds β_{m1}, and vice versa. The change in the rate of interest in turn lowers or raises spending depending on whether the interest elasticity of spending—$\gamma_s(\eta_{cw} - \sigma)$—is positive or negative. Finally, the fourth effect is the wealth effect—which is the product of the wealth elasticity of spending, η_{cw}, and the percentage change in real wealth induced by the appreciated value of the domestic production of importables. This value of the domestic production of importables appreciates in each period t ($t = 0, 1$) by the magnitude $\beta_{mt}\mu_{mt}$. The rise in real wealth associated with each period appreciation is obtained by multiplying this magnitude by the weight of the corresponding period spending in real wealth (these weights are $1 - \gamma_s$ for period zero and γ_s for period one). Hence the percentage change in real wealth is a weighted average of $\beta_{mt}\mu_{mt}$ ($t = 0, 1$).

As is evident from equations (6.16) through (6.18), the net effect of changes in the terms of trade on the balance of trade depend on the relative magnitudes of the four aforementioned effects. To sharpen the analysis, consider the case in which the utility function is homothetic, and the expenditure shares and output-consumption ratios are constant over time (i.e., let $\eta_{cw} = 1$, $\beta_{m0} = \beta_{m1} = \beta_m$, and $\mu_{m0} = \mu_{m1} = \mu_m$). In that case equations (6.16) through (6.18) become

$$\frac{\partial(TA_c)_0}{\partial \log p_0} = \beta_m[(1 - \mu_{c0}) + \gamma_s(\mu_m + \sigma - 1)]C_0, \qquad (6.16a)$$

$$\frac{\partial(TA_c)_0}{\partial \log p_1} = -\beta_m\gamma_s(\mu_m + \sigma - 1)C_0, \qquad (6.17a)$$

$$\frac{\partial(TA_c)_0}{\partial \log p} = \beta_m(1 - \mu_{c0})C_0. \qquad (6.18a)$$

In interpreting these results, consider first equation (6.18a) corresponding to a permanent deterioration in the terms of trade. This equation shows that the key criterion determining the direction of the change in the balance of trade is whether at the initial terms of trade the trade account is in deficit or surplus (i.e., whether μ_{c0}, exceeds or falls short of unity). If at the initial terms of trade the trade account is in deficit, then the permanent deterioration in the terms of trade improves the balance of trade, and vice versa. Finally, if initially the trade account is balanced, then the permanent deterioration in the terms of trade is neutral in its effect on the balance of trade. In that case the equiproportional fall in real GDP and in real spending implies that both fall by the same magnitude, and therefore the difference between them (the trade account) remains unchanged.

There are two key differences between the effects of permanent and temporary (current or future) deteriorations in the terms of trade. First, temporary changes alter the intertemporal pattern of real GDP in a manner similar to that of temporary negative supply shocks (analyzed in section 5.3). This change in the intertemporal pattern of real GDP, taken by itself, induces a trade-account deficit in the case of a current deterioration of the terms of trade and a trade-account surplus in the case of a future deterioration in the terms of trade. These trade-account adjustments are induced by the consumption-smoothing effects and are reflected by the term $\beta_m \gamma_s (1 - \mu_m)$ which appears negatively in equation (6.16a) and positively in equation (6.17a).

The second difference between the effects of permanent and temporary deteriorations in the terms of trade reflects the induced changes in the real rate of interest. If the terms of trade deteriorate permanently, then, with constant expenditure shares, the real rate of interest does not change. This is reflected in equation (6.18a) by the absence of terms relating to intertemporal substitution. In contrast, a current deterioration raises the rate of interest and induces substitution away from current spending toward future spending. This consumption-tilting effect is reflected by the positive term $\beta_m \gamma_s \sigma$ in equation (6.16a). Analogously, a future deterioration in the terms of trade lowers the real rate of interest and induces substitution toward current spending. This is reflected by the negative term $-\beta_m \gamma_s \sigma$ in equation (6.17a).

The foregoing analysis of the effects of temporary deteriorations in the terms of trade shows that the induced change in the intertemporal pattern of real GDP influences the trade account in a manner opposite to that of the induced change in the real rate of interest. As shown by equations (6.16a) and (6.16b), the net effect depends on whether the intertemporal elasticity of substitution, σ, exceeds or falls short of the ratio of imports to consumption of importables, $1 - \mu_m$. For values of σ smaller than this import-consumption ratio, the qualitative effects of temporary deteriorations in the terms of trade (starting from an initial balance in the trade account) are similar to those exerted by temporary negative supply shocks. On the other hand, for values of σ larger than this import-consumption ratio, the qualitative effects of temporary deteriorations in the terms of trade on the balance of trade are the opposite of those induced by negative supply shocks.

Before concluding, it is worth recalling that throughout the analysis we have expressed the balance of trade in terms of the consumption basket. Since changes in the terms of trade impact on the price index, the choice of the units of measurement is material. As an example, suppose that the trade account is measured in terms of exportables. By definition, the trade account measured in terms of exportable, TA, is related to its value measured in terms of the consumption basket, TA_c, according to $TA = P_0 TA_c$. Since the price index, P_0, depends only on the current price of importables, p_0, and not on the future price, p_1, it is obvious that changes in the two measures of the trade account may differ from each other only if the current terms of trade change. In that case, using our previous notations, the change in $(TA)_0$ is

$$\frac{\partial (TA)_0}{\partial \log p_0} = \left[\frac{\partial (TA_c)_0}{\partial \log p_0} + \beta_{m0}(\mu_{c0} - 1)C_0 \right] P_0. \tag{6.19}$$

Substituting equation (6.16) into (6.19) yields the expression indicating the effect of a current deterioration of the terms of trade on the trade account measured in terms of exportables. In order to derive the effect of a rise in p_1 on $(TA)_0$, we first note that a future deterioration in the terms of trade does not alter P_0. It follows that the expression (6.17), multiplied by P_0, yields the corresponding effect of a future rise in the price of importables. Obviously the effect of a permanent deterioration in the terms of trade on the trade account measured in terms of exportables is the sum of these two expressions.

As is evident, changes in the current terms of trade may result in different inferences concerning the direction of the change in the two measures of the trade account only if at the initial terms of trade the trade account is unbalanced. For example, if the current rise in the price of importables worsens the trade account TA_c (measured in terms of the consumption basket), and if at the initial terms of trade there is a relatively large surplus in the trade account ($\mu_{c0} > 1$), then, as seen in equation (6.19), the trade account TA (measured in terms of exportables) improves. Obviously under such circumstances the trade account measured in terms of importables must worsen. This phenomenon of a J-curve effect is exclusively an artifact of the arbitrary choice of units of measurements. As indicated previously, we have chosen to express the values of real spending, real GDP, and thereby the real trade balance in terms of the consumption basket in order to obtain information that is more amenable for a welfare analysis.

We note that an additional mechanism through which changes in the terms of trade influence the balance of trade operates through the effects of capital gains or losses on external debt commitments. These gains or losses depend on the units in terms of which debt is denominated. Specifically, unless the economy's external debt is fully linked to the consumption-based price index, any change in the terms of trade alters the real value of its initial debt commitment. This alters wealth and exerts an additional independent influence on spending and on the trade balance.

Figure 6.1 demonstrates the effects of a temporary deterioration in the terms of trade on the consumption-based trade balance. At the initial equilibrium point A, the current account is balanced. A current rise in the relative price of importables relocates the budget line: the consumption-based wealth falls and the consumption-based real rate of interest rises. The new endowment point is shown by B and the new consumption point is shown by A'. Thus, the trade account position is in a deficit.

Table 6.1, based on Mendoza 1991a, illustrates the role of the trade balance as a shock absorber. The trade balance is more volatile than output and the terms of trade. Excluding Canada and the

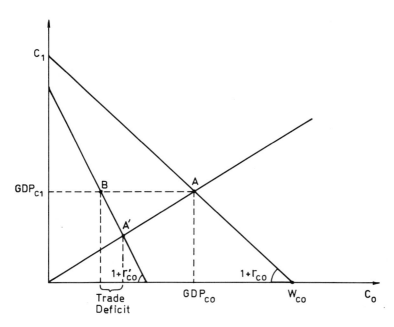

Figure 6.1
The effects of temporary deterioration of the terms of trade on the trade deficit

United States, the trade balance and the terms of trade are positively correlated, in line with the Harberger-Laursen-Metzler effect. However, the stylized relationships uncovered in the table yield no direct support for the prediction of the intertemporal model, since more persistent output and terms of trade shocks do not weaken the comovements between the trade balance and the terms of trade, or output. Consequently, a more structural econometric approach is required to assess the validity of the intertemporal approach.

Table 6.1
Statistical properties of output, the trade balance, and the terms of trade in the seven largest industrialized countries

Country	GDP		Terms of trade			Trade balance[a]			
	σ	ρ (persistence)	σ	ρ (persistence)	$\rho_{tot,\gamma}$	σ	ρ	$\rho_{tb,\gamma}$	$\rho_{tb,tot}$
United States	2.17	0.446	4.00	0.263	0.197	7.99	0.377	−0.227	−0.363
United Kingdom	1.98	0.524	4.41	0.551	−0.230	6.32	0.509	−0.538	0.731
France	1.49	0.654	3.46	0.341	0.287	4.43	0.132	−0.019	0.566
Germany	1.92	0.439	4.37	0.490	0.239	4.78	0.424	−0.299	0.346
Italy	2.17	0.537	5.03	0.504	0.112	8.73	0.305	−0.210	0.404
Canada	2.01	0.540	3.09	0.469	−0.034	4.75	0.394	−0.709	−0.102
Japan	3.58	0.812	10.98	0.583	0.559	10.99	0.275	0.054	0.527

Sources: Mendoza (1991a). International Monetary Fund, *International Financial Statistics*, and data base for the *World Economic Outlook*.

Note: Data for the terms of trade and the trade balance are for the period 1960–1989, and for GDP for the period 1965–1989, expressed in per-capita terms and detrended using the Hodrick-Prescott filter with the smoothing parameter set at 100. The GDP is at constant domestic prices from National Income Accounts, the terms of trade are the ratio of U.S. dollar unit value of exports to U.S. dollar unit value of imports, the trade balance is exports minus imports of merchandise from the balance of payments expressed at constant import prices (the detrended trade balance corresponds to detrended exports minus detrended imports).

a. σ is the percentage standard deviation, ρ is the first-order serial autocorrelation, $\rho_{tot,\gamma}$ is the correlation of the terms of trade with GDP, $\rho_{tb,\gamma}$ is the correlation of the trade balance with GDP, and $\rho_{tb,tot}$ is the correlation of the trade balance with the terms of trade.

7

Current-Account Dynamics

The past decade has witnessed the development of a large theoretical literature on the dynamic-optimizing (or intertemporal) approach to the current account. The models developed have typically emphasized the effects on the current-account balance of real factors such as productivity, the terms of trade, and government spending and taxes, which operate through intertemporal substitution in consumption, production, and investment.[1] But how important is the role of intertemporal substitution? Might this micro-based theory indeed be wrong? We can answer this question by deriving the empirical implications of the theory and by proving or disproving the importance of the role played by intertemporal substitution. Although the following discussion does not engage in formal statistical testing, the numbers it presents and analyzes shed light on the validity of the intertemporal theories' key testable hypotheses.

The Mundell-Fleming approach to the macroeconomic modeling of an open economy (as in chapters 3 and 4) treats the trade balance as a side show, important only for its effect on current output. This is perhaps because it pays little attention to capital and debt accumulation. At center stage are the exchange rate, output, and employment. Recall that under a flexible exchange rate, a current transitory fiscal expansion, which does not alter expectations about the future value of the exchange rate, induces a rightward shift of the IS schedule, raising the level of output (under the Keynesian assumption of price rigidity) and raising the domestic interest rate.

To maintain interest parity, the rise in the interest rate must result in the appreciation of the domestic currency. The current account must deteriorate because output has risen and the domestic currency has appreciated. Under a fixed exchange rate, interest arbitrage ensures equality between the domestic and foreign interest rates. Consequently a fiscal expansion that induces a rightward shift of the IS schedule gains full potency in raising the level of output, since there is no currency appreciation to offset it. The current account must deteriorate in this case too. Yet the links between the fiscal deficit and the trade deficit, on the one hand, and between the trade deficit and the value of the domestic currency, on the other, are empirically weak (e.g., see Kotlikoff 1992, ch. 3).

In contrast with this standard static model, the modern intertemporal optimizing approach provides a framework suitable for positive and normative analyses of current-account dynamics. The predictive content of the model is enhanced by taking explicit account of the intertemporal budget constraint and of optimization by individual households and firms.

The key factors governing the nature of the macroeconomic equilibrium differ drastically across the two models. In the static income-expenditure model, the nature of the macroeconomic equilibrium reflects the relative magnitudes of parameters measuring the effects of changes in income on spending and the demand for money. In the intertemporal model, by contrast, the nature of the equilibrium reflects parameters measuring the effects of intertemporal substitution and the debt-income position. What might we learn about certain recent episodes by following the intertemporal approach rather than the less rigorous Mundell-Fleming approach? Income-expenditure models of the Mundell-Fleming sort suggest a simple relation between the government budget and economic activity: A cut in the government deficit depresses consumption and output. In many countries, however, large cuts in government spending carried out as part of stabilization programs have led to expansions rather than contractions in economic activity and have resulted in improvements in the current-account balance (e.g., see Giavazzi and Pagano 1990; Bertola and Drazen 1993; Razin and Sadka 1996). In Denmark in the early 1980s and in Ireland in the late 1980s, the government deficit was large relative to GDP, and public debt was growing rapidly. Giavazzi and Pagano (1990) show, however, that the consumption-to-GDP ratio rose and the current account improved in the aftermath of stabilization programs that made large budget cuts. The distinct feature of the mid-1985 disinflation program in Israel was a major and severe fiscal and monetary restraint. The public sector domestic deficit fell to about 0 to 2 percent of GNP from about 12 percent prior to the stabilization. Similarly Razin and Sadka (1996) show that the fiscal consolidation resulted surprisingly in consumption and output booms. These results are inconsistent with the predictions of income-expenditure models but are quite consistent with the predictions of intertemporal models.

A basic assumption that characterizes all intertemporal models is capital mobility. If there is no such mobility, a country cannot engage in intertemporal substitution, and there can be no meaningful intertemporal approach. It is suggestive to think in terms of a dichotomy between perfect and imperfect capital mobility. Perfect capital mobility seems to prevail, more or less, between developed countries, whereas imperfect capital mobility seems to prevail between developed and less developed countries. To the extent that this observation is true, we should expect the intertemporal model to perform better in explaining current-account fluctuations among developed countries (those belonging to the OECD) than among less developed countries.

7.1 Current-Account Theory

The intertemporal approach, like the income-expenditure approach, begins with the national-income identity. Unlike earlier approaches, however, it models investment and consumption (saving) in ways that focus on intertemporal optimization and the differing effects of various shocks. It distinguishes, in particular, among four types of shocks: those that are transitory in duration, those that are persistent, those that are country specific, and those that are common across countries. Each type of shock has distinct effects on the dynamics of a country's saving-investment balance. Thus its current-account balance is driven by different shocks in distinctly different ways.

The benchmark model we use to illustrate the intertemporal approach assumes the existence of riskless assets that are traded freely, a single representative agent, and perfect competition in the goods market. Nevertheless, the main findings about the different effects of the various shocks carry over also to intertemporal models with risky assets, heterogeneous populations, and imperfect competition. The conclusions depends importantly, however, on the implicit assumption, maintained throughout, that only noncontingent borrowing is possible, since that assumption rules out diversification against country-specific shocks (see Obstfeld 1995, who examines the theory and evidence on diversification).

By the national account identity, the current-account balance is given by

$$CA_t = Y_t - Z_t - C_t + (R - 1)F_{t-1},$$

where CA_t, Y_t, Z_t, C_t, R_t, and F_{t-1}, stand for period t current-account surplus, output, investment, consumption, (gross) interest rate (one plus the world rate of interest), and lagged foreign assets, respectively. (Note that F is the negative of foreign [one period] debt B in equation 5.6 in chapter 5.) We look first at the modeling of investment and then at the modeling of consumption (saving).

Investment

Consider a small open economy, producing a single aggregate tradable good (see Leiderman and Razin 1991; Mendoza 1991; Glick and Rogoff 1992). The production function for that good Y is Cobb-Douglas:

$$Y_t = AK_t^\alpha, \tag{7.1}$$

where A, α, and K denote the productivity level, the distributive share of capital, and the capital stock, respectively. We assume that productivity shocks follow a first-order autoregressive stochastic process:

$$(A_t - \bar{A}) = \rho(A_{t-1} - \bar{A}) + \varepsilon_t, \qquad 0 \leqslant \rho \leqslant 1, \tag{7.2}$$

where ρ and ε denote the persistence parameter and an i.i.d. term, with mean zero, respectively, and $\bar{A}$ is the steady state productivity level.

Firms maximize the expected value of the discounted sum of profits subject to the available production technology and to a cost-of-adjustment investment technology. According to the latter, gross investment Z is specified as

$$Z_t = I_t \left(1 + \frac{g}{2} \frac{I_t}{K_t} \right), \tag{7.3}$$

where $I_t = K_{t+1} - K_t$, and g denote net capital formation (assuming zero depreciation) and the cost-of-adjustment coefficient, respectively. Thus, in the presence of costs of adjustment, gross investment typically exceeds net capital formation because of the reorganization and retraining costs associated with the installation of new capital equipment (similar to the specification 5.1 in chapter 5).

The optimal-investment rule implies that the cost of investing an additional unit of capital in the current period must be equal to the expected present value of the next period's marginal productivity of capital *plus* the next period's induced fall in the adjustment cost of investment resulting from the enlarged stock of capital (i.e., the derivative of equation 7.3 with respect to K) plus the residual value in the next period of the capital remaining for the entire future:

$$E_t R^{-1} \left[\alpha A_{t+1} K_{t+1}^{\alpha-1} + \frac{g}{2} \left(\frac{I_{t+1}}{K_{t+1}} \right)^2 + q_{t+1} \right] = q_t, \tag{7.4}$$

where E_t is the expectation operator based on period t information, $q_t = 1 + g(I_t/K_t)$ is the firm's market value per unit of capital (the Tobin q measure), and R is the gross interest rate. Observe that $I_t = (q_t - 1)K_t/g$; therefore $I_t \geqslant 0$ as $q_t \geqslant 1$. Thus q_t is the (marginal) Tobin q measure. Note also that $q_t K_t$ represents value of the firm so that q_t is also the average Tobin q measure (see Hayashi 1982).

At the deterministic steady state, $I_t = 0$, and the investment rule reduces to an equality between the rate of interest and the marginal productivity of capital:

$$R - 1 = \alpha \bar{A}(\bar{K})^{\alpha-1}, \tag{7.5}$$

where $\bar{A}$ and $\bar{K}$ are the steady-state levels of productivity and the stock of capital, respectively.

Linearizing (7.4) around the steady state yields

$$k_t + a_0 E_t k_{t+1} + a_1 E_t k_{t+2} = b_0 - b E_t A_{t+1}, \tag{7.6}$$

where $k = K - \bar{K}$ denotes the deviation of the capital stock from its steady-state level,

$$a_0 = \frac{(R-1)(\alpha-1) - g(1+R)}{Rg},$$

$$a_1 = \frac{1}{R},$$

$$b_0 = \frac{\bar{K}}{g}\left(\frac{R-1}{R}\right),$$

$$b = \frac{\alpha \bar{K}^{\alpha}}{kg}.$$

The solution for k_t (see appendix A) is given by

$$k_t = \lambda_1 k_{t-1} + \lambda_1 b \sum_{i=0}^{\infty} \left(\frac{1}{\lambda_2}\right)^i E_t A_{t+1+i} + \frac{b_0}{1 - \lambda_2}, \tag{7.7}$$

where $\lambda_1 < 1$ and $\lambda_2 > 1$ are the roots of the quadratic equation $1 + a_0 \lambda + a_1 \lambda^2 = 0$, with $\lambda_1 + \lambda_2 = a_0$ and $\lambda_1 \lambda_2 = a_1$.[2] Lagging (7.7) by one period and subtracting it from the period t equation yields the corresponding solution for the desired investment flow:

$$Z_t \cong I_t = \lambda_1 I_{t-1} + \lambda_1 b \sum_{i=1}^{\infty} \left(\frac{1}{\lambda^2}\right)^{i-1} [E_t A_{t+i+1} - E_{t-1} A_{t+i+1}]. \tag{7.8}$$

The first term on the right-hand side of (7.8) captures the effects on period t investment of lagged productivity shocks, and the second term captures the revisions of expectations about future productivity shocks (revisions based on the change in information from period $t-1$ to period t). Such persistent shocks convey new information about future shocks.

Substituting (7.2) into (7.8) yields

$$I_t = \lambda_1 I_{t-1} + \left(\frac{\lambda_1 \lambda_2 b \rho}{\lambda_2 - \rho}\right) \Delta A_t, \tag{7.8}'$$

where $\Delta A_t = A_t - A_{t-1}$. If the shocks are *country specific* and *permanent*, ρ in equation (7.2) is equal to 1, and we have a random walk. Substituting $\rho = 1$ into (7.8) yields

$$I_t = \lambda_1 I_{t-1} + \left(b\frac{\lambda_1 \lambda_2}{\lambda_2 - 1}\right) \Delta A_t. \tag{7.9}$$

Subtracting I_{t-1} from both sides yields

$$\Delta Z_t \cong \Delta I_t = (\lambda_1 - 1)\Delta I_{t-1} + \left(b\frac{\lambda_1 \lambda_2}{\lambda_2 - 1}\right)\Delta A_t. \tag{7.10}$$

Thus current investment is shown to be positively correlated with a permanent country-specific productivity shock.

If instead $\rho = 0$ in (7.8), the country-specific shocks are only *transitory*. Recomputing the change in investment yields

$$\Delta Z_t \cong \Delta I_t = (\lambda_1 - 1)\Delta I_{t-1}. \tag{7.11}$$

Hence a transitory productivity shock has no impact whatsoever on current investment.

Consider now what happens if productivity shocks are *common* to all countries. The shock will raise the world rate of interest, $R-1$, whether or not the shock is persistent. If it is persistent, it will tend to raise current investment by raising future productivity, but the rise in the cost of capital will outweigh the expected rise in future productivity, thereby weakening the effect on current investment. If it is not persistent, it will affect current investment only marginally through its impact on world saving and thereby on the world rate of interest.

Consumption

We now turn to the modeling of consumption (saving). Consider the key elements of consumption behavior, based on the familiar permanent-income hypothesis (which holds only when the representative consumer has full access to world capital markets). The representative agent chooses a consumption path so as to maximize his/her lifetime utility (assumed quadratic)

$$E_t \sum_{i=0}^{\infty} \delta^i u(C_{t+i}),$$

$$u(C) = hC - \frac{1}{2}C^2, \tag{7.12}$$

subject to the constraint

$$C_t + F_t = Y_t + RF_{t-1}, \tag{7.13}$$

where δ and F denote the subjective discount factor and the stock of foreign assets, respectively. Net output Y accounts for the resources used up in investment (i.e., Z_t has been subtracted from Y_t). Assuming, for simplicity, no consumption tilting ($\delta R = 1$), the solution to the consumer's optimization problem is given by

$$C_t = \beta W_t, \quad \beta = \frac{R-1}{R}, \tag{7.14}$$

where W_t denotes wealth so that $W(R-1)/R$ represents the corresponding permanent income flow. Wealth consists of the expected discounted flow of domestic income *plus* income from the initial stock of foreign assets:

$$W_t = E_t \sum_{i=0}^{\infty} \left(\frac{1}{R}\right)^i Y_{t+i} + RF_{t-1}. \tag{7.15}$$

The general-equilibrium aspect of our framework is reflected by the fact that the representative agent's wealth depends on the economy-wide output stream, which is in turn determined by investment behavior. Accordingly, the realized sequence of current and future productivity shocks (and the induced investment path) are the driving forces behind consumption spending. Specifically the linear approximation of the production function around the steady state yields

$$Y_t = d_0 + d_K K_t + d_A A_t,$$ (7.16)

where $d_0 = \bar{Y} = \bar{A}\bar{K}^\alpha$, $d_K = k - 1$, and $d_A = \bar{K}^\alpha$. Substituting (7.16), together with (7.2) and (7.7), into the wealth term in (7.14) and (7.15) yields the closed-form solution for current consumption spending as a function of the observable (current and past) productivity levels and of foreign asset holdings as follows (see appendix B):

$$C_t = Y_{t-1} + \frac{R}{R - \lambda_1} d_K I_{t-1} + \left(\frac{R-1}{R-\rho} d_A + \frac{d_K}{k-\lambda_1} \frac{\lambda_1 \lambda_2 b \rho}{\rho_2 - \rho} \right) \Delta A_t$$

$$+ \frac{\rho - 1}{k - \rho} d_A (A_{t-1} - \bar{A}) + (R - 1)F_{t-1}.$$ (7.14)'

Consider the effects on consumption of *persistent* country-specific productivity shocks, representing persistence by the extreme case $\rho = 1$. Writing (7.16) in first-difference form and substituting (7.2) and (7.9) into the resulting expression yields

$$\Delta Y_t = (\lambda_1 - 1)d_K \Delta I_{t-1} + \left(\frac{\lambda_1 \lambda_2}{\lambda_2 - 1} b d_K + d_A \right) \Delta A_t.$$ (7.17)

Writing (7.14)' in first-difference form for $\rho = 1$ yields

$$\Delta C_t = \left\{ \frac{\lambda_1 \lambda_2}{\lambda_2 - 1} b d_K \left(1 + \frac{\lambda_1}{R} \frac{(R-1)}{(R-\lambda_1)} \right) + d_A \right\} \Delta A_t$$

$$+ (R - 1)\Delta F_{t-1}.$$ (7.18)

Observe that the coefficient of ΔA_t in (7.18) is larger than the corresponding coefficient in (7.17). The economic intuition is straightforward. The effect of a productivity change (ΔA_t) on current consumption is subject to two reinforcing influences: First, if investment is held constant in response to the shock, current income and current consumption should rise by equal amounts; this effect is captured by the term $\lambda_1 \lambda_2 bd_K/(\lambda_2 - 1) + d_A$ in (7.17) and (7.18); second, the productivity shock (ΔA_t), however, raises the entire expected future investment path and thus leads to a larger future capital stock and larger future income. Consequently permanent income (and, along with it, current consumption) should rise by more than current income. This effect is captured by the term $\{\lambda_1(R - 1)/[R(R - \lambda_1)]\}[\lambda_1 \lambda_2 bd_K/(\lambda_2 - 1)]$ in (7.18).

Consider, instead, a *transitory* productivity shock $(\rho = 0)$. It follows from (7.11) that investment is not affected at all, and the change in wealth must therefore equal the transitory increment to current income with no change in future expected income. Indeed, substituting $\rho = 0$ into (7.14)' yields

$$\Delta C_t = (R - 1)\left(\Delta F_{t-1} + \frac{d_A}{R} \Delta A_t \right). \tag{7.19}$$

Now, comparing (7.18) and (7.19), it is evident that transitory shocks have relatively weak effects on current consumption. This is also in line with standard consumption theory.

It is noteworthy that disturbances other than productivity shocks, such as changes in government spending, can be incorporated by making only slight modification in the framework. Recall that even under Ricardian assumptions, government spending can have real effects in an intertemporal framework. Under Ricardian equivalence, an increase in government spending that is fully anticipated reduces a household's wealth and consumption and thus affects the current account. Its effects are weaker in the absence of Ricardian equivalence or when the increase is not fully anticipated (see also Backus, Kehoe, and Kydland 1992, which looks at the effects of temporary and permanent changes in government spending.)

Current Account

Substituting the solutions for Y_t, C_t, and Z_t into the definition of the current-account balance, we get

$$CA_t = -\lambda_1 \left(\frac{d_k}{R - \lambda_1} - 1 \right) I_{t-1}$$

$$- \left[\frac{\rho - 1}{R - \rho} d_A + \frac{\lambda_1 \lambda_2 b \rho}{\lambda_2 - \rho} \left(\frac{d_K}{R - \lambda_1} + 1 \right) \right] \Delta A_t$$

$$- \frac{\rho - 1}{R - \rho} d_A (A_{t-1} - \overline{A}). \tag{7.20}$$

With $\rho = 1$, the effects on the current account of persistent country-specific shocks are given by

$$\Delta CA_t = \left\{ -\frac{\lambda_1 \lambda_2}{\lambda_2 - 1} b d_K \frac{\lambda_1}{R} \frac{(R - 1)}{(R - \lambda_1)} - \frac{\lambda_1 \lambda_2}{\lambda_2 - 1} b \right\} \Delta A_t$$

$$+ (R - 1) CA_{t-1} - \lambda_1 \left(\frac{d_K}{R - \lambda_1} - 1 \right) \Delta I_{t-1}. \tag{7.21}$$

The coefficient of ΔA_t in (7.21) is negative. Consequently a permanent country-specific productivity-enhancing shock must, for two reasons, worsen the current account. First, it causes investment spending to rise. Second, it causes current consumption spending to rise by more than the current rise in output. This means that the current account has to be negatively correlated with persistent country-specific productivity shocks.

When shocks of this sort are *not* persistent ($\rho = 0$), however, consumption responds only weakly, and investment does not respond at all. Substituting $\rho = 0$ into (7.20) yields

$$\Delta CA_t = \frac{d_A}{R} \Delta A_t + (R - 1) CA_{t-1} - \lambda_1 \left(\frac{d_K}{R - \lambda_1} - 1 \right) \Delta I_{t-1}. \tag{7.22}$$

The positive coefficient of the productivity term implies that a positive transitory productivity shock tends to move the external balance into surplus. This means that the current account has to be positively correlated with nonpersistent country-specific shocks.

We have shown that an extreme transitory country specific shock ($\rho = 0$) generates a positive correlation between current account position and domestic output, whereas an extreme permanent shock

($\rho = 1$) leads to a negative correlation. In practice, we do not have either one of the two extreme degrees of persistence. To determine the condition under which such correlation is positive or negative, we calculate a critical value of ρ, ρ^*, which generates a zero correlation. From (7.20) define

$$F(\rho) = -\frac{\rho - 1}{R - \rho} - \frac{\rho \alpha}{(\lambda_2 - \rho)g}\left[\frac{R - 1}{R - \lambda_1} + 1\right].$$

Observe that $F(0) > 0$ and $F(1) < 0$. Then $F(\rho^*) = 0$. If $\rho > \rho^*$, the current-account–output correlation is negative, while, if $\rho < \rho^*$, the correlation is positive.

A *global* shock that affects all countries should have a significantly different impact on the external balance than would a country-specific shock. A persistent productivity-enhancing shock common to all countries will raise the world rate of interest. The rise in the interest rate should dampen the increases in current consumption and investment spending that would be produced by a comparable country-specific shock. Thus the response of the current account to a persistent global shock must be smaller than the response to a country specific shock. In a world of identical countries, in fact, the ultimate change in the world rate of interest produced by a global productivity-enhancing shock must rule out any observable change in any country's current-account balance, since all countries cannot experience simultaneous improvements in their current accounts. A global nonpersistent positive shock generates excess world saving and thereby exerts a downward pressure on the world rate of interest, which in turn will stimulate current spending. Consequently the response of the current account to a transitory global shock must be weaker than the response to a transitory country-specific shock. The compositional point holds here as well, for, if all countries were identical, the ultimate change in the world interest rate in response to a global shock would be just large enough to prevent any change in any country's current account. A printout of a computer program, which can assist in simulating dynamic paths of the current account, is included at the end of the book.

7.2   Correlations between Saving and Investment

The typical impulse response of saving (i.e., the difference between output and consumption), investment, and the trade balance to a positive, but not fully persistent, productivity shock is presented in figure 7.1. This pattern of saving, investment and trade balance is consistent with the behavior of output (7.16), consumption (7.14)′, investment (7.8)′, and the current account balance (7.20). There is a positive impact effect on saving and a downward monotonic adjustment back to the initial equilibrium, reflecting the fact that consumption is smoothed relative to output. The impulse response of investment shown in the figure indicates a large positive impact effect, followed by a sharp drop and a monotonic convergence to the initial equilibrium reflecting the intertemporal substitution in investment induced by the shock. The trade balance fluctuates, first deteriorating, then improving, and finally converging to the initial equilibrium, reflecting the alternating positions of saving and investment.

These patterns explain why the covariance between saving and investment is typically *positive* under the assumption of perfect

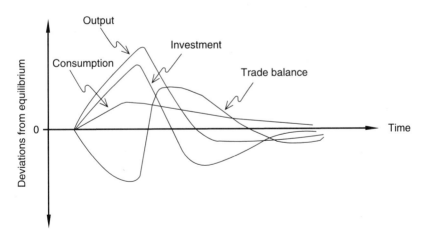

Figure 7.1
Saving-investment balance: Impulse response to productivity shock

capital mobility (see Obstfeld 1986). To see this, recall that the covariance expression includes a quadratic term, the product of saving and investment. Therefore observations involving large deviations from the initial equilibrium, such as the positive impact effects, take on large weights in the covariance formula, and the covariance becomes positive when the time spent at each point on the impulse function is the same. By implication, a positive covariance between saving and investment should not necessarily be interpreted as an indication of capital immobility, as was argued by Feldstein and Horioka (1980). In fact the narrow differentials between interest rates on offshore and onshore assets denominated in the same currency indicate that capital mobility is more nearly perfect than zero among the developed countries. Thus, the observed positive covariance does not pose a challenge to the intertemporal approach because it is in fact predicted by that approach.

7.3   Real-Exchange-Rate Theory

Up to this point, we have assumed that all goods are traded in world markets. In this subsection, we introduce goods that are not traded; their relative prices are determined exclusively in the domestic economy. In this case macroeconomic shocks have domestic effects additional to those discussed in the previous section because they affect the relative prices of nontraded goods (i.e., the inverse of the real exchange rate).

The intertemporal approach provides important insights into the time-series properties of the real exchange rate, the relative price of tradable in terms of nontradable. Following recent intertemporal models of the trade balance and the real exchange rate (see Razin 1984; Mendoza 1992; Rebelo 1992a; see especially Rogoff 1992), we assume a stylized two-sector model of a small open economy. Preferences over consumption of tradables, C^T, and nontradables, C^N, are represented by a Cobb-Douglas intratemporal utility function (similar to the specification in chapter 6):

$$V(C^T, C^N) = (C^T)^{1-\gamma}(C^N)^{\gamma}. \tag{7.23}$$

Equality between the marginal rate of substitution between tradables and nontradables and their corresponding relative price implies that

$$P = \frac{(1 - \gamma)C^N}{\gamma C^T},$$ (7.24)

where P denotes the relative price of nontradables in terms of tradables and is thus the real exchange rate.

The representative agent is infinitely lived and seeks to maximize

$$U = \sum_{t=0}^{\infty} \beta^t \left[\frac{1}{1 - \sigma}(V_t^{1-\sigma} - 1) \right].$$ (7.25)

Sectoral outputs are represented by Cobb-Douglas production functions:

$$Y^T = A^T(K^T)^{1-\alpha}(L^T)^{\alpha},$$ (7.26)

$$Y^N = A^N(K^N)^{1-v}(L^N)^{v}.$$ (7.27)

Intersectoral Factor Mobility

The classic model of the real exchange rate, which was developed by Balassa (1964) and Samuelson (1964), assumes that capital and labor can move freely between sectors and that capital is internationally mobile. The model thus represents an economy in a long-run equilibrium, with free capital flows. Given the common wage and rental rates in the two sectors and the fact that the rental rate of capital in the tradable sector is nailed down by the world rate of interest, the standard profit-maximization conditions imply that

$$dp = \left(\frac{v}{\alpha}\right)da^T - da^N,$$ (7.28)

where a lowercase letter denotes the logarithm of a variable indicated by the corresponding uppercase letter (for derivation of 7.28, see appendix C). This equation asserts that the path of the logarithm of the real exchange rate is completely determined by the productivity shocks da^T and da^N, regardless of the aggregate-demand conditions. Thus a productivity increase in the tradable sector leads to a real appreciation. Under purchasing-power parity holding for tradable goods, the domestic inflation rate is driven exclusively by shocks to the outputs of tradables and nontradables, as indicated by (7.27). Therefore intersectoral factor mobility implies that the real exchange rate is highly sensitive to shocks to the output of the traded good, and only to the extent that these shocks are transitory, the real exchange rate will display a relatively low degree of persistence.

Sector-Specific Factors

The polar opposite to the above-mentioned case is that in which factors are intersectorally immobile. That case can be viewed as describing an economy in short-run equilibrium and thus explaining month-to-month fluctuations of the real exchange rate. As has been emphasized by Rogoff (1992), the equilibrium real exchange rate responds in the short run mainly to aggregate demand shocks in a way that is akin to the behavior of consumption, which smooths out transitory shocks to income.

The intertemporal smoothing of expected marginal utility implies that

$$(x_t)^{1-\gamma}(V_t)^{-\sigma} = \beta R E_t (x_{t+1})^{1-\gamma}(V_{t+1})^{-\sigma}, \quad x = \frac{C^N}{C^T}. \tag{7.29}$$

Setting aside shocks to the supply of nontradable goods (so that equilibrium C^N is constant) and assuming no consumption tilting (so that $\delta R = 1$), we substitute (7.24) into (7.29) to get

$$P_t^{1-\gamma(1-\sigma)} = E_t P_{t+1}^{1-\gamma(1-\sigma)}. \tag{7.30}$$

Approximating the exponential term P^x for any parameter x by the linear term $(1 + xp)$, where p denotes the logarithm of P, we can rewrite (7.30) as

$$p_t = E_t p_{t+1}.$$

Thus the logarithm of the real exchange rate will follow a random walk, regardless of the underlying shocks to the traded-goods sector.[3] Intersectoral factor mobility therefore implies that the time series of the real exchange rate will display a relatively high degree of persistence.

7.4 Evidence of Persistence and the Commonality of Shocks

Having set out the theory to highlight the relevant issues, we will proceed in this subsection to look at some evidence. We will be concerned with two types of empirical work, which identify the nature of shocks and the testable implications of the dynamic-optimizing (intertemporal) approach.

Drawing on Razin and Rose (1992), we provide some evidence on the time-series nature of the shocks that operate on output, consumption, and investment. (For similar work, focused on segregating global and country-specific shocks, see Glick and Rogoff 1992.) The data set comprises 138 countries and spans the period from 1950 to 1988. It is taken from the Penn World Tables, documented in Summers and Heston (1991).

Persistence

To address the issue of persistence, Razin and Rose (1992) computed simple Dickey-Fuller tests for (the logarithms of) each of our variables. At conventional levels of statistical significance, the data typically do not reject the hypothesis that a single unit root exists in the univariate representations of output, consumption, and investment. Razin and Rose ran separate tests for consumption, output, and investment and for each of the 138 countries; of these, 18 tests (4.5 percent) rejected the null hypothesis of a unit root at the 5 percent significance level, and five tests (1.3 percent) rejected the null hypothesis at the 1 percent significance level. These results are quite close to what would be expected under the null hypothesis, implying that the data are consistent with the existence of unit roots in the autoregressive representations of the variables.

It is well known that such tests have low power against stationary alternatives and that there are serious problems in interpreting the test results as demonstrating a high degree of persistence. Thus we should view the findings as being consistent with a high degree of persistence in shocks but by no means as definitive.

Commonality of Shocks

The models developed earlier in this chapter indicate that the dynamics of the saving-investment balance should depend critically on whether shocks are country specific or common across countries. Accordingly, Razin and Rose (1994) tested for the nature of the shocks using standard factor-analytic techniques. The factor analysis was performed across countries on the detrended measures of output, consumption, and investment. The results are given in table 7.1. Because the national-accounts data in the Penn World Tables are sometimes unavailable for the entire 1950–88 period, table 7.1 provides results for two sets of countries: those with at least 20 annual observations and those with at least 35 observations; results for the different sets of countries are quite comparable.

Factor-analysis results depend critically on the method of detrending. When the variables are detrended by using the standard linear trend (TS) method, four factors (those corresponding to the

Table 7.1
Cross-country factor analysis of shocks (proportions of total variance explained)

	Output		Consumption		Investment	
	TS	DS	TS	DS	TS	DS
Countries with at least 20 annual observations						
1 factor	43	20	37	16	35	19
4 factors	85	49	80	45	78	53
Countries with at least 35 annual observations						
1 factor	41	18	38	15	35	15
4 factors	79	41	74	37	68	39

largest four eigenvalues) typically account for around three-quarters of the variation in all three series; the first factor alone accounts for over one-third of the total variation. This finding may indicate that only a small number of important shocks have been common across countries. The fractions fall by approximately one-half, however, when the first-differencing (DS) method of detrending is employed (a method that implicitly adopts a random-walk model of trend).

To summarize, the evidence indicates that many business-cycle shocks are both persistent and common to many countries.

Volatility, Persistence, and Correlations

Intertemporal models predict that the degree of capital-market integration and the nature of shocks are key determinants of the volatility of consumption (saving), investment, and the current account. In this subsection we provide time-series evidence on current-account dynamics so as to shed some light on the empirical importance of the effects identified by the theoretical models discussed in sections 7.1 through 7.3.

Volatility measures for the current account (as a percentage of GDP) and for the logarithms of per capita GDP are exhibited in figure 7.2 for a sample of 58 countries. The data pertain to the period 1967 to 1990; as before, they come from the Penn World Tables (Mark 5). To measure volatility, we use the standard deviation of the (first-difference) detrended variable. Each country is identified by the first two or three letters of its name.

There is a cluster of mainly developed countries and fastest-growing less developed countries that show relatively low current-account and output volatility; this group includes countries such as Japan and Indonesia. The group with high current-account volatility and low output volatility includes countries such as Venezuela and Iran, which are major oil producers.

Two major conclusions can be gleaned from figure 7.2. The less developed countries show more current-account and output volatility than do the developed countries, and the ratio of current-account volatility to output volatility (measured by the slope of a ray from

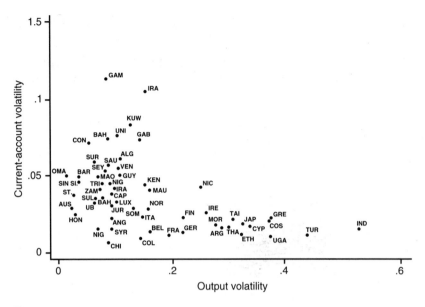

Figure 7.2
Current-account and output volatility (detrending: first difference)

the origin that fits the cluster of observations) is not markedly different for less developed and developed countries.

Table 7.2 provides a set of statistics describing the time-series
properties of the trade balance, output, the terms of trade, the real
effective exchange rate, and the interest rate for each of the seven
largest developed countries and for a sample of less developed countries. It reports measures of volatility and persistence and the correlations between pairs of variables (see also Mendoza 1992). Observe
that relative price changes (e.g., changes in the terms of trade, the
real exchange rate, and the rate of interest) cause income effects
for the country akin to shifts in output, in addition to the direct substitution effects. For example, because a deterioration in the terms of
trade means that, with the same quantity of exports, the country is
able to import reduced amounts of goods and services from abroad,
real income falls. The distinction between temporary and permanent
changes is as relevant here as for the case of output shocks. The
temporary versus permanent distinction is also relevant for the inter-

temporal substitution effect (e.g., as in Svensson and Razin 1983 and Obstfeld 1982).

The main regularities shown in table 7.2 can be summarized as follows:

1. There is a significant degree of persistence in output, the terms of trade, and the real exchange rate, a finding similar to our earlier conclusion based on the Penn World Tables.

2. The trade balance is in most cases more volatile than the terms of trade or output.

3. The trade balance and the terms of trade are positively correlated for most of the countries, in line with the Harberger-Laursen-Metzler effect. Recall that this proposition predicted that a deterioration of the terms of trade would reduce saving. According to the intertemporal approach, a temporary deterioration of the terms of trade will induce substitution from current to future consumption (i.e., will increase saving), but a permanent deterioriation will not.

4. Looking across countries, one cannot detect the link predicted by the theory between the persistence of output or terms-of-trade shocks and the correlation between the trade balance, on the one hand, and the terms of trade or output, on the other. It seems that a more structural, econometric approach is needed to test the validity of this implication of the intertemporal approach. It should be noted, however, that Mendoza (1992) reproduced the expected relationship by a different method. He constructed two benchmark economies to characterize a "typical" developed country and a "typical" less developed country. Conditioning them with empirically based parameters pertaining to terms-of-trade shocks, he was able to simulate the Harberger-Laursen-Metzler effect whereby the persistence parameter of the terms-of-trade shocks is positively associated with the correlation between the trade balance and the terms of trade.

5. The real rate of interest and terms of trade are more volatile for less developed than for developed countries, and the volatility of the trade balance is also significantly larger for less developed than for developed countries.

Table 7.2
Statistical properties of key variables in selected countries

Seven largest developed countries: Standard deviation and persistence[a]

	GDP		Terms of trade		Trade balance		Real effective exchange rate		Real rate of interest	
	σ	ρ	σ	ρ	σ	ρ	σ	ρ	σ	ρ
United States	2.17	0.446	7.11	0.776	9.00	0.509	12.68	0.814	2.46	0.694
United Kingdom	1.98	0.524	4.56	0.460	7.98	0.685	10.83	0.799	3.57	0.676
France	1.49	0.654	5.38	0.683	4.59	0.183	6.11	0.695	2.24	0.449
Germany	1.92	0.439	7.69	0.766	6.19	0.640	6.58	0.751	1.73	0.241
Italy	2.17	0.537	7.83	0.764	10.20	0.496	5.62	0.720	2.84	0.268
Canada	2.01	0.540	3.64	0.577	5.37	0.532	7.76	0.682	2.08	0.565
Japan	3.58	0.812	14.77	0.820	13.48	0.546	9.66	0.670	3.21	−0.166

Seven largest developed countries: Correlations[a]

	$\rho_{tb.tot}$	$\rho_{tot.e}$	$\rho_{tot.r}$	$\rho_{tb.e}$	$\rho_{tb.r}$	$\rho_{e.r}$	$\rho_{tb.y}$	$\rho_{tot.y}$
United States	−0.378	0.393	−0.039	−0.481	0.078	0.712	−0.277	0.197
United Kingdom	0.634	0.499	0.539	0.690	0.816	0.681	−0.538	−0.230
France	0.351	−0.463	−0.530	−0.372	−0.356	−0.183	−0.019	0.287
Germany	0.590	0.458	−0.351	0.299	−0.083	−0.324	−0.299	0.239
Italy	0.572	0.426	−0.231	−0.034	0.021	0.050	−0.210	0.112
Canada	−0.026	−0.312	0.286	0.012	0.430	0.067	−0.709	−0.034
Japan	0.600	0.287	−0.264	0.075	0.122	−0.358	0.054	0.559

Less developed countries: σ, δ, correlations[a]

	Terms of trade		Trade balance		Real rate of interest		Correlations		
	σ	ρ	σ	ρ	σ	ρ	$\rho_{tb.tot}$	$\rho_{tot.r}$	$\rho_{tb.r}$
Argentina	10.64	0.295	26.84	0.347	57.44	−0.020	0.179	0.271	0.321
Brazil	14.17	0.614	27.33	0.679	37.14	0.053	0.031	−0.110	0.004
Chile	13.62	0.518	18.86	0.435	8.27	0.127	0.277	−0.540	−0.084
Mexico	14.20	0.741	30.84	0.718	11.50	−0.219	0.368	0.290	0.142
Peru	10.77	0.337	26.57	0.572	13.56	0.385	0.304	−0.016	0.337
Venezuela	35.07	0.786	28.04	0.386	7.72	0.231	0.291	0.341	0.544
Israel	5.94	0.667	11.77	0.490	367.08	−0.574	0.313	0.112	−0.344
Egypt	9.78	0.413	17.35	0.665	3.35	0.092	−0.157	−0.133	0.378
Taiwan	10.44	0.699	13.82	0.575	7.08	−0.023	0.556	−0.063	−0.054
India	10.05	0.667	18.29	0.723	2.55	−0.131	0.439	−0.183	0.114
Indonesia	29.17	0.817	12.35	0.268	3.08	−0.367	0.337	0.181	0.137
Korea	10.56	0.778	16.19	0.574	9.03	0.527	0.243	0.332	0.188
Philippines	13.68	0.815	13.93	0.377	7.69	−0.037	0.444	0.103	−0.002
Thailand	9.76	0.586	13.16	0.551	4.05	0.388	−0.339	−0.491	−0.206
Algeria	35.59	0.761	23.83	0.343	2.70	0.052	0.181	−0.288	−0.450
Cameroon	22.70	0.812	17.25	0.467	2.94	0.322	0.421	0.334	−0.016
Zaire	19.14	0.647	18.97	0.723	16.80	−0.241	0.390	0.276	0.069
Kenya	9.94	0.450	16.05	0.374	4.42	0.416	0.204	−0.064	0.226

Table 7.2 (continued)

Less developed countries: σ, δ, correlations[a]

	Terms of trade		Trade balance		Real rate of interest		Correlations		
	σ	ρ	σ	ρ	σ	ρ	$\rho_{tb.tot}$	$\rho_{tot.r}$	$\rho_{tb.r}$
Morocco	10.46	0.582	15.86	0.659	3.21	0.207	0.259	0.135	0.192
Nigeria	39.95	0.785	31.33	0.527	9.10	0.181	-0.217	0.022	-0.025
Tunisia	24.09	0.852	12.50	0.452	2.29	0.304	-0.138	-0.620	0.047

Sources: IMF, *International Financial Statistics*, and data base for *World Economic Outlook*.

Note: Data for the terms of trade and the trade balance are for 1960 to 1989, and for GDP for 1965 to 1989, expressed in per capita terms and detrended using the Hodrick-Prescott filter with the smoothing parameter set at 100. GDP is at constant domestic prices from National Income Accounts, the terms of trade are the ratio of U.S. dollar unit value of exports to U.S. dollar unit value of imports, the real effective exchange rate is the ratio of unit value of exports to GDP, the trade balance is exports minus imports of merchandise from the balance of payments expressed at constant import prices (the detrended trade balance corresponds to detrended exports minus detrended imports).

a. σ is the percentage standard deviation, ρ is the first-order serial autocorrelation, $\rho_{tb.tot}$ is the correlation of the trade balance with the terms of trade, $\rho_{tot.e}$ is the correlation of the terms of trade with the real effective exchange rate, $\rho_{tot.r}$ is the correlation of the terms of trade with the real of interest, $\rho_{tb.e}$ is the correlation of the trade balance with the real effective exchange rate, $\rho_{tb.r}$ is the correlation of the trade balance with the real rate of interest, and $\rho_{e.r}$ is the correlation between the real effective exchange rate and the real of interest.

6. The correlation between the rate of interest and the trade balance is positive for most countries. This is consistent with the presence of intertemporal substitution; the current-account balance will improve if a rise in the interest rate reduces current spending on consumption and investment and augments future spending.

7. The real exchange rate is only weakly correlated with the trade balance. In contrast to the Mundell-Fleming model, the intertemporal model does not make a clear prediction concerning this correlation.

8. The real exchange rate shows a high degree of persistence and a relatively low correlation with the terms-of-trade shocks. This may support the validity of the consumption-smoothing model of the real exchange rate discussed in the second part of section 7.3.

9. Finally, and most important, the trade balance is in most cases negatively correlated with output. Recall that a permanent country-specific shock worsens the trade balance for two reasons. First, it raises investment; second, it causes current consumption to rise by more than the current rise in output. This finding is therefore in line with the predictions of the intertemporal model in sections 7.1 and 7.2.

Sachs (1981) investigated nonstructural regressions describing the behavior of the current account for both developed and less developed countries. He emphasized that most of the explanatory power of his regressions was the result of an investment surge that led to current-account deficits; saving rates changed little. Further developments in theory and methodology have facilitated structural testing.

Structural Testing

A full-blown optimizing model is difficult to estimate because it is often impossible to reduce it to a small number of tractable equations. There have been, however, a few attempts at empirical implementation.

The intertemporal model predicts that shocks that are persistent and common to all countries (that is, formed by a GNP-weighted average of the individual productivity measures) have no effect on the trade balance. To test this proposition, Glick and Rogoff (1992) computed the Solow residuals for each country and broke them down into country-specific and global shocks and into transitory and persistent shocks. They found that the various shocks enter current-account regressions with the predicted signs. The hypothesis stood up to the annual data of eight developed countries for the period 1960 to 1990. In particular, Glick and Rogoff found that the coefficient of the productivity variable in their trade-balance equation was, as predicted, larger than the corresponding coefficient in their investment equation. They, however, did not rigorously incorporate the cross-equation restrictions implied by the theory, and the fit of their regression equations was weak in several cases.

Leiderman and Razin (1991) estimated an intertemporal model for Israel using monthly data for the 1980s. They found strong evidence in favor of consumption smoothing (indicated by an offsetting response of private saving to changes in government saving and only a small proportion of liquidity-constrained consumers), as well as a strong response of investment to country-specific productivity shocks.

Mendoza (1991, 1992) provides recursive simulations based on a calibrated model with empirically based parameters that lend support to the emphasis that the intertemporal approach attaches to the persistence of shocks and to consumption smoothing.

Razin and Rose (1992) provide indirect tests of the intertemporal approach. The approach predicts that capital-market integration will lower consumption volatility while raising investment volatility to the extent that productivity shocks are idiosyncratic and nonpersistent. They use a unique panel data set (ranging from the 1950s to the late 1980s and covering developed as well as less-developed countries); it includes indicators of barriers to trade in goods and (financial) capital. The results of their study are inconclusive, for they did not find a strong link between business-cycle volatility and openness. Countries with greater capital mobility (i.e., fewer barriers to trade in financial assets), for instance, do not appear to have systematically smoother consumption streams or more volatile investment behavior.

Finally, the usefulness and limitations of the intertemporal approach to the current account in providing a benchmark for the discussion of "excessive imbalances" and the sustainability of persistent external imbalances is analysed in Chapter 17.

7.5   Conclusion

As described in chapter 1, in recent years we have seen large, unsynchronized changes in national fiscal policies, and these have resulted in substantial budgetary imbalances, volatile real rates of interest and real exchange rates, and large current-account imbalances. The intertemporal approach provides a framework for analyzing these fiscal (and productivity) shocks and offers a coherent theory that can potentially account for the observed diversity of current-account balances. This chapter has illustrated the use of this approach in analyzing current-account dynamics and has reviewed the evidence supporting it.

The intertemporal approach begins with the national-income identity and with detailed descriptions of the intratemporal and intertemporal budget constraints faced by the decision-making units. It models investment and consumption (saving) in ways that emphasize intertemporal optimization and the differing effects of various shocks and shows the importance of distinguishing among four types of shocks. These can be transitory or persistent in duration, country-specific or common across countries. Because different shocks have different effects on the saving-investment balance, they have different effects on the trend and volatility of the current-account balance.

Are there easier ways to explain current-account behavior? Can one take shortcuts that are simpler to implement than the rigorous modern approach? A popular method of applied analysis is to regress the current-account balance on such "price" variables as the real exchange rate and interest rates and on such "income" variables as output, government spending, tax-burden indicators, government debt, and money creation. The typical regression uses mostly current variables, except that lagged output is added to function jointly with current output as a proxy for permanent income. Most applied work, however, still emphasizes income and price elasticities of demand for exports and imports, a practice that can be rationalized only by invoking a one-period partial-equilibrium model.

Traditional studies test debt neutrality by asking whether regression coefficients on taxes and debt are significantly different from zero. Similarly they test whether the exchange rate is effective in improving the trade deficit by the sign and statistical significance of the coefficient of the real exchange rate, allowing possibly for simultaneous-equations bias by the use of instrumental variables. This sort of reduced-form analysis, however, omits all of the variables suggested by the intertemporal model. It also fails to distinguish between the different types of shocks or between types of taxation (i.e., taxes on capital income, labor income, or consumption). Accordingly, reduced-form regression analyses of the trade balance are not likely to provide relevant information on the validity of debt neutrality, the sensitivity of the current account to exogenous or policy-induced changes in the exchange rate or the rate of interest, or on a host of other policy-related issues. That is, they ignore an important possibility. If current taxes are a good predictor of future government spending, a tax coefficient significantly different from zero will be consistent with the neutrality proposition and contrary to the traditional interpretation. Furthermore a large positive current-output coefficient may indicate the presence of persistent productivity shocks, which play no role in the traditional approach.

The empirical implementation of the intertemporal approach has not been widespread, since intertemporal models are inherently intractable and demand much data. Nevertheless, there have been recent attempts to test some of the key hypotheses of this approach, and as indicated in this chapter, the results are quite encouraging.

A drawback of other existing approaches is their inability to account for changes in the fiscal or monetary regime. An increase in the stock of government bonds, for example, may signal a future increase in taxes, since an increase will be needed to service the new debt. But the increase in debt may also signal a future fall in government spending or forthcoming monetary accommodation and inflation. Current econometric methods cannot distinguish between different types of regime change, with different implications for the debt-neutrality question and other important hypotheses. Innovations in the theory of endogenous policy should prove useful for this purpose.

7.6 Appendix A: Solution to Second-Order Stochastic Difference Equations

This appendix reproduces the backward- and forward-expansion solution methods for second-order stochastic difference equations (based on Sargent 1987). These methods are useful for solving a variety of stochastic dynamic problems and are applied in this chapter.

A typical second-order stochastic difference equation (SDE) takes the following form:

$$E_t Y_{t+1} - a_1 Y_t - a_2 Y_{t-1} = b_1 + b_2 E_t X_{t+1}. \tag{A.1}$$

Define the lag (or backward-shift) operator by $L^n Z_t = Z_{t-n}$ for $n = 1, 2, 3, \ldots$. Then the above equation can be rewritten

$$(1 - a_1 L - a_2 L^2) E_t Y_{t+1} = b_1 + b_2 E_t X_{t+1}. \tag{A.2}$$

Factorizing the polynomial expression in parenthesis on the left-hand side yields

$$1 - a_1 L - a_2 L^2 = (1 - \lambda_1 L)(1 - \lambda_2 L),$$

where λ_1 and λ_2 are the roots of the polynomial, with $\lambda_1 + \lambda_2 = a_1$ and $-\lambda_1 \lambda_2 = a_2$. If these are distinct roots with $\lambda_1 < 1$ (stable) and $\lambda_2 > 1$ (unstable), we can apply the factorization to (A.2) by dividing both sides by $1 - \lambda_2 L$ to get

$$(1 - \lambda_1 L) E_t Y_{t+1} = \frac{1}{1 - \lambda_2 L} (b_1 + b_2 E_t X_{t+1}). \tag{A.3}$$

Notice that, formally,

$$\frac{1}{1 - \lambda_2 L} = \frac{-(\lambda_2 L)^{-1}}{1 - (\lambda_2 L)^{-1}}$$

$$= \frac{-1}{\lambda_2 L}\left[1 + \left(\frac{1}{\lambda_2}\right)L^{-1} + \left(\frac{1}{\lambda_2}\right)^2 L^{-2} + \cdots\right]$$

$$= -\left(\frac{1}{\lambda_2}\right)L^{-1} - \left(\frac{1}{\lambda_2}\right)^2 L^{-2} - \left(\frac{1}{\lambda_2}\right)^3 L^{-3} - \cdots.$$

Applying this expansion to the right hand side of (A.3) yields

$$(1 - \lambda_1 L)E_t Y_{t+1} = \frac{b_1}{1 - \lambda_2} - b_2 E_t\left[\sum_{i=0}^{\infty} \lambda_2^{-i} X_{t+1+i}\right] + c\lambda_2^{t+1}. \qquad \text{(A.4)}$$

Imposing the transversality condition, the constant c has to be set to zero. Applying the backward shift, using the stable root λ_1 on the left hand side of (A.4), and moving this term to the right hand side yields the final solution to (SDE) as follows:

$$E_t Y_{t+1} = \lambda_1 Y_t + \frac{b_1}{1 - \lambda_2} - b_2 E_t\left[\sum_{i=0}^{\infty} \lambda_2^{-i} X_{t+1+i}\right]. \qquad \text{(A.5)}$$

7.7   Appendix B: Derivation of the Optimal Consumption Rule (7.14)′

In this appendix we derive the optimal consumption rule (7.14)′. Rewrite the Y_{t+i} term in the wealth equation (7.15) as

$$Y_{t+i} = Y_t + \sum_{j=1}^{i} \Delta Y_{t+j}.$$

Substituting this into (7.15) (ignoring the foreign asset term), we get

$$W_t = \frac{R}{R - 1}\left(Y_t + E_t \sum_{j=1}^{\infty} \frac{\Delta Y_{t+j}}{R^j}\right). \qquad \text{(A.6)}$$

Lagging (7.16) by one period and subtracting it form (7.16) yields

$$Y_t = Y_{t-1} + d_k I_{t-1} + d_A \Delta A_t. \tag{A.7}$$

Substituting this into (A.6), we get

$$\frac{R-1}{R} W_t = Y_t + d_k E_t \sum_{i=1}^{\infty} \frac{I_{t+i-1}}{R^i} + d_A E_t \sum_{i=1}^{\infty} \frac{\Delta A_{t+i}}{R^i}. \tag{A.8}$$

Decomposing ΔA_{t+j} as $(A_{t+j} - A) - (A_{t+j+1} - A)$ and substituting it along with (7.8)′ into (A2.3), we have

$$\frac{R-1}{R} W_t = Y_t + \frac{d_k}{R} \sum_{i=1}^{\infty} \frac{I_t \lambda_1^i}{R^i}$$

$$+ d_A E_t \left(\sum_{i=1}^{\infty} \frac{(A_{t+i} - \bar{A})\rho^i}{R^i} - \sum_{i=1}^{\infty} \frac{(A_{t+i-1} - \bar{A})\rho^i}{R^i} \right).$$

Expanding the geometric series and writing $A_t - \bar{A}$ as $(\Delta A_t + A_{t-1} - \bar{A})$, we obtain

$$C_t = \frac{R-1}{R} W_t = Y_t + \frac{d_k}{R - \lambda_1} I_t + \frac{\rho - 1}{R - \rho} d_A (\Delta A_t + A_{t-1} - \bar{A}).$$

Substituting (7.8)′ and (A.7) into this equation yields the optimal consumption rule (7.14)′ in the text.

7.8 Appendix C: Derivation of the Balassa-Samuelson Effect (7.28)

In this appendix we derive the Balassa-Samuelson effect as revealed by (7.28). Denoting the wage and rental rates by W and R, respectively, we have from the Cobb-Douglas production functions (7.26) and (7.27) and the profit-maximizing conditions

$$W^T = \alpha A^T \left(\frac{K^T}{L^T} \right)^{1-\alpha}, \tag{A.9}$$

$$R^T = (1 - \alpha) A^T \left(\frac{K^T}{L^T} \right)^{-\alpha}, \tag{A.10}$$

$$W^N = v A^N \left(\frac{K^N}{L^N} \right)^{1-v}, \tag{A.11}$$

$$R^N = (1 - v)A^N \left(\frac{K^N}{L^N}\right)^{-v}. \tag{A.12}$$

Intersectoral factor mobility implies that

$$W^T = PW^N, \tag{A.13}$$

$$R^T = PR^N. \tag{A.14}$$

The international mobility of capital implies that

$$R^T = R^*, \tag{A.15}$$

where R^* is the world rate of interest.

Substituting (A.10) into (A.15) to solve for K^T/L^T, we get

$$\frac{K^T}{L^T} = \left(\frac{(1 - \alpha)A^T}{R^*}\right)^{1/\alpha}. \tag{A.16}$$

Substituting (A.12) and (A.15) into (A.14) yields

$$\alpha A^T \left(\frac{(1 - \alpha)A^T}{R^*}\right)^{(1-\alpha)/\alpha} = PvA^N \left(\frac{(1 - v)A^N P}{R^*}\right)^{(1-v)/v}. \tag{A.17}$$

Substituting (A.16) into (A.9) and (A.17) into (A.11) and the resulting expressions into (A.13), we have

$$\frac{K^N}{L^N} = \left(\frac{(1 - v)A^N P}{R^*}\right)^{1/v}. \tag{A.18}$$

Taking logs and collecting terms, we get

$$p = \frac{v}{\alpha}a^T - a^N + v\left(\frac{1 - v}{v} - \frac{1 - \alpha}{\alpha}\right)r^* + \text{constant}. \tag{A.19}$$

Taking first differences while keeping the world rate of interest constant yields (7.28) in the text.

Problems

1. Consider the small open economy model of chapter 5 in which there is a single aggregate tradable commodity. Agents receive endowments of this good in each period and for simplicity assume that the investment technology is such that it is never profitable to augment the endowment through investment. Consumers face an exogenous world discount factor, which we denote here by $R = 1/(1 + r)$, where r is the world interest rate prevailing between the two periods. For simplicity, we assume there is no historically given debt commitment so that initial trade and current account balances are equal. The utility function of the representative consumer is taken to be

$$U = \frac{C_1^{1-1/\sigma} + DC_2^{1-1/\sigma}}{1 - 1/\sigma},$$

where C_t denotes consumption in period t, D is the subjective discount factor, and σ is a positive parameter. The budget constraint of the consumer is

$$C_1 + RC_2 = Y_1 + RY_2 \equiv W,$$

where Y_t denotes the endowment in period t and W is the present value of the endowment stream or wealth.

a. Determine the levels of C_1 and C_2 that maximize utility, subject to the budget constraint.

b. Suppose that the endowment in period 1 falls and that the endowment in period 2 rises in such a way that W is unchanged. Find the effect on the current-account balance between periods 1 and 2.

c. Suppose now that the endowment in period 1 falls with no change in the endowment in period 2. Find the effect on the current-account balance. How does it compare to your finding in part b?

d. Suppose that there is an exogenous change in the world discount factor, R. Find the effect of such a change on the current-account balance. What role does the parameter σ play in your answer? You may assume, in this part of the question, that the world discount factor R and the subjective discount factor D are equal in the initial equilibrium and that the endowment is constant over time.

2. Consider a small open economy with preferences as described in the previous exercise, with a positive endowment in the second period only and no endowment in period 1. As before, assume that this economy has free access to the world capital market and faces a given world discount factor, which is taken to be equal to the subjective discount factor in the initial equilibrium. Assume also that there is no investment or historically given debt commitment.

a. Write down the expression for the current account deficit in period 1.

b. The government decides to impose a (small) tax on international borrowing, namely on all loans taken out in period 1 for repayment in period 2. For simplicity assume that the interest rate inclusive of the tax on borrowing is r, with associate discount factor R, while the world interest rate is r^* with corresponding discount factor R^*. Assume that any revenue collected as a result of this tax is redistributed to private agents in a lump-sum fashion. Also assume that in the initial equilibrium $R = R^* = D$. What is the budget constraint faced by the representative consumer in this case?

c. What is the effect of the tax on foreign borrowing on the current-account balance?

3. Consider the two-country version of the model outlined in exercise 1. The representative consumer in the home country has preferences

$$U = \frac{C_1^{1-1/\sigma} + DC_2^{1-1/\sigma}}{1 - 1/\sigma},$$

while the consumer in the foreign-country has the corresponding utility function

$$U^* = \frac{C_1^{*\,1-1/\sigma^*} + D^* C_2^{*\,1-1/\sigma^*}}{1 - 1/\sigma^*},$$

where a superscripted asterisk denotes a foreign economy variable, and all other notation is as in exercise 1. As before, agents in each country receive endowments of the single aggregate consumption good in each period, and we assume that there is no investment. There are no impediments to trade in goods or capital, and to simplify we assume that no historical debt commitment. Initially we assume that the subjective discount factors, D and D^*, are equal to one another. From the argument presented in chapter 4, the common value of the subjective discount factor must also be equal to the equilibrium world discount factor, which we denote as before by R. Finally, for the purpose of evaluating comparative statics results in the remainder of this exercise, it may be assumed that initially the profile of output (endowments) is flat in each country, $Y_1 = Y_2$ and $Y_1^* = Y_2^*$.

a. What is the effect on the world discount factor R of an increase in world output in period 1, $Y_1 + Y_1^*$? How does an increase in world output in the second period affect R? Prove that an increase in the growth rate raises the equilibrium interest rate. What role does intertemporal substitution play in your answer?

b. Suppose that output both at home and abroad grows by a given percentage in period 1. How does this affect the home country's current-account position in period 1? Provide a condition involving the relative magnitudes of σ and σ^* under which the home country's current account necessarily improves.

4. Consider the setup of the previous exercise. The utility functions of the representative agents in each country are, respectively,

$$U = \frac{C_1^{1-1/\sigma} + D C_2^{1-1/\sigma}}{1 - 1/\sigma},$$

and

$$U^* = \frac{C_1^{*\,1-1/\sigma^*} + D^* C_2^{*\,1-1/\sigma^*}}{1 - 1/\sigma^*},$$

with notation as described previously. In addition there is a government in each country that purchases goods and finances its expenditures via lump-sum taxation.

a. Write down the budget constraint of the representative consumer and the government in each country.

b. Under the same simplifying assumptions as the previous exercise (no output growth, and subjective and world discount factors initially equal), find the effect of a transitory increase in government spending on the world discount factor. What is the effect of an anticipated future increase in government spending? Compare your answer to the one obtained in part a of the previous exercise. What is the intuition?

c. Suppose that government spending is initially the same fraction of GDP in each economy and identical across periods. Assume that governments in both countries undertake a coordinated fiscal expansion whereby they raise their expenditures in proportion to GDP by the same amount in period 1 only. Will the impact of such a policy be neutral insofar as the current account is concerned? What assumptions on the behavioral parameters would ensure that the current account neither worsens nor improves as a result of such a policy?

5. Consider a simplified version of the model of chapter 5 in which there is no domestic endowment of the importable good and no domestic consumption of the exportable good. Agents receive a constant endowment Y of the exportable good in each period which is sold in world markets at a constant price equal to unity. The import good is also purchased in world markets at a constant world price of unity. Agents can borrow and lend in world capital markets at a constant world interest rate equal to the domestic rate of time preference; the common value of the subjective and world discount factors is denoted by D. Agents have logarithmic utility given by

$$U = \log C_0 + D \log C_1,$$

where C_t denotes consumption of importables in period $t = 0, 1$.

a. Consider an initial equilibrium in which there is in place a constant ad valorem tariff at rate $t > 0$ levied on imports. Moreover assume that the government rebates any collected tariff revenues in a lump-sum fashion and that there is no government consumption. Compare the utility level enjoyed by the representative agent in this case to a situation in which there is free trade, $t = 0$, in both periods. Note that this is not a comparative statics exercise; you are not asked to compute the effects on utility of small tariff changes. Rather, you need to solve for the utility level associated with a strictly positive tariff and the utility level associated with free trade. Explain the intuition of your answer.

b. Consider the situation with a strictly positive tariff t in both periods. The government decides to lower the tariff to zero in period 0 and maintain the same level t in period 1. Is the representative consumer better or worse off than when there is a constant tariff at rate t in both periods? (Note again this is *not* a comparative statics exercise.) Provide an intuitive explanation for the effect of a temporary liberalization on welfare.

6. Consider the model of chapter 5 in which agents consume importables and exportables and receive endowments of importables and exportables in each period. Assume that there is no investment and that world prices are constant and, for convenience, equal to unity in each period. Assume that the world interest rate is equal to the domestic rate of time preference, and denote the common value of the world discount factor and subjective discount factor by D. Utility is assumed to be a logarithmic function of present and future consumption indices where the latter are themselves Cobb-Douglas functions of importables and exportables consumption in each period:

$$U = \log[c_{x0}^b c_{m0}^{1-b}] + D \log[c_{x1}^b c_{m1}^{1-b}],$$

where $0 < b < 1$.

Consider an initial equilibrium of free trade. Determine the effects on the trade balance measured in constant world prices of the following policies:

a. A temporary export tax imposed in period 0.
b. A temporary import tariff imposed in period 0.
c. A permanent export tax.
d. A permanent import tariff.

Assume in all cases that revenues from tax collections are rebated to consumers in a lump-sum fashion and that there is a no government consumption.

Are any of these policies equivalent policies. Lerner's symmetry theorem states that import and export taxes are equivalent policies. Is this theorem valid here?

7. Consider the model of chapter 5 where the representative agent consumes and receives endowments of importables and exportables in each period. There is no investment. Letting C_t denote the sub-utility index in period t, assume that agents maximize

$$U = \frac{C_1^{1-1/\sigma} + DC_2^{1-1/\sigma}}{1 - 1/\sigma},$$

where

$$C_t = \frac{c_{xt}^{1-1/\varepsilon} + c_{mt}^{1-1/\varepsilon}}{1 - 1/\varepsilon}, \qquad t = 0, 1,$$

and where D is the subjective discount factor assumed to be equal to the world discount factor, and c_{xt} and c_{mt} denote, respectively, consumption of exportables and importables in period t, $t = 0, 1$. The parameter σ denotes the intertemporal elasticity of substitution, while the parameter ε denotes the intratemporal elasticity of substitution between exportables and importables.

In this economy the government levies a constant ad valorem tariff on imports in amount T in each period. The government redistributes the revenues from tariff collections to consumers in a lump-sum fashion. There is no government consumption.

a. Solve for the demands for C_t (the real spending functions) as a function of wealth, the discount factor, and the within-period consumer price indices.

b. Solve for the demand $c_{x,t}$ and $c_{m,t}$ as functions of within-period spending $P_t C_t$ and the within-period relative price. In this regard, you may assume that the world relative price is constant and equal to unity. You need not solve explicitly for P_t but you should recall from the chapter that its elasticity with respect to the within-period relative price is equal to the expenditure share.

c. Consider the effect on the period zero trade balance (measured in constant world prices) of an increase in the tariff in period zero (with no change in the tariff in period 1). You may assume that the initial equilibrium is stationary in the sense that the expenditure share on importables (denoted by $1 - b$) and the price index P_t are constant through time. (Recall that the tariff rate T and world prices are constant in the initial equilibrium.) Does the temporary tariff cause the trade balance to "improve" or "deteriorate"? On what parameters of the utility function does your answer depend? Compare your answer to the one you got in the previous exercise in which the parameters σ and ε were both assumed to be equal to unity.

8. This exercise focuses on the effects of permanent terms-of-trade shocks on consumption, which is an important ingredient into the Laursen-Metzler effect discussed in chapter 5. We extend the model of that chapter to a setting in which the terms of trade are subject to random shocks (see section 4.5 for further technical details). Since shocks are assumed to be of a permanent nature, and since it will prove convenient to work in a continuous-time framework, it is natural to think of the terms of trade as following the continuous-time version of a random walk, namely Brownian motion.

Accordingly, consider a small open economy that receives a constant endowment y of an export good which, in order to simplify the analysis, we assume is not consumed domestically. The representative agent in this country consumes an imported good c (of which there is no domestic endowment). The relative price of the export good in terms of the import good is called p and evolves according to

$$dp_t = \mu\, dt + \sigma\, dz,$$

where μ is a drift parameter and z is a standard Weiner process with zero mean and unitary standard deviation. The consumer has preferences

$$U_t = E_t \int_t^\infty e^{-\delta(s-t)} u(c_s)\, ds,$$

where

$$u(c_s) = -\eta^{-1} e^{-\eta c_s}$$

and η is the Arrow-Pratt measure of absolute risk aversion. Asset accumulation is specified as

$$dA_t = (rA_t - c_t) + yp_t,$$

where r is the constant (nonrandom) real interest rate.

a. Solve for the consumption function in this case.

b. How do innovations in the terms of trade (dz in equation 1) affect consumption and the trade balance?

9. Consider the infinite horizon model of a small open economy introduced in section 5.5. Assume that stochastic innovations dz of the returns q_i in risky assets are increments of a standard Wiener process z:

$$q_i = \mu_i\, dt + \sigma_i\, dz_i, \qquad i = 1, 2, \ldots, n,$$

so that asset i has mean μ_i and standard deviation σ_i. For simplicity suppose that households receive no labor income. Also assume that the government follows a balanced budget policy and taxes households in proportion to their beginning-of-period wealth and at a constant tax rate τ. The stochastic innovations in τ are modelled as increments of a Wiener process with

$$d\tau = \mu_g\, dt + \sigma_g\, dz_g.$$

a. What determines a household's allocation of wealth among different risky assets? Are the optimal portfolio shares independent of a household's wealth? Show that if some risky assets had identical means and variances, domestic households would hold a larger share of the asset whose return has a higher covariance with government spending.

b. Assume domestic households have a power utility function of the form

$$u(c) = \left(\frac{1}{\eta}\right)c^{\eta}, \qquad 0 < \eta < 1.$$

Show that under the optimal consumption rule, if it exists, a household consumes a constant fraction of beginning-of-period wealth in each period. In this case, are the portfolio allocations independent of a household's wealth? What are the necessary transversality conditions for a well-defined solution? Suppose that there is only one risky asset. Define a countercyclical (procyclical) fiscal policy where, ceteris paribus, government spending is negatively (positively) correlated with asset returns. What are the effects of countercyclical and procyclical fiscal policies on the optimal consumption level?

10. Consider a two-country, two-period stock market model. In the first period agents allocate their initial wealth among three assets: a riskless bond offering a return R, a domestic equity offering an uncertain pre-tax return R_1, and foreign equity with stochastic pre-tax return R_2. Aside from the equity returns, domestic and foreign taxes form a second source of uncertainty. These are levelled on dividends from equity holdings in the second period with tax rates based on the country in which the equity was issued (source principle).

For simplicity, and unlike the model in section 5.5, suppose that consumption of a single consumer good is confined to the second period. Also assume that the agents expected utility function can be represented by a mean-variance preference function (see Levy and Markowitz 1979):

$$E\{V_h\} - \frac{1}{2\tau_h}\operatorname{var}\{V_h\},$$

where E denotes the expectation operator, Var the variance, and V_h is the home country's after-tax return on its portfolio. A similar function characterizes the foreign consumer's preferences. The parameter τ_j ($j = h, f$ and $\tau_j > 0$) may differ across countries and is a measure of the agent's "risk tolerance," the marginal rate of substitution between variance and expected return.

a. Derive the necessary equilibrium conditions for the world stock market. Show that the after-tax excess returns can be described by a capital asset pricing model (CAPM) relationship.

b. Demonstrate that domestic and foreign agents will hold shares in the same world market portfolio. Also prove that if domestic agents have a higher risk tolerance ($\tau_h > \tau_f$) and if the riskless asset is in zero net supply, the domestic agents will be a net borrower of the riskless asset.

c. Discuss how asset returns respond to changes in the stochastic properties of domestic taxes.

11. Consider the two-country, two-period open economy model of section 5.5. Assume that there are two assets, a domestic and a foreign equity share, and that markets are complete.

a. Describe the government's optimal resource allocation across time and states if it maximizes a separable part of the private agent's expected utility function.

b. Assume that preferences of the representative domestic consumer can be described by the following expected utility function:

$$U = \frac{1}{1 - \sigma} [c_{ho}^{1-1/\sigma} + \delta\pi_0 c(0)_{h1}^{1-1/\sigma} + \delta\pi_1 c(1)_{h1}^{1-1/\sigma}] + U_g,$$

where U_g represents the utility derived from government consumption and π_s is the probability of state $s = 0, 1$. Assume that U_g and the representative foreign consumer's preferences are also described by power utility functions, although with possibly different substitution parameters σ, with $\sigma > 1$. Derive the optimal consumption plans for private agents and the government. Explain the implications for state-contingent prices of a redistribution of incomes from the private sector to the government.

c. Describe the effects of alternative tax paths across time and states on asset prices.

12. Consider a two-country, two-period stock market model. In the first period agents allocate their initial wealth among three assets: a riskless bond offering a return R, a domestic equity offering an uncertain return R_1, and foreign equity with stochastic return R_2. Aside from the equity returns, domestic and foreign taxes form a second source of uncertainty. These are leveled on dividends from equity holdings in the second period with tax rates based on the country of residence of the investor (destination or residence principle).

For simplicity, suppose that consumption of a single consumer good is confined to the second period. Also assume that the agent's expected utility function can be represented by a mean-variance preference function:

$$E\{V_h\} - \frac{1}{2\tau_h}\,\mathrm{var}\{V_h\},$$

where E denotes the expectations operator, Var the variance, and V_h is the home country's after-tax return on its portfolio. A similar function characterizes the foreign consumer's preferences. The parameter τ_j ($j = h, f$ and $\tau_j > 0$) may differ across countries and is a measure of the agent's risk "tolerance," the marginal rate of substitution between variance and expected return.

a. Derive the necessary equilibrium conditions for the stock market.

b. Demonstrate that domestic and foreign agents will, in general, *not* hold shares in the same world market portfolio. Compare this result with exercise 2 where, under otherwise the same set-up, taxation was based on the source principle.

c. As a special case, suppose that the domestic tax factor is a constant fraction of the foreign tax factor: $(1 - \tau_1) = \gamma(1 - \tau_2)$, where $\gamma > 0$ and τ_i ($i = h, f$) denotes the tax rate for the domestic or foreign resident. Also assume that the riskless after-tax return differs by the same factor γ across countries. Show that under these conditions domestic and foreign agents will hold shares in the same world market portfolio.

13. Consider the model in section 7.1. Compute the correlation coefficient between savings $(Y_t - C_t)$ and investment Z_t motivated by

the Feldstein-Horioka puzzle. Based on the computed coefficient, discuss alternative tests that can discriminate between the Feldstein-Horioka segmented capital market hypothesis and the integrated capital market hypothesis underlying the model of section 7.1.

14. Consider the model in section 7.1. Recall that ρ^* is defined as the critical value of the persistence parameter that generates a zero correlation between the trade balance and output. Show how ρ^* depends on the deep parameters of the model: R, α, and g. Provide an economic interpretation.

15. Consider the model in section 7.3 with intersectoral labor mobility. Derive the relation between real wages and the productivity shocks in the traded and nontraded goods sectors. Compare this relation to (7.28), and provide an interpretation.

16. Consider the real-exchange-rate smoothing property reflected in (7.30). Design an empirical test for this property. How are deviations from this property related to intersectoral wage differences?

17. Consider a small open economy that faces a fixed world interest rate (assumed, for simplicity, to be equal to the fixed rate of time preference) as in section 7.1. The (infinitely lived) representative consumer is assumed to maximize

$$\sum_{r=0}^{\infty} \beta^t u(c_r),$$

where β is the subjective discount factor. The agent's stock of assets evolves according to

$$b_t = (1 + r)b_{t-1} + q_t - i_t - c_t - g_t,$$

where b is the stock of foreign assets, $(1 + r)$ is the fixed world interest rate, q_t, i_t, c_t, g_t are GDP, investment, and private and government consumption, respectively. (The budget constraint assumes that the government has access to lump-sum taxation and the Ricardian equivalence holds.) Given that Fisherian separability holds in this setup (since the economy is small and takes the world interest rate as given), investment will be exogenous to the consumption decision (though it may still be chosen optimally to maximize expected wealth).

a. Under the assumption of a quadratic period utility function, solve for the optimal consumption function.

b. Solve for the optimal current account balance.

c. On the basis of your answer to part b, what would be the optimal response of the current account to permanent, transitory, or anticipated shocks to national cash flow, defined as output net of investment and government spending?

18. Consider an economy with the same setup as in the previous problem, except that now, instead of quadratic utility, the utility function has a positive third derivative. Specifically, assume that the utility function exhibits constant (absolute) risk aversion:

$$u(c_t) = -\left(\frac{1}{\alpha}\right)e^{-\alpha c_t}$$

where $\alpha > 0$ is the Arrow-Pratt measure of (absolute) risk-aversion.

a. Write down the first order condition (Euler equation) governing optimal consumption choice over time.

b. Under the assumption that the innovations to national cash flow (output net of investment and government spending) are normally distributed, what is the form of the consumption function in this case?

c. What is the solution for the current account in this case, and how does this solution compare to the one you obtained in the previous problem in the case of a quadratic utility function?

19. Consider the economy described in the setup of problem 17. Suppose that you have time-series data on GNP, GDP, private consumption, investment, and government consumption for a particular country.

a. Show that by estimating a bivariate (first-order, for simplicity) autoregression in national cash flow (output net of investment and government consumption) and the current account, you can use the parameter estimates to write out a formula for the expected present value of future declines in national cash flow as a weighted average of national cash flow and the current account.

b. Under the null hypothesis that the actual current-account balance is equal to the optimal consumption-smoothing current account balance (i.e., the one you solved for in problem 9 referring to chapter 7), what will the weights be?

c. How would you interpret deviations between your time series for the optimal current account and the actual behavior of the current account in a particular country?

20. Consider the setup with the constant-absolute risk-aversion utility function in problem 18.

a. Can the empirical methodology described in the previous problem be used to estimate a time series for the optimal current account in this case?

b. How would you judge whether the more complicated setting here is appropriate or if the assumption of quadratic utility is satisfactory?

IV

An Intertemporal Approach to Fiscal Policies in the World Economy

8

Government Spending: Volume and Composition

Up to now we have disregarded the role of government. In this chapter we extend the analysis by incorporating government into the model. There are various layers through which the introduction of government impacts on the economic system. First, from the perspective of the representative individual the public goods provided by the government enter directly into the utility function. Further, the taxes used to finance government spending enter directly into the individual's budget constraint. Second, from the perspective of the economy as a whole, the activities of the government absorb resources and provide public consumer and producer goods. Thereby the government alters the amount of resources available to the private sector, and the availability of public goods may alter the intertemporal pattern of private consumption and production. Third, from the perspective of the rest of the world, the activities of the government are transmitted internationally through its direct and indirect effects on world goods and capital markets. In what follows we examine the implications of government spending as they operate through the various layers. We start with the formal analytical framework.

8.1 The Analytical Framework

In the presence of government the representative individual's utility function, U, is $U(C_0, C_1, G_0, G_1)$, where G_0 and G_1 denote government spending in periods zero and one, respectively. For ease of exposition we assume that the utility function U takes the form of

$U(C_0, G_0) + \delta U(C_1, G_1)$, where as before δ denotes the subjective discount factor. To highlight the pure effects of government spending, we abstract from possible distortionary effects arising from government finance. Thus throughout this chapter we assume that the government finances its budget with lump-sum taxes T_0 and T_1. Hence the individual seeking to maximize lifetime utility solves the following problem:

$$V(G_0, G_1, T_0, T_1) = \max_{\{C_0, C_1\}} U(C_0, G_0) + \delta U(C_1, G_1) \tag{8.1}$$

subject to

$$C_0 + \alpha_1^p C_1 = (\overline{Y}_0 - T_0) + \alpha_1^p(\overline{Y}_1 - T_1) - (1 + r_{-1}^p)B_{-1}^p = W_0, \tag{8.2}$$

where α_1^p denotes the present-value factor applicable to the private sector. The formulation in equation (8.1) indicates that, as usual, the individual who chooses the utility-maximizing path of consumption $\{C_0, C_1\}$ treats the paths of government spending $\{G_0, G_1\}$, and taxes $\{T_0, T_1\}$ as given. The function $V(\cdot)$ denotes the maximized value of utility given the paths of spending and taxes. The lifetime constraint in equation (8.2) indicates that the discounted sum of life-time consumption equals the discounted sum of lifetime disposable income net of initial private debt commitment $(1 + r_{-1}^p)B_{-1}^p$. For simplicity we assume that there is no investment.

The specification of equation (8.2) indicates that as long as the discounted sum of taxes $(T_0 + \alpha_1^p T_1)$ remains unchanged, the timing of taxes does not influence the individual's behavior.

As usual, the first-order condition for utility maximization requires that the marginal rate of substitution between consumption in two consecutive periods equals the reciprocal of the market discount factor applicable to the private sector. It is important to emphasize, however, that in the present case the marginal rate of substitution also reflects the interaction between government spending and private consumption. Hence

$$\frac{U_c(C_0, G_0)}{\delta U_c(C_1, G_1)} = \frac{1}{\alpha_1^p}, \tag{8.3}$$

where U_c denotes the marginal utility of consumption. It can also be shown (using the envelope relations obtained by constructing the Lagrangian form associated with equation 8.1 and the implied first-order conditions) that

$$\frac{\partial V(\cdot)}{\partial G_0} = U_G(C_0, G_0), \quad \frac{\partial V(\cdot)}{\partial G_1} = \delta U_G(C_1, G_1),$$

$$\frac{\partial V(\cdot)}{\partial T_0} = -U_c(C_0, G_0), \quad \frac{\partial V(\cdot)}{\partial T_1} = -\delta U_c(C_0, G_0).$$

(8.4)

These equalities state that the change in the maximized level of utility induced by a marginal change in government spending and by a marginal change in taxes equals, respectively, the marginal utility of public goods and the negative of the marginal utility of ordinary consumption.

The foregoing analysis treated the levels of government spending and taxes as given. The two, however, are linked to each other through the requirement that the government in its various activities must be solvent. The government budget constraints specify that in each period government outlays be financed by taxes or by debt issue, and solvency requires that in the last period all debt be repaid without issuing new liabilities. In our two-period model these constraints are

$$G_0 = B_0^g + T_0 - (1 + r_{-1}^g)B_{-1}^g,$$

$$G_1 = T_1 - \frac{1}{\alpha_1^g}B_0^g,$$

(8.5)

where B^g denotes government debt, and thus $(1 + r_{-1}^g)B_{-1}^g$ is the government debt commitment on the historically given initial government debt position. The formulation in (8.5) embodies the possibility that the rate of interest applicable to the government may differ from the one applicable to the private sector. Hence the government budget constraint is specified in terms of the present-value factor applicable to the government, α_1^g, rather than in terms of α_1^p.

Analogously to the procedure applied previously to consolidate the private sector's periodic budget constraints into a single present-value budget constraint, we can also consolidate the government constraints into a single present-value constraint. Applying this procedure to the constraints in (8.5) yields

$$G = G_0 + \alpha_1^g G_1 = T_0 + \alpha_1^g T_1 - (1 + r_{-1}^g)B_{-1}^g, \tag{8.6}$$

where G denotes the discounted sum of government spending.

The fully informed forward-looking individuals are presumed to "see through" the government budget constraint and thereby to recognize the precise dependence between the levels of government spending and the implied tax liabilities. Hence they incorporate the implications of the government budget constraint into their own. Incorporating the government budget constraint (8.6) into the private-sector constraint (8.2) yields

$$C_0 + \alpha_1^p C_1 = (\overline{Y}_0 + \alpha_1^p \overline{Y}_1) - (G_0 + \alpha_1^p G_1) - (\alpha_1^g - \alpha_1^p)(G_1 - T_1)$$
$$+ (r_{-1}^p - r_{-1}^g)B_{-1}^g - (1 + r_{-1}^p)B_{-1}, \tag{8.7}$$

where B_{-1} denotes the historically given value of the economy's external debt position, which in turn equals the sum of the corresponding private-sector and government debts (i.e., $B_{-1} = B_{-1}^p + B_{-1}^g$). The right-hand side of equation (8.7) specifies the value of private-sector wealth which incorporates the government budget constraints as perceived (correctly) by the private sector. As may be seen, the value of wealth is composed of three items: the discounted sum of GDP net of government spending (discounted by the private sector's market interest rates), terms that are proportional to the discrepancy between private and government interest rates, and finally the historically given value of the economy's external debt commitment.

Equation (8.7) reveals that changes in taxes that satisfy the government budget constraint and that are not associated with changes in government spending alter private-sector wealth if the discount factors applicable to the private and to the public sectors differ from each other. Likewise, changes in the historical value of government debt that are not associated with corresponding changes in the economy's external debt position or in government spending alter private-sector wealth if there is a discrepancy between the historical rates of interest applicable to the private and to the public sectors.

Consider, for example, the effect of a government budget deficit arising from a current tax cut. Obviously, as indicated by the government budget constraint (8.6), a deficit arising from a fall in T_0, as long as it is not accompanied by a change in government spending, must be accompanied by an equal future surplus (in present-value terms) arising from a rise in future taxes, T_1. Equation (8.7) shows that if for reasons such as finite life the discount factor applicable to the government exceeds the discount factor applicable to the private sector (i.e., $\alpha_1^q - \alpha_1^p > 0$), then the deficit raises private-sector wealth, and thereby influences behavior and alters the real equilibrium of the system. The opposite holds if $\alpha_1^q < \alpha_1^p$. These examples highlight the considerations underlying the famous *Ricardian equivalence* proposition, according to which the timing of taxes and the size of government debt do not influence private sector's behavior and the real equilibrium as long as government spending and the size of foreign debt remain unchanged. In our case the Ricardian proposition emerges if the private and the public rates of interest are equal to each other (i.e., if $\alpha_1^q = \alpha_1^p = \alpha_1$ and $r_{-1}^g = r_{-1}^p = r_{-1}$). With such equalities the private-sector budget constraint (8.7) becomes

$$C_0 + \alpha_1 C_1 = (\overline{Y}_0 - G_0) + \alpha_1(\overline{Y}_1 - G_1) - (1 + r_{-1})B_{-1}. \qquad (8.8)$$

Equation (8.8) shows that if both the private and the public sector can lend and borrow freely in the world capital market (at the same terms) and if all taxes are nondistortionary, then private-sector's wealth consists of the discounted sum of GDP net of government spending and of the initial external debt commitment. This is the case in which the internalization of government activities by the private sector eliminates the influence of the details of public finance.

8.2   Government Spending in a Small Open Economy

The foregoing analysis examined the factors underlying the effects of public finance (with nondistortionary taxes) on private-sector wealth. We turn next to analyze the effects of changes in government spending, starting with the case of a small open economy facing a given world rate of interest. In this context we highlight the role of timing by distinguishing between changes in government spending that are temporary (current or future) and changes that are permanent.

As indicated earlier, government spending influences the private sector through two channels. First, government activities absorb resources that otherwise would have been available to the private sector, and second, government spending may influence the marginal evaluations of private goods. The first channel is reflected in the terms $(\overline{Y}_0 - G_0)$ and $(\overline{Y}_1 - G_1)$ on the right-hand side of the budget constraint (8.8). We refer to this channel as the *resource-withdrawal* channel. The second channel is reflected in equation (8.3) by the dependence of the marginal rate of substitution between consumption in two consecutive periods on the levels of government spending. We refer to this channel as the *consumption-tilting* channel.

In operating through the resource-withdrawal channel, the influence of government spending is similar to that of supply shocks: both alter the size of *net* GDP (GDP net of government spending). Therefore our previous analysis of temporary (current or future) and permanent positive supply shocks (in section 5.3) also applies to the effects of temporary (current or future) and permanent reductions in government spending, operating through the resource-withdrawal channel.

In analyzing the effects of government spending as they operate through the consumption-tilting channel, we note that the dependence of the marginal rate of substitution of consumption in two consecutive periods on the levels of government spending reflects the characteristics of the utility function. If private consumption and government spending are complements (i.e., if the marginal utility of consumption rises with the level of government spending), then a temporary rise in current government spending raises the marginal rate of substitution in equation (8.3), whereas a temporary rise in future government spending lowers the marginal rate of substitution. In the former case the consumption expansion locus tilts toward current consumption, and in the latter case it tilts toward future consumption. The opposite holds if private consumption and government spending are substitutes. In the neutral case the marginal utility of private consumption (and therefore the marginal rate of substitution of consumption between consecutive periods) is independent of the level of government spending. In that case government spending does not induce consumption-tilting effects. Finally, we note that the effect of a permanent change in government spending on the marginal rate of substitution in consumption combines the effects of current and future changes in government spending. As was shown (except for the neutral case), the two effects tend to tilt the intertemporal consumption patterns in opposite directions. In fact, as is evident from equation (8.3), if the initial patterns of consumption and government spending are stationary, then the two effects exactly offset each other. It follows that in that case a permanent change in government spending does not induce a tilt in the intertemporal pattern of consumption. We conclude that the influence of the intertemporal pattern of government spending on the marginal rate of substitution of consumption are akin to the consumption-tilting effects analyzed in section 5.3.

   In summary, the impact of government spending on the equilibrium of the system reflects the combination of the effects operating through the resource-withdrawal channel and through the consumption-tilting channel. In the neutral case, in which the marginal rate of substitution of consumption in two consecutive periods is independent of the level of government spending, the impact of government spending operates only through the resource-withdrawal channel. In that case our analysis of the effects of supply shocks (in section 5.2) is fully applicable to the analysis of the effects of government spending.

8.3   Government Spending and the World Rate of Interest

Up to now we considered the case in which the economy is small in the world capital markets. To examine the effects of government spending on the rest of the world, we turn now to an extension of the analysis to a two-country model of the world economy. To simplify exposition, we consider the case in which government spending enters the utility function in a separable way and the utility functions are homothetic. The separability assumption implies that the marginal rate of substitution between consumption in different periods does not depend on the level of government spending. Thus in what follows government spending operates only through the resource-withdrawal channel, and not through the consumption-tilting channel.

Consider, first, the effects of a current transitory rise in the home country's government spending. At the initial rate of interest this rise in spending creates an excess demand for current-period goods. This excess demand arises from the fact that the private sector (whose taxes have risen in order to finance government spending) lowers its demand for current goods by less than the rise in government demand since the private sector's marginal propensity to spend is smaller than unity. This excess demand is eliminated by a rise in the relative price of present goods in terms of future goods, that is, by a rise in the rate of interest. This analysis is illustrated in figure 8.1 in which it is assumed that the home country's propensity to consume present goods relative to future goods exceeds the foreign country's corresponding propensity. As before, the dimensions of the box measure the present and the future levels of world GDP. At the initial equilibrium the international and intertemporal pattern of world consumption is represented by point A which denotes the intersection between the home and the foreign countries' consumption-expansion loci OA and O^*A, respectively. These loci correspond to the equilibrium rate of interest, r_0.

If the level of government spending on present goods is G_0, then the size of the box (corresponding to world GDP net of government spending) diminishes. Accordingly, in figure 8.1 the length of the

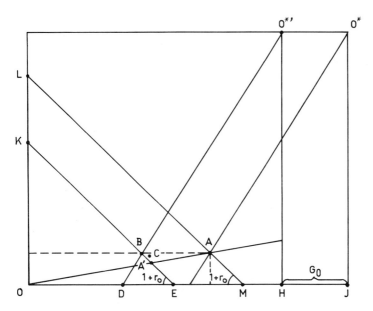

Figure 8.1
The effect of a temporary rise in current government spending on the world
rate of interest

horizontal axis measuring the supply of current goods net of government spending is reduced from OJ to OH. At the prevailing
interest rate foreign demand remains unchanged, as represented in
figure 8.1 by point B. This point is located on the foreign consumption-expansion locus displaced to the new origin $O^{*\prime}$. By construction, the parallel line segments $O^{*\prime}B$ and O^*A are of equal length.
Analogously, as long as the initial rate of interest remains unchanged, the consumption-expansion locus of the domestic residents
remains unchanged, but in view of the lower level of wealth (induced by the fall in disposable income), the new level of desired
consumption is represented by point A' instead of point A. Diagrammatically, point A' designates the intersection of the domestic
consumption-expansion locus and the line KE; the latter is obtained
by a leftward (parallel) shift of the initial budget line LM by
the magnitude of government spending G_0 (i.e., by construction,
$HJ = EM$). As seen, the desired bundles of domestic and foreign

consumption (indicated by points A' and B, respectively) represent an excess world demand for current goods and a corresponding excess world supply of future goods. Therefore the rate of interest (the relative price of current goods) must rise. The higher rate of interest induces substitution away from current consumption and toward future consumption. This substitution rotates both countries' consumption-expansion loci toward future goods and results in a new equilibrium (corresponding to their intersection) at a point such as C. Because of this rotation the new equilibrium point must lie to the left of point A' and to the right of point B. It follows that foreign current consumption must fall. Hence part of the rise in domestic government spending is "financed" through the crowding out of foreign consumption.

If we characterize the international transmission mechanism in terms of the correlations between contemporaneous levels of domestic and foreign private-sector consumption, then the temporary rise in current government spending is transmitted *positively* to the rest of the world. This inference follows since both domestic and foreign private-sector consumption fall. It is also noteworthy that this conclusion concerning the effects of a temporary rise in government spending does not depend on the assumption (implicit in figure 8.1) that the domestic subjective rate of time preference exceeds the foreign rate. Independent of the relation between the domestic and foreign subjective rate of time preference the temporary rise in current government spending must raise the rate of interest and must crowd out both domestic and foreign private-sector consumption of current goods.

The rise in the world rate of interest transmits the effects of the rise in government spending to the rest of the world. The higher rate of interest lowers the discounted sum of foreign disposable incomes, and thereby lowers foreign wealth. These changes in the interest rate and in wealth alter foreign consumption and impact on welfare. In the case shown in figure 8.1, point C indicates a fall in foreign welfare since in the initial equilibrium the bundle of goods represented by point C was affordable but B was chosen. Hence by the principle of revealed preference we conclude that in the case shown, the rise in the home country's government spending lowers foreign welfare. This result, however, is not general since point C could have been located to the southwest of the line segment A'B. In that case foreign welfare would have risen. The key factor determining whether the rise in the rate of interest lowers or raises foreign welfare is the initial current account position, reflecting the initial differences between domestic and foreign *average* saving propensities. A rise in the rate of interest lowers foreign welfare if the foreign country was a net borrower in the world economy (i.e., if it ran a current account deficit), and vice versa. In addition to these considerations the impact of government spending on the home country's welfare also depends on both the reduced consumption of private goods and the increased consumption of public goods.

A similar analysis applies to the effects of a transitory rise in *future* government spending. In that case, however, the change in government spending induces an excess world demand for future goods and a corresponding excess supply of current goods. To restore equilibrium, the relative price of current goods—that is, the rate of interest—must fall. The fall in the rate of interest initiates the mechanism that transmits the effects of government spending to the rest of the world. It induces a rise in foreign wealth and impacts on foreign consumption and welfare in a manner opposite to the one discussed earlier when government spending rose in the present.

The analyses of the effects of transitory increases in current or in future government spending provide the ingredients relevant for determining the effects of a *permanent* rise in government spending. Since in that case there is a rise in government demand for both current and future goods, the rate of interest may rise or fall depending on the relative change in private-sector demand for current and future goods. In general, if the extent of the fall in private-sector demand for current goods is large relative to the fall in the demand for future goods, then the rate of interest falls, and vice versa. The key factor determining the relative reductions in private-sector demands for current and future goods is the difference between the domestic and the foreign marginal saving propensities. If the domestic saving propensity falls short of the foreign propensity (i.e., if the domestic subjective rate of time preference exceeds the foreign rate), then, at the prevailing rate of interest, the permanent rise in government spending raises world savings and necessitates a fall in the rate of interest. On the other hand, if the domestic saving propensity exceeds the foreign, the permanent rise in government spending lowers world savings and induces a rise in the rate of interest.

These results are illustrated in figure 8.2a and b. Panel a corresponds to the case in which the domestic subjective rate of time preference exceeds the foreign rate ($\rho > \rho^*$), and panel b corresponds to the opposite case in which $\rho^* < \rho$. The initial equilibrium is specified by point A. The permanent rise in government spending withdraws resources from the world economy in both the present and the future periods. Diagrammatically, this rise in the share of world output, which is absorbed by the government, is reflected in an equiproportional decline in the dimensions of the box. Hence, following the permanent rise in domestic government spending, the foreign country's origin shifts along the diagonal of the box from point O^* to point $O^{*\prime}$. At the prevailing rate of interest foreign consumption (measured from $O^{*\prime}$) is represented by point B (where the distance $O^*A = O^{*\prime}B$), and domestic consumption is represented by point A' along the initial consumption-expansion locus. Point A' is obtained by subtracting from the domestic private-sector budget the resources needed to finance the rise in government spending, G_0 and G_1, respectively. Geometrically, we note that by construction the distance $O^*O^{*\prime}$ equals the distance AB and that the slope of the line connecting points A' and B is one plus the prevailing rate of interest. As is evident, the consumption bundles represented by points A' and B indicate an excess supply of current goods in panel a and an excess demand for current goods in panel b. It follows that in the former case the rate of interest must fall, but in the latter case the rate of interest must rise.

As an interpretation of this result, we note that for the case in which $\rho > \rho^*$ (shown in figure 8.2a), the intertemporal pattern of spending of the domestic private sector (relative to the pattern of the foreign private sector) is biased toward current goods. The permanent rise in government spending lowers domestic private disposable income

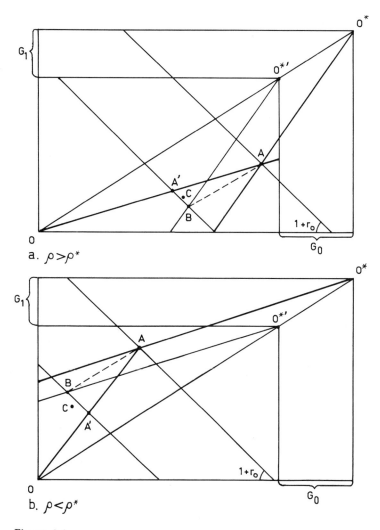

Figure 8.2
The effect of a permanent rise in government spending on the world rate of interest

and reduces the relative weight of domestic private spending in world private spending. As a result world private spending is less biased toward current goods, and the rate of interest must fall. An analogous interpretation pertains to the case in which $\rho < \rho^*$ (shown in figure 8.2b) in which the pattern of the intertemporal spending of the domestic private sector is relatively biased toward future goods.

As already indicated, the international transmission mechanism operates through the integrated world capital market, and the change in the rate of interest serves to transmit the effects of the rise in government spending to the rest of the world. The change in the rate of interest induced by the permanent rise in government spending rotates both countries' consumption-expansion loci and brings about a new equilibrium at a point like point C. This new equilibrium point must lie inside the rectangle whose opposite vertexes are A' and B, implying a rise in foreign current consumption and a fall in foreign future consumption; the opposite holds in panel b in which point C must lie to the southeast of point B.

The effects of changes in domestic government spending on the level of foreign private-sector consumption are summarized in table 8.1 (which also contains a summary of the other results). As may be seen, depending on its timing and on the relation between the domestic and the foreign marginal propensities to save (which is governed by the relation between ρ and ρ^*), the rise in government spending may crowd out or crowd in foreign private consumption. Since domestic private consumption must always be crowded out, it follows that the sign of the correlation between changes in domestic and foreign private-sector consumption induced by changes in domestic government spending also depends on the time pattern of government spending and on the difference between the two private sectors' subjective rates of time preference.

8.4 Government Spending and the Terms of Trade in a Two-Country World

The preceding analysis of government spending was conducted under the assumption of a single composite-commodity world. As

Table 8.1
Effects of a rise in domestic government spending on the world rate of interest, levels of consumption, and the trade account

Rates of time perference	r_0	$C_{0'}$	$C_{0'}^*$	$(TA)_0$
Effects of a current rise in government spending on				
$\rho > \rho^*$	+	−	−	−
$\rho < \rho^*$	+	−	−	−
Effects of a future rise in government spending on				
$\rho > \rho^*$	−	−	+	+
$\rho < \rho^*$	−	−	+	+
Effects of a permanent rise in government spending on				
$\rho > \rho^*$	−	−	+	+
$\rho < \rho^*$	+	−	−	−

Note: The case in which $\rho > \rho^*$ indicates that the domestic marginal propensity to save out of wealth falls short of the foreign propensity, and vice versa.

a result government spending influenced the world economy only through its impact on the *intertemporal* terms of trade (the rate of interest). In general, of course, if the economy is large enough in the world markets for goods, then changes in the level and commodity composition of government purchases also alter the *temporal* terms of trade (the relative price of importables in terms of exportables). Such changes in the temporal terms of trade provide an additional mechanism through which the effects of government spending are transmitted internationally.

In this section we extend the analysis by considering the effects of government spending on both the temporal and the intertemporal terms of trade. In order to identify the key principles, we first analyze the effects that government spending exert on the commodity terms of trade in isolation from the intertemporal repercussions induced by possible changes in the rate of interest. We then consider the other extreme by reexamining the effects that government spending exerts on the intertemporal terms of trade in isolation from the temporal repercussions induced by possible changes in the commodity terms of trade. Finally, we consider some aspects of the interactions between the temporal and the intertemporal terms of trade.

We start by focusing on the relation between the temporal terms of trade and the commodity composition of government spending. For this purpose consider a benchmark case in which the transmission mechanism operates exclusively through the commodity terms of trade and not through the rate of interest. Accordingly, we assume that the utility functions are homothetic, that in each country the composition of outputs (net of government purchases) does not vary over time, and that the domestic and foreign subjective rates of time preference are equal to each other. Also we assume that the time profiles of government and private consumption spendings are identical. These assumptions ensure (as implied by the analysis in chapter 6) that the domestic and the foreign (consumption-based) real rates of interest are equal to each other and that both are equal to the common rate of time preference (adjusted for growth, as in equation (5.14). As a result, in each country income equals spending. Thus in this benchmark case a *permanent* rise in government spending does not impact on the world rate of interest, and its effects are absorbed exclusively by induced changes in the (temporal) relative price of goods.

The diagrammatic analysis of the effects of a rise in government spending in this benchmark case can be carried out with the aid of a relabeled version of figure 8.2. The relabeling replaces the two periods by the two commodities, the intertemporal terms of trade by the temporal terms of trade, and the international differences between the marginal propensities to spend out of wealth in the two periods (indicated by the difference between the domestic and the foreign marginal rates of time preference) by the international differences in the marginal shares of expenditures on the two goods. Thus in figure 8.2 the dimensions of the box correspond to the world supply of the two goods net of government spending on these goods. The vertical axis measures good x—the home country's exportables—and the horizontal axis measures good m—the home country's importables. In the initial equilibrium the commodity composition of the domestic and foreign private-sector demands are indicated by the slopes of the rays OA and O^*A, respectively. The initial equilibrium obtains at point A, at which the relative price of importables, p_m, is the common slope of the domestic and foreign indifference curves at point A (not drawn). Thus the angle indicated by $1 + r_0$ in figure 8.2 now measures the relative price of goods, p_m. The case shown in panel a differs from the one shown in panel b. Panel a corresponds to a situation in which the domestic pattern of the commodity composition of spending is relatively biased toward importables so that the domestic expenditure share β_m exceed the foreign share, β_m^*, whereas panel b corresponds to the opposite case in which the domestic spending patterns are relatively biased toward exportables so that $\beta_m < \beta_m^*$. (In that case the composition of domestic output is even more biased in favor of good x, which therefore is the export good.)

Consider first the case of an equiproportional rise in government spending on both goods (indicated in figure 8.2 by G_0 on importables and G_1 on exportables). This lowers world output net of government spending and reduces the dimensions of the box. It changes the foreign-country origin along the diagonal from point O^* to point $O^{*\prime}$. At the initial terms of trade the desired domestic consumption basket is indicated by point A', and the corresponding foreign consumption basket (measured from the origin $O^{*\prime}$) is indicated by point B. As is evident, if β_m exceeds β_m^* (as in panel a), this configuration represents excess supply of importables and a corresponding excess demand for exportables, and vice versa if β_m falls short of β_m^* (as in panel b). In the former case p_m falls so that the terms of trade of the domestic country improve, and in the later case p_m rises so that the domestic terms of trade worsen. These changes in the terms of trade bring about a new equilibrium pattern of world consumption as indicated in figure 8.2 by a point located within the square whose opposite vertexes are points B and A', such as point C.

This example of the terms-of-trade effects of an equiproportional rise in government spending indicates the analogy between the intertemporal analysis of the effects of permanent government spending and the temporal analysis of an equiproportional rise of government purchases of goods. In order to derive the general principle governing the effects of government spending on the terms of trade, we define the marginal share of government expenditure on importables by $\beta_m^g = p_m G_m / (p_m G_m + G_x) = 1/[1 + (G_x / p_m G_m)]$, where G_m and G_x denote the rise in government purchases of importables and exportables, respectively (from an initial position where both quantities are zero). With this definition the basic criterion determining the effects of a rise in government spending on the terms of trade involves a comparison between the expenditure shares of the private sector and of the government. If β_m^g *exceeds* β_m, *then the rise in government spending induces a deterioration of the terms of trade, and conversely if* β_m^g *falls short of* β_m.

The dependence of the change in the terms of trade on the relative magnitudes of β_m and β_m^g is shown in figure 8.3, which illustrates the case of a borderline situation in which the change in government spending does not alter the terms of trade. In the case shown, the

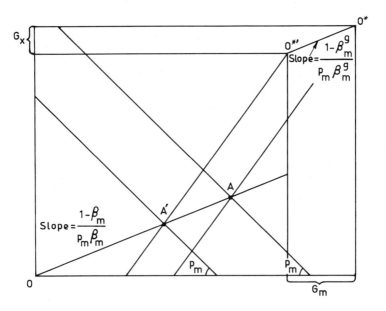

Figure 8.3
The effect of the commodity-composition of government spending on the terms of trade

government expenditure share β_m^g is assumed to be equal to the domestic expenditure share β_m. The rise in government spending shifts the origin O^* to $O^{*'}$ and alters the equilibrium point from point A to point A'. In the figure the rays OA and $O^*O^{*'}$ are drawn parallel to each other due to the assumed equality between β_m^g and β_m. As is evident, in the move from the initial equilibrium point, A, to the new equilibrium point, A', the terms of trade have not changed.

The interpretation of this result is given in terms of the transfer-problem criterion. In the present case the transfer of income from the domestic private sector to the government (a transfer associated with the taxes levied to finance the rise in government spending) does not alter the commodity composition of the domestic *national* spending (private sector plus government) since it involves a transfer of income between units with identical spending patterns. Therefore the transfer does not alter the levels of world demand and supply, and the terms of trade do not change. This borderline case implies that if β_m^g exceeds β_m, then the rise in government spending tilts the composition of national spending toward importables and results in a deterioration of the domestic terms of trade. Conversely, if $\beta_m^g < \beta_m$, the rise in government spending tilts the composition of national spending toward exportables, and the terms of trade improve.

We turn next to reexamine the effects of the time profile of government spending on the intertemporal terms of trade, and we consider another benchmark case in which the transmission mechanism operates exclusively through the intertemporal terms of trade and not through the commodity terms of trade. For that reason we assume that the composition of output (net of government purchases) does not vary over time and that the government as well as the domestic and the foreign expenditure shares are equal to each other. These assumptions ensure that the commodity terms of trade are fixed and do not depend on the time pattern of government spending. Under these assumptions we can aggregate the two goods into a single composite commodity. This aggregation reduces the multiple good model to its single-good counterpart of section 8.3.

As in the previous analysis of the effects of government spending on the temporal terms of trade, there is a general principle that governs the effects of government spending on the intertemporal terms of trade. This principle can also be stated in terms of a transfer-problem criterion; it involves a comparison between the saving propensities of the private sector and the government. For this we define the government marginal propensity to save out of government "wealth" (the discounted sum of government spending) by $\gamma_s^g = \alpha_{x1} G_1/(G_0 + \alpha_{x1} G_1)$; we recall that the private sector marginal propensity to save out of wealth is $\gamma_s = \alpha_{x1} z_1/(z_0 + \alpha_{x1} z_1)$, where $z_t (t = 0, 1)$ denotes private-sector spending in terms of good x. The effect of a rise in government spending on the rate of interest depends on whether the time profile of the rise in government spending is such that the implied saving propensity, γ_s^g, exceeds or falls short of the private saving propensity, γ_s. *If γ_s^g exceeds γ_s, then a rise in government spending lowers the rate of interest (raises α_{x1}), and conversely if γ_s^g falls short of γ_s.* As with the analysis of the temporal terms of trade, the transfer-problem criterion provides the interpretation of this result. Accordingly, if γ_s^g exceeds γ_s, the rise in government spending transfers wealth from a low saver (the private sector) to a higher saver (the government), and thereby raises *national* (private-sector plus government) saving. This induces excess world savings and necessitates a fall in the rate of interest. The opposite holds if $\gamma_s^g < \gamma_s$. Finally, in the borderline case in which $\gamma_s^g = \gamma_s$, the rise in government spending redistributes wealth between economic units with identical saving propensities. Therefore in that case national and world saving do not change, and the rate of interest remains intact.

Before proceeding, it is relevant to note that the definitions of saving used in the preceding analysis, which provided the key criterion for determining the effect of government spending on the intertemporal terms of trade, differ from those used in the national income accounts. In particular, we have defined the government propensity as the ratio of future government spending (in present value) to the discounted sum of current and future taxes. In contrast, the national income accounts define government saving in terms of the difference between contemporaneous taxes and spending. A similar remark applies to the definition of private saving.

It is noteworthy that the analysis of the effects of temporary (current or future) and permanent changes in government spending (conducted in the previous sections) can be viewed as specific illustrations of the general principle. Accordingly, a transitory current rise in government spending corresponds to the case $\gamma_s^g = 0$ (and hence $\gamma_s > \beta_s^g$). An anticipated future rise in government spending corresponds to the case $\gamma_s^g = 1$ (and hence $\gamma_s < \gamma_s^g$). Finally, a permanent rise in government spending (which raises permanently the relative share of government spending in world output) corresponds to the case in which the government-saving propensity, γ_s^g, equals the world private-sector-saving propensity, γ_s^w, which is defined as the ratio of the discounted sum of future net world output to the discounted sum of current and future world net output. Thus

$$\gamma_s^w = \frac{\alpha_1(\overline{Y}_1 - G_1 + \overline{Y}_1^* - G_1^*)}{[(\overline{Y}_0 - G_0) + (\overline{Y}_0^* - G_0^*)] + \alpha_1[(\overline{Y}_1 - G_1) + (\overline{Y}_1^* - G_1^*)]}.$$

We further note that γ_s^w is a weighted average of the saving propensities of the domestic and foreign private sectors, γ_s and γ_s^*. It follows that if $\gamma_s^* > \gamma_s$, then $\gamma_s^g > \gamma_s$—and conversely, if $\gamma_s^* < \gamma_s$, then $\gamma_s^g < \gamma_s$. Our previous analysis showed that the effects of a permanent change in government spending depend on differences between the saving propensities of the domestic and the foreign private sectors. This dependence, however, reflects the more general principle stated in terms of the relation between the saving propensities of the domestic government and the *domestic* private sector, since with a permanent change in government spending the relation between γ_s^g and γ_s can be cast in terms of the relation between γ_s^* and γ_s.

The foregoing analysis isolated the two mechanisms through which the effects of government spending are transmitted to the rest of the world. These two mechanisms operate through the induced changes in the temporal terms of trade (the relative price of exportables in terms of importables) and through the induced changes in the intertemporal terms of trade (the rate of interest).

The two benchmark cases were designed to distinguish between the two mechanisms of adjustment. In general, however, if the subjective rates of time preference and the expenditure shares differ across countries, changes in government spending alter both the temporal and the intertemporal terms of trade. In that case the generalization of the transfer-problem analysis implies that the changes in the two terms of trade are governed by a multitude of transfer-problem criteria involving comparisons between the private-sector and the government temporal spending propensities —indicated by the expenditure shares β_m and β_m^g—and intertemporal spending propensities—indicated by the saving ratios γ_s and γ_s^g.

To illustrate the interactions between the temporal and the intertemporal terms of trade, consider the logarithmic utility function

$$U = [\beta_{m0} \log c_{m0} + (1 - \beta_{m0}) \log c_{x0}]$$
$$+ \delta[\beta_{m1} \log c_{m1} + (1 - \beta_{m1}) \log c_{x1}]. \tag{8.9}$$

With this utility function it is shown in the appendix that for each period the consumption-based temporal price index (defined in section 6.1) can be written as

$$P_0 = (p_{m0})^{\beta_{m0}} \quad \text{and} \quad P_1 = (p_{m1})^{\beta_{m1}}. \tag{8.10}$$

Using these price indexes, the (consumption-based) real discount factor $\alpha_{c1} = \alpha_{x1}(P_1/P_0)$ is

$$\alpha_{c1} = \frac{1}{1 + r_{c0}} = \frac{1}{1 + r_{x0}} \frac{P_1}{P_0}, \tag{8.11}$$

and the (consumption-based) wealth deflator, P_w (the intertemporal "true" price index) is defined by

$$P_w = P_0^{(1-\gamma_s)}(\alpha_{x1} P_1)^{\gamma_s}. \tag{8.12}$$

In general, government spending influences both the temporal and the intertemporal terms of trade, and thereby alters both the (consumption-based) real discount factor and the real wealth deflator. In the appendix we show that, in general, the effects of government spending can be characterized in terms of a multitude of transfer-problem criteria. Accordingly, at the prevailing prices a rise in government spending alters the temporal and the intertemporal pattern of the domestic national demand (private sector plus government) only if the saving propensity and the expenditure shares of the government differ from the corresponding magnitudes of the domestic private sector. In the absence of such differences, changes in government spending do not create an excess demand or supply and do not necessitate a change in the initial equilibrium prices.

It is shown in the appendix that the rise in government spending creates excess demands only if the government's marginal propensities to spend on importables out of government wealth (i.e., government lifetime spending) differ from that of the domestic private sector. Formally, the rise in government spending does not create excess demands only if

$$\beta_{m0}(1 - \gamma_s) = \beta_{m0}^g(1 - \gamma_s^g) \tag{8.13}$$

and

$$\beta_{m1}\gamma_s = \beta_{m1}^g\gamma_s^g. \tag{8.14}$$

In the absence of such equalities, the induced excess demands must alter the prevailing prices. The precise changes in the equilibrium prices depend on differences among the saving propensities of the domestic and foreign private sectors, on differences among the temporal expenditure shares of the two private sectors, and on the relative shares of the two private sectors in world demands and supplies.

As is evident, the complex structure of the model implies that, in general, the effects of government spending on the temporal and the intertemporal terms of trade—and thereby on the (consumption-based) real rates of interest and wealth deflator—depend on numerous transfer-problem criteria involving comparisons among the value of parameters characterizing the behavior of the domestic government, the domestic private sector, and the foreign private sector. In order to focus on the differences between the private and the public sectors, we examine the special case in which in the initial equilibrium the domestic and the foreign economies are identical in terms of production and consumption patterns. In this case the effects of the rise in the domestic government spending reflect only the differences in the behavioral patterns of the domestic private and public sectors.

Table 8.2 summarizes the effects of government spending on the (consumption-based) real rate of interest, r_{c0}, and on the real wealth deflator, P_w. The results reported in the table are based on the analysis in the appendix. It shows that if the government propensity to spend on exportables in the current period, $(1 - \gamma_s^g)(1 - \beta_m^g)$, falls short of the corresponding private-sector saving propensity, $(1 - \gamma_s)(1 - \beta_m)$, then the rise in the domestic government spending raises the real wealth deflator (which is the "true" price of lifetime spending). Conversely, if the government propensity to spend on exportables in the current period exceeds the corresponding private sector's propensity, then the rise in government spending lowers the real wealth deflator. If the two spending propensities are equal to each other, then the transfer-problem criterion implies that the rise in government spending does not alter the real wealth deflator.

The second row (r_{c0}) in table 8.2 shows the effects of the rise in government spending on the (consumption-based) real rate of interest. As is evident, in this multicommodity world the key factor governing the direction of the induced change in the real rate of interest remains the transfer-problem criterion applied to a comparison between the saving propensities of the domestic government and the domestic private sector. Accordingly, if the private-sector-saving propensity, γ_s, exceeds the government-saving propensity, γ_s^g, then (at the prevailing prices) a rise in government spending redistributes wealth from the private to the public sectors and lowers national savings. To restore equilibrium, the level of savings must be raised. The necessary rise in savings is brought about through changes in the temporal and in the intertemporal prices. These price changes yield a higher (consumption-based) real rate of interest. The opposite holds if the saving propensity of the private sector falls short of the corresponding propensity of the domestic

Table 8.2
The effects of a rise in government spending on the (consumption-based) real rate of interest and real wealth deflator

Effects on	Relation between private and public spending propensities		
	$(1 - \beta_m)(1 - \gamma_s) > (1 - \beta_m^g)(1 - \gamma_s^g)$	$(1 - \beta_m)(1 - \gamma_s) = (1 - \beta_m^g)(1 - \gamma_s^g)$	$(1 - \beta_m)(1 - \gamma_s) < (1 - \beta_m^g)(1 - \gamma_s^g)$
P_w	+	0	−
r_{c0}	$\gamma_s > \gamma_s^g$	$\gamma_s = \gamma_s^g$	$\gamma_s < \gamma_s^g$
	+	0	−

Note: r_{c0} is the (consumption-based) real rate of interest, and P_w is the (consumption-based) real wealth deflator (the intertemporal price index). The symbols +, 0, and − indicate, respectively, that the rise in the domestic government spending raises, leaves unchanged, or lowers P_w or r_{c0}. The underlying assumption is that the private sectors in the two countries are identical, that the initial equilibrium is autarkic, and that initially government spending in both countries is zero.

government. In the borderline case for which the two saving propensities are equal to each other so that $\gamma_s = \gamma_s^g$, the transfer-problem criterion implies that the rise in government spending does not alter national savings, and therefore the (consumption-based) real rate of interest remains intact.

Finally, it is relevant to note that the assumed similarity between the two countries' private sectors implies that the changes in the foreign (consumption-based) real rate of interest and real wealth deflator are the same as those occurring in the domestic economy.

8.5   Government Spending and Investment

Up to this point our analysis of the effects of government spending on the world economy abstracted from investment. The stylized facts, on the other hand, suggest a close correlation between public-sector spending and investment. In what follows we extend the analysis and allow for endogenous investment. In order to focus on the essentials, we return to the single composite-commodity world. As seen earlier, government spending influences the level of the equilibrium rates of interest. These changes in interest rates alter the profitability of domestic and foreign investment and influence the evolution of world output.

The analysis is conducted with the aid of figure 8.4, in which the upward-sloping schedule, S^w, describes the ratio, z, of current to future world GDP net of investment and government spending as an increasing function of the rate of interest. Formally, using the previous notation,

$$z = \frac{\overline{Y}_0 - I_0(r_0) + \overline{Y}_0^* - I_0^*(r_0) - G_0 - G_0^*}{\overline{Y}_1 + F[I_0(r_0)] + \overline{Y}_1^* + F^*[I_0^*(r_0)] - G_1 - G_1^*}. \tag{8.15}$$

The positive dependence of z on the rate of interest reflects the fact that investment falls when the rate of interest rises.

The downward-sloping schedules in figure 8.4 plot the desired ratio of current to future consumption as a decreasing function of the rate of interest. The assumption that the utility functions are

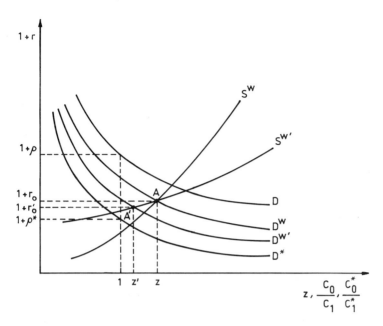

Figure 8.4
The effect of a permanent rise in domestic government spending on the rate of interest and investment

homothetic enables us to express the various demand schedules in terms of desired consumption ratios. The domestic and foreign private-sector relative demands are denoted by D and D^*, and their values at the point in which $(C_0/C_1) = (C_0^*/C_1^*) = 1$ indicate, respectively, the subjective rates of time preference ρ and ρ^*. The elasticities of the relative demand schedules are the corresponding intertemporal elasticities of substitution in consumption. The world relative demand, D^w, is a weighted average of the two private sectors' relative demands, D and D^*:

$$\frac{C_0 + C_0^*}{C_1 + C_1^*} = \mu\frac{C_0}{C_1} + (1 - \mu)\frac{C_0^*}{C_1^*}, \tag{8.16}$$

where

$$\mu = \frac{C_1}{C_1 + C_1^*}.$$

The initial equilibrium is described by point A in figure 8.4, at which the rate of interest is r_0.

Consider the effect of a permanent rise in domestic government spending. This permanent rise alters both the supply schedule and the world demand schedule in figure 8.4. We define a permanent rise in government spending as an equal rise in the relative share of the domestic government in world net output in both the present and the future. It follows that such a change in current and future government spending does not alter the initial ratio on the supply schedule. As a matter of arithmetic it is obvious that this rise in government spending rotates the supply schedule around the initial equilibrium of point A. As a result the supply schedule associated with the permanently higher level of government spending is $S^{w'}$ instead of S^w. The rise in government spending also alters the world demand schedule. Specifically, since at the prevailing rate of interest domestic disposable income must fall (in order to finance the growth of government), it follows that the relative weight μ attached to the domestic schedule D falls. This change in relative weights shifts the world (weighted-average) demand schedule closer to D^* and results in a new world demand schedule $D^{w'}$.

The new equilibrium obtains at point A'. The equilibrium rate of interest falls from r_0 to r_0', and as may be seen, in the new equilibrium the world rate of interest is closer to the foreign rate of time preference ρ^*. In the new equilibrium aggregate private spending is less biased toward present goods, reflecting the lower weight attached to the lower saving pattern of the home country's private demand. The lower rate of interest encourages investment in both countries according to the properties of the investment functions $I_0(r_0)$ and $I_0^*(r_0)$. This rise in investment raises future outputs according to the properties of the investment opportunity functions $F(\cdot)$ and $F^*(\cdot)$.

It is relevant to note that the effect of the permanent rise in government spending on the balance of trade is ambiguous since it reflects the possibly different responses of domestic and foreign investment and future outputs. This should be contrasted with the situation analyzed earlier in figure 8.2a in which investment was absent. In that case the permanent rise in government spending lowered interest rates and induced a deficit in the first-period balance of trade.

The foregoing analysis of the effects of permanent changes in government spending was conducted under the assumption that (in comparison with the rest of the world) the home country's spending patterns are biased toward the consumption of present goods. This relative bias reflected the assumption that the domestic rate of time preference, ρ, exceeds the corresponding foreign rate, ρ^*. In the opposite case, for which $\rho < \rho^*$, the permanent rise in government spending raises the (weighted-average) world relative demand curve in figure 8.4 and results in a higher world rate of interest and in lower levels of investment.

Similar principles can be applied to the analysis of the effects of transitory (current or future) changes in the levels of government spending. Corresponding to our previous analysis, it follows that a transitory rise in current government spending lowers domestic and foreign investment since it raises the rate of interest, whereas a transitory rise in future government spending raises domestic and foreign investment since it lowers the rate of interest. These results are summarized in table 8.3. The key point underscored by this table is that whether government spending crowds out or crowds in private investment depends on the timing of government spending and on the difference between the domestic and the foreign private sectors' marginal propensities to save. Alternatively, cast in terms of the general rule, if γ_s exceeds γ_s^g, then, by raising the world rate of

Table 8.3
The effects of a rise in domestic government spending on the levels of investment

Rates of time preference	Current rise	Future rise	Permanent rise
$\rho > \rho^*$	−	+	+
$\rho < \rho^*$	−	+	−

Note: The case in which $\rho > \rho^*$ indicates that the domestic marginal propensity to save out of wealth falls short of the foreign propensity, and vice versa.

interest, government spending crowds out domestic and foreign private-sector investment, and conversely if γ_s falls short of γ_s^g.

8.6   The Optimal Size of Government

Throughout the previous analysis we have treated the level of government spending as exogenous, and we have examined the effects of various changes in the time profile of spending. In this section we extend the analysis and examine the optimal path of government spending. This extension facilitates a more complete analysis of the welfare implications of fiscal policies.

In order to determine the optimal size of government, we use the private sector's utility function and recognize that the provision of public goods influences the level of welfare. Thus we use the maximized level of utility (defined in equation 8.30) together with the government budget constraint (defined in equation 8.35). In order to focus on the determination of the optimal path of government spending and abstract from issues concerning the optimal path of taxes, we assume that the private and the public sectors face the same world rate of interest so that $\alpha_1^g = \alpha_1^p = \alpha_1$. This assumption introduces the Ricardian irrelevance property into the model. Formally, the government maximization problem is

$$\tilde{V} = \max_{\{G_0, G_1, T_0, T_1\}} V(G_0, G_1, T_0, T_1) \tag{8.17}$$

subject to

$$G_0 + \alpha_1 G_1 = T_0 + \alpha_1 T_1 - (1 + r_{-1})B_{-1}^g.$$

Carrying out the maximization and using the conditions specified in equation (8.4) yields the first-order conditions:

$$\frac{U_G(C_0, G_0)}{U_C(C_0, G_0)} = \frac{U_G(C_1, G_1)}{U_C(C_1, G_1)} = 1. \tag{8.18}$$

As usual for a two-good economy, equation (8.18) states the requirement that in each period the marginal rate of substitution between the two goods equals the marginal rate of transformation (which in the present specification equals unity). Since the two goods are a private good and a public good, the equality between the marginal rate of substitution and the marginal rate of transformation reflects the implicit assumption of a single-consumer economy; in general, the Samuelson condition requires equality between the *sum* of the individual marginal rates of substitution and the economy's marginal rate of transformation.

The formal specification of the government maximization problem embodies the utility-maximizing conditions of the private sector. Hence in addition to the *temporal* condition (8.18) the solution contains the intertemporal condition (8.3) stating the *intertemporal* marginal rate of substitution between consumption of private goods as well as between consumption of public goods equals one plus the rate of interest. These equilibrium conditions along with the economy's consolidated budget constraint (8.2) determine the optimal path of government spending as part of the general equilibrium solution of the model.

The symmetric treatment of private and public goods suggests that the question of the optimal size of government can also be cast in terms of the utility-maximizing demand functions for current and future consumption of private and public goods. As usual, these demand functions are expressed as functions of prices and wealth. In our case the relevant temporal price of public goods in terms of private goods is unity, the intertemporal price is α_1, and the relevant concept of wealth is the discounted sum of GDP net of the historically given initial external debt commitment; that is, $\overline{Y}_0 + \alpha_1 \overline{Y}_1 - (1 + r_{-1})B_{-1}$. Formally, these demand functions are

$$C_t = C_t[\alpha_1; \overline{Y}_0 + \alpha_1 \overline{Y}_1 - (1 + r_{-1})B_{-1}],$$
$$G_t = G_t[\alpha_1; \overline{Y}_0 + \alpha_1 \overline{Y}_1 - (1 + r_{-1})B_{-1}] \qquad t = 0, 1,$$

$$(8.19)$$

where we have suppressed the temporal prices that are equal to unity.

The equations in (8.19) can be used to analyze the effects of supply shocks on the optimal path of government spending. For this purpose we assume that the private and the public goods are normal goods. Consider the effect of a temporary supply shock that raises the value of current GDP, $\overline{Y}_0$. Since all goods (including future goods) are normal, it is obvious that in order to "finance" a rise in future consumption (C_1 and G_1), the induced rise in current consumption of both goods (C_0 and G_0) must be smaller than the rise in $\overline{Y}_0$. Thus, since not all new output is absorbed by current consumption, it follows that the current-period supply shock induces an improvement in the economy's balance of trade. Analogously, if the temporary supply shock is expected to occur in the future, normality implies that the rise in $\overline{Y}_1$ raises consumption of all four goods, including current goods. In that case the economy's trade balance deteriorates in the early period. The foregoing examples demonstrate that the consumption-smoothing motive that characterizes private consumption in the absence of public goods also extends to the broader concept of consumption that includes both private and public goods, if the supply of the latter is optimal. Consequently the qualitative trade-balance effects of temporary supply shocks also remain intact.

Finally, consider the effects of a permanent supply shock. For ease of exposition suppose that the historically given initial external debt position, B_{-1}, is zero, that the utility function over all four goods is homothetic, and that the level of GDP is stationary. In that case the initial trade balance is zero, and an equiproportional rise in current and future GDP raises the consumption of all goods (including public goods) by the same proportion and leaves the trade balance unchanged. This outcome is the analogue to the neutral-supply shock analyzed in figure 8.3 for the case in which public goods were absent.

A key proposition of the foregoing analysis is that in the presence of both private and public goods, supply shocks induce a positive correlation between the levels of consumption of private and public goods if the latter are optimally supplied. The symmetric treatment of private and public goods reveals that the optimal supply of public goods (as reflected by the level of government spending) responds to expected future events in a manner similar to that of the consumption of private goods. Therefore the optimal level of government spending need not be synchronized with supply shocks, and as a result the contemporaneous correlation between government spending and GDP may be low. This property reflects the role of government as a supplier of public goods and not as an instrument of stabilization policies. Allowance for the latter role would introduce countercyclical elements to the path of government spending and would thereby contribute to a negative correlation between contemporaneous changes in GDP and government spending.

8.7   Fiscal Policies and the Real Exchange Rate

Up to this point we have assumed that all goods are internationally tradable in world markets. This characteristic implies that fiscal policies that alter the relative price of goods directly affect the rest of the world. In this section we extend the analysis by allowing for goods that are nontradable internationally; their relative prices are determined exclusively in the domestic economy. In that case the effects of domestic fiscal policies and their international transmission also operate through changes in the relative price of nontradable goods (the inverse of the real exchange rate). In what follows we examine the role of the real exchange rate in the analysis of fiscal policies. After introducing the analytical framework, we study the effects of government spending and then analyze the implications of budget deficits arising from tax cuts.

The analytical framework employs a general-equilibrium intertemporal approach for a two-country model of the world economy. Throughout we assume that there are two composite goods: an internationally tradable good denoted by x, and a nontradable good denoted by n. To allow for intertemporal considerations we assume, for simplicity, a two-period model, periods 0 and 1. The relative price of the nontradable good (the inverse of the real exchange rate) in period t is p_{nt}, the exogenously given output of that good is Y_{nt}, government purchases of the nontradable good are G_{nt}, and private-sector demand is $c_{nt}(t = 0, 1)$. The private-sector lifetime budget constraint is

$$(c_{x0} + p_{n0}c_{n0}) + \alpha_{x1}(c_{x1} + p_{n1}c_{n1})$$
$$= (\overline{Y}_{x0} + p_{n0}\overline{Y}_{n0}) + \alpha_{x1}(\overline{Y}_{x1} + p_{n1}\overline{Y}_{n1})$$
$$- (T_0 + \alpha_{x1}T_1) - (1 + r_{x,-1})B^p_{-1} \equiv W_0, \tag{8.20}$$

where $\alpha_{x1} = 1/(1 + r_{x0})$ denotes the discount factor in terms of tradable goods and where T_t, c_{xt}, and $\overline{Y}_{xt}$ denote, respectively, the level of lump-sum taxes, the level of consumption, and the exogenously given level of production of tradable goods in period t ($t = 0, 1$). W_0 denotes wealth, r_{xt} ($t = -1, 0$) denotes the world interest rate, and B^p_t denotes private-sector debt in period t ($t = -1, 0$). The values of taxes, wealth, debt, and the interest rates are measured in terms of tradable goods.

The individual maximizes lifetime utility subject to the lifetime budget constraint (8.20). We assume that the lifetime utility function can be expressed as a function of two linearly homogeneous sub-utility functions $C_0(c_{x0}, c_{n0})$ and $C_1(c_{x1}, c_{n1})$. Hence lifetime utility is $U(C_0, C_1)$. The maximization of this utility function subject to the lifetime budget constraint (8.20) is carried out in two stages, where the first stage optimizes the composition of spending within each period and the second stage optimizes the intertemporal allocation of spending between periods.

The optimization of the intertemporal allocation of the (consumption-based) real spending yields the demand functions for real spending in each period, $C_t = C_t(\alpha_{c1}, W_{c0})$, where α_{c1} is the (consumption-based) real wealth. Expressed in terms of tradable goods, the level of spending in each period is $P_t C_t$, where P_t is the consumption-based price index (the "true" price deflator). Thus $\alpha_{c1} = \alpha_{x1}P_1/P_0$ and $W_{c0} = W_0/P_0$. Clearly the price index in each period depends on the temporal relative price p_{nt} with an elasticity that equals the relative share of expenditure on nontradable goods, β_{nt}. Within each period the utility-maximizing allocation of spending between goods depends on the relative price p_{nt}.

The market for nontradable goods must clear in each country during each period. Accordingly,

$$c_{n0}[p_{n0}, P_0 C_0(\alpha_{c1}, W_{c0})] = \overline{Y}_{n0} - G_{n0} \tag{8.21}$$

and

$$c_{n1}[p_{n1}, P_1 C_1(\alpha_{c1}, W_{c0})] = \overline{Y}_{n1} - G_{n1}, \tag{8.22}$$

where the left-hand sides of these equilibrium conditions show the demand functions and the right-hand sides show the supply net of government purchases.[1] As we have seen, the demand functions depend on the relative price, p_{nt}, and on spending, $P_t C_t$, where P_t is the (consumption-based) price index, and C_t is (consumption-based) real spending. Real spending in turn depends on the (consumption-based) real discount factor α_{c1}. We assume that the utility function is homothetic, so that the elasticity of consumption demand with respect to spending, as well as the elasticity of spending with respect to wealth, is unity.

8.8 Spending Policies

In analyzing the effects of government spending, we obtain the equilibrium value of wealth, W_0, by substituting the government present-value budget constraint

$$(G_{x0} + p_{n0} G_{n0}) + \alpha_{x1}(G_{x1} + p_{n1} G_{n1})$$

$$= T_0 + \alpha_{x1} T_1 - (1 + r_{-1}) B^g_{-1},$$

where G_{xt} and G_{nt} denote government purchases of tradable and nontradable goods and B^g_t government debt in period t, into the corresponding private-sector budget constraint. Accordingly,

$$W_0 = [p_{n0}(\overline{Y}_{n0} - G_{n0}) + (\overline{Y}_{x0} - G_{x0})]$$

$$+ \alpha_{x1}[(\overline{Y}_{n1} - G_{n1}) + (\overline{Y}_{x1} - G_{x1})] - (1 + r_{x,-1}) B_{-1}. \tag{8.23}$$

Thus, as usual, government spending absorbs resources that otherwise would have been available to the private sector. We assume that the public goods generated by these policies do not tilt the private-sector relative demand for private goods.

Next we determine the effects of government spending on the path of private-sector consumption of tradable goods. Analogously to the previous specification, the demand function for tradable goods in period t is

$$c_{xt} = c_{xt}[p_{nt}, P_t C_t(\alpha_{c1}, W_{c0})], \qquad t = 0, 1. \tag{8.24}$$

Clearly, in contrast to the markets for nontradable goods, the consumption of tradable goods in any given period is not limited by the available domestic supply. It is shown in appendix A that the *intertemporal-consumption ratio* of tradable goods, c_{x0}/c_{x1}, depends on the world discount factor according to

$$\frac{d \log(c_{x0}/c_{x1})}{d \log \alpha_{x1}} = \frac{\sigma_{nx}\sigma}{\beta_n\sigma + (1 - \beta_n)\sigma_{nx}}, \tag{8.25}$$

where β_n denotes the relative share of private-sector spending on nontradable goods and σ and σ_{nx} denote, respectively, the intertemporal and the temporal elasticities of substitution.[2] Equation (8.25) (which incorporates the induced change in the path of the real exchange rate) shows that the only factors governing the change in the intertemporal-consumption ratio are pure temporal and intertemporal substitution effects. The absence of wealth effects reflects the homotheticity assumption. The foreign economy is assumed to be characterized by a structure of demand and supply similar to that of the domestic economy.

To determine the equilibrium in the world economy, we need to consider the factors governing world demand and world supply of tradable goods. The analysis is carried out with the aid of figure 8.5. Panel I of figure 8.5 shows the *relative* intertemporal domestic, D, foreign, D^*, and world D^w, demands for tradable goods. The world relative demand is a weighted average of the domestic and foreign relative demands:

$$D^w = \frac{c_{x0} + c_{x0}^*}{c_{x1} + c_{x1}^*} = \mu_d \frac{c_{x0}}{c_{x1}} + (1 - \mu_d)\frac{c_{x0}^*}{c_{x1}^*}, \tag{8.26}$$

where $\mu_d = c_{x1}/(c_{x1} + c_{x1}^*)$. The relative-demand schedules relate the desired consumption ratio of tradable goods to the interest rate. Their slope reflects the negative relationship embodied in equation

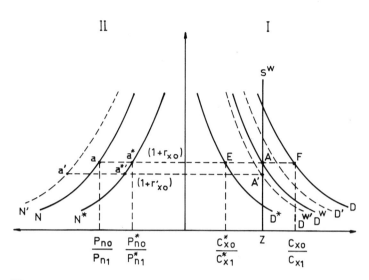

Figure 8.5
The effects of government spending on the world interest rate and on the paths of real exchange rates

(8.25). These demand schedules are drawn for a given level of government spending. Analogously, the relative world supply of tradable goods net of government purchases, z, is

$$z = \frac{(\overline{Y}_{x0} - G_{x0}) + (\overline{Y}_{x0}^* - G_{x0}^*)}{(\overline{Y}_{x1} - G_{x1}) + (\overline{Y}_{x1}^* - G_{x1}^*)}. \tag{8.27}$$

The relative-supply schedule, S^w, is drawn with a zero interest elasticity, since we abstract from investment. This schedule is also drawn for a given level of government spending.

The schedules N and N^* in panel II of figure 8.5 show the relationship between the world interest rate and the internal relative-price structure (the path of the real exchange rate) in each country. The elasticity of these schedules is given by equation (8.28), which is derived in appendix B:

$$\frac{d\log(p_{n0}/p_{n1})}{d\log\alpha_{x1}} = \frac{\sigma}{\beta_n\sigma + (1 - \beta_n)\sigma_{nx}}. \tag{8.28}$$

Equation (8.28) indicates that changes in the world interest rate influence the path of the real exchange rate only through the intertemporal substitution effect. Accordingly, a rise in the world interest rate (a fall in α_{x1}) induces intertemporal substitution of spending toward the future. It thereby lowers the current price of nontradable goods relative to the future price (i.e., it decelerates the rate of increase in the real exchange rate from period 0 to period 1). As before, the homotheticity assumption accounts for the absence of the wealth variable in equation (8.28).

The initial equilibrium is described in panel I by point A, in which the world interest rate is r_{x0}. The domestic and foreign intertemporal consumption ratios are indicated by points F and E. The periodic percentage changes of the domestic and the foreign real exchange rates associated with the initial equilibrium are shown in panel II by points a and a^*.

Consider the effects of a rise in the level of domestic-government spending.[3] This change alters the domestic relative demand and the domestic country weight, μ_d (thereby the world relative demand), as well as the world relative supply. A rise in the level of domestic-government spending influences world relative demand in two ways: (8.20) through its effect on domestic relative demand, and (8.21) through its effect on the domestic-country weight, μ_d. The effect of the rise in government spending on the domestic relative demand (derived in appendix B) is given by

$$\frac{d\log(c_{x0}/c_{x1})}{dG} = \frac{\beta_n\beta_n^g O_n(1-\gamma_s)(\sigma_{nx}-\sigma)}{\beta_n\sigma+(1-\beta_n)\sigma_{nx}}\left[\frac{(1-\gamma_s^g)}{(1-\gamma_s)}-\frac{\gamma_s^g}{\gamma_s}\right], \qquad (8.29)$$

where ϕ_n denotes the inverse of the value of private consumption of nontradable goods in period 0, that is, $\phi_n = 1/p_{n0}c_{n0}$. The intertemporal and temporal allocations of government spending are governed by the government saving propensity, γ_s^g, defined as the ratio of future government spending (in present-value terms) to the discounted sum of spending, and by the relative share of government spending on nontradables in total government spending in period t, β_n^g. Finally, γ_s, defined as the ratio of private-sector future consumption (in present-value terms) to the discounted sum of private-sector spending, denotes the private-sector saving propensity.

As shown in equation (8.29), the direction of the change in the relative-demand schedules depends on the *government-induced bias* in the intertemporal net supply of nontradable goods and on the *temporal-intertemporal substitution bias* in private-sector demand. Indeed, if either σ equals σ_{nx} or γ_s equals γ_s^g, the change in government spending does not alter the position of the relative-demand schedule.

The direction of the change in the world demand due to the induced change in the weight μ_d, while maintaining c_{x0}/c_{x1} constant, is equal to

$$\frac{d\log[(c_{t0} + c_{x0}^*)/(c_{x1} + c_{x1}^*)]}{dG}$$

$$= \frac{1}{(c_{x0} + c_{x0}^*)}(1 - \mu_d)(1 - \beta_n)\gamma_s\left[\frac{1 - \gamma_s^*}{\gamma_s^*} - \frac{1 - \gamma_s}{\gamma_s}\right]. \qquad (8.30)$$

Note that this effect vanishes if γ_s equals γ_s^*.

To determine the direction of the change in the relative-supply schedule, we differentiate equation (8.27) with respect to government spending. Accordingly,

$$\frac{d\log z}{dG} = \lambda_x^g(1 - \beta_n^g)(1 - \gamma_s^g)\frac{\gamma_s^g}{1 - \gamma_s^g}$$

$$- \mu_d\frac{\gamma_s}{1 - \gamma_s} - (1 - \mu_d)\frac{\gamma_s^*}{1 - \gamma_s^*}, \qquad (8.31)$$

where λ_x^g denotes the reciprocal of the world output of tradable goods net of government purchases of these goods in period 1. Thus $\lambda_x^g = 1/[(\overline{Y}_x - G_x) + (\overline{Y}_x^* - G_x^*)]$. Equation (8.31) indicates that the direction of the change in the relative supply reflects the bias in the intertemporal allocation of government spending on tradable goods. For example, a temporary *current* rise in government spending ($\gamma_s^g = 0$) induces a leftward shift of the relative-supply schedule, whereas a temporary *future* rise in government spending ($\gamma_s^g = 1$) induces a rightward shift of the relative supply.

Similar considerations apply to the effects of government spending on the paths of the domestic and foreign real exchange rates. For a given value of the world interest rate (measured in terms of tradable goods), the effects of the rise in government spending on the time path of the real exchange rate, p_{n0}/p_{n1}, is found by differentiating equations (8.21) and (8.22) around $G = 0$, subtracting the resulting equations from each other, and using the Slutsky decomposition. This yields

$$\frac{d \log(p_{n0}/p_{n1})}{dG} = \frac{\beta_n^g \phi_n (1 - \gamma_s)}{\beta_n (\beta_n \sigma + (1 - \beta_n)\sigma_{nx})}\left[\frac{1 - \gamma_s^g}{1 - \gamma_s} - \frac{\gamma_s^g}{\gamma_s}\right]. \tag{8.32}$$

Equation (8.32) reveals that the direction of the change in the path of the real exchange rate depends on the temporal and the intertemporal allocations of government demand for nontradable goods relative to the corresponding allocations of private-sector demand. If the ratio of the relative share of government spending on nontradable goods in the current period, $\beta_n^g(1 - \gamma_s^g)$, to the private-sector share, $\beta_n(1 - \gamma_s)$, exceeds the corresponding ratio in the future period, $\beta_n^g \gamma_s^g / \beta_n \gamma_s$, then a rise in government spending raises the percentage rate of change of the real exchange rate, and vice versa.

This result can be interpreted in terms of a transfer-problem criterion relating the temporal and intertemporal spending patterns of the government and the domestic private sector. Accordingly, the rise in government spending raises the current price of nontradable goods relative to its future price if the pattern of government spending is biased toward current nontradable goods in comparison with the pattern of private-sector spending. As indicated by equation (8.31), depending on the temporal and intertemporal spending patterns of the government, the rise in government spending may induce a rightward or leftward shift of the N schedule in panel II of figure 8.5.

To illustrate the working of the model, we consider in figure 8.5 the effects of government spending for a benchmark case in which the intertemporal elasticity of substitution, σ, exceeds the temporal elasticity, σ_{nx}; the ratio of the shares of government spending to private spending in the current period, $(1 - \gamma_s^g)/(1 - \gamma_s)$, exceeds the corresponding ratio of future spending, γ_n^g/γ_s; government spending falls entirely on nontradable goods (so that $\beta_n^g = 1$); and the domestic private sector's saving propensity equals the foreign propensity. As indicated by equation (8.29), in this benchmark case the domestic, and thereby the world, relative-demand schedules shift leftward from the position indicated by D and D^w to the position indicated by D' and $D^{w'}$, respectively. Further, as indicated by equation (8.31), with $\beta_n^g = 1$ the relative supply of world tradable goods does not change. It follows that in this case the equilibrium point shifts from point A to point A' in panel I of figure 8.5, and the world interest rate falls from r_{x0} to $\tilde{r}'_{x0}$.

In panel II of figure 8.5 we show the effects of the rise in government spending on the paths of the domestic and foreign real exchange rates. As indicated by equation (8.32), in this benchmark case the N schedule shifts outward and, given the new lower world interest rate, the domestic and foreign equilibrium points shift from a and a^* to a' and $a^{*'}$, respectively. Accordingly, the percentage change (per unit of time) in the real exchange rates increases in both countries. In concluding the presentation of this benchmark case, we note that since the world interest rate (measured in terms of tradable goods) falls, and since in both countries the time paths of the real exchange rates steepen, it follows that in both countries the consumption-based real interest rates fall (even though, in general, the magnitude of this decline need not be the same for both countries).

We chose this specific benchmark case in which the rise in government spending lowers the world interest rate in order to highlight the implications of government spending on nontradable goods. In fact, if government spending falls entirely on tradable goods (so that $\beta_n^g = 0$), then the rise in spending does not alter the relative-demand schedules in figure 8.5, as seen from equation (8.29) with $\beta_n^g = 0$, but it induces a leftward shift of the relative-supply schedule, as seen from equation (8.31) for the case $\gamma_s^g < \gamma_s$, $\beta_n^g = 0$. Thus, under such circumstances, the rise in government spending raises the equilibrium interest rate. This case underlies the simple transfer-problem criterion described in the introduction to this chapter.

Table 8.4
The effects of a rise in government spending on the world interest rate in a model with nontradable goods

Relationship between temporal and intertemporal elasticities of substitution	Intertemporal and temporal allocations of government spending			
	$\gamma_s > \gamma_s^g$		$\gamma_s < \gamma_s^g$	
	$\beta_n^g = 0$	$\beta_n^g = 1$	$\beta_n^g = 0$	$\beta_n^g = 1$
$\sigma_{nx} > \sigma$	$+$	$+$	$-$	$-$
$\sigma_{nx} = \sigma$	$\geqq$	0	$-$	0
$\sigma_{nx} < \sigma$	$+$	$-$	$-$	$+$

Note: The world rate of interest is measured in terms of internationally tradable goods. This table assumes that initially $\gamma_s = \gamma_s^*$.

The more general configurations of the effects of government spending on the world interest rate, as implied by equations (8.27) and (8.29), are summarized in table 8.4, where we assume that initially $\gamma_s = \gamma_s^*$. The table demonstrates that if the commodity composition of government spending is strongly biased toward goods that are internationally tradable (so that β_n^g is small), then the key factor determining the direction of the change in the world interest rate is the intertemporal allocation of government and private-sector spending. If government spending is biased toward the current period relative to private-sector spending, so that γ_s exceeds γ_s^g, then the world interest rate rises, and vice versa. On the other hand, if the commodity composition of government spending is strongly biased toward nontradable goods (so that β_n^g is close to unity), then the direction of the change in the interest rate depends on the interaction between the intertemporal allocation of government spending relative to the private sector and the difference between the temporal and the intertemporal elasticities of substitution of the domestic private sector. In fact, since in this case the effects of government spending operate only through changes in the relative-demand schedules, the interest rate rises if $(\sigma_{nx} - \sigma)(\gamma_s - \gamma_s^g)$ is positive, and vice versa.

Table 8.5
The effects of a rise in government spending on the paths of domestic and foreign real exchange rates

Relationship between temporal and intertemporal elasticities of substitution	The real exchange rate in the	Intertemporal and temporal allocations of government spending			
		$\gamma_s > \gamma_s^g$		$\gamma_s < \gamma_s^g$	
		$\beta_n^g = 0$	$\beta_n^g = 1$	$\beta_n^g = 0$	$\beta_n^g = 1$
$\sigma_{nx} > \sigma$	domestic economy	−	?	+	?
	foreign economy	−	−	+	+
$\sigma_{nx} = \sigma$	domestic economy	−	+	+	−
	foreign economy	−	0	+	0
$\sigma_{nx} < \sigma$	domestic economy	−	+	+	−
	foreign economy	−	+	+	−

Note: The paths of the real exchange rates are measured by p_{n0}/p_{ni} and p_{n0}^*/p_{n1}^*. This table assumes that initially $\gamma_s = \gamma_s^*$.

The various possibilities concerning the relative magnitudes of the key parameters also imply that the effects of government spending on the time path of the domestic and foreign real exchange rates are not clear-cut. The possible outcomes are summarized in table 8.5. The results show that if the commodity composition of government spending is strongly biased toward internationally tradable goods (so that β_n^g is about zero), then, as implied by equation (8.32), the change in government spending does not materially displace the N schedule in panel II of figure 8.5. Therefore the induced change in the path of the domestic real exchange rate mirrors only the change in the interest rate, since it involves a movement along the given N schedule. It follows that, with a small β_n^g, the change in the time path of the domestic real exchange rate is inversely related to the change in the world interest rate. This inverse relationship is verified from a comparison between the entries appearing in tables 8.4 and 8.5 in the columns corresponding to the case of $\beta_n^g = 0$. Indeed, in this case the direction of the change in the path of the real exchange rate depends only on the simple transfer-problem criterion involving the saving propensities of the domestic private and public sectors.

In the other extreme case, in which government spending falls mainly on nontradable goods (so that β_n^g is close to unity), then the key factor determining whether the path of the real exchange rate steepens or flattens is the intertemporal allocation of government spending, as long as the temporal elasticity of substitution, σ_{nx}, does not exceed the intertemporal elasticity of substitution, σ. If government spending is biased toward the current period relative to private-sector spending, so that γ_s exceeds γ_s^g, the rise in spending accelerates the time path of the real exchange rate, and vice versa. On the other hand, if σ_{nx} exceeds σ, the time path of the real exchange rate is influenced by two conflicting forces, the one operating through a movement along the N schedule (induced by the change in the interest rate) and the other operating through a shift in the N schedule (induced by the direct effect of government spending on the relative supply of nontradable goods).

Finally, note that the foreign schedule, N^*, is not affected by domestic-government spending, so that the time path of the foreign real exchange rate, p_{n1}^*/p_{n1}^*, is always related negatively to the world interest rate. But since the correlation between the time path of the domestic real exchange rate and the world interest rate may be positive, zero, or negative (as can be verified by comparing the results reported in tables 8.4 and 8.5), it follows that the cross-country correlations between the paths of the real exchange rates and between the (consumption-based) real interest rates may also be negative, zero, or positive. The analysis underlying tables 8.4 and 8.5 identifies the main factors governing the signs of the various cross-country correlations.

8.9 Summary

In this chapter we incorporated the government into the model. For this purpose we extended the specification of the utility function and the budget constraints so as to include public goods and taxes. We showed that there are two channels through which government spending influences the equilibrium of the economic system: the resource-withdrawal channel and the consumption-tilting channel.

The former reflects the combination of changes in net output (induced by government purchases of goods and services) and in private-sector wealth (induced by the nondistortionary taxes used for government finance). The latter reflects the temporal-intertemporal substitution-complementarity relations between public and private consumption and production.

In analyzing the effects of domestic government spending on the two-country world economy, we focused on the induced changes in the temporal and intertemporal terms of trade and on the cross-country comovement of private sectors' spending. We cast the analysis in terms of various transfer-problem criteria familiar from the theory of international transfers. In the present context these criteria involve comparisons between the domestic country's private and public sector's saving and spending propensities. Accordingly, if the government's propensity to spend on importables (out of expenditure) exceeds the corresponding private-sector propensity, then a rise in the domestic government's spending raises the relative price of importables, and thereby worsens the domestic country's temporal terms of trade, and vice versa. Likewise, if the domestic government's saving propensity exceeds the corresponding private-sector propensity, then the rise in the domestic government's spending lowers the world rate of interest—the intertemporal terms of trade, and vice versa. In this context both the private and the public sector's saving propensities reflect the relation between the present value of future consumption and the discounted sum of current and future consumption. This transfer-problem criterion underscores the significance of the timing of government spending, being transitory or permanent.

In our multicommodity world there is a complex interaction between the temporal and the intertemporal terms of trade. To allow for this interaction, we defined the appropriate (consumption-based) real rate of interest and real wealth deflator, and applied the transfer-problem criterion to determine the effects of the commodity composition and the time pattern of government spending on these variables.

In regards to investment, we showed that the key factor determining whether government spending crowds in or crowds out private-sector investment at home and abroad is again the relation between the domestic private and public sector's saving propensities.

A brief analysis of the optimal size of government showed that the consumption-smoothing motive characterizing private consumption in the absence of public goods extends to the broader concept of consumption that includes both private and public goods, if the supply of the latter is optimal. A key proposition emerging from this consumption-smoothing feature is that with an optimal provision of public goods, supply shocks induce a positive correlation between the levels of consumption of private and public goods.

We have also dealt here with the effects of government spending on the world economy. Using the modern international-intertemporal approach, our analysis has shown the precise manner in which the effects of government spending depend critically on two biases: the bias in the *intertemporal* allocation of government spending relative to the domestic private sector, and the bias in the commodity *composition* of government purchases relative to the domestic private sector. When government spending is strongly biased toward purchases of tradable goods, the key factor determining whether the world interest rate rises or falls is the intertemporal pattern of government spending relative to the private sector: if the government intertemporal pattern is biased toward current spending, the interest rate rises, and vice versa.

The analysis has also provided information about the time paths of the domestic and foreign real exchange rates. When the share of government spending on tradable goods is relatively high, a rise in government spending decelerates the rates of change of the domestic and foreign real exchange rates if the intertemporal allocation of government spending (relative to the private sector) is biased toward the present. But if the intertemporal allocation of government spending (relative to the private sector) is biased toward the future, the rates of change of the real exchange rates accelerate. It follows that, in this case, government spending induces positive cross-country correlations between the time paths of the real exchange rates as well as between the (consumption-based) real interest rates.

In contrast, if the commodity composition of government spending is strongly biased toward purchases of nontradable goods, the interest-rate effects depend on the interaction between the bias in the intertemporal allocation of government spending relative to the private sector and the temporal-intertemporal substitution bias of the domestic private sector. It is important to emphasize that, even though there is no presumption concerning the precise effects of government spending on the world interest rate and on the time paths of the real exchange rates, we identify the key (estimatable) parameters whose relative magnitudes determine these effects.

In analyzing government spending policies, one could examine the effects of tax policies under alternative tax systems—consumption tax and income tax systems. It could be shown that with consumption taxes a budget deficit raises the world interest rate and lowers the domestic effective interest rate applicable to domestic consumption decisions. In addition, the deficit decelerates the rate of change of the domestic real exchange rate and accelerates the corresponding foreign rate of change. The deficit thereby lowers the domestic (consumption-based) effective real interest rate and raises the corresponding foreign real interest rate. These changes result in a negative cross-country correlation between the (consumption-based) real effective interest rates. In contrast, under an income tax system, the same budget deficit *lowers* the world interest rate and raises the domestic effective rate applicable to intertemporal labor-supply decisions. The deficit accelerates the rate of growth of the domestic real wage and decelerates the corresponding foreign growth rate.

Similarly, an analysis of budget deficits arising from tax cuts could be designed to illuminate the effects of revenue-neutral tax-conversion schemes. One could demonstrate that the effects of such shifts between income and consumption tax systems *raise* the world interest rate if the current-account position is in deficit. The revenue-neutral tax conversions *lower* the world interest rate if the current-account position is in surplus.

We conclude by reiterating one of the principal implications of this study. A proper analysis of the effects of fiscal policies on the world economy cannot be carried out on the basis of a single aggregate measure of the fiscal stance such as the budget deficit. It must be based on more detailed and specific information on government spending and taxes. On the spending side, such information must specify the distribution of spending between tradable and nontradable goods and its intertemporal allocation. On the revenue side, the information must specify the characteristics of the tax system, including the timing of taxes and the types of taxes used to finance the budget.

8.10   Appendix A: Government Spending and Terms of Trade

In this appendix we provide a formal analysis of the effects of government spending on the temporal and the intertemporal terms of trade. Throughout we assume logarithmic utility functions. We start with a derivation of the consumption-based price indexes corresponding to the specific utility function.

The maximization problem is

$$\tilde{U} = \max_{\substack{c_{m0}, c_{x0} \\ \{c_{m1}, c_{x1}\}}} \beta_{m0} \log c_{m0} + (1 - \beta_{m0}) \log c_{x0}$$

$$+ \delta[\beta_{m1} \log c_{m1} + (1 - \beta_{m1}) \log c_{x1}] \tag{A.1}$$

subject to

$$z_0 + \alpha_{x1} z_1 = W_0,$$

where

$$z_0 = (p_{m0} c_{m0} + c_{x0}),$$

$$z_1 = (p_{m1} c_{m1} + c_{x1}).$$

The solution to this maximization problem yields the following demand functions:

$$c_{m0} = \frac{\beta_{m0} W_0}{(1 + \delta)P_{m0}}, \qquad c_{m1} = \frac{\beta_{m1} W_0}{(1 + \delta)\alpha_{x1} P_{m1}},$$

$$c_{x0} = \frac{1}{1 + \delta}(1 - \beta_{m0}) W_0, \quad c_{x1} = \frac{\delta(1 - \beta_{m1}) W_0}{(1 + \delta)\alpha_{x1}}.$$

(A.2)

Substitution of the demand functions into the utility function yields the indirect utility function

$$\tilde{U} = a + \log\left(\frac{W_0^{(1+\delta)}}{p_{m0}^{\beta_{m0}} p_{m1}^{\beta_{m1}\delta} \alpha_{x1}^\delta}\right),$$

(A.3)

where a is a constant.

Recalling the definition of γ_s—the private sector propensity to save out of wealth—and using the definitions of spending and the demand functions from (A.2) yields

$$\gamma_s = \frac{\alpha_{x1} z_1}{z_0 + \alpha_{x1} z_1} = \frac{\delta}{1 + \delta}.$$

(A.4)

Substituting (A.4) for δ into (A.3) yields

$$\tilde{U} = a + \log\frac{W_0^{1/(1-\gamma_s)}}{P_w^{1/(1-\gamma_s)}} = a + \left(\frac{1}{1 - \gamma_s}\right)\log\left(\frac{W_0}{P_w}\right),$$

(A.5)

where

$$P_w = (P_0)^{1-\gamma_s}(\alpha_{x1} P_1)^{\gamma_s},$$

(A.6)

$$P_0 = p_{m0}^{\beta_{m0}},$$

$$P_1 = p_{m1}^{\beta_{m1}}.$$

Equation (A.6) defines the "true" utility-based *temporal* price indexes P_0 and P_1 and the "true" utility-based *intertemporal* price index P_w. As seen from (A.5), P_w is the price index relevant for welfare analysis.

Equilibrium in the world economy requires that in each period world private-sector demand for the two goods equals the corresponding supply net of government purchases. Thus

$$\beta_{m0} = \frac{1}{1+\delta} W_0 + \beta_{m0}^* \frac{1}{1+\delta} W_0^*$$

$$= p_{m0}[\overline{Y}_{m0} - G_{m0} + (\overline{Y}_{m0}^* - G_{m0}^*)], \tag{A.7}$$

$$(1 - \beta_{m0}) \frac{1}{1+\delta} W_0 + (1 - \beta_{m0}^*) \frac{1}{1+\delta^*} W_0^*$$

$$= (\overline{Y}_{x0} - G_{x0}) + (\overline{Y}_{x0}^* - G_{x0}^*), \tag{A.8}$$

$$\beta_{m1} \frac{\delta}{1+\delta} W_0 + \beta_{m1}^* \frac{\delta^*}{1+\delta^*} W_0^*$$

$$= \alpha_{x1} p_{m1}[(\overline{Y}_{m1} - G_{m1}) + (\overline{Y}_{m1}^* - G_{m1}^*)], \tag{A.9}$$

$$(1 - \beta_{m1}) \frac{\delta}{1+\delta} W_0 = (1 - \beta_{m1}^*) \frac{\delta^*}{1+\delta^*} W_0^*$$

$$= \alpha_{x1}[(\overline{Y}_{x1} - G_{x1}) + (\overline{Y}_{x1}^* - G_{x1}^*)], \tag{A.10}$$

where

$$W_0 = p_{m0}(\overline{Y}_{m0} - G_{m0}) + (\overline{Y}_{x0} - G_{x0})$$

$$+ \alpha_{x1}[p_{m1}(\overline{Y}_{m1} - G_{m1}) + (\overline{Y}_{x1} - G_{x1})],$$

$$W_0^* = p_{m0}(\overline{Y}_{m0}^* - G_{m0}^*) + (\overline{Y}_{x0}^* - G_{x0}^*)$$

$$+ \alpha_{x1}[p_{m1}(\overline{Y}_{m1}^* - G_{m1}^*) + (\overline{Y}_{x1}^* - G_{x1}^*)].$$

By Walras's law we omit, in what follows, equation (A.10).

Differentiating totally the system (A.7) through (A.9) around $G = 0$, we get

$$[\lambda_{m0}(1 - \gamma_s)\beta_{m0}\mu_{m0} + \lambda_{m0}^*(1 - \gamma_s^*)\beta_{m0}^*\mu_{m0}^* - 1]\hat{p}_{m0}$$

$$+ [\lambda_{m0}\gamma_s\beta_{m1}\mu_{m1} + \lambda_{m0}^*\gamma_s^*\beta_{m1}^*\mu_{m1}^*]\hat{p}_{m1}$$

$$+ [\lambda_{m0}\gamma_s\mu_1 + \lambda_{m0}^*\gamma_s^*\mu_1^*]\hat{\alpha}_{x1}$$

$$= g_{m0}[\beta_{m0}(1 - \gamma_s) - \beta_{m0}^g(1 - \gamma_s^g)]dG, \tag{A.11}$$

$$[\lambda_{x0}(1 - \gamma_s)\beta_{m0}\mu_{m0} + \lambda_{x0}^*(1 - \gamma_s)\beta_{m0}^*\mu_{m0}^*]\hat{p}_{m0}$$

$$+ [\lambda_{x0}\gamma_s\beta_{m1}\mu_{m1} + \lambda_{x0}^*\gamma_s^*\beta_{m1}^*\mu_{m1}^*]\hat{p}_{m1}$$

$$+ [\lambda_{x0}\gamma_s\mu_1 + \lambda_{x0}^*\gamma_s^*\mu_1^*]\hat{\alpha}_{x1}$$

$$= g_{x0}[(1 - \beta_{m0})(1 - \gamma_s) - (1 - \beta_{m0}^g)(1 - \gamma_s^g)]\,dG, \tag{A.12}$$

$$[\lambda_{m1}(1 - \gamma_s)\beta_{m0}\mu_{m0} + \lambda_{m1}^*(1 - \gamma_s^*)\beta_{m0}^*\mu_{m0}^*]\hat{p}_{m0}$$

$$+ [\lambda_{m1}\gamma_s\beta_{m1}\mu_{m1} + \lambda_{m1}^*\gamma_s^*\beta_{m1}^*\mu_{m1}^* - 1]\hat{p}_{m1}$$

$$+ [\lambda_{m1}\gamma_s\mu_1 + \lambda_{m1}^*\gamma_s^*\mu_1^* - 1]\hat{\alpha}_{x1}$$

$$= g_{m1}[\beta_{m1}\gamma_s - \beta_{m1}^g\gamma_s^g]\,dG, \tag{A.13}$$

where λ denotes the share of spending on a given good by the corresponding unit in world net output of the given good (net of government purchases). For example, λ_{m0} denotes the share of domestic private-sector spending on good m (in period zero) in world net output of good m in period zero; that is, $\lambda_{m0} = c_{m0}/[(\overline{Y}_{m0} - G_{m0}) + \overline{Y}_{m0}^* - G_{m0}^*)]$. Initially, with $G = 0$, $\lambda_{m0} = c_{m0}/(\overline{Y}_{m0} + \overline{Y}_{m0}^*)$, and in this case $\mu_{m1} = \overline{Y}_{m1}/c_{m1}$. The terms g_{m0}, g_{x0}, and g_{m1} denote, respectively, the reciprocals of the world production of good m_0, x_0, m_1 (net of government purchases of the good). The rest of the variables are defined in the text.

The system (A.11) through (A.13) can be solved to yield the effects of G on p_{m0}, p_{m1}, and α_{x1}. As is obvious by inspection of the coefficients of dG in equations (A.11) through (A.13), changes in the level of domestic government spending influence the temporal and the intertemporal terms of trade according to the principles known from the analysis of transfers. Thus changes in government spending influence the equilibrium only if the various spending propensities of the private sector differ from the corresponding propensities of the government. Indeed, in the special case in which these propensities are equal to each other so that $\beta_{m0} = \beta_{m0}^g$, $\beta_{m1} = \beta_{m1}^g$, and, $\gamma_s = \gamma_s^g$, changes in government spending do not influence the equilibrium temporal and intertemporal prices.

As is evident, the complex structure of the model implies that, in general, the effects of government spending on the temporal and intertemporal terms of trade depend on a multitude of transfer-problem criteria, involving comparisons among the marginal propensities to save of the private sector and of the government as well as comparisons among the periodic expenditure shares of the domestic and the foreign private sectors and the government.

In order to focus on differences between the private and the public sectors, suppose that the various shares do not vary over time and that the domestic and the foreign private sectors are identical in their marginal propensities to save, in their expenditure shares, and in their relative shares in world private demand. In that case $\lambda_m = \lambda_m^*$, $\beta_m = \beta_m^*$, and $\gamma_s = \gamma_s^*$, where the time subscript is omitted due to the assumption that the various propensities and shares are constant over time. We further assume that initially the ratios of output to private-sector spending are equal across countries so that $\mu_m = \mu_m^*$ and $\mu_1 = \mu_1^*$. This implies that the initial equilibrium is autarkic, so that $\mu_1 = \mu_m = 1$. With these assumptions the solution for the effect of government spending on the consumption-based intertemporal price index (the utility-based wealth deflator), P_w, is

$$\frac{d \log P_w}{dG} = \frac{1}{\overline{Y}_x + \overline{Y}_x^*}[(1 - \beta_m)(1 - \gamma_s) - (1 - \beta_m^g)(1 - \gamma_s^g)]. \quad (A.14)$$

Equation (A.14) shows that, as usual, the direction of the effect of a rise in government spending on the utility-based wealth deflator depends only on the various transfer-problem criteria.

Similarly, under the same assumptions the effect of a rise in government spending on the consumption-based real discount factor, $\alpha_{c1} = \alpha_{x1} P_1 / P_0$, is

$$\frac{d \log \alpha_{c1}}{dG} = \frac{\beta_m}{\gamma_s p_m (\overline{Y}_m + \overline{Y}_m^*)}[\beta_m(1 - \gamma_s) - \beta_m^g(1 - \gamma_s^g)]$$

$$+ \frac{(1 - \beta_m)c_m}{\gamma_s c_x (\overline{Y}_m + \overline{Y}_m^*)}[(1 - \beta_m)(1 - \gamma_s) + (1 - \beta_m^g)(1 - \gamma_s^g)].$$

Using the equality $p_m c_m / c_x = \beta_m / (1 - \beta_m)$, we have

$$\frac{d \log \alpha_{c1}}{dG} = \frac{\beta_m}{\gamma_s p_m (\overline{Y}_m + \overline{Y}_m^*)} (\gamma_s^g - \gamma_s).$$ (A.15)

Equations (A.14) through (A.15) underly the results reported in table 8.2 of the text.

8.11 Appendix B: The World Interest Rate, Tradable-Goods Consumption, and the Real Exchange Rate

In this appendix, we derive the effects of the world discount factor on the growth rate of consumption of tradable goods and on the path of the real exchange rate. Recall that the market for nontradable goods must clear during each period. The equilibrium conditions indicated by equations (8.21) to (8.22) of the text are

$$c_{n0}[p_{n0}, P_0 C_0(\alpha_{c1}, W_{c0})] = \overline{Y}_{n0} - G_{n0}$$ (A.16)

and

$$c_{n1}[p_{n1}, P_1 C_1(\alpha_{c1}, W_{c1})] = \overline{Y}_{n1} - G_{n1}$$ (A.17)

Using these equations and the Slutsky decomposition, the percentage changes in $p_{nt}(t = 0, 1)$ for a given percentage change in the world discount factor are

$$\hat{p}_{n0} = \left[\frac{\gamma_s \sigma}{\beta_n \sigma + (1 - \beta_n) \sigma_{nx}} + \frac{\gamma_s(\mu_1 - 1)}{(1 - \beta_n) \sigma_{nx}} \right] \hat{\alpha}_{x1}$$ (A.18)

and

$$\hat{p}_{n1} = \left[\frac{-(1 - \gamma_s) \sigma}{\beta_n \sigma + (1 - \beta_n) \sigma_{nx}} + \frac{\gamma_s(\mu_1 - 1)}{(1 - \beta_n) \sigma_{nx}} \right] \hat{\alpha}_{x1},$$ (A.19)

where a circumflex (ˆ) denotes percentage change of a variable and μ_1 denotes the ratio of future net output to private consumption. Subtracting (A.19) from (A.18) yields equation (A.20), which is equation (8.28) of the text:

$$\frac{d \log(p_{n0}/p_{n1})}{d \log \alpha_{x1}} = \frac{\sigma}{\beta_n \sigma + (1 - \beta_n) \sigma_{nx}}.$$ (A.20)

In determining the percentage change in c_{xt} ($t = 0, 1$), we differentiate equation (8.24) in the text and use the Slutsky decomposition. This yields

$$\hat{c}_{x0} = \beta_n(\sigma_{nx} - \gamma_s\sigma)\hat{p}_{n0} + \beta_n\gamma_s\sigma\hat{p}_{n1} + \gamma_s(\sigma + \mu_1 - 1)\hat{a}_{x1} \qquad (A.21)$$

and

$$\hat{c}_{x1} = \beta_n(1 - \gamma_s)\sigma\hat{p}_{n0} + \beta_n[\sigma_{nx} - (1 - \gamma_s)\sigma]\hat{p}_{n1}$$
$$- [(1 - \gamma_s\sigma - \gamma_s(\mu_1 - 1)]\hat{a}_{x1}. \qquad (A.22)$$

We can use these equations to determine the elasticity of the consumption ratio, c_{x0}/c_{x1}, with respect to the growth rate of the real exchange rate, p_{n0}/p_{n1}. This yields

$$\frac{d\log(c_{x0}/c_{x1})}{d\log(p_{n0}/p_{n1})} = \beta_n(\sigma_{nx} - \sigma). \qquad (A.23)$$

Equation (A.23) shows that the qualitative effects of the changes in the price ratio p_{n0}/p_{n1} on the consumption ratio of tradable goods, c_{x0}/c_{x1}, depend only on whether the temporal elasticity of substitution, σ_{nx} exceeds or falls short of the intertemporal elasticity of substitution, σ. A rise in the relative price of nontradable goods, p_{nt}, induces substitution of consumption of tradable goods for nontradable goods *within* period t. The magnitude of this temporal substitution is indicated by σ_{nx}. Further, if p_{n0} rises by more than p_{n1} (so that the ratio p_{n0}/p_{n1} also rises), the extent of the temporal substitution within the current period exceeds the corresponding substitution within the future period. As a result the ratio of current to future consumption of tradable goods rises. This is reflected by the positive term $\beta_n\sigma_{nx}$ in equation (A.23). The same rise in the intertemporal price ratio p_{n0}/p_{n1} raises the (consumption-based) real interest rate (and lowers the corresponding real discount factor, α_{c1}). This rise in the real interest rate induces substitution of spending *between* periods: from the present to the future period. The magnitude of this intertemporal substitution is indicated by the negative term $-\beta_n\sigma$ in equation (A.23). Finally, we note that the change in the intertemporal consumption ratio does not depend on private wealth. This reflects the homotheticity assumption, which implies that the tax-induced fall in wealth lowers current and future demand for tradable goods by the same proportion.

To determine the elasticity of tradable-goods consumption with respect to the discount factor we substitute equations (A.18) and (A.19) into (A.21) and (A.22), and obtain

$$\hat{c}_{x0} = \gamma_s \left[\frac{\sigma_{nx}\sigma}{\beta_n\sigma + (1 - \beta_n)\sigma_{nx}} + \frac{\mu_1 - 1}{1 - \beta_{nx}} \right] \hat{\alpha}_{x1} \qquad (A.24)$$

and

$$\hat{c}_{x1} = \left[\frac{-(1 - \gamma_s)\sigma_{nx}\sigma}{\beta_n\sigma + (1 - \beta_n)\sigma_{nx}} + \frac{\gamma_s(\mu_1 - 1)}{1 - \beta_n} \right] \hat{\alpha}_{x1}. \qquad (A.25)$$

Subtracting (A.25) from (A.24) yields equation (A.26), which is equation (8.25) of the text:

$$\frac{d \log(c_{x0}/c_{x1})}{d \log \alpha_{x1}} = \frac{\sigma_{nx}\sigma}{\beta_n\sigma + (1 - \beta_n)\sigma_{nx}}. \qquad (A.26)$$

Finally, combining equations (8.32) and (A.23) yields equation (8.29) of the text.

9

Budget Deficits with Nondistortionary Taxes: The Pure Wealth Effect

In this chapter we develop an analytical framework for the analysis of the effects of budget deficits in an undistorted economy. In such a framework, it is the induced wealth effects that constitute the primary mechanism by which budget deficits influence the economy. This mechanism supplements the one outlined later (in chapter 11) where we allowed for distortionary taxes. With such taxes budget deficits influence the economy through temporal and intertemporal substitution effects induced by the distortions.

To conduct a meaningful analysis of budget deficits in the absence of distortions, our analytical framework departs from the pure Ricardian model in which the timing of taxes and government debt issue plays no role as long as the path of government spending is given. We depart from that model by allowing for differences between the time horizons relevant for individual decision making and for the society at large. These differences result in discrepancies between the private and public sectors' costs of borrowing, which in turn implies that the equilibrium is no longer invariant with respect to the timing of taxes. The specification that we use to yield differences between the horizons relevant for the individual and the society relies on the assumption that individuals have finite life. In contrast, the society at large has an infinite horizon due to the continuous entry of newly born generations.

A significant portion of this chapter is devoted to the development of the analytical framework underlying the overlapping-generations model. In this context we specify in detail the procedure by which the individual behavioral functions are aggregated into the corresponding aggregate behavioral functions. This procedure constitutes a key building block which is used in the next chapter.

Following the development of the model, we devote the remainder of this chapter to the analysis of the effects of budget deficits on aggregate consumption and debt accumulation in an economy facing given world rates of interest. The wealth effects induced by budget deficits stem from differences between the effective interest rates that individuals use in discounting future taxes and the corresponding market interest rates that govern public sector behavior.

9.1   The Aggregate Consumption Function

We start with a specification of the individual decision problem and derive the individual consumption function. The dynamic character of the overlapping-generations society necessitates great care in the specification of the aggregate behavior. Accordingly, we discuss in detail the procedures underlying the aggregation of the individual consumption functions into the aggregate private-sector consumption function.

Let $c_{a,t}$ denote the level of consumption in period t of an individual of age a, and suppose that the utility function of this individual in period t is

$$U = \frac{1}{1-\theta} \sum_{v=0}^{\infty} \delta^v c_{a+v,t+v}^{1-\theta}, \tag{9.1}$$

where δ denotes the subjective discount factor and θ is the reciprocal of the intertemporal elasticity of substitution, σ (thus $\theta = 1/\sigma$). Assume that the individual maximizes *expected utility*, which is computed on the basis of his or her probability of survival. We denote the probability that an individual survives from one period to the next by γ, which, in order to facilitate the aggregation, is assumed to be independent of the individual's age. Thus the probability that an individual survives the next v periods is γ^v. Accordingly, the probability as of period t that an individual of age a will be alive in period

$t + v$ and enjoy the utility level $[1/(1 - \theta)]c_{a+v,t+v}^{1-\theta}$ is γ^v. Therefore, using equation (9.1), the expected utility can be written as

$$\frac{1}{1 - \theta} E_t \sum_{v=0}^{\infty} \delta^v c_{a+v,t+v}^{1-\theta} = \frac{1}{1 - \theta} \sum_{v=0}^{\infty} (\gamma\delta)^v c_{a+v,t+v}^{1-\theta}. \tag{9.2}$$

Equation (9.2) is the *certainty equivalent* utility function with an effective discount factor that is equal to $\gamma\delta$. Thus, by reducing the effective discount factor, the probability of death raises the effective subjective discount rate and (in and of itself) tilts consumption toward the present period.

We assume that because of uncertain lifetime, all loans require in addition to regular interest payments a purchase of life insurance. In case of death, the estate is transferred to the life insurance company which, in turn, guarantees to cover outstanding debts. It is assumed that there is a large number of individuals in each cohort so that the frequency of those who survive equals the survival probability, γ. Furthermore we assume that there is competition among insurance companies. Under such circumstances the zero-profit condition ensures that the percentage insurance premium equals the probability of death, $1 - \gamma$. To verify this relation, consider a given population composed of many individuals who, in the aggregate, borrow one dollar. The insurance company's income associated with this loan transaction is the percentage premium, π, which, if invested at the market rate of interest, r, yields at the end of the period $\pi(1 + r)$. On the other hand, since a fraction $(1 - \gamma)$ of this population does not survive, the commitment to cover the outstanding debts costs the company $(1 - \gamma)(1 + r)$ dollars. The zero-profit condition guarantees that $\pi = 1 - \gamma$. An alternative institutional arrangement to the requirement that each loan is associated with a purchase of life insurance is a direct surcharge imposed on the loan. Under such an arrangement it is assumed that in case of death the lender has no claim on the outstanding debt. In this case, in order to secure a safe return, $1 + r$, on a given one-dollar loan, the competitive lender charges $(1 + r)/\gamma$ dollars. Since the fraction of the borrowers who survive to repay the loan is γ, the safe return is $\gamma[(1 + r)/\gamma] = 1 + r$.

Thus the *effective* cost of borrowing relevant for individual decision making is $(1 + r)/\gamma$.

Consider an individual who is of age a in period zero. His periodic budget constraints are

$$c_{a,0} = y_0 + b_{a,0} - \left(\frac{1 + r_{-1}}{\gamma}\right) b_{a-1,-1},$$

$$c_{a+1,1} = y_1 + b_{a+1,1} - \left(\frac{1 + r_0}{\gamma}\right) b_{a,0}, \tag{9.3}$$

$$c_{a+2,2} = y_2 + b_{a+2,2} - \left(\frac{1 + r_1}{\gamma}\right) b_{a+1,1}, \quad \text{etc.,}$$

where the budget constraint applicable to period t is

$$c_{a+t,t} = y_t + b_{a+t,t} - \frac{1 + r_{t-1}}{\gamma} b_{a+t-1,t-1} \tag{9.3a}$$

and where y_v and $b_{a+v,v}$ are the individual's disposable income and new (one-period) borrowing in period v ($v = 0, 1, \ldots$). The formulation in (9.3) also presumes that disposable income is the same across all individuals regardless of age. This assumption is made to facilitate the aggregation.

Following procedures similar to those in previous chapters, the periodic budget constraints can be consolidated into a single present-value lifetime constraint. For this purpose we define a present-value factor. The present-value factor, whose inverse is composed of one-period rates of interest compounded from period zero up to period $t - 1$, is denoted by α_t, and therefore the ratio α_t/α_{t+1} is the *market* discount factor, which is equal to one plus the market rate of interest in period t (i.e., $1 + r_t$). Accordingly, $\alpha_0 = 1$. Analogously, the market risk rate is $\gamma^t/\gamma^{t+1} = 1/\gamma$. It follows that the *effective* interest factor faced by individuals is $\alpha_t/\gamma\alpha_{t+1}$, and correspondingly the effective interest rate is $[(1 + r_t)/\gamma] - 1$.

Using this notation, the consolidated present-value constraint is

$$\sum_{v=0}^{\infty} \gamma^v \alpha_v c_{a+v,v} = \sum_{v=0}^{\infty} \gamma^v \alpha_v y_v - \frac{1 + r_{-1}}{\gamma} b_{a-1,-1} = w_{a,0}, \tag{9.4}$$

where $w_{a,0}$ is the wealth of an individual of age a at period zero. Finally, in deriving equation (9.4), we have made use of the solvency requirement that in the limit, as v approaches infinity, the present value of debt commitment is zero. That is,

$$\lim_{v \to \infty} \gamma^v \alpha_v b_{a+v,v} = 0. \tag{9.5}$$

As seen from the consolidated budget constraint in equation (9.4), the individual's wealth is composed of two components. The first, which is the discounted sum of income, is referred to as *human* wealth, and the second, which is the interest plus principal payments on past debt (which may be positive or negative), is referred to as *financial* (nonhuman) wealth. The key characteristic of human wealth is that it is attached to a specific individual. As a result the individual's human wealth disappears from the system once the individual is not alive.

The individual's problem is to maximize the expected utility, given by equation (9.2), subject to the budget constraint (9.4). Formally, the maximization problem can be written

$$\max_{\{c_{a+v,v}\}} \frac{1}{1-\theta} \sum_{v=0}^{\infty} (\gamma\delta)^v c_{a+v,v}^{1-\theta} + \lambda \left(w_{a,0} - \sum_{v=0}^{\infty} \gamma^v \alpha_v c_{a+v,v} \right), \tag{9.6}$$

where λ denotes the Lagrange multiplier associated with the budget constraint. The first-order condition of maximization implies that

$$(\gamma\delta)^v c_{a+v,v}^{-\theta} - \lambda(\gamma^v \alpha_v) = 0 \qquad \text{for } v = 0, 1, \ldots. \tag{9.7}$$

Equation (9.7) shows that the finiteness of life, reflected by γ, influences both the subjective and the market-effective present-value factors, $(\gamma\delta)^v$ and $\gamma^v \alpha_v$, in the *same* manner. It follows therefore that the marginal rates of substitution between the levels of consumption in two consecutive periods equal the *market* (risk-free) discount factor, $1/(1 + r)$, independent of γ. In other words, even though there is a discrepancy between the effective (risk-adjusted) rates of interest applicable to the individual choice and the market (risk-free) rate of interest applicable to the society at large, this discrepancy does not distort the intertemporal allocations of consumption. This property ensures that in the absence of other distortions, the equilibrium obtained is Pareto efficient. In the subsequent discussion we assume that taxes are nondistortionary. As a result the mechanism through which budget deficits influence the real equilibrium does not operate through the distortion effects analyzed in chapter 11. We will return to these issues later on.

Using the budget constraint (9.4) and substituting the solution for $c_{a+v,v}$ from (9.7), we have $w_{a,0} = \sum_{v=0}^{\infty} \gamma^v \alpha_v c_{a+v,v} = \lambda^{-\sigma} \sum_{v=0}^{\infty} \gamma^v \alpha_v (\delta^v/\alpha_v)^\sigma$. In this case we recall that the elasticity of substitution, σ, is equal to $1/\theta$. Accordingly, the solution for the value of the marginal utility of wealth is

$$\lambda = [(1 - s_0)w_{a,0}]^{-1/\sigma}, \tag{9.8}$$

and the consumption function is

$$c_{a+t,t} = (1 - s_0)\left(\frac{\delta^t}{\alpha_t}\right)^\sigma w_{a,0} \qquad \text{for } t = 0, 1, \ldots, \tag{9.9}$$

where

$$1 - s_0 = \left\{\sum_{v=0}^{\infty} (\gamma^v \alpha_v)^{1-\sigma}[(\gamma\delta)^v]^\sigma\right\}^{-1}.$$

In equation (9.9) the term $1 - s_0$ denotes the marginal propensity to consume out of wealth in period zero. Thus for $t = 0$, $c_{a,0} = (1 - s_0)w_{a,0}$. It is seen that the propensity to consume depends, in general, on the *entire path* of effective rates of interest (indicated by the effective present-value factor $\gamma^v \alpha_v$) and on the effective present-value factor $(\gamma\delta)^v$. In the special case for which the utility function is logarithmic, the elasticity of substitution is unity, and the marginal propensity to spend depends only on the effective subjective discount factor, $\gamma\delta$, and not on the path of the effective rates of interest. In that case $1 - s_0 = 1 - \gamma\delta$. This special case may be viewed as intermediate between two extreme cases. In one extreme case the elasticity of substitution is zero, and in the other extreme case the elasticity of substitution is infinite. With no substitution, the marginal propensity to spend depends only on the effective present-value factor $\gamma^v \alpha_v$. In that case consumption is fixed over time (so that the consumption smoothing motive is absolute), and using the budget constraint, the marginal propensity to spend is $1/\sum_{v=0}^{\infty} \gamma^v \alpha_v$. In the other extreme case, with perfect substitution, the marginal propensity to spend is zero if δ^v exceeds α_v, and it is unity if δ^v falls short of α_v. In the general case, as seen from equation (9.9), the spending propensity falls with the rate of interest if the elasticity of substitution exceeds unity, and vice versa if the elasticity of substitution is smaller than unity.

The saving propensity, s_0, is the key parameter linking the value of wealth in period zero with the value of wealth in period one. Analogous to the definition of period-zero wealth of an individual who is of age a at period zero, $w_{a,0}$ (equation 9.4), the value of wealth in period one of the same individual, $w_{a+1,1}$, is defined as

$$w_{a+1,1} = \sum_{v=1}^{\infty} \gamma^{v-1}(1 + r_0)\alpha_v y_v - \frac{1 + r_0}{\gamma} b_{a,0}. \tag{9.10}$$

Using the fact that consumption in period zero is proportional to period zero wealth (with $1 - s_0$ being the proportionality factor), it follows from the definitions of $w_{a,0}$ and $w_{a+1,1}$, and from the budget constraint applicable to period zero (equation 9.3), that

$$w_{a+1,1} = \frac{1 + r_0}{\gamma} s_0 w_{a,0}. \tag{9.11}$$

Equation (9.11) shows that if the individual survives from period zero to period one, then his wealth equals the fraction of wealth not consumed in period zero, $s_0 w_{a,0}$ adjusted by the *effective* rate of interest.

Thus far we have specified the utility-maximizing saving propensity for period zero, s_0, as derived from period-zero maximization problem (9.6). A similar maximization problem can be formulated for an individual of age a in period t. With this formulation the resultant utility-maximizing consumption function for period t, $c_{a,t}$, is

$$c_{a,t} = (1 - s_t)w_{a,t}, \tag{9.12}$$

where

$$1 - s_t = \left\{ \sum_{v=t}^{\infty} \left(\gamma^{v-t} \frac{\alpha_v}{\alpha_t} \right)^{1-\sigma} [(\gamma\delta)^{v-t}]^{\sigma} \right\}^{-1},$$

$$w_{a,t} = \sum_{v=1}^{\infty} \gamma^{v-t} \frac{\alpha_v}{\alpha_t} y_t - \frac{1 + r_{-1}}{\gamma} b_{a-1,t-1}.$$

The spending propensity $1 - s_t$ is the generalization of the expression for period-zero propensity, $1 - s_0$, in equation (9.9), and as is evident, it depends on the entire path of the rates of interest. In general, if the rates of interest vary over time, the saving propensity s_t is not constant, except for the special case in which the elasticity of substitution, σ, is unity. In that case the spending propensity is a constant (equal to $1 - \gamma\delta$). Independent, however, of whether the elasticity of substitution equals to or differs from unity, the spending propensity does not depend on the *age* of the individual. This property (which reflects the assumption that the probability of survival does not depend on age) permits a simple aggregation of the *individual* consumption functions into the *aggregate* consumption function.

We now turn to the derivation of the *aggregate* consumption function. Population is normalized so that at birth every cohort consists of one individual who is assumed to be born without debt. Due to death the size of each cohort of age a becomes γ^a. The equality between the probability of survival of a given cohort and its frequency relative to its initial size stems from the law of large numbers. Since at each period there are γ^a members of a cohort of age a, the (constant) aggregate size of population is

$$\sum_{a=0}^{\infty} \gamma^a = \frac{1}{1 - \gamma}.$$

Aggregate consumption in period t is the sum of consumption of individuals from all cohorts. Since consumption of a cohort of age a is $\gamma^a c_{a,t}$, per-capita aggregate consumption, C_t, is

$$C_t = (1 - \gamma) \sum_{a=0}^{\infty} \gamma^a c_{a,t}. \tag{9.13}$$

Disposable income, y_t, is assumed to be the same across all individuals regardless of age. Therefore the per-capita value of aggregate income, Y_t, is equal to the individual disposable income, y_t. In what follows Y_t is referred to as per-capita income. The per-capita aggregate consumption function (9.13) together with the individual consumption function and the definition of wealth from equation (9.12) yields

$$C_t = (1 - s_t)W_t, \tag{9.14}$$

where

$$W_t = H_t - (1 + r_{-1})B^p_{t-1},$$

$$H_t = (1 - \gamma) \sum_{a=0}^{\infty} \gamma^a \sum_{v=t}^{\infty} \gamma^{v-t} \frac{\alpha_v}{\alpha_t} y_v = \sum_{v=t}^{\infty} \gamma^{v-t} \frac{\alpha_v}{\alpha_t} y_v,$$

$$B^p_{t-1} = (1 - \gamma) \sum_{a=0}^{\infty} \gamma^{a-1} b_{a-1,t-1}.$$

Equation (9.14) is the per-capita *aggregate* consumption function in which W_t, H_t, and B^p_{t-1} denote, respectively, the per-capita values of aggregate total wealth, aggregate human wealth, and aggregate private sector indebtedness. The per-capita value of aggregate human wealth is defined as the discounted sum of per-capita income computed by using the effective (risk-adjusted) rates of interest. As formulated in equation (9.14), the per-capita value of total aggregate wealth in period t, W_t, equals the value of human wealth in that period net of interest and principal payments on past private-sector per-capita debt. As is evident, the rate of interest applicable to the (per-capita value of) aggregate private-sector debt is the (risk-free) market rate of interest. This should be contrasted with the formulation of the *individual* wealth in equation (9.14) in which the rate of interest applicable to the computation of individual debt service is the (risk-adjusted) effective rate. We also note that as indicated earlier, the invariance of the individual spending propensity with respect to age is reflected in the equality between the individual and the aggregate spending propensities in equations (9.12) and (9.14).

Finally, the specification in equation (9.14) defines the per-capita magnitudes of aggregate consumption and wealth. Obviously, as long as the demographic parameter, γ, is given, the size of the population is constant, and therefore the distribution between per-capita and aggregate quantities is inconsequential. In the limit, as γ approaches unity, the magnitude of the aggregate quantities (e.g., population, consumption, and wealth) is boundless, but the per-capita quantities are well defined according to equation (9.14).

9.2   Aggregate Wealth and Its Composition

The analysis of per-capita aggregate consumption specified the behavior of the economy at a point in time as a function of per-capita aggregate wealth. In order to characterize the behavior of the economy over time so as to be able to deal with the dynamic effects of fiscal policies, we need to determine the evolution of per-capita aggregate wealth through time. Since, as will be shown later, the two components of wealth (human and nonhuman wealth) are governed by different laws of motion, we need to study them separately. Throughout, we analyze the evolution of the per-capita aggregate quantities, but, for short, we omit in what follows an explicit mention of the term "per capita." We start with an analysis of the dynamics of human wealth. Lagging the expression for H_t from equation (9.14) by one period yields an analogous expression for H_{t-1} which, together with equation (9.14), yields

$$H_t = \frac{1 + r_{t-1}}{\gamma}(H_{t-1} - Y_{t-1}). \tag{9.15}$$

Equation (9.15) describes the evolution of aggregate human wealth as a function of the difference between its own lagged value and the lagged value of aggregate income Y_{t-1}. It is important to note that both the definition of aggregate human wealth and its law of motion employ the *effective* rates of interest that include the life insurance premium associated with the probability of death. This feature is specific to the human wealth component and does not play a role in the computation of the other component of wealth to which we turn next.

The evolution of aggregate private debt, B_t^p, can be obtained by aggregating equation (9.3a) across individuals. Accordingly,

$$B_t^p = C_t - Y_t + (1 + r_{t-1})B_{t-1}^p. \tag{9.16}$$

In contrast with the law of motion governing the accumulation of human wealth (in equation 9.15) and *individual* debt (in equation 9.3a), the accumulation of *aggregate* private debt is governed by the *market* rate of interest $(1 + r_{-1})$ rather than the *effective* rate of interest $(1 + r_{t-1})/\gamma$. The absence of the life-insurance premium from the law of motion governing aggregate debt accumulation in equation (9.16) stems from the fact that from the perspective of the society at large, the life-insurance premia represent transfers within the society that do not alter the social rates of return.

Having determined the evolution of the human and financial components of wealth, we can now combine the two in order to characterize the evolution of aggregate wealth. Substituting equations (9.15) and (9.16) into the definition of wealth in equation (9.14), and using the consumption function $C_{t-1} = (1 - s_{t-1})W_{t-1}$, we obtain

$$W_t = (1 + r_{t-1})s_{t-1}W_{t-1} + (1 - \gamma)H_t. \tag{9.17}$$

Equation (9.17) expresses the value of wealth in period t in terms of its value in period $t - 1$ and in terms of its human wealth component. The dependence of the path of aggregate wealth on its composition reflects the asymmetry between human and nonhuman wealth. This asymmetry, which arises from the uncertainty concerning the length of life, disappears if the probability of survival is unity. Thus, with $\gamma = 1$, the value of wealth becomes

$$W_t = (1 + r_{t-1})s_{t-1}W_{t-1}. \tag{9.18}$$

In this case the evolution of wealth depends on its *aggregate* value and not on its *composition*.

As indicated by the aggregate consumption function, for any given path of the rate of interest, the evolution of aggregate consumption depends exclusively on the evolution of aggregate wealth. Thus we can use equations (9.14) and (9.17) in order to characterize the evolution of aggregate consumption. Accordingly, the dependence of current consumption on the lagged value thereof is characterized by

$$C_t = s_{t-1}(1 + r_{t-1})\frac{1 - s_t}{1 - s_{t-1}}C_{t-1} + (1 - \gamma)(1 - s_t)H_t. \qquad (9.19)$$

Thus, analogously to the characteristics of the evolution of aggregate wealth, aggregate consumption in period t depends on its lagged value as well as on the composition of wealth. In the special case for which $\gamma = 1$, equation (9.19) reduces to

$$C_t = \left[s_{t-1}(1 + r_{t-1})\frac{1 - s_t}{1 - s_{t-1}} \right] C_{t-1}. \qquad (9.19a)$$

In that case (for a given path of the rates of interest) aggregate consumption in period t depends only on its lagged value. The comparison between (9.19) and (9.19a) reveals the role that the finiteness of the individual's horizon plays in determining the dynamics of aggregate consumption. As seen in (9.19a), given the rates of interest, the only variable relevant for predicting future consumption is current consumption. In particular, once current consumption is known, knowledge of wealth is not required for the prediction of future consumption. In the general case, however, as indicated by equation (9.19), once $\gamma < 1$, knowledge of current consumption is not sufficient for the prediction of future consumption, and one needs to know the detailed path of the composition of wealth. In the appendix we modify assumptions underlying equation (9.19) and obtain an empirically estimable form. In the next section we analyze in greater detail the factors governing aggregate consumption. This analysis will then be used in interpreting the effects of fiscal policies.

9.3   Dynamics of Aggregate Consumption

To facilitate the exposition, we assume in this section that the world rate of interest faced by the small economy is stationary so that $r_t = r$. In this case the saving propensity defined in equation (9.12) is constant, and can be written as

$$s = \left(\frac{\gamma}{R}\right)^{1-\sigma}(\gamma\delta)^{\sigma} = \gamma\delta^{\sigma}R^{\sigma-1}, \tag{9.20}$$

where $R = 1 + r$. As is evident, the saving propensity is a function of the effective cost of borrowing, R/γ, and the effective subjective discount factor, $\gamma\delta$; the weights of these two factors are $1 - \sigma$ and σ, respectively. In the special case in which the intertemporal elasticity of substitution is unity, the saving propensity equals $\gamma\delta$; in that case the saving propensity is independent of the cost of borrowing.

To determine the dynamics of consumption, we need to characterize the dynamics of wealth. For expositional simplicity suppose that the path of future disposable incomes is stationary so that $Y_t = Y$ for $t > 0$. In that case current and future human capital can be written with the aid of equation (9.14) as

$$H_0 = Y_0 + \frac{\gamma}{R - \gamma}Y,$$

$$\tag{9.21}$$

$$H_t = \frac{R}{R - \gamma}Y \qquad \text{for } t > 0.$$

Accordingly, using equations (9.14), (9.19), and (9.21), we obtain the levels of current and future consumption

$$C_0 = (1 - s)\left[\left(Y_0 + \frac{\gamma}{R - \gamma}Y\right) - RB_{t-1}^p\right],$$

$$\tag{9.22}$$

$$C_t = RsC_{t-1} + (1 - \gamma)(1 - s)\frac{R}{R - \gamma}Y \qquad \text{for } t > 0.$$

The equations in (9.22) characterize the evolution of consumption through time. These consumption dynamics are illustrated in figure

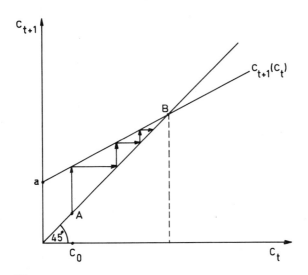

Figure 9.1
Consumption dynamics in the overlapping-generations model: The stable case

9.1. The schedule $C_{t+1}(C_t)$ plots the values of C_{t+1} as a function of C_t. The equation of this schedule is shown in (9.22). As seen, the slope of the schedule is Rs, and the case drawn in figure 9.1 corresponds to the situation in which $Rs < 1$. In this case the system converges to a steady state with positive consumption. Accordingly, if the initial equilibrium is associated with consumption level C_0 (shown by point A in figure 9.1), the long-run equilibrium is associated with a steady-state level of consumption C (shown by point B in figure 9.1). The arrows in the figure indicate the path along which the level of consumption evolves through time.

To clarify the role played by the finiteness of the horizon, we note that the intercept of the $C_{t+1}(C_t)$ schedule (indicated by point a) depends on the value of γ. Specifically, with infinite lifetime, $\gamma = 1$ and $a = 0$. In that case the $C_{t+1}(C_t)$ schedule emerges from the origin, and the system does not converge to a long-run steady state with positive consumption. The saving propensity is $\delta^\sigma R^{\sigma-1}$, and the slope of the consumption schedule is $(R\delta)^\sigma$. Thus, if $R\delta$ exceeds unity, consumption grows without a bound, and if $R\delta$ falls short of unity, consumption shrinks to zero. It follows that in order to allow for the possibility of a steady-state equilibrium with positive levels of consumption, the model must allow for a finite horizon.

The steady-state trade-balance surplus depends on the discrepancy between output, Y, and consumption C. Using (9.22), the steady-state level of consumption is

$$C = \left(\frac{1-\gamma}{R-\gamma}\right)\left(\frac{1-s}{1-Rs}\right)RY. \tag{9.23}$$

Using this equation along with equation (9.20), the steady-state trade-balance surplus is

$$Y - C = \frac{\gamma(R-1)Y}{(R-\gamma)(1-Rs)}[1 - (R\delta)^\sigma].$$

It can be seen that the economy runs a steady-state trade-balance surplus if $R\delta < 1$. This surplus is necessary in order to service the debt accumulated during the transition toward the steady state during which (on average) the economy consumed in excess of its GDP. On the other hand, if $R\delta$ exceeds unity, then the transition toward the steady state is characterized by trade-balance surpluses as the economy produces (on average) in excess of its consumption. In that case the economy reaches the steady state as a net creditor. As a result its steady-state level of consumption exceeds its GDP, and the steady-state trade balance is in deficit.

The foregoing analysis presumed that Rs is smaller than unity so that the economy converges to a long-run equilibrium with a positive level of consumption. To complete the analysis, we show in figure 9.2 the case in which Rs exceeds unity. In that case consecutive increments to the levels of consumption rise over time, and as a result consumption increases without a bound.

The level of consumption can be solved (by forward iteration of equation 9.22) to yield

$$C_t = (Rs)^t(C_0 - C) + C, \tag{9.24}$$

where C_0 and C are defined in equations (9.22) and (9.23). As seen, if $Rs < 1$, the first term in equation (9.24) approaches zero with the

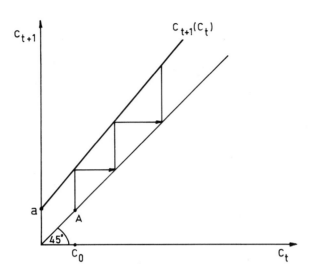

Figure 9.2
Consumption dynamics in the overlapping-generations model: The unstable case

passage of time, and consumption converges to its steady-state level C. On the other hand, if $Rs > 1$, the level of consumption grows over time without bound since in that case (as indicated by equations 9.22 and 9.23) $C_0 - C$ must be positive.

The foregoing analysis of the dynamics of consumption will prove useful in the subsequent section where we analyze the effects of budget deficits.

9.4   Wealth Effects of Budget Deficits

In this section we use the analytical framework of the small open economy for the analysis of the effects of a budget deficit arising from a current cut in lump-sum taxes. In order to focus on the essentials underlying aggregate saving and current-account adjustments, we abstract from capital accumulation and from multiple goods. We continue to assume that government spending is financed by taxes or by debt issue. Accordingly, the government budget constraint for period t is

$$G_t = T_t + B_t^g - (1 + r_{t-1})B_{t-1}^g, \tag{9.25}$$

where G_t, T_t, and B_t^g denote, respectively, the per-capita values of government spending, lump-sum taxes, and new government borrowing in period t. As is evident from equation (9.25), in analogy with the evolution of aggregate private debt in equation (9.26), the law of motion governing the accumulation of government debt depends on the *market* rate of interest.

Consolidating the temporal budget constraints (9.25) and imposing the requirement that over time government spending obeys the intertemporal solvency constraint implies that

$$\sum_{v=0}^{\infty} \alpha_v(T_v - G_v) = (1 + r_{t-1})B_{-1}^g. \tag{9.26}$$

Equation (9.26) states that the value of government debt commitment (interest plus principal payments) at the beginning of period zero must equal the discounted sum of current and future budget surpluses.

Prior to analyzing the effects of current budget deficits, we note for future use that the sum of private debt, B^p, and government debt, B^g, equals the value of the economy's external debt, B. Hence, using equations (9.16) and (9.25), the evolution of the external debt is governed by the current-account position according to

$$B_t - B_{t-1} = (C_t + G_t - Y_t) + r_{t-1}B_{t-1}. \tag{9.27}$$

To examine the role of government budget deficits, suppose that the government changes the time pattern of taxes and debt issue while holding the path of spending unchanged. Specifically, consider the situation in which taxes are reduced in period j but are raised in a more distant period u so as to satisfy the government intertemporal solvency constraint. To find the effects of the change in the time profile of taxes on the level of current (period-zero) consumption and thereby on the trade balance, we need to determine the change in current wealth, W_0. Since the only component of wealth affected by the tax policy is the current value of human wealth, H_0, it is sufficient to determine the effect of the change in the timing of taxes on current human wealth. Using equation (9.14), current human wealth is

$$H_0 = \sum_{v=0}^{\infty} \gamma^v \alpha_v (Y_v - T_v), \tag{9.28}$$

and the change in current value of human wealth is

$$dH_0 = -(\gamma^j \alpha_j dT_j + \gamma^u \alpha_u dT_u). \tag{9.29}$$

From the government solvency requirement (9.26) we note that

$$dT_u = \frac{\alpha_j}{\alpha_u} dT_j, \tag{9.30}$$

and therefore the change in current human wealth is

$$dH_0 = -(1 - \gamma^{u-j})\gamma^j \alpha_j dT_j. \tag{9.31}$$

Equation (9.31) shows that a tax cut in period j (in the more distant period, u, followed by a corresponding tax rise, $dT_j < 0$ and $u > j$) raises the current value of human wealth. This positive wealth effect is stronger, the longer the period of time elapsing between the tax cut and the corresponding tax hike. The key factor responsible for the positive wealth effect induced by the tax policy is the finiteness of the individual horizon. At the limit, as γ approaches unity, the wealth effects disappear. In that case the Ricardian proposition re-emerges, and once the path of government spending is given, the time pattern of taxes and government debt issue is irrelevant.

The foregoing analysis demonstrated that both a current budget deficit or an anticipated future deficit must raise current period wealth as long as it is financed by a subsequent rise in taxes. The rise in wealth stimulates current period consumption and worsens the trade balance.

The explanation for this result can be given as follows: If the probability of survival, γ, is unity, then the rise in future taxes (which is equal in present value to the reduction in current taxes) leaves wealth unchanged. On the other hand, the same change in the pattern of taxes raises wealth if each individual knows that there is a positive probability that he or she will not survive to pay these higher future taxes. Under such circumstances the current reduction in taxes constitutes net wealth. Equivalently, the explanation can be stated in terms of the difference between the market and the effective interest factors. For example, in the case of a current tax cut the government solvency requirement implies that changes in current taxes must be made up for by α_u times the offsetting change in future taxes. On the other hand, individuals discount these future taxes by $\gamma^u \alpha_u$. Therefore, as long as $\gamma < 1$, the current budget deficit raises human wealth. Yet another interpretation may be given in terms of a transfer-problem criterion familiar from the theory of international transfers. Accordingly, the budget deficit exerts real effects because it redistributes wealth from those who have not yet been born, and whose marginal propensity to consume current goods is obviously zero, to those who are currently alive and whose marginal propensity to consume current goods is positive. As a result the budget deficit raises private-sector spending.

The foregoing analysis showed that a change in the time profile of taxes in favor of the present generation raises current consumption and worsens the balance of trade. To characterize the dynamic effects of the tax policy, we use the formulation of section 9.3 and examine the dynamic effects of a current tax cut which is accompanied by a permanent rise in future taxes. Using equation (9.30), the implied changes in current and future disposable incomes are

$$d(Y_0 - T_0) = -\frac{1}{R-1} d(Y - T). \tag{9.32}$$

With such changes in the time profile of disposable income, the change in current consumption (obtained from equation 9.22) is

$$\frac{dC_0}{dT_0} = -\frac{(1-\gamma)(1-s)R}{R-\gamma}. \tag{9.33}$$

Similarly, if the steady state exists (i.e., if $Rs < 1$), then the change in the steady-state level of consumption (obtained from equation

9.23) is

$$\frac{dC}{dT_0} = (R - 1)\frac{(1 - \gamma)(1 - s)R}{(R - \gamma)(1 - Rs)}. \tag{9.34}$$

As is evident from inspection of (9.33) and (9.34), the current budget deficit raises current consumption, C_0, and lowers the long-run level of consumption, C.

The changes in current and future consumption can be illustrated in terms of figure 9.1. Accordingly, a unit rise in current disposable income resulting from a tax cut induces a downward displacement of the $C_{t+1}(C_t)$ schedule by the magnitude $(R - 1)(1 - \gamma)(1 - s)R/(R - \gamma)$. As seen in figure 9.1, such a displacement lowers the long-run level of consumption and displaces the long-run equilibrium point B leftward along the 45° line. In addition, by raising current consumption, the budget deficit displaces the initial equilibrium point, A, rightward along the 45° line. The fall in long-run consumption is necessary in order to finance the larger steady-state debt service resulting from the tilting of the path of consumption in favor of the current generation.

The precise effect of the budget deficit on the level of consumption in any period, t, is obtained from equation (9.24) along with equations (9.33) and (9.34). Accordingly,

$$\frac{dC_t}{dT_0} = -\frac{(1 - \gamma)(1 - s)R}{(R - \gamma)(1 - Rs)}[R(1 - s)(Rs)^t - (R - 1)]. \tag{9.35}$$

As is evident, the current budget deficit raises the levels of consumption in periods that are close to the present, but it lowers the levels of consumption in periods that are more distant from the present. It can be shown from equation (9.35) that the period $\bar{t}$, in which the level of consumption following the tax policy equals the level obtained in the absence of such policy, is

$$\bar{t} = \frac{\log[(R - 1)/(1 - s)R]}{\log Rs}. \tag{9.36}$$

Equation (9.36) shows that a higher saving propensity (induced by a higher value of γ or δ) lowers the length of time during which the level of consumption exceeds the level obtained in the absence of the tax policy. Finally, we note that in the periods immediately following the tax cut, the level of consumption exceeds the level obtained in the absence of such policy, even through disposable income is lower. This consumption pattern reflects the consumption-smoothing motive of the members of the generation enjoying the rise in wealth consequent on the tax cut. Mortality reduces the size of this generation, and birth of new generations implies that the weight in aggregate consumption of the generation benefiting from the tax cut falls over time. Hence aggregate consumption is increasingly dominated by the reduced wealth of the future generations' incurring the rise in taxes, and eventually, after period $\bar{t}$, aggregate consumption falls below the level obtained prior to the tax policy.

9.5 Summary

In this chapter we developed an analytical framework suitable for the analysis of the effects of budget deficits in an undistorted economy. In that framework the principal mechanism through which tax policy influences economic behavior operates through the induced wealth effects. These wealth effects stem from the difference between the *effective* interest rate that individuals use in discounting future taxes and the corresponding *market* interest rates governing government behavior. In the present analysis the specific reason responsible for the difference between the two interest rates arises from differences between the time horizons relevant for private and public-sector decisions. This provides a rationale for our formulation in chapter 8 where we allowed for differences between the private and the public sectors' rates of interest. It is relevant to note that in contrast with the formulation in chapter 11, in which the difference between the intertemporal terms of trade governing the private and the public sectors arises from distortionary taxes, here the interest differential neither reflects nor results in a distortion.

To gain an intuitive feel into the quantitative implications of the finiteness of the horizon, it is instructive to examine the effects of a

Table 9.1
Current-consumption multiplier for alternative length of current tax-cut periods

Length of current tax-cut period	Life expectancy			
	∞ ($\gamma = 1$)	90 ($\gamma = 0.90$)	38 ($\gamma = 0.85$)	20 ($\gamma = 0.80$)
1	0	0.19	0.28	0.36
3	0	0.35	0.49	0.59
5	0	0.48	0.63	0.75
7	0	0.58	0.74	0.84

Note: The multipliers reported are equal to $(1 - \gamma\delta)[(R/(R - \gamma)](1 - \gamma^s)$, where s is one plus the length of the period for which the current tax cut is in effect. Life expectancy of the economic decision maker equals $\sum_{a=1}^{\infty} a\gamma^a = \gamma/(1 - \gamma)^2$. The computations assume that $R = 1.05$.

current tax cut on current consumption for alternative assumptions concerning the life expectancy of the economic decision maker. Consider a current period unit tax cut lasting for $s - 1$ periods and followed by a permanent rise in taxes that maintains the discounted sum of taxes. The rise in wealth induced by this tax-shift policy equals $[R/(R - \gamma)](1 - \gamma^s)$, and the change in current consumption equals the marginal propensity to consume $(1 - \gamma\delta)$ times this change in wealth. The resulting consumption multiplier is shown in table 9.1 for alternative values of life expectancy and of length of tax-cut period. As is evident, with immortality the multipliers are zero, and the Ricardian proposition emerges. On the other hand, with low life expectancy, for example, twenty years, the multipliers associated with tax cuts lasting one and three periods are, respectively, 0.36 and 0.59. The relatively low life expectancy would seem to correspond to economies in which the average age of the economic decision maker (being roughly the difference between life expectancies at birth and at that age) is relatively high.

An implicit assumption underlying the analytical framework is the absence of a bequest motive. Accordingly, each individual's utility function does not contain as arguments the levels of utility of the subsequent generations. Otherwise, individuals could be thought of as immortal through their offspring up to the indefinite future. In that case the Ricardian proposition reemerges, and budget deficits arising from changes in the time profile of taxes do not alter the real equilibrium. We could of course allow for a bequest motive as long as it does not extend into the indefinite future or, alternatively, as long as there is uncertainty about survival of each dynastic family. In that case the effective life expectancy of the dynastic family decision-making unit may be significantly longer than that of any given individual.

Finally, we note that a similar (nondistorting) mechanism by which budget deficits exert pure wealth effects on the existing generation could also be present under circumstances in which individuals are immortal or, equivalently, are endowed with a bequest motive linking them to their offspring up to the indefinite future. This would be the case if over time there is growth in the number of individuals and entry of new families. Under such circumstances the future tax base is broader, and the burden of the future tax hike associated with the current deficit falls in part on the new members of the society that do not enter into the bequest considerations of the existing families. With this mechanism, the growth-adjusted rates of interest of the society at large (i.e., of the government) is lower than the corresponding rates used by individuals and families.

In case of growth the interest differential depends on the growth rate in a manner similar to its dependence on the mortality rate in the case of finite horizons. In both cases the wealth effects induced by budget deficits are similar.

The analysis in this chapter illustrates the wealth effects induced by changes in the timing of taxes for a given path of the world rates of interest. In the next chapter we use this model to determine the effects of budget deficits on the world rates of interest. Such changes in the world rate of interest constitute the key mechanism for the international transmission of budget deficits in an undistorted world economy.

9.6 Appendix

In this appendix we modify three of the assumptions underlying the consumption equation (9.19) of the text. We allow for an uncertain income stream and for durable goods, and we replace the homothetic utility function by a quadratic function. These modifications yield on empirically estimable form of the consumption equation. Accordingly, the individual's objective function on the right-hand side of equation (9.2) of the text is replaced by

$$E_t = \sum_{v=0}^{\infty} (\gamma\delta)^v u(c_{a+v,t+v}),$$ (A.1)

where E_t is the conditional-expectation operator reflecting the uncertain income stream. With durable goods, we modify the periodic budget constraint (9.3a) of the text to become

$$c_{a+t,t} = (1 - \phi)c_{a+t-1,t-1} + x_{a+t,t},$$ (A.2a)

$$x_{a+t,t} = y_t + b_{a+t,t} - \frac{R}{\gamma}b_{a+t-1,t-1},$$ (A.2b)

where c denotes the *stock* of consumer goods, x denotes the *flow* of consumption purchases, ϕ denotes the rate of depreciation of the stock, and $R = 1 + r_{t-1}$ is assumed to be constant. The flow of income, y_t, is stochastic. Equations (A.2) and (A.2b) reduce to (9.3a) in the special case for which $\phi = 1$ and y_t is deterministic. The utility function is assumed to be quadratic:

$$u(c_{a+v,t+v}) = \alpha c_{a+v,t+v} - \frac{1}{2}c_{a+v,t+v}^2,$$ (A.3)

where $\alpha > 0$ and $c_{a+v,t+v} < \alpha$. This ensures that the marginal utility of consumption is positive and diminishing. To simplify the notation, we suppress in what follows the subscripts a and v; thus we replace $c_{a+v,t+v}$ by c_t, and so on.

The maximization problem can be expressed in dynamic programming terms by the value function v as

$$v\left(y_t - \frac{R}{\gamma}b_{t-1}\right) = \max_{x_t} \left\{ u[x_t + (1 - \phi)c_{t-1}]\right.$$

$$\left. + \gamma\delta E_t v\left[y_{t+1} + \frac{R}{\gamma}\left(y_t - x_t - \frac{R}{\gamma}b_{t-1}\right)\right]\right\}. \quad (A.4)$$

Differentiating the right-hand side of (A.4) and equating to zero yields

$$u'(c_t) - \delta RE_t v'(\cdot) = 0, \quad (A.5)$$

where the primes denote derivatives. Totally differentiating (A.4) yields

$$v'\left(y_t - \frac{R}{\gamma}b_{t-1}\right) = [u'(c_t) - \delta RE_t v'(\cdot)]\frac{dx_t}{dy_t} + \delta RE_t v'(\cdot),$$

$$= \delta RE_t v'(\cdot), \quad (A.6)$$

where use has been made of (A.5). Equations (A.5) and (A.6) imply that

$$u'(c_t) = \delta RE_t u'(c_{t+1}). \quad (A.7)$$

Using the specification in (A.3), we can express (A.7) as

$$\alpha - c_t = \delta RE_t(\alpha - c_{t+1}). \quad (A.8)$$

Expected human wealth is expressed as

$$E_t h_t = E_t \sum_{v=0}^{\infty} \left(\frac{\gamma}{R}\right)^v y_{t+v}. \quad (A.9)$$

From equation (A.9) we obtain

$$y_t = E_t h_t - \frac{\gamma}{R}E_t h_{t+1}. \quad (A.10)$$

For the purpose at hand, it is convenient to define expected (durability-adjusted) wealth as

$$E_t \tilde{w}_t = E_t h_t - \frac{R}{\gamma}b_{t-1} + (1 - \phi)c_{t-1}. \quad (A.11)$$

The constraints (A.2a) and (A.2b), together with (A.10), imply that

$$ac_t = E_t \tilde{w}_t - \left(\frac{\gamma}{R}\right) E_t \tilde{w}_{t+1}, \tag{A.12}$$

where

$$a = 1 - \left(\frac{\gamma}{R}\right)(1 - \varphi).$$

We proceed by postulating that the solution to the maximization problem is of the form

$$c_t = (\beta_0 + \beta_1 E_t \tilde{w}_t). \tag{A.13}$$

In what follows we show that this is indeed the solution, and we provide explicit expressions for the coefficients β_0 and β_1. We first note that equations (A.12) and (A.13) imply that

$$E_t \tilde{w}_{t+1} = \frac{R}{\gamma}[-\beta_0 a + (1 - \beta_1 a) E_t \tilde{w}_t]. \tag{A.14}$$

Substituting (A.13) into (A.8) yields

$$\alpha - (\beta_0 + \beta_1 E_t \tilde{w}_t) = \delta R[\alpha - (\beta_0 + \beta_1 E_t \tilde{w}_{t+1})]. \tag{A.15}$$

Likewise substituting (A.14) into (A.15) yields

$$\alpha - (\beta_0 + \beta_1 E_t \tilde{w}_t)$$

$$= \delta R \left[\alpha - \left\{ \beta_0 + \beta_1 \frac{R}{\gamma}[-\beta_0 a + (1 - \beta_1 a) E_t \tilde{w}_t] \right\} \right]. \tag{A.16}$$

Rearranging terms in equation (A.16) yields

$$\left\{ (1 - \delta R)\alpha - \left[1 - \delta R\left(1 - \frac{R}{\gamma}\beta_1 a\right)\right]\beta_0 \right\}$$

$$+ \left[-1 + \frac{\delta R^2}{\gamma}(1 - \beta_1 a)\right]\beta_1 E_t \tilde{w}_t = 0. \tag{A.17}$$

The solution specified in equation (A.13) is confirmed if (A.17) holds for all $E_t \tilde{w}_t$. This requirement is fulfilled if each of the bracketed terms in (A.17) equals zero. Thus equating these terms to zero yields

$$\beta_1 = \frac{1}{a}\left(1 - \frac{\gamma}{\delta R^2}\right), \tag{A.18}$$

$$\beta_0 = \alpha \frac{\gamma(1 - \delta R)}{\delta R(R - \gamma)}, \tag{A.19}$$

where from (A.12) the parameter a (and thus β_1) depends on the depreciation coefficient, ϕ. The consumption function (A.13) whose coefficients are given in equations (A.18) and (A.19) is the analogue to the consumption function in equation (9.8).

We turn next to derive a consumption equation suitable for empirical estimations. Using (A.11) in (A.13), aggregating the resultant individual consumption function over all cohorts, and dividing by the size of population yields the per-capita aggregate consumption C_t, where

$$C_t = \beta_0 + \beta_1\left[E_t \sum_{v=0}^{\infty} \left(\frac{\gamma}{R}\right)^v Y_{t+v} - RB^p_{t-1} + \gamma(1 - \phi)C_{t-1}\right]. \tag{A.20}$$

Aggregating (A.2b) over all cohorts, the per-capita flow aggregate budget constraint (in period $t - 1$) is

$$B^p_{t-1} = X_{t-1} - Y_{t-1} + RB^p_{t-2}, \tag{A.21}$$

where X_t denotes aggregate per-capita purchases. This equation is the analogue to equation (9.16). Substituting (A.2a), (A.10), and (A.20) into (A.21) yields

$$B^p_{t-1} = \beta_0 + (\beta_1 - 1)E_{t-1}h_{t-1} + \frac{\gamma}{R}E_{t-1}h_t + R(1 - \beta_1)B^p_{t-2}$$

$$+ \gamma(1 - \phi)(\beta_1 - 1)C_{t-2}. \tag{A.22}$$

Define

$$\tilde{E}_t \tilde{W}_t = E_t h_t - RB^p_{t-1} + \gamma(1 - \phi)C_{t-1}$$

$$= E_{t-1}h_t - RB^p_{t-1} + \gamma(1 - \phi)C_{t-1} + \varepsilon^*_t, \tag{A.23}$$

where $\varepsilon^* = (E_t h_t - E_{t-1} h_t)$. Substituting (A.22) into (A.23) yields

$$E_t \tilde{W}_t = (1 - \gamma) E_{t-1} h_t - R\beta_0 - R(\beta_1 - 1) E_{t-1} \tilde{W}_{t-1}$$
$$+ \gamma(1 - \phi) C_{t-1} + \varepsilon_t^*. \tag{A.24}$$

Equation (A.20) can be rewritten as

$$C_t = \beta_0 + \beta_1 E_t \tilde{W}_t. \tag{A.20a}$$

Lagging (A.20a) and rearranging yields

$$E_{t-1} \tilde{W}_{t-1} = \frac{1}{\beta_1} (C_{t-1} - \beta_0). \tag{A.25}$$

Substituting (A.25) into (A.24) yields

$$E_t \tilde{W}_t = (1 - \gamma) E_{t-1} h_t + \gamma(1 - \phi) C_{t-1} - R\beta_1$$
$$- \frac{R(\beta_1 - 1)}{\beta_1} (C_{t-1} - \beta_0) + \varepsilon_t^*, \tag{A.26}$$

which can be substituted into (A.20a) to yield

$$C_t = \beta_0(1 - R) + \beta_1(1 - \gamma) E_{t-1} h_t$$
$$+ [\gamma(1 - \phi)\beta_1 - R(\beta_1 - 1)] C_{t-1} + \varepsilon_t,$$

where $\varepsilon_t = \beta_1 \varepsilon_t^*$ is a stochastic (zero-mean) residual term.

Equation (A.27) is the analogue to equation (9.19). Using the facts that aggregate consumption purchases, X_t, are related to the aggregate stock, C_t, according to $X_t = C_t - (1 - \phi) C_{t-1}$, while $C_{t-1} = \sum_{\tau=0}^{\infty} (1 - \phi)^\tau X_{t-1-\tau}$, we can express (A.27) in terms of the current and the lagged values of *observable* purchases. This form therefore is readily applicable for empirical estimation of the key parameters, particularly, the finite-horizon coefficient γ.

10

An Exposition of the Two-Country Overlapping-Generations Model

In this chapter we extend the overlapping-generations model of chapter 9 to a two-country model of the world economy. We develop a simple diagrammatic exposition which is used in the analysis of the international effects of fiscal policies. The key channel through which the effects of fiscal policies are transmitted internationally is the world rate of interest. As in chapter 9, in the absence of distortionary taxes, the mechanism responsible for the real effects of budget deficit operates through the pure wealth effects. These effects stem from the intergenerational redistribution of income consequent on budget deficits.

We also extend the analysis by allowing a more refined commodity aggregation, distinguishing between tradable and nontradable goods. The incorporation of nontradable goods permits an examination of the consequences of budget deficits on the real exchange rate, as they operate through the mechanism of the pure wealth effect.

The exposition in this chapter is based on the assumption that the utility function is logarithmic. Under this assumption, as shown in chapter 9 the marginal propensity to save is $\gamma\delta$ (where γ denotes the survival probability and δ denotes the subjective discount factor). Accordingly, the per-capita aggregate consumption function is

$$C_t = (1 - \gamma\delta)W_t, \tag{10.1}$$

where, as before, per-capita aggregate wealth, W_t, equals the sum of human wealth and financial wealth. Human wealth is the discounted sum of disposable income, computed by using the *effective* rates of interest. Since this chapter deals with the interaction between the domestic economy and the rest of the world, we need to specify the behavioral functions of the foreign economy. In what follows variables pertaining to the foreign economy are denoted by an asterisk (*), and it is assumed that the foreign consumption function has the same form as the domestic consumption function.

10.1   World Equilibrium

In this section we analyze the determination of the equilibrium path of world rates of interest in the two-country world economy. As before, we assume that world capital markets are fully integrated and therefore individuals and governments in both countries face the same *market* rates of interest. This feature provides for the key channel through which policies undertaken in one country affect economic conditions in the rest of the world.

World equilibrium requires that in each period the given supply of world output equals the demand. To facilitate the exposition, we divide the horizon into two periods: the present, which is denoted by $t = 0$, and the future ($t = 1, 2, \dots$). The detailed procedure of time aggregation is specified in the appendix. In aggregating the future into a composite single period, we need to compute the present values of the various flows. Assuming that outputs, government spending, and taxes do not vary across future periods ($t = 1, 2, \dots$), we define an *average* interest rate, r. This average interest rate, which may be thought of as the yield on current investment lasting up to the indefinite future, represents the entire path of rates of interest that actually *do change* over time. For further reference r may be termed a "constancy-equivalent" interest rate.

The equilibrium conditions include the specification of the initial values of domestic and foreign wealth as well as the requirement that present and future goods-markets clear. These conditions are given in equation (10.2) through (10.5):

$$W_0 = (Y_0 - T_0) + \frac{\gamma}{R - \gamma}(Y - T) + (1 + r_{-1})(B^g_{-1} - B_{-1}),$$

$$(10.2)$$

$$W_0^* = (Y_0^* - T_0^*) + \frac{\gamma}{R - \gamma}(Y^* - T^*) + (1 + r_{-1})(B^{g*}_{-1} - B_{-1}),$$

$$(10.3)$$

$$(1 - \gamma\delta)W_0 + (1 - \gamma\delta^*)W_0^* = (Y_0 - G_0) + (Y_0^* - G_0^*), \qquad (10.4)$$

$$\left[\gamma\delta W_0 + \frac{(1 - \gamma)}{(R - 1)}\frac{R}{(R - \gamma)}(Y - T)\right]$$

$$+ \left[\gamma\delta^* W_0^* + \frac{(1 - \gamma)}{(R - 1)}\frac{R}{(R - \gamma)}(Y - T)\right]$$

$$= \frac{1}{R - 1}[(Y - G) + (Y^* - G^*)], \qquad (10.5)$$

where $R = 1 + r$, and where we have assumed that $\gamma = \gamma^*$.

Equations (10.2) and (10.3) specify the initial equilibrium values of domestic and foreign wealth owned by the existing population. In this specification private wealth is expressed as the sum of present values of current and future disposable incomes plus the net asset positions. In these equations the term $\gamma/(R - \gamma)$ denotes the present value of an annuity (commencing at period $t = 1$) evaluated by using the effective constancy-equivalent interest rate. These equations also embody the requirement that the home country's initial external indebtedness, B_{-1}, equals the foreign country's initial net creditor position.

Equation (10.4) is the requirement that world demand for goods in period $t = 0$ equal world supply. The left-hand side of this equation shows the sum of domestic and foreign per-capita private sector consumption (as implied by equation (10.1) and its foreign counterpart), and the right-hand side is the sum of per-capita domestic and foreign outputs (Y_0 and Y_0^*) net of government spending. The equality between γ and γ^* ensures that sizes of the population of the two countries are equal to each other. As a result aggregate world demand and supply can be expressed in terms of an equality between the *unweighted* sum of the individual country per-capita demand and the unweighted sum of the corresponding per-capita supply.

Equation (10.5) specifies the requirement that the discounted sum of per-capita domestic and foreign private demand for future goods equal the discounted sum of per-capita future world outputs net of government spending. These discounted sums are computed as of period $t = 0$ with the aid of the constancy-equivalent interest rate. The interpretation of the various terms follows. Consider the first bracketed term on the left-hand side of equation (10.5). In this expression the term $\gamma \delta W_0$ represents the per-capita savings of the population *present* in $t = 0$; these savings ultimately must be spent on future goods. The second term represents the per-capita wealth of those who will be born in all *future* periods from $t = 1$ onward; this wealth will be spent on future goods. To verify that this is indeed the meaning of the second term, we note that $(Y - T)$ is the disposable income of each individual at the time of birth and its product with $R/(R - \gamma)$ is the present value of such an annuity. Therefore the term $[R/(R - \gamma)](Y - T)$ denotes each individual's wealth at the time of birth, and since by our normalization the size of each cohort at birth is one individual, this term also represents the cohort's wealth at birth. Since in each period in the future there is a new cohort whose wealth at birth is computed similarly, the discounted sum of all future cohorts' wealth (as of period $t = 1$) is obtained by multiplying the term $[R/(R - \gamma)](Y - T)$ by $R/(R - 1)$, which denotes the present value of an annuity (commencing at $t = 1$) evaluated by using the constancy-equivalent interest rate. The resulting expression is then discounted to the present (period $t = 0$) through a division by R. This yields $[R/(R - 1)(R - \gamma)](Y - T)$. Multiplying this term by $(1 - \gamma)$ converts this aggregate wealth into the corresponding per-capita wealth. Equivalently, the first bracketed term on the left-hand side of equation (10.5) can also be obtained as the discounted sum of per-capita consumption, expressed by an equation analogous to equation (9.24). A similar interpretation applies to the second bracketed term on the left-hand side of equation (10.5). Finally, the right-hand side of equation (10.5) is the discounted sum of all future domestic and foreign outputs net of government spending. As a manifestation of Walras's law the system (10.2) through (10.5) is linearly dependent. This property is used in the subsequent analysis.

In addition to equations (10.1) through (10.5) the equilibrium conditions also include the requirements that both governments be solvent. Expressed in terms of the constancy-equivalent interest rate, these requirements are

$$(T_0 - G_0) + \frac{1}{R - 1}(T - G) = (1 + r_{-1})B^g_{-1} \tag{10.6}$$

and

$$(T_0^* - G_0^*) + \frac{1}{R - 1}(T^* - G^*) = (1 - r_{-1})B^{g*}_{-1}. \tag{10.7}$$

This system of equations can be solved for the equilibrium values of W_0 and W_0^* and R for any given values of the parameters. As shown in the appendix, the solutions obtained for the equilibrium values of wealth, W_0 and W_0^*, are the same as those that may be obtained from the original system (without the specific time aggregation) for which the rates of interest within the future may now vary. The use of the constancy-equivalent interest rate thus simplifies the analysis considerably, and it provides complete information about the impact of policies on the precise *current* values of all key variables including wealth, consumption, and debt accumulation, as well as on the average value of the rate of interest (computed as of time zero).

Using the government budget constraints, substituting $C_0 / (1 - \gamma\delta)$ for W_0, and omitting equation (10.2) by Walras's law, the complete system of equations can be reduced to two basic market-clearing equilibrium conditions, one for present goods and another for future goods. These conditions are

$$C_0 + (1 - \gamma\delta^*)\left[(Y_0^* - G_0^*) + \frac{\gamma}{R - \gamma}(Y^* - T^*)\right.$$

$$\left. + \frac{1}{R - 1}(T^* - G^*) + (1 + r_{-1})B_{-1}\right]$$

$$= [(Y_0 - G_0) + (Y_0^* - G_0^*)], \tag{10.8}$$

$$\left[\frac{\gamma\delta}{(1 - \gamma\delta)}C_0 + \frac{(1 - \gamma)}{R - 1}\frac{R}{(R - \gamma)}(Y - T)\right]$$

$$+ \left\{\gamma\delta^*\left[(Y_0^* - G_0^*) + \frac{\gamma}{R - \gamma}(Y^* - T^*)\right.\right.$$

$$\left. + \frac{1}{R - 1}(T^* - G^*) + (1 + r_{-1})B_{-1}\right]$$

$$\left. + \frac{(1 - \gamma)}{R - 1}\frac{R}{(R - \gamma)}(Y^* - T^*)\right\}$$

$$= \frac{1}{R - 1}[(Y - G) + (Y^* - G^*)]. \tag{10.9}$$

Equation (10.8) is the reduced-form market-clearing condition for present goods, with the left-hand side showing the sum of domestic and foreign private sector demands and the right-hand side showing the world supply of outputs net of government spending. Equation (10.9) is the reduced-form market-clearing condition for future goods, with analogous interpretations applied to the terms on its left and right-hand sides. These market-clearing conditions are used later in the diagrammatic exposition of the world equilibrium.

Throughout we assume that the foreign government follows a balanced-budget policy and that initially the domestic budget is balanced. This ensures that changes in world rates of interest that result from domestic fiscal deficits do not impact on the solvency of the foreign government and therefore do not necessitate secondary changes in fiscal policies.

Figure 10.1 shows the equilibrium of the system. In panel I the *PP* schedule describes combinations of R and C_0 that maintain equilib-

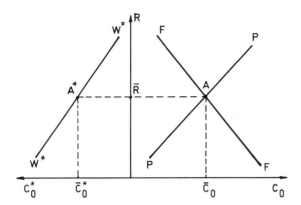

Figure 10.1
Equilibrium consumption and the rate of interest in the world economy

rium in the market for *present* goods. It is positively sloped since, as seen from equation (10.8), a fall in the rate of interest raises foreign wealth and induces a rise in foreign spending on present goods; therefore domestic consumption must fall in order to induce an offsetting reduction in demand. The *FF* schedule describes combinations of R and C_0 that maintain equilibrium in the market for *future* goods. Its slope is negative since a fall in R creates an excess supply of world future output which is eliminated by an offsetting rise in demand induced by a rise in domestic wealth that is associated with the rise in C_0. Panel II of figure 10.1 portrays the negatively sloped W^*W^* schedule describing the equilibrium relationship between R and C_0^* as implied by the foreign consumption function and by the negative dependence of W^* on R (from equation 10.3). The equilibrium is described by points A and A^* at which the values of the variables are $\bar{C}_0$, $\bar{C}_0^*$, and $\bar{R}$.

10.2 Effects of Current Budget Deficits

In this section we analyze the effects of budget deficits on the world rates of interest and on the levels of domestic and foreign private-sector spending. To focus on the impact of deficits rather than the impact of government spending, we assume that the deficits result from changes in taxes and that the path of government spending is given. Since government spending remains unchanged, solvency requires that current changes in taxes be accompanied by offsetting changes in future taxes. The present value of these tax changes must equal each other. The initial balance in the domestic budget ensures (from equation 10.6) that a change in current taxes, dT_0, must be related to the future change, dT, according to

$$dT_0 = -\frac{1}{R-1}dT, \tag{10.10}$$

where $1/(R-1) = 1/r$ is the annuity value of a unit tax change commencing from period $t = 1$ and evaluated in period $t = 0$. The rate of interest used in computing this annuity value is the constancy-equivalent rate of interest.

Figure 10.2 is used to determine the effects of a budget deficit. A deficit induced by a current tax cut of $-\Delta T_0$ necessitates (as long as government spending remains unchanged) a corresponding rise in future taxes by $(R-1)\Delta T_0$ according to equation (10.10). These tax changes do not impact on the PP schedule, but as seen from equation (10.9), they induce a fall in demand for future goods. To restore

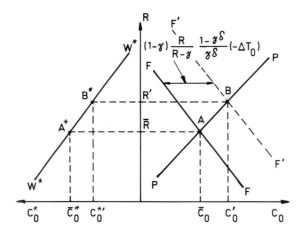

Figure 10.2
The effects of a current budget deficit

equilibrium at the given rate of interest, W_0 must rise so as to raise demand for future goods. Associated with such a rise in wealth is a rise in current consumption C_0. Thus the FF schedule shifts to the right by $(1 - \gamma)R(1 - \gamma\delta)/[\gamma\delta(R - \gamma)]\Delta T_0$. As a result the new equilibrium is reached at points B and B^* and $C_0' > \bar{C}_0$, $R' > \bar{R}$, and $C_0^{*'} < \bar{C}_0^*$.

Thus a budget deficit arising from a reduction in domestic taxes raises the world interest rate. Likewise, the domestic budget deficit raises the equilibrium value of domestic consumption, C_0, and lowers the corresponding value of foreign consumption, C_0^*. It follows that domestic budget deficits are transmitted *negatively* to the rest of the world. The international transmission mechanism is effected through the rate of interest. The rise in the world interest rate lowers foreign wealth and mitigates the initial rise in domestic wealth. These changes in wealth raise domestic spending, lower foreign spending, and worsen the domestic current account of the balance of payments. In the present context the direction of the international transmission is measured in terms of the comovements of current levels of domestic and foreign spending. It is relevant to note, however, that the level of current spending may not be a sufficient indicator for welfare changes.

As may be seen, if the probability of survival, γ, is unity, then budget deficits do not alter interest rates and consumption. In that case the model yields the familiar Ricardian proposition according to which the timing of taxes, and thereby the timing of deficits, do not influence the real equilibrium of the system as long as the path of government spending remains intact. In terms of figure 10.2, in that case the FF schedule does not shift in response to such tax changes. In the general case, however, with $\gamma < 1$, budget deficits exert real effects.

10.3   Effects of Current and Future Government Spending

The diagrammatic apparatus developed in the previous section can also be applied to illustrate the effects of government spending. In order to focus on the effect of changes in the level of government spending rather than on the effects of budget deficits, we assume (as in earlier chapters) that government budgets are balanced. The basic mechanism through which balanced-budget changes in government spending influence the economy do not depend, of course, on whether or not the model conforms with the Ricardian equivalence proposition. Accordingly, the results illustrated in this section are similar to those shown in chapter 8. These results are repeated here as a useful application of the diagrammatic apparatus.

Anticipating the results we recall from chapter 8 that, in general, the effects of balanced-budget changes in government spending on private-sector spending and on the world rate of interest depend on the comparison between the time pattern of government spending, as reflected by its saving propensity and the time pattern of domestic private-sector spending, as reflected by its saving propensity. Specifically, if the saving propensity of the government, γ_s^g, exceeds the private-sector saving propensity, γ_s, then a rise in the discounted sum of government spending creates an excess demand for future goods and necessitates a fall in the rate of interest, and vice versa. In the present case the government saving propensity is the fraction of the discounted sum of government spending that falls on future goods:

$$\gamma_s^g = \frac{G/(R-1)}{G_0 + G/(R-1)}. \tag{10.11}$$

Likewise, the corresponding private-sector-saving propensity, $\gamma_{s'}$, is the fraction of the discounted sum of private-sector spending that falls on future goods. Using the terms pertaining to domestic private-sector spending from equations (10.4) and (10.5), we obtain

$$\gamma_s = \frac{\gamma \delta W_0 + [(1-\gamma)R]/[(R-1)(R-\gamma)](Y-T)}{W_0 + [(1-\gamma)R]/[(R-1)(R-\gamma)](Y-T)}. \tag{10.12}$$

The expression in (10.11) and (10.12) define the average saving propensities, while our general principle is stated in terms of a comparison between the *marginal* saving propensities. If, however, the initial levels of debt, government spending, and taxes are zero, if the

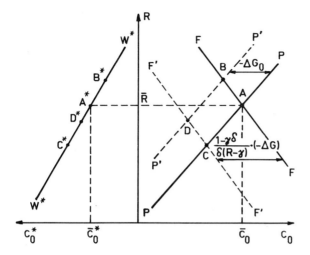

Figure 10.3
Changes in external debt, domestic and foreign consumption, and the world rate of interest

initial path of output is stationary and if the government maintains balanced budgets then the average and the marginal propensities are equal to each other. In the following exposition we identify the expressions in equations (10.11) and (10.12) with the corresponding marginal saving propensities.

The implications of this general principle are illustrated in figure 10.3 where we analyze the effects of alternative time patterns of government spending. In figure 10.3 the initial equilibrium obtains at points A and A^* at which the levels of domestic and foreign consumption are $\bar{C}_0$ and $\bar{C}_0^*$ and the rate of interest is indicated by $\bar{R}_0$. A transitory balanced-budget rise in *current* government spending of ΔG_0 creates an excess demand for present goods and necessitates a corresponding fall in private-sector spending. As implied by equation (10.8), the PP schedule shifts to the left by ΔG_0 to $P'P'$, and the new equilibrium obtains at points B and B^*. In that case the equilibrium world rate of interest rises and the levels of domestic and foreign private-sector consumption fall. This result conforms with the general principle since, as seen from equations (10.11) and (10.12), with a transitory rise in current government spending, the saving propensity of the government, γ_s^g, is zero while the corresponding propensity of the domestic private sector is positive.

Consider next a transitory balanced-budget rise in *future* government spending by ΔG. Such a rise creates an excess demand for future goods and necessitates a corresponding fall in private-sector demand for future goods. Such a reduction results from a decline in wealth that also induces (for any given rate of interest) a corresponding reduction in C_0. As implied by equation (10.9), the FF schedule shifts to the left by $(1 - \gamma\delta)/[\delta(R - \gamma)]\Delta G$ to the position indicated by $F'F'$. The new equilibrium obtains at points C and C^*. In that case the equilibrium world rate of interest falls, domestic private-sector consumption falls, and foreign consumption rises. This result also illustrates the general principle since, as seen from equations (10.11) and (10.12), with a transitory rise in future government spending, γ_s^g is unity while γ_s is smaller than unity.

The foregoing analysis provides the ingredients necessary for determining the effects of a *permanent* balanced-budget rise in government spending. Such a rise in government spending (with $\Delta G_0 = \Delta G$) raises demand for *both* present and future goods and shifts both schedules in figure 10.3 leftward. The impact on the rate of interest depends on the *relative* excess demands in both markets. Diagrammatically, the difference between the horizontal leftward shifts of the PP and the FF schedules is $(\delta R - 1)/[\delta(R - \gamma)]\Delta G$. Accordingly, if δR falls short of unity, then the leftward shift of the FF schedule exceeds that of the PP schedule. This situation is shown in figure 10.3 where the new equilibrium obtains at point D and D^*. At this equilibrium the world rate of interest falls, and domestic private-sector consumption falls while foreign consumption rises. If, on the other hand, δR exceeds unity, then the leftward shift of the PP schedule exceeds that of the FF schedule. In that case the world rate of interest rises and the levels of domestic and foreign private-sector consumption fall.

In interpreting these results, we note that if δR exceeds unity, then the desired level of consumption by individuals in the domestic economy rises over time. In and of itself this contributes to a surplus in the current account of the domestic balance of payments during the early periods. Of course the counterpart to this surplus is a corresponding deficit in the foreign current account of the balance of payments. Thus, if $\delta R > 1$, then (at the margin) the domestic economy is a net saver in the world economy and the permanent rise in government spending raises the world rate of interest. The opposite holds if the domestic economy is a net dissaver in the world economy, that is, if R falls short of unity.

The dependence of the interest-rate effects of a permanent rise in government spending on whether δR exceeds or falls short of unity conforms with the general principle expressed in terms of a comparison between the domestic private- and public-sector-saving propensities. To verify this conformity, we substitute equation (10.2) for W_0 into equation (10.12); assuming the absence of initial debt as well as balanced budgets and stationary paths of output and government spending, it can be shown that γ_s^g exceeds or falls short of γ_s according to whether δR falls short or exceeds unity.

To gain further insights, we apply the relative demand—relative supply diagrammatic apparatus of chapter 8 to determine the effects of balanced-budget changes in government spending on the rates of growth of domestic and foreign per-capita consumption. Since the qualitative effects of the analysis do not depend on whether the survival probability is unity or not, we assume that the value of γ is unity so that individuals have an infinite horizon. This assumption permits the use of this diagrammatic device.

Figure 10.4 shows the domestic (D), the foreign (D^*), and the world (D^w) relative demand schedules as functions of the rate of interest. In the figure, g_c, g_c^*, and g_c^w denote the ratios of the discounted sum (as of period one) of future consumption to current consumption of the domestic, the foreign, and the world private sector, respectively. These magnitudes are indicators of the corresponding growth rates of consumption. The model contained in equations (10.1) through (10.5) implies that if $\gamma = 1$ then $g_c = \delta R$ and $g_c^* = \delta^* R$. Hence in the present case the downward-sloping relative demand schedules are rectangular hyperbolas. As in the previous chapters, the D^w schedule is a weighted average of D and D^*. Accordingly,

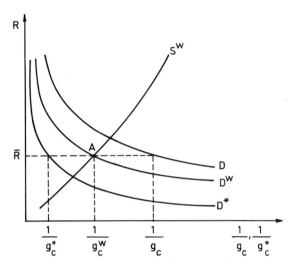

Figure 10.4
Government spending; domestic, foreign, and world growth rates of consumption; and the world rate of interest

$$\frac{1}{g_c^w} = \mu \frac{1}{g_c} + (1 - \mu) \frac{1}{g_c^*}, \tag{10.13}$$

where μ is the fraction of the discounted sum of future domestic consumption in the discounted sum of world future output net of government spending.

The S^w schedule in figure 10.4 portrays the ratio of current to (the discounted sum of) future world output net of government spending. This schedule is positively sloped since a rise in the rate of interest lowers the discounted sum of future outputs. The initial equilibrium is shown by point A at which the world relative demand equals the corresponding supply. At this point the equilibrium rate of interest is indicated by $\bar{R}$, and the relative world consumption is indicated by $1/g_c^w$. Associated with this rate of interest, the corresponding values of domestic and foreign relative consumption are indicated by $1/g_c$ and $1/g_c^*$, respectively.

A transitory balanced-budget rise in current government spending lowers the relative supply and induces a leftward displacement of the S schedule. Further the rise in taxes that is necessary to balance the budget lowers private-sector consumption and, as indicated by equation (10.13), reduces the weight of the domestic relative demand in the world relative demand. This induces a displacement of the D^w schedule toward the foreign schedule D^* (whose relative weight has risen). The case shown in figure 10.4 corresponds to the situation in which $\delta < \delta^*$ so that the domestic saving propensity falls short of the foreign one. In that case the domestic schedule D lies to the right of D^*, and the rise in the domestic government spending induces a leftward displacement of the D^w schedule. Specifically, if the relative supply schedule shifts leftward by 1 percent, then the world relative demand schedule shifts leftward by only μ percent. As a result the equilibrium rate of interest rises, and the growth rates of consumption in both countries rise. The same qualitative results apply to the situation in which the saving-propensities condition is reversed so that $\delta > \delta^*$. In that case the D schedule lies to the left of the D^* schedule and the rise in the domestic government induces a rightward shift of the D^w schedule. In that case the rate of interest rises to a larger extent.

A similar analysis applies to the effects of a transitory rise in future government spending. In that case the relative supply schedule shifts to the right, and as before, the world relative demand schedule shifts to a position closer to that of the foreign relative demand schedule. The new equilibrium is associated with a lower rate of interest and a higher growth rate of domestic and foreign consumption. These qualitative results are independent of the relative magnitudes of δ and δ^* since even if the relative world demand shifts in the same direction as the supply, the proportional horizontal displacement of the S schedule, exceeds the corresponding displacement of the D^w schedule.

Finally, a permanent rise in government spending that does not alter the relative share of government spending in world GDP leaves the S schedule intact and displaces the D^w schedule toward the foreign schedule D^*. Hence, if δ exceeds δ^*, the world relative demand schedule shifts to the right, the rate of interest rises, and the growth rates of consumption fall. The opposite holds for the case in which δ falls short of δ^*. Since the equilibrium value of $1/R$ lies in between δ and δ^*, it is evident that the dependence of the effects of a permanent rise in government spending on the saving-propensities condition (i.e., on whether δ exceeds or falls short of δ^*) can be expressed equivalently in terms of whether δR exceeds or falls short of unity. Indeed, the previous analysis in this section was cast in terms of the latter condition.

10.4   Effects of Past Government Spending

We proceed with the exposition in this chapter by applying the diagrammatic apparatus to the analysis of the effects of past balanced-budget rises in government spending. Other things equal, the higher level of past transitory government spending was associated with a worsened past current-account position. Therefore, from the perspective of the current generations, the higher level of past government spending is reflected in a larger size of the initial external debt.

To analyze the effect of the size of the initial external debt position, consider a redistribution of world debt from the home country to the rest of the world. Suppose that this transfer is represented by increasing $(1 + r_{-1})B_{-1}$ by ΔB. This redistribution of world debt lowers domestic demand for both present and future goods and induces a corresponding rise in foreign demand. From equation (10.8) it is seen that the PP schedule shifts to the left by $(1 - \gamma \delta^*)\Delta B$, and from equation (10.9) it is seen that the FF schedule shifts to the left by $(1 - \gamma \delta)(\delta^*/\delta)\Delta B$. From equation (10.3) and the foreign consumption function the transfer also shifts the W^*W^* schedule to the left by $(1 - \gamma \delta^*)\Delta B$. As a result the equilibrium of the system shifts from points A and A^* to points B and B^*.

The effect of the transfer on the new equilibrium rate of interest reflects the usual considerations underlying the transfer-problem criterion. In terms of figure 10.5 the rate of interest falls if the horizontal displacement of the FF schedule exceeds the corresponding displacement of the PP schedule, and vice versa. As can be seen, the difference between the horizontal shifts of the FF and the PP

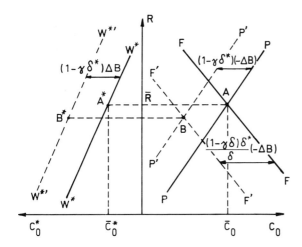

Figure 10.5
Changes in external debt, domestic and foreign consumption, and the world rate of interest

schedules is proportional to $(\delta^* - \delta)/\delta$. If the saving-propensities condition is such that $\delta < \delta^*$, then the transfer raises world savings and necessitates a fall in the rate of interest so as to restore the initial level of world savings. This is the case illustrated in figure 10.5. If, however, $\delta > \delta^*$, then the transfer lowers world savings and induces a rise in the world rate of interest. In general, independent of the direction of the change in the rate of interest, the redistribution of world debt in favor of the foreign country lowers domestic consumption and raises foreign consumption.

10.5   Welfare Aspects

The analysis in the preceding sections indicated the effects of fiscal policies on interest rates and wealth. Knowledge of these effects was sufficient for determining the impact of policies on the paths of aggregate consumption which, in turn, govern the evolution of the key economic variables in the world economy. It is obvious, however, that because of the structure of the overlapping-generations model, the analysis of *normative* questions is much more complex.

Specifically, it is evident that the welfare effects of fiscal policies cannot be inferred from knowledge of the resulting changes in aggregate private wealth. In the first place changes in intertemporal prices (rates of interest) also impact on the level of welfare in addition to their effects on wealth. More important, complexities arise from the fact that not all generations share equally in the benefits of tax cuts and in the burdens of tax levies. Furthermore, in designing optimal fiscal policies, one needs to define a social welfare function. This raises the conceptual issues concerning the proper weighting of current and prospective generations in the social welfare function and the possible implication for the time consistency of government policies.

In this section we illustrate some of these issues by examining the effects of a current budget deficit on the welfare of the population existing in the period of the tax cut. It is convenient to focus the analysis on the individual born in the period of the tax cut, but since the survival probability is the same for all individuals, the direction of the change in welfare is the same for everyone else who is alive during the period of the tax cut. Therefore the qualitative results apply to the entire population that is alive during the period of the deficit. Recalling that each individual is born with no debt and that therefore his wealth consists of the properly discounted value of lifetime disposable income, the per-capita wealth is

$$w_0 = (Y_0 - T_0) + \frac{\gamma}{R - \gamma}(Y - T). \tag{10.14}$$

With the assumed logarithmic utility function, the individual's expected utility is given by

$$\sum_{t=0}^{\infty} (\gamma\delta)^t \log c_t, \tag{10.15}$$

and correspondingly, his consumption (computed with the aid of the constancy-equivalent interest rate) is

$$c_t = (1 - \gamma\delta)(\delta R)^t w_0. \tag{10.16}$$

Using these expressions, it can be shown that the individual's *indirect* expected utility, v, is represented by

$$v = \log \frac{w_0}{R^{-\gamma\delta/(1-\gamma\delta)}} = \log \left[\frac{(Y_0 - T_0) + \gamma/(R - \gamma)(Y - T)}{R^{-\gamma\delta/(1-\gamma\delta)}} \right], \quad (10.17)$$

where the second equality follows from equation (10.14) and $R^{-\gamma\delta/(1-\gamma\delta)}$ is the real-wealth deflator which is the intertemporal price index (in terms of current consumption) appropriate for evaluating the real value of wealth. Thus utility is a function of *real* wealth. As seen in equation (10.17), current budget deficits impact on the level of utility directly through the effects of the reduction in T_0 and the accompanying rise in T and, indirectly through the effect of changes in the rate of interest. The latter in turn operates through its impact on the present value of future disposable income and on the intertemporal price index. As is evident, in the extreme case with $\gamma = 1$, the direct effects induced by the changes in current and future taxes offset each other (since $dT_0 + dT/[R - 1] = 0$), and since with $\gamma = 1$ the rate of interest does not change, the indirect effect of the tax shift is also zero. Obviously in that case a budget deficit does not impact on the individual's utility level. In the other extreme for which γ is very small, the individual is concerned mainly with his or her current level of income and consumption and therefore changes in the rate of interest exert small effects on his welfare. In that case the weight, $\gamma\delta/(1 - \gamma\delta)$, of future prices in the real-wealth deflator as well as the weight of future disposable income in w_0 are small, and therefore a current tax cut raises welfare. In general, since the budget deficit raises both the value of wealth and the rate of interest (as shown formally in the appendix), it follows that it raises the level of welfare of the existing population. The preceding analysis examined the impact of current budget deficits on the level of welfare of the existing population. Of course the future rise in taxes and the associated changes in the rates of interest also impact on the utility level of the yet unborn generations.

Turning to the evaluation of foreign welfare, we note that the changes in the rates of interest impact on the welfare of the existing foreign population according to whether the foreign country is a net saver or dissaver. Thus, as far as the existing foreign population is concerned, the direction of changes in their current wealth and consumption (which was emphasized in our preceding positive analysis) is not the relevant indicator for welfare changes. Therefore, in assessing whether the international transmission mechanism is positive or negative, a distinction should be drawn between positive measures of transmission expressed in terms of current consumption and wealth and normative measures expressed in terms of welfare.

In concluding this section, it is relevant to note that throughout the discussion we have not inquired into the motives underlying the adaption of a budget-deficit policy. In this context the possibility that the existing population gains from current deficits raises the question as to what factors limit the introduction of further tax cuts at the expense of future generations, and possibly at the expense of foreigners (if they are net borrowers). In general, considerations that may operate to limit current tax cuts include (1) governments that are also concerned with future generations' welfare, (2) the possibility that the welfare loss imposed on foreigners through the domestic tax cuts may stimulate retaliation and result in a costly "fiscal war," (3) the existence of an upper limit to the feasible rise in future taxes, (4) the existence of distortionary taxes and costly fiscal management that sets an upper limit to the benefits that current tax cuts yield to the future population, and (5) the possibility that a significant rise in debt introduces the probability of default and may raise the cost of external borrowing. In connection with this final consideration we recall that throughout the analysis individuals were assumed to be mortal, whereas government commitments were implicitly assumed to be immortal. In general, of course, the probability that governments and their commitments survive indefinitely is also less than unity. Under such circumstances the interest-rate differential on private and public sectors' loans, and thereby the impact of budget deficits, is governed by the relation between the default probabilities of individuals and government commitments. It is noteworthy, however, that allowing for the possibility that governments renege on their commitments (in the context of designing optimal policies) introduces to the analysis new dimensions associated with the issues of time-consistent policies.

10.6   Budget Deficits and Real Exchange Rates: The Two-Country World

In this section we extend the analysis to the two-country case. As in previous chapters such an extension illuminates the nature of the international transmission mechanism of tax policies. In our analysis we continue to assume that all taxes are nondistortionary. As a result the mechanism responsible for the real consequences of budget deficits operates through the wealth effects. We adopt the general features of the model outlined in section 10.1 but modify the classification of commodities so as to allow for the existence of nontradable goods at home and abroad. This extension introduces the domestic and foreign real exchange rates as key variables adjusting to the budget deficits.

To simplify the exposition, we follow a similar procedure as in section 10.1 and divide the horizon into two the current period and the future period. All quantities pertaining to the current period are indicated by a zero subscript, and the paths of the exogenous variables are assumed stationary across future periods.

Equilibrium necessitates that in the current period world output of tradable goods is demanded and the discounted sum of future outputs of tradable goods equals the discounted sums of future domestic and foreign demands. Likewise, in each country current and future period outputs of nontradable goods must be demanded. In what follows we outline the complete two-country model. The aggregate consumption functions at home and abroad are $Z_t = (1 - s)W_t$ and $Z_t^* = (1 - s^*)W_t^*$, where as before the propensities to save, s and s^*, are equal to $\gamma\delta$ and $\gamma\delta^*$ (where the survival probability, γ, is assumed to be equal across countries). Domestic and foreign wealth are defined as

$$W_0 = (\bar{Y}_{x0} + p_{n0}\bar{Y}_{n0} - T_0) + \frac{\gamma}{R - \gamma}(\bar{Y}_x + p_n\bar{Y}_n - T)$$

$$+ (1 + r_{x,-1})(B^g_{-1} - B_{-1}) \tag{10.18}$$

and

$$W_0^* = (\bar{Y}_{x0}^* + p_{n0}^*\bar{Y}_{n0}^* - T_0^*) + \frac{\gamma}{R - \gamma}(\bar{Y}_x^* + p_n^*\bar{Y}_n^* - T^*)$$

$$+ (1 + r_{x,-1})(B_{-1}^{*g} + B_{-1}). \tag{10.19}$$

As seen, equations (10.18) and (10.19) express wealth as the sum of the present values of current and future disposable incomes plus net asset positions. Also it is recalled that in these equations the term $\gamma/(R - \gamma)$ denotes the present value of an annuity (commencing at period $t = 1$) evaluated by using the discount factor relevant for private decision making, γ/R.

The market-clearing conditions for the domestic nontradable goods require that

$$\beta_n(1 - s)W_0 = p_{n0}[\bar{Y}_{n0} - \beta_n^g(1 - \gamma_s^g)G] \tag{10.20}$$

and

$$\beta_n\left[sW_0 + \frac{1 - \gamma}{R - 1}\frac{R}{R - \gamma}(\bar{Y}_x + p_n\bar{Y}_n - T)\right]$$

$$= \frac{1}{R - 1}[p_n\bar{Y}_n - \beta_n^g\gamma_s^gG], \tag{10.21}$$

where, as before, G denotes the discounted sum of government spending and where β_n^g and γ_s^g indicate the government's temporal and intertemporal spending pattern. Equation (10.20) specifies the equilibrium condition in the current-period market, and equation (10.21) states that the discounted sum of domestic demand for future nontradable goods equals the discounted sum of future supply net of government absorption.

Analogously, equations (10.22) and (10.23) describe the corresponding equilibrium conditions in the foreign markets for nontradable goods.

$$\beta_n^*(1 - s^*)W_0^* = p_{n0}^* \bar{Y}_{n0}^* - \beta_n^{*g}(1 - \gamma_s^{*g})G^* \tag{10.22}$$

and

$$\beta_n^* \left[s^*W_0^* + \frac{1 - \gamma}{R - 1} \frac{R}{R - \gamma}(\bar{Y}_x^* + p_n^*\bar{Y}_n^* - T^*) \right]$$

$$= \frac{1}{R - 1}[p_n^*\bar{Y}_n^* - \beta_n^{*g}\gamma_s^{*g}G^*]. \tag{10.23}$$

Finally, the equilibrium conditions in the *world* market for tradable goods are specified in equations (10.24) and (10.25), where the first of the two pertains to the current period and the second pertains to the discounted sums of demand and supply in all future periods:

$$(1 - \beta_n)(1 - s)W_0 + (1 - \beta_n^*)(1 - s^*)W_0^*$$

$$= \bar{Y}_x - (1 - \beta_n^g)(1 - \gamma_s^g)G + \bar{Y}_x^* - (1 - \beta_n^{*g})(1 - \gamma_s^{*g})G^* \tag{10.24}$$

and

$$(1 - \beta_n) \left[sW_0 + \frac{1 - \gamma}{R - 1} \frac{R}{R - \gamma}(\bar{Y}_x + p_n\bar{Y}_n - T) \right]$$

$$+ (1 - \beta_n^*) \left[s^*W_0^* + \frac{1 - \gamma}{R - 1} \frac{R}{R - \gamma}(\bar{Y}_x^* + p_n^*\bar{Y}_n^* - T^*) \right]$$

$$= \frac{1}{R - 1}[\bar{Y}_x - (1 - \beta_n^g)\gamma_s^g G + \bar{Y}_x^* - (1 - \beta_n^{*g})\gamma_s^{*g}G^*]. \tag{10.25}$$

The system of equations (10.18) through (10.25) can be solved for the equilibrium values of the domestic and foreign current-period wealth, W_0 and W_0^*, current and future prices of nontradable goods (the inverse of the corresponding real exchange rates), p_{n0}, p_{n0}^*, p_n, p_n^*, and for the world rate of interest, $R - 1$. As usual, the eight-equation system (10.18) through (10.25) is linearly dependent, and thus, by Walras's law, one of these equations can be left out. In what follows we leave out equation (10.18) specifying the equilibrium value of domestic wealth.

We can reduce the complete model to two basic equilibrium conditions. These conditions state that the world markets for tradable goods clear in both the current period as well as in the (consolidated) future period. These equations, derived explicitly in the appendix, are reduced-form equations—they incorporate the requirement that in each country and in all periods the markets for nontradable goods clear. Accordingly,

$$(1 - \beta_n)(1 - \gamma\delta)W_0 + (1 - \beta_n^*)(1 - \gamma\delta^*)W_0^* = \overline{Y}_x + \overline{Y}_x^*, \quad (10.26)$$

$$(1 - \beta_n)\left[\gamma\delta W_0 + \frac{(1 - \gamma)R}{(R - 1)(R - \gamma)}I(R, W_0, T)\right]$$

$$+ (1 - \beta_n^*)\left[\gamma\delta^* W_0^*(R) + \frac{(1 - \gamma)R}{(R - 1)(R - \gamma)}I^*(R)\right]$$

$$= \frac{1}{R - 1}(\overline{Y}_x + \overline{Y}_x^*), \quad (10.27)$$

where we replaced s and s^* by $\gamma\delta$ and $\gamma\delta^*$, respectively.

Equation (10.26) states that the sum of world private demand for current tradable goods equals world supply. In this equation $(1 - \beta_n)(1 - \gamma\delta)W_0$ is the home country's private demand, and $(1 - \beta_n^*)(1 - \gamma\delta^*)W_0^*$ is the corresponding foreign demand. The foreign wealth is expressed as a negative function of the rate of interest reflecting the role of the latter in discounting future incomes and in influencing the real exchange rate used to evaluate the income streams. It is noteworthy that this reduced-form functional dependence of wealth on the rate of interest is not shown explicitly for the domestic wealth since we have omitted the explicit domestic-wealth equation (10.18) by Walras's law. This choice makes the equilibrium determination of domestic wealth (along with the world rate of interest) the focus of the subsequent analysis.

The second reduced-form equation (10.27) states that the discounted sum of domestic and foreign demands for future tradable goods equals the discounted sum of future world supply. The first term is the product of the consumption share of tradable goods $(1 - \beta_n)$ and total domestic future consumption. The latter equals the sum of the savings of those alive in period zero, $\gamma \delta W_0$, and the discounted sum of the demand for future goods of those who will be born in the future and whose disposable income in each period is I. This reduced-form future disposable income (in terms of tradable goods) is expressed as a negative function of future taxes, T, and a positive function of the future relative price of nontradable goods. The latter in turn depends negatively on R (through its effect on future wealth of those yet unborn) and positively on W_0 (through its effect on the demand of those alive). An analogous interpretation applies to the foreign disposable income, I^*. The dependence of I^* on R only reflects the assumption that foreign taxes are zero and incorporates the negative dependence of W_0^* on R. Before proceeding, it is relevant to note that in the absence of nontradable goods, $\beta_n = \beta_n^* = 0$, $I(R, W_0, T) = Y - T$, $I^*(R) = Y^*$, $\overline{Y}_n = \overline{Y}_n^* = 0$, and $W^*(R) = Y^* + Y^*/(R - 1) + R(B_{-1}^g + B_{-1})$. Thus in this special case equations (10.26) and (10.27) reduce to equations (10.8) and (10.9).

Equations (10.26) and (10.27) yield the equilibrium values of the home country's initial wealth, W_0, and the world rate of interest, $r_x = R - 1$, for any given values of the parameters. In equilibrium the demand for nontradable goods $\beta_n(1 - \gamma\delta)W_0$ equals the value of the supply, $p_{n0}\overline{Y}_n$. Hence the equilibrium price (the inverse of the real exchange rate) is

$$p_{n0} = \frac{\beta_n(1 - \gamma\delta)W_0}{\overline{Y}_n}. \tag{10.28}$$

The equilibrium of the system is analyzed by means of figure 10.6. The PP schedule drawn in panel I of figure 10.6 shows combinations of r_x and p_{n0} that clear the market for present tradable goods. It is positively sloped since a rise in the rate of interest lowers foreign demand (by lowering W_0^*), and a rise in p_{n0} raises domestic demand (by raising W_0). The future tradable-goods market clears along the FF schedule. This schedule is negatively sloped since

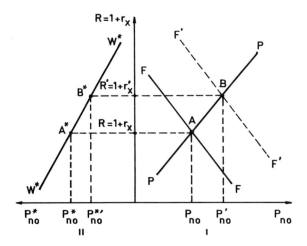

Figure 10.6
Budget deficits, the real exchange rates, and the real rate of interest

a rise in the rate of interest creates an excess demand for future tradable goods which must be offset by a fall in W_0 (and therefore p_{n0}). Panel II of the figure shows the negative relation between the equilibrium rate of interest and the foreign relative price of nontradable goods. This relation is based on equation (10.29) which is the foreign-country analogue to equation (10.28):

$$p_{n0}^* = \frac{\beta_n^*(1 - \gamma\delta^*)}{\overline{Y}_n} W_0^*(R). \tag{10.29}$$

The equilibrium of the system is shown by point A in panel I and point A^* in panel II of figure 10.6. Accordingly, the current equilibrium relative price of domestic tradable goods is p_{n0}, the foreign equilibrium relative price is p_{n0}^*, and the corresponding equilibrium rate of interest is r_x. In what follows we analyze the effects of a domestic budget deficit on the world rate of interest and on the equilibrium real exchange rates. The formal derivations of the results are contained in the appendix.

A domestic budget deficit arising from a current tax cut necessitates a corresponding rise in future taxes, T. As seen from equation (10.27), the rise in future taxes lowers future domestic disposable income, I, and thereby lowers the demand for future goods. For a given world rate of interest the fall in demand can be eliminated by a rise in W_0. As implied by equation (10.28) the rise in W_0 is associated with a rise in p_{n0}. Thus the FF schedule shifts to the right to $F'F'$. As is evident the horizontal shifts of the FF schedule is proportional to $(1 - \gamma)$; if $\gamma = 1$ the position of the schedule as well as the characteristics of the initial equilibrium remain intact (the Ricardian equivalence case). In general, as indicated in panel I, the new equilibrium obtains at point B with a *higher rate of interest, a higher domestic relative price of nontradable goods, p_{n0}, and a higher level of domestic wealth and consumption. The new equilibrium is indicated in panel II by point B^*, where it is seen that the higher rate of interest lowers foreign wealth and consumption and reduces the foreign relative price of nontradable goods.* Thus on the basis of the correlations between domestic and foreign private-sector spending and between domestic and foreign real exchange rate, *the international transmission of the budget deficit is negative.* As an interpretation we note that the wealth effects induced by the domestic budget deficit creates an excess demand for present tradable goods resulting in a rise in their *inter-temporal* relative price—the rate of interest. Likewise, it creates an excess demand for domestic nontradable goods and an excess supply of foreign nontradable goods. These excess demands and supplies alter the *temporal* relative price of these goods—the real exchange rates.

10.7 Summary

In this chapter we provided an exposition of the two-country over-lapping-generations models of the world economy. We developed a simple diagrammatic exposition of the model by focusing on the markets for present and future goods. To reduce the high dimensionality of the model, we have constructed a composite of future goods and defined the concept of a constancy-equivalent rate of interest used in the definition of this composite good. This procedure facilitated the exposition and simplified the analysis considerably without loss of pertinent information.

The diagrammatic apparatus was applied to the analysis of the effects of current budget deficits and to the effects of various time patterns of balanced-budget changes in government spending. In this context we focused on the effects of these fiscal policies on the world rate of interest and on the levels and growth rates of domestic and foreign private-sector spending.

The diagrammatic exposition provided in this chapter illustrates the general principles of the various transfer-problem criteria developed in previous chapters. It illustrates that the interest-rate effects of various time patterns of government spending can be determined by simple comparison between the properly defined marginal saving propensities of the domestic private and public sectors. Likewise, the effects of changes in the time profile of taxes are interpreted in terms of a comparison between the marginal spending propensities of current and future generations. Finally, the effects of a redistribution of world debt arising from past balanced-budget changes in government spending depend on the relative magnitudes of the marginal saving propensities of domestic and foreign residents.

We followed the exposition with a brief analysis of welfare implications of budget deficits. This discussion was cast in terms of the effects of budget deficits on wealth and on the wealth deflator. It was shown that the budget deficit raises the level of welfare of the existing domestic population. The welfare of the foreign population rises if the foreign economy is a net saver in the world economy, and vice versa. We also outlined some of the checks that may limit the incentives for the adoption of budget deficits.

We concluded the exposition with an analysis of the consequences of budget deficits on the real exchange rate operating through the mechanism of the pure wealth effect. To focus on this mechanism rather than the mechanism of substitution effects, we assumed that all taxes are nondistortionary. In that case the finiteness of the horizon implies that budget deficits induce a positive wealth effect.

Our analysis of the two-country case focused on the consequences of budget deficits on the domestic and the foreign real exchange rates. In this case the international transmission mechanism operates through the effects of the budget deficit on the world rate of interest. Accordingly, the wealth effect induced by the budget deficit raises the domestic demand for present-period goods, and thereby lowers the domestic real exchange rate and raises the world rate of interest. This rise transmits the effects of the domestic deficit to the rest of the world: it lowers foreign spending and raises the foreign real exchange rate. Accordingly, the budget deficit induces negative cross-country correlations between the levels of private-sector spending as well as between the real exchange rates.

The pattern of the cross-country correlations between real exchange rates and the effects of budget deficits on the world rate of interest reflect the mechanism of the pure wealth effect set in place in the absence of distortionary taxes. These results should be contrasted with those obtained in chapter 8 where it was shown that with distortionary taxes the effects of budget deficits depend on the specific taxes that are altered. In this context we also note that the interest-rate and real exchange-rate effects of a balanced-budget rise in government spending (analyzed in chapter 8) carry over to the infinite-horizon model used here.

The analysis can be reinterpreted by viewing leisure as the nontradable good and the real wage as the reciprocal of the real exchange rate. With such a reinterpretation the analysis in this chapter yields insights into the effects of budget deficits on real-wage dynamics, and on cross-country correlations of real wages.

10.8 Appendix

The Time-Aggregation Procedure

The aggregation procedure and the use of the constancy-equivalent rate of interest which underlie equations (10.2) through (10.5) is justified as follows. From equation (9.14) and its foreign-country counterpart, the market-clearing condition for period $t = 0$ is shown in equation (A.1) and the corresponding definitions of wealth are shown in equations (A.2) and (A.3). Thus

$$(1 - s_0)W_0 + (1 - s_0^*)W_0^* = (Y_0 - G_0) + (Y_0^* - G_0^*), \qquad \text{(A.1)}$$

$$W_0 = \sum_{t=0}^{\infty} \gamma^t \alpha_t (Y_t - T_t) + (1 + r_{-1})(B_{-1}^g - B_{-1}), \qquad \text{(A.2)}$$

$$W_0^* = \sum_{t=0}^{\infty} (\gamma^*)^t \alpha_t (Y_t^* - T_t^*) + (1 + r_{t-1})(B_{-1}^{g*} + B_{-1}), \qquad \text{(A.3)}$$

where

$$s_0 = 1 - \left\{ \sum_{t=0}^{\infty} (\gamma^t \alpha_t)^{1-\sigma} [(\gamma \delta)^t]^{\sigma} \right\}^{-1},$$

$$s_0^* = 1 - \left\{ \sum_{t=0}^{\infty} [(\gamma^*)^t \alpha_t]^{1-\sigma^*} [(\gamma^* \delta^*)^t]^{\sigma^*} \right\}^{-1}.$$

The value of s_0 is taken from equation (9.9), and s_0^* is the corresponding foreign-country counterpart.

Under the conditions that $Y_t - T_t = Y - T$, $Y_t^* - T_t^* = Y^* - T^*$ (for $t = 1, 2, \ldots$), $\sigma = \sigma^* = 1$, and $\gamma = \gamma^*$, equations (A.1) through (A.3) can be solved for the equilibrium values of W_0, W_0^*, and $\sum_{t=1}^{\infty} \gamma^t \alpha_t$. In the text we define $\sum_{t=1}^{\infty} \gamma^t \alpha_t$ by $\gamma/(R - \gamma)$, where $r = R - 1$ is the constancy-equivalent rate of interest. With these substitution equations (A.1) through (A.3) become equations (10.2) through (10.4).

It can be readily verified that adding equation (10.5) to the system (10.2) through (10.4) yields a linearly dependent system of equations. Therefore, as a manifestation of Walras's law the *equilibrium* values of W_0, W_0^*, and R can be solved from any subset of three equations from the four-equation system.

The Impact of Budget Deficits

In this part of the appendix we consider the impact of current budget deficits. The quantitative impacts of changes in domestic taxes on R, W_0, and W_0^*, (evaluated around an initial balanced budget and initial stationary paths of output, taxes, and government spending) can be obtained from any three equations of the system (10.2) through (10.5) along with the implications of the government budget constraint (10.10). These changes are

$$\frac{dW_0}{dT_0} = -(1-\gamma)(1-\gamma\delta^*)\lambda^* \frac{R^2}{(R-\gamma)^2} < 0, \tag{A.4}$$

$$\frac{dW_0^*}{dT_0} = (1-\gamma)(1-\gamma\delta)\lambda^* \frac{R^2}{(R-\gamma)^2} > 0, \tag{A.5}$$

$$\frac{dR}{dT_0} = -(1-\gamma)\frac{(1-\gamma\delta)\lambda^* R^2}{\gamma(Y^*-G^*)} < 0, \tag{A.6}$$

where λ^* is the relative share of foreign output net of government spending in the corresponding world quantity; that is,

$$\lambda^* = \frac{Y^*-G^*}{Y-G+Y^*-G^*},$$

and where use has been made of the market-clearing condition by which

$$(1-\gamma\delta)\frac{R}{R-\gamma}(Y-T) + (1-\gamma\delta^*)\frac{R}{R-\gamma}(Y-T)$$

$$= Y-G+Y^*-G^*.$$

Thus a current budget deficit arising from a reduction of domestic taxes ($dT_0 < 0$) raises the rate of interest and domestic wealth and lowers foreign wealth. Multiplying these changes in wealth by the propensities to consume, $(1-\gamma\delta)$ and $(1-\gamma\delta^*)$, yields the corresponding changes in domestic and foreign consumption. These changes vanish if $\gamma = 1$.

In this part of the appendix we first derive the reduced-form equations (10.26) and (10.27). Throughout we omit equation (10.18) by Walras's law. Using equations (10.21) and (10.23) and solving for the future values of production of nontradable goods yields

$$p_n \overline{Y}_n = A\left[(R-1)sW_0 + \frac{(1-\gamma)R}{R-\gamma}(\overline{Y}_x - T)\right], \tag{A.7}$$

$$p_n^* \overline{Y}_n^* = A^*\left[(R-1)s^*W_0^* + \frac{(1-\gamma)R}{R-\gamma}(\overline{Y}_x^* - T^*)\right], \tag{A.8}$$

where

$$\theta = \frac{\beta_n^g \gamma_s^g G}{p_n \overline{Y}_n},$$

$$\theta^* = \frac{\beta_n^* \gamma_s^{*g} G^*}{p_n^* \overline{Y}_n^*},$$

$$A = \frac{\beta_n}{(1-\theta) - \beta_n(1-\gamma)R/(R-\gamma)},$$

$$A^* = \frac{\beta_n^*}{(1-\theta^*) - \beta_n^*(1-\gamma)R/(R-\gamma)}.$$

The requirement that in equilibrium there is positive consumption of nontradable goods that command a positive price imposes the feasibility condition according to which

$$A \geqslant 0, \quad A^* \geqslant 0. \tag{A.9}$$

Substituting (A.8) and equation (10.22) into equation (10.29) yields

$$W_0^* = D^*\left[\overline{Y}_x^* - T_0^* + \frac{\gamma}{R-\gamma}\left(1 + A^*\frac{(1-\gamma)R}{R-\gamma}\right)(\overline{Y}_x^* - T^*)\right.$$

$$\left. + (1 + r_{x,-1})(B_{-1}^{*g} + B_{-1})\right], \tag{A.10}$$

where

$$D^* = (1-\theta^*)\left\{(1-\theta^*)\right.$$

$$\left. - \beta_n^*\left[\frac{(R-1)\gamma s^*}{(1-\theta^*)(R-\gamma) - \beta_n^*(1-\gamma)R} + \frac{1-s^*}{1-\theta^*}\right]\right\}^{-1}.$$

The requirement that in equilibrium wealth is positive imposes the additional feasibility constraint according to which

$$D^* \geqslant 0. \tag{A.11}$$

Substituting equation (A.10) into equation (10.24) yields

$$(1 - \beta_n)(1 - s)W_0 + (1 - \beta_n^*)D^* \left\{ \overline{Y}_x^* - T_0^* \right.$$

$$+ \frac{\gamma}{R - \gamma} \left[1 + A^* \frac{(1 - \gamma)R}{R - \gamma} \right](\overline{Y}_x^* - T^*)$$

$$+ (1 + r_{x, -1})(B_{-1}^{*g} + B_{-1}) \right\}$$

$$= \overline{Y}_x - (1 - \beta_n^g)(1 - \gamma_s^g)G + \overline{Y}_x^* - (1 - \beta_n^{*g})(1 - \gamma_s^{*g})G^*. \tag{A.12}$$

Substituting equations (A.7) and (A.8) for $p_n \overline{Y}_n$ and $p_n^* \overline{Y}_n^*$ into equation (10.25) yields

$$(1 - \beta_n) \left[sW_0 + \frac{(1 - \gamma)R}{(R - 1)(R - \gamma)} \left\{ A(R - 1)sW_0 \right. \right.$$

$$+ \left[1 + A \frac{(1 - \gamma)R}{R - \gamma} \right](\overline{Y}_x - T) \right\} \right]$$

$$+ (1 - \beta_n^*) \left[s^*W_0^* + \frac{(1 - \gamma)R}{(R - 1)(R - \gamma)} \left\{ A^*(R - 1)s^*W_0^* \right. \right.$$

$$+ \left[1 + A^* \frac{(1 - \gamma)R}{R - \gamma} \right](\overline{Y}_x^* - T^*) \right\} \right]$$

$$= \frac{1}{R - 1} [\overline{Y}_x - (1 - \beta_n^g)\gamma_s^g G + \overline{Y}_x^* - (1 - \beta_n^{*g})\gamma_s^{*g}G^*]. \tag{A.13}$$

The system of equations (A.10), (A.12), and (A.13) can be used to solve for the equilibrium values of W_0, W_0^*, and R.

To derive the more compact formulation of the reduced-form equilibrium conditions of the text, we focus on the role of domestic tax policy by assuming that $G = G^* = T^* = 0$. We first note that for a given value of the parameters the equilibrium value of foreign wealth shown in equation (A.10) can be expressed implicitly as

$$W_0^* = W_0^*(R), \quad \frac{\partial W_0^*}{\partial R} < 0. \tag{A.14}$$

Equation (A.14) expresses foreign current wealth as a negative function of the rate of interest. This reduced-form relationship incorporates the equilibrium conditions in the markets for current and future nontradable goods. The negative dependence on the rate of interest reflects the role of the rate of interest in discounting future incomes and in influencing the real exchange rates used to evaluate the income streams. Next we define the domestic and foreign reduced-form future disposable incomes

$$I(R, W_0, T) = (R - 1)A\gamma\delta W_0 + \left[1 + \frac{(1 - \gamma)RA}{R - \gamma}\right](\bar{Y}_x - T) \tag{A.15}$$

and

$$I^*(R) = (R - 1)A^*\gamma\delta^* W_0^*(R) + \left[1 + \frac{(1 - \gamma)RA^*}{R - \gamma}\right]\bar{Y}_x^*. \tag{A.16}$$

Equation (A.15) expresses disposable income (in terms of tradable goods) as a negative function of future taxes, T, and a positive function of the relative price of nontradable goods, p_n. The latter in turn depends negatively on R through its effect on future wealth of those yet unborn) and positively on W_0 (through its effect on the demand of those alive). An analogous interpretation applies to the foreign disposable income, I^*, where in (A.47) we incorporate the functional dependence of W_0^* on R and the assumption that foreign taxes are zero.

Substituting equations (A.15) and (A.16) into (A.12) and (A.13) together with the assumption that $G = G^* = T^* = 0$ yields

$$(1 - \beta_n)(1 - \gamma\delta)W_0 + (1 - \beta_n^*)(1 - \gamma\delta^*)W_0^*(R) = \bar{Y}_x + \bar{Y}_x^*, \tag{A.17}$$

$$(1 - \beta_n)\left[\gamma\delta W_0 + \frac{(1 - \gamma)R}{(R - 1)(R - \gamma)} I(R, W_0, T)\right]$$

$$+ (1 - \beta_n^*)\left[\gamma\delta^* W_0^*(R) + \frac{(1 - \gamma)R}{(R - 1)(R - \gamma)} I^*(R)\right]$$

$$= \frac{1}{R - 1}(\bar{Y}_x + \bar{Y}_x^*). \tag{A.18}$$

Equations (A.17) and (A.18) are the reduced-form equilibrium conditions (10.26) and (10.27). These equations underlied the diagrammatical analysis of the text.

We turn next to a more formal analysis of the comparative statics results reported in the text. For this purpose we return to the complete model outlined in equations (10.18) through (10.24), omitting equation (10.25) by Walras's law. We continue to assume that $G = G^* = T^* = 0$. Substituting (A.7) and equation (10.20) into equation (10.19) yields

$$W_0 = D\left\{\bar{Y}_x - T_0 + \frac{\gamma}{R - \gamma}\left[1 + A\frac{(1 - \gamma)R}{R - \gamma}\right](\bar{Y}_x - T)\right.$$

$$\left. + (1 + r_{x,-1})(B_{-1}^g - B_{-1})\right\}, \tag{A.19}$$

where

$$D = \left\{1 - \beta_n\left[\frac{(R - 1)\gamma^2\delta}{(R - \gamma) - \beta_n(1 - \gamma)R} + (1 - \gamma\delta)\right]\right\}^{-1}.$$

Likewise, with zero foreign government spending and taxes, equation (A.10) becomes

$$W_0^* = D^*\left\{\bar{Y}_x^* + \frac{\gamma}{R - \gamma}\left[1 + A^*\frac{(1 - \gamma)R}{R - \gamma}\right]\bar{Y}_x^*\right.$$

$$\left. + (1 + r_{x,-1})(B_{-1}^{*g} + B_{-1})\right\}, \tag{A.20}$$

where

$$D^* = \left\{ 1 - \beta_n^* \left[\frac{(R-1)\gamma^2\delta^*}{(R-\gamma) - \beta_n^*(1-\gamma)R} + (1 - \gamma\delta^*) \right] \right\}^{-1},$$

and feasibility requires that $D \geqslant 0$ and $D^* \geqslant 0$. Finally, using equation (10.24), we get

$$(1 - \beta_n)(1 - \gamma\delta)W_0 + (1 - \beta_n^*)(1 - \gamma\delta^*)W_0^* = \overline{Y}_x + \overline{Y}_x^*. \qquad (A.21)$$

The system of equations (A.19) through (A.21) solves for the equilibrium values of W_0, W_0^*, and R. Differentiating this system, and noting that from the government budget constraint $dT_0 = -[1/(R-1)]\,dT$, yields

$$\frac{dW_0}{dT} = -(1 = \gamma)\frac{J_1 J_2}{\Delta}(1 - \beta_n^*)(1 - \gamma\delta^*) > 0, \qquad (A.22)$$

$$\frac{dW_0}{dT} = (1 = \gamma)\frac{J_1 J_2}{\Delta}(1 - \beta_n)(1 - \gamma\delta) < 0, \qquad (A.23)$$

$$\frac{dR}{dT} = -(1 - \gamma)\frac{J_2}{\Delta}(1 - \beta_n)(1 - \gamma\delta) > 0, \qquad (A.24)$$

where

$$\Delta = -\left\{ (1 - \beta_n^*)^2(1 - \gamma\delta^*)\frac{\gamma[1 - \beta_n^*(1-\gamma)]\overline{Y}_x^* D^{*2}}{[(R-\gamma) - \beta_n^*(1-\gamma)R]^2} \right.$$

$$\left. + (1 - \beta_n)^2(1 - \gamma\delta)\frac{\gamma[-\beta_n(1-\gamma)]\overline{Y}_x D^2}{[(R-\gamma) - \beta_n(1-\gamma)R]^2} \right\} < 0,$$

$$J_1 = \frac{(1 - \beta_n^*)\gamma[1 - \beta_n^*(1-\gamma)]\overline{Y}_x^* D^{*2}}{[(R-\gamma) - \beta_n^*(1-\gamma)R]^2} > 0,$$

$$J_2 = \frac{(1 - \beta_n)RD}{(R-1)[(R-\gamma) - \beta_n(1-\gamma)R]} > 0.$$

Using (A.22) and (A.24) together with equations (10.28) and (10.29) yields

$$\frac{dp_{n0}}{dT} = -(1 - \gamma)\frac{J_1 J_2}{\Delta \overline{Y}_n} \beta_n (1 - \gamma\delta)(1 - \beta_n^*)(1 - \gamma\delta^*) > 0, \qquad (A.25)$$

$$\frac{dp_{n0}^*}{dT} = (1 - \gamma)\frac{J_1 J_2}{\Delta \overline{Y}_n^*} \beta_n^* (1 - \gamma\delta^*)(1 - \beta_n)(1 - \gamma\delta) < 0. \qquad (A.26)$$

The results reported in (A.22) through (A.26) justify the diagrammatic analysis of the text. They show that a current budget deficit (necessitating a future rise in taxes so that $dT > 0$) raises domestic wealth, lowers foreign wealth, raises the world rate of interest, lowers the domestic current real exchange rate (the reciprocal of p_{n0}), and raises the foreign current real exchange rate. All of these real effects vanish if the value of γ approaches unity. In that case the pure wealth effects of budget deficits do not exist.

A similar computation reveals that the effects of the budget deficit on the future value of the real exchange rates are ambiguous. This ambiguity reflects the conflicting forces exercised by the wealth and substitution effects induced by the change in the rate of interest that in the home country supplements the direct wealth effects of the tax policy. It can be shown, however, that the budget deficit decelerates the rate of increase of the foreign real exchange rate between the present and the future period.

11

Fundamental Relations in International Taxation

This chapter is about the most fundamental relations among different combinations of fiscal instruments.[1] Taxes themselves may vary in many apparently significant respects, such as who pays them, what country collects them, when the taxes are collected, and whether the fiscal instruments are even thought of as taxes, yet many of these differences vanish with the households and firms. The resulting equivalences have an important bearing on the design and effectiveness of tax policy. They suggest that a given objective may be accomplished in a variety of ways, some perhaps more feasible or politically acceptable than others. Another implication, however, is that a tax policy may be subverted by the failure to coordinate such equivalent channels. These implications can have considerable economic significance, and there is ample evidence that they, as well as the equivalences themselves, are of prime relevance for policymaking.

For example, one fundamental equivalence we discuss is of combinations of trade-based (border) taxes on exports and imports and domestic taxes on production and consumption. A second equivalence concerns *direct* and *indirect* taxation. As Anthony Atkinson (1977) puts it, direct taxes are taxes that can be based on specific characteristics of individuals and households (e.g., marital status, number of dependents, or age) or businesses (e.g., type of industry). The main forms of direct taxes are personal and corporate income taxes, wealth taxes, and inheritance taxes. Indirect taxes are taxes based on *transactions* such as consumption, exports, or imports.

As we argue below, the relevance of these tax equivalences can be demonstrated using the economic integration of the countries of the European Community (EC, now the European Union, EU). Among the goals of the 1992 process of economic integration in Europe was a harmonization of national tax systems, aimed at eliminating the adverse incentives for the movement of capital, goods, and production activity that may derive from the conflicting national objectives of independently designed national tax systems.

Economic integration obviously requires limits on the ability of countries to tax or subsidize exports or imports within the integrated community. In addition, in recognition of the relevance of domestic taxation to export and import incentives, two types of domestic indirect taxation are dealt with in the harmonization provisions. An important indirect tax used in the EU is the value-added tax (VAT) that applies to the domestic consumption of goods and services. The coverage, rates, and method of calculation of such taxes vary extensively among the member countries. The difference in tax rates gives rise to incentives to move reported sales from high-tax to low-tax countries. Because of differences in tax base definitions, some sales across national borders may be taxed in more than one country. The harmonization proposals would attack these problems by reducing the extent of tax rate variation and standardizing the tax base definition. In addition, the excise duties currently levied at very different rates among countries on specific commodities such as alcoholic beverages, cigarettes, and gasoline would be entirely harmonized at uniform tax rates for each commodity.

The apparent motivation for these provisions is that they will facilitate the elimination of fiscal frontiers with the EU. This exclusive focus on indirect taxation is also found in the provisions of the General Agreements on Tariffs and Trade, (GATT, now the World Trade Organization, WTO), which restrict tax-based trade barriers. The discussion in this chapter implies, however, that there is little theoretical basis for such an approach. Just as domestic and trade-based indirect taxes have similar effects that require coordination, so too do direct and indirect taxes.

To provide the intuition for certain tax equivalences, we begin with a simple model in which many different types of tax policy are assumed to be the same and then show the conditions under which some of these very basic equivalences carry over to much more refined models that are better suited for guiding policy actions.

11.1 One-Period Model

We consider a one-period model of a small open economy with a single representative consumer. The country produces two goods in domestically owned industries, and both goods are consumed domestically. One good, X, is exported as well as being domestically consumed. The other good, M, is imported as well as being domestically produced. Each good is produced using two factors of production, labor, L, and capital, K. Let C_i be the domestic consumption of good i; L_i and K_i the levels of labor and capital allocated to industry i, respectively; w and r the factor returns of labor and capital, respectively; and π_i the pure profits generated for the household sector by industry i $(i = X, M)$. Let the world price of the export good be normalized to unity, with the relative world price of the imported good equal to p_M. In the absence of taxes the household's budget constraint is

$$C_X + p_M C_M = wL_X + wL_M + rK_X + rK_M + \pi_X + \pi_M. \tag{11.1}$$

Equation (11.1) states simply that spending equals income.

This budget constraint may be derived in an alternative way via the production and trade sectors of the economy. Starting with the production sector accounts, which require that production in sector i, Z_i, equal factor payments plus profits, we obtain

$$p_i Z_i = wL_i + rK_i + \pi_i, \qquad i = X, M. \tag{11.2}$$

To this we add the requirement that trade must be balanced; that is, exports must equal imports:

$$p_M(C_M - Z_M) = Z_X - C_X. \tag{11.3}$$

Equation (11.3) is a requirement imposed by the model's single-period assumption. No country will be willing to "lend" goods to the rest of the world by running a trade surplus; because there will be no subsequent period in which the debt can be repaid via a trade deficit. Using equation (11.2) in equation (11.3) yields equation (11.1), which can be then viewed as the overall budget constraint of the economy.

Let us now introduce to this model a variety of taxes including consumption taxes, income taxes, and trade taxes. In practice, consumption taxes may take a variety of forms, including retail sales taxes and VATs on consumption goods. In this simple model, with no intermediate production, the two types of taxes are identical. One could also impose a direct consumption tax at the household level. Although there has been considerable theoretical discussion of personal consumption taxes, no country has yet adopted such a tax.

Simple Equivalences

Let the tax on good i be expressed as a fraction τ_i of the producer price. (A basic and familiar feature concerning excise taxes is that it is irrelevant whether the tax is paid by the producer or the consumer.) The tax appears on the left-hand side of the budget constraint (11.1), and the export good's domestic consumer price becomes $1 + \tau_x$, and the import good's domestic consumer price becomes $(1 + \tau_M)p_M$. The producer domestic prices are $p_x = 1$ and p_M, respectively.

The first very simple equivalence to note is that the taxes could also be expressed as fractions $(\tau_i', i = X, M)$ of the consumer prices, in which case the consumer prices would become $p_i/(1 - \tau_i')$. This distinction is between a tax, τ, that has a *tax-exclusive* base and one, τ', that has a *tax-inclusive* base. If $\tau' = \tau/(1 + \tau)$, then the two taxes have identical effects on the consumer and producer and provide the same revenue to the government. Yet, when tax rates get reasonably high, the nominal difference between tax-exclusive and tax-inclusive rates becomes quite substantial. A tax-inclusive rate of 50 percent, for example, is equivalent to a tax-exclusive rate of 100 percent.

We consider now income taxes on profits and returns to labor and capital. Rather than raising consumer prices, these taxes reduce the resources available to consume. In practice, such taxes are assessed both directly and indirectly. There are individual and business income taxes, but also payroll taxes, for example. By the national income identity, a uniform VAT on all production is simply an indirect tax on domestic factor incomes, both payrolls and returns to capital and profits.

We note, as in the case of consumption taxes, that it does not matter whether the supplier of a factor, in this case the household, or the user, in this case the firm, must actually remit the tax. A factor tax introduced in equation (11.2) or (11.1) has the same effect. The same point holds in regard to tax-exclusive versus tax-inclusive tax bases. We also observe from inspection of (11.1) that a uniform tax on income is equivalent to uniform tax on consumption. Each tax reduces real income. Imposition of a tax-inclusive consumption tax at rate τ divides the left-hand side of (11.1) by the factor $(1 - \tau)$, whereas a tax-inclusive income tax (the way an income tax base is normally defined) at the same rate multiplies the right-hand side of (11.1) by $(1 - \tau)$. Because dividing one side of an equation by a certain factor is equivalent to multiplying the other side by the same factor, the equivalence between a uniform consumption tax and a uniform income tax is established in a one-period model.

Despite their simplicity, these basic equivalences are useful in understanding the potential effects of various policies. For example, the EU tax harmonization provisions would narrow differences in rates of VAT among member countries, but these provisions say nothing about income taxes. But our results suggest that a uniform consumption tax or any type of uniform income tax would be equivalent to a uniform VAT. Thus, a country with a VAT deemed too high could accede to the provisions of the harmonization process by lowering its VAT and raising other domestic taxes, with no impact on its own citizens nor, moreover, on the citizens of other countries either. We must conclude that either these proposals have not taken adequate account of simple equivalences or that the simple equivalences may break down in more complicated situations, a possibility we explore next.

International Trade Equivalences

We turn now to taxes explicitly related to international trade. We say *explicitly*, of course, because an obvious theme of this chapter is to recognize the equivalences that make some policies, not specifically targeted at trade, perfect substitutes for others that are.

Tax-based trade policies may involve border taxes, such as tariffs on imports or export subsidies, but may also be industry-specific taxes aimed, for example, at making trade-sensitive industries more competitive. It is well known that quantity restrictions may in some cases be used to replicate the effects of trade-based taxes. The most familiar case is the use of import quotas instead of tariffs. Other alternatives to explicit tax policies are discussed later.

The first equivalence we note among trade-based tax policies is between taxes on exports and taxes on imports. One might imagine that these policies would work in opposite directions, because the first appears to encourage a trade deficit (a decline in exports not of imports), whereas the second appears to discourage one. However, it must be remembered that this one-period model *requires* balanced trade. Hence, there can be no trade deficit or surplus; only the *level* of balanced trade may be influenced. Once this is recognized, the equivalence of these two policies can be more rapidly understood; each policy discourages trade by driving a wedge between the buyer's and seller's prices of one of the traded goods. This is the well-known Lerner's symmetry proposition.

Algebraically, the equivalence is straightforward. An import tax at a tax-exclusive rate of τ causes the domestic price of the imported good to equal the world price, p_M, multiplied by the factor $1 + \tau$. Note that because the import tax does not apply to the domestic producer, then $p_M(1 + \tau)$ is the domestic price not only for the consumer but also for the domestic producers. If we denote by w and r the equilibrium factor returns to labor and capital, respectively, the four-tuple

$$(p_M(1 + \tau); 1, w, r) \tag{11.4}$$

is an equilibrium domestic price vector with an import tax at a tax-exclusive rate of τ. On the other hand, an export tax at the same tax-exclusive rate of τ causes the exporting firm to receive only $1/(1 + \tau)$ for every unit of the export good sold at the export price of one. The rest, $\tau/(1 + \tau)$, equals what the tax exporters must pay, which is the tax rate times the net price received, $1/(1 + \tau)$. Note that $1/(1 + \tau)$ becomes also the domestic price of the export good, as an exporter can either sell domestically or abroad and must therefore receive the same net price at home and abroad. Multiplying the price vector (11.4) by $1/(1 + \tau)$, we obtain another price vector

$$\left(p_M, \frac{1}{(1 + \tau)}, w', r' \right), \tag{11.5}$$

where $w' = w/(1 + \tau)$, and $r' = r/(1 + \tau)$. Notice that the price vectors (11.4) and (11.5) represent the same *relative* prices. As only relative prices matter for economic behavior, the two price vectors, (11.4), and (11.5), support the same equilibrium allocation. Put differently, multiplying p_M on the left-hand side of the household's budget constraint by $1 + \tau$ (an import tax) is equivalent to multiplying all other prices in that equation (and the profits π_M and π_X) by $1/(1 + \tau)$ (an export tax). Thus, the equivalence between an import tax at a tax-exclusive rate of τ (which generates the equilibrium price vector (11.4)) and an export tax at the same tax-exclusive rate of τ (which generates the equilibrium price vector (11.5)) is established.

It is important to point out that this symmetry of trade taxes makes no assumption about whether the taxing country is small or large, that is, whether its policies can affect the relative world price of the two goods. The equivalence indicates that these two policies are really one.

Equivalences between Trade and Domestic Policies

The next class of policy equivalences we study is between trade policies and combinations of domestic policies. We have already shown that an import tariff at a tax-exclusive rate τ causes the domestic price of the imported good to equal the world price, p_M, multiplied by the factor $1 + \tau$. We also noted that $p_M(1 + \tau)$ is the domestic price for both the consumer and the producer. If instead of an import tax at a tax-exclusive rate of τ, the government imposes an excise (consumption) tax at the same tax-exclusive rate of τ, then the consumer price of the import good becomes $p_M(1 + \tau)$, but the producer price remains the world price of p_M. However, the producer will be indifferent between the import tax [which generates a producer price of $p_M(1 + \tau)$] and the excise tax (which generates a producer price of only p_M) if the excise tax is accompanied by a subsidy at a rate τ to domestic production that raises the price for the producer back to $p_M(1 + \tau)$. An immediate implication is that one cannot control tax-based trade barriers without also controlling domestic taxes and that controlling only domestic sales or consumption taxes alone is still not enough. It is possible to convert a perfectly domestic sales tax into an import tariff by subsidizing domestic production of the commodity in question at the rate of consumption tax already in place.

11.2   A Multiperiod Model: Double Taxation of Savings

Many of the equivalences just demonstrated hold in very general models. Even those that do not may "break down" in much more limited ways than one might think. Furthermore, the conditions under which such equivalences do fail provide insight into the channels through which different tax policies operate. Perhaps the most important extension of the simple model we have used is the addition of several periods during which households may produce and consume. This permits the appearance of saving, investment, and imbalances of both the government and trade accounts, the "two deficits."

In fact, we may go quite far toward such a model simply by reinterpreting the previous one. We consider once again the basic model of equations (11.1)–(11.3). We originally interpreted this as a one-period model, with capital and labor as primary factors supplied to the production process and p_M, w, and r the one-period relative prices of imports, labor, and capital. Let us consider instead a multiperiod economy. What would the budget constraint of a household choosing consumption and labor supply over several periods look like? We know that the household planning on bequests would equate the present value of its lifetime consumption to the present value of its lifetime labor income plus the initial value of its tangible wealth. What is this initial wealth? It equals the present value of all future profits plus the value of the initial capital stock. The value of the initial capital stock, in turn, may also be expressed as the present value of all future earnings on that capital. Thus we may replace expression (11.1) with

$$PV(C_X + p_M C_M) = PV(wL_X + wL_M) + PV(rK_X + rK_M)$$
$$+ PV(\pi_X + \pi_M), \tag{11.6}$$

where $PV(\ )$ represents the present value of a future stream rather than a single period quantity, K_i is the initial capital stock of industry i, and L_i and π_i are the flows of industry i's labor input and profits in period i.

In (11.6) we have made the transition to a multiperiod budget constraint. Note that this budget constraint no longer requires that income equal consumption in any given period, only that lifetime income (from labor plus initial wealth) equal lifetime consumption, in present value. Thus there may be saving in some periods and dis-saving in others.

Similar adjustments are needed to equations (11.2) and (11.3) to complete the transition to a multiperiod model. Just as a household need not balance its budget in any given year, a country need not have balanced trade in any given year. Over the entire horizon of the model, however, trade must be balanced in present value, following the argument used for balance in the one-period model. That is, each country will give up no more goods and services, in present value, than it receives. The dates of these matching exports and imports may be different, of course, and this is what causes single-period trade deficits and surpluses. Thus equation (11.3) becomes

$$PV[p_M[C_M - Z_M)] = PV[Z_X - C_X]. \tag{11.7}$$

The last equation in need of reinterpretation is (11.2). The natural analogue in the multiperiod context is

$$PV(p_i Z_i) = PV(wL_i) + PV(rK_i) + PV(\pi_i), \qquad i = X, M, \qquad (11.8)$$

which says that the present value of output in each industry equals the present value of the streams of payments to labor and profits plus the payments to the *initial* capital stock. However, this condition requires further explanation, because one might expect returns to all capital over time, and not just the initial capital stock, to appear on the right-hand side of the expression.

The explanation is that new investment and its returns are subsumed by the "final form" relationship between final outputs and primary inputs given in (11.8). Stated differently, Z_i is the output that is available for final uses outside the production sector (that is, for either domestic consumption or exports). We may think of capital goods produced after the initial date and then used in production as intermediate goods. Normal production relations represent each stage of production. In a two-period model, for example, we would depict first-period capital and consumption as being produced by initial capital and first-period labor, and second-period consumption as being produced by initial capital plus capital produced during the first period, and second-period labor. Inserting the first-period production relation into the second-period production relation allows us to eliminate first-period capital from the equation, giving us a single "final form" relating each period's consumption to each period's labor input and the initial stock of capital. This approach may be applied recursively in the same manner for multiperiod models, leading to the type of relationship given in (11.8). In fact, if the capital goods produced in one industry are used in the other, then (11.8) does not hold for each industry separately—only when the two conditions are summed together. This is still consistent with conditions (11.6) and (11.7).

Given the similarity of the multiperiod model (11.6)–(11.8) and the single-period model (11.1)–(11.3), it is not surprising that several of the one-period equivalences carry over to the multiperiod model. First, a permanent tax on consumption is equivalent to a permanent tax on labor income plus profits plus the returns to the initial capital stock. A permanent consumption tax at a tax-exclusive rate of τ causes expression (11.6) to become

$$PV[(1 + \tau)(C_X + p_M C_M)] = PV(wL_x + wL_M) + PV(rK_X + rK_M)$$

$$+ PV(\pi_X + \pi_M). \tag{11.9}$$

Multiplying this equation by $1 - \tau' = 1/(1 + \tau)$, we obtain

$$PV(C_X + p_M C_M) = PV[(wL_x + wL_M)(1 - \tau')]$$

$$+ PV[(rK_K + rK_M)(1 - \tau')]$$

$$+ PV[(\pi_M + \pi_X)(1 - \tau')]. \tag{11.10}$$

Equation (11.10) is obtained from (11.6) when a permanent tax at a tax-inclusive rate of τ' is imposed on labor income plus profits plus the returns to the initial stock of capital. Thus the equivalence between the latter tax and a consumption tax is established. Clearly this equivalence holds only if the tax rates are *constant* over time, so that the tax terms can be taken outside the present value operators $PV(\ )$. One may be tempted to interpret this result as showing that consumption taxes and income taxes are equivalent in multiperiod models with saving, but it is important to recognize that the type of income tax imposed here is not the income tax as normally conceived. The tax here is on wage income plus capital income attributable to initial wealth. It excludes from the tax base the income attributable to capital generated by saving done during the model's periods. Were such income also taxed, there would be an additional change to both sides of (11.6): the present-value operator, $PV(\ )$, which aggregates future streams of income and consumption, would now be based on the after-tax interest rate, $r(1 - \tau')$, rather than on the market interest rate, r. Transferring resources from one period to a subsequent one would now increase the household's tax burden. Indeed, this *double taxation* of saving has traditionally been emphasized in distinguishing income taxation from consumption taxation.

On the other hand, it is also no longer true that labor-income taxation and consumption taxation are equivalent. The equivalence we have uncovered is between consumption taxation, and labor-income taxation *plus* taxes on profits and the returns to the initial capital stock. This distinction between consumption taxes and labor-income taxes has been misleadingly termed a "transition" issue by some, because only the capital income from initial assets is concerned. However, such income is large, even in present value. For example, if the economy's capital to output ratio is 3, and the ratio of output to consumption is 1.5 (realistic values for the United States), then a permanent consumption tax of, say, 20 percent, which attaches 20 percent of these assets' flows and hence 20 percent of their value, will raise additional revenue equal to 90 percent (0.2 × 3 × 1.5) of one year's consumption.

The equivalence between export and import taxes also carries over to the multiperiod case. Inspection of (11.7) shows that the imposition of a permanent import tariff at rate τ multiplies the terms inside the present-value operator on the left-hand side by $(1 + \tau)$, whereas an export tax divides each of the terms inside the present-value operator on the right-hand side by $(1 + \tau)$. Again, if the tax rates are constant over time, one may take them outside the present-value operators, and the logic of the one-period model then applies. Clearly the equivalence would not hold for time-varying tax rates. For example, a single-period import tax would be expected not only to discourage trade overall but also to shift imports to other periods. Likewise an export tax would not only discourage trade but also shift exports to other periods. Thus one would expect the first policy to lead to a greater trade surplus *in the period of taxation* than the second.

A similar outcome for temporary taxation would hold in the previous case of consumption taxes and taxes on labor income plus returns to initial assets. It has been argued that a VAT should be more favorable to the development of trade surpluses because of its use of the destination principle rather than the origin principle of taxation. Indeed, for a one-period tax, this will be so, because a one-period consumption tax (destination-based VAT) will shift consumption to other periods, whereas a one-period income tax will shift production to other periods.

Thus the primary requirements for the basic one-period equivalences to carry over to the multiperiod context are that rates be permanent and the returns to savings not be taxed. (Even the basic equivalences depend on our implicit assumption that there are no additional nominal constraints on the system—for example, that it is just as easy for a real wage reduction to be accomplished through a fall in the nominal wage as a rise in the price level.) Yet it is unrealistic to assume that governments wish to keep taxes constant over time or that, even if they did, they could bind themselves to do so. Likewise the taxation of new saving and investment plays an extremely important role not only in the domestic policy context but also increasingly in the international area, as world capital markets become more integrated and the transactions and information costs to investment abroad decline. It is important that we go beyond the previous analysis to consider the effects of changing tax rates and the taxation of savings and investment.

11.3   Tax Equivalences in a Two-Period Model and Cash-Flow Taxation

To allow a tractable treatment of more general tax policies and yet maintain the dynamic aspect of the multiperiod model, we consider a two-period model with a single consumption good, no pure profits, and fixed labor supply, with the input in each period normalized to unity. In such a model there can no longer be exports and imports in the same period, but issues of trade can still be discussed because there can be exports in one period and imports in another. Because we wish to consider time-varying tax policies and capital-income taxation, we must explicitly treat capital accumulation, including foreign as well as domestic investment. This is most easily exposited by representing separately the budget constraints the household faces in each of the two periods, taking account of first-period savings decisions.

In the absence of taxes the household's budget constraints in periods zero and one for this model are

$$C_0 = w_0 + \rho_0 K_{D0} + \rho_0^* K_{F0} - K_{D1} - K_{F1}, \tag{11.11}$$

$$C_1 = w_1 + \rho_1 K_{D1} + \rho_1^* K_{F1}, \tag{11.12}$$

where C_i is period i consumption, w_i is the wage in period i, ρ_i is the return to capital in the home country in period i, ρ_i^* is the return to capital in the foreign country in period i, K_{Di} is the stock of domestic capital owned by the household in period i, and K_{Fi} is the stock of foreign capital owned by the household in period i. In terms of the multiperiod model previously considered, K_{D1} and K_{F1} are stocks of initial capital. Capital fully depreciates in each period. There are no costs of adjustment of investment. The only savings decisions involve the levels of second-period capital purchased.

Now let us introduce taxes to this model. In addition to the consumption taxes and labor income taxes discussed previously, we consider several taxes on capital income. We make three important distinctions with respect to these capital-income taxes: whether they are assessed at home or abroad, whether they are assessed on the firm or the household, and whether they apply to capital invest-ment or capital income. These three binary distinctions give rise to eight types of capital-income tax. Although such a number of tax instruments may seem excessive, each of these taxes has differ-ent economic effects, and all have significant real-world representa-tions. Indeed, there are still important restrictions implicit in this characterization.

The eight instruments are denoted τ_{RD}, τ_B, τ_{RF}, τ_{NB}^*, τ_{HS}, τ_I, τ_{RFC}, and τ_I^*. The first four apply to capital income, and they may be different in periods zero and one. The last four apply to capital investment and hence are relevant only in period zero. We now define each of these taxes and offer real-world examples:

τ_{RD} = household-level domestic tax on income from domestic investment, such as taxes on interest and dividend income from domestic sources.

τ_B = firm-level domestic tax on income from domestic invest-ment, such as domestic corporate income taxes.

τ_{RF} = household-level domestic tax on income from foreign investment, such as taxes on interest and dividend income from foreign sources (net of foreign tax credits).

τ_{NB}^* = firm level foreign tax on income from foreign investment, such as foreign corporate income taxes.

τ_{HS} = household-level domestic rate of deduction for domestic investment.

τ_I = firm-level domestic rate of deduction for domestic investment, such as domestic investment tax credit.

τ_{RFC} = household-level domestic rate of deduction for foreign investment, such as tax-deductible pension saving abroad.

τ_I^* = firm-level foreign rate of deduction for foreign investment, such as foreign investment tax credit.

Note that the two tax instruments denoted by an asterisk are applied by foreign governments to investment and capital income owned by the domestic household in the foreign countries. This tax classification scheme does not include domestic taxes on foreign corporate income. For simplicity we assume that all investment abroad is portfolio investment by domestic households rather than foreign direct investment by corporations. We adopt this restriction not because foreign direct investment is unimportant empirically (for this is not the case) but because the effects of taxation on foreign investment can be described adequately using the instruments already specified. Likewise we ignore the fact that such portfolio income may in some countries be taxed by the host country at the individual as well as firm levels before being repatriated.

In any particular country several of these eight capital tax instruments might be absent. For example, if a country integrated its personal and corporate income tax systems, a policy often recommended but never fully adopted, all separate firm-level taxes would vanish. If a country's tax rules called for taxation of foreign-source capital income, the tax rate τ_{RF} could be low or even zero if the home country credited foreign taxes on such income. In such a scheme the tax on foreign-source income is

$$\tau_{RF} = \frac{(\tau - \tau^*)}{(1 - \tau^*)},$$

where τ and τ^* are the statutory rates of income tax in the home and foreign countries, respectively. Thus, if $\tau = \tau^*$, $\tau_{RF} = 0$.

To introduce these taxes into the budget constraints (11.11) and (11.12) in a realistic manner, we need one additional element of notation. Most countries that tax household capital income emanating from firms do so only on a *realization* basis. Households are taxed on dividends and interest received, but not on corporate retained earnings. This has important implications concerning the cost of capital and the market value of corporate assets. To represent the fact that retained earnings are not taxed at the household level, we let R_0 and R_0^* be earnings retained in period 0 by domestic and foreign corporations owned by domestic households and assume that household-level taxes on corporate income are levied on earnings net of these values.

Letting τ_{ci} be the tax-exclusive consumption tax and τ_{Li} the labor income tax in period i, we rewrite the budget constraints (11.11) and (11.12) to account for the capital-income tax treatment just considered as

$$(1 + \tau_{C0})C_0 = (1 - \tau_{L0})w_0 + (1 - \tau_{RD0})[(1 - \tau_{B0})\rho_0 K_{D0} - R_0]$$
$$+ (1 - \tau_{RF0})[(1 - \tau_{NB0}^*)\rho_0^* K_{F0} - R_0^*]$$
$$- (1 - \tau_{HS})[(1 - \tau_I)K_{D1} - R_0]$$
$$- (1 - \tau_{RFC})[(1 - \tau_I^*)K_{F1} - R_0^*] \tag{11.13}$$

and

$$(1 + \tau_{C1})C_1 = (1 - \tau_{L1})w_1 + (1 - \tau_{RD1})(1 - \tau_{B1})\rho_1 K_{D1}$$
$$+ (1 - \tau_{RF1})(1 - \tau_{NB1}^*)\rho_1^* K_{F1}. \tag{11.14}$$

Despite its apparent complexity this system is useful in demonstrating a variety of tax equivalences.

We begin with a special case. Suppose that there are no taxes at the firm level, and that tax rates for deductions on investment at home and abroad, τ_{HS} and τ_{RFC}, equal the corresponding taxes on investment income, τ_{RD} and τ_{RF}, respectively. The budget constraints (11.13) and (11.4) then become

$$(1 + \tau_{C0})C_0 = (1 - \tau_{L0})w_0 + (1 - \tau_{RD0})(\rho_0 K_{D0} - K_{D1})$$

$$+ (1 - \tau_{RF0})(\rho_0^* K_{F0} - K_{F1}) \tag{11.15}$$

and

$$(1 + \tau_{C1})C_1 = (1 - \tau_{L1})w_1 + (1 - \tau_{RD1})\rho_i K_{D1}$$

$$+ (1 - \tau_{RF1})\rho_1^* K_{F1}. \tag{11.16}$$

Note that in this case the consumption tax in each period is equivalent to a combination of taxes in the same period at the same rate on labor income, domestic capital income, and foreign capital income, net of domestic and foreign investment. This is a new result, but it is closely related to one derived in the previous section. If, in addition, we assume that the tax rates are constant over time, and the rates of return ρ_1 and ρ_1^* are equal (as would be the case if foreign and domestic investments were taxed at the same rate and investors chose to hold each), we may combine (11.15) and (11.16) to obtain

$$(1 + \tau_C)\left(C_0 + \frac{C_1}{\rho_1}\right) = (1 - \tau_L)\left(w_0 + \frac{w_1}{\rho_1}\right) + (1 - \tau_{RD})\rho_0 K_{D0}$$

$$+ (1 - \tau_{RF})\rho_0^* K_{F0}, \tag{11.17}$$

which gives the previous multiperiod result, confirming the equivalence of a constant consumption tax to taxes at the same rate on labor income and the income from initial assets.

Even when tax rates differ across periods, we have identified an important period-by-period equivalence between consumption and income taxes. A consumption tax can be replicated by a tax on labor income plus taxes on domestic plus foreign capital income, net of new investment. This is in no way inconsistent with our previous intuition that a consumption tax does not impose a tax on new savings: a constant tax on capital income, net of investment, imposes no tax in present value on the income from new investment.

Although the entire return from such investment is taxed, its entire cost is deducted at the same rate. Thus, the government is simply a fair partner in the enterprise (although because of its passive role in the actual operation of the firm it is sometimes called a "sleeping" partner). Only income from capital already in place at the beginning of period one is subject to a true tax, and this tax was previously seen to be part of the income tax-equivalent scheme.

These foreign and domestic taxes on capital income less investment are sometimes called *cash-flow* taxes, because they are based on net flows from the firm. In the case of the foreign tax, the cash-flow tax is a tax on net capital inflows. In this sense it is equivalent to a policy of taxing foreign borrowing and interest receipts and subsidizing foreign lending and payments of interest. In the domestic literature on taxation much has been made of the equivalence between labor-income taxes plus business cash-flow taxes and consumption taxes. But in an open economy this equivalence also requires the taxation of cash flows from abroad; otherwise, the destination-based consumption tax will include an extra piece that is absent from the tax on labor and domestic capital income net of domestic investment.

We turn next to issues related to the level of capital-income taxation, business versus household. In the real world, some payments by firms to suppliers of capital are taxed only at the investor level, without being subject to a business-level tax. These are interest payments, which are treated as tax-deductible business expenses. Other payments—dividends—are typically either partially deductible or not deductible at all. One may think of the tax rates τ_B and τ_{NB}^* as representing weighted-average tax rates of the positive tax rate on dividends and the zero tax rate on interest. (Again it is typical for the *individual* tax rates on these two forms of capital income to differ, but not as significantly. We ignore such differences in our model.)

One would expect these tax provisions to affect firms' incentives with respect to retained earnings, R and R^*. Indeed, it is clear from the budget constraint (11.13) that the optimal policy will be to maximize (minimize) R if $\tau_{RD} > (<) \tau_{HS}$; likewise, for foreign investment R^* should be maximized (minimized) if $\tau_{RF} > (<) \tau_{RFC}$. In the "normal" case that savers do not receive a full immediate deduction for funds supplied to the firm, firms will retain earnings until constrained from doing so. This would presumably be when they had financed all their investment, $(1 - \tau_I)K_{D1}$, or exhausted all available internal funds, $(1 - \tau_B)\rho_0 K_{D0}$. Were τ_{RD} to equal τ_{HS}, households would be indifferent: payments made to them by the firm and then immediately sent back would have no tax consequences. Following the same logic, a more generous rate of savings deduction would lead firms to distribute as much as possible to allow savers the opportunity to return the funds and reduce their net taxes. The lower limit on retentions would be zero, as dividends cannot be negative.

We thus have three cases domestically (and analogously three cases with respect to foreign savings):

1. $\tau_{RD} > \tau_{HS}$ and $R = \min[(1 - \tau_I)K_{D1}, (1 - \tau_B)\rho_0 K_{D0}]$.
2. $\tau_{RD} = \tau_{HS}$ and $\min[(1 - \tau_I)K_{D1}, (1 - \tau_B)\rho_0 K_{D0}] > R > 0$.
3. $\tau_{RD} < \tau_{HS}$ and $R = 0$.

For each of these cases we may substitute the optimal value of R into equation (11.13) to obtain a budget constraint in which R does not explicitly appear. In the normal case (1) and the intermediate case (2), this procedure yields

$$(1 + \tau_{C0})C_0 = (1 - \tau_{L0})w_0$$
$$+ (1 - \tau_{DS0})[(1 - \tau_{B0})\rho_0 K_{D0} - (1 - \tau_I)K_{D1}]$$
$$+ (1 - \tau_{FL0})[(1 - \tau_{NB}^*)\rho_0^* K_{F0} - (1 - \tau_I^*)K_{F1}],$$
$$(11.13a)$$

where

$$\tau_{DS} = \begin{cases} \tau_{HS} & \text{if } (1 - \tau_{B0})\rho_0 K_{D0} < (1 - \tau_I)K_{D1}, \\ \tau_{RD} & \text{if } (1 - \tau_{B0})\rho_0 K_{D0} > (1 - \tau_I)K_{D1}, \end{cases}$$

$$\tau_{FL} = \begin{cases} \tau_{RFC} & \text{if } (1 - \tau_{NB}^*)\rho_0^* K_{F0} < (1 - \tau_I^*)K_{F1}, \\ \tau_{RF} & \text{if } (1 - \tau_{NB}^*)\rho_0^* K_{F0} > (1 - \tau_I^*)F_{F1}. \end{cases}$$

The value of τ_{DS} depends on whether the firm is in a regime in which it is paying dividends at the margin and hence financing marginal investment from retained earnings, τ_{RD}, or not paying dividends and financing new investment through issues of new shares, τ_{HS}. In either case, however, the behavior of the optimizing firm induces a household-level cash-flow tax. This implies that the economy may be closer to cash-flow taxation than might appear from the statutory tax treatment of household capital income. In particular, the *effective* tax burden on capital income at the household level is zero in present value, even if there are dividends and $\tau_{RD} > \tau_{HS}$. This is another equivalence, of existing systems of household capital income taxation to household cash-flow taxation.

A final equivalence involving the two levels of capital income taxation is *between* taxes at the two levels. In a variety of situations a tax at the firm level is equivalent to one at the household level. Consider, for example, the case in which all capital income taxes are cash-flow taxes. This is like the situation considered in equation (11.15) but with cash-flow business taxes added. In this case the first-period budget constraint is

$$(1 + \tau_{C0})C_0 = (1 - \tau_{L0})w_0 + (1 - \tau_{RD0})(1 - \tau_{B0})(\rho_0 K_{D0} - K_{D1})$$

$$+ (1 - \tau_{RF0})(1 - \tau_{B0}^*)(\rho_0^* K_{F0} - K_{F1}). \qquad (11.13b)$$

(The second-period budget constraint [11.14] is unaffected.) It is clear from this equation that it is irrelevant from the household's viewpoint whether taxes are collected from firms or individuals. The tax rate τ_B is a perfect substitute for τ_{RD}, and τ_B^* is one for τ_{RF}. In the first case, with both taxes collected by the same government, the equivalence is complete; government is indifferent as well. In the second case this would not be so, unless a tax treaty existed that directed capital income taxes collected on specific assets to specific countries regardless of who actually collected the taxes.

Even in the domestic case, the taxes might *appear* to have different effects due to their different collection points. For example, measured rates of return from the corporate sector would be net of tax were the taxes collected from firms, but gross of tax were they collected from households.

11.4 Present-Value Equivalences and the Measurement of Public Deficits

In discussing cash-flow taxation, we have made a point that has a more general application: that tax policies may change the timing of tax collections without changing their burden, in present value. A constant-rate cash-flow tax exerts no net tax on the returns to marginal investment, giving investors an initial deduction equal in present value to the ultimate tax on positive cash flows the investment generates.

In our two-period model, a cash-flow tax at a constant rate collects revenue equal in present value only to the cash flows from the first-period capital stock. Thus, an initial wealth tax on that stock would be equivalent from the viewpoint of both household and government. For example, consider the simple case with no firm-level taxes and constant tax rates examined previously. This is the example in which the first-period and second-period budget constraints can be combined as in the multiperiod model of the previous section. These three budget constraints (first-period, second-period, and combined) are under cash-flow taxation (assuming that $\rho = \rho^*$):

$$(1 + \tau_C)C_0 = (1 - \tau_L)w_0 + (I - \tau_{RD})(\rho_0 K_{D0} - K_{D1})$$

$$+ (1 - \tau_{RF})(\rho_0^* K_{F0} - K_{F1}), \tag{11.15a}$$

$$(1 + \tau_C)C_1 = (1 - \tau_L)w_1 + (1 - \tau_{RD})\rho_1 K_{D1} + (1 - \tau_{RF})\rho_1^* K_{F1}, \tag{11.16a}$$

and

$$(1 + \tau_C)\left(C_0 + \frac{C_1}{\rho_1}\right) = (1 - \tau_L)\left(w_0 + \frac{w_0}{\rho_1}\right) + (1 - \tau_{RD})\rho_D K_{D0}$$

$$+ (1 - \tau_{RF})\rho_0^* K_{F0}. \tag{11.17a}$$

Here, if the terms K_{D1} and K_{F1} appearing in the first- and second-period budget constraints were no longer multiplied by $1 - \tau_{RD}$ and $1 - \tau_{RF}$, respectively, cash-flow tax would be replaced by a first-period tax on the returns to existing capital—a wealth tax—yet there would be no impact at all on the household's combined budget constraint. Its *measured* saving would be affected, but not its consumption.

Just as measured household saving would be affected, so would there also be apparent differences between the levels of government debt in the two cases. In the cash-flow tax case the government's revenue would be lower in the first and higher in the second period, and it would have a smaller first-period budget deficit. At the same time, firm values would be lower, to account for the larger impending second-period cash-flow tax payments. Indeed, these differences exactly offset each other. One could imagine the cash-flow tax policy as being a combination of the wealth tax policy plus a decision by the government to lend in the first period and force firms to accept loans of equal value at the market interest rate, to be repaid in the same period. Firms would require fewer funds from the household sector, leaving households just enough extra money to purchase the bonds floated by the government.

Thus, the explicitly measured government debt is not an accurate indicator of policy, because it may vary considerably between the two equivalent situations. One may think of the "forced loans" of the cash-flow tax system as being off-budget assets that cause the deficit to be overstated, assets that can be brought on budget by recalling the loans, paying back the debt, and shifting to the wealth tax.

One can imagine many similar examples of present-value equivalences, none of which go beyond the bounds of the realistic tax policies we have already considered. The government can arbitrarily change the measured composition of a household's wealth between government debt and tangible capital (and indeed between government debt and human capital, through changes in the time pattern of labor-income taxation) simply by introducing offsetting levels of debt and forced loans attached to these other assets. This is true whether or not the asset owners are domestic residents or not. Foreign owners of a domestic corporation that is suddenly hit with a cash-flow tax on *new* investment (i.e., excluding the wealth-tax effect on preexisting capital) will spend less of their funds on the domestic firms and the remainder on other assets—quite possibly the government debt—but not on the country's external debt, that is, the aggregate value of domestic assets owned by foreigners.

It is noteworthy that the government's ability to shift such asset values of foreigners is more circumscribed than its ability with respect to domestic residents. It cannot, for example, cause a reduction in the value of a foreigner's human capital offset by a loan to the foreigner (by cutting labor-income taxes today and raising them in the future), because it cannot tax the foreigner's labor income. All adjustments with respect to external debt must be through the tax treatment of foreign-owned domestic assets.

Problems

1. Consider a two-country model of the world economy as in chapter 6. In each period t, the home country is completely specialized in the production of good X_t and similarly, the foreign country is completely specialized in the production of good M_t, $t = 1, 2$. Let p_t denote the relative price of good X_t, i.e., the terms of trade of the home country and let M_t serve as numeraire throughout. Let R denote the world discount factor in terms of the foreign good. The budget constraint of the representative consumer living in the home country is

$$p_1 c_{x1} + c_{m1} + R(p_2 c_{x2} + c_{m2})$$
$$= p_1(X_1 - I_1 - T_1) + Rp_2[X_2(K_1 + I_1) - T_2],$$

where I_1 represents the level of domestic investment; c_{xt} and c_{mt} denote consumption of home and foreign goods in period t; K_1 is the initial capital stock and the technology $X_2(\cdot)$ satisfies $X_2' > 0$ and $X_2'' < 0$. Tax liabilities in period t are denoted T_t. A corresponding constraint holds for the representative consumer living in the foreign country:

$$p_1 c_{x1}^* + c_{m1}^* + R(p_2 c_{x2}^* + c_{m2}^*)$$
$$= (M_1 - I_1^* - T_1^*) + R[M_2^*(K_1^* + I_1^*) - T_2^*],$$

where an asterisk denotes a corresponding foreign variable and where the technology $M_2(\cdot)$ satisfies $M_2' > 0$ and $M_2'' < 0$.

a. Show that I_1 is an increasing function of the domestic discount factor Rp_2/p_1 while I_1^* is an increasing function of the foreign discount factor R.

b. Suppose that the representative consumer in the home country has the following utility function:

$$U = \frac{C_1^{1-1/\sigma} + DC_2^{1-1/\sigma}}{1 - 1/\sigma},$$

where $C_t = c_{xt}^b c_{mt}^{1-b}$ and D is the subjective discount factor. The utility function in the foreign country is also CES and the period-utility function Cobb-Douglas. Assume that preferences are identical so that $D = D^*$, $\sigma = \sigma^*$, and $b = b^*$ (where b^* denotes the expenditure share on good x). Consider an initial equilibrium in which government spending levels in both countries are optimally set (i.e., government spending is zero in both countries). What is the effect of a temporary current period increase in government spending undertaken by the home country on domestic and foreign investment levels? Consider both the cases where the government spends on domestic goods and on foreign goods.

2. Consider the two-country model developed in the previous exercise. Can a temporary fiscal expansion lead to a negative comovement between consumption growth rates at home and abroad? Discuss your answer.

3. Consider a two-country model of the world economy. In each period t, each country receives endowments of two goods X_t and M_t for the home country X_t^* and M_t^* for the foreign country, where the first good is assumed to be exported by the home country and the second is imported by the home country, and $t = 1, 2$. The world relative price of importables is denoted p_t and the world discount factor is R. The numéraire is the home country's exportable. There is no investment. The budget constraint of the representative consumer living in the home country is

$$c_{x1} + p_1(1 + \tau_1)c_{m1} + R[c_{x2} + p_2(1 + \tau_2)c_{m2}]$$

$$= [X_1 + p_1(1 + \tau_1)M_1 + G_1] + R[X_2 + p_2(1 + \tau_2)M_2 + G_2]$$

$$= W,$$

where τ_t is an ad valorem tariff levied by the government of the home country on imports $(c_{mt} - M_t)$ and G_t denotes government spending on transfers, which consumers take as given. The government's budget constraint satisfies

$$G_1 + RG_2 = \tau_1 p_1 c_{m1} + R\tau_2 p_2 c_{m2}.$$

In the foreign country the consumer's budget constraint is given by

$$c_{x1}^* + p_1 c_{m1}^* + R(c_{x2}^* + p_2 c_{m2}^*) = (X_1^* + p_1 M_1^*) + R(X_2^* + p_2 M_2^*)$$
$$= W^*,$$

where it has been assumed that there is no tariff in the foreign country, and where an asterisk denotes a corresponding foreign-economy variable. Suppose that preferences in the home country are given by

$$U = \log[c_{x1}^b c_{m1}^{1-b}] + D\log[c_{x2}^b c_{m2}^{1-b}],$$

where $0 < b < 1$ and D is the subjective discount factor. Assume that preferences in the foreign country are of the same form and that $b = b^*$ and $D = D^*$.

a. Beginning from an initial equilibrium of free trade (i.e., $\tau_2 = \tau_2 = 0$), find the effect on relative prices p_1 and p_2 of the imposition of a permanent tariff (i.e., $d\tau_1 = d\tau_2 = d\tau > 0$).

b. Find the effect on the period 1 trade balance of the permanent tariff. You may assume that initially the trade account balance is equal to zero. How does your answer compare to the answer you got in exercise 6 in part III for the case of a small country? Discuss this.

4. Consider an endowment economy where dynasties, in contrast to the model in chapter 9, have infinite lives. Suppose that new cohorts enter the economy in each period, say due to immigration, and that the total population grows at a constant rate n. While new entrants have no initial debt they are otherwise identical to existing dynasties. In particular, all agents have identical endowments ("labor incomes") and are subject to the same lump-sum taxes. Suppose that

preferences of an agent born at time s can be described by a log-utility function:

$$U(s) = \sum_{\delta}^{\infty} \delta^t \ln\{c(s, t)\},$$

where δ denotes the subjective discount factor $(0 < \delta < 1)$ and $c(s, t)$ is consumption in period t of an agent born at time s $(s \geq t)$.

a. Describe the optimal consumption path and debt allocation for agents born in period s.

b. Find the *aggregate* consumption path and the law of motion for the different types of wealth. Explain why the relevant private-sector discount rates are different for human capital and financial assets/debt.

c. Show that for $n > 0$ Ricardian neutrality does not hold even though agents have infinite horizons.

5. Consider the infinite horizon overlapping generations model with nonzero population growth that was developed in exercise 4. Suppose that the government enacts a temporary tax cut followed by future tax increases that leave government's spending path unchanged. Calculate the value of the current-consumption multiplier for alternative length of the tax-cut period and different values of the population growth rate. Assume that the interest rate factor $R = 1.05$, the subjective discount factor $\delta = 0.95$, and let the time interval for the tax cut range from 1 to 7 periods. Compare the results to the effects of varying life expectancies in the model of chapter 9.

6. Consider the overlapping-generations model of chapter 9 where agents have a constant survival probability γ. In an extension to the model, suppose that new cohorts arrive each period as described in exercise 4. Consequently total population is growing at a constant rate n. For simplicity assume that an agent's preferences can be described by a logarithmic expected utility function.

a. Derive the optimal consumption path and the laws of motion for different types of wealth.

b. Explain the conditions for debt neutrality. Show that the results in chapter 9 and exercise 4 emerge as special cases.

7. Consider the two-country overlapping generations model of chapter 10. Suppose that preferences of domestic and foreign agents can be represented by logarithmic utility functions and that the planning horizon is identical for individuals in both countries ($\gamma = \gamma^* < 1$). Let the foreign government's budget be balanced in all periods. Assume that the path of domestic government expenditure remains unaffected by the following modifications to the budget deficit:

a. Suppose that all future periods are aggregated into a single period. In this two-period model, derive the effects of an anticipated future budget deficit on the "constancy equivalent" interest rate.

b. Let future periods be divided into two separate intervals, a "near" future and a "distant" future. Suppose that the domestic government alters taxes in the near future and offsets the revenue effects by changing taxes in the distant future, leaving current period taxes unchanged. For simplicity assume initial debt, taxes, and government spending are zero and that outputs are stationary. Show that a deficit in the near future will increase the future interest rate. Also demonstrate that the effect on the interest rate between the current period and the near future depends on a familiar transfer criterion.

8. Consider a small open economy version of the model in chapter 10. Suppose that the country produces both tradable and nontradable goods and that the output levels of either good are fixed over time. Agents have a finite planning horizon as a result of their finite lifespans and incomplete bequest motives. Assume that the consumer's preferences can be represented by a logarithmic expected utility function. The government buys tradable and nontradable goods, and its purchases are financed with lump-sum taxes. Finally, assume that the small country faces a constant interest rate, r_x, in terms of the tradable good, the numéraire in the analysis.

a. Show that the private propensity to save is independent of the real exchange rate.

b. Suppose that the government implements an unanticipated tax cut in the current period followed by a tax increase in the subsequent period, leaving government spending patterns unchanged.

Prove that the unanticipated current-period tax cut leads to an increase in today's nontradable price and a lower nontradable goods price in the next period. Also describe the effects of the unanticipated deficit on consumption and the economy's external debt.

9. Consider a monetary version of the model in Chapter 10. Assume that domestic and foreign goods are internationally tradable and perfect substitutes. At the *beginning* of each period, financial markets are open, and agents acquire their desired asset portfolios. As part of these transactions, they purchase domestic and foreign currencies based on the planned consumption purchases *during* the period (i.e., at a time when the financial markets are closed). Accordingly, goods purchases are subject to a cash-in-advance constraint. It is assumed that cash payments have to be conducted in terms of the seller's country currency. At the end of each period, which is equivalent to the beginning of the next period, domestic firms redistribute their receipts to domestic residents and foreign firms to foreign residents. For simplicity assume that the domestic country pegs its exchange rate at a unified level for all transactions and faces a given interest rate and price level in terms of the foreign currency. As in chapter 10 individuals have finite lives with a constant probability of survival γ, and their preferences are characterized by a logarithmic expected utility function.

a. Describe the equilibria in the goods and asset markets.

b. Show that exchange-rate interventions affect the individual's wealth (for $\gamma < 1$), and thereby the consumption opportunity set, but leave intertemporal prices unchanged. Thus one can interpret exchange-rate management as a lump-sum tax policy.

V

Economic Growth and International Convergence

12

Exogenous Growth under International Capital and Labor Mobility

The world economy is characterized by diverse levels of income and patterns of growth across countries and across time. To understand the evolution of such diversity and whether there are tendencies toward cross-country equality, we have to study the mechanics of the growth process in each country individually and in the world equilibrium at large. To provide a systematic analysis of such process, we devote this chapter to a simplified world where the engine of growth is exogenously determined. As a natural extension, this growth engine will be endogenized in the next chapter.

Evidently, factor mobility could potentially influence the convergence/divergence tendencies across countries within a growing world economy. We therefore focus our analysis on the roles that capital mobility and labor mobility can play in such a process. In addition we examine the potential welfare gains that capital and labor mobility can generate. Also studied are the effects of factor mobility on the speed of adjustment to long run equilibria and on the rate of convergence (if any) across countries.

We also cast our exogenous growth model in a stochastic framework and derive some important time-series properties useful for empirical analysis. A printout of computer programs to simulate stochastic dynamic general equilibrium models is provided at the end of the book. These programs are especially useful for our analysis in part V.

12.1 The Closed Economy

In this section we provide an exposition of the standard growth model that emphasizes the role of saving and physical capital accumulation in driving short run output growth and that of (exogenous) human capital accumulation in driving long run growth.[1]

Consider a closed economy with a Cobb-Douglas technology that transforms physical capital, K_t, and human capital, H_t, into a single composite good, Y_t:

$$Y_t = A_t K_t^{1-\alpha} H_t^{\alpha}. \tag{12.1}$$

The productivity level A_t is, in general, time-varying and can be a source of growth and fluctuations. To make things simple at this stage, we assume that $A_t = A$, a deterministic constant. In section 12.4 we will assume it to follow a stochastic process in order to analyze growth under uncertainty.[2] Human capital H_t is a product of the size of the labor force N_t (treated synonymously with the size of population, assuming constant labor force participation and inelastic work hours) and their skill level, h_t. An important feature of this model is constant returns to scale technology.[3] While increasing returns to scale will give rise to unbounded growth (which is thus inconsistent with the existence of a stable long-run equilibrium), decreasing returns to scale cannot generate sustainable long run growth (see appendix A).

Physical and human capital are accumulated according to the following laws of motion, respectively:

$$K_{t+1} = I_t + (1 - \delta_k)K_t \qquad \text{given } K_0, \tag{12.2}$$

where I_t is gross investment in, and δ_k the rate of depreciation of, physical capital.

$$H_{t+1} = (1 + g_H)H_t \qquad \text{given } H_0, \tag{12.3}$$

where g_H is the exogenous rate of growth of human capital. Since $H_t = N_t h_t$ and both N_t and h_t are assumed to grow at exogenous constant rates g_N and g_h, we can decompose (12.3) into $N_{t+1} =$

$(1 + g_N)N_t$ and $h_{t+1} = (1 + g_h)h_t$, with $(1 + g_N)(1 + g_h) = 1 + g_H$ given N_0 and h_0.

The representative consumer is the owner of both physical and human capital. He/she accumulates these two forms of capital over time, and supplies them as factor inputs to the representative firm for production at the competitive wage, w_t, and rental, r_{kt}, rates, period by period. To derive its demand for physical capital, K_t^d, and human capital, H_t^d, the firm in turn solves a static profit maximization problem:[4]

$$\max_{\{K_t^d, H_t^d\}} A(K_t^d)^{1-\alpha}(H_t^d)^\alpha - w_t H_t^d - r_{kt} K_t^d.$$

This yields the standard marginal productivity-factor price relations

$$w_t = \alpha A X_t^{1-\alpha},$$

$$r_{kt} = (1 - \alpha)A X_t^{-\alpha}, \tag{12.4}$$

where X_t is the ratio of physical capital to human capital, K_t/H_t.

Preferences of the dynastic head of the family are given by an isoelastic utility function:

$$U = \sum_{t=0}^{\infty} \beta^t N_t \left(\frac{c_t^{1-\sigma}}{1 - \sigma} \right), \tag{12.5}$$

where $0 < \beta < 1$ is the subjective discount factor and $\sigma > 0$ the reciprocal of the intertemporal elasticity of substitution in consumption, c_t. In the limiting case where $\sigma = 1$, the utility function is logarithmic. The household derives wage income from the supply of human capital, $w_t H_t$, and rental income from the supply of physical capital, $r_{kt}K_t$. He/she can either consume, $N_t c_t$, or save these incomes in the form of physical capital, $K_{t+1} - (1 - \delta_k)K_t$. He/she can also borrow B_{t+1} at the rate of interest r_{t+1} in any period t, and repay $(1 + r_t)B_t$ for his/her borrowing B_t from the previous period $t - 1$.[5] The household's net saving is therefore given by $[K_{t+1} - (1 - \delta_k)K_t] - [B_{t+1} - (1 + r_t)B_t]$. His/her period t budget constraint can thus be written

$$N_t c_t + [K_{t+1} - (1 - \delta_k)K_t] = w_t H_t + r_{kt}K_t + [B_{t+1} - (1 + r_t)B_t]. \tag{12.6}$$

The consumer chooses $\{c_t, K_{t+1}, B_{t+1}\}$ to maximize (12.5) subject to (12.2), (12.3), and (12.6). The first-order conditions for this problem imply that

$$R_{B_{t+1}} = \frac{1}{\beta}\left(\frac{c_{t+1}}{c_t}\right)^\sigma = R_{k_{t+1}}, \tag{12.7}$$

where $R_{B_{t+1}} = 1 + r_{t+1}$ and $R_{k_{t+1}} = 1 + r_{kt+1} - \delta_k$. Recall that, as in chapter 5, in making his/her borrowing decision, the consumer equates the gross rate of interest ($R_{B_{t+1}}$) to his/her intertemporal marginal rate of substitution (IMRS). In addition, as an owner of physical capital, he/she also equates the return on physical capital ($R_{k_{t+1}}$) to the same IMRS. Arbitrage through capital market forces will drive equality between the interest rate and rental rate on capital (net of depreciation), that is, $r_{t+1} = r_{kt+1} - \delta_k$.

The equilibrium values of the wage rate, rental rate, and interest rate are determined by the following market-clearing conditions: $H_t = H_t^d$ in the labor market, $K_t = K_t^d$ in the physical capital market, and $B_{t+1} = 0$ in the financial capital market.[6] By the Walras law, the consumer budget constraint (12.6), the profit-maximizing conditions (12.4), and these market-clearing conditions together imply the economywide resource constraint

$$N_t c_t + K_{t+1} - (1 - \delta_k)K_t = F(K_t, H_t). \tag{12.8}$$

That is, output is split between consumption and saving/investment.

The Mechanics of Economic Growth

The dynamics of our example economy are driven by the two fundamental laws of motion (12.2) and (12.3), which can be combined to yield a single difference equation in the physical capital–human capital ratio (or the capitals ratio X_t):

$$X_{t+1} = \left(\frac{A}{1 + g_H}\right) s_t X_t^{1-\alpha} + \left(\frac{1 - \delta_k}{1 + g_H}\right) X_t, \tag{12.9}$$

where s_t is the saving rate at time t, defined as the ratio between saving S_t (gross and net) and output Y_t (i.e., I_t/Y_t, since $S_t = I_t$ in the closed economy equilibrium). In general, the equilibrium saving rate is determined by solving the consumer's intertemporal optimization problem and imposing the market clearing conditions. We spell out the dynamics of the system in appendix B, and illustrate how the saving rate is derived in an example economy in appendix C.

We can express per capita output as y_t $(= Y_t/N_t) = A(X_t)^{1-\alpha} h_t$, where $h_t = h_0(1 + g_h)^t$. Evidently, the dynamic path of y_t depends on that of X_t and h_t. In particular, the growth rate of $y_t (g_{yt})$ can be approximated, using $\ln(1 + g) = g$, by

$$\ln\left(\frac{y_{t+1}}{y_t}\right) = (1 - \alpha)\ln\left(\frac{X_{t+1}}{X_t}\right) + \ln\left(\frac{h_{t+1}}{h_t}\right)$$

$$= (1 - \alpha)\ln\left[\left(\frac{A}{1 + g_H}\right) s_t X_t^{-\alpha} + \frac{1 - \delta_k}{1 + g_H}\right] + g_h$$

$$= (1 - \alpha)\{\ln[As_t X_t^{-\alpha} + (1 - \delta_k)] - g_N\} + \alpha g_h. \tag{12.10}$$

Observe that g_{yt} depends positively on the saving rate, s_t, and the skill growth rate, g_h, and negatively on the capitals ratio, X_t, and the population growth rate, g_N. If, however, the economy converges to a long-run time-invariant equilibrium where $X_{t+1} = X_t$ so that $\ln(X_{t+1}/X_t) = 0$, then g_y will converge to g_h.

Steady-State Growth and Transitional Dynamics: Policy Implications

While equation (12.9) describes the entire growth path of the capitals ratio X_t, it can conveniently be divided into two components: the transition path (from an initial state to the steady state) and the steady-state growth path. *Steady-state* growth is defined as the particular pattern of growth where growth rates of all variables are constant over time, but possibly different from one another.

(It is sometimes called "*balanced* growth" as well.) The constant-returns-to-scale assumption, combined with isoelastic preferences (which implies equality between the average and marginal propensities to consume), are necessary for the existence of such long-run equilibrium. With $X_t = X_{t+1} = \hat{X}$ and $s_t = s_{t+1} = \hat{s}$ (where the hats ^ denote steady state values). In the steady state, the capitals rati and the level of per-capita output can be expressed as (positive) functions of the saving rate as follows:

$$\hat{X} = \left(\frac{sA}{g_H + \delta_k}\right)^{1/\alpha},$$

$$\hat{y}_t = \left(\frac{s}{g_H + \delta_k}\right)^{(1-\alpha)/\alpha} A^{1/\alpha} h_0 (1 + g_h)^t.$$

The capital–(raw) labor ratio $\hat{k}_t$ ($= K_t/N_t$) is equal to $\hat{X}h_t = \hat{X}h_0(1 + g_h)^t$. Observe that $\hat{y}_t$ and $\hat{k}_t$ both grow at the same rate g_h along the steady-state growth path, implying that the capital–output ratio must be constant. Since the rate of return on capital, $\hat{r}_{kt}$, is given by $(1 - \alpha)\hat{y}_t/\hat{k}_t$, it must also be constant. Indeed these steady-state properties of $\hat{y}_t$, $\hat{k}_t$, and $\hat{r}_{kt}$ are all consistent with a set of empirical regularities about patterns of growth established by Kaldor (1963).

Another component of the growth path exhibits transitional dynamics described by equation (12.9) for $X_t \neq X_{t+1} \neq \hat{X}$ and portrayed by figure 12.1. For any initial stocks of physical and human capital (K_0 and H_0, hence X_0), the capitals ratio in the next period (X_1) can be read off the concave curve for the corresponding equilibrium value of the saving rate (s_0, e.g., s'). Given X_1, the capitals ratio in the period after (X_2) can be obtained from a point on the concave curve corresponding to the equilibrium saving rate in period 1 (s_1, say, s''). Eventually the capitals ratio will converge to the steady state at the intersection between the 45° line and the concave curve with constant saving rate $\hat{s}$ (point A). As shown in the example in appendix C, the Solow (1956) model is a special case of our model (when $\sigma = \delta_k = 1$), where the saving rate is time invariant (e.g., $\hat{s}$). In this case for $X_t < \hat{X}$, $X_{t+1} > X_t$ (as indicated by the arrows

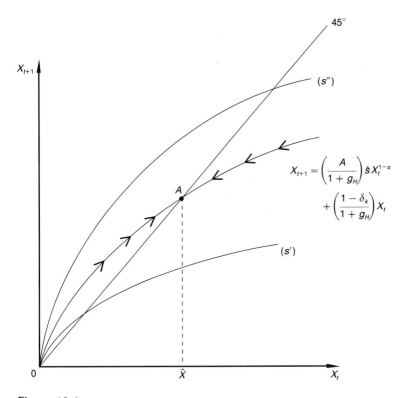

Figure 12.1
Transitional dynamics and the steady state

pointing to the right), and for $X_t > \hat{X}$, $X_{t+1} < X_t$ (as indicated by the leftward-pointing arrows).

In appendix B we derive two measures of the speed of convergence to the long-run equilibrium. The first one measures the half-life of the dynamical system, that is, the time it takes to reach half of the distance between the initial position and the steady state. The second one, analogous to Barro and Sala-i-Martin (1992), measures the ratio between the deviations of output from its steady-state value in two consecutive periods.

From the arguments just presented, it should now be evident that, in the exogenous growth paradigm, policies that target saving rates (e.g., taxation of capital income) can influence growth only along the transition path but not in the long-run steady-state equilibrium. They can nonetheless affect the long-run level of output per capita. In other words, these policies only have *level* effects, but no *growth* effects.

12.2   The Open Economy: Capital Mobility

From a global perspective there is an issue as to whether countries with different levels of initial income will converge (with income gaps narrowing) over time. We have just shown that income convergence can occur even among isolated economies if the long run (capital-account autarky) steady-state positions they converge to are similar. This entails similar technologies (A, α, and δ_k), preferences (β and σ), and, most important, similar exogenous growth rates (g_H, or g_N and g_h).

When the economies are open, it is more likely that such convergence will take place because openness can potentially enhance technology transmission. Moreover, when capital markets are integrated into the world capital market, the process of convergence (its speed as well as the particular transition path) will likely be altered. International borrowing and lending can facilitate consumption smoothing and create additional investment opportunities, which will improve the efficiency in the allocation of consumption over time and the allocation of capital across countries. For these reasons capital market integration may generate welfare gains as well. In this section therefore we introduce capital mobility in order to study its role for the growth process and for international convergence of income levels.

Perfect Capital Mobility

Consider integration of our example economy into the world capital market. Assume free trade in commodities. With a single composite good here, a country can either export or import (but will not do both) within any given period. But it can definitely engage in intertemporal trade in this single commodity (exporting in some periods and importing in others). This implies mobility in financial capital (in the form of various financial securities, loans, etc.). Naturally, trade in goods can occur in the form of investment goods as well. In other words, physical capital also becomes internationally mobile.

Accordingly, we modify the consumer budget constraint (12.6) as follows:

$$N_t c_t + (K_{t+1}^H + K_{t+1}^{H*}) - (1 - \delta_k)(K_t^H + K_t^{H*})$$

$$= w_t H_t + r_{kt} K_t^H + r_k^* K_t^{H*} + (B_{t+1}^H + B_{t+1}^{H*} - B_{t+1}^{*H})$$

$$- (1 + r_t)(B_t^H + B_t^{H*}) + (1 + r^*)B_t^{*H}. \tag{12.11}$$

K^H and B^H denote the domestic consumer's claims on physical capital residing in the home country and domestic debt respectively. Likewise K^{H*} and B^{H*} ($-B^{*H}$) stand for the domestic consumer's claims on physical capital residing in the foreign country and (net) foreign debt, where B^{H*} represents the flow of debt issued by the home (H) country to the foreign ($*$) country, and B^{*H} the reverse flow. The domestic rate of interest and rental rate are denoted by r and r_k, and their foreign counterparts by r^* and r_k^*, respectively.

Similarly the resource constraint of the domestic economy (12.8) will have to be modified:

$$N_t c_t + (K_{t+1}^H + K_{t+1}^{H*}) - (1 - \delta_k)(K_t^H + K_t^{H*})$$

$$= F(K_t, H_t) + r_k^* K_t^{H*} - r_{kt} K_t^{*H} + (B_{t+1}^{H*} - B_{t+1}^{*H})$$

$$- [(1 + r_t)B_t^{H*} - (1 + r^*)B_t^{*H}], \tag{12.12}$$

where $K = K^H + K^{*H}$, the latter being the stock of foreign direct investment in the domestic economy. K^{H*} and K^{*H} are defined similarly as B^{H*} and B^{*H}.

We can rearrange terms in (12.12) in order to derive the country's balance-of-payments accounts $CA_t + KA_t = 0$ as follows:

$$CA_t = GNP_t - N_t c_t - I_t^H$$

$$= [F(K_t, H_t) + (r^* B_t^{*H} - r_t B_t^{H*}) + (r_k^* K_t^{H*} - r_{kt} K_t^{*H})]$$

$$- N_t c_t - [K_{t+1}^H - (1 - \delta_k)K_t^H],$$

$$KA_t = -(FDI_t + FPI_t)$$
$$= -[K_{t+1}^{H*} - (1 - \delta_k)K_t^{H*}] + [(B_{t+1}^{*H} - B_t^{*H}) - (B_{t+1}^{H*} - B_t^{H*})].$$

Here CA stands for the current-account balance, KA the capital-account balance, FDI foreign direct investment, and FPI foreign portfolio investment.

In this deterministic setting, capital flows will be unidirectional, the direction being determined by the relative magnitudes of the domestic and foreign rates of interest. Furthermore, since $r = r_k - \delta_k$ and $r^* = r_k^* - \delta_k$ in equilibrium, physical capital and financial capital are perfect substitutes. Assume without loss of generality that $r > r^*$ so that $r_k > r_k^*$. Then $B^{*H} = 0$ and $K^{H*} = 0$.

To highlight the role of capital mobility for international convergence of per-capita output levels, we assume that the rest of the world is initially in a long-run steady-state growth equilibrium of the sort studied in the previous section, whereas the home economy starts initially with a lower physical capital-human capital ratio ($X_0 < X_0^* = \hat{X}^*$).

Assume further that the rest of the world is large so that the home country is a price-taker in the world market. Capital market integration then ensures that $r_t = r^*$ ($= (1 - \alpha)A(\hat{X}^*)^{-\alpha} - \delta_k$ from equation 12.4). As a result the capital inflow will generate an immediate convergence in the capitals ratio ($X_1 = \hat{X}^*$) and hence convergence in output per-capita human capital (i.e., $\hat{y}_t/h_t = \hat{y}_t^*/h_t^*$ for all $t \geq 1$). But per-capita GDPs will not converge in general (i.e., $\hat{y}_t \neq \hat{y}_t^*$) unless the initial stocks of knowledge are identical across countries (i.e., $h_0 = h_0^*$). From (12.7) we can verify that the consumption growth rate will converge at the same time to its long-run value g_h. Per-capita consumption and GNPs will not converge for two reasons: (a) the capital inflow will fail to equalize labor income between the home country and the rest of the world, and (b) the former will start with a lower X_0 and thus accumulate different amounts of external assets during the transition. Evidently, the home economy reaps all the benefits from the intertemporal trade—since prices in the rest of the world remain unchanged while, for the domestic economy, the initial marginal productivity of capital net of depreciation exceeds the world rate of interest. Therefore the consumption ratio c_t/c_t^* will initially rise, and then stay constant thereafter (given equality between their consumption growth rates).[7]

Free capital flows must generate welfare gains from intertemporal trade, akin to the standard gains from trade argument. Obviously the magnitude of the gains is directly related to the difference in the initial capitals ratios between the home country and the rest of the world. (Recall that this is assumed to be the only source of heterogeneity in our analysis.) In appendix D we compute such gains for the case of log utility (i.e., $\sigma = 1$) and relate them to the initial cross-country difference. These gains are measured in utility terms. An alternative welfare concept ω, measured in terms of compensating variations in consumption, is defined implicitly by

$$\sum_{t=0}^{\infty} \beta^t U(c_t^{\text{autarky}}(1 + \omega)) = \sum_{t=0}^{\infty} \beta^t U(c_t^{k\,\text{mobility}}).$$

Constrained-Capital Mobility

Free capital mobility is an extreme situation based on ideal market structure with full information and absence of risk, default, and time-inconsistent behavior (both for private agents and governments). When such elements are taken into account, borrowing and lending may be subject to significant constraints and regulations. To account for these possibilities in our aggregative model, we now introduce an upper bound on financial capital flows. No such bound is imposed, however, on foreign direct investment.

We assume that households (in their capacity as owners of the firms) can only borrow up to a certain limit. The limit is the collateral based on the ownership by the domestic households of the domestic firm's net worth, which is equal to K_t^H.[8] Recall, however, that an increase in domestic consumption can come from three sources: international borrowing, domestic output net of returns to FDI, and reduction in investment by domestic residents in domestic capital. Therefore, if borrowing from abroad is constrained, domestic consumers can still offset the effect of this constraint by reducing their investment in domestic capital. Only when a lower bound on that form of investment is imposed will the consumption boom following the opening-up of the international capital market become constrained. We therefore make the realistic assumption that gross investment of this kind be nonnegative. (This constraint will effectively eliminate the possibility of using the domestic firm's capital stock, which is partly owned by foreigners, as an additional collateral for borrowing from abroad to finance domestic consumption.) If binding, these two constraints (viz., $B^{H*} = K^H$ and $K_{t+1} - (1 - \delta_k)K_t = 0$) together with the resource constraint (12.12) and the Euler theorem will imply that

$$N_t c_t = w_t H_t + [K^H_{t+1} - (1 - \delta_k)K^H_t]. \tag{12.12a}$$

At the same time the domestic rate of interest will not be set equal to the world rate of interest because of the borrowing constraint. From the intertemporal condition (12.7) we have $c_{t+1}/c_t > [\beta(1 + r^*)]^{1/\sigma}$. In comparison to the free capital mobility case, therefore, while the jump in consumption immediately following the opening-up of international capital markets is smaller, the consumption growth rate is higher as long as the constraints remain binding. Thus, while the borrowing constraint lengthens the transitional dynamics, it generates a more accelerated rate of growth in consumption and income during that phase compared to the long-run growth rate. Eventually the constraints will become slack, and the growth rate will converge to the same long-run value, g_h.

This is a stylized example of real world constraints that tend to slow down the adjustment process. The welfare gains from the opening up of credit markets will evidently be lower than those under free capital mobility.

12.3   Open Economy: Labor Mobility

Since both labor and physical capital are primary inputs in production, labor mobility is expected to play a similar role in the growth process as capital mobility. By "labor mobility" we mean a situation where workers retain their source country residence while working in another country (cf. "migration," by which we mean a permanent change of country residence). Since skill levels are typically embodied in labor, we have international transfer of skills and human capital as an integral part of labor mobility.

We now open up the home country to free labor flows. For simplicity we assume that capital (financial as well as physical) is immobile internationally. As before the rest of the world is assumed to be in the long-run steady state initially, whereas the home economy starts with a lower physical capital–human capital ratio ($X_0 < X_0^* = \hat{X}^*$). This implies that $w_0 < w_0^* = \hat{w}^*$. We retain the assumption that the rest of the world is large so that the home country is a price-taker in the world market. Labor market integration then ensures that $w_t = \hat{w}^*$ ($= \alpha A(\hat{X}^*)^{1-\alpha}$ from equation 12.4). As a result of the labor outflow, we obtain an immediate convergence in the capitals ratio ($X_1 = \hat{X}^*$) and hence convergence in output per-capita human capital (i.e., $\hat{y}_t/h_t = \hat{y}_t^*/h_t^*$ for all $t \geq 1$), but not convergence in per-capita GDPs. At the same time the consumption growth rate will again converge to its long-run value, g_h, because wage-rate equalization implies interest-rate equalization. Per-capita GNPs and consumption will not converge for similar reasons as in the capital mobility case. Evidently, the home economy reaps all the benefits from the intertemporal trade, since prices in the rest of the world remain unchanged while the initial marginal productivity of labor in the domestic economy falls short of the world wage rate. Therefore the consumption ratio c_t/c_t^* will initially rise and stay constant thereafter (given equality between their consumption growth rates). What we have just shown is that labor mobility is a perfect substitute for capital mobility, with the same welfare implications.

The assumption of free labor flows abstracts, however, from the significant costs of adjustment associated with such mobility (e.g., cultural, ethnic, family, and other differences). When such costs are accounted for, labor mobility becomes a less efficient convergence mechanism in comparison with capital mobility (even after incorporating the above-mentioned borrowing constraints).

12.4   Stochastic Growth

So far we have been assuming that growth is deterministic. To highlight the effects of random shocks on the growth dynamics, we introduce in this section stochastic elements. We simplify the analysis by reverting to the closed economy setting developed in section 12.1. The complexity in characterizing the stochastic dynamics excludes the possibility of an analytic inspection of the growth mechanism except for relatively low-dimensional cases, one of which is elegantly analyzed by Campbell (1994) and is presented in this section. At the same time, however, we develop here tools of analysis that will be useful for analyzing higher-dimensional problems such as those in an open economy. These techniques will be further developed in chapter 13.

To incorporate random disturbances into the model of section 12.1, we assume that the productivity level a_t $(= \ln(A_t))$ follows a first-order autoregressive process:

$$a_{t+1} = \rho a_t + \varepsilon_{t+1}, \tag{12.13}$$

where ε_{t+1} is an i.i.d. shock with zero mean and constant variance, and $0 \le \rho \le 1$ measures the persistence of the shock. In the presence of such shocks, the expectation operator will have to be inserted into equations (12.5) and (12.7).

Defining $X = K/H$ and $Z = c/h$, we can rewrite the two dynamic equations (12.7) and (12.8) in K and c as (A.2) and (A.3) in appendix B. Together with equation (12.13) these two laws of motion form a system of nonlinear expectational difference equations in (Z_t, X_t, A_t). To get a handle on the solution, we take a loglinear approximation of this nonlinear system around its deterministic steady state (with $\varepsilon_t = 0$) to obtain a linear system of expectational difference equations in x_t $(= \ln(X_t))$ and z_t $(= \ln(Z_t))$. Details of the solution procedure are laid out in appendix E, from which we derive the approximate dynamic behavior of the economy as a function of the shock as follows:

$$a_t = \frac{1}{(1 - \rho L)} \varepsilon_t. \tag{12.14}$$

$$x_{t+1} = \frac{\eta_{xa}}{(1 - \eta_{xx}L)(1 - \rho L)} \varepsilon_t. \tag{12.15}$$

$$z_t = \frac{\eta_{za} + (\eta_{zx}\eta_{xa} - \eta_{za}\eta_{xx})L}{(1 - \eta_{xx}L)(1 - \rho L)} \varepsilon_t. \tag{12.16}$$

$$\ln\left(\frac{y_t}{h_t}\right) = (1 - \alpha)x_t + a_t = \frac{1 + [(1 - \alpha)\eta_{xa} - \eta_{xx}]L}{(1 - \eta_{xx}L)(1 - \rho L)} \varepsilon_t. \tag{12.17}$$

In these equations L denotes the lag operator, and η_{zx}, η_{za}, η_{xx}, and η_{xa} represent the partial elasticities of z_t with respect to x_t, z_t with respect to a_t, x_{t+1} with respect to x_t, and x_{t+1} with respect to a_t. The explicit expressions for these elasticities in terms of the fundamental parameters are spelled out in appendix E. Observe from equations (12.15)–(12.17) that the logarithm of the ratio between physical capital and human capital, x_t, follows an AR(2) process, while the logarithm of the ratio between consumption and human capital, z_t, as well as the logarithm of the ratio between output and human capital, $\ln(y_t/h_t)$, follow an ARMA(2, 1) process. Note also that they have identical autoregressive roots η_{xx} and ρ.

We now flesh out some properties of the partial elasticities:

1. η_{zx}, which measures the effect on current consumption of an increase in the capital stock for a fixed level of productivity, naturally does not depend on the persistence of the productivity shock ρ.

2. η_{za}, which measures the effect on current consumption of a productivity increase with a fixed stock of physical capital, is increasing in ρ for low values of σ but decreasing for high values of σ. The initiution behind this is as follows: When substitution effects are weak (small σ), the consumer responds mostly to income effects, which are stronger the more persistent the shock. When substitution effects are strong (high σ), a persistent shock which raises the furture rate of interest will stimulate saving at the expense of current consumption, making the response in consumption small.

3. η_{xx}, which measures the effect on the future level of capital stock of an increase in the current level of capital stock with a fixed level of productivity, does not depend on ρ but declines with σ. In fact in our model of section (12.1) where technology is time-invariant, $1 - \eta_{xx}$ reflects the speed of convergence to the steady state, similar to our second measure of convergence at the end of that section.

Turning to the general equilibrium implications of the persistence parameter ρ, observe that if productivity follows a random walk ($\rho = 1$), we have $\eta_{zx} + \eta_{za} = 1$ and $\eta_{xx} + \eta_{xa} = 1$. Consequently capital, consumption, and output will follow cointegrated random walk processes, and the difference between any two of them is stationary.

12.5   Appendix A: Returns to Scale and Long-Run Growth

Consider a Cobb-Douglas production function that allows for decreasing, increasing, and constant returns to scale.

$$Y_t = AK_t^\beta H_t^\alpha, \tag{A.1}$$

where $\beta + \alpha$ can be < 1, > 1, or $= 1$.

Following Solow (1956), assume for simplicity a constant saving rate s, so that investment, I_t, is equal to sY_t. The physical capital–human capital ratio, X_t, can be shown to evolve according to

$$X_{t+1} = \left(\frac{s}{1 + g_H}\right) AX_t^\beta H_t^{\alpha+\beta-1} + \left(\frac{1 - \delta_K}{1 + g_H}\right) X_t.$$

If $\alpha + \beta > 1$ (increasing returns), we will have unbounded growth in the long run. If $\alpha + \beta < 1$ (decreasing returns), the economy will vanish over time.

12.6   Appendix B: Local Dynamics of Our Example Economy

The dynamics of our example economy is governed by the system of difference equations (12.2), (12.3), and (12.7) in c_t, K_t, H_t, and A_t.

For the sake of the analysis in section 12.4, the productivity level A is allowed to be time-varying. Defining X_t as K_t/H_t as before and Z_t as c_t/h_t, we can combine (12.2) and (12.3) as one single difference equation in X_t:

$$(1 + g_H)X_{t+1} = A_t X_t^{1-\alpha} + (1 - \delta_k)X_t - Z_t. \tag{A.2}$$

Dividing (12.7) throughout by h_t yields a difference equation in Z_t:

$$Z_t^{-\sigma} = \beta E_t[(1 + g_h)Z_{t+1}]^{-\sigma}[(1 - \alpha)A_{t+1}X_{t+1}^{-\alpha} + (1 - \delta_k)]. \tag{A.3}$$

In the steady state, $A_t = A_{t+1} = A$, $X_t = X_{t+1} = \hat{X}$, and $Z_t = Z_{t+1} = \hat{Z}$. These steady-state values are given by

$$\hat{X} = \left[\frac{(1 - \alpha)A}{(1 + g_h)^{\sigma}/\beta - (1 - \delta_k)} \right]^{1/\alpha},$$

$$\hat{Z} = A\hat{X}^{1-\alpha} - (g_H + \delta_k)\hat{X}.$$

Log-linearizing (A.2) and (A.3) around the steady state $(\hat{Z}, \hat{X})$ yields

$$s_z \left(\frac{dZ_t}{Z_t} \right) + s_x(1 + g_H)E_t \left(\frac{dX_{t+1}}{X_{t+1}} \right) - s_x(1 - \delta_k) \left(\frac{dX_t}{X_t} \right)$$

$$= (1 - \alpha) \left(\frac{dX_t}{X_t} \right) + \frac{dA_t}{A_t}, \tag{A.4}$$

where

$$s_x = \frac{\hat{X}}{\hat{Y}} = \frac{\hat{X}^{\alpha}}{A} = \frac{1 - \alpha}{r + \delta_k},$$

$$s_z = \frac{\hat{Z}}{\hat{Y}} = 1 - (g_H + \delta_k)s_x = 1 - \frac{(1 - \alpha)(g_H + \delta_k)}{r + \delta_k},$$

$$\sigma \left[E_t \left(\frac{dZ_{t+1}}{Z_{t+1}} \right) - \frac{dZ_t}{Z_t} \right] = \left(\frac{r + \delta_k}{1 + r} \right) E_t \left[\left(\frac{dA_{t+1}}{A_{t+1}} \right) - \alpha \left(\frac{dX_{t+1}}{X_{t+1}} \right) \right]. \tag{A.5}$$

We can group (A.4) and (A.5) into a matrix difference equation as follows:

$$AE_t \begin{bmatrix} \dfrac{dX_{t+1}}{X_{t+1}} \\[2mm] \dfrac{dZ_{t+1}}{Z_{t+1}} \end{bmatrix} = B \begin{bmatrix} \dfrac{dX_t}{X_t} \\[2mm] \dfrac{dZ_t}{Z_t} \end{bmatrix} + CE_t \left(\dfrac{dA_{t+1}}{A_{t+1}} \right) + D \left(\dfrac{dA_t}{A_t} \right), \qquad (A.6)$$

where the matrices A, B, C, and D are given by

$$A = \begin{bmatrix} s_x(1 + g_H) & 0 \\[2mm] \dfrac{\alpha(r + \delta_k)}{1 + r} & \sigma \end{bmatrix}, \quad B = \begin{pmatrix} (1 - \alpha) + s_x(1 - \delta_k) & -s_z \\[2mm] 0 & \sigma \end{pmatrix},$$

$$C = \begin{bmatrix} 0 \\[2mm] \dfrac{r + \delta_k}{1 + r} \end{bmatrix}, \quad D = \begin{pmatrix} 1 \\ 0 \end{pmatrix}.$$

Equation (A.6) can be rewritten

$$E_t \begin{bmatrix} \dfrac{dX_{t+1}}{X_{t+1}} \\[2mm] \dfrac{dZ_{t+1}}{Z_{t+1}} \end{bmatrix} = W \begin{bmatrix} \dfrac{dX_t}{X_t} \\[2mm] \dfrac{dZ_t}{Z_t} \end{bmatrix} + RE_t \left(\dfrac{dA_{t+1}}{A_{t+1}} \right) + Q \left(\dfrac{dA_t}{A_t} \right), \qquad (A.7)$$

where $W = A^{-1}B$, $R = A^{-1}C$, and $Q = A^{-1}D$.

To study the deterministic dynamics of this system, we revert to the case where A is time-invariant (hence the expectation operators and the terms dA_t/A_t and dA_{t+1}/A_{t+1} can be dropped from equation (A.7). We can then compute the eigenvalues (call them λ_1 and λ_2) by solving the equation $\det(W - \lambda I) = 0$, which is a quadratic equation in λ. The values of the two roots λ_1 and λ_2 are complicated functions of the parameters α, σ, β, A, δ_k, r, and g_H. One can show that λ_1 and λ_2 satisfy the following conditions:

$$\lambda_1 \lambda_2 = \frac{1 + r}{1 + g_H},$$

$$\lambda_1 + \lambda_2 = 1 + \left(\frac{1}{1 + g_H}\right)\left\{(1 + r) + \left(\frac{\alpha}{\sigma}\right)\left[\frac{r + \delta_k}{1 - \alpha} - (g_H + \delta_k)\right]\right.$$
$$\left.\times \left(\frac{r + \delta_k}{1 + r}\right)\right\}.$$

Of the two eigenvalues of the fundamental matrix W, one exceeds unity (unstable root) and the other is less than unity (stable root, call it λ). Imposing the transversality condition: $\beta(1 + g_H)^{1-\sigma} = (1 + g_H)/(1 + r) < 1$, we can eliminate the unstable root from the solution to obtain

$$x_t - \hat{x} = (x_0 - \hat{x})\lambda^t, \tag{A.8}$$

$$z_t - \hat{z} = (z_0 - \hat{z})\lambda^t, \tag{A.9}$$

where $x = \ln(X)$ and $z = \ln(Z)$.

The dynamics in the vicinity of the steady state can be portrayed graphically by a "phase diagram" shown in figure 12.2.[9] The stationary schedules corresponding to $x_t = x_{t+1}$ and $z_t = z_{t+1}$ are given by the vertical curve and the inverted U-curve, respectively. The steady state $(\hat{z}, \hat{x})$ is attained at the intersection of these schedules. The unstable trajectories diverge from the vicinity of this steady state in the northeast and southwest directions, while the stable trajectories approach the steady state from the northwest and southeast directions. The equilibrium transitional dynamics correspond to movements along the stable paths, described by equations (A.8) and (A.9).

As a measure of the speed of adjustment to the steady state, we use the concept of half life, t^*, defined as

$$\frac{x_{t^*} - \hat{x}}{x_0 - \hat{x}} = \frac{1}{2} = \frac{z_{t^*} - \hat{z}}{z_0 - \hat{z}}.$$

Substituting from (A.8) and/or (A.9) and solving for t^*, we get $t^* = -\ln(2)/\ln(\lambda)$.

Alternatively, we can measure the speed of convergence from the implied ratio of $y_{t+1} - \hat{y}_{t+1}$ to $y_t - \hat{y}_t$:

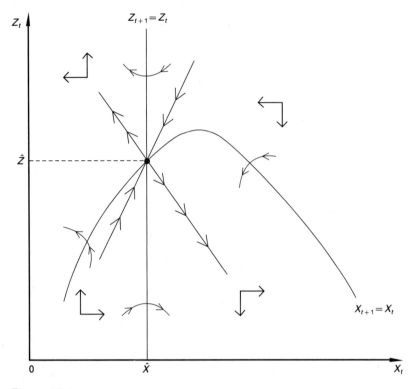

Figure 12.2
Phase diagram of the consumption-capital trajectories

$$\frac{y_{t+1} - \hat{y}_{t+1}}{y_t - \hat{y}_t} = (1 + g_h)\left(\frac{X_{t+1}^{1-\alpha} - \hat{X}^{1-\alpha}}{X_t^{1-\alpha} - \hat{X}^{1-\alpha}}\right)$$

$$\approx (1 + g_h)\left(\frac{[1 + (1 - \alpha)X_{t+1}] - [1 + (1 - \alpha)\hat{X}]}{[1 + (1 - \alpha)X_t] - [1 + (1 - \alpha)\hat{X}]}\right)$$

$$= (1 + g_h)\lambda,$$

where we have used $y_t = A(X_t)^{1-\alpha}h_0(1 + g_h)^t$ in the first equality and the approximation $X^{1-\alpha} = 1 + (1 - \alpha)X$ in the second equality. This is the discrete-time analogue of the convergence rate, β, in Barro and Sala-i-Martin (1995)'s continuous time setup, where

$$\ln\left(\frac{y_t}{\hat{y}_t}\right) = e^{-\beta t}\ln\left(\frac{y_0}{\hat{y}_0}\right).$$

12.7   Appendix C: An Example Economy with Full-fledged Solution

To show the mechanics of growth in this model, we simplify it by setting $\sigma = \delta_k = 1$. From equations (12.4) and (12.7) we get

$$\frac{c_{t+1}}{\beta c_t} = (1 - \alpha)AX_{t+1}^{-\alpha} = (1 - \alpha)\frac{Y_{t+1}}{K_{t+1}}. \tag{A.10}$$

We can write $c_t = (1 - s_t)Y_t/N_t$ and $K_{t+1} = s_t Y_t$. Denoting $\beta(1 + g_N)$ by $\tilde{\beta}$ and substituting these into (A.10) yields

$$\frac{1 - s_{t+1}}{\tilde{\beta}(1 - s_t)} = \frac{1 - \alpha}{s_t}.$$

This can be restated as a first-order difference equation in s_t, with an unstable root. Thus the unique (economically plausible) solution is a constant saving rate $s = \tilde{\beta}(1 - \alpha)$. Substituting this saving rate into (12.9) gives the following fundamental difference equation in X_t:

$$X_{t+1} = \left[\frac{\tilde{\beta}(1 - \alpha)A}{1 + g_H}\right]X_t^{1-\alpha}. \tag{A.11}$$

We display this dynamic equation graphically in figure 12.1. The concave curve, depicting the right-hand side of (A.11) with $\hat{s} = \tilde{\beta}(1 - \alpha)$, intersects the 45° line at two points to produce two steady states, at the origin (unstable) and A (stable). For any given initial value $X_0 > 0$, the economy must converge to the long-run equilibrium point A along the trajectories as indicated by the arrows. At A the steady-state value of the ratio between the two capital stocks is given by $\hat{X} = \{[\tilde{\beta}(1 - \alpha)A]/(1 + g_H)\}^{1/\alpha}$.

Given this closed form solution, it is straightforward to compute the consumer's utility along the entire growth path. Recursive substitution of the log transformation of (A.11) implies that

$$\ln(X_t) = \left[\frac{1 - (1 - \alpha)^t}{\alpha}\right]\ln\left[\frac{\tilde{\beta}(1 - \alpha)A}{1 + g_H}\right] + (1 - \alpha)^t \ln(X_0).$$

Substituting this into $c_t = [1 - \tilde{\beta}(1 - \alpha)]AX_t^{1-\alpha}h_0(1 + g_h)^t$ and then the resulting expression into the utility function, we get

$$U = \sum_{t=0}^{\infty} \tilde{\beta}^t \ln(c_t)$$

$$= \left(\frac{1 - \alpha}{1 - \tilde{\beta}(1 - \alpha)}\right)\ln(X_0) + \left(\frac{1}{1 - \tilde{\beta}}\right)\left[\ln\{[1 - \tilde{\beta}(1 - \alpha)]Ah_0\}\right.$$

$$\left. + \left(\frac{\tilde{\beta}(1 - \alpha)}{1 - \tilde{\beta}(1 - \alpha)}\right)\ln\left(\frac{\tilde{\beta}(1 - \alpha)A}{1 + g_H}\right) + \frac{\tilde{\beta}g_h}{1 - \tilde{\beta}}\right].$$

This welfare measure will be used in the capital mobility section to evaluate the gains from intertemporal trade.

12.8   Appendix D: Welfare Gains from Free Capital Flows

To evaluate the welfare gains from capital flows, we first compute the equilibrium consumption path under such regime. From the intertemporal condition (12.7), we have $c_t = c_0[\beta(1 + r^*)]^t$, where c_0 can be solved from the consumer's present-value budget constraint, obtainable by consolidating the flow budget constraint in (12.11):

$$\sum_{t=0}^{\infty} \frac{N_t c_t}{(1 + r^*)^t} = \sum_{t=0}^{\infty} \frac{Y_t}{(1 + r^*)^t} + K_0.$$

As we make clear in the text, the capitals ratio will jump to its steady state in one period. Consequently output per capita is given by

$$Y_t = AX_t^{1-\alpha}H_t = \begin{cases} AX_0^{1-\alpha}H_0, & t = 0, \\ A(\hat{X})^{1-\alpha}H_0(1 + g_H)^t, & t > 0. \end{cases}$$

Substituting this and $c_t = c_0[\beta(1 + r^*)]^t$ into the present value budget constraint, we have

$$c_0 = (1 - \tilde{\beta})H_0\left[X_0 + AX_0^{1-\alpha} + A\hat{X}^{1-\alpha}\left(\frac{1 + g_H}{r^* - g_H}\right)\right].$$

Substituting into the utility function yields

$$U = \sum_{t=0}^{\infty} \tilde{\beta}^t \ln(c_t)$$

$$= \left(\frac{1}{1-\tilde{\beta}}\right)\left\{\ln(1-\tilde{\beta})H_0[X_0 + AX_0^{1-\alpha}\right.$$

$$\left. + A\hat{X}^{1-\alpha}\left(\frac{1+g_H}{r^*-g_H}\right)\right]\right) + \left(\frac{\tilde{\beta}}{1-\tilde{\beta}}\right)\ln[\beta(1+r^*)]\right\},$$

where

$$r^* = \frac{1+g_H}{\tilde{\beta}} - 1.$$

12.9   Appendix E: Stochastic Dynamics

We follow Campbell (1994) by solving the equilibrium dynamics of the system of equations (A.4), (A.5), and (12.13) by the method of undetermined coefficients. We guess a solution for z_t ($= \ln(Z_t)$) of the form

$$z_t = \eta_{zx}x_t + \eta_{za}a_t, \tag{A.12}$$

where η_{zx} and η_{za} are unknown fixed coefficients, and $a_t = \ln(A_t)$. To verify this solution, substitute (A.12) into (A.4) and (A.5), and rearrange to get

$$x_{t+1} = \eta_{xx}x_t + \eta_{xa}a_t,$$

where

$$\eta_{xx} = \frac{1+r}{1+g_H} + \left[(g_H + \delta_k) - \frac{r+\delta_k}{1-\alpha}\right]\eta_{zx}, \tag{A.13}$$

$$\eta_{xa} = \frac{r+\delta_k}{(1-\alpha)(1+g_H)} + \left[(g_H + \delta_k) - \frac{r+\delta_k}{1-\alpha}\right]\eta_{za},$$

$$\eta_{zx}E_t(x_{t+1} - x_t) + \eta_{za}E_t(a_{t+1} - a_t) = \sigma\left(\frac{r+\delta_k}{1+r}\right)E_t(a_{t+1} - x_{t+1}). \tag{A.14}$$

Substituting (A.13) into (A.14) and using the fact that $E_t a_{t+1} = \rho a_t$

from (12.13), we arrive at one equation in x_t and a_t:

$$\eta_{zx}(\eta_{xx} - 1)\eta_{zx}x_t + [\eta_{zx}\eta_{xa} + \eta_{za}(\rho - 1)]a_t$$

$$= \sigma\left(\frac{r + \delta_k}{1 + r}\right)[(\rho - \eta_{xa})a_t - \eta_{xx}x_t]. \tag{A.15}$$

Recall from (A.13) that η_{xx} is a linear function of η_{zx} and η_{xa} is a linear function of η_{za}. Comparing the coefficients on x_t on the two sides of equation (A.15), we obtain a quadratic equation in η_{zx}:

$$Q_2\eta_{zx}^2 + Q_1\eta_{zx} + Q_0 = 0,$$

where

$$Q_2 = (g_H + \delta_k) - \frac{r + \delta_k}{1 - \alpha},$$

$$Q_1 = \frac{r - g_H}{1 + g_H} + \sigma\left(\frac{r + \delta_k}{1 + r}\right)\left[(g_H + \delta_k) - \frac{r + \delta_k}{1 - \alpha}\right], \tag{A.16}$$

$$Q_0 = \frac{\sigma(r + \delta_k)^2}{(1 - \alpha)(1 + r)}.$$

Imposing the transversality condition (which implies that $r > g_H$), we know that η_{zx} must be positive. Taking only the positive root, we have

$$\eta_{zx} = -\frac{1}{2Q_2}(Q_1 + \sqrt{Q_1^2 - 4Q_0Q_2}). \tag{A.17}$$

Given this solution for η_{zx}, we can compare the coefficients on a_t on the two sides of equation (A.15) to solve for η_{za}:

$$\eta_{za} = \frac{-\dfrac{\eta_{zx}(r + \delta_k)}{(1 - \alpha)(1 + g_H)} + \sigma\left(\dfrac{r + \delta_k}{1 + r}\right)\left(\rho - \dfrac{r + \delta_k}{(1 - \alpha)(1 + g_H)}\right)}{(\rho - 1) + \left[(g_H + \delta_k) - \left(\dfrac{r + \delta_k}{1 - \alpha}\right)\right]\left[\eta_{zx} + \sigma\left(\dfrac{r + \delta_k}{1 + r}\right)\right]}. \tag{A.18}$$

The last two coefficients η_{xx} and η_{xa} can be backed out from (A.13), given (A.17) and (A.18).

13

Endogenous Growth under International Capital and Labor Mobility

In this chapter we provide an extension of the exogenous growth model developed in the previous chapter. The standard model assumes that human capital accumulation, which drives long-run growth, is exogenously determined. Our extension involves endogenizing the rate of human capital formation by deriving it from the optimizing decisions of private households. The extended model emphasizes the role of saving (broadly defined to include investment in both physical and human capital) in the entire (short- and long-run) growth process. Cast in a stochastic framework, the engine of growth in this model (human capital) generates interesting time-series properties with a unique feature; that is, transitory shocks will have long-lasting level and growth effects.

In an integrated world economy, capital and labor mobility are potentially key elements in equalizing differences in levels and rates of growth of income across countries. Are labor mobility and capital mobility substitutes or complements for cross-country convergence? These issues are subject matters of the analysis in this chapter.

13.1   The Closed Economy

We extend the closed economy model of chapter 12 in a dimension pertaining to the accumulation of human capital as described by (12.3). More specifically, we can rewrite (12.3) as $H_{t+1} = N_{t+1}h_{t+1} = [(1 + g_N)N_t][(1 + g_{ht})h_t] = (1 + g_H)H_t$. Expressing $1 + g_{ht}$ as a function of the time invested in human capital (e_t for education) and the rate of depreciation in human capital, δ_h, we have

$$h_{t+1} = Be_t^\gamma h_t + (1 - \delta_h)h_t, \qquad (13.1)$$

where $Be^\gamma h$ is the human capital production function, B the knowledge efficiency coefficient, and γ the productivity parameter.

As implicitly assumed before, each household is endowed with one unit of time in each period. But instead of spending it only on work, n_t, and education, e_t, so that $n_t + e_t = 1$. Taking this into account, the consumer budget constraint can be rewritten

$$N_t c_t + K_{t+1} - (1 - \delta_k)K_t = w_t(1 - e_t)N_t h_t + r_{kt}K_t + B_{t+1}$$

$$- (1 + r_t)B_t. \qquad (13.2)$$

Denoting the consumer's earned income as $Y_t = w_t(1 - e_t)N_t h_t + r_{kt}K_t$, we define two saving rates: (1) physical-capital saving rate, $s_{Kt} = [K_{t+1} - (1 - \delta_k)K_t]/Y_t$, and (2) human-capital saving rate, $s_{Ht} = w_t e_t N_t h_t/Y_t$. These two saving rates will have an important role to play in the long-run growth process.

The consumer chooses $\{c_t, e_t, B_{t+1}, K_{t+1}, h_{t+1}\}$ to maximize his/her utility (12.5) subject to the above budget constraint (13.2) and the law of motion of human capital (13.1). The endogeneity of human capital decision is captured by two additional first-order conditions corresponding to the choice of e_t and h_{t+1}. Combining them with the first-order conditions for c_t, K_{t+1}, and B_{t+1} yields an analogue of (12.7):

$$\frac{1}{\beta}\left(\frac{c_{t+1}}{c_t}\right)^\sigma = R_{Bt+1} = R_{Kt+1} = R_{Ht+1}, \qquad (13.3)$$

where the gross rate of interest on bonds $R_{Bt+1} = 1 + r_{t+1}$, the gross rate of return on physical capital $R_{Kt+1} = 1 + r_{kt+1} - \delta_k$, and the gross rate of return on human capital R_{Ht+1} is given by

$$R_{Ht+1} = \left(\frac{w_{t+1}}{w_t}\right)(1 + g_N)\gamma Be_t^{\gamma-1}.$$

This expression of R_{Ht+1} shows its dependence on wage growth, population growth, and the marginal productivity of schooling time.

These three rates of return are equalized through arbitrage among the three forms of investment.

Long-Run Growth

The most crucial element of this extended model is the possibility of having sustainable long-run growth that is endogenously determined through human capital accumulation. Recall that $g_{ht} = Be_t^\gamma - \delta_h$. Assume for simplicity complete depreciation so that $\delta_k = \delta_h = 1$. We can thus show (see appendix A) that the steady-state value of the time invested in human capital, $\hat{e}$, satisfies

$$1 + \gamma\left(\frac{1 - e}{e}\right) = (1 + g_N)(Be^\gamma)^{1-\sigma}. \tag{13.4}$$

It is necessary to place restrictions on the parameters σ, g_N, γ, and B in order to guarantee the existence of a solution to the above equation with $0 < \hat{e} < 1$, and to yield a positive rate of growth of human capital g_h from (13.1).[1]

This long-run growth rate can be related to the saving rates as

$$g_h = \left[\frac{s_K}{\beta(1 - \alpha)(1 + g_N)}\right]^{1/(1-\sigma)} - 1,$$

$$g_h = B\left(\frac{s_H}{\alpha + s_H}\right)^\gamma - 1.$$

These expressions reveal that the long-run growth rate is positively related to the human-capital saving rate but positively related, negatively related, or totally unrelated to the physical-capital saving rate (depending on whether $\sigma < 1$, $\sigma > 1$, or $\sigma = 1$). This justifies labeling human capital as the "engine of growth." Consequently policies that target the human-capital saving rate (e.g., through education subsidies) can directly affect the long-run growth rate of the economy.[2]

In a world of isolated economies with similar preferences and technology but possibly different initial endowments of physical and human capital (hence different initial incomes), our analysis implies

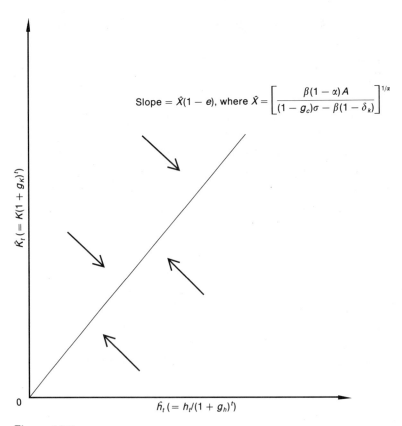

Slope $= \hat{X}(1 - e)$, where $\hat{X} = \left[\dfrac{\beta(1 - \alpha)A}{(1 - g_c)\sigma - \beta(1 - \delta_k)} \right]^{1/\alpha}$

$\hat{K}_t (= K(1 + g_K)^t)$

$\hat{h}_t (= h_t/(1 + g_h)^t)$

Figure 13.1
Convergence in the absence of human capital externality

that they will converge over time to the same long-run steady-state
growth path with the same growth rates. Just as the exogenous
growth model of the previous chapter, these economies will have
the same detrended income levels. This is illustrated in figure 13.1
portraying the steady-state relation between the detrended stocks of
physical and human capital. Since the ratio between these two forms
of capital, $\hat{X}$, is constant in the long run, this relation is represented
by a ray from the origin with slope equal to $\hat{X}(1 - e)$. Countries
can start from any initial position on the $\hat{h}_t - \hat{K}_t$ plane. The arrows
in the figure show how they move from their respective initial
positions to possibly different long-run positions on the ray, implying different levels of income. But since they all end up on the

ray with the same capitals ratio, $\hat{X}$, their detrended levels of income, $\hat{y}_t/h_t$, will be equalized in the long run, similar to the exogenous growth case.

Human-Capital Externality

In analyzing cross-country differences in wage rates and rates of return on capital, we follow Lucas (1988, 1990) in isolating an important element in human-capital formation. This element captures the possibility that through investment in human capital, the individual not only enhances his/her earning ability (if he/she turns out to be the most knowledgeable/skillful guy/gal in the population) but also generates an external effect by contributing to the aggregate level of productivity.[3] This external effect is modeled as

$$Y_t = AK_t^{1-\alpha}[(1 - e_t)N_t h_t]^\alpha \bar{h}_t^\varepsilon, \tag{13.5}$$

where $\bar{h}_t$ is the level of human capital of the smartest guy/gal (i.e., the upper tail of the skill distribution) in the population and ε (> 0) the externality parameter. While this production function exhibits increasing returns in K_t, H_t, and $\bar{h}_t$ (since $1 - \alpha + \alpha + \varepsilon > 1$), it still retains the constant-returns property in the two private inputs K_t and H_t. In equilibrium, $\bar{h}_t = h_t$.

Under this specification of technology, the intertemporal condition becomes $(c_{t+1}/c_t)^\sigma = \beta[(1 - \alpha)A(K_{t+1}/H_{t+1})^{-\alpha}\bar{h}_{t+1}^\varepsilon + (1 - \delta_k)]$. Along the steady-state growth path the constancy of c_{t+1}/c_t and e_{t+1} requires that $(K_t/N_t h_t)^{-\alpha}\bar{h}_t^\varepsilon$ be constant. This implies that K_t must grow at the same rate as $N_t h_t^\zeta$, where $\zeta = 1 + \varepsilon/\alpha$ (> 1), and the equilibrium condition $\bar{h}_t = h_t$ is imposed. Rearranging terms, we write

$$\hat{K}_t = \left[\frac{\beta(1 - \alpha)A}{(1 + g_c)^\sigma - \beta(1 - \delta_k)} \right]^{1/\alpha} N_0(1 - e)\hat{h}_t^\zeta,$$

where $1 + g_c$ can be shown to equal $(1 + g_h)^\zeta$. This equation is represented by the convex curve between $\hat{K}_t$ and $\hat{h}_t$ in figure 13.2. Observe that, at $t = 0$, the detrended variables are equal to their

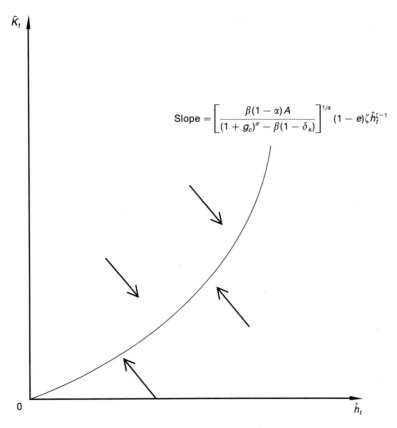

Figure 13.2
Convergence in the presence of human-capital externality

original (undetrended) values (i.e., $\hat{K}_0 = K_0$ and $\hat{h}_0 = h_0$). In the presence of knowledge spillovers ($\zeta > 1$), countries starting from different initial positions on the $\hat{h}_t$–$\hat{K}_t$ plane will converge to different long-run positions on the curve, implying different levels of income. However, unlike the no-externality case, the slope of the ray varies (increases) with $\hat{h}_t$, thus implying that the capitals ratio $\hat{X}$ will, in general, be different across countries. Their detrended levels of income, $\hat{y}_t/h_t$, will not be equalized in the long run, in sharp contrast to the exogenous growth case. The external effect is therefore a fundamental force behind long-run income diversity.

13.2   The Open Economy: Capital Mobility

From a global perspective there is an important issue as to whether countries with different income levels will exhibit similar rates of growth or whether the low-income countries exhibit higher growth rates so that they can catch up with the high-income countries over time. We have shown in the previous section that in the presence of knowledge spillovers that are somehow confined within national boundaries, if cross-country differences are due to differences in initial positions, then growth rates will converge but levels will not.

In the absence of externality, international capital mobility will speed up the convergence to the steady state as in the exogenous growth model. In this section we ask whether, in the presence of externality, capital mobility will also bring about convergence in long-run income levels across countries.

Consider, as before, a small open economy that is integrated into the world capital market. The rest of the world is assumed to be traveling along its long-run steady-state growth path. Opening up the capital market implies an immediate equalization of returns on both financial and physical capital (net of depreciation). Accordingly, from the intertemporal condition (13.3), the home country consumption growth rate will converge in one period to the consumption growth rate in the rest of the world. This also implies equalization of income growth rates (i.e., $g_y = g_y^*$) in the long run but with no implications for level convergence. The fact that $r_{kt} - \delta_k = r^*$ implies that $K_t/N_t h_t^\zeta$ is constant and equal to its steady-state value. This is the main difference between the autarky and capital mobility cases.

But the long-run detrended levels and rates of growth of output are the same in both cases, given the similarity in preferences and technology.[4]

13.3   Open Economy: Labor Mobility

In the exogenous growth case, labor mobility and capital mobility are perfect substitutes. In this section we examine whether this property will still hold under conditions of endogenous growth. If not, can labor mobility achieve convergence in income levels, something that is not achievable under capital mobility?

Consider again two isolated economies that have identical preferences and technologies, but possibly different endowments of physical and human capital. Even without capital mobility, interest rates will be equalized across these two economies in the long run (i.e., along their autarky balanced growth paths) as their steady-state physical capital-human capital ratios converge to the same value. In the presence of knowledge spillovers, wage rates in these two economies will differ as long as the skill levels of their workers are different. With labor mobility, workers will naturally move from low-wage (human-capital-poor) countries (e.g., the home country) to high wage (human-capital-rich) countries (e.g., the rest of the world). Since labor will flow from the home country to the rest of the world, the fraction of native effective labor working in the rest of world, n^*, equals 1, and the corresponding fraction in the home country, n, lies between 0 and 1. The effective work force in the home country is $nN_t h_t$ and that in the rest of the world is $N_t^* h_t^* + (1 - n)N_t h_t$.

Suppose that while some workers from the home country choose to work in the rest of the world, they continue to accumulate their human capital in their own country. Although the extent of knowledge spillovers may be limited by national boundaries, labor mobility provides an indirect channel of raising the productivity of labor in the labor-exporting country. This is because, as a result of labor mobility and wage equalization, guest workers in the foreign country will immediately enjoy an upward shift in their wage profile and so will "those left behind" working in the home country. This will provide the incentive for the home population to increase their rate of human capital accumulation (while that in the foreign population remains unchanged). In this sense workers from the home country enjoy the fruits of the knowledge externality (i.e., equal pay) while working with the more skilled workers in the rest of the world, and these benefits will get transmitted to their countryfolk. It is in this sense that these workers can be viewed as "messengers" of technological progress. Over time this knowledge transmission will lead to equalization in the levels of human capital and income per capita in the whole world.

In more formal terms the above level-equalizing argument can be stated as a proposition:

PROPOSITION   Along the steady-state growth path with nonzero labor flows and $\varepsilon > 0$, $g_h = g_h^*$ and $\hat{h} = \hat{h}^*$.

Proof   See Appendix B.

In the two earlier sections we showed that the spillovers associated with human capital formation are essential for generating diversity in the long-run income level. In their absence, (detrended) income levels of countries similar in preferences and technology will converge. In this section we show that a combination of human capital externality and labor mobility is essential for restoring level convergence. Thus knowledge spillovers are both a source of divergence (in the absence of labor mobility) and a source of convergence (in the presence of labor mobility).

13.4   Stochastic Growth and Time-Series Implications

The stochastic version of the endogenous growth model has important implications for empirical implementations. To highlight its time-series implications, we recast the closed economy model in a stochastic environment without externality, similar to that of section 12.4.

Assume that productivity is subject to random shocks, which evolve according to the following law of motion:

$$a_{t+1} = \rho a_t + \varepsilon_{t+1},$$

where $a = \ln(A)$ and ε is an i.i.d. disturbance. (Recall that A is the productivity level in the production function.) Similar law of motion can be introduced for the human-capital productivity level, B.

The stochastic Euler equations (first-order conditions) look similar to their deterministic counterparts spelled out in appendix A except for the addition of expectation operators on future values of the variables. In appendix C we describe the log-linearization technique that can generate solutions for consumption c_t, education e_t, physical capital K_{t+1}, and human capital h_{t+1} in terms of past and present realizations of the shock ε_t and the initial values of the capital stocks K_0 and h_0. In other words, we get reduced form equations in these variables that can be used as regression equations for empirical analysis. The coefficients of these regressions can be related explicitly to the deep structural parameters $(\beta, \sigma, \alpha, \delta_k, B, \gamma, \delta_h, \rho)$ of the model.

A key feature of the growth model is the existence of a unit root in the reduced form regression equations. To see this, consider the law of motion of the growth engine, human capital, in its detrended form:

$$(1 + g_h)^{t+1}\hat{h}_{t+1} = B\hat{e}_t^\gamma(1 + g_h)^t\hat{h}_t + (1 - \delta_h)(1 + g_h)^t\hat{h}_t.$$

Upon simplification, this can be expressed as

$$(1 + g_h)\hat{h}_{t+1} = [B\hat{e}_t^\gamma + (1 - \delta_h)]\hat{h}_t. \tag{13.6}$$

At the deterministic steady state (around which the nonlinear stochastic dynamical system is linearized), $\hat{h}_{t+1} = \hat{h}_t$ and $\hat{e}_t = \hat{e}$ constant, so $1 + g_h = B\hat{e}^\gamma$. Log-linearizing this equation around the steady state yields

$$\Delta \ln(\hat{h}_{t+1}) = \Delta \ln(\hat{h}_t) + \left[\frac{\gamma B\hat{e}^\gamma}{B\hat{e}^\gamma + (1 - \delta_h)}\right]\Delta \ln(\hat{e}_t), \tag{13.7}$$

where $\Delta \ln(x) = \Delta x/x$. Equation (13.7) reveals that the evolution of the (detrended) engine of growth, $\hat{h}$, is characterized by a unit root. This feature reflects the growth-sustainability property of the human capital engine. This unit root feature in turn implies that any transitory shocks will generate persistent effects on equilibrium values of all the detrended variables. Obviously the same applies to these variables in their original nondetrended forms as well. (For an empirical application of this idea, see Jones 1995.)

13.5   Appendix A: Derivation of Equation (13.4)

The consumer's first-order conditions with respect to c_t, e_t, B_{t+1}, K_{t+1}, and h_{t+1} are given by

$$c_t^{-\sigma} = \mu_t, \tag{A.1}$$

$$\mu_{h_t} \gamma B e_t^{\gamma-1} = \mu_t w_t N_t, \tag{A.2}$$

$$\mu_t = \beta \mu_{t+1}(1 + r_{t+1}), \tag{A.3}$$

$$\mu_t = \beta \mu_{t+1}(1 + r_{kt+1} - \delta_k), \tag{A.4}$$

$$\mu_{h_t} = \beta[\mu_{h_{t+1}} B e_{t+1}^{\gamma} + \mu_{t+1} w_{t+1}(1 - e_{t+1})N_{t+1}], \tag{A.5}$$

where μ_t and μ_{ht} are the Lagrange multipliers (μ for multipliers) at time t associated with the consumer budget constraint (13.2) and the law of motion of human capital (13.1), respectively. The firm's first-order conditions are

$$w_t = \alpha A \left(\frac{X_t}{1 - e_t}\right)^{1-\alpha}, \tag{A.6}$$

$$r_{kt} = (1 - \alpha)A \left(\frac{X_t}{1 - e_t}\right)^{-\alpha}. \tag{A.7}$$

The equilibrium conditions in the labor and capital markets are

$$(1 - e_t)N_t h_t = H_t^d, \tag{A.8}$$

$$K_t = K_t^d. \tag{A.9}$$

Substituting (A.6) and (13.1) with $\delta_h = 1$ into (A.2), we get

$$\frac{\gamma \mu_{ht} h_{t+1}}{e_t} = \frac{\alpha \mu_t Y_t}{1 - e_t}. \tag{A.10}$$

Along the balanced growth path, time allocations are constant (i.e., $e_t = e_{t+1}$), so (A.10) implies that

$$\frac{\beta \mu_{h_{t+1}} h_{t+2}}{\mu_{h_t} h_{t+1}} = \frac{\beta \mu_{t+1} Y_{t+1}}{\mu_t Y_t}, \tag{A.11}$$

where the two terms in (A.11) are given, respectively, by

$$\frac{\mu_{ht} h_{t+1}}{\beta \mu_{h_{t+1}} h_{t+2}} = 1 + \alpha \left(\frac{\mu_{t+1} Y_{t+1}}{\mu_{h_{t+1}} h_{t+2}} \right) \tag{A.12}$$

from (13.1), (A.5), and (A.6), and by

$$\frac{\mu_t Y_t}{\beta \mu_{t+1} Y_{t+1}} = \frac{1}{\beta (1 + g_N)(Be^{\gamma})^{1-\sigma}} \tag{A.13}$$

from (A.4) and (A.7), with $\delta_k = 1$. Combining (A.10)–(A.13) yields equation (13.4) in the text.

13.6   Appendix B: Proof of the Labor-Mobility–Level Convergence Proposition

For any two countries A and B with labor flowing from B to A, we state in more technical terms:

PROPOSITION   Along the steady-state growth path with nonzero labor flows and $\varepsilon > 0$, $g_h^A = g_h^B$ and $h^A = h^B$.

Proof   Along the global steady-state growth path, $g_K^i = g_Y^i$ ($i = A, B$), and the ratios of the cross-border labor income $w^A(1 - n^B)N^B h^B$ to both GDP^A and GDP^B must be constant. Given the Cobb-Douglas production function, these balanced growth conditions imply that $(1 + g_N^A)(1 + g_h^A) = (1 + g_N^B)(1 + g_h^B)$ and

$$\frac{1 + g_Y^A}{1 + g_Y^B} = \left(\frac{1 + g_h^B}{1 + g_h^A} \right)^{\varepsilon/(1-\alpha)}.$$

From the Cobb-Douglas function and the equality $g_K^i = g_Y^i$ ($i = A, B$), we also have

$$\frac{1 + g_Y^A}{1 + g_Y^B} = \left(\frac{1 + g_h^A}{1 + g_h^B} \right)^{\varepsilon/\alpha}.$$

Combining the two conditions above, we have $g_h^A = g_h^B$. Along the equilibrium balanced path, the fundamental growth equation à la Rebelo (1992) can be expressed as

$$\left(\frac{1 + g_c}{1 + g_c^*}\right)^{\sigma} = \left(\frac{1 + g_h^A}{1 + g_h^B}\right)^{\sigma\zeta} = \frac{r_k^A}{r_k^B} = \frac{x^B}{x^A},$$

where

$$x^A = \frac{K^A}{N^A h^A + N^B h^B (1 - n^B)},$$

$$x^B = \frac{K^B}{N^B h^B n^B}.$$

The first equality reflects the balanced growth condition between c_t and h_t^ζ, implied by (13.2) and (13.5). The second equality follows from the intertemporal condition (13.3). The third equality is derived from the relation between the rental rate of capital and the wage rate (i.e., $r_k^i = (1 - \alpha)w_t^i / \alpha x_t^i$, $i = A, B$, and the wage equality condition $w_t^A = w_t^B$.[5]

Equality of growth rates ($g_h^A = g_h^B$) implies equality of interest rates ($r_k^A = r_k^B$) and hence capital–effective-labor ratios (x_t^A and x_t^B). From the wage equality condition ($w^A = \alpha(x^A)^{1-\alpha}(h^A)^{\varepsilon} = \alpha(x^B)^{1-\alpha}(h^B)^{\varepsilon} = w^B$), we have $x^A = x^B$, which in turn implies that $h^A = h^B$. This concludes the proof of the proposition.[6]

13.7   Appendix C: Log-linearization of the Stochastic Growth Model

In this appendix we follow King, Plosser, and Rebelo (1988) and Campbell (1994) by providing a log-linear approximation of the stochastic growth model to derive expressions for the endogenous variables in terms of the underlying exogenous shocks.

To reduce the dimension of the problem, we substitute the firm's first-order conditions, (A.6) and (A.7), and the market-clearing conditions, (A.8) and (A.9), into the consumer's first-order conditions, stochastic versions of (A.1)–(A.5), to eliminate the factor prices, w_t and r_{kt}. The result is a set of six equations in the two control variables (c_t and e_t), the two state variables (K_{t+1} and h_{t+1}), and the two co-state variables (the Lagrange multipliers μ_t and μ_{ht}).

Since we want to linearize the stochastic dynamical system around its deterministic steady state, we need to first detrend the set of six equations in order to solve for its steady state in the absence of shocks. Direct inspection of the original nonlinear dynamical system suggests the following detrending rules:

$$\hat{c}_t = \frac{c_t}{(1 + g_h)^{\sigma t}}, \quad \hat{e}_t = e_t,$$

$$\hat{K}_t = \frac{K_t}{(1 + g_N)(1 + g_h)^t}, \quad \hat{h}_t = \frac{h_t}{(1 + g_h)^t},$$

$$\hat{\mu}_t = \mu_t(1 + g_h)^{\sigma t}, \quad \hat{\mu}_{h_t} = \frac{\mu_{h_t}(1 + g_h)^{\sigma t}}{(1 + g_N)^t},$$

where g_h is the steady-state growth rate of human capital. Naturally this detrended system has the property that in the steady state all the detrended ("hat") variables are time invariant.

Using the above detrending rules, we can rewrite the equilibrium system in terms of these detrended variables. Shutting down the shocks and dropping the expectation terms and the time subscripts yields a set of six nonlinear deterministic steady-state equations in $\{\hat{c}, \hat{e}, \hat{K}, \hat{h}, \hat{\mu}, \hat{\mu}_h\}$. We then log-linearize the set of six original stochastic nonlinear dynamical equations around its deterministic steady state.

Solving the linearized version of the control equations for $(\hat{c}_t, \hat{e}_t)$ as functions of $(\hat{K}_{t+1}, \hat{h}_{t+1}, \hat{\mu}_t, \hat{\mu}_{ht})$ and substituting them into the state and co-state equations, we obtain a linear system with four difference equations in the state and co-state variables $(\hat{K}_{t+1}, \hat{h}_{t+1}, \hat{\mu}_t, \hat{\mu}_{ht})$.

14

International Taxation and Exogenous Growth

The increased integration of the world capital markets has strong implications for the taxation of income from capital. In general, if factors become more mobile they are potentially less desirable as a source for government revenue.[1] In the extreme case, such as the federal system (in the United States and Germany), the ability of individual states to tax capital income is severely constrained, for capital can move freely across state borders.

This chapter addresses the issue of the taxation of capital income for a growing small open economy completely integrated into the world capital markets.[2] We bring together in a simple growth model three major considerations. First, as shown by Chamley (1986) and Judd (1985), it is not efficient to tax capital income in a steady state of a closed economy, since capital has essentially a perfectly elastic supply in the steady state. This result is extended to a small open economy by appealing to the efficiency of a residence-based taxation (e.g., Frenkel, Razin, and Sadka 1991). Such steady-state analysis can only provide limited guidance for policymaking.

Second, when enforceability of taxation of foreign-source income is not feasible and containing capital flight is impossible, it would be efficient to tax exempt capital income from domestic sources as well (see Razin and Sadka 1991). This result has important policy implications, for it holds at any moment and not only if a steady state is reached.

Third, even though it is efficient to let capital flow freely in and out of the country when such a flow does not undermine the ability to tax foreign-source income, it is efficient to restrict capital export and reinstate capital taxation when foreign source income cannot effectively be taxed (see Razin and Sadka 1991).

14.1   Principles of International Taxation

The diverse structures of the national tax systems have important implications for the direction and magnitude of international flows of goods and capital and consequently for the worldwide efficiency of resource allocation in the integrated world economy. Although no country adheres strictly to a pure principle of international taxation, two polar principles with a wide application can be detected in direct and indirect taxation: the *residence* (of taxpayer) principle and the *source* (of income) principle. According to the residence principle, residents are taxed on their worldwide income uniformly, regardless of the source of income (domestic or foreign), while nonresidents are not taxed on income originating in the country[3] and, according to the source principle, income is taxed at the source regardless of the residence (domestic or foreign).

To better understand the issue of tax arbitrage that arises under the integration of capital markets, consider the familiar two-country (home and foreign) model with perfect capital mobility. Denote interest rates in the home country and in the foreign country by r and r^*, respectively. In general, the home country may have three different effective tax rates applying to capital (interest and dividend) income:

τ_D = tax rate levied on residents on their domestic source income.

τ_A = effective rate of the *additional* tax levied on residents on foreign-source income (over and above the tax paid in the foreign country).

τ_N = tax levied on income of nonresidents.

Correspondingly, the foreign country levies similar taxes, denoted by τ_D^*, τ_A^*, and τ_N^*.[4]

At equilibrium the home country residents must be indifferent between investing at home or investing abroad. This implies that

$$r(1 - \tau_D) = r^*(1 - \tau_N^* - \tau_A). \tag{14.1}$$

Similarly at the equilibrium the residents of the foreign country must be indifferent between investing in their home country (the foreign country) or investing abroad (the home country). Thus

$$r^*(1 - \tau_D^*) = r(1 - \tau_N - \tau_A^*). \tag{14.2}$$

For the interest rates r and r^* to be positive (in which case we say that the capital market equilibrium is viable), the two equations (14.1) and (14.2) must be linearly dependent:

$$(1 - \tau_D)(1 - \tau_D^*) = (1 - \tau_N - \tau_A^*)(1 - \tau_N^* - \tau_A). \tag{14.3}$$

This constraint, which involves tax rates of the two countries, implies that even though the two countries do not explicitly coordinate their tax systems between them, each one must nevertheless take into account the tax system of the other in designing its own tax system.[5]

It is noteworthy that if both countries adopt one of the two aforementioned polar principles of taxation, residence or source, then condition (14.3) is fulfilled. To see this, observe that if both countries adopt the residence principle, then

$$\tau_D = \tau_A, \quad \tau_D^* = \tau_A^*, \quad \tau_N = \tau_N^* = 0. \tag{14.4}$$

If both countries adopt the source principles, then

$$\tau_D = \tau_N, \quad \tau_D^* = \tau_N^*, \quad \tau_A = \tau_A^* = 0. \tag{14.5}$$

Evidently, the joint constraint (14.3) is fulfilled if either (14.4) or (14.5) holds. However, if the two countries do not adopt the same polar principle (or do not adopt either one of the two polar principles), then, in general, condition (14.3) is not met, and a viable equilibrium may not exist.

The structure of taxation also has important implications for the international allocation of investments and savings. If all countries adopt the residence principle (condition 14.4 holds), then it follows from either (14.1) or (14.2), the rate-of-return arbitrage conditions, that $r = r^*$. That is, the pre-tax rates of return to capital are equated internationally. As the gross return to capital is equal to the marginal product of capital, it follows that the marginal product of capital is equated across countries. Thus the world (future) output is maximized and worldwide production efficiency prevails.[6] If, however, the tax rate on capital income is not the same in all countries (i.e., $\tau_D \neq \tau_D^*$), then the after-tax return on capital would vary across countries. As the net return to capital is equal to the consumer's (intertemporal) marginal rate of substitution, it follows that the intertemporal marginal rates of substitution are not equated internationally. Thus the international allocation of world savings is inefficient.

Alternatively, if all countries adopt the source principle (condition 14.5 holds), then it follows from either (14.1) or (14.2) that $r(1 - \tau_D) = r^*(1 - \tau_D^*)$. Thus the intertemporal marginal rate of substitution is equated internationally, and the allocation of world savings is efficient. If, however, the tax rate on income from capital is not the same in all countries, then $r \neq r^*$. That is, the marginal product of capital varies across countries and the worldwide allocation of investment is inefficient.

14.2   Optimal Capital Taxation in a Small Open Economy

Optimal taxation of capital income is usually subject to two conflicting forces. On the one hand, the income from existing capital is a pure rent, and taxing all of it away must be efficient. On the other hand, the taxation of the returns on current and future investment in capital may retard growth and thus may be an inefficient policy.

Following Lucas (1990), consider a small open economy with an infinitely lived representative agent, endowed with one unit of human capital input (divisible into leisure and labor) and K_0 units of capital. Assume for simplicity that the exogenous growth rates of population and skills are zero. Unlike chapter 12, this chapter is based on the convention that investment in physical capital is done by the firm rather than the household. The maximization problem of the representative agent is specified by

$$\max_{(c_t, L_t)} \sum_{t=0}^{\infty} \beta^t u(c_t, L_t) \qquad (14.6)$$

subject to $\sum_{t=0}^{\infty} P_t[\overline{w}_t(1 - L_t) - c_t] \geqslant 0,$

where β denotes the subjective discount factor, c_t and L_t consumption of goods and leisure in period t, respectively, P_t the consumer (post-tax) present-value factor from period t to period 0, $\overline{w}_t$ the post-tax wage rate in period t, and u the instantaneous utility function of the household. The Lagrangean expression for this problem is

$$L = \sum_{t=0}^{\infty} \{\beta^t u(c_t, L_t) + \lambda P_t[\overline{w}_t(1 - L_t) - c_t]\},$$

where $\lambda \geqslant 0$ is a Lagrange multiplier.

Underlying the specification in (14.6) is the idea that households sell their endowments of capital to firms at $t = 0$, and at this point of time the government confiscates these incomes, since they amount to lump-sum incomes.[7] Consequently the lifetime budget constraint implies that the discounted flow of consumption must be equal to the discounted flow of labor income. In other words, income originating from the existing capital should appear nowhere in the household optimization problem, while income originating from new capital is incorporated into the household budget constraint, as the latter is expressed in present-value terms.

First-order conditions are given by

$$\beta^t u_c(c_t, L_t) - \lambda P_t = 0, \qquad (14.7a)$$

$$\beta^t u_x(c_t, L_t) - \lambda P_t \overline{w}_t = 0. \qquad (14.7b)$$

These conditions, substituted into the budget constraint in (14.6), generate the household's implementability constraint for the optimum tax problem, as follows:

$$\sum_{t=0}^{\infty} \beta^t [u_L(c_t, L_t)(1 - L_t) - u_c(c_t, L_t)c_t] = 0. \qquad (14.8)$$

Assume that the representative firm is equipped with a constant-returns-to-scale production function, $F(K_t, H_t)$; where K_t is the capital stock and H_t the employment of labor in period t. Denote the rate of corporate income tax in period t by τ_t. The firm's objective is to maximize the present value of its net cash flows. Thus the firm chooses (K_t, H_t) so as to maximize

$$\sum_{t=0}^{\infty} q_t\{(1 - \tau_t)F(K_t, H_t) - [K_{t+1} - (1 - \delta_K)K_t]$$

$$+ \tau_t\delta_K K_t - (1 - \tau_t)w_t H_t\}, \tag{14.9}$$

where q_t denotes the tax-adjusted present value factor from period t to period 0, δ_K the rate of physical capital depreciation, and w_t the pre-tax wage rate in period t. The net cash flow of the firm in period t consists of the after-tax value of output, $(1 - \tau_t)F_t$, minus gross investment, $K_{t+1} - (1 - \delta_K)K_t$, plus the tax saving resulting from the depreciation allowance, $\tau_t\delta_K K_t$, minus the tax-adjusted wage bill $(1 - \tau)w_t L_t$.[8] The present-value factor, q_t, associated with the tax-adjusted domestic rate of interest, evolves according to the familiar relation:

$$\frac{q_t}{q_{t+1}} = 1 + (1 - \tau_{t+1})r_{t+1}, \tag{14.10}$$

where r_{t+1} is the pre-tax rate of interest from period t to period $t + 1$. Since the depreciation allowance for tax purposes is equal to the true economic depreciation and the firm finances its investment entirely by issuing debt (rather than equity), the corporate tax does not affect the firm's behavior. This can be seen from the following first-order conditions for the firm's optimization problem:

$$F_H(K_t, H_t) = w_t \tag{14.11}$$

and

$$F_K(K_t, H_t) - \delta_K = r_t. \tag{14.12}$$

These last two conditions generate the firm's implementability constraint for the optimum tax problem.

The optimal tax problem for the benevolent government can now be specified as follows: The government chooses c_t, $H_t(=1-L_t)$, K_t, w_t, and r_t so as to maximize the household utility function

$$\sum_{t=0}^{\infty} \beta^t u(c_t, L_t)$$

subject to the present-value resource constraint of the small open economy,

$$\sum_{t=0}^{\infty} [1 + r^*(1 - \tau_N^*)]^{-t} \{ F(K_t, 1 - L_t)$$

$$- [K_{t+1} - (1 - \delta_K)K_t] - c_t - g_t \},$$

and to the implementability conditions (14.8), (14.11), and (14.12), where g_t denotes government spending in period t. Notice that in this optimal tax problem, w_t and r_t appear only in constraints (14.11) and (14.12). Hence the two control variables w_t and r_t and the two constraints (14.11) and (14.12) may be omitted initially from the tax optimization problem. Once the problem is solved, we can employ (14.11) and (14.12) in order to set w_t and r_t. The Lagrangean expression for the optimal tax problem is then

$$L = \sum_{t=0}^{\infty} \beta^t u(c_t, L_t) + \phi \sum_{t=0}^{\infty} \beta^t [u_L(c_t, L_t)(1 - L_t) - u_c(c_t, L_t)c_t]$$

$$+ \mu \sum_{t=0}^{\infty} [1 + r^*(1 - \tau_N^*)]^{-t}$$

$$\cdot \{ F(K_t, 1 - L_t) - [K_{t+1} - (1 - \delta_K)K_t] - c_t - g_t \}, \qquad (14.13)$$

where $\phi \geq 0$ and $\mu \geq 0$ are Lagrange multipliers. The resource constraint for the small open economy is equal to the discounted (using the world net of tax interest rate, $r^*(1 - \tau_N^*)$) sum of output flows F_t minus gross investment $K_{t+1} - (1 - \delta_K)K_t$, private consumption c_t, and public consumption g_t.[9]

Setting the derivative of (14.13) with respect to K_{t+1} equal to zero yields

$$-[1 + r^*(1 - \tau_N^*)]^{-t+1}$$

$$+ [1 + r^*(1 - \tau_N^*)]^{-t}[F_K(K_t, 1 - L_t) + 1 - \delta_K] = 0.$$

Hence

$$F_K(K_t, 1 - L_t) - \delta_K = r^*(1 - \tau_N^*). \tag{14.14}$$

Equation (14.14) implies that under the optimum tax regime the net (after depreciation) marginal product of capital must be equal to the world rate of interest (net of foreign tax) in each period of time. As was already pointed out in the preceding section, if individual residents can freely invest abroad, they must earn the same net return whether investing at home or abroad:

$$r_t(1 - \tau_{Dt}) = r^*(1 - \tau_N^* - \tau_{At}). \tag{14.15}$$

Matching up conditions (14.12), (14.14), and (14.15), we see that under the optimal tax regime the government in the small open economy must let capital move freely in and out of the country and must employ the *residence principle* of taxation, $r_t = r^*(1 - \tau_N^*)$ and $\tau_{Dt} = \tau_{At}$. Thus, at the optimum, investment is *efficiently* allocated between the home country and the rest of the world: the production efficiency result.[10]

Other first-order conditions (with respect to c_t and L_t) for the optimal tax problem are given by

$$\beta^t\{u_c(c_t, L_t) - \phi[u_{cc}(c_t, L_t)c_t + u_c(c_t, L_t) - u_{cL}(c_t, L_t)(1 - L_t)]\}$$

$$= \mu[1 + r^*(1 - \tau_N^*)]^{-t}, \tag{14.16}$$

$$\beta^t\{u_c(c_t, L_t) - \phi[u_{cL}(c_t, L_t)c_t - u_{cc}(c_t, L_t)(1 - L_t) + u_L(c_t, L_t)]\}$$

$$= \mu[1 + r^*(1 - \tau_N^*)]^{-t}F_H(K_t, 1 - L_t). \tag{14.17}$$

Consider now a unique parameter configuration that yields a *steady state* for the optimal tax problem. For a small open economy this requires a specific relation between the discount factor and the (net-of-tax) world rate of interest (absence of consumption tilting; see chapter 5):

$$\beta[1 + r^*(1 - \tau_N^*)] = 1,$$

or

$$r^*(1 - \tau_N^*) = \beta^{-1} - 1. \tag{14.18}$$

Notice that β^{-1} is the intertemporal marginal rate of substitution in the steady state (where $c_{t+1} = c_t$ and $L_{t+1} = L_t$). Utility maximization implies that $\beta^{-1} - 1$ is equated to

$$\left(\frac{P_t}{P_{t+1}}\right) - 1 = (1 - \tau_{Dt+1})r_{t+1}$$

(see condition 14.10). Thus

$$(1 - \tau_D)r = \beta^{-1} - 1 = r^*(1 - \tau_N^*)$$

by equation (14.18). Comparing with the optimality principle of residence-based taxation, we have

$$\tau_D = \tau_A = 0.$$

We can conclude that in the steady state the tax on capital income, from either domestic or foreign sources, *vanishes* entirely from the optimum tax menu. This is essentially the result of Chamley (1986) and Judd (1985).

14.3   Zero Tax at Any Moment

A considerable degree of coordination among countries is required to tax effectively worldwide income. International coordination takes the form of an exchange of information among the tax authorities, withholding arrangements, with possible breachments of bank secrecy laws, and the like. This coordination enables each country to effectively tax its residents on capital income that is invested in the other country.

However, if international coordination with the rest of the world is lacking, governments cannot tax the income from capital that is invested in the rest of the world. We show that in this case it will be efficient to abolish the tax on capital income altogether if capital mobility cannot be restricted.

To see this, note that with no tax on foreign source income ($\tau_A = 0$), the arbitrage condition (14.15) becomes

$$(1 - \tau_{Dt})r_t = (1 - \tau_N^*)r^*. \tag{14.19}$$

Matching up (14.19) with (14.12) and (14.14) implies that

$$\tau_{Dt} = 0, \qquad t = 0, 1, 2, \ldots.$$

Thus the optimal tax rule for a country that cannot enforce taxes on foreign source income is to abstain entirely from capital income taxation. This capital flight possibility, leading to full tax exemption of capital income, captures the essence of a problem hindering many countries in the integrated world economy.

14.4 Reinstating the Tax on Capital Income

When foreign-source income cannot be taxed, another possibility is to try to contain capital of residents within the national boundaries and tax it. Can such "nonliberal" policy be efficient?

The answer is in the affirmative! Starting from a case where capital is freely mobile and hence efficiently untaxed, the net marginal product of domestic capital is equal to the world rate of interest (net of foreign tax); see equation (14.14). At this point the domestic economy loses nothing in terms of GNP by marginally shifting the capital of home residents from abroad to home (by introducing a quota on capital exports). On the other hand, such a shift increases the capital income tax base, thereby allowing a reduction of the tax rates on all other sources for a given level of public consumption (and consequently for given tax revenue needs). Such a reduction in the tax rates must raise welfare. Put differently, a forced reduction in capital exports starting from this initial point amounts essentially to a lump-sum transfer of income from the representative consumer to the government, brought about by the expansion in the tax base. Such a transfer must improve welfare because with distortionary finance the social value of a marginal dollar in the hands of the government must exceed the social value of this dollar in the hands of private consumers.

How severe should the restrictions on capital exports be? Should capital exports be banned altogether? If r_t is close to $r^*(1 - \tau_N^*)$ under autarky, then there is little gain for society as a whole from investing abroad because this gain is equal only to the difference between $r^*(1 - \tau_N^*)$ and r_t. However, the private sector can still gain considerably from investing abroad if $r_t(1 - \tau_D)$ is considerably below $r^*(1 - \tau_N^*)$. Therefore a significant quantity of capital may fly abroad, and the government will lose a significant amount of tax revenues from such an outflow of capital. In this case it may be efficient to totally disallow exports of capital.

No capital-income tax can efficiently be imposed by a small open economy if capital flight to the rest of the world cannot be effectively stopped. Consequently all of the tax burden falls on the internationally immobile factor, such as labor, property, and land. The resulting equilibrium is a *constrained* optimum, relative to the set of tax instruments that is available. Since, however, the set of tax instruments in this case is more restricted than if taxes on foreign sources of income are enforceable, it follows that the constrained optimum (in the case of capital-flight) is inferior to the second-best optimum that could be reached if worldwide income taxation is implementable. Countries therefore should have strong incentives to coordinate their tax collection activities so as to enforce taxation of foreign-source income. In the absence of such coordination, each country may do well by trying to contain its residents' capital within its national borders, at least partially. These considerations are not restricted to the Chamley-Judd steady-state framework, which has limited relevance for policy design. Rather they apply to the ongoing policymaking.

15

International Taxation and Endogenous Growth

Lucas (1988) posed the *problem of economic development* as the problem of accounting for "the observed pattern, across countries and across time, in levels and rates of growth of per capita income . . . ." Assuming symmetry in preferences and technology across countries, the growth literature has been successful in explaining income *level* differences in terms of asymmetry in initial factor endowments (as a transitory short-run phenomenon in exogenous growth models and as a sustainable long-run phenomenon in endogenous growth models). The explanation of growth *rate* differences is a much harder challenge —especially in exogenous growth models where the natural growth rate is an unalterable given. In the context of recent models of endogenous growth, one explanation that has been widely explored lies in differences in national (especially tax) policies.[1] Such asymmetry can generate differential effects on the private agents' incentives to invest in growth-enhancing activities and hence the rates of productivity growth in different countries.[2]

With increasing global integration of the world economy, factor mobility opens a room for cross-border spillovers of policy effects, with policy changes in one country exerting an impact on resource allocation and growth in another country through changes in factor price differentials. In this chapter we examine whether the tax-driven diversity in income growth rates can be preserved when (1) factors of production are freely mobile across national borders and (2) the factor incomes earned in the foreign country are potentially subject to double taxation by both the home and foreign governments and are thus affected by both domestic and foreign tax policies. In particular, is international income taxation a growth-diverging force? How do factor mobility and cross-country tax structures interact to determine growth differentials?

15.1   Tax-Driven Divergence in a Closed Economy

Consider the closed economy endogenous growth model of chapter 13. Suppose now that there is a fiscal authority that levies flat rate taxes on labor income, τ_{wt}, and capital income, τ_{rt}. We allow for tax-deductibility of depreciation expenses for physical capital, $(\tau_{rt}\delta_k K_t)$, and possibly human capital, $\phi\tau_{wt}\delta_h e_t N_t h_t$, with $\phi = 1$ if deductible and $\phi = 0$ otherwise. If depreciation of human capital is tax-deductible and if income taxation is comprehensive and uniform so that the tax rates on labor and capital incomes are equal, the tax treatment of the two forms of capital becomes symmetric. As usual, in order to focus on the distortionary effects of taxation, we assume that the tax proceeds are rebated in a lump-sum fashion to the households. The consumer budget constraint, the counterpart of (13.2), is given by

$$N_t c_t + [K_{t+1} - (1 - \delta_k)K_t] - [B_{t+1} - (1 + r_t)B_t] - T_t$$

$$= \Omega_{wt} w_t (1 - e_t)N_t h_t + \phi\tau_{wt}\delta_h w_t N_t h_t + \Omega_{rt} r_{kt} K_t + \tau_{rt}\delta_k K_t, \quad (15.1)$$

where T_t is the lump-sum rebate, and the tax wedges are defined as $\Omega_{rt} = 1 - \tau_{rt}$ and $\Omega_{wt} = 1 - \tau_{wt}$.

The optimization problem facing the household is to choose $\{c_t, e_t, K_{t+1}, h_{t+1}, B_{t+1}\}_{t=0}^{\infty}$ to maximize utility (12.1) subject to the human-capital accumulation equation (13.1) and the budget constraint (15.1), given $\{w_t, r_t, \tau_{wt}, \tau_{rt}\}_{t=0}^{\infty}$.

Following similar steps in appendix A of chapter 13, we can derive the following steady-state equation in the time allocated to education, e:

$$1 = \beta(1 + g_h)^{1-\sigma}(1 + g_N)\left\{1 + \gamma\left(\frac{1-e}{e}\right)\left(\frac{g_h + \delta_h}{1 + g_h}\right)\right.$$

$$\left. \times \left[1 + \phi\delta_h\left(\frac{\tau_w}{\Omega_w}\right)\left(\frac{1}{1-e}\right)\right]\right\}, \quad (15.2)$$

where

$$g_h = Be^\gamma - \delta_h.$$

Given the solution for e from (15.2), the ratio of the stocks of physical capital to human capital $\tilde{k}(= K/Nh)$ can be solved from

$$(1 + g_h)^\sigma = \beta\left\{1 + \Omega_r\left[(1 - \alpha)A\left(\frac{\tilde{k}}{1 - e}\right)^{-\alpha} - \delta_k\right]\right\}. \qquad (15.3)$$

Direct inspection of (15.2) reveals that the intertemporal (capital) tax wedge (Ω_r) has no effect on the allocation of time between work and education, hence growth rates, in the steady state. The source of this neutrality lies in the fact that in the simplified model, there are no other time-consuming activities (e.g., leisure), and physical capital is not required for the production of human capital.

In the absence of depreciation allowance for human capital ($\phi = 0$), the intratemporal (labor) tax wedge (Ω_w) will have no effect on long run time allocation (hence growth rate) either. This can be understood from Boskin's (1975) argument that increase in the *constant* tax rate on labor income along the balanced growth path will reduce both the returns (in terms of future wage earnings) and costs (in terms of forgone earnings) of investment in human capital equally at the margin.[3] When depreciation of human capital is tax-deductible ($\phi = 1$), however, the reduction in returns in terms of future wage earnings due to the wage tax are exactly offset by this allowance. Thus, since only the costs in terms of income forgone are reduced, the labor income tax is no longer neutral.

In reality, tax-deductibility of depreciation of human capital does not exist in the exact form as modeled here, but it can be viewed as mimicking the effects of two common provisions of taxation: tax progressivity and subsidized health care.[4] This is proxied by $0 < \phi < 1$ in our model. On the other hand, our simplified setup has abstracted from modeling other time-consuming activities, such as leisure or child-rearing (a driving force behind population growth), and the use of physical capital as an input in the production of human capital. Adding these features to our model will strengthen the effects of the labor income tax on the growth rate of human capital (and population) and introduce a channel through which the capital income tax may affect the growth rate as well.

In our simplified world, countries with similar preferences and technology but different labor income tax rates will have different long-run growth rates. Differences in capital income tax rates, however, will not lead to divergence in growth rates.

15.2   Tax Divergence in an Open Economy: Capital Mobility

We now integrate our economy into the world capital market. We continue to assume that tax rates are different across countries. If the residence principle of international taxation is adopted universally, then (as shown in chapter 14) the pre-tax marginal products of physical capital will be equalized across countries. The after-tax marginal products will differ, however, if the capital income tax rates vary across countries. The interest-equalization arbitrage-based relation $(1 - \tau_{rD})r = (1 - \tau_{rA} - \tau_{rN}^*)r^*$ can be viewed as an additional condition (relative to the autarky case) in the set of world equilibrium conditions. Since the other equilibrium conditions remain the same as in the closed economy, the analogue of the time equation (15.2) indicates that the steady-state growth rate of human capital also remains unchanged. This implies that countries with different (the same) labor income tax rates will grow at different (the same) rates—implication 1.

If net capital flows are nonzero in the long run, the size of this flow can, in principle, be determined from the arbitrage-based condition. However, in the steady state, these flows should grow at the same rate as the outputs in both the home country and the rest of the world. Thus, if they exhibit identical (exogenous) rates of growth of population (as we have been assuming so far), they must also have the same growth rates in human capital (or income per capita). But this contradicts implication 1, implying that either the steady state is nonexistent or capital flows are zero.

Suppose then that net capital flows are zero in the steady state. In the absence of barriers to capital flows, the arbitrage-based condition will continue to hold even when no capital flows exist in equilibrium. From (15.3) we can write

$$\left(\frac{1 + g_y}{1 + g_y^*}\right)^\sigma = \frac{1 + (1 - \tau_{rD})(r_k - \delta_k)}{1 + (1 - \tau_{rA}^* - \tau_{rN})(r_k - \delta_k)}. \tag{15.4}$$

As explained in chapter 14, the residence principle implies that $\tau_{rN} = 0$ and $\tau_{rA}^* = \tau_{rD}^*$. This implies that g_y and g_y^* are different (equal) as long as $\tau_{rD} \neq (=) \tau_{rD}^*$, thus ruling out zero capital flow as a steady-state equilibrium phenomenon from implication 1 (unless the two countries have strong similarities across the two tax bases). As a result a steady state will not exist, in general, in the presence of tax differences. In other words, capital mobility will drive countries off the world steady-state growth path.[5]

To restore the possibility of a steady state, we introduce an additional source of growth which, similar to human capital, involves time-consuming activities: endogenous population growth.

Given the close connection between population growth and income growth in the development process and as a broadening of the definition of the *problem of development*, we will devote equal emphasis to accounting for the observed diversity in the growth of (per capita and aggregate) *income* as well as *population*. When population growth is determined exogenously, taxes can only affect income growth through the growth engine (human capital), with indistinguishable effects on the growth of per capita income and aggregate income. Endogenizing population growth will introduce a new channel through which taxes can affect per capita income growth and aggregate income growth differently.

For the above reasons we think that it is important to examine the interaction between taxation and (population and income) growth in the presence of factor mobility. To accomplish this, we need to extend the model in three dimensions: preferences for the quantity and quality of children, the time constraint, and the law of motion of population.

Consider the home country as a dynastic family with N_t identical members in each period ($t = 0, 1, 2, \ldots$) and two engines of growth (human capital and population). The typical household cares about his/her own consumption c_t and the other family members N_t. His/her preferences are given by

$$\sum_{t=0}^{\infty} \beta^t N_t^{\xi} \left(\frac{c_t^{1-\sigma}}{1 - \sigma} \right),$$

(15.5)

where $\xi \in (0, 1)$ is an altruism parameter.[6] As long as $\xi > 0$, altruism is reflected not only in preference for "quantity" but also "quality" of children (i.e., consumption per capita, or standard of living)— since with positive ξ there is weight given to quantity, but the weight on the consumption term is magnified as well. Observe that if $\xi > 1 - \sigma$, then there will be a relative bias in preference toward quantity, whereas if $\xi < 1 - \sigma$, the bias will be in the opposite direction. When $\xi = 1 - \sigma$, the representative agent is said to be "fairly altruistic" in the sense that he cares only about the size of the total pie $(N_t c_t)$ to be shared among all family members, but is indifferent to the exact sharing arrangement.

In each period t there are N_t members in the representative family (given N_0 at $t = 0$). As before, each household member is endowed with one unit of non-leisure time in each period t. But instead of splitting it between work and education, he/she can now divide the unit time among three time-consuming activities: work (n_t for number of work hours), learning in schools (e_t for education), and child-rearing (v_t, for vitality), i.e., $n_t + e_t + v_t = 1$. The child-rearing activity gives rise to population growth:

$$N_{t+1} = D(v_t^{\eta})N_t + (1 - \delta_N)N_t,$$

(15.6)

where $D > 0$ and $\eta \in (0, 1]$ are the fertility efficiency coefficient and productivity parameter, respectively. One can think of N_{t+1}/N_t as one plus the number of children per family (when the number of parents is normalized to unity). Since the child-rearing cost v is increasing with the number of children, Dv^{η} can be thought of as the inverse function of this cost-quantity relation. This completes the description of the new elements of the model.

The Role of Capital Mobility in Growth Rate Convergence

As in chapter 12, under free capital mobility, the law of diminishing returns implies that capital will move from capital-rich (low marginal product of capital, MPK) countries to capital-poor (high MPK) countries. Over time such cross-border capital flows will equalize the MPKs (pre-tax or post-tax, depending on the international tax principle) prevailing in all countries. In the long run an empirically relevant steady-state world equilibrium will involve positive net capital flows from some countries to some other countries.

Without further restrictions, two other situations are possible in the long run: (1) all capital in the world resides in one single country, and (2) no cross-border capital flows (i.e., back to autarky). Both are unrealistic cases. We make sufficient assumptions to eliminate them even as theoretical possibilities. Case 1 will not occur if the MPK becomes infinitely high when the capital remaining in any capital-exporting country gets sufficiently small (i.e., the Inada conditions can rule out this corner solution). Case 2 will not occur as long as the countries are heterogeneous in some fundamentals. (If they were homogeneous in all respects, capital flows would not have taken place in the first place.) Since we want to investigate the role of taxes on growth, we will assume that asymmetry in capital income tax rates is the factor that first induced cross-border capital flows. Suppose further that these countries were traveling along their steady-state growth paths initially. Should these taxes remain different, the driving force that initiated capital movement to begin with will be reactivated if the countries revert to their long-run autarky growth paths. As such case 2 can also be ruled out. The only empirically interesting case that remains is the one that involves nonzero flows. In that case we should expect the direction of capital flows to be from low after-tax MPK countries to high after-tax MPK countries.

Let us now try to understand how capital mobility may affect the convergence in long-term growth rates across countries. In the world steady-state equilibrium, the nonzero net capital flow of each country must be growing at the same rate as its total income. But since the capital inflow of one country is equal to the capital outflow of another country, the steady-state (balanced growth) restriction forces the total income growth rates to be uniform across countries in the long run:

PROPOSITION 1 Along the steady-state growth path with nonzero net capital flows, the growth rates of (total but not necessarily per-capita) GDP must be equal across countries.

To prove this, suppose without loss of generality that capital flows from the rest of the world to the home country (since, in our full certainty model, equilibrium capital flows will be unidirectional.) Consider the resource constraint facing the home country with all the growing variables detrended by dividing the whole equation through by $N_t h_t$:

$$c + [(1 + g_N)(1 + g_h)]K^H$$

$$= F(K^H + K^{*H}, n) - (1 - \tau_{rN})rK^{*H}\left(\frac{N_t^* h_t^*}{N_t h_t}\right).$$

The steady-state growth rate of per capita GDP, g_y, is equal to g_h, so the steady-state growth rate of GDP is $g_Y = (1 + g_N)(1 + g_h) - 1$, and similarly for the rest of the world. We can rewrite the last term as

$$-(1 - \tau_{rN})rK^{*H}\left(\frac{N^* h^*}{Nh}\right)\left(\frac{(1 + g_N^*)(1 + g_h^*)}{(1 + g_N)(1 + g_h)}\right)^t,$$

where $N \equiv N_t/(1 + g_N)^t$ and $h \equiv h_t/(1 + g_h)^t$ are the detrended steady-state levels of population and human capital, respectively, in the home country, and similarly in the rest of the world. Note that this term is time-varying unless $(1 + g_N)(1 + g_h) = (1 + g_N^*)(1 + g_h^*)$, implying equality of the growth rates of (total) GDP g_Y^i in the two countries along the steady-state growth path.

We can decompose the *total* income growth rates into the *per-capita* income growth rates and *population* growth rates: $(1 + g_Y) = (1 + g_N)(1 + g_y)$. Together with the total growth equalization result, this decomposition implies that $(1 + g_N)(1 + g_y) = (1 + g_N^*)(1 + g_y^*)$. Two empirical implications follow:

1. Long-term rates of growth of population and per capita incomes should be negatively correlated across countries.[7]

2. Total income growth rates should exhibit less variation than per-capita income growth rates across countries.

Some empirical support for these and other related implications is provided by Razin and Yuen (1995c).

The Role of International Capital Taxation in Growth Rate Convergence

When capital is mobile, the choice of international tax principle and tax rates levied on capital incomes earned by residents and nonresidents at home and abroad will affect the after-tax rates of return on capital and, indirectly, the rates of growth of per capita consumption and population (g_c and g_N) across countries through the intertemporal conditions:

$$(1 + g_N)^{1-\xi}(1 + g_c)^\sigma = 1 + (1 - \tau_{rD})(r_k - \delta_k),$$

$$(1 + g_N^*)^{1-\xi}(1 + g_c^*)^\sigma = 1 + (1 - \tau_{rD}^*)(r_k^* - \delta_k).$$

Along the steady-state growth path, $g_c = g_y$ and $g_c^* = g_y^*$, and as we have just shown, $(1 + g_N)/(1 + g_N^*) = (1 + g_y^*)/(1 + g_y)$. The arbitrage-based condition implies that $(1 - \tau_{rD}^*)(r_k^* - \delta_k) = (1 - \tau_{rA}^* - \tau_{rN})(r_k - \delta_k)$. Substituting these conditions into the above equations, and dividing one equation by the other, we get

$$\left(\frac{1 + g_y}{1 + g_y^*}\right)^{\xi-(1-\sigma)} = \frac{1 + (1 - \tau_{rD})(r_k - \delta_k)}{1 + (1 - \tau_{rA}^* - \tau_{rN})(r_k - \delta_k)}. \tag{15.7}$$

This equation shows how the relative (per capita) income growth rates in the two countries depend on their capital tax rates and relative bias in preference toward quantity versus quality of children (ξ versus $1 - \sigma$).

Recall that under perfect capital mobility the no-arbitrage restrictions will force the after-tax rates of return on capital, $\bar{r}$, to be equalized across countries under the source principle. Equation (15.7) therefore implies convergence in both the per capita and total income growth rates if the *source* principle prevails (when $\tau_{rA}^* = 0$ and $\tau_{rN} = \tau_{rD}$). Under the alternative *residence* principle (when $\tau_{rN} = 0$), since the after-tax interest rates are not equalized by capital mobility, asymmetry in $\bar{r}$'s (due to the asymmetry between τ_{rD} and τ_{rD}^*) implies in turn asymmetry in growth rates.

Equation (15.7) also indicates that under residence-based taxation when $\xi \neq 1 - \sigma$, asymmetric tax rates may have differential effects on the growth of per capita income and population. In particular, when people are more biased toward quality than quantity ($\xi < 1 - \sigma$), the country with a higher capital tax rate will exhibit faster growth in per capita income and slower growth in population. The reverse is true when people are more biased toward quantity than quality ($\xi > 1 - \sigma$).[8] Other things equal, the country with a higher capital tax rate will have less incentive to invest in physical capital and more to invest in child quality if $\xi < 1 - \sigma$ or in child quantity if $\xi > 1 - \sigma$. We summarize these results as follows:

PROPOSITION 2   Under capital mobility and international capital income taxation,

1. when both countries adopt the source principle, they will exhibit identical rates of growth of per capita income and population if $\xi \neq 1 - \sigma$ irrespective of international tax differences;

2. when both countries adopt the residence principle, they will exhibit different rates of growth of per-capita income and population in general. In particular, $g_y \gtrless g_y^*$ and $g_N \lessgtr g_N^*$ as $\tau_{rD} \lessgtr \tau_{rD}^*$ if $\xi > 1 - \sigma$, and $g_y \lessgtr g_y^*$ and $g_N \gtrless g_N^*$ as $\tau_{rD} \lessgtr \tau_{rD}^*$ if $\xi < 1 - \sigma$.[9]

While asymmetry in tax rates can induce differential growth rates when both countries adopt the residence principle, we note that the adoption of asymmetric international tax principles by different countries can also generate disparity in growth rates. Note also from equation (15.7) that in cases intermediate between the source and residence principles (i.e., without complete exemption from taxes on foreign-source capital income to be paid to the domestic and/or foreign governments), the relative magnitudes of the tax wedges (with respect τ_{rD}, τ_{rA}, and τ_{rN}) matter. In those cases it will also be important to distinguish between the differential growth effects of the credit system that we have been assuming here and the alternative deduction system.

15.3 Tax Divergence in an Open Economy: Labor Mobility

Let us now turn to the other extreme case where labor is freely mobile but capital is not. In the absence of taxes, it is evident that the role of labor mobility in growth rate convergence is no different than that of capital mobility. In the presence of taxes, the absence of arbitrage opportunities ensures the equalization of after-tax marginal products of labor (MPH or wage rates) for any worker who can choose to work in either country under perfect labor mobility. In particular, $(1 - \tau_{wDt})\text{MPH}_t = (1 - \tau_{wAt} - \tau^*_{wNt})\text{MPH}^*_t$, implying that $\text{MPK}_t = \Lambda_t \text{MPK}^*_t$. The fundamental relative growth equation (15.7) can be rewritten as

$$\left(\frac{1 + g_y}{1 + g^*_y}\right)^{\xi - (1 - \sigma)} = \frac{1 + (1 - \tau_{rD})(r_k - \delta_k)}{1 + (1 - \tau^*_{rD})(\Lambda r_k - \delta_k)},$$

where

$$\Lambda = \left(\frac{1 - \tau_{wA} - \tau^*_{wN}}{1 - \tau_{wD}}\right)^{\alpha/(1-\alpha)}. \tag{15.8}$$

Note that $\tau_{wD} = \tau_{wA}$ and $\tau_{wN} = 0$ (implying that $\Lambda = 1$) under the residence principle of wage taxation, and $\tau_{wD} = \tau_{wN}$ and $\tau_{wA} = 0$ (implying that $\Lambda \gtrless 1$ as $\tau_{wD} \gtrless \tau^*_{wD}$) under the source principle. For cases where $\delta_k = 1$ and depreciation is not tax-deductible, or $\delta_k = 0$, the proposition below should be transparent.[10]

PROPOSITION 3   Under labor mobility and international labor income taxation,

3. when both countries adopt the source principle, they will exhibit different rates of growth of per capita income and population in general. In particular, $g_y \gtrless g^*_y$ and $g_N \lessgtr g^*_N$ as $(1 - \tau_{rD})^{1-\alpha}(1 - \tau_{wD})^\alpha \gtrless (1 - \tau^*_{rD})^{1-\alpha}(1 - \tau^*_{wD})^\alpha$ if $\xi > 1 - \sigma$, and $g_y \lessgtr g^*_y$ and $g_N \gtrless g^*_N$ as $(1 - \tau_{rD})^{1-\alpha}(1 - \tau_{wD})^\alpha \gtrless (1 - \tau^*_{rD})^{1-\alpha}(1 - \tau^*_{wD})^\alpha$ if $\xi < 1 - \sigma$.

4. when both countries adopt the residence principle, they will exhibit different rates of growth of per capita income and population in general. In particular, $g_y \gtreqless g_y^*$ and $g_N \lesseqgtr g_N^*$ as $\tau_{rD} \lesseqgtr \tau_{rD}^*$ if $\xi > 1 - \sigma$, and $g_y \lesseqgtr g_y^*$ and $g_N \gtreqless g_N^*$ as $\tau_{rD} \lesseqgtr \tau_{rD}^*$ if $\xi < 1 - \sigma$.

Contrary to what we find in the capital mobility case, condition 3 shows that the source principle is not necessarily growth equalizing. Although the post-tax MPHs are equalized under territorial taxation, the post-tax MPKs are not unless the weighted tax wedges $(1 - \tau_{rD})^{1-\alpha}(1 - \tau_{wD})^\alpha$ are uniform across countries. So, in contrast to condition 1, wage tax asymmetry matters here as much as interest tax asymmetry. Like condition 2, though, condition 4 implies that asymmetry in capital tax rates can be a source of growth disparity under worldwide taxation. As before, we can show that asymmetry in the international income tax principle can also be another source of growth rate differences.

In chapter 13, we have seen how labor mobility combined with knowledge spillovers can bring about convergence in income levels in the absence of tax differences. When tax rates do differ across countries, however, the resulting differences in growth rates (as shown in conditions 3 and 4 above) imply that level convergence can no longer be achieved. We can therefore view cross-country tax asymmetry as both a growth-diverging and level-diverging force.

With knowledge spillovers, the absence of arbitrage opportunities ensures the equalization of after-tax marginal products of labor (MPHs or wage rates) for any worker who can choose to work in either country under perfect labor mobility. In particular, $(1 - \tau_{wDt})\text{MPH}_t = (1 - \tau_{wAt} - \tau_{wNt}^*)\text{MPH}_t^*$. This arbitrage-based relation is used in appendix B to derive the following fundamental relative growth equation.[11]

$$\left(\frac{1 + g_y}{1 + g_y^*}\right)^{\xi - (1 - \sigma)} = \frac{1 + (1 - \tau_{rD})(r_k - \delta_k)}{1 + (1 - \tau_{rD}^*)(\Gamma r_k - \delta_k)},$$

where

$$\Gamma = \Lambda \left(\frac{\overline{h}^*}{\overline{h}} \right)^{\varepsilon/\alpha},$$

$$\Lambda = \left(\frac{1 - \tau_{wA} - \tau_{wN}^*}{1 - \tau_{wD}} \right)^{\alpha/(1-\alpha)}. \tag{15.9}$$

Equation (15.9) reveals that in the presence of tax differences, growth rates and levels are not in general equalized across countries.

To see more specifically which country will achieve higher level of income, we consider the following cases: Suppose that there is preference bias toward child quantity in all countries (i.e., $\xi > 1 - \sigma$).[12] Consider first the case that either the residence principle is applied to labor taxation or that labor income taxes are source based and symmetric across countries (so that $\Lambda = 1$). If the home country taxes capital more heavily than the foreign country (i.e., $\tau_{rD} > \tau_{rD}^*$), then we can observe from equation (15.9) that $g_y < g_y^*$ and $\overline{h} < \overline{h}^*$. Thus, regardless of the initial income level differentials, the (detrended) steady-state income level of the home country will be lower than that of the foreign country. The converse will be true if $\tau_{rD} < \tau_{rD}^*$. Consider next the case where $\tau_{rD} = \tau_{rD}^*$ and labor income taxes are source based and asymmetric across countries. In particular, suppose that home country levies higher tax rates on labor than the foreign country (i.e., $\tau_{wD} > \tau_{wD}^*$). Then inspection of equation (15.9) reveals that $g_y < g_y^*$ and $\overline{h} < \overline{h}^*$ so that the home country's (detrended) steady-state income level will be lower than that of the foreign country, regardless of initial conditions. The converse holds if $\tau_{wD} < \tau_{wD}^*$. Note that in all these cases we may have the possibility that a country that starts from a lower income level may overtake an initially higher income country in the long run due to tax advantages.

15.4 Summary

Let us first summarize the answers to the several questions posed at the beginning of this chapter, and then make some concluding remarks:

1. *Is factor mobility a growth-equalizing force?* Yes, for *aggregate* income growth rates, but not necessarily for *per capita* income growth rates.

2. *Are capital mobility and labor mobility perfect substitutes as growth-equalizing forces?* Yes, in the absence of international tax differences.

3. *Can tax-driven diversity in growth rates be preserved under factor mobility and international income taxation?* Yes, (a) under residence-based taxation with either capital or labor mobility; (b) under source-based taxation if labor is mobile; (c) if different countries adopt different international tax principles; and (d) if different international tax principles are applied to capital incomes and labor incomes separately.

4. *Are the growth effects of taxes symmetric under capital mobility and labor mobility?* Yes, under the residence principle; no, under the source principle, or when different countries follow different international tax principles.

In a nutshell, we have identified two sources of disparity in income and population growth rates across countries. They are (1) asymmetry in factor income tax rates and (2) asymmetry in international income tax principles, as adopted by different countries or applied to different factors of production. We have also shown how the growth effects of capital mobility and labor mobility can differ under these two cases and how they are related to the relative bias in preferences towards quantity and quality of children. Although these differences can easily be eliminated if enough symmetry is assumed between the two factors (e.g., uniform taxation of incomes from both factors), we believe that the asymmetries examined here are very real. In fact the unequal barriers to the cross-border movements of the two factors can be another real source of asymmetry that is nonetheless ignored in our analysis.

15.5 Policy Implications

Europe has reached almost complete integration in capital markets through the 1992 "single-market" initiative. Risk-adjusted and currency-adjusted rates of return on capital are, to a large extent, equalized across countries/regions in Europe. However, the European labor markets are still very much segmented across regions and countries. Compared with the U.S. as a benchmark, a key difference for the European single market lies in the degree of labor mobility and the speed of adjustment of the labor markets to regional disturbances. Three examples of barriers to labor mobility in Europe are housing regulations (e.g., rent control and high taxes on house purchases), the nonportability of pensions, and the country-specificity of social security schemes.

Per-capita income levels are significantly different between North and South Europe. We believe that labor mobility can act as an important (possibly essential) channel through which convergence in income levels can be achieved. If this is the case, it remains as a challenge for the European Union to design policies to facilitate the movement of labor across different regions.

Evidently there is a significant wage differential between North and South Europe. With identical technologies, when labor has a higher marginal product (effective wage) in the North, capital must have a higher marginal product (rate of return) in the South. We thus have a puzzle: Why capital from the North does not flow into the South so as to equate the marginal product of capital, especially since capital is freely mobile within Europe? A resolution of the puzzle would emphasize the existence of knowledge spillovers that are confined to regional borders. That is, there is no essential difference between the marginal products of capital between the North and South. Instead, there is only a productivity difference that is generated by an external effect in human capital.

The interaction between such knowledge spillovers and labor mobility can have important implications for the speed of growth in each European country and the European Union at large and the convergence in income levels across North and South Europe. This is an important feature of our analytical framework in section 13.3.

Another characteristic of the integration of European markets is the implementation and process of tax harmonization across member countries. Relative to other economic entities (e.g., the states within the United States, where income tax rates are more or less the same across states), however, the tax burden among the European countries is unevenly distributed. This is a feature of our analytical framework in sections 15.2–15.3.

Four related issues of capital mobility, labor mobility, uneven tax burden, and growth are the subject matter of part V. We consider a human-capital-based growth model featuring knowledge spillover effects. Using this model, we analyze the following regimes: closed isolated economies, economies integrated within a world capital market, and economies connected through labor flows. For all these regimes we look at the effects of various taxes and consider the role of tax asymmetry for the equality of income across countries that start off from different initial income levels.

Based on our analysis in part V, we can sketch a proposal for Europe comprising three principles:

1. *Lifting implicit barriers to labor mobility*, which is shown to be an income-equalizing force across countries in the presence of knowledge spillovers that are somehow confined within national borders. Evidently, explicit barriers to labor mobility do not exist within Europe, but significant implicit restrictions on labor flows are prevalent. More specifically, privatizing pension schemes and moving towards portable social security and unemployment benefits schemes will facilitate labor mobility.

2. *Harmonizing labor income tax rates and capital income tax rates across European countries*, so as to sustain the income-equalization objective. In the absence of tax harmonization, income level convergence is in general not achievable.

3. *Internalizing the knowledge spillovers* (through subsidies to education) either in isolation or in coordination can be shown to achieve efficient growth across Europe.

15.6   Appendix A: Derivation of the Tax-Growth Relation in the Closed Economy

In this appendix we derive equations (15.2) and (15.3) in the text. The consumer's first-order conditions with respect to c_t, e_t, K_{t+1}, and h_{t+1} are given by

$$c_t^{-\sigma} = \mu_t, \tag{A.1}$$

$$\mu_{h_t} \gamma B e_t^{\gamma-1} = \mu_t \Omega_{wt} w_t N_t, \tag{A.2}$$

$$\mu_t = \beta \mu_{t+1} [1 + \Omega_{r_{t+1}} (r_{t+1} - \delta_k)], \tag{A.3}$$

$$\mu_{h_t} = \beta \{ \mu_{h_{t+1}} [B e_{t+1}^{\gamma} + (1 - \delta_h)]$$
$$+ \mu_{t+1} w_{t+1} N_{t+1} [\Omega_{w_{t+1}} (1 - e_{t+1}) + \phi \tau_{w_{t+1}} \delta_h] \}. \tag{A.4}$$

The Lagrange multipliers (μ for multipliers) at time t associated with the consumer budget constraint and the law of motion of human capital are denoted by μ_t, and μ_{ht}, respectively. Assuming that the capital income tax rate τ_{rt} applies uniformly to both financial and physical capital, the arbitrage condition implies that $r_t = r_{kt} - \delta_k$. The firm's first-order conditions are

$$w_t = \alpha A \left(\frac{K_t}{H_t} \right)^{1-\alpha}, \tag{A.5}$$

$$r_t = (1 - \alpha) A \left(\frac{K_t}{H_t} \right)^{-\alpha}. \tag{A.6}$$

The equilibrium conditions in the labor and capital markets are

$$N_t h_t = H_t^d, \tag{A.7}$$

$$K_t = K_t^d. \tag{A.8}$$

Substituting (13.1) and (A.5) into (A.2), we get,

$$\frac{\gamma \mu_{h_t} [h_{t+1} - (1 - \delta_h) h_t]}{e_t} = \frac{\alpha \mu_t \Omega_{w_t} Y_t}{1 - e_t}. \tag{A.9}$$

Along the balanced-growth path, time allocations and tax rates are constant; that is, $e_t = e_{t+1}$, $\Omega_t = \Omega_{t+1}$, $\Omega_{wt} = \Omega_{wt+1}$, and $\Omega_{rt} = \Omega_{rt+1}$. Human capital and consumption will grow at the same constant rate g_h and output at the rate $(1 + g_N)(1 + g_h) - 1$, respectively, so (A.1) and (A.9) imply that

$$\frac{\mu_{h_{t+1}} h_{t+2}}{\mu_{h_t} h_{t+1}} = \frac{\mu_{t+1} Y_{t+1}}{\mu_t Y_t} = (1 + g_N)(1 + g_h)^{1-\sigma}. \tag{A.10}$$

Multiplying (A.4) throughout by h_{t+1} and dividing the resulting expression by $\beta \mu_{ht+1} h_{t+2}$, we get

$$\frac{\mu_{h_t} h_{t+1}}{\beta \mu_{h_{t+1}} h_{t+2}} = 1 + \left(\frac{\mu_{t+1} Y_{t+1}}{\mu_{h_{t+1}} h_{t+2}}\right) \alpha \left[\Omega_w + \phi \delta_h \tau_w \left(\frac{1}{1-e}\right)\right],$$

where

$$\frac{\mu_{t+1} Y_{t+1}}{\mu_{h_{t+1}} h_{t+2}} = \left(\frac{\gamma}{\alpha \Omega_w}\right)\left(\frac{1-e}{e}\right)\left(\frac{g_h + \delta_h}{1 + g_h}\right). \tag{A.11}$$

Combined with (A.10), this yields equation (15.2) in the text.

Equation (15.3) can be derived by combining (A.1) and (A.3) and imposing the steady-state restrictions.

15.7 Appendix B: Derivation of the Relative Growth Equation

Rates of growth of per-capita consumption and population (g_c and g_N) are related to the rates of return on physical capital through the intertemporal conditions:

$$(1 + g_N)^{1-\xi}(1 + g_c)^\sigma = 1 + (1 - \tau_{rD})(r_k - \delta_k),$$

$$(1 + g_N^*)^{1-\xi}(1 + g_c^*)^\sigma = 1 + (1 - \tau_{rD}^*)(r_k^* - \delta_k).$$

Along the steady-state growth path, $g_c = g_y$ and $g_c^* = g_y^*$ and, as we have shown in section 15.2, $(1 + g_N)/(1 + g_N^*) = (1 + g_y^*)/(1 + g_y)$. Substituting these conditions into the above equations, and dividing one equation by the other, we get

$$\left(\frac{1 + g_y}{1 + g_y^*}\right)^{\xi - (1-\sigma)} = \frac{1 + (1 - \tau_{rD})(r_k - \delta_k)}{1 + (1 - \tau_{rD}^*)(r_k^* - \delta_k)}.$$

The arbitrage-based relation, $(1 - \tau_{wDt})MPH_t = (1 - \tau_{wAt} - \tau_{wNt}^*) MPH_t^*$, implies that $MPK_t^* = \Gamma_t MPK_t$, where Γ_t is as defined in the text. Substituting this into the above yields equation (15.9) in the text.

Problems

1. Consider the closed economy example in appendix C of chapter 12 (with $\sigma = \delta_k = 1$). Suppose there is a time-invariant tax, τ_r, levied on capital income, $r_{kt} K_t$, and that the tax proceeds are rebated as lump-sum transfers to the households. Show how this tax rate will affect the saving rate, s_t, the speed of adjustment to the long-run equilibrium, and the levels and rates of growth of per-capita output in that equilibrium.

2. In the previous problem, how will your answers be affected if the tax proceeds, $\tau_r r_{kt} K_t$, are used to finance government spending, g_t, in each period?

3. Consider the case of labor mobility described in section 12.3.
a. Show how the opening up of the international labor market will alter the specification of the consumer budget constraint (12.6), the resource constraint of the domestic economy (12.8), and the dynamics of the capitals ratio (X_t, redefined as the ratio between physical capital and domestically employed labor).
b. Consider a labor importation quota set by the receiving country (the rest of the world). Is it possible to set the quota level (Q_t in each period t) in such a way as to make the constrained-labor mobility regime equivalent to the constrained-capital mobility regime?

4. Consider a special case of the closed economy model in section 13.1 with a single capital input in the production function: $Y_t = AK_t$. The accumulation of this input follows the same law of motion

as that of physical capital in (12.2). Find the long-run steady state, and describe the transitional dynamics. What if the production function takes the form $Y_t = A(1 - e_t)N_t h_t$, and the capital input h_t follows the law of motion of human capital in (13.1)? How does the growth rate depend on the saving rate in these cases?

5. Consider the closed-economy model in section 13.1, with $\sigma = \gamma = \delta_k = \delta_h = 1$. How will the presence of the Lucas externality as specified in (13.5) affect the long-run equilibrium growth rate of human capital in the steady state? Compare this with the efficient growth rate where the external effect is fully internalized (i.e., solution to the social planner's problem). Show also that, in both cases, $1 + g_c = (1 + g_h)^\zeta$ in the steady state.

6. Consider a case of external economies of scale in which technology at the firm level exhibits constant returns to scale in its firm-specific capital (k_t) and labor inputs, but its productivity depends on the level of economywide average stock of capital (K_t), that is, $y_t = A k_t^{1-\alpha}[(1 - e_t)N_t h_t]^\alpha K_t^\varepsilon$. At the competitive equilibrium, $k_t = K_t$ and $y_t = Y_t$. Compare the long-run growth rates and the ratios between physical and human capital between two symmetric economies (in preferences and technology) that start from different initial positions. Can these two economies achieve growth rate convergence? Income level convergence? What if barriers to capital flows between these two economies are lifted? Compare to the labor mobility case discussed in the text (in the presence of the Lucas externality).

7. Consider the model in section 13.4. Assume for simplicity that g_h is given as in the exogenous growth model. Solve explicitly the log-linearized system. Show whether transitory shocks will have permanent effects on output.

8. Consider the tax-growth model in chapter 14. Assume that instead of fully confiscating the household income derived from selling their initial endowment of capital to the firms, the government faces an upper bound (e.g., of 100 percent) on the tax rate it levies on this income. Using a log utility function, evaluate the pattern of

optimal capital income tax along the dynamic path. Compare it with that in the closed economy with no cross-border capital flows.

9. Consider a two-period model of a small open economy with one composite consumption-investment good. In the first period, the economy possesses an initial endowment of the good (y_0), and individuals can decide how much of it to consume (c_1) and how much of it to save. Savings are allocated either to investment at home (in the form of domestic capital K) or to investment abroad (in the form of foreign capital B). Foreign investment generates a rate of return equal to the world interest rate r^*. In the second period, output (produced from capital accumulated from the first period and other fixed inputs through a constant-returns-to-scale technology) and income from foreign investment are allocated between private and public consumption (c_2 and g). The government finances its (public) consumption by taxing profits (π) and capital income (rK) in the second period. In the context of this model, derive formally the result concerning the reinstatement of the tax on capital income in section 14.4.

10. Consider the closed economy model of section 15.1 with an additional time-consuming activity, leisure L_t. The time constraint is specified as $L_t + n_t + e_t = 1$. The utility function is rewritten as

$$U = \sum_{t=0}^{\infty} \beta^t N_t \left(\frac{(c_t^\eta L_t^{1-\eta})^{1-\sigma}}{1-\sigma} \right).$$

Assume for simplicity that $\phi = 0$ and $\delta_k = \delta_h = 1$. Analyze the effects of capital and labor income taxes (with lump-sum rebates) on the steady-state growth rate of income for two special cases:
a. Inelastic labor (i.e., $n_t = n$ constant).
b. Fixed time input in human capital formation (i.e., $e_t = e$ constant).

11. Consider the closed economy model of section 15.1 with an additional time-consuming activity, child-rearing v_t, which gives rise to endogenous population growth. The time constraint is specified as $v_t + n_t + e_t = 1$. The utility function is given by (15.5), and the law of motion of population by (15.6). Assume for simplicity that

$\phi = 0$, $\delta_k = \delta_h = \delta_N = 1$, and $\tau_r = 0$. Analyze the effects of capital and labor income taxes (with lump-sum rebates) on the steady-state growth rate of income for two special cases:

a. Inelastic labor (i.e., $n_t = n$ constant).

b. Fixed time input in human capital formation (i.e., $e_t = e$ constant).

12. Consider the capital mobility model with endogenous population in section 15.2. Explain how the effects of international capital income taxation on cross-country growth rates will change if the home country adopts the source principle while the rest of the world adopts the residence principle.

13. Consider the labor mobility model without knowledge spillovers in section 15.3. Explain how the effects of international labor income taxation on cross-country growth rates will change if the home country adopts the source principle while the rest of the world adopts the residence principle.

14. Suppose that capital and labor are both internationally mobile. Examine how the effects of international capital and labor income taxation on cross-country growth rates will change if the source principle is applied to the taxation of labor income and the residence principle to the taxation of capital income in both countries. Assume for simplicity that knowledge spillovers do not exist.

15. In the presence of knowledge spillovers, consider a social planner who maximizes dynastic utility subject to the law of motion of human capital and the resource constraint. Unlike the private agent who ignores his/her own potential contribution to the uppermost skill level in the economy, the planner internalizes the human capital externality by equating the skill level of the smartest guy/gal ($\bar{h}$) to that agent's skill level (h) in solving the social planning problem. Attach $s_t e_t - T_t$ as an extra source of income to the right-hand side of the consumer budget constraint (13.2), where s_t is the rate of educational subsidy and T_t lump-sum taxes raised to finance the subsidy. Derive the equilibrium conditions under this policy, and compare them with the optimality conditions of the social planner. Express explicitly the optimal subsidy in the following cases:

a. Closed economy.

b. A two-country world economy with labor mobility and without policy coordination between their governments.

16. Solve problem 15 for the case where the average skill level substitutes the upper tail of the skill distribution as an argument in the knowledge spillover function ($\bar{h}^e$). This spillover effect is termed human capital externality à la Lucas (1988).

VI

Epilogue

16

Analytical Overview: Traditional versus Modern Approaches

In parts II to IV of this book we have attempted to develop a unified conceptual framework suitable for the analysis of the effects of government expenditure and tax policies on key macroeconomic aggregates in the interdependent world economy. The analysis was motivated by the major developments occurring in the world economy during the 1980s and the first half decade of the 1990s: Changes in national fiscal policies were unsynchronized, real rates of interest were high and volatile, and real exchange rates exhibited diverging trends and were subject to large fluctuations. Furthermore large fiscal imbalances resulted in drastic changes in public debt and were associated with large imbalances in current-account positions and with significant changes in the international allocations of debt. Though these real-world developments provide the impetus for the analysis, the orientation of the book is theoretical. It aims at clarifying the complex economic mechanisms underlying the international transmission of the effects of macroeconomics policies. An empirical implementation of the theory developed throughout the book is highly complex. Without attempting to launch on such a challenging endeavor, we provide in section 16.1 some illustrative computations of the intertemporal model and compare the results with the actual data. Section 16.2 highlights key differences between the income-expenditure and the intertemporal models as reflected in the economic mechanisms underlying, the main channels of the international transmission of fiscal policies. Finally, section 16.3 contains a brief discussion of suggested extensions.

16.1 An Illustrative Computation

In this section we use the analytical model developed in part III
to compute the predicted paths of domestic and foreign consumption, which are implied by the actual paths of the exogenous macroeconomic variables. We then compare these predicted paths of
consumption with the paths that have actually been followed. In
addition we compute the correlations between the predicted paths
of consumption and the actual paths of the other variables and
compare these correlations with those actually observed in the data.
Though these computations should not be viewed as the empirical
counterpart to the theoretical model, they nevertheless are suggestive of the potential applicability of the theoretical approach.

The illustrations used in this section center around the paths of
consumption since the comovements of these paths with the other
key economic variables were the focus of the theoretical analysis. In
performing the computations, we have assumed specific values for
the key parameters. These parameter values along with the actual
paths of the exogenous variables were substituted into the model
yielding the solution paths of the endogenous variables.

Tables 16.1 and 16.2 report the actual and the predicted annual
growth rates of private-sector consumption in the United States and
in the rest of the world for the period 1956 to 1984. For this
illustration the rest of the world is defined as the Group of Seven
major industrial countries excluding the United States. This group
comprises Canada, France, Italy, Japan, the United Kingdom, and
West Germany. The computation of the model necessitates the conversion of all data for various countries into common currency units.
In view of the sharp changes in exchange rates that have occurred
during the sample period, the choice of the common numéraire may
have significant consequences for the relations among the various
time series. Therefore, to allow for this possibility, we have computed all series for two alternatives. The first expresses the data in
constant German prices, and the second in constant U.S. prices.

The growth rates reported in both tables exhibit considerable
correlation between the actual and the predicted time series. For

example, the actual mean annual growth rate of U.S. private-sector consumption (in constant German prices) is 2.84 percent with a standard deviation of 7.4 percent, whereas the predicted mean and standard deviation are 2.24 percent and 7.60 percent, respectively. The correlation between the predicted and actual rates of growth of consumption is 0.75. A similar pattern (with a somewhat lower correlation) emerges for the series that are based on constant U.S. prices. In that case the means of the actual and of the predicted growth rates are reasonably close to each other, being 2.99 and 3.10 percent, respectively, but the standard deviations of the two series are further apart from each other, being 2.23 and 6.36 percent, respectively. The correlation coefficient corresponding to these two series is 0.61.

The relation between the actual and the predicted growth rates of private-sector consumption in the rest of the world is shown in table 16.2. When expressed in constant U.S. prices, the mean and the standard deviation of the actual series are 4.49 and 6.73 percent, respectively, whereas the corresponding mean and standard deviation of the predicted data are 3.32 and 6.88, respectively. The correlation between the actual and the predicted series is also significant, being 0.72. When the data are expressed in constant German prices, the correlation between the two series is also relatively high (even though somewhat less pronounced), being 0.61.

The correlations between the growth rates of private-sector consumption and the growth rates of the key economic variables are shown in tables 16.3 and 16.4. In these tables we report the correlations between the *actual* growth rates of consumption and the other macroeconomic variables and compare these correlations with the corresponding correlations between the *predicted* growth rates of consumption and the same macroeconomic variables. As is evident, especially for growth rates of series expressed in constant German prices, there is considerable similarity between the actual and the predicted correlations. This similarity which is exhibited by figures pertaining to U.S. consumption (in table 16.3) and to the rest-of-the-world consumption (in table 16.4) is reflected in both the relative magnitudes and signs of the various correlations.

Table 16.1
Predicted and actual U.S. consumption: 1956–1984 (annual percentage growth rates)

Year	In constant German prices		In constant U.S. prices	
	Actual	Predicted	Actual	Predicted
1956	2.21	1.97	3.21	1.89
1957	3.26	−1.30	1.99	−1.46
1958	1.00	−7.96	0.30	−6.30
1959	6.23	8.74	6.25	7.97
1960	2.94	5.91	3.03	6.61
1961	−3.29	−8.45	1.95	−0.95
1962	2.17	−1.22	4.76	1.96
1963	2.34	3.66	3.96	5.03
1964	4.37	7.38	5.62	8.91
1965	4.01	5.46	5.62	6.89
1966	4.30	−1.63	4.66	−1.14
1967	3.68	−4.95	2.52	−6.47
1968	7.51	3.44	4.97	1.18
1969	4.72	6.23	2.72	6.97
1970	−4.33	−8.42	0.95	1.40
1971	−1.88	−5.11	3.65	2.50
1972	−5.30	0.82	5.81	11.27
1973	−14.69	−2.08	3.75	16.69
1974	−0.95	−6.65	−1.43	−5.29
1975	−1.34	−5.63	0.68	−3.60
1976	8.50	14.36	4.83	9.93
1977	−1.15	2.95	4.20	8.81
1978	−6.02	2.93	3.82	14.58
1979	−1.97	0.57	0.62	5.78
1980	4.07	2.56	−2.53	−0.34
1981	25.97	23.23	0.41	−4.07
1982	9.06	0.29	1.19	−8.20
1983	10.10	12.09	5.07	6.41
1984	16.73	15.80	4.06	2.86
Mean	2.84	2.24	2.99	3.10

Table 16.1 (continued)

	In constant German prices		In constant U.S. prices	
Year	Actual	Predicted	Actual	Predicted
Standard deviation	7.40	7.62	2.23	6.36
RMSE		5.25		5.21
Correlation		0.75		0.61

Note: In aggregating the six non-U.S. countries into the rest of the world, we have used two alternative methods. The first expressed all quantities in German marks deflated by the German GDP deflator; the second expressed all quantities in U.S. dollars deflated by the U.S. GDP deflator. The parameters used in forming the predicted series are $\gamma = \gamma^* = 0.99$, $\delta = \delta^* = 0.95$, $\varepsilon_n = \varepsilon_n^* = \beta_n = \beta_n^* = 0.40$, and $\theta = \theta^* = 0.25$.

Overall, the computations reported in tables 16.1 through 16.4 indicate considerable conformity between the actual and predicted growth rates. They exhibit similar patterns of correlations between the actual growth rates of consumption and of key macroeconomic variables, on the one hand, and between the predicted growth rates of consumption and the same variables, on the other hand. These results indicate the potential usefulness of the analytical framework developed in this book. It is important to reiterate, however, that the purpose of these computations has only been illustrative and should not be viewed as a substitute for a thorough empirical implementation of the model.

16.2   Interest Rates and Terms of Trade: Differences between Models

In this section we highlight some of the key differences between the predictions of, and the economic mechanisms underlying, the income expenditure model and the intertemporal model. The integration of both goods and capital markets in the world economy implies that the key channels through which the effects of fiscal policies are transmitted internationally are the temporal and the

Table 16.2
Predicted and actual rest-of-the-world consumption: 1956–1984 (annual percentage growth rates)

Year	In constant German prices		In constant U.S. prices	
	Actual	Predicted	Actual	Predicted
1956	6.14	2.84	7.13	2.55
1957	5.23	−0.38	3.96	−0.75
1958	2.05	−5.74	1.36	−4.20
1959	1.72	9.39	1.73	8.30
1960	7.76	7.17	7.85	7.57
1961	1.73	−7.04	6.97	0.33
1962	5.27	−0.12	7.86	2.90
1963	6.76	4.49	8.38	5.67
1964	6.45	8.28	7.70	9.60
1965	6.02	6.98	7.63	8.20
1966	5.08	0.70	5.44	0.98
1967	5.78	−2.17	4.62	−3.91
1968	4.45	6.01	1.91	3.41
1969	6.42	8.32	4.43	8.62
1970	0.15	−5.84	5.43	3.57
1971	3.49	−2.21	9.02	5.02
1972	5.43	3.20	16.54	13.25
1973	−1.82	−1.55	16.62	16.57
1974	1.06	−7.30	0.58	−5.98
1975	5.12	−5.54	7.14	−3.52
1976	3.54	13.18	−0.14	9.38
1977	2.02	3.66	7.37	9.78
1978	6.43	3.46	16.27	14.88
1979	1.31	−2.57	3.90	1.95
1980	5.75	−2.66	−0.86	−6.72
1981	11.85	18.54	−13.71	−8.01
1982	−1.60	−2.02	−9.47	−10.46
1983	4.24	8.96	−0.78	3.32
1984	7.92	16.41	−4.74	3.93
Mean	4.34	2.63	4.49	3.32

Table 16.2 (continued)

Year	In constant German prices		In constant U.S. prices	
	Actual	Predicted	Actual	Predicted
Standard deviation	2.99	6.87	6.73	6.88
RMSE	5.73		5.11	
Correlation	0.61		0.72	

Note: The rest of the world comprises a weighted average of the non-U.S. G7 countries (Canada, France, Italy, Japan, the United Kingdom, and West Germany). See the note to table 16.1.

Table 16.3
Correlations between annual growth rates of U.S. consumption and key economic variables: 1956–1984

Actual growth rates in	In constant German prices		In constant U.S. prices	
	Actual	Predicted	Actual	Predicted
Y	0.98	0.81	0.84	0.69
I	0.81	0.90	0.81	0.76
C	1.00	0.75	1.00	0.61
G	0.93	0.53	0.03	−0.47
T	0.84	0.75	0.37	0.39
WPI/CPI	−0.50	−0.23	−0.18	0.27
Y^*	0.62	0.73	0.32	0.65
I^*	0.30	0.48	0.32	0.62
C^*	0.57	0.57	0.39	0.61
G^*	0.50	0.39	0.11	0.45
T^*	0.35	0.29	0.05	0.45
WPI^*/CPI^*	−0.40	−0.28	−0.24	0.04
$C + C^*$	0.97	0.78	0.62	0.71

Note: See the note to table 16.1.

Table 16.4
Correlations between annual growth rates of rest-of-the-world consumption and key economic variables: 1956–1984

Actual growth rates in	In constant German prices		In constant U.S. prices	
	Actual	Predicted	Actual	Predicted
Y	0.60	0.76	0.36	0.73
I	0.58	0.92	0.33	0.78
C	0.57	0.70	0.39	0.72
G	0.53	0.47	0.01	−0.33
T	0.65	0.73	0.20	0.40
WPI/CPI	−0.27	−0.28	0.37	0.21
Y^*	0.92	0.75	0.98	0.74
I^*	0.69	0.55	0.90	0.72
C^*	1.00	0.61	1.00	0.72
G^*	0.81	0.34	0.94	0.53
T^*	0.49	0.24	0.82	0.51
WPI^*/CPI^*	−0.48	−0.28	−0.01	0.02
$C + C^*$	0.75	0.75	0.96	0.83

Note: See the note to table 16.2.

intertemporal prices—that is, the world rates of interest and the commodity terms of trade. Accordingly, in what follows we choose to illustrate the differences between the two approaches developed in the preceding chapters by focusing on, and summarizing, the interest-rate and the terms-of-trade effects of fiscal policies. The different predictions of the two alternative models concerning the effects of fiscal policies on the current world rate of interest and on the current terms of trade are summarized, respectively, in tables 16.5 and 16.6.

The interest-rate effects are shown in table 16.5. The results pertaining to the income-expenditure model are based on the analysis in chapter 3 and those pertaining to the intertemporal model are based on the analysis in chapter 10 extended (on the basis of chapter 9) to allow for a finite horizon. The key characteristics emerging from table 16.5 are the significant differences in the predic-

Table 16.5
The effects of fiscal policies on the current rate of interest: Income-expenditure and intertemporal models

Effects of	Income-expenditure model		Intertemporal model	
	Fixed exchange rates	Flexible exchange rates	Tradable goods	Nontradable goods
Debt-financed rise in government spending				
Current	+ (for $A > 0$) − (for $A < 0$)	+	+	+ (for $\sigma_{nx} > \sigma$) − (for $\sigma_{nx} < \sigma$)
Future	0	0	−	− (for $\sigma_{nx} > \sigma$) + (for $\sigma_{nx} < \sigma$)
Permanent	+	+	+ (for $CA > 0$) − (for $CA < 0$)	$\left.\begin{array}{c} + \\ - \end{array}\right\}a$
Tax-financed rise in government spending				
Current	+ (for $A > 0$) − (for $A < 0$)	0	+	+ (for $\sigma_{nx} > \sigma$) + (for $\sigma_{nx} < \sigma$)
Future	0	0	−	− (for $\sigma_{nx} > \sigma$) + (for $\sigma_{nx} < \sigma$)
Permanent	+ (for $A > 0$) − (for $A < 0$)	0	+ (for $CA > 0$) − (for $CA < 0$)	$\left.\begin{array}{c} + \\ - \end{array}\right\}a$
Current tax cut	+	+	+	+

Note: A rise in the world rate of interest is indicated by a +, and a fall by a −. The signs corresponding to the income-expenditure model are based on the assumption that exchange-rate expectations are static and that there are no revaluation effects; those pertaining to the intertemporal model presume that taxes are nondistortionary. $A = s/M_y - s^*/M_y^*$, CA denotes the current-account position, and a indicates that the result depends on the interactions between the current-account position and the sign of the difference between the intertemporal elasticity of substitution, σ, and the temporal elasticity of substitution, σ_{nx}.

Table 16.6
The effects of fiscal policies on the current terms of trade: Income-expenditure and
intertemporal models

Effects of	Income-expenditure model	Intertemporal model
Debt-financed rise in government spending		
Current	$+$ (for $\tilde{B} > 0$) $-$ (for $\tilde{B} < 0$)	$+$ (for $J > 0$) $-$ (for $J < 0$)
Future	0	$-$
Permanent	$+$ (for $\tilde{B} > 0$) $-$ (for $\tilde{B} < 0$)	$\left.\begin{array}{c}+\\-\end{array}\right\} a$
Tax-financed rise in government spending		
Current	$+$	$+$ (for $J > 0$) $-$ (for $J < 0$)
Future	0	$-$
Permanent	$+$	$\left.\begin{array}{c}+\\-\end{array}\right\} a$
Current tax cut	$+$ (for $\tilde{D} > 0$) $-$ (for $\tilde{D} < 0$)	0

Note: A rise in the relative price of importables in terms of exportables is indicated by a $+$, and a fall by a $-$. The signs corresponding to the income expenditure model are based on the assumptions that the exchange rate is flexible, that
exchange-rate expectations are static, and that there are no revaluation effects.
The signs pertaining to the intertemporal model are based on the assumption
that all goods are internationally tradable. $\tilde{B} = e_t(M_y/M_r)[\tilde{a}^* + \tilde{s}^*(1 - a^g)] -
(M_{y^*}^*/M_{r^*}^*)[\tilde{a} + \tilde{s}a^g]$, $\tilde{D} = e_t(M_y/M_r)(\tilde{a}^* + \tilde{s}^*) - (M_{y^*}^*/M_{r^*}^*)\tilde{a}$, $J = \beta_m^g - \beta_m(1 - \gamma_s)$,
and a indicates that the result depends on the interactions between the current-
account position and the sign of the difference between the shares of importables
of the private sector, β_m, and of the government, β_m^g.

tions of the various models. Furthermore, for those cases in which a
given policy may either raise or lower the rate of interest, the key
factors governing the actual outcome differ drastically across the
two models. In the income-expenditure model these key factors
reflect relative magnitudes of parameters measuring the effects of
changes in income on spending and on money demand. In contrast,
in the intertemporal model the key factors reflect intertemporal
parameters, both the temporal/intertemporal substitution elasticities
and the current-account positions. It is also relevant to note that for

the cases in which the *directions* of predicted interest-rate changes do not differ across the two models, the *magnitudes* of the changes may differ sharply since the mechanisms that operate in the two models are not the same.

A similar inference applies to the comparison of the predictions of the two models concerning the terms-of-trade effects of fiscal policies, shown in table 16.6. Due to the assumed fixity of GDP deflators in the income-expenditure model, the changes in the terms of trade pertaining to this model arise from exchange-rate changes (under the flexible exchange-rate regime) and are based on the analysis in chapter 3. The results pertaining to the intertemporal model are based on those analyzed in chapter 10 extended (on the basis of chapter 9) to allow for a finite horizon. As examples of the difference, consider the effects of a debt-financed rise in current government spending on the current terms of trade. Both models imply that the current terms of trade may either rise (deteriorate) or fall (improve). However, the factors determining the actual outcome differ significantly. In the income-expenditure model the actual result depends on the relative sensitivities of the domestic and the foreign rates of interest to income changes (arising from the fiscal policy). These relative sensitivities underly the sign of the parameter $\tilde{B}$. In contrast, in the intertemporal model the actual result depends on the difference between the government and private-sector's propensity to spend on current importables out of wealth. These propensities underly the sign of the parameter J.

The examples shown in tables 16.5 and 16.6 were based on simplified versions of the models chosen to highlight differences between some of their predictions. The more complex versions analyzed in the preceding chapters allow for mechanisms and factors that may generate additional differences. These include debt revaluation effects arising from terms-of-trade changes, exchange-rate expectations in the income-expenditure model of chapter 3, details of the nominal exchange rate regime and distortionary taxes. The latter factor is of special interest, since it plays a unique role in determining the effects of tax policy in the intertemporal model. Specifically, as shown in chapters 10–11, the various types of taxes can be classified into those for which a current tax cut raises the world rate of interest (e.g., as a value-added tax) and those for which a current tax cut lowers the world rate of interest (e.g., an income tax).

For ease of exposition, the summary provided in tables 16.5 and 16.6 considers only the effects of policies on the *current* values of the interest rate and the terms of trade. As such it focuses on the current channels of the international transmission of fiscal policies. Throughout the discussion in this book we emphasized that current policies also have profound effects on the *future* values of the interest rates and the terms of trade. The two models also differ sharply in their predictions of these future values. The differences reflect the fundamental distinction between the models. The intertemporal model is based on forward-looking behavior of individuals and governments whose current and future decisions must obey intertemporal budget constraints. No such features characterize the dynamics of the income-expenditure model.

Finally, the analysis in this book also highlights differences between the models that are not summarized in tables 16.5 and 16.6. These differences are reflected in the current and the future levels (and growth rates) of domestic and foreign private-sector consumption, investment, outputs, and real exchange rates.

16.3 Conclusions and Extensions

The Modern Intertemporal Approach

A key feature of the modern approach to the analysis of fiscal policies in open economies is the great attention given to microeconomic foundations, in which behavior is forward looking. Intertemporal considerations, therefore, play a major role in determining the effects of fiscal policies. In contrast with the traditional approach, the modern intertemporal optimizing approach also provides a framework suitable for a normative analysis of the domestic and international welfare implications of government spending and tax policies.

The stylized model of a small open economy that underlies the neoclassical theory of fiscal policy in open-economy macroeconom-

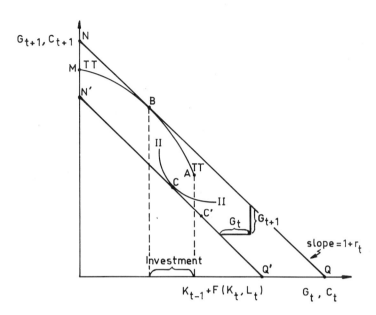

Figure 16.1
The general equilibrium of consumption, investment, and the trade balance

ics is presented in figure 16.1. Investment spending is measured in a leftward direction, from the point measuring the endowment of the country (consisting of the sum of current period GDP, $F(K_t, L_t)$, and previous-period capital stock, K_{t-1}). The economy can produce present (public and private) consumption, G_t and C_t, according to the transformation schedule, TT. Point A represents zero current investment while point M represents an economy which fully mobilizes its resources for investment. The intermediate point, B, represents the efficient level of investment, at which the domestic marginal rate of transformation is equal to the corresponding world marginal rate of transformation (one plus the rate of interest). The (public and private) consumption possibility frontier is portrayed by the line NBQ, whose slope is equal to one plus the world rate of interest, r_t. Subtracting from the consumption frontier a vector consisting of present and next period public consumption yields the private consumption possibilities frontier, $N'Q'$. An efficient consumption allocation point is the one at which the intertemporal marginal rate of substitution is equal to the world marginal rate of transformation, point C. If taxes are not distortionary, the stylized model yields the celebrated Ricardian equivalence proposition, which states that government finance, namely the debt-tax composition of the government budget, is irrelevant (see Barro 1974).

Government spending influences the private sector through two channels: it absorbs resources that otherwise would have been available for consumption (the "tax effect"), and it may influence the marginal evaluations of private goods (the "consumption tilting effect"). In operating through the resource-withdrawal channel, government spending policies generate a transfer of purchasing power between the private and public sectors and the international economic effects of the fiscal policy are therefore akin to the "transfer problem," familiar from the international trade literature (see Samuelson 1952). A temporary rise in government spending implies a transfer from a sector with high saving propensity (the private sector) to a sector with low saving propensity (the government), since the temporary government spending can be viewed as an intertemporal shift in the pattern of government spending toward the present. Consequently, national savings falls and the current account of the balance of payment must deteriorate. If the country enjoys some market power in the world capital markets the world rate of interest must rise. If, on the other hand, the rise in government spending is viewed as permanent, national saving would not be affected (provided that the intertemporal composition of public and private consumptions are the same), since the transfer then involves sectors with equal saving propensities (see Frenkel and Razin 1987b).

The stylized intertemporal model features government debt neutrality, stating that shifts between lump-sum taxes and debt have no real consequences. With intergenerational altruism this property is extended to infinite horizon models (see Barro 1974). The requirements for the Ricardian equivalence of interior transfers may not, however, be satisfied, and consequently shifts from tax finance to debt finance may not be neutral. Furthermore, even if interior intergenerational transfers take place, strategic behavior implies that income distributions across generations are not neutral even with intergenerational altruism (see Kotlikoff, Razin, and Rosenthal 1990). Evidently the use of distortionary taxes weakens the key implication of the neutrality proposition, the private-sector saving offsets changes in public-sector saving, and the current account balance is not significantly affected by budgetary imbalances.

The predictions of the Mundell-Fleming model concerning the effects of budget deficits on relative prices, employment, and deficits on the current account contrast sharply with the implications of the international-intertemporal model. Within the context of the latter model, if taxes are lump-sum and nondistortionary, it follows that the timing of taxes and the path of budget deficits do not affect the real equilibrium. In contrast, in the Mundell-Fleming framework with fixed exchange rates budget deficits are a powerful instrument of policy.

Budget deficits play a meaningful role in the international-intertemporal model if an overlapping-generations structure is incorporated into the model (see Samuelson 1958) or distortionary taxes are admitted. Blanchard (1985) demonstrates that a tax cut tends to raise the current account deficit through a wealth effect if the overlapping generations have finite horizons (see also Frenkel and Razin 1987b for two-country extensions that also involve relative price adjustments). Similarly, Weil (1987) analyses a variant of the overlapping-generations model with a growing population. In these models, budget deficits in effect generate a transfer between generations with unequal saving propensities. With finite horizons a tax cut followed by a future tax rise (so as to maintain the government solvent) amounts to a transfer from the future generation (whose propensity to consume in the present is zero) to the current generation (whose propensity to consume in the present is positive). Consequently current absorption must rise and the current account position must deteriorate. A similar mechanism (akin to the transfer problem criterion) also operates with population growth if there are weak altruistic links between old and young generations, as in Weil (1987).

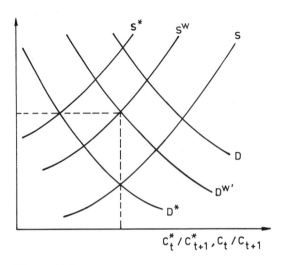

Figure 16.2
The effects of budget deficits under alternative tax systems

The effects of budget deficits on the current account operate
through a different mechanism if taxes are distortionary. To demonstrate this point consider alternatively consumption and income tax
systems. If a current tax cut, followed by a future tax hike (to
maintain government solvency), is carried out under a consumption
tax system, the budget deficit policy operates through an intertemporal substitution of consumption to advance consumption spending
from the future to the present. Consequently the current account
position deteriorates. Figure 16.2 portrays the domestic, D, foreign,
D^*, and the world, D^W, relative demand curves, that is, ratios of
present and future consumption spending, for a two-country world
economy. The corresponding relative supply curves are denoted by
S, S^*, and S^W. Schedule D^W is a weighted average of schedules D
and D^*, while schedule S^W is a weighted average of schedules S and
S^*. The effects of domestic budget deficit policies under the income
tax system can be demonstrated by a rightward shift in the domestic
and world relative demand curves, resulting in a deterioration in the
domestic current account position and a rise in the world rate of
interest, r_t. If, however, the budget deficit arises under the income

tax system, the effect on the current account operates through intertemporal substitution in investment, creating incentives to raise current output net of investment, at the expense of the corresponding future net output. Consequently the current account position improves. In terms of the diagram in figure 16.1 the domestic budget deficit policy would cause a rightward shift in the domestic and world relative supply curves, resulting in an improvement in the domestic external balance and a fall in the world rate of interest (see Frenkel and Razin 1987b).

International Taxation

The objectives of fiscal policies may be accomplished in a variety of ways and means. A leading example is the elimination of fiscal frontiers in Europe of 1992. The trade-creating incentives that can result may, however, be mitigated if domestic-based taxes that exert equivalent effects are changed in an offsetting manner (e.g., Gordon and Levinsohn 1990). The international taxation literature has uncovered a long list of such tax equivalences which have important policy implications (see chapter 11). Notable examples are the equivalence between import and export taxes (for static models, see Lerner 1936, and for dynamic models, Razin and Svensson 1983); the equivalence between consumption taxes and taxes on income from labor, profits, and returns on the pre-existing capital (Atkinson 1977); and the equivalence between indirect taxes (e.g., source-based value-added tax) and income taxes (such as cash-flow income tax).

The economic integration of the world goods market and capital markets transforms tax bases from national to global, although each national tax jurisdiction remains independent. Imports and exports of goods and services may be subject to double taxation, first at the origin and second at the destination, even if border tax adjustments (e.g., import tariffs or export taxes) are not allowed. Broadly based indirect taxation, such as the value-added tax, could be levied by both the importing and the exporting country. Similarly, even if international borrowing and lending taxes are allowed, foreign-source capital income of a country's residents may be subjected to taxes by the home country while the same income may be taxed at the source by the foreign country. The interactions between sovereign jurisdictions in an integrated world economy have immensely important implications for the allocation of savings and investment among countries, as well as for the location of production and consumption of goods and services.

To alleviate the problem of double taxation, the various tax systems in most of the industrialized countries follow one of the two dual principles: the residence and the source principles (in the case of income taxation) and the destination and origin principle (in the case of indirect taxation). According to the residence (destination) principle, foreign-source incomes of residents (imports of goods) are taxed by the home country, while they are exempt by the foreign country, which is the source (origin) country. According to the source and origin principles, foreign-source income and imports of goods are tax-exempt by the home country, while they are subject to the income tax and indirect taxes by the foreign country, respectively. Giovannini (1989) and Frenkel, Razin, and Sadka (1991) show that the residence principle, if used universally (with country-specific income tax rates to accommodate the country revenue needs), generates an efficient allocation of world investment among countries. At the same time, however, the allocation of world saving is inefficient. Similarly the destination principle of indirect taxation generates an efficient allocation of the production of goods and services across countries, but the geographical distribution of consumption may be inefficient. In contrast, the source principle of income taxation and the origin principle of indirect taxation, if adopted universally (but with country-specific rates), distort the international allocation of investment and production while maintaining an efficient international allocation of world saving and consumption. These basic principles are useful as a guide for the design of optimal tax systems.

The optimal taxation model (see Diamond and Mirrlees 1971) yields the aggregate production-efficiency result. It specifies that the tax-ridden economy must operate on its consumption possibilities frontier, TT, in figure 16.2. Optimal tax wedges should be used to separate consumers' marginal rates of substitution from producers' marginal rates of transformation but not to separate marginal rates of transformation across production units. The equilibrium of the optimum tax system is shown by points B and C' in figure 16.2. Based on this model the key implications of optimal taxation for international economic policies are that (1) impediments to trade in goods and services and capital flows should be removed, (2) direct taxation should adopt the residence principle, and (3) indirect taxation should adopt the destination principle.

Due to the distortions caused by direct and indirect taxation in a world economy with uncoordinated national fiscal authorities, an important issue is whether there are gains from harmonizing tax policies of the individual tax authorities. Evidently if fiscal authorities can manipulate the terms of trade to gain national advantages the resulting Nash equilibrium must be inefficient, as known from the prisoner's dilemma game (see Dixit 1985). However, in an integrated world economy each individual country may not enjoy significant market power. Frenkel, Razin, and Sadka (1991) demonstrate that if the world prices are beyond the influence of an individual country, then in a Nash equilibrium each government adopts the residence-based taxation as an optimizing strategy. Thus the competition among national tax authorities generates an efficient allocation of the world stock of capital. If, instead of competing, national fiscal authorities jointly determine the optimal design of taxes, the most that they can achieve with the distortionary taxes at their disposal is an efficient allocation of capital, as implied from the production efficiency proposition. Such an allocation is, however, achieved anyway through tax competition. Thus there are no gains from an international tax harmonization if governments cannot manipulate the terms of trade in the design of their tax systems.

Deviations from this benchmark could, however, arise if domestic authorities cannot enforce taxes on the foreign source income of their residents. Such enforcement failure generates incentives to restrict capital exports (see Frenkel. Razin, and Sadka 1991).

Dynamic Inconsistency and Fiscal Policy

Fiscal policy is dynamically inconsistent if in absence of new information, future policies deviate from the original plan due to altered
incentives on the part of the government. Kydland and Prescott
(1977) and Calvo (1978) first demonstrated that the supply elasticities of capital, or money balances, vary during the process of asset
accumulation, and consequently government incentives to tax income from assets vary over time, leading to dynamically inconsistent tax policies.

In a dynamically inconsistent setting a Phillips curve monetary
policy game has been developed by Barro and Gordon (1983) to
explain inflationary biases. In the Barro-Gordon, one-period game
the private sector chooses first the expected inflation (through the
wage contract). Once the private sector has committed itself to this
rate, the government may choose the rate of inflation so as to
minimize a loss function, featuring inflation and unemployment.
If the government target level of output exceeds the natural rate
(the private-sector target), then the Nash equilibrium, in which the
inflation expected by the private sector is in fact implemented by the
government, is an inflationary-biased solution for the game.

Dynamic inconsistency is invoked to explain situations in which
international harmonization may be inferior to the international
competitive equilibrium (which is also less costly to implement). An
important example is developed by Rogoff (1985), who applies the
Barro-Gordon framework to the issue. The inflationary effects associated with exchange rate depreciations, which arise only if monetary expansions are uncoordinated, tend to restrain the government
in its pursuit of the high-employment—low-inflation objective. In
comparison, if monetary expansions are coordinated, depreciations
of the exchange rate are absent. Consequently coordinated-policy
inflation rates exceed the noncoordinated rates, while output levels
are the same. In this example coordination is therefore undesirable.

Kehoe (1989) provides a similar example where the ability to
coordinate policies would exacerbate the credibility problem of each
government vis-à-vis its own private sector for the case of fiscal

policy. Using a standard two-period neoclassical model, in which the objective function of each country's policymaker coincides with the objective function of its residents, Kehoe assumes that national tax authorities make the policy decision before the private-sector decisions on the precise international allocation of its saving are made. He demonstrates that with international policy coordination the joint policy must tax away all the return on savings. Anticipating the low return prospect, investors would not invest at all. In the alternative case of international tax competition, low taxes on income from saving are used by each government to attract world saving. It then follows that taxes on the returns on savings would be relatively low and forward-looking investment must be high. Thus international cooperation is again undesirable.

Canzoneri and Diba (1991) consider the beneficial effects of international coordination. They show that if governments have access to the world capital market a rise in government spending generates a smaller increase in the rate of interest compared to the financial autarkic situation. Consequently the amount by which the payment on existing debt rises is smaller, and the costs associated with the rise in taxes to finance the increase in spending are diminished, relative to financial autarky. Thus financial integration of the capital markets induces a government spending bias. This mechanism generates the classic benefits from coordination, since if an individual government makes its spending decisions it internalizes the costs to other governments associated with debt servicing.

Evidence on the Twin Deficits

In testing the hypothesis about the irrelevance of the timing of taxes and the neutrality of government debt, the traditional approach is to regress the current account deficit on real exchange rates, interest rates (as "price variables") and output, government spending, taxes, government debt and money creation (as "income variables"). The typical regression uses mostly current variables, except that lagged output is added so that with current output they both form a proxy of permanent income. Traditional studies test debt neutrality by the restriction that the coefficients of taxes and debt are not significantly different from zero. However, none of the future expected variables suggested by the intertemporal model are explicitly included in the estimated equation.

The reduced-form equation of the current-account surplus is not likely to provide the relevant information on the validity of the debt neutrality proposition because, if current taxes are good predictors of future government spending, the fact that the tax coefficient is significantly different from zero is evidently in line with the neutrality proposition; this is contrary to the above-mentioned interpretation.

A more recent approach in empirical tests of the proposition is based on rational expectation estimations of structural (saving-investment balance) models (e.g., Aschauer 1985; Leiderman and Razin 1990). In these models the behavior equations arising from the intertemporal optimization of consumers are estimated jointly with the underlying exogenous stochastic processes that characterize the behavior of spending and taxes. The null hypothesis is specified by a set of cross-equation nonlinear restrictions on the parameters, as implied by the theory.

So far the empirical findings about the neutrality of government debt are mixed. Although there exists substantial evidence that private-sector savings tend to offset, to some extent, changes in public-sector saving, a full offset (indicated by government-debt neutrality) is rejected.

A drawback of existing approaches is the inability to account for fiscal regime changes. An increase in the stock of government bonds may signal future increases in taxes, so as to service the new debt. But the rise in debt may also signal future monetary accommodation, or future fall in government spending. The current econometric approach cannot distinguish between the different forms of regime change, and thus it is incapable of providing more decisive answers to the debt-neutrality puzzle (see Blejer and Leiderman 1988).

Evidence on International Policy Coordination

The interdependence among economies highlighted by the theoretical models has been subjected to numerous econometric examinations employing large-scale models of the world economy. While results differ across models, the fundamental point that fiscal actions undertaken by a large country are transmitted to the rest of the world is evident. In most international macroeconometric models a fiscal expansion by the United States worsens the U.S. balance of trade, appreciates the foreign exchange value of the U.S. dollar, puts upward pressures on interest rates, and stimulates foreign output (see Bryant et al. 1988).

The interdependence among economies, which intensified with the growing integration of world capital markets, has led to the development of the international policy coordination process of the Group of Seven industrial countries (G7), as well as to an intensification of multilateral surveillance through the International Monetary Fund (IMF). The coordination process is aided by the use of "objective indicators" related to policy actions and economic performance (e.g., fiscal positions, GNP and demand growth, monetary conditions, and the balance of payments). The indicators can be used ex ante in formulating objectives and policies, as well at ex post in monitoring progress and assessing outcomes.

The literature on the costs and benefits from international policy coordination is abundant (e.g., see Branson, Frenkel, and Goldstein 1990). Among the obstacles that are frequently cited are that countries do not share the same objectives, they are not subject to the same political constraints, their economic systems differ from each other, policy instruments of some are the policy objectives of others, the econometric models are not viewed as a reliable guide for policies, policy commitments are hard to enforce, and the like. Nevertheless, a consensus emerges that the highly integrated world economy requires some degree of policy coordination, at least in the form of an ongoing process of cooperation in which information is exchanged to yield a joint assessment of the economic situation and prospects.

Gauging the effects of policy coordination, the literature compares the value of a welfare function under the assumption that each country maximizes welfare independently, with the value obtained under the alternative assumption that the countries maximize a joint welfare function. The early findings reveal that the gains from coordination are likely to be small (see Oudiz and Sachs 1984), and if policymakers cannot precommit themselves to a policy rule, then coordination could be counterproductive (see Canzoneri and Henderson 1988; Kehoe 1989; Rogoff 1985). More generally, if coordination attempts to reinforce "bad" policies, it will be welfare-reducing (see Feldstein 1988). However, some of the negative findings obtained by this strand of analysis need to be qualified. First, the relevant comparison is frequently between suboptimal uncoordinated policies with suboptimal coordinated policies rather than between optimal coordinated and uncoordinated policies. Second, some of the gains from coordination may be unobservable and spread beyond the area of fiscal policies. Third, empirical estimates of gains from coordination have typically compared policies that do not exploit the incentive governments may have not to adhere to agreements in the light of changed circumstances, on one hand, and the incentives to stick to agreements to enhance their reputation, on the other hand.

The debate on the need for, and the modalities of, coordination of fiscal policies within Europe has come to the fore with the progress toward the creation of a single market within Europe as part of the 1992 process of European economic integration. Two notable examples are tax harmonization and the constraints that a European Monetary Union imposes on the conduct of fiscal policies. The key issue in the debate on tax harmonization arises from the great diversity of tax rates among the members of the European Community and the diverging welfare implications of a greater convergence of tax rates (see Frenkel, Razin, and Sadka 1991). The key issues in the debate on the fiscal consequences of a European Monetary Union are the constraints that need to be imposed on member countries' fiscal deficits, including the "no bail-out" guarantee and the prohibition on monetizing deficits, fiscal transfers among member states designed to reconcile the gap between the international incidence of economic shocks and the increased centralization of policy, and the distribution of seignorage from centralized money creation.

17

Policy Overview: Current-Account Sustainability

This chapter is about the current-account balance as a policy target. What persistent level of current-account deficits should be considered sustainable? Conventional wisdom is that current-account deficits above 5 percent of GDP flash a red light, in particular, if the deficit is financed with short-term debt or foreign exchange reserves, and if it reflects high consumption spending. How seriously should such thresholds be taken? Which other factors should be considered in the evaluation of sustained current account imbalances? A cursory look at historical episodes suggests that countries such as Australia, Ireland, Israel, and South Korea were able to sustain persistent current-account deficits close to this threshold for several years, while Chile and Mexico, for example, suffered severe external crises.

The natural question that comes to mind in evaluating the viability of external imbalances is whether the country is solvent, that is, whether it has the ability to generate sufficient trade surpluses in the future to repay existing debt. We argue that this notion of solvency, which is satisfied when the country meets its debt obligations, is not always appropriate in evaluating the sustainability of external imbalances. First, it considers only the ability to pay, but abstracts from the willingness to pay. The present value of trade surpluses may theoretically be sufficient to repay the country's external debt, but it may not be politically feasible to divert output from domestic to external use in order to service the debt. Second, this notion of solvency often relies on the assumption that foreign investors are willing to lend to the country on current terms. This assumption, however, may be unrealistic, in particular, when there is uncertainty about the country's willingness to meet its debt obligations. In the presence of other market imperfections, availability of foreign funds imposes constraints on the sustainability of current account imbalances in addition to those imposed by pure intertemporal solvency.

In section 17.1 we consider a notion of current-account sustainability that explicitly takes into account willingness to pay and willingness to lend in addition to intertemporal solvency analysis. We find that it provides a better framework for understanding the variety of country experiences with protracted current-account imbalances. We use this notion in the study of a selected number of countries, with the purpose of identifying the major determinants of current-account sustainability. Some of these countries experienced an external crisis, while others were able to sustain persistent current-account imbalances. Besides the burden of external debt service (adjusted for growth and real-exchange-rate changes), we show that among the most important operational indicators of current-account sustainability are the size of the export sector and the level of international competitiveness, the level of domestic savings, the composition of external liabilities, the strength of the financial system, and the degree of political stability. In addition fiscal consolidation is often a key feature of the adjustment required to generate trade surpluses.

Section 17.2 discusses more fully sustainability of current-account imbalances. Section 17.3 considers intertemporal solvency, which links current-account imbalances with intertemporal consumption and investment decisions, in terms of simple relations derived from national accounting identities. Section 17.4 examines key determinants of willingness to pay and to lend by way of a simple model of international portfolio allocation and moral hazard. Section 17.5 develops a set of operational indicators of sustainability, based on the theoretical analysis of the previous sections, and section 17.6 discusses the role of these factors in a few actual country experiences. We relate these experiences to the theoretical discussion, and in section 17.7 we try to distill some policy lessons. Section 17.8 presents some concluding remarks.

17.1 The Notion of Sustainability

The current-account deficit (or surplus) is the positive (negative) increment to the stock of external liabilities of the economy. An evaluation of persistent current-account imbalances has to take into account their contribution to the buildup of this stock. Three related questions are frequently asked in relation with an economy's external imbalances: Is a debtor country *solvent*? Are current-account imbalances *sustainable*? Is the current-account deficit *excessive*? We focus on the first two questions, and discuss briefly the third.

Solvency and Sustainability

Solvency is theoretically defined in relation to an economy's present-value budget constraint. In this sense an economy is solvent if the present discounted value of future trade surpluses equals current external indebtedness. In the case of public finances, solvency implies that the present discounted value of future budget surpluses is equal to the current public debt. The practical applicability of the theoretical definition is hampered by the fact that it relies on future events/policy decisions without imposing any "structure" on them. For example, in the case of fiscal imbalances, if future surpluses are sufficiently large, virtually any deficit path can be consistent with intertemporal solvency. Therefore researchers have attempted to define a baseline for future policy actions. In the case of public sector solvency, this has typically been done by postulating a continuation into the indefinite future of the current policy stance *and* no change in the relevant features of the macroeconomic environment.[1] This process gives rise to the notion of "sustainability"—the current policy stance is "sustainable" if its continuation in the indefinite future does not violate solvency (budget) constraints.

The definition of sustainability based on solvency considerations is simpler for fiscal imbalances, given that these can be associated (at least to some degree) with direct policy decisions on taxation and government expenditure. Defining sustainability is more complex in the case of current-account imbalances, given that these reflect the interaction between savings and investment decisions of the government and domestic private agents, as well as the lending decisions of foreign investors. While government decisions can, to a first approximation, be taken as given, this is not the case for private sector decisions. Furthermore a key relative price—the exchange rate—is a forward-looking variable that by definition depends on the future evolution of policy variables.

An alternative way of formulating the question of whether current-account imbalances are "sustainable" is the following: Is a continuation of the current policy stance and/or of the present private sector behavior going to entail the need for a "drastic" policy shift (e.g., a sudden policy tightening causing a large recession), or to lead to a "crisis" (e.g., an exchange rate collapse leading to an inability to service external obligations)? If the answer is yes, we have a case of unsustainability. This drastic change in policy or crisis situation can be triggered by a domestic or an external shock, that causes a shift in domestic and foreign investors' confidence and a reversal of international capital flows.[2] Note that the shift in foreign investors' confidence may relate to their perception of a country's *inability* or *unwillingness* to meet its external obligations.

To give some meaningful content to the definition of current-account sustainability, two related issues must be addressed. First, if a continuation in the indefinite future of current government policy implies the violation of budget constraints, forward-looking private agents will anticipate that a "policy shift" has to occur. For example, if external borrowing is growing without bound under the current policy stance, private agents' expectations will reflect the anticipation of a policy reversal, which could take the form of debt default, a drastic devaluation and/or fiscal adjustment. Ignoring these expectations and their reflections on private sector behavior (as is commonly the practice in "baseline scenarios") can lead to forecasting errors and overestimation of the durability of such unsustainable policy. Private sector's anticipations of future policy changes are reflected, for example, in interest rate differentials (when the exchange rate is pegged), and capital flight, both reflecting expectations of a future devaluation or—for capital flight—of future taxation of domestic assets.

The second issue concerns the "trigger" that will give rise to the policy reversal. The evaluation of a policy scenario based on a model that incorporates the expectations of forward-looking private agents needs a specification of the "event" that will trigger a policy shift. For example, this event could be a given combination of a level of the external debt to GDP ratio and the realization of a negative shock. Evidently, private agents' behavior and its implications for the future path of the economy will depend on the particular "trigger." The event that would trigger a policy shift is, in principle, different across countries and may reflect different degrees of vulnerability to external shocks, or a difference in the capacity to undertake adjustment policies. An example of the first would be the degree of diversification of the export base that makes a country more or less vulnerable to terms of trade shocks; an example of the second is the political-economic situation that will affect the ability of the government to implement drastic changes in policy without causing social and political upheaval.[3]

"Excessive" Current-Account Imbalances

The question whether given current-account balances are "excessive" can be answered only in the context of a model that yields predictions about the "equilibrium" path of external imbalances. Actual imbalances can then be compared to the theoretically predicted ones in order to judge whether or not they have been excessive. For example, a benchmark for defining what constitutes excessive deficits can be based on a representative agent model, with consumption behavior based on the permanent income hypothesis, in the presence of free capital mobility and investment adjustment costs (see chapter 7).

Two main approaches to the empirical implementation of this model have been used. The first approach (see Leiderman and Razin 1991; Glick and Rogoff 1995; Razin 1995) relies on structural estimation of the model and focuses, in particular, on estimated responses to various types of shocks (permanent and transitory, country-specific, and global). The estimated responses can be used to evaluate the persistence of current account imbalances. The second approach (e.g., see Ghosh and Ostry 1995) uses vector autoregression analysis to estimate the consumption-smoothing current account, which is equal to minus the present discounted value of expected changes in national cash flow (output minus investment minus government spending). The predicted current-account behavior is then used as a benchmark to evaluate "excessive" current-account imbalances.

The three concepts of solvency, sustainability and "excessive" current account deficits imply an increasing order of restrictiveness. The first concept, based on the intertemporal budget constraint, can accommodate a variety of future behavior patterns. The second is based on a continuation of the current policy stance, and therefore imposes more structure on future behavior. Within the notion of sustainability, we can also include cases in which a timely reversal of the current policy stance is sufficient to prevent a "hard landing". The notion of "excessive" current account deficits is instead based on deviations from an "optimal" benchmark, derived under the assumption of perfect capital mobility and efficient financial markets.

17.2 Intertemporal Solvency

In this section we use standard accounting identities to present the notion of intertemporal solvency, emphasizing in particular the role of growth, interest rates, and the real exchange rate.

Intertemporal Budget Constraints

We define intertemporal solvency as a situation in which the country as a whole and each economic unit within the country, including the government, obey their respective intertemporal budget constraints. In the context of the overall economy's resource constraint, the current account plays a crucial role, since it measures the change in the net foreign asset position of the country. In an accounting framework the current-account balance, CA, is defined as follows:

$$CA_t \equiv F_t - F_{t-1} = Y_t + rF_{t-1} - C_t - I_t - G_t$$

$$= S_{pt} + S_{gt} - I_t, \tag{17.1}$$

where F is the stock of net foreign assets, Y is GDP, r is the world interest rate (assumed for simplicity to be constant), C is private consumption, G is government current expenditure, I is total investment (private and public), S_p is private savings, and S_g is public savings. As the second equality in (17.1) shows, the current-account balance is also equal to the difference between the economy's total savings and total investment.

Following Sachs (1982), we calculate the annuity values of each form of income and spending, Y_t, C_t, G_t, and I_t, which we identify with the superscript p.[4] Government solvency requires equality between the permanent level of government consumption and the annuity value of public sector wealth, which is given by the PDV of taxes plus the initial net asset position of the government:

$$G^p = \frac{r}{1+r}\left[(1+r)F_{gt-1} + \sum_{s=t}^{\infty}\left(\frac{1}{1+r}\right)^{s-t}T_s\right], \tag{17.2}$$

where F_g is the public sector's level of net assets. The net foreign asset position of the country, F, is given by $F_p + F_g$, since government net liabilities vis-à-vis the private sector cancel out.

Using (17.2) and (17.2b) together with the economy's resource constraint (17.1), we obtain the following expression for the current account:

$$CA_t = (Y_t - Y_t^p) - (C_t - C_t^p) - (I_t - I_t^p) - (G_t - G_t^p). \tag{17.3}$$

Therefore current-account imbalances in an intertemporally solvent economy reflect deviations of output, consumption, investment, and/or government spending from their "permanent" levels. Of course, to evaluate the effects on the current-account balance of deviations of, say, government spending from its permanent level, it is necessary to have a model that specifies the behavior of consumption, investment, and output. For example, with full consumption smoothing the level of consumption C_t would always be equal to C^p. Assuming that investment decisions are driven by technology and world real interest rates and that the capital stock and labor force are fully utilized in production, a positive deviation of government spending G_t from its permanent level G^p would generate a current account deficit. This deficit is the result of private agents' decisions to smooth consumption by borrowing from abroad during periods of temporarily high government spending. If, instead, output is above its permanent level, consumption smoothing would imply a current-account surplus. In a Keynesian setting, however, focusing on deviations between actual and potential output, positive deviations of output from its potential level are associated with current account deficits.

Growth, the External Debt Burden, and the Real Exchange Rate

We now turn to the examination of how relative price changes, the level of real interest rates and the rate of economic growth interact with trade imbalances in shaping the evolution of the ratio of external debt to GDP, the measure of the external debt burden.

Assume that the domestic economy grows at a given rate $\gamma < r$,[5] let s_t, p_t, p_t^* and i_t^* be the nominal exchange rate, the domestic GDP deflator, the foreign GDP deflator, and the world nominal interest rate, respectively, and define the real exchange rate q_t as $p_t/s_t p_t^*$. We can then rewrite the current-account identity (17.1) as

$$s_t p_t^* F_t - s_t p_{t-1}^* F_{t-1} = p_t(Y_t - C_t - G_t - I_t) + i^* s_t p_{t-1}^* F_{t-1}, \qquad (17.4)$$

where F_t is now the stock of foreign assets denominated in foreign goods.[6] Let the foreign assets to output ratio f_t be equal to $F_{t-1}/q_t Y_t$. Dividing both sides of (17.4) by nominal GDP, $p_t Y_t$, and rearranging terms, we obtain

$$f_{t+1} - f_t = \frac{1}{(1 + \gamma_t)(1 + \varepsilon_t)} [tb_t + f_t(r^* - \varepsilon_t - \gamma_t - \gamma_t \varepsilon_t)], \qquad (17.5)$$

where $f_t = F_{t-1}/Y_t$, other lowercase letters indicate the ratio of the respective variables to GDP, and ε is the rate of real appreciation of the domestic currency. This expression simply says that changes in the ratio of foreign assets to GDP are driven by trade imbalances *and* by a "debt dynamics" term proportional to $f(r^* - \gamma - \varepsilon)$.[7] The latter term rises with the world rate of interest and falls with the rate of real exchange rate appreciation and the rate of growth of the domestic economy.

Consider now an economy in steady state, in which consumption, investment, public expenditure, and the stock of foreign assets (liabilities) are constant as a fraction of GDP. What is the long-run net resource transfer (trade surplus) that an indebted country must undertake in order to keep the debt-to-output ratio constant? From equation (17.5) we get

$$tb = 1 - i - c - g = -f(r^* - \varepsilon - \gamma), \tag{17.6}$$

where tb is the long-run trade balance. This expression highlights the role played by the average future value of world interest rates, domestic growth, and the long-run trend in the real exchange rate in determining the resource transfers necessary to keep the debt to GDP ratio from increasing.[8] Consider the case in which the long-run real exchange rate is constant ($\varepsilon = 0$). Condition (17.6) then indicates that the country's long-run absorption can be higher than its income only if the country is a net creditor. In this case the country will run a trade deficit, equal to $(r - \gamma)f$, but a current-account surplus equal to γf, thanks to the interest it earns on its foreign assets. In other words, in the presence of economic growth, permanent current-account deficits can be consistent with solvency even when the growth rate is below the world interest rate, provided they are accompanied by sufficiently large trade surpluses.

Clearly, if the long-run growth rate of the economy is zero, the current account must be balanced in order for the foreign debt (assets) to GDP ratio to be constant. In this case a country that is a debtor in the long run will have to run a trade surplus, equal to $-rf$, to pay the interest on its external liabilities, while a country that is a long-run creditor will run a trade deficit.

In the long run the dynamics of the real exchange rate can be assumed to be driven by the evolution of productivity differentials between the traded and nontraded goods in the domestic economy and in the rest of the world (the Balassa-Samuelson effect). Define d as the (log of the) relative price of traded goods across countries, and a^T (a^N) as (the log of) the productivity level in the traded (nontraded) sector. As shown in appendix I, we can then express the changes in the real exchange rate as

$$\varepsilon = \dot{d} + (1 - \beta)\left[\frac{v}{\alpha}(\dot{a}_T - \dot{a}_T^*) - (\dot{a}_N - \dot{a}_N^*)\right],\tag{17.7}$$

where a dot indicates time derivative, a star indicates "foreign" variables, $\alpha(v)$ is the labor share in the traded (nontraded) goods sector, and β is the share of traded goods in the price index used for the calculation of the real exchange rate.[9] For given behavior of productivity in the nontraded good sectors, countries with more rapid productivity increases in the traded goods sector than its trading partners will, ceteris paribus, experience a real-exchange-rate appreciation and therefore can sustain a larger debt to output ratio.

17.3   Willingness to Pay and Willingness to Lend

So far we have considered a world in which market imperfections such as asymmetric information, moral hazard, and absence of bankruptcy arrangements do not play a role in shaping international borrowing and lending. These problems, however, are particularly relevant for country borrowers characterized by shallower financial markets, higher vulnerability to terms of trade shocks, and higher political uncertainty. In this section we focus on the factors that determine international investors' willingness to lend to a given country. To highlight this issue in a simple way, we present a simple (static) model of international portfolio diversification with moral hazard. An international investor has to decide its optimal portfolio allocation by choosing investment projects across $J + 1$ countries, indexed by j. The rate of return in the home country $(j = H)$ expressed in foreign currency follows an i.i.d. process with mean ρ_H and variance σ_H^2. The remaining J countries (the rest of the world) are symmetric and have rates of return r^j, which follow a random i.i.d. process with mean ρ and variance σ^2.

Assume that the international investor has a portfolio of size W, and denote by θ the share of the investor's portfolio allocated to the home country. Her/his portfolio's expected return is given by

$$W[\theta\rho_H + (1 - \theta)\rho]\rho_H = i_H - \frac{\dot{s}}{s}, \tag{17.8}$$

and the variance is given by

$$W^2\left(\theta^2\sigma_H^2 + \frac{(1 - \theta)^2}{J}\sigma^2\right), \tag{17.9}$$

where i_H is the rate of return in the home country's currency, s is the exchange rate between the home country and the rest of the world, and a dot indicates a time derivative. The variance on the rate of return σ_H^2 represents the combined effect of exchange rate risk and domestic interest rate risk. Clearly both ρ_H and σ_H^2 are endogenous, since they depend on the government's policy choices. This endogeneity is made explicit below (see equation 17.15). The international investor is assumed to have constant absolute risk aversion, with a coefficient γ. Thus expected utility U is given by

$$U = W[\theta\rho_H + (1 - \theta)\rho] - \frac{\gamma W^2}{2}\left[\theta^2\sigma_H^2 + \frac{(1 - \theta)^2}{J}\sigma^2\right]. \tag{17.10}$$

Maximizing expected utility with respect to θ and denoting the foreign currency value of home country's indebtedness θW by B_H, we obtain

$$B_H = \left(\sigma_H^2 + \frac{\sigma^2}{J}\right)^{-1}\left[\frac{i_H - \dot{s}/s - \rho}{\gamma} + W\frac{\sigma^2}{J}\right]. \tag{17.11}$$

Figure 17.1 depicts the supply of external finance B_H as a function of the mean rate of return in the home country ρ_H, which will be

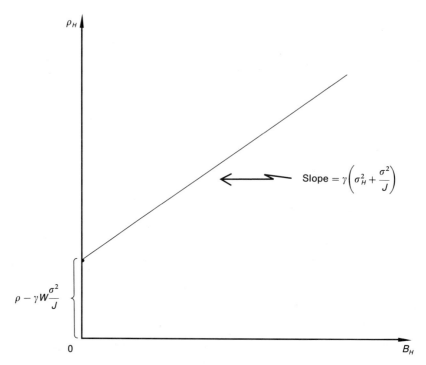

Figure 17.1
Supply of external funds

identified as the cost of foreign borrowing. From equation (17.11) we can verify that the supply schedule is upward-sloping; that is, the country has to raise the rate of interest (adjusted for expected exchange rate changes) in order to elicit more capital from abroad. Furthermore the supply schedule shifts upwards as (1) the opportunities for international diversification (J) rise (as in the case of "emerging markets"); (2) the country's credit and exchange rate risk (σ_H^2) increases; (3) the rate of interest in the rest of the world (ρ) increases. It shifts downwards as (4) the riskiness of the rest of the world's investment projects (σ) rises, and (5) the size of the world's portfolio (W) increases.

As highlighted in figure 17.1, at the given level of external liabilities B_H, in order to elicit external funding a country must pay the rate of interest ρ_H, which is determined as the intersection between the supply-of-external-funds schedule and the vertical line originating at B_H. If a "bad" shock that shifts the supply schedule upwards occurs, there will be an increase in the country's cost of external borrowing ρ_H. This increase may force the country to drastically change its policy stance in order to generate the additional flow of resources necessary to service external liabilities.[11]

So far we have assumed that there is symmetric information about the characteristics of the countries' investment projects. We now turn to the case where information is asymmetric, so borrowers are better informed about the riskiness of projects than international investors. As shown in Stiglitz and Weiss (1981) in the context of bank lending, this informational structure can lead to credit rationing. The fundamental factor is that the rate of interest a bank charges may itself affect the riskiness of loans by either (1) affecting the action of borrowers (moral hazard or incentive effect) or (2) sorting potential borrowers (the adverse selection effect). We now illustrate the first channel.

Suppose that the country is risk neutral and that, if it borrows an amount B, expressed in foreign currency, it is charged an interest rate r_H. The country will have an incentive to default on its loan if the real return on its project Y plus the real collateral C are insufficient to repay the promised amount:

$$C + Y < \frac{s}{p} B(1 + r_H), \tag{17.12}$$

where p is the domestic price level, so s/p is the real exchange rate. In a strict sense, collateral can be identified with the "equity" of the country in the project. Alternatively, it could be interpreted as loan guarantees or as those country assets that can be seized by the lender in the event of a default. In a more general sense, it could include the present value of the cost of penalties imposed on a defaulting country, such as trade disruptions and isolation from international capital markets, and an evaluation of the "reputation cost" associated with default.

A surprise real depreciation of the domestic currency (e.g., due to a negative terms of trade shock) increases, ceteris paribus, the probability of default. Furthermore investors' perception of the policy instruments the government will use to meet external obligations is influenced by political economy considerations. For example, capital flight driven by fear of direct taxation or exchange rate depreciation can increase external debt, B, beyond the accumulated level of past current account imbalances.[12] The existence of implicit or explicit bailout clauses can worsen moral hazard problems, in an analogous fashion to a decline in collateral. In practice, the international financial community may be unwilling to let a country default on its debt obligations, because of the trade and capital markets disruptions this could induce or for protection of foreign investors (e.g., Mexico in 1994). Moral hazard problems may be exacerbated by the implicit or explicit bailout clauses *within* a debtor country: for example, excessive borrowing by the banking sector can be induced by expectations of a government bailout should the sector run into financial difficulties.

To illustrate the effect of moral hazard problems on the supply of external funds, suppose that the country can choose between two investment projects, 1 and 2, and assume for simplicity that purchasing power parity holds so that $s/p = 1$. The expected return to the i project is

$$\pi_i = E[\max(Y_i - (1 + r_H)B, -C)], \qquad i = 1, 2. \tag{17.13}$$

The derivative of the expected return with respect to the rate of interest is given by

$$\frac{d\pi_i}{dr_H} = -B[1 - F_i((1 + r_H)B - C)], \tag{17.14}$$

where $F_i(\cdot)$ is the probability of default using project i. If, for some r, $\pi_1 = \pi_2$, then an increase in r_H would lower the expected return from the project with the higher probability of repaying the loan by more than the other project. Thus the increase in the interest rate results in the country preferring the project with the higher probability of default.

The expected rate of return to the international investor and its variance will be given by

$$\rho_H = (1 - F_i)r_H + F_i\frac{C}{B},$$

$$\sigma_H^2 = \frac{F_i}{1 - F_i}\left(\rho_H - \frac{C}{B}\right)^2.$$

(17.15)

Consider first the expected rate of return. By raising the interest rate r_H, the probability of default, F_i, rises *for a given project*. Furthermore, as a consequence of the interest rate increase, the firm is more likely to choose a riskier project, thereby further increasing the probability of default. Even if the foreign investor were risk neutral, it could find it optimal to "ration" credit supply at a given interest rate, rather than raising the rate in the face of excess demand for credit. This would happen if the expected return from the loan actually fell with an increase in r_H, due to the increase in the probability of default. The possibility of credit rationing is enhanced by the foreign investor's risk aversion. Indeed credit rationing could occur even when the expected return ρ_H increases with r_H because the variance of returns rises as well (see 17.15).

For our purposes we can consider (17.15) as establishing a positive relation between the mean rate of return ρ_H and its variance σ_H^2. This implies that the credit supply curve for the country will be even steeper than in figure 17.1 (see equation 17.11), and that it may entail credit rationing, with the foreign investor unwilling to lend to the country more than a given amount at an interest rate at which the country would demand more funds.

The foregoing analysis underscores the possibility that external funds would "dry up" when an economy is hit by a negative shock of the type 1–5, listed below equation (17.11). The trigger of a crisis could come from the foreign investor's perception of condition (17.12)—that is, from the likelihood that the debt burden $B(1 + r_H)$ will exceed $C + Y$. This can be caused by factors such as an increase in world interest rates, a negative supply shock such as a terms-of-trade decline, a change in the perceived solvency of the financial sector that would call for a government bailout, or a change in the perceived political costs of default.[13] Similar to, but more dramatic than in, the case of symmetric information, the pre-existing policy can turn out to be unsustainable.

In addition to the case considered above, in which a shock can change the perception of a country's ability to meet its external obligations, debt-driven balance of payments crises can be generated by a fundamental inconsistency in macroeconomic policy, such as expansionary monetary policy under a fixed exchange rate or persistent fiscal imbalances, which result in protracted current account deficits. Appendix B presents two examples, that highlight the role of external debt accumulation and external borrowing constraints respectively.

17.4   Sustainability Indicators

This section discusses possible operational indicators of current-account-sustainability based the analysis of solvency and willingness-to-lend considerations identified in sections 17.3 and 17.4, respectively. We focus in particular on the economy's structure, macroeconomic policy, and political economy factors, and link them with the evolution of external imbalances.

Structural Features

1. *Investment/savings.* The current-account balance is determined by the difference between national savings and domestic investment. For a given current-account balance, the *levels* of savings and investment can have implications for the sustainability of the external position, for a given current-account imbalance. High levels of investment imply, ceteris paribus, higher future growth through the buildup of a larger productive capacity, and therefore they enhance intertemporal solvency (see equation 17.6).[14] High savings and investment ratios can also act as a signal of creditworthiness to international investors, because they raise the perceived ability to service and reduce external debt.[15]

2. *Economic growth.* Fast-growing countries can sustain persistent current account deficits without increasing their external indebt-

edness relative to GDP, as can be seen, for example, from equations (17.5) and (17.6). In addition to the accumulation of physical capital through investment, stressed in the previous paragraph, high growth is driven by other factors such as the accumulation of human capital and increases in total factor productivity.

3. *Openness*. The degree of openness can be defined as the ratio of exports to GDP. To service and reduce external indebtedness, a country needs to rely on traded goods' production as a source of foreign exchange. Clearly countries with a large exports sector can service external debts more easily because debt service will absorb a lower fraction of their total export proceeds. To generate the foreign exchange necessary to service external debt in case of an interruption in capital flows, a country needs to engineer a resource shift toward the exports sector. This sectoral shift is likely to be more costly in a closed economy. Furthermore, since this shift cannot occur instantly, sharp import compression may become necessary, with adverse consequences on the domestic industries relying on "essential" imported inputs (Sachs 1985 and Sachs and Warner 1995).

Clearly trade disruptions associated with debt default are more costly for an open economy. Consequently sudden reversals of capital inflows will be less likely because foreign investors will perceive the country, ceteris paribus, as less risky.[16]

The commodity *composition* of trade can be an important indicator of vulnerability. Fluctuations in commodity prices have a larger impact on the terms of trade for countries with a narrow export base, and those particularly dependent on raw materials for their imports, as shown in equation (17.20). Terms of trade fluctuations can weaken the ability of the economy to sustain current account deficits.[17]

The sectoral composition of growth may be an additional indicator of potential external difficulties. In particular, low export growth could reflect an exchange rate misalignment, which would point to the need of a policy reversal. A related argument is that for a small open economy large external trade can imply a more diversified input base for production, and hence higher productivity growth. A positive impact on productivity can also come from access to technology embodied in internationally traded goods.[18]

4. *Composition of external liabilities.* The composition of external liabilities may have an impact on the ability of a country to absorb
smoothly a shock. In general terms, we can distinguish between
"debt" and "equity" instruments. In principle, equity financing allows asset price adjustments to absorb at least part of negative
shocks, so that part of the burden is borne by foreign equity investors. In contrast, in the case of foreign currency debt financing, the
country bears most of the burden, provided it does not default.[19]
The structure of equity and debt liabilities is also important in order
to evaluate a country's vulnerability to shocks. With regard to equity, portfolio investment is potentially more volatile than foreign
direct investment. With regard to debt, its maturity structure, currency composition, and any fixed or floating interest all affect vulnerability to shocks. The risk of external shocks is enhanced by
short-term maturities, foreign currency denomination, and variable
interest because the impact on the debt burden is magnified.

5. *Financial structure.* In developing countries, financial intermediation is typically dominated by banks: Bank deposits are the most
important form of private savings and bank loans the main source of
finance for firms.[20] The disciplinary effect of competition with alternative forms of financial intermediation is limited, and therefore the
role of bank supervision is essential. The fact that it is more likely
that banks will be bailed out by the central bank (government),
relative to other financial institutions, can also imply more risk-
taking behavior in a bank-dominated financial system. Problems are
likely to surface when the central bank itself is involved in direct
lending, financed through high reserve requirements, because of the
conflict this implies with the arm's length supervision role. A financial structure with poor bank supervision, weak monitoring of borrowers make a country more vulnerable to external shocks, and
more prone to experience balance of payments crises.

Macroeconomic Policy Stance

1. *Monetary and exchange rate policy.* The level of the real exchange
rate is an important indicator of sustainability. A persistent real-

exchange-rate appreciation can be driven by "fundamental" factors such as high productivity growth in the traded goods sector, or favorable terms of trade shocks. However, in the context of a fixed or managed exchange rate system, it could reflect a fundamental inconsistency between the monetary policy stance and exchange rate policy, giving rise to "overvaluation."

In this case the overvaluation would typically be maintained by high domestic interest rates and/or by the presence of capital controls. An overvalued exchange rate would encourage a decline in savings as domestic residents intertemporally substitute present for future consumption. It can also cause a decline in economic activity, both because of the high interest rates needed to maintain the exchange rate peg and because the traded goods sector is "priced out" of world markets. These effects would contribute to a widening of current-account imbalances and loss of foreign exchange reserves. The drain of foreign reserves can be reinforced by expectations of a future devaluation that encourage capital outflows.[21] Finally, the weakening of the export sector hinders the ability of the country to sustain external imbalances.

There is also the possibility, however, that a real-exchange-rate appreciation would result from large capital inflows; to the extent that these are not driven by long-term fundamentals, they can result in an overvaluation. Weaknesses in domestic financial intermediation and supervision (which we discuss below) can hinder the efficient allocation of capital inflows between consumption and investment, and contribute to the overvaluation.[22]

2. *Fiscal policy.* To examine the relation between fiscal and external imbalances, we start from a benchmark "debt neutrality" case (Barro 1974) where there is no correlation between the public sector deficit and current-account imbalances. This can be seen most easily in the context of the intertemporal framework of chapter 7 and section 17.2 (see equation 17.3): The current account is independent of the time profile of taxation, and therefore of the budget deficit.[23] Among other things, the debt neutrality result relies on the fact that consumption depends only on lifetime income and that taxes are not distortionary. In the context of equation (17.3), distortionary taxes

would have an effect on the level of output and investment, and would therefore affect the current account. Furthermore, if consumption depends also on disposable income, for example, because some consumers are unable to borrow at the same terms as the government, lower taxes today would induce higher consumption (see Jappelli and Pagano 1989). Similarly for the firms, the effective easing of borrowing constraints associated with lower present taxes could induce an increase in investment. Analogous effects would obtain if future tax obligations are not expected to fall entirely on current period taxpayers.[24]

All the effects discussed so far would imply, among other things, a positive correlation between budget deficits and current-account deficits. The discussion also suggests that the strength of this correlation may depend on the degree of development of domestic financial markets. Namely, in countries with underdeveloped or highly regulated financial markets, we would expect to find stronger links between the fiscal stance and the current-account balance, and therefore between government budget solvency and current account sustainability.

The degree of private-sector saving offset to a given increase in public-sector saving may also depend on the level of public debt. With low public debt the current generation could view a future debt stabilization policy (via fiscal surpluses) as remote; thus the future tax liabilities are perceived to be small and fiscal adjustments affect aggregate demand and savings. In contrast, with high public debt the future debt stabilization looks imminent and the debt neutrality is at a full force. The link between the twin deficits may therefore be stronger the lower is the level of public debt. Another implication of this line of reasoning is that the effects of fiscal stabilization on aggregate demand are weaker the higher is the public debt burden.[25]

3. *Trade policy.* Countries with a protectionist trade policy are more likely to have a limited export base. Consequently they are more vulnerable to shocks, and their current-account deficits less sustainable. A process of trade liberalization typically necessitates shifts in relative prices; under these circumstances a devaluation of the ex-

change rate would encourage a transfer of resources to the traded goods sector (e.g., see Edwards 1989). It would also facilitate containment of external imbalances during the transition.

4. *Capital-account policy regime.* When the capital account is very open, *de jure* or *de facto*, a country is more vulnerable to sudden reversals in the direction of capital flows. This reversal may concern not only foreign capital, but also domestic capital.[26] Clearly the degree of de facto opening of the capital account is endogenous, and depends in particular on the strength of the incentives to export capital (risk-adjusted rate of return differentials due to domestic policy misalignments, political instability, etc.). Capital controls are a distortion that puts a wedge between rates of return on capital in the domestic economy and abroad. They can also affect the consistency of the macroeconomic policy stance: For example, capital controls can allow a government to temporarily pursue an expansionary monetary policy with a fixed exchange rate, thereby weakening the current account. An open capital account can provide a disciplining device, since this policy inconsistency would result in the collapse of the peg.

A related argument is that an open capital account could serve as a signal of a country's commitment to the pursuit of "sustainable" policies, and thereby raise foreign investors' perception of the country's creditworthiness. This would contribute to reducing the cost of capital for the country and/or to increase the supply of foreign funds (e.g., see, Bartolini and Drazen 1994). On the other side, economic research and practical experience have also highlighted the potential dangers associated with poor financial supervision and a weak banking system when the capital account is open (e.g., see Díaz-Alejandro 1985).

Political Economy Factors

Numerous empirical studies have documented the detrimental macroeconomic effects of political instability.[27] In the context of current-account sustainability, political instability can be important for various reasons. Domestic and foreign investors become more susceptible to the risk of a sudden policy reversal—for example, a government favoring free capital mobility may be replaced by one more prone to the imposition of capital controls or more prone to default. This makes the occurrence of capital outflows more likely. Political instability is often driven by distributional conflict, which can cause capital flight as a response to the fear of capital taxation (e.g., see Alesina and Tabellini 1989). Indicators of this type of political instability are, for example, the historical frequency of changes in government and/or attempted coups and measures of industrial strife.

The political situation can affect the sustainability of external liabilities for different reasons. For example, a "weak" government may have difficulties in undertaking economic adjustment that may be needed in response to a shock because of the difficulty inherent in gathering sufficient political support. Also a government facing an election may be reluctant to implement adjustment measures for fear of jeopardizing its electoral chances. Indicators of this form of "policy rigidity" are the degree of support of the government in Parliament, the party composition of government (coalition vs. majority) and the timing of elections.

Market Expectations

So far we have discussed economic, structural, and political economy factors that may affect the sustainability of persistent current account imbalances. A key issue of course is whether it is possible to rely on a set of indicators that help signal the likelihood of a major policy shift and/or a crisis situation. As mentioned in section 17.1, private agents' behavior is affected by their anticipation of future policy shifts. The behavior of capital flows and foreign exchange reserves are the most obvious indicator of domestic and foreign investors' perceptions of a country's creditworthiness. Bond prices or interest rate spreads on international loans and bonds (such as Brady bonds) also provide a useful measure of international investors' perceptions of the country's ability to service its external obligations. There is a danger, however, that these market-based indicators would fail to signal problems ahead of time;[28] it is therefore essential to take into consideration the more general set of factors discussed earlier in this section.

17.5   Country Episodes

So far we have discussed conceptual aspects of current-account sustainability, emphasizing the role of overall foreign indebtedness, vulnerability to shocks, and government solvency. We now turn to a description of the experience of a selected group of countries with persistent current-account imbalances. These experiences are divided into "good" and "bad" ones. We define "good" experiences as those in which crises did not occur, either because of a fundamental consistency in economic policy or because of a timely policy reversal. By contrast, we define "bad" experiences as those in which a crisis did occur so that a policy reversal was forced by the crisis. We attempt to characterize these different experiences in terms of the factors discussed in the previous section: macroeconomic policy stance, structural characteristics of the economy, political factors, and balance-of-payments shocks.

The countries we consider in this section are Australia, Chile, Ireland, Israel, Mexico, and South Korea. The experiences of these countries can be broadly characterized as follows: Chile (1982) and Mexico (1976, 1982, 1994) suffered external crises. Other countries, such as Ireland (1982, 1987), Israel (1985), and South Korea (1980) had a policy reversal that prevented potential external crises, while Australia (1990−95) has sustained persistent current account deficits with no drastic policy change.[29] We will look for common factors in the above experiences in order to draw some tentative policy lessons. The short "case studies" are accompanied by Charts describing the evolution of the current account, investment, savings, and the real exchange rate.

Australia, 1981−94

Australia has run almost uninterrupted current-account deficits for the past 40 years (the exception being 1973), and the impact of persistent current-account imbalances has been at the center of the economic policy debate for a long time.[30] The average size of current-account deficits has been close to 5 percent of GDP since the early 1980s, a considerably higher figure than in the previous decades.

As figure 17.2 shows, at the end of the 1970s, Australia's net external position was characterized by low external debt (6 percent of GDP, or 25 percent of Australia's net external liabilities), since the capital inflows that financed the current-account imbalances took mainly the form of equity. Australia experienced a recession in 1982–83, but a rapid recovery thereafter, with output growth averaging 4.5 percent for the rest of the decade. At the end of 1983 the exchange rate, which had followed a crawling peg since 1976, was floated. Following a negative terms of trade shock in 1985–86, current-account imbalances worsened, with a deficit close to 6 percent of GDP in 1985 and 1986. As terms of trade improved, the current-account deficit narrowed somewhat during the following two years, but it widened again considerably in 1989. The increase in current-account imbalances took place notwithstanding a fiscal policy tightening that started in 1984 and led to the emergence of a surplus by 1989. The increase in public savings was offset by an increase in private spending, in particular, on investment. The persistent current-account imbalances and the shift toward debt financing resulted in an increase in the ratio of external debt to GDP to over 30 percent by the end of 1989, with debt service absorbing 20 percent of total export receipts.

The 1990s started with a recession, triggered by a fall in business investment, a depreciation in the real exchange rate, and a decline in commercial property prices, which resulted in a sharp increase in unemployment. Output recovered in 1992 and 1993, driven mainly by increases in private consumption and net exports, as the real exchange rate continued to depreciate. Growth accelerated in 1994 to around 5 percent, driven by buoyant domestic demand. The investment share of GDP, however, failed to regain the levels reached in the 1980s. The fiscal balance, that had

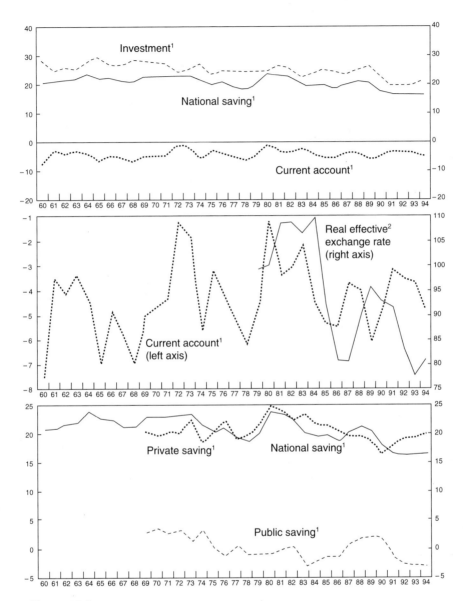

Figure 17.2
Australia. (1) Ratio to GDP. (2) Index, 1980 = 100; based on consumer prices.
Source: IMF, *World Economic Outlook and Information Notices System*.

registered a surplus until 1990, returned to a deficit, which was close to 6 percent in 1993, and current-account imbalances widened again, and they are forecasted to exceed 5 percent of GDP in 1995.

What are the main characteristics of Australia's external position? During the 1980s, following the worldwide deregulation of financial markets and the removal of capital controls, capital flows took mainly the form of debt. During the last five years, instead, current-account imbalances were mainly financed by net equity flows, while debt accumulation was quite modest. Indeed Australia stands out among OECD countries for the large fraction of external liabilities that take the form of equity. The external debt to GDP ratio stood at 36 percent at the end of 1994, with two-thirds of the debt reflecting private obligations.[31] A significant fraction of this debt (over 40 percent) is denominated in Australian dollars, making the external position less vulnerable to fluctuations in the exchange rate.

A salient feature of the economy is the floating exchange rate regime, which makes them less vulnerable to a balance-of-payments crisis. The real effective exchange rate is currently more depreciated than its historical average. The degree of openness has increased over time, with the export ratio rising from 15 percent in the early 1980s to around 20 percent in 1994. The composition of exports has been changing, with the importance of wool and other agricultural products declining and with exports of minerals and manufactures increasing; nevertheless, the economy remains vulnerable to swings in the terms of trade. The investment ratio, which averaged 24 percent over the 1980s, has declined to an average of 20 percent over the period 1990–94; the GDP share of national savings (that averaged 16.5 percent during the latter period) has also declined. The growth rate has exceeded the OECD average over the past ten years. There is no political instability and the financial system is well developed. In terms of our range of indicators, these factors point to a sustainable current-account position, notwithstanding the decline in savings and investment.

Chile: 1977–82

The first half of the 1970s was a turbulent period for Chile, both politically and economically. The coup in 1973 ousted Allende's socialist government and installed a military regime, with radically different economic policies. In particular, after a period during which the role of government in the economy had steadily increased, the new regime strived for balancing the budget, privatization, and financial and trade liberalization. During this period the economy endured a severe recession (1974–75; see figure 17.3), resulting from a combination of external shocks (fall in the price of copper and increase in the price of oil) and domestic policy tightening.

By 1978 yearly inflation was reduced from over 400 percent in 1973 to 30 percent, the public sector was in surplus (1.5 percent of GDP), and the economy was growing at 8 percent. However, the pickup in investment and the low level of private savings implied a large current-account deficit (5.2 percent of GDP). Furthermore the unemployment rate stood above 14 percent. Following the adoption of a schedule of preannounced devaluations of the nominal exchange rate (the *tablita*) for a year and a half, the government decided to use the exchange rate as a full-fledged nominal anchor in the disinflation process, and fixed the rate vis-à-vis the dollar in June 1979. The following years were characterized by a continuation of strong recovery. Inflation, however, declined slowly, with full backward-looking indexation providing inertial momentum (Edwards and Cox-Edwards 1987). This inflationary process was sustained by monetary growth due to large capital inflows, reflecting private sector external borrowing to finance investment in the wake of financial liberalization.[32] Consequently the real exchange rate appreciated rapidly, and the current-account balance deteriorated, with the ratio of the deficit to GDP reaching double digits in 1981.[33]

By late 1981 wholesale prices were falling, but the magnitude of the cumulative real appreciation caused expectations of a devaluation and therefore a widening of interest rate spreads between peso- and dollar-denominated assets. Output began to decline, and unemployment increased. In 1982 a sequence of external events—a

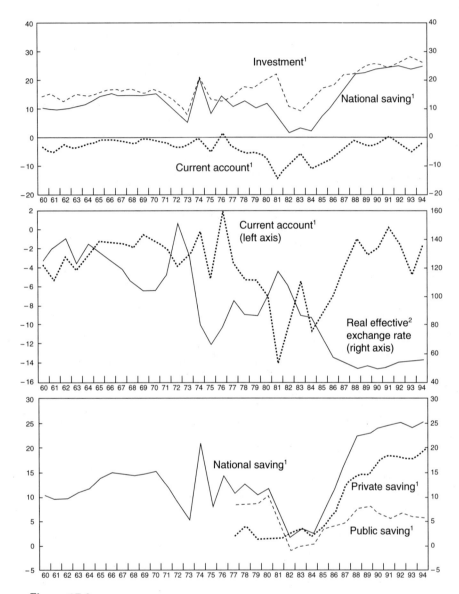

Figure 17.3
Chile. (1) Ratio to GDP. (2) Index, 1980 = 100; based on consumer prices.
Sources: For 1979 to 1994, IMF, *World Economic Outlook and Information Notices System*; prior to 1979, Central Bank of Chile and IMF, *International Financial Statistics*.

sharp decline in the terms of trade, the large increase in world interest rates, and a drying up of external sources of financing following the Mexican debt crisis—forced the government to abandon its exchange rate peg. In June 1982 the exchange rate was devalued by 18 percent and the wage indexation scheme was abandoned. This, however, was not sufficient. As in Mexico in 1994, speculation against the peso increased and reserves declined rapidly. Toward the end of 1982, in the wake of an impending financial crisis, the government imposed capital controls and import surcharges. By June 1983 the peso had been devalued in nominal terms by close to 100 percent with respect to its June 1982 level.

The crisis caused widespread bankruptcies in the private sector, and the government was forced to liquidate banks but also to bail out several other financial and nonfinancial institutions. In particular, the central bank intervened in support of the banking system, giving rise to a large quasi-fiscal deficit (Larrañaga 1989). The absence of government guarantees on private foreign borrowing notwithstanding, the government assumed responsibility for a large fraction of the private sector's foreign liabilities. The government's overall fiscal balance deteriorated for additional reasons—namely the revenue effects of the recession, and especially the reform of the social security system that had been undertaken in 1981.[34] The crisis was extremely severe: Output fell by 14 percent in 1983 alone, and unemployment rose dramatically to close to 20 percent (Corbo and Fischer 1994). Inflation rebounded to its "historical" level of 27 percent, and the management of the crisis caused an initial policy reversal with respect to exchange rate policy, wage indexation, current- and capital-account openness, and privatization. Starting in 1984, however, the government resumed its policy of trade liberalization, privatization, and deregulation, and the adjustment of the Chilean economy, although painful, was relatively rapid. Growth resumed in 1984 and has averaged over 6 percent over the last ten years.

It should be noted that not all the indicators discussed in the previous section pointed to a likely crisis. The economy was experiencing fast economic growth. The fiscal balance was in surplus throughout this period; indeed the government had been reducing its external liabilities. Investment was growing rapidly, albeit from a low base, and so were exports (until 1981). However, Which factors can then explain the 1982 crisis?

1. The size of external debt. External indebtedness had reached 50 percent of GDP in 1981, with interest payments totalling 6 percent of GDP.

2. An overvalued real exchange rate. Inflation failed to converge rapidly to world levels due to the effects of lagged wage indexation, as well as to increased demand for nontradables fueled by foreign borrowing. Investment was stimulated by the reduced the price of imported capital goods, as well as by the possibility to get financing on world markets at the world rate of interest, given the pegged exchange rate.

3. Low level of savings. National savings averaged only 10 percent of GDP during the period 1978–81. Their decline was particularly significant in 1981, possibly reflecting intertemporal substitution effects.

4. Weak financial system/overborrowing. "Overborrowing" by the private sector was fueled by the availability of foreign credit (following the recycling of oil exporters' surpluses) and facilitated by weak supervision of the banking sector, which encouraged risk-taking behavior (see Diaz-Alejandro (1985)). In this context, de la Cuadra and Valdes-Prieto (1991) stress the negative role played by the government's extension to the private sector of exchange rate and interest rate risk guarantees.

5. Severe external shocks: the large increase in world interest rates, the drying up of foreign financing, and a decline in the terms of trade.[35]

Interestingly, the fiscal burden of the crisis turned out to be extremely large. Indeed it reflected not only the increase in the real debt burden following the real depreciation of the peso and the increase in world interest rates, and the fall in revenues due to the crisis, but also the cost of assuming a large fraction of private external debt.

Ireland: 1980—94

Ireland is an interesting case of a country with persistently large current-account imbalances, leading to a large external debt that has achieved a remarkable turnaround in its external accounts. As in the Israeli case, this turnaround was the result of a drastic fiscal stabilization plan aimed at reversing the increasing trend of the public debt to GDP ratio.

In the late 1970s Ireland's external imbalances worsened dramatically following the second oil shock. Although exports had increased throughout the decade, imports had risen more rapidly: By 1979 the current-account deficit was around 13 percent of GDP, and it remained above 10 percent of GDP over the next three years. This worsening reflected a continuing decline in the ratio of public savings to GDP, as well as a fall in private savings (see figure 17.4), that more than offset a decline in the GDP share of investment. As a result the government's external public debt doubled as a fraction of GDP from 22 percent of GDP in 1979 to 45 percent in 1982. Inflation rose to over 20 percent in 1981, and the fiscal deficit reached 12 percent of GDP. To face these growing macroeconomic imbalances, in 1982 the government implemented a fiscal adjustment plan, which was accompanied by a sharp disinflation strategy centered on the pegging of the Irish punt within the EMS. By 1984 the full-employment primary deficit had been reduced by more than 7 percentage points of GDP, thanks primarily to tax increases (Giavazzi and Pagano 1990), but not eliminated, and inflation had fallen below 10 percent. Private consumption and investment fell dramatically, but exports rose rapidly, by more than 10 percentage points of a GDP. The export boom was driven by large increases in manufacturing exports, which are mainly produced by foreign firms.[36] This resulted in a remarkable turnaround in the trade balance, from a deficit of over 12 percent of GDP in 1981 to a surplus of 1 percent of GDP in 1984.

During this period the high interest burden and the appreciation of the U.S. dollar implied an increase in the ratio of public external debt to GDP to almost 60 percent by 1984.[37] Notwithstanding the

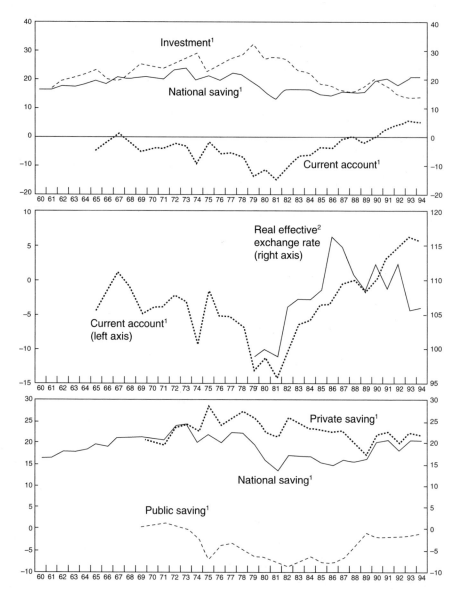

Figure 17.4
Ireland. (1) Ratio to GDP. (2) Index, 1980 = 100; based on consumer prices.
Sources: IMF, *World Economic Outlook and Information Notices System*, and *International Financial Statistics*.

fiscal adjustment effort, the domestic public debt also kept rising, and the ratio of total debt to GDP reached 130 percent in 1987. In that year another drastic fiscal stabilization plan was implemented. This time the plan relied more heavily on expenditure cuts than the previous plan. This time the fiscal contraction was preceded by an exchange rate devaluation, in order to stimulate exports. The fiscal stabilization reduced fiscal imbalances by 9 percentage points of GDP (8 of which consisting of primary balance) between 1986 and 1989, reversing the increasing trend of the public debt to GDP ratio.[38] The economy, spurred by very favorable external developments, grew at an average rate of over 4 percent between 1988 and 1994, and gross public debt declined to around 90 percent by 1994.

The stabilization was accompanied by another drastic improvement in the current-account balance, thanks to an increase in the trade surplus to over 10 percentage points of GDP. Once again exports of manufactures expanded rapidly: They now account for over 40 percent of GDP. As a result Ireland ran a current-account surplus for the first time in 20 years.

Some specific features of the Irish experience should be pointed out. Foreign direct investment has clearly played a very important role and has decisively contributed to the increase in export orientation and to the change in the composition of exports away from agricultural goods toward manufactured goods.[39] By 1990 foreign firms accounted for around one-half of Ireland's manufacturing gross output and over 75 percent of its manufacturing exports (OECD, 1993). As a consequence the current-account balance shows a sizable deficit in net factor income due to interest on foreign borrowing, and especially, profit repatriation.[40] This deficit is in part compensated by large net current transfers, in particular, from the European Union, which amounted to over 6 percent of GNP in 1993.

In summary, Ireland's large external imbalances in the early and mid-1980s were clearly associated with an unsustainable fiscal policy stance. The drastic contraction in fiscal policy was accompanied by strong export-led growth that helped reverse the pattern of large persistent external deficits.[42] The increase in exports was itself stimulated by the 1987 devaluation that made the real exchange rate competitive. Favorable external conditions (the boom in the United Kingdom and the United States, the fall in commodity prices, and world interest rates) also played an important role. The large increase in unemployment, only partly reabsorbed, and the large decline in the investment share (from over 30 percent in the late 1970s to 15 percent in 1993) are the lingering negative aspects of a successful adjustment strategy.

Israel: 1979–85

Throughout its short history Israel has run persistent current-account deficits, notwithstanding large unilateral transfers from abroad, with the exception of the period 1986–89. Economic growth, sustained by periodic waves of immigration and by high investment rates, averaged 10 percent until the early 1970s, a pace that was resumed in the early 1990s. During the 1970s and the 1980s, however, growth was much more modest, and the issue of sustainability of external imbalances came to the forefront, especially in two episodes. The first episode (Israel I), in 1973–74, was characterized by the increase in oil prices and by the Yom Kippur war; the second (Israel II), started in 1979 but lasted until the mid-1980s. We will focus on the second episode.

During the period 1979 to mid-1985, the Israeli economy experienced low growth, high inflation, large fiscal imbalances (around 15 percent of GNP), and large current-account deficits. As a result domestic and foreign public debt accumulated rapidly, reaching levels of about 110 percent and 84 percent of GNP, respectively, in 1984. The dramatic acceleration of inflation in 1984 to over 400 percent per year underscored the need for drastic stabilization measures. In June of the following year, an inflation stabilization plan was implemented. Its main characteristics were the fixing of the exchange rate after a big devaluation, monetary tightening, and a massive fiscal adjustment (expenditure cuts, tax increases, and increased transfers from abroad) that led to an elimination of the budget deficit. Inflation declined abruptly to the 15–20 percent range. An additional "payoff" of the stabilization plan was a remarkable turnaround in external accounts. The current account, which showed an average deficit of over 7 percent of GNP over the previous three years, turned to a surplus of 5 percent of GNP in 1985. This adjustment defused the risk of excessive external indebtedness: The foreign public debt to GDP ratio was rapidly reduced from 84 percent of GDP in 1984 to around 30 percent by 1990. (48 percent [1984] to 28 percent [1991] for net external debt over GDP).[42]

What accounted for the turnaround in the current-account balance? Investment declined sharply, while national savings and international transfers increased. In the following years, international transfers fell as a proportion of GNP, investment rates remained low, and national savings stable but at a higher level than during the inflationary period. The competitiveness of the export sector was at a historical peak, enhanced by the upfront exchange rate depreciation, the de-indexation of wages, and the fiscal consolidation (see figure 17.5). More generally, the degree of openness of the economy was high and favored by free trade agreements with the European Community and the United States. Clearly the increase in international transfers facilitated the adjustment of the Israeli economy to a low-inflation environment by obviating the need for even more drastic fiscal adjustment measures. The consumption boom following the exchange rate–based stabilization plan reduced private savings as a proportion of GNP, but by less than the increase in public savings, despite the fact that substantial budget cuts were implemented.

In contrast to other countries in our sample, the fiscal/current-account adjustment process was not triggered by unfavorable external shocks. Indeed the adjustment was actually facilitated by external developments (the increase in transfers and the decline in the price of oil in 1986). The fiscal adjustment process was an example of "expansionary fiscal consolidation," and unemployment did not increase (Razin and Sadka 1996).[43]

Korea: 1978–88

During the 1960s the Korean economy was characterized by rapidly rising savings, investment, and exports (see figure 17.6). Foreign

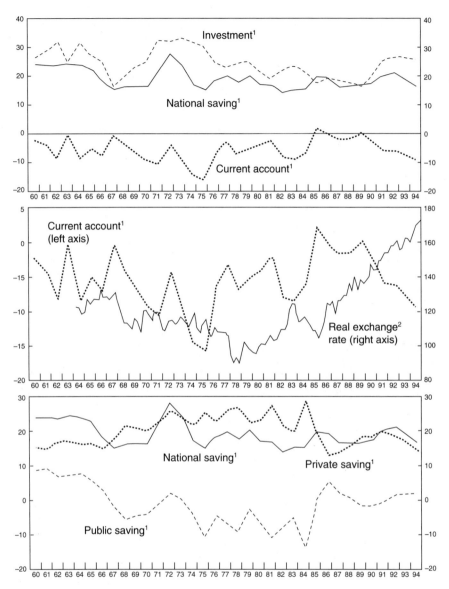

Figure 17.5
Israel. (1) Ratio to GDP. (2) Index, 1980 = 100; ratio of GDP deflator and exports
deflator. Source: IMF, *World Economic Outlook,* and *International Financial Statistics.*

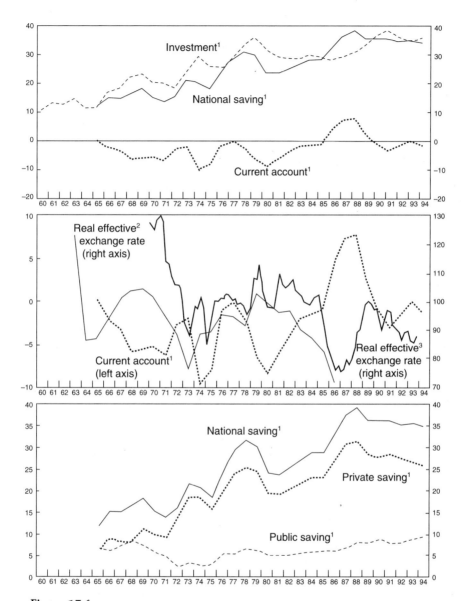

Figure 17.6
Korea. (1) Ratio to GDP. (2) Index, 1980 = 100; based on relative prices. Source: NBER, *Developing Country Debt and Economic Performance*, vol. 3 (1989). (3) Index, 1980 = 100; based on consumer prices. Source: IMF, *Information Notices System*.

borrowing was used to supplement domestic savings in financing investment, which was the key element in the growth-oriented strategy of the Korean government. The ratio of foreign indebtedness to GDP rose rapidly, especially in the second half in the decade, reaching 28 percent by 1970.

In the wake of the first oil shock, Korean foreign indebtedness rose sharply because of the high dependence of the country on imported energy and raw materials. The policy response of the government was to continue with the growth-oriented strategy while forgoing monetary stability. Thanks to the high growth rate and low or negative real interest rates in 1976–78, the foreign debt to GDP ratio remained at around 32 percent. The second oil shock hit the Korean economy at a particularly delicate juncture. It coincided with a period of political instability, following the assassination of President Park in October 1979, and with a bad harvest, and was following a period of real exchange rate appreciation, due to high domestic inflation coupled with a fixed nominal exchange rate vis-à-vis the US dollar. The current-account deficit rose to over 8 percent of GDP in 1980 as household savings declined sharply. A deep recession and a large nominal devaluation caused the ratio of foreign debt to GDP to increase to 44 percent in 1980; it further rose to 49 percent in 1981 and 52 percent in 1982, following the large rise in world interest rates in the wake of the debt crisis.[44]

The policy response to these external shocks was different from the one adopted at the time of the first oil shock. Namely the government relied on tight monetary and fiscal policy and on a large nominal exchange rate adjustment. Their objective was a sharp reduction in the foreign debt to GDP ratio. By 1984 the government had succeeded in eliminating inflation and fiscal imbalances, and the current-account deficit was reduced to less than 2 percent of GDP. During this period investment and economic growth remained strong, unlike in other highly indebted countries after the debt crisis. Savings increased, thanks to a rebound in household savings, while government savings remained high and corporate savings were a stable fraction of GDP (Collins and Park 1989).

The second half of the 1980s was characterized by more favorable external developments such as the fall in the price of oil and the depreciation of the dollar, by a more flexible exchange rate policy, and by a large real depreciation until 1986 and a sharp appreciation thereafter. The current account showed large surpluses in the years 1985–89, averaging $5\frac{1}{2}$ percent of GDP, allowing the government to pre-pay a large portion of the external debt. By the end of the decade, the foreign debt to GDP ratio was down to 14 percent in 1989, also thanks to rapid economic growth.

What lessons can be drawn from the Korean experience? Clearly the situation at the beginning of the 1980s was difficult. The policies pursued in the wake of the first oil shock had led to a loosening of monetary policy and to an overvalued real exchange rate, and the second oil shock occurred in a period of political instability, which made it more difficult for the government to react as rapidly as it had done in the past. External debt had increased rapidly and was perceived as a threat to macroeconomic stability.

After the deep recession of 1980, the policy response was swift and comprehensive, acting on the monetary, fiscal and exchange rate side.[45] The adjustment was facilitated by high economic growth that resumed in 1981. Korea's exchange rate policy after the second oil shock constitutes a notable shift with respect to previous years. After the 1980 devaluation the real exchange rate was allowed to appreciate modestly in 1981–82 in order to dampen price increases. After 1983 the real exchange rate was allowed to depreciate substantially in order to generate the large trade surpluses necessary to an early repayment of foreign debt.[46] The large current-account deficits of 1979–80 had reflected a decline in private savings, and the ensuing rapid adjustment was characterized by a rebound in savings, with investment remaining relatively stable. According to Soon (1983) the Korean financial sector, although relatively underdeveloped, managed to sustain the tight monetary and fiscal policies that were pursued in response to the external shocks thanks to its strengthening during the previous decade.[47]

Mexico: 1958–95

The experience of Mexico during the last two decades is particularly interesting because the country experienced three balance-of-payments crises driven by large current-account imbalances (1976, 1982, and 1994), which we will refer to as Mexico I, II, and III. It is interesting to observe that each crisis occurred in an election year, although—with the exception of 1988 and 1994—the country had basically a one-party system. The "political cycle" is also reflected in the path of the real exchange rate, which tends to appreciate in election years, with an adjustment after the election.

Mexico I
The Mexican economy experienced a long period of sustained economic growth and low, stable inflation during the post–World War II period (see figure 17.7). Between 1958 and 1972 economic growth averaged 6.7 percent, inflation never rose above 6 percent, and fiscal imbalances were moderate (Buffie 1989). Throughout this period the exchange rate vis-à-vis the dollar was fixed. The economy was fairly closed, with a relatively underdeveloped export sector and a "modestly protectionist" trade regime by the standards of LDCs (Buffie 1989). The beginning of the 1970s saw a shift in economic policy that led to an increasingly important role for the public sector. Public expenditure rose from 20 percent of GDP in 1971 to 32 percent in 1976, reflecting in particular the growing importance of state-owned enterprises. During this period inflation accelerated, reaching double digits in 1973. The resulting real-exchange-rate appreciation, together with the large increase in public sector investment, induced rapid growth of imports, especially intermediate inputs and capital goods, while exports stagnated. This caused a rapid accumulation of external debt.

In 1976 the exchange rate peg collapsed because of the mounting balance-of-payments pressures; the peso was devalued by almost 100 percent, import controls were imposed, and later in the year an agreement on a stabilization package was reached with the IMF. The fiscal deficit was reduced in 1977, and real fixed capital formation

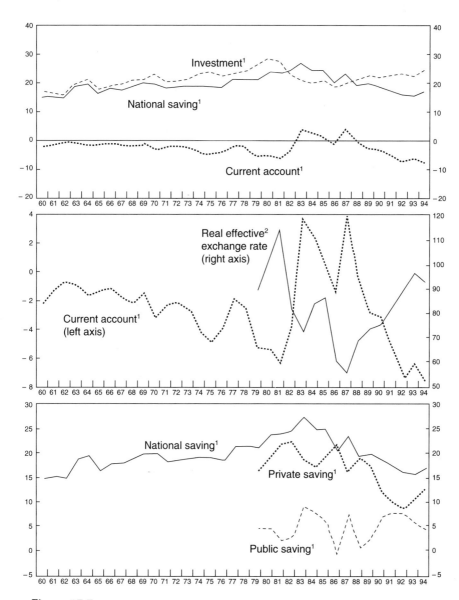

Figure 17.7
Mexico. (1) Ratio to GDP. (2) Index, 1980 = 100; based on consumer prices.
Sources: For 1979 to 1994 IMF, *World Economic Outlook and Information Notices System*; prior to 1979, WEFA Group Intline Database and IMF, *International Financial Statistics*.

declined as the price of imported capital goods was raised by a series of currency devaluations.

Mexico II

The policy stance changed again as a result of the increase in the amount of proven oil reserves increased from 6.4 billion barrels in 1975 to 16 billion barrels in 1977. As a result the constraints on foreign borrowing were lifted as foreign banks started to compete to lend to Mexico on very attractive terms. On the domestic policy front, public expenditure once again increased dramatically from 29.5 percent of GDP in 1977 to 41.3 percent in 1981, with state-owned enterprises taking an important role in public investment. During 1978–81 public and private investment rose rapidly, and growth was above 8 percent. Private savings rose rapidly, but public sector savings experienced a significant decline; this, together with the investment boom, was reflected in large current-account deficits (over 6 percent of GDP in 1981. As a result external debt almost doubled in dollar terms between 1979 and 1981.

Although domestic inflation exceeded 20 percent, the nominal exchange rate was being devalued at a slower rate, resulting in a large real appreciation. During 1981 it became clear that the earlier assumptions regarding the rate of increase of oil export revenues were unrealistic. This fueled speculation that the peso would be devalued, causing massive capital flight. To stem the drain of foreign exchange reserves, the government increased its external borrowing by over 20 billion dollars; the terms of the debt, however, began to worsen with an increase in the spreads over LIBOR (at a time when the LIBOR itself was increasing) and a shortening of maturity.

The crisis worsened in 1982 as a result of external shocks (e.g., the increase in world real interest rates and the world recession) and increasing fiscal imbalances. A 40 percent devaluation of the peso in February stemmed capital flight only briefly, and the government had to borrow an additional 5.7 billion dollars in medium-term syndicated loans. In August a dual exchange rate system was established. Shortly thereafter dollar deposits at Mexican commercial banks were converted into pesos at an unfavorable exchange rate, and on September 1 the banking system was nationalized. During the last four months of the year, there was a de facto moratorium on foreign debt service, until a December agreement with foreign commercial banks to reschedule $23 billion of debt amortization was reached.

In 1983 the new De la Madrid administration implemented a drastic adjustment plan, characterized by a fiscal contraction, a lifting of previously adopted trade restrictions, and a reduction in real wages. The turnaround in the current account was immediate—it registered a surplus, although this came at a heavy price. Output contracted by over 5 percent in 1983, with public and private investment falling drastically.

Aside from external shocks and the high level of external indebtedness, what were the key aspects of the 1982 Mexican crisis?[48]

1. *Real-exchange-rate appreciation.* Between 1977 and 1981 Mexico's exchange rate appreciated by 30 percent in real terms vis-à-vis the dollar (Buffie 1989). This appreciation stimulated a boom in imports that increased much faster than oil exports. The perceived unsustainability of the exchange rate led to large capital flight during the years preceding the crisis, as well as in the following years.

2. *Large fiscal imbalances.* Unlike Chile, in Mexico most of the debt accumulation reflected public sector external borrowing. The increase in public expenditure during the late 1970s and early 1980s was extremely large, and it came on top of another large increase in the early 1970s. Furthermore it financed not only increased public investment but also growing public consumption. Notwithstanding the large revenue increase coming from oil, total revenues failed to keep up with expenditures, causing large fiscal deficits to emerge. The government's external position was worsened by the fact that public sector external borrowing went to finance not only fiscal imbalances but also private capital flight, as foreign exchange reserves were rapidly depleted.

3. *Misperceptions regarding oil wealth.* Policy design in Mexico was based on an overoptimistic assessment of future oil prices; when the

expected price increases failed to materialize, the government did not introduce alternative measures to limit fiscal imbalances.

4. *Weakness of the financial system.* The Mexican system was characterized by financial repression, with high reserve requirements that had the main purpose of facilitating the financing of public sector deficits.

Mexico III

The Mexican economy experienced large structural changes toward the end of the 1980s: A change in monetary and fiscal policy stance was followed by restructuring of the external debt, privatization, and trade liberalization. The results of these changes were remarkable: Economic growth averaged $3\frac{1}{2}$ percent in the period 1989–92, inflation fell from 160 percent in 1987 to single digits in 1993, the overall balance of the public sector improved by 13 percentage points of GDP, foreign debt declined in relation to GDP from 50 percent in 1988 to 22 percent in 1992, thanks to the debt restructuring agreement, real-exchange-rate appreciation, and economic growth. The disinflation process was undertaken using the exchange rate as a nominal anchor: In real effective terms, the exchange rate appreciated by over 60 percent from the end of 1987 to the end of 1992. The banking system, which had been nationalized in 1983, was privatized during 1991 and 1992.

In the aftermath of the debt-restructuring agreement, Mexico regained access to international capital markets: Net capital inflows increased dramatically in the period 1990–93, totaling over $90 billion (an average of 6 percent of GDP per year), or roughly one-fifth of all net inflows to developing countries. Net foreign direct investment during this period was about $17 billion, or around 4.5 percent of 1993 GDP. In contrast to the period prior to the debt crisis of 1992, most of the inflows occurred in the form of portfolio investment (a total of over $60 billion). Between 1991 and 1993, $22 billion flowed into the Mexican stock market (IMF 1995b).

Gross domestic investment recovered from around 19 percent of GDP in 1987 to close to 23 percent in 1992. Notwithstanding a large increase in government savings, however, national savings fell sharply, reaching the low level of 16 percent of GDP in 1992. As a result the current-account deficit reached 6.8 percent of GDP in 1992. The capital-account surplus, however, was more than sufficient to finance the deficit: foreign exchange reserves rose from $6 billion in 1988 to $19 billion in 1992. Imports grew rapidly throughout the period, as did non-oil exports: Total export growth had larger fluctuations, with rapid growth in 1988–89 and more modest increases in 1991 and 1992.

During 1993 the Mexican economy experienced a slowdown, with output growth falling below 1 percent and investment declining to 20.6 percent of GDP.[49] The current-account deficit remained large, at 6.4 percent, as national savings stalled. In 1994, however, the economy recovered, with output growing at 3.5 percent, sustained by rapid export growth (over 14 percent in dollar terms). Imports, however, continued to grow more rapidly, and the current-account deficit widened to 8 percent of GDP. 1994 was a turbulent year, characterized by a series of domestic and external shocks, and a change in the policy stance in the run-up to the August 1994 presidential election. The peasant revolt in Chiapas in January, the assassination of the ruling party's presidential candidate Colosio in March, and the increase in U.S. interest rates in the early part of the year caused loss of confidence in international financial markets and a reversal in capital flows. The real exchange rate was allowed to depreciate within its band, and the Central Bank sterilized the impact of the loss of reserves on money supply. Subsequently, reserves remained fairly stable until October, as capital inflows resumed somewhat during the third quarter.

Between March and October, the authorities reacted to an increase in the interest differential between peso- and dollar-denominated short-term public debt (Cetes and Tesobonos, respectively) by changing the debt composition. The share of dollar-denominated Tesobonos in total government debt outstanding increased from 6 percent at the end of February to 50 percent at the end of November.

The crisis unfolded very quickly. At the end of November tensions resurfaced on foreign exchange markets, and the Bank of Mexico lost reserves. The fluctuation band of the peso was widened by 15 percent on December 19 in an attempt to stem foreign exchange pressures. This was, however, insufficient. The peso reached the new edge of the band within two days, and reserves were drained trying to maintain the exchange rate at the band's edge. On December 22, it was announced that the peso would be allowed to float against the U.S. dollar. The crisis was very severe: The peso lost another 20 percent by the end of the year. Notwithstanding an international rescue package put together at the end of January, 1995 has been a very difficult year for the Mexican economy, with widespread bankruptcies, generalized financial distress and a sharp decline in economic activity.

There are several, to some degree complementary, explanations of the Mexican crisis.[50] It was not clear that the crisis was one of overall sustainability of external imbalances. Indeed the foreign debt to GDP and the debt to exports ratio (34.7 and 184 percent, respectively) were not excessively high by historical terms and also in comparison with other heavily indebted middle-income developing countries. Furthermore fiscal policy, a clear culprit of the previous two Mexican crises, had been restrained for the past four years. It has been argued that the use of the peso as a nominal anchor in the disinflation process had led, in the presence of sticky prices, to overvaluation and large current-account deficits that were ultimately unsustainable. According to this view, an exchange rate correction was overdue (e.g., see Dornbusch and Werner 1994; Dornbusch, Goldfajn, and Valdes 1995). The domestic political shocks and the external shocks simply exposed the vulnerability of the Mexican economy.

Dornbusch et al. recognize that the current-account deficit and the real exchange rate appreciation were, at least to some degree, the logical consequence of the productivity increases facilitated by the implementation of large market-oriented reforms, the access to NAFTA, the reduction of inflation and of the size of the public sector. In this context the increase in permanent income would lead private agents to raise their consumption level, as in the textbook intertemporal model of the current account (Razin 1995). The increase in output would take some more time to surface because of the lags associated with investment and the intersectoral reallocation of resources induced by trade liberalization and changes in relative prices. The issue is to what degree the real appreciation reflected a misalignment.

An alternative, but possibly complementary view, stresses policy inconsistencies that emerged in 1994: In particular, the monetary policy stance and the management of the public debt. Once capital inflows stopped in the second quarter of 1994, because of the increase in U.S. interest rates and political events in Mexico, reserves started to drop because of the current-account deficit. The sterilization of reserve losses by the Bank of Mexico, however, prevented interest rates from exerting an impact on the direction of capital flows and, through a dampening of economic activity, on the current-account balance.[51] Furthermore the large conversion of short-term domestic currency into short-term dollar-denominated public debt (e.g., see, Sachs, Tornell, and Velasco 1995; Calvo and Mendoza 1995) implied an increasing stock of short-term liabilities denominated in foreign exchange that could be "redeemed" at the central bank in exchange for reserves.

What were the fundamental factors behind this crisis? Exports, still low as a fraction of GDP,[52] were going strongly in 1994, albeit not as much as imports, but the national savings rate had declined to very low levels (13.7 percent). Furthermore there is general consensus that the exchange rate was overvalued, at least to some degree, although there is less agreement on what would have been the appropriate way to "unwind" the overvaluation. Finally, the banking system was having difficulties. This is important because increases in domestic interest rates to stem reserve losses were likely to further weaken banks. The impending election made it more difficult to undertake policy adjustments in response to the series of severe domestic and external shocks that hit the economy during 1994.

17.6 Policy Lessons

The main lesson that we draw from these episodes is that it is necessary to consider a combination of factors, rather than single variables, in order to gauge the likelihood that persistent imbalances will be sustainable. Table 17.1 provides a set of sustainability indicators for the various country episodes.

A first factor, directly related to solvency, is the implied resource transfer needed to prevent the external debt to output ratio from rising. This resource transfer is equal to the debt service ratio, adjusted for growth and real-exchange-rate changes (equation 17.6). In the crisis episodes we examined, this measure of the external burden was indeed high with respect to the other episodes.

A second factor that seems to play an important role is the ratio of exports to GDP. Countries that successfully adjusted after experiencing large current-account imbalances, such as Korea, Ireland, and Israel, had a large export share. By contrast, the export to GDP ratio was lower in Mexico (especially in 1982) and in Chile, although it should be pointed out that exports were rising rapidly prior to all three crisis episodes considered (Mexico II and III; Chile).[53] This finding is in line with results presented in Sachs (1985), who compares East Asian and Latin American countries at the time of the debt crisis. The finding is theoretically plausible—the shift in resources needed to achieve sustained trade surpluses is easier in countries with a large traded goods sector, and the vulnerability to trade disruptions in case of default is larger.

A third factor is the real exchange rate. The three crisis episodes we consider are all characterized by an appreciated real exchange rate (with respect to historical averages) in the period leading up to the crisis. The appreciation was accompanied by very rapid growth of imports. It is interesting to note that an exchange rate devaluation was undertaken by all countries under consideration—for some it was forced by events, while for others it was preventive.

A fourth factor is the savings ratio, which was very low (and declining) in Mexico 1994 and, especially, in Chile in the run-up to the crisis. Savings were also low in Ireland and Israel, but their

Table 17.1
Sustainability indicators

	Australia 1990–94	Chile 1979–81 (1982–83)	Ireland 1979–86 (1987–90)	Israel 1982–84 (1985–86)	Korea 1977–82 (1983–88)	Mexico II 1977–81 (1982–83)	Mexico III 1991–94
CA balance*	−4.9	−7.7 (−7.6)	−8.5 (−0.6)	−7.0 (3.0)	−5.4 (2.6)	−5.0 (0.2)	−7.1 (−1.0)
Savings*	18.3	9.3 (5.8)	16.0 (15.7)	15.0 (21.0)	25.6 (31.6)	18.7 (22.0)	14.0 (—)
Investment*	23.2	17.0 (13.5)	24.5 (16.3)	22.0 (18.0)	31.0 (29.0)	23.7 (21.8)	21.0 (—)
Exports*	17.0	20.7 (21.7)	52.4 (60.0)	33.0 (34.0)	32.5 (36.9)	10.6 (17.2)	16.5 (20.0)
Debt/GDP**	36.0	50.0 (78.0)	58.4 (40.9)	46.0 (45.0)	52.3 (14.8)	32.6 (66.6)	35.5 (39.0)
Debt service Burden**	2.1	6.0 (11.0)	—	4.0 (4.0)	5.8 (1.7)	4.1 (7.0)	2.2 (—)
Fiscal balance*	−2.2	2.1 (−3.3)	−11.8 (3.5)	−13.0 (2.0)	−2.8 (0.0)	−8.0 (−18.0)	0.7 (0.5)
Real exchange rate*a	81.0	124.1 (118.5)	97.9 (103.4)	103.5 (94.3)	103.5 (92.2)	126.4 (103.5)	113.0 (98.3)
Growth*	3.0	7.9 (−7.4)	2.8 (56.7)	2.0 (4.0)	5.8 (10.7)	7.5 (−2.4)	2.6 (−6.9)
Political uncertainty	No	No	Moderate	Election	Yest	Yes (election)	Yes (election)
Financial structure	Strong	Weak	Strong	Fair	Fair	Very week	Weak

Note: * Average level during the period. ** Last year of the period.
a. 100 is the historical mean.

export ratios were considerably higher. Economic theory suggests that for a given current-account deficit, high savings are an indicator of intertemporal solvency and therefore creditworthiness, since they imply high investment and therefore an enhanced capacity to repay debt in the future. Furthermore the necessary adjustment during a crisis does not require to reduce investment to very low levels. It is interesting to observe that in both Chile and Mexico III the low savings rates were not attributable to public-sector imbalances but rather to high private-sector consumption. In both Ireland and Israel the low savings rates reflected large public-sector imbalances; these experienced a dramatic turnaround as a result of the adjustment process. In Korea the savings rate was higher than in the other countries we consider.

A fifth factor, the fiscal policy stance, does not seem to play a defining role that would allow us to systematically signal crisis episodes ahead of time. In Chile and in Mexico III the current-account deficits prior to the crisis were not associated with large fiscal imbalances, while they were in Mexico II. It is important to point out, however, two aspects. First, the crises entailed, ex post, a large fiscal cost for the government in the form of bailouts of banks and firms, as well as the shouldering by the budget of private external debt. Second, among our "good" episodes, the turnaround in external accounts in Israel and Ireland came as a result of a policy shift in which fiscal consolidation played a major role.

A sixth factor is the degree of political instability or uncertainty. This played a role in all three Mexican external crises: 1976, 1982, and 1994 were all electoral years in Mexico. In all these cases signs of a possible crisis were already surfacing, but the imminence of an election made the government reluctant to undertake severe adjustment measures. In Korea the 1980 recession was probably accentuated by the difficult political situation following the assassination of President Park; in Israel 1984 was an election year, and the economic policy stance was considerably loose, leading to a larger fiscal deficit and further acceleration of inflation. The successful adjustment in 1985 was undertaken by a "national unity" government. In Ireland the fiscal adjustment in 1982 was made more difficult by instability in the governing coalition. Interestingly, the successful adjustment of 1987 was undertaken by a minority government, albeit with general political support. In Chile political instability did not play a role.

A seventh factor is the composition of capital inflows. Australia has relied more heavily on equity than the developing countries we have examined, and Ireland has received substantial inflows of foreign direct investment. This implies that the risk of domestic and external shocks is shared between foreign investors and the country, reducing the vulnerability of the external position. Furthermore in countries such as Ireland and Australia, which have a more developed bond market, a significant fraction of external debt is denominated in domestic currency, making them less vulnerable to a real-exchange-rate changes. Another aspect of foreign currency debt obligations that has played an important role is the determination of the interest rate. At the time of the debt crisis, most of the external debt in Mexico and Chile (but not in Korea) was at a floating interest rate, making the external position more vulnerable to interest rate shocks.

Finally, an eighth factor is the quality of financial intermediation and especially the fragility of the banking system. This factor played an important role in all the crises we have considered, and it has made the adjustment process more painful. Weaknesses in banking system supervision, distortions in the incentive structure of banks, and lack of competition within the banking sector and from nonbank financial institutions imply inefficiencies in the intermediation of external funds associated with large current-account deficits. For a given size of current-account imbalances, these inefficiencies make the economy more vulnerable to changes in foreign investors' sentiment or other shocks.

17.7 Concluding Remarks

Persistent current-account imbalances are often viewed as a sign of weakness, implying a need for policy action. Economic theory suggests, however, that intertemporal borrowing and lending are a natural vehicle to achieve faster capital accumulation, a more efficient allocation of investment, and the smoothing of consumption. In this chapter we have considered to what degree persistent current-account imbalances can be taken as a signal of a potential "hard lending," or crisis ahead. We have argued that traditional sustainability measures, based only on the notion of intertemporal solvency, may not be always appropriate because they sidestep the issue of a country's willingness to repay its external obligations and the related issue of foreign investors' willingness to continue lending on current terms. We have therefore proposed an alternative notion of sustainability that emphasizes these two issues, in addition to pure solvency.

We have considered a list of operational indicators that can help shed light on the sustainability of external imbalances. In the light of these considerations, we have examined the experiences of a number of countries that ran persistent current account imbalances, some of which experienced an external crisis. A formal econometric analysis, while desirable, is difficult at this stage because of the number and nature of the episodes and the indicators being considered. We have nonetheless distilled from the case studies a number of stylized facts that could help evaluate the sustainability of external imbalances.

We conclude that a specific threshold on persistent current-account deficits (e.g., 5 percent of GDP for three to four years) is not per se a sufficiently informative indicator of sustainability. The size of current-account imbalances should be considered in conjunction with exchange rate policy and structural factors, such as the level and composition of external liabilities, the degree of openness and the composition of trade, the level of savings and investment. Persistent current-account deficits should flash a red light if the export sector is small, debt service is large, savings are low, the financial sector is dominated by banks under weak supervision, and equity financing is small.

17.8 Appendix A: Balance-of-Payments Crisis; Two Examples

In a seminal paper, Krugman (1979) showed how a sudden attack on foreign exchange reserves can force the abandonment of a fixed exchange rate in a country running a monetary policy inconsistent with the peg. Furthermore his explanation does not rely on any form of irrationality in foreign exchange markets: The crisis is simply the natural resolution of a fundamental inconsistency in economic policy setting. We draw on Calvo (1995) to illustrate an extension of the basic Krugman framework that focuses on the possibility of a "double attack"—a run on external debt *and* on foreign exchange reserves.

Consider an economy that is financing budget deficits with external indebtedness, without any recourse to monetary expansion:

$$\dot{b}_t = d_t + i^*b_t, \qquad\qquad\qquad\qquad (A.1)$$

where b_t is external debt, d_t is the primary budget deficit (assumed to be constant), i^* is the foreign interest rate, and a dot over a variable indicates its time derivative. Debt is assumed to have instantaneous maturity.[54] All variables are expressed in real terms (denominated in foreign currency), and PPP holds.

The country is endowed with a stock of foreign exchange reserves R_0 and maintains a fixed exchange rate. Without loss of generality, reserves are assumed to earn no interest.[55] Since domestic credit is not expanding, there is no change in the stock of foreign exchange reserves as long as the peg is maintained. However, with foreign debt growing without bounds (see equation 17.5), the budgetary situation is ultimately unsustainable.[56] This implies the need for a "policy switch" at some point in the future. With perfect foresight and in the absence of default on foreign liabilities, the policy switch must occur *before* foreign liabilities, b_t, exceed foreign exchange reserves, R_0. Otherwise, the country would be unable to meet its external liabilities if a sudden run on its (short-term) debt happens. It is assumed that the only source of revenue the government can rely on to service/repay the debt is seigniorage. Given PPP, the country cannot use the inflation tax without abandoning the peg.

Could an attack occur at the time the stock of short-term foreign debt equals foreign exchange reserves? It is easy to understand that this cannot be the case. The reason is that once inflation becomes positive, there is a discrete drop in money demand. Domestic residents holding "excess" money balances will want to convert them into foreign exchange reserves, analogously to bond holders, but would be unable to do so if reserves cover the redemption of short-term debt only. This implies that reserves at the time of the attack have to cover both bond redemption and the sellout of excess money balances. Thus the attack will take place *before* debt reaches the level R_0. Indeed there will be a "double attack" on foreign exchange reserves, driven by a debt run and conversion of domestic money balances. While the former has no effect on the money supply (since it involves a repayment of foreign liabilities through a reduction in the consolidated public sector's foreign assets), the latter involves a reduction in the money supply (since the central bank "buys back" domestic money in exchange for its remaining stock of foreign exchange reserves).

Let T be the time of the attack. Equilibrium in the money market requires the drop in money demand to equal the contraction in the money supply, which is given by the initial stock of foreign exchange reserves net of bond redemption, $R_0 - b_T$:

$$R_0 - b_T = L(i^*) - L(i^* + \pi), \qquad (A.2)$$

where π is the rate of inflation (and of exchange rate depreciation) after the country abandons the peg. How is π determined? Clearly the inflation rate must allow the government to raise enough seigniorage to finance its budgetary needs so that

$$\pi L(i^* + \pi) = d. \qquad (A.3)$$

Using equations (A.1) and (A.2), we can determine the level of debt at the time of the attack b_T and the postattack inflation rate π.[57] Equation (A.3) can then be used to pin down the timing of the attack T.

In the simple model we have presented, the balance-of-payments crisis is a reflection of a fundamental fiscal imbalance. The "unpleasant monetarist arithmetic" (Sargent and Wallace 1981) implies that eventually debt liabilities that are not covered by regular taxation have to be monetized, which implies that the exchange rate peg is ultimately not sustainable. This fiscal imbalance has been temporarily financed by current-account deficits, and the fiscal crisis comes together with an inability to roll over maturing external debt.

A second example is due to Atkeson and Rios-Rull (1995). In their model government and consumers face limits on their international borrowing as a result of risk of default inherent in international capital markets. If the private sector perceives an increase in its permanent income, for example, because of structural reforms, trade deficits will ensue, and at some point private and public sectors will hit their international borrowing constraints. When these international borrowing constraints are reached, the inflow of international capital stops. At this point the sale of central bank's stock of foreign exchange reserves is the only way that the country can continue to finance its trade deficits. In other words, when the international borrowing constraints bind, the private sector will sell to the central bank its holdings of government debt in exchange for the country's international reserves. Consequently the central bank, left with only limited policy options, has to abandon the exchange rate pegging and raise the rate of interest, and the country's trade balance then moves into a surplus.

18

History of Thought: Selected Bibliographical Notes

Throughout this book we have not dealt with the large body of literature bearing on the subjects covered in the various chapters. In this chapter we provide selected bibliographical notes. We do not present a comprehensive survey of the voluminous work underlying the development of economic thought and analysis of fiscal policies in the world economy. Rather, our purpose is to indicate some linkages between the ideas and concepts developed in this book and the work that precedes it. We do not refer here to our own earlier work which is cited in the preface to the book.

Part II of the book was devoted to the presentation of traditional approaches to international macroeconomics, with special emphasis given to the role of fiscal policies. It opened with a model of international economic interdependence which is based on the Keynesian analysis of the foreign-trade multiplier as developed, among others, by Metzler (1942a), Machlup (1943), and Robinson (1952).

Throughout the book we have analyzed the international mechanism of adjustment in terms of the transfer-problem criterion. This criterion was developed originally in the context of post-World War I discussions about the German reparations, and it was debated among Keynes (1929), Ohlin (1929), and Rueff (1929). This concept was further clarified by Metzler (1942b), Meade (1951), Samuelson (1952), Johnson (1956), and Mundell (1960).

The basic model used throughout our analysis of the traditional approach to international macroeconomics is the income-expenditure model. In specifying this model, we have employed elements from the absorption approach to the balance of payments, as developed by Alexander (1952), and from the monetary approach to the balance of payments, as presented by Polak (1957), Johnson (1958), Prais (1961), Mundell (1964), Frenkel and Johnson (1976), and IMF (1977).

The increased integration of world capital markets led to the development of models in which international capital mobility plays a pivotal role. A pioneering treatment of international capital mobility appears in Iversen (1935). The incorporation of capital movements into the main corpus of international macroeconomics was carried out in a series of classic articles in the 1960s by Mundell (collected in Mundell 1968 and 1971), and by Fleming (1962). The so-called Mundell-Fleming model is still the main workhorse of traditional open-economy macroeconomics. This model has been extended in several directions. Among them is a long-run analysis by Rodriguez (1979); a stock (portfolio) specification of capital mobility by McKinnon (1969), Floyd (1969), Branson (1970), and Frenkel and Rodriguez (1975); an analysis of the debt-revaluation effects induced by exchange-rate changes by Boyer (1977) and Rodriguez (1979); and an analysis of expectations and exchange-rate dynamics by Kouri (1976) and Dornbusch (1976). A critical evaluation of the Mundell-Fleming model is provided by Purvis (1985).

Expositions of the income-expenditure models for alternative exchange-rate regimes and for different degrees of international capital mobility are presented in Swoboda and Dornbusch (1973) and Mussa (1979). The diagrammatic analysis used in chapters 2 and 3 builds in part on these two expositions.

Surveys of various issues covered by the traditional approaches to open-economy macroeconomics are contained in Frenkel and Mussa (1985), Kenen (1985), Marston (1985), and Obstfeld and Stockman (1985), and a comprehensive treatment is provided in Dornbusch (1980).

The usefulness of the Mundell-Fleming model for empirical research has been advanced by casting it in a stochastic rational expectations framework, an exposition of which is given in chapter 4. One of the first contributions to this branch of literature is Mussa (1976).

A recent empirical work based on this approach is Clarida and Gali (1995). Flood and Marion (1982) develop a model similar to the one in chapter 4 to analyze the effects of various exchange rate regimes on aggregate supply.

Part III of the book (chapters 5 to 7) has provided an exposition of the basic elements of intertemporal macroeconomics. The intertemporal approach extends Fisher's (1930) analysis to the entire spectrum of macroeconomic decision making, including saving, investment, and labor. Examples of such extensions in the context of consumption-savings decisions are Modigliani and Brumberg (1954), Friedman (1957), and Hall (1978). Examples in the context of investment theory are Lucas (1967), Uzawa (1968), Tobin (1969), Lucas and Prescott (1971), Abel (1979), Hayashi (1982), and Abel and Blanchard (1986). Other examples in the context of dynamic labor supply and demand are Lucas and Rapping (1969), Heckman (1974), Ghez and Becker (1975), and Sargent (1978). Integrations of the various elements into a general equilibrium model of closed-economy business-cycle theory are contained in Barro (1981a) and Lucas (1981).

Elements of the intertemporal approach that we developed in chapter 4 have been used in the context of open economies, with special emphasis given to the theory of international borrowing and the current account of the balance of payments. Examples of writings in this approach are Bruno (1976, 1982), Eaton and Gersovitz (1981), Sachs (1981, 1984), Razin (1984), and Penati (1987). In chapter 6 we developed the relations between temporal and intertemporal prices and their effects on the time profile of spending and the current account. This analysis is based on Obstfeld (1982), Dornbusch (1983), and Svensson and Razin (1983), who in turn reexamine the older problem of the effects of changes in the terms of trade on savings as analyzed by Harberger (1950) and Laursen and Metzler (1950).

For empirical applications the intertemporal approach to the current account of the balance of payments has been cast in a stochastic dynamic framework, distinguishing between shocks of various kinds (transitory versus persistent, country-specific versus global), by Leiderman and Razin (1991), Mendoza (1991), and Glick and Rogoff (1992). Chapter 7 provides an exposition of the stochastic dynamics of the intertemporal approach to the current account.

The intertemporal approach to fiscal policies in the world economy was presented in part IV of the book (chapters 8 through 11). Our analysis of the effects of government spending in chapter 8 builds on a model embodying the Ricardian neutrality property, according to which intertemporal shifts of lump-sum taxes do not influence the economic system. Typically, this proposition is ascribed to Ricardo, even though, as documented by O'Driscoll (1977), Ricardo himself while anticipating its logic denied its practical validity. Analyses of elements underlying the Ricardian proposition originate in Buchanan (1958), Modigliani (1961), Bailey (1962), and Patinkin (1965), and its modern revival is due to Barro (1974).

Early discussion of the long-term effects of fiscal policies in a Keynesian closed-economy context is contained in Blinder and Solow (1973). In the context of the intertemporal approach Barro (1981a) highlights the distinction between permanent and transitory government spending.

Our discussion of budget deficits (chapters 9 and 10) has dealt with the dynamic effects of fiscal policies in models of overlapping generations. The first formulation of the model in a closed-economy context is due to Samuelson (1958), and the detailed analysis of public debt and capital accumulation within this model is found in Diamond (1965). Examples of open-economy applications of this model are Buiter (1981), Dornbusch (1985), and Persson and Svensson (1985). Aspects of welfare are high-lighted in Fried (1980) and Persson (1985). In chapter 10 we adopted another formulation of the overlapping generations model, based on Yaari (1965) and due to Blanchard (1985). In this model the finiteness of the horizon stems from lifetime uncertainty. An application of the model to a two-country framework is found in the first edition of this book (Frenkel and Razin (1987) and in Buiter (1987). The role of population growth in a similar model is treated by Weil (1987). An important implication of this line of reasoning is that the effects of fiscal stabilization on aggregate demand are weaker, the higher the public debt burden, as shown in Sutherland (1995).

The literature has also dealt with the analysis of the effects of current and anticipated future fiscal policies on the term structure of the world rate of interest and the dynamics of the real exchange rates. Examples of related works dealing with similar issues are Blanchard (1984), Branson (1986), Dantas and Dornbusch (1986), and Helpman and Razin (1987). Dynamic patterns of real exchange rates induced by resource changes rather than fiscal policies are analyzed in the context of the so-called "Dutch Disease." Early examples of such analyses are Gregory (1976), Corden and Neary (1982), and Purvis and Neary (1985).

Chapter 11 considered the international effects of distortionary taxes. The exposition of tax equivalences in the open economy in the chapter draws on Auerbach, Frenkel, and Razin (1988). The symmetry of import and export taxes was first noted by Lerner (1933). An extension of the symmetry argument to dynamic setting is found in Razin and Svensson (1983). Kotlikoff (1989) addressed the issue of tax equivalences in the context of debt-tax finance. He argues that in many policy-relevant circumstances measured budget deficits may not be an economically meaningful concept. Gordon and Levinsohn (1990) provide an empirical analysis of the use of domestic tax instruments to offset the reduction in border taxes. Another useful equivalence, the relationship between taxes on international borrowing and the dual exchange rate system, is analyzed in Frenkel and Razin (1988) and Mendoza (1990).

Our discussion of distortionary taxes in chapters 11 through 15 is related to earlier research emphasizing intertemporal considerations in a closed economy framework. Examples of such research are Diamond (1970, 1975), Diamond and Mirrlees (1971), Mirrlees (1972), Barro (1974, 1979, 1981b), Feldstein (1974, 1977), Atkinson and Stern (1974), Atkinson and Stiglitz (1976), Sadka (1977), Dutton, Feldstein, and Hartman (1979), Kydland and Prescott (1980), Brock and Turnovsky (1981), Balcer and Sadka (1982), Dixit (1985), King (1983), Lucas and Stokey (1983), Gordon (1986), and Judd (1987). In the international context examples of analyses of various aspects of distortionary taxes are found in Razin and Svensson (1983), Aschauer and Greenwood (1985), Greenwood and Kimbrough

(1985), Kimbrough (1986), and van Wijnbergen (1986). An important implication is that expansionary effects of fiscal consolidation could come from a decline in the present value of future taxes. This can occur for two reasons: permanent reductions in government spending and the reduction in the present value of the excess burden of taxation due to a restoration of tax smoothing (Giavazzi and Pagano 1990).

Uncertainty elements appear in various branches of economics and play a central role in financial economics and in modern macroeconomics. Arrow (1963–64) emphasized the role of elementary securities in the allocation of risk. Following Arrow's insight, Diamond (1967) developed a general-equilibrium model of a stock market economy. Helpman and Razin (1978) applied the stock market model to international trade in the presence of uncertainty. Examples of relevant literature in finance, using stochastic processes in the analysis of markets for equity and debt, are Merton (1971), Pitchford and Turnovsky (1977), Ingersoll (1987), Svensson (1988), and Faig (1991).

Among the literature bearing on dynamic simulation analyses of international spillovers of fiscal policies are Auerbach and Kotlikoff (1987), Cnossen and Shoup (1987), Pechman (1988), Tait (1988), Tanzi and Bovenberg (1989), and Perraudin and Pujol (1991).

Part V was concerned with international convergence in levels and growth rates of income in the growing world economy. There has been a renewed interest among economists and policymakers about whether or not the levels of income in different countries converge over time. This has been a subject of both intensive and extensive empirical research recently. The initial empirical strategy was to relate average income growth rates of countries to their initial income levels. A negative coefficient on initial income levels that has almost invariably been found in the data is taken to imply convergence (see Baumol 1986; De Long 1988). These studies use essentially international cross-sectional data (although some of them augment these data by a few time-series observations.) Baumol (1986) and Baumol and Wolff (1988) conclude that levels of income across industrial countries seem to have converged, mid-income countries to exhibit moderate convergence, and low-income countries to have diverged.

Barro and Sala-i-Martin (1991, 1992) spark off a renewed interest in the convergence issue by extending the scope of empirical analysis. They address the key economic issue of whether poor countries or regions tend to grow faster than rich ones. They also use the Solow-type exogenous growth model as a framework to structure their empirical analysis and to study the speed of convergence. Their findings seem to support convergence of both regions and countries, with a relatively robust estimate of the speed of convergence. These findings are still based on essentially cross-sectional data with limited number of time-series observations.

There is a difficulty in the interpretation of the negative correlation between average annual income growth rates and initial income levels, based almost exclusively on cross-sectional observations. Friedman (1992) and Quah (1993) question whether the negative coefficient on initial income levels should be taken as indication of convergence. Very much like Hotelling's (1933) criticism on a similar evidence purporting to show that business enterprises were tending to converge in size, this level convergence analysis may suffer from the classical Galton fallacy of "regression toward the mean." Expanding on different meanings of convergence, Quah (1993) puts forward the notion of whether the cross-sectional dispersion of per-capita incomes diminishes over time. The key message from his calculations is that cross-sectional distributions of incomes do not appear to be collapsing; they seem to be fluctuating over time.

Ben David (1994) follows Quah (1993) by examining the dispersion of per-capita incomes across countries within three income groups: high, middle, and low. He finds that the group of wealthy countries is characterized by "upward convergence," where the poor members catch up with the richer members in the group. The group of extremely poor countries exhibits "downward convergence," where the richer members dwindle down to join the poorer members in the group. Notwithstanding the progress made in the empirical analysis of this issue, the kind of evidence on level convergence is still mixed at this stage. In contrast to the rich body of empirical work on convergence in income levels, the empirical evidence on convergence in income growth rates is still in its infancy.

The mechanism by which income levels and growth rates may converge or diverge in the long run is the subject matter of chapters 12, 13, and 15. This mechanism is analyzed in the context of both exogenous and endogenous growth models. The standard exogenous growth model was pioneered by Solow (1956) with inelastic saving, and extended later by Cass (1965) and Koopmans (1965) to incorporate elastic saving behavior based on optimization. Indeed, much earlier, the first growth model was developed by Ramsey (1928). Most of these and later models assume that human-capital accumulation, which drives long-run growth, is exogenously determined. Uzawa (1965) and Razin (1972) represent the first-generation analysis which endogenizes the investment in human capital in the growth framework. Its second-generation counterpart is initiated by Lucas (1988, whose human capital–based growth model is identical to the one in Razin 1972). A reinterpretation and an emphasis on the sustainability of long-run growth and the convergence issues are the main novelty of the second-generation growth models. Indeed this reorientation also brings out new directions such as the interaction between trade on the one hand, and technological innovations, product quality, and product diversity on the other (see Grossman and Helpman 1992).

The stochastic growth sections in chapters 12 and 13 have presented what has now become a workhorse for macroeconomic analysis, dealing with an economy subject to random variations in the productivity level, government spending, and the like. Brock and Mirman (1972) were the first to characterize analytically the optimal growth path under uncertainty. Kydland and Prescott (1982) showed how to take a linear-quadratic approximation of the original nonlinear stochastic growth model around its deterministic steady state in order to calibrate the model to real world data by mimicking the real business cycle properties of the major macroeconomic variables. King, Plosser, and Rebelo (1988) developed an alternative approximation method, on which our computer programs are based. Reliance on numerical computations can often mask the salient properties of the cycle and growth mechanisms. Realizing this difficulty, Campbell (1994) proposed a simple analytical approach, suitable for low-dimensional growth models, in order to inspect the underlying mechanism.

Chapter 14 was devoted to the taxation of capital income in the open economy. A comprehensive treatise of various aspects of international taxation is found in Frenkel, Razin, and Sadka (1991). Examples of the literature bearing on this subject are Chamley (1986), Dixit (1985), Gordon (1986), Musgrave (1987), Giovannini (1990), Judd (1985), Lucas (1990), Sinn (1990), and Yuen (1991).

Many authors have started to explore the role of political distortions in explaining actual fiscal policymaking. A recent, yet growing, literature elaborated the idea that political distortions may lead governments to follow systematic policies of excessive borrowing. There are at least five classes of political models of fiscal deficits: (1) the public choice approach (Buchanan), (2) models of government weakness and decentralized government, (3) distributional conflicts models, (4) models of strategic public debt choice, and (5) political business cycle models. The findings of the empirical literature testing these models are very encouraging, for they successfully provide evidence of the importance of political factors in explaining the size of the deficits (as well as seigniorage and inflation rates) for many industrial and developing countries. See Buchanan, Rowley, and Tollison (1986), Roubini and Sachs (1989a, 1989b), Cukierman and Meltzer (1989), Alesina and Drazen (1991), Alesina and Tabellini (1990), Tabellini and Alesina (1990), Nordhaus (1975), Rogoff (1990), Rogoff and Sibert (1989), Aghion and Bolton (1990). Open economy formulations of these models include Alesina and Tabellini (1989) and Velasco (1993). For a more systematic survey of this literature, see Corsetti and Roubini (1993), Alesina and Perotti (1994), and Persson and Tabellini (1990).

Chapter 16 of part VI of the book has provided a summary of the intertemporal approach to international economics and extensions in three areas: (1) international taxation, (2) dynamic inconsistency, and (3) the evidence on the twin deficits and international fiscal policy coordination. Examples of the literature on international taxation are

Frenkel, Razin, and Sadka (1991), Giovannini (1990), Gordon (1986), Sinn (1990), and Slemrod (1988).

The constraints on the conduct of fiscal policies may give rise to difficulties associated with time inconsistency of government actions. Such issues are dealt with in Calvo (1978), Kydland and Prescott (1977), Lucas and Stokey (1983), Fischer (1986), Calvo and Obstfeld (1988), and Persson and Svensson (1986). A related issue concerns the formulation of a positive theory of government policy, as analyzed by Barro and Gordon (1983) in the context of an inflation-biased economy. Accordingly, in situations for which policy makers are unable to commit their course of future actions, the game-theoretic equilibrium may be suboptimal, as in the well-known "prisoner's dilemma" game. Recent literature adopts the intertemporal approach and develops a positive theory of economic policy in an alternative institutional environment. Examples of this political economy literature are Persson and Tabellini (1990) and Metzer, Cukierman, and Richards (1991).

Empirical analyses of the effects of fiscal policies on private-sector spending are ample. Examples are Kochin (1979), Feldstein and Horioka (1980), Barro (1981), Feldstein (1982), Kormendi (1983), Aschauer (1985), Aschauer and Greenwood (1985), Leiderman and Razin (1989, 1991), and Mendoza (1991). A survey of key issues relevant for empirical testing is Leiderman and Blejer (1988). Simulations of models based on consumers with finite horizons are found in Blanchard and Summers (1984), Hubbard and Judd (1986), and Poterba and Summers (1986). The intertemporal approach to macroeconomics has also been subjected to numerous empirical tests. Examples are Hall (1978), MaCurdy (1981), Altonji (1982), Mankiw, Rothemberg, and Summers (1985), and Leiderman and Razin (1985). A modification of saving behavior allowing for life cycle characteristics is contained in Auerbach and Kotlikoff (1987) and Modigliani (1987). A further modification of the saving behavior arising from an altruistic bequest motive that is not operative is examined by Barro (1974), Drazen (1978), Feldstein (1986), Nerlove, Razin, and Sadka (1988), and Kotlikoff, Razin, and Rosenthal (1990).

Kydland and Prescott (1982) simulate a theoretical dynamic model, using assumed parameter values, and are able to generate stochastic behavior that closely resembles economic time series. For an application to international economics, see Mendoza (1991).

The interdependencies among countries provide incentives for strategic behavior by individual countries. Analysis of the implications of such strategic behavior is contained in Hamada (1976, 1985). The interdependencies among countries may call for harmonization and coordination of economic policies. Early analyses of these issues are contained in Cooper (1968, 1985). Examples of analyses of this issue within a game-theoretic approach are Oudiz and Sachs (1984), Rogoff (1984, 1986), Canzoneri and Gray (1983), and Canzoneri and Henderson (1987). Additional examples of the empirical literature on the costs and benefits from international policy coordination are contained in Branson, Frenkel, and Goldstein (1990).

The 1982 debt problem generated renewed interests in the analytics of international debt management. Examples of the ample literature on this issue are Eaton and Gersovitz (1981), Kletzer (1984), Sachs (1984, 1985), Cohen and Sachs (1986), Krugman (1985, 1990), Bulow and Rogoff (1988), Dooley (1990), and Helpman (1990).

Notes

Chapter 4

1. To guarantee the existence of a long-run (steady-state) equilibrium for our system, the deterministic growth rates of output on both the supply and demand sides (g_y) are assumed to be identical.

2. Problem 8 at the end of the chapter considers also effects of transitory shocks.

Chapter 5

1. See also Caballero (1991).

Chapter 6

1. An alternative (dual) way to characterize the price index, P, is as follows:

$$\min_{\{c_x, c_m\}} z = c_x + pc_m \quad \text{subject to } C(c_x, c_m) \geq \bar{C}.$$

Necessary conditions for a minimum are

$$1 - \lambda C_1(c_x, c_m) = 0,$$

$$p - \lambda C_2(c_x, c_m) = 0,$$

$$C(c_x, c_m) = \bar{C},$$

where λ is the Lagrange multiplier that is associated with the constraint in the minimum problem.

Thus the minimum cost of obtaining utility level $\bar{C}$ is $z = c_x + pc_m = \lambda[c_x C_1(c_c, c_m) + c_m C_2(c_x, c_m)] = \lambda\bar{C}$, and λ is therefore equal to the corresponding *unit* cost, the price index, $P(p)$.

It is easy to check that $\partial z/\partial p = c_m$. Thus $[dP(p)/P(p)]/[dp/p] = [d(z/c)/dp]/[p/(z/c)] = pc_m/z$. Accordingly, the price elasticity of $P(p)$ is equal to the share of importables in consumption.

Chapter 7

1. To derive a linear approximation to equation (7.4), rewrite (7.4) using the definition of q_t ($= 1 + g(I_t/K_t)$) and the definition of I_t ($= K_{t+1} - K_t$) as

$$E_t R^{-1} \left[\alpha A_{t+1} K_{t+1}^{\alpha-1} + \frac{g}{2} \left(\frac{K_{t+2} - K_{t+1}}{K_{t+1}} \right)^2 + 1 + g \left(\frac{K_{t+2} - K_{t+1}}{K_{t+1}} \right) \right]$$

$$= 1 + g \left(\frac{K_{t+1} - K_t}{K_t} \right).$$

In the deterministic steady state, $k_t = k_{t+1}$, and $R - 1 = \alpha \bar{A} \bar{K}^{\alpha-1}$. Applying the Taylor expansion (up to the first order) around the steady state using $k = K - \bar{K}$ to the above equation yields (7.6) in the text.

2. Define $h(\lambda) = 1 + a_0 \lambda + a_1 \lambda^2 = 0$. Note that $h(1) < 0$ and $h(0) > 0$. Therefore $0 < \lambda_1 < 1 < \lambda_2$. This guarantees that the solution (7.7) is unique. Note also that since $\lambda_1 \lambda_2 = 1/R$, $0 < \lambda_1 < 1 < R < \lambda_2$.

3. If P_t follow a log normal distribution, then (7.30) will imply that p_t must follow a random walk exactly.

Chapter 8

1. The government present-value intertemporal budget constraint is

$$(G_{x0} + p_{n0} G_{n0}) + \alpha_{x1}(G_{x1} + p_{n1} G_{n1}) = T_0 + \alpha_{x1} T_1 - (1 + r_{x-1}) B_{-1}^g,$$

where G_{xt} and G_{nt} denote, respectively, government purchases of tradable and nontradable goods, and where B_t^g denotes government debt in period t. Consolidating the private-sector lifetime constraint (1) with that of the government (2) and imposing equality between consumption and production of nontradable goods in each period yields the economy's consolidated constraint:

$$c_{x0} + \alpha_{x1} c_{x1} = (\bar{Y}_{x0} - G_{x0}) + \alpha_{x1}(\bar{Y}_{x1} - G_{x1}) - (1 + r_{x-1}) B_{-1},$$

where $B_t = B_t^p + B_t^g$ denotes the economy's external debt in period t.

2. In general, these parameters may vary over time because they may depend on the time-varying relative prices. Equation (8.25) corresponds to an initial situation in which relative prices are stationary. In what follows, we consider the case in which the temporary elasticity of substitution, σ_{nx}, is close to unity, so that changes in relative prices do not have an appreciable effect on the expenditure share, β_n. Clearly under such circumstances we can fully characterize the world economic system in terms of percentage rates of growth of the endogenous variables (prices and quantities).

3. Here and in what follows we assume that the initial level of government spending is zero, and we denote the rise in the discounted sum of government spending by dG.

4. This interpretation suggests that the effects of government spending on the interest rate and on the time path of real wages depend critically on the relative importance of wages in the government budget. For the remainder of this section we continue to assume zero government spending.

5. Thus the expression specifying the world relative supply is the analogue to equation (8.27) modified to allow for a variable labor supply with zero government spending.

6. Again in the present case the N and N^* schedules are adjusted for the dependence of the relative output of nontradable goods on the percentage growth rate of the real exchange rate.

7. This can be verified by recalling that the effective discount factors are $\alpha_{xt1} = [(1 + \tau_{c1})/(1 + \tau_{c0})]\alpha_{x1}$ and $\alpha_{nt1} = [(1 - \tau_{y1})/(1 - \tau_{y0})]\alpha_{c1}$.

Chapter 11

1. This chapter draws on Alan Auerbach, Jacob A. Frenkel, and Assaf Razin, "Notes on International Taxation," IMF, January 1989. We thank Alan Auerbach for the permission to reproduce the work.

Chapter 12

1. Solow (1956) interprets this factor as labor-augmenting technological progress.

2. On the other hand, we can also allow A_t to follow a deterministic growth trend, say, $A_{t+1} = (1 + g_A)A_t$ (Hicks-neutral technological progress). We choose not to specify it this way because such process has already been subsumed under the accumulation process of human capital. In other words, one can interpret $1 + g_H = (1 + g_A)^{1/\alpha}$; that is, technological progress is labor-augmenting.

3. Indeed, in most of the discussions below, we need not specialize the production function to the Cobb-Douglas form. We choose this specific form in order to simplify the exposition.

4. An equivalent specification, as in chapter 7, assumes that the firm is the owner of physical capital and makes its investment and production decision by solving an intertemporal profit maximization problem.

5. Note that the time convention in our notations in this chapter is slightly different from that used in chapter 5. In this chapter, we denote current period (t) borrowing by B_{t+1} rather than B_t and the corresponding rate of interest by r_{t+1} instead of r_t. This change is done in order to be consistent with the time convention for factor accumulation.

6. In the closed economy, equilibrium in the financial capital market implies that gross saving (saving in the form of physical capital) amounts to consumer's net saving.

7. If the rest of the world starts from an off-steady-state position initially, the economies will immediately converge and then grow together at the same rates toward a common long run steady state in terms of per-capita GDP.

8. Barro, Mankiw, and Sala-i-Martin (1995) consider similar international borrowing constraints. Their model focuses on the impossibility of financing investment in human capital through borrowing.

9. Strictly speaking, the phase diagram apparatus applies only to continuous time dynamics described in terms of a system of differential equations. The discrete time dynamics that we examine here are just approximations to their continuous time counterparts.

Chapter 13

1. Since $\hat{e} = [(1 + g_h)/B]^{1/\gamma}$ from (13.1), (13.4) can be restated in terms of g_h as

$$(1 + g_N)(1 + g_h)^{1-\sigma} = 1 + \gamma \left[\left(\frac{B}{1 + g_h} \right)^{1/\gamma} - 1 \right].$$

The parameter restrictions on σ, B, γ, and g_N for a positive g_h are implicit in the solution to the above equation. In the log utility case, $B[\gamma/(\gamma + g_N)]^\gamma > 1$ gives such restriction for $g_h > 0$.

2. This suggests that the AK-style model, which lumps all forms of capital into one broad aggregate and applies a single saving rate that drives the accumulation of this all-encompassing capital, may lead to imprecise policy implications. One potential reason to target the human capital saving rate has to do with the Lucas (1988) externality.

3. This external effect is similar, but not exactly identical, to the Lucas (1988) type of externality, which is captured by the economywide average level of human capital. Despite their differences, they both imply that without barriers, capital and labor will move in the same direction, contrary to the prediction of the standard theory (in the absence of the external effect). Atkeson and Bayoumi

(1993) provide evidence from U.S. regions that is consistent with this framework. They compare measures of interregional capital flows (as indicated by differences between regional income and product levels) and interregional population movements. Their data show that, by and large, population flows mirror the flows of capital. It appears therefore that labor and capital have been flowing to the same areas for the past two decades rather than moving in opposite directions as the standard theory predicts. (See their tables 2 and 3.) In the context of international labor mobility, the movement of labor from low-skill economies to high-skill economies would reduce the average level of skill in the labor-receiving countries but not their uppermost skill levels. Thus the productivity level of the latter countries will be reduced under the Lucas externality but not under our specification. Therefore the Lucas externality will generate resistance to labor inflows from lower-skill countries but not in ours. We owe this observation to Se-Jik Kim.

4. Note, however, that as in the exogenous growth case, the long-run detrended level of consumption under capital mobility will not be equal to their counterpart in the autarky case.

5. Even though there may not exist any labor flows along the steady-state growth path due to the symmetry in preferences and technology between the home country and the rest of the world, the absence of barriers to labor mobility guarantees the cross-country wage equality:

$$w_t = \alpha x_t^{1-\alpha} h_t^\varepsilon = \alpha x_t^{*1-\alpha} \bar{h}_t^{*\varepsilon} = w_t^*.$$

6. We conjecture that, even without symmetry in technology and preferences across countries, labor mobility combined with knowledge spillovers will be a level-equalizing force although complete equalization of income levels will not be achieved.

Chapter 14

1. See Christiansen, Hagen, and Sandmo (1994) for an interesting discussion of the scope of taxation in an open economy.

2. For related analysis see Giovannini (1990), Gordon (1986), Musgrave (1987), and Sinn (1990).

3. A tax credit is usually given against taxes paid abroad on foreign-source income so as to achieve a uniform *effective* tax rate on income from all sources. The residence principle means that the home country does not levy additional taxes on incomes of nonresidents over and above what they will have to pay in their country of residence. Therefore the "zero-tax" reference points for nonresidents would mean "same tax", as the tax levied on nonresidents in the country of

residence. See Frenkel, Razin, and Sadka (1991) for a modern treatise of international taxation.

4. We assume that these tax rates apply symmetrically to both interest income and interest expenses.

5. The issue of tax arbitrage is not unique to open economies. Tax arbitrage emerges also in closed economies if the relative tax treatment of various assets differ across individuals. In the open-economy case tax arbitrage becomes more serious if different types of financing are treated differently. This enables individuals and corporations to arbitrage across different statutory tax rates. Another factor that increases the scope of the tax arbitrage is the interaction between inflation and exchange rates, on the one hand, and differential tax treatments of inflation and exchange rate gains and losses, on the other.

6. Efficiency emerges when corporate and individual taxes are fully integrated and interest income faces the same tax rate as equity income. Evidently a nonuniform treatment of different components of the capital income tax base would violate efficiency.

7. It is well-known that the solution obtained depends on the credibility of government, which must promise never again to tax away all of the existing capital income. That is, it is a full-commitment solution.

8. This specification of the net cash flow of the firm assumes that the depreciation allowance for tax purposes is equal to the true economic depreciation (δ_k).

9. For simplicity, it is assumed that the foreign tax rate (τ_N^*) and the world rate of interest (r^*) are constant over time.

10. If rents cannot be fully taxed or if the country can manipulate world prices, the choice of whether to adopt the source principle or the residence principle (or a mixture of the two principles) would depend on the interest rate elasticities of saving and investment; see Giovannini (1989). See also Gordon (1986), Musgrave (1987), and Sinn (1990). Dixit (1985) demonstrates a related result by showing that the production efficiency proposition implies no border taxes, such as import or export taxes.

Chapter 15

1. Two other explanations include (1) multiple steady states—economies with different initial endowments can evolve along the same equilibrium growth path, but in different directions, thus converging to different long-run positions (e.g., see Becker, Murphy, and Tamura 1990; Azariadis and Drazen 1990); (2) multiple equilibria—economies with the same initial endowment can follow different

equilibrium growth paths and converge to different long-run positions (e.g., see Benhabib and Perli 1994; Xie 1994).

2. See, for example, Rebelo (1991) and Jones and Manuelli (1990) for a qualitative analysis, Easterly and Rebelo (1995) for an empirical examination, and King and Rebelo (1990), Lucas (1990), and Stokey and Rebelo (1995) for a quantitative assessment of the effects of tax changes on long-run growth rates in models with capital formation (human and physical) as the source of growth.

3. This argument applies to substitution effect between education and work. The potential income effect of taxes is absent in this case due to the homotheticity of preferences.

4. The progressivity of income tax implies that the tax rate that could have been applied to forgone income is smaller than the tax rate that is actually applied to the increase in future labor earnings due to human capital investment. Subsidized health care in the form of tax-deductibility of medical expenses is equivalent to the depreciation allowance for human capital associated with health.

5. Another way to see this is to observe that with zero capital flows, the number of unknowns falls short of the number of equilibrium conditions.

6. See Razin and Ben-Zion (1975) for similar setup. As in Becker and Barro (1988), the altruism parameter ξ dictates the extent to which the marginal utility of children diminishes as the number of children is increased. Note that σ does not only reflect the elasticity of substitution in consumption but also the preference weight attached to child quality (relative to quantity). We thus restrict σ to be less than unity to ensure that children command positive marginal utility, which implies a different restriction on its value for the existence of steady state than that specified in section 13.1. The utility function from previous chapters is altered by dropping the -1 from the numerator to ensure that, under endogenous population growth, consumption will grow at the same rate as human capital in the steady state. The objective function (15.5) can also be interpreted as a social welfare function. In terms of the utilitarian approach, it is a Millian (average utility) social welfare criterion when $\xi = 0$. When $\xi = 1$, it becomes a Benthamite (sum of utilities) criterion. See Razin and Yuen (1995a) for details.

7. This implication means that in a small and large economy world, the small economy will "disappear" relative to the large economy in terms of population, but its aggregate income will still grow at the same rate as the latter's in the limit. This need not be true if capital is not mobile across these two economies or if they do not have current-account imbalances in the long run.

8. The tax rate τ_{rD}, rather than the after tax MPK, matters here because the cross-country MPKs will be equalized under the residence principle anyway.

9. We require tax symmetry across countries $\tau_{rD} = \tau_{rD}^*$, so $(1 + g_N)(1 + g_y) = (1 + g_N^*)(1 + g_y^*)$ for the existence of world steady-state growth if $\xi = 1 - \sigma$. This condition is not required, however, in (15.1) when $\xi = 1 - \sigma$.

10. We require $\Omega = \Omega^*$ in case 1 and $\tau_{rD} = \tau_{rD}^*$ in case 2, so $(1 + g_N)(1 + g_y) = (1 + g_N^*)(1 + g_y^*)$ for the existence of balanced growth if $\xi = 1 - \sigma$.

11. Note that $\tau_{wD} = \tau_{wA}$ and $\tau_{wN} = 0$ (implying that $\Lambda = 1$) under the residence principle of wage taxation, and $\tau_{wD} = \tau_{wN}$ and $\tau_{wA} = 0$ (implying $\Lambda \gtrless 1$ as $\tau_{wD} \gtrless \tau_{wD}^*$) under the source principle.

12. In Razin and Yuen (1996) we find in the context of a calibrated model for the G7 countries that $\xi > (1 - \sigma)$.

Chapter 17

This chapter draws on Milesi-Ferretti and Razin (1996a,b). We thank Gian Maria Milesi-Ferretti for the permission to reproduce an extended version of this work, which was presented at the IMF conference on International Capital Flows, held in Washington, DC, on December 13–14, 1995.

1. See, for example, Corsetti and Roubini (1991).

2. In the presence of uncertainty, the definition of solvency and sustainability rely to some degree on expected values, implying that in some states of the world insolvency will occur. Under these circumstances the issue becomes how likely will a "bad" scenario occur, and how vulnerable is a country to external shocks (which depends, among other things, on the expected distribution of the shock).

3. Another implication is that the probability private agents attribute to a policy shift is state contingent and can be taken to be a measure of sustainability. For a more thorough discussion of this issue, see, for example, Horne (1991). A different notion of sustainability was put forward by Krugman in the context of the dollar overvaluation in the mid-1980s (Krugman 1985, 1988). He extrapolated the future path of the exchange rate using interest rate parity and evaluated at this exchange rate the implied future path of the U.S. current-account balance. Having found an explosive path of U.S. external liabilities, he concluded that the level of the dollar (and its market forecasted path) was unsustainable.

4. The annuity value is calculated from the sum of the present discounted values (PDV) of present and future flows; it is given by

$$X^p = \frac{r}{1 + r} \sum_{s=t}^{\infty} \left(\frac{1}{1 + r} \right)^{s-t} X_s, \qquad X = Y, C, G, I. \tag{17.2a}$$

To ensure solvency of the private sector, the PDV of lifetime consumption should be equal to the PDV of lifetime disposable income (private sector wealth). Accordingly, the permanent (solvent) level of private consumption must equal the annuity value of private sector wealth:

$$C^p = \frac{r}{1+r}\left[(1+r)F_{pt-1} + \sum_{s=t}^{\infty}\left(\frac{1}{1+r}\right)^{s-t}(Y_s - I_s - T_s)\right], \tag{17.2b}$$

where F_p is the private sector's level of net assets (domestic and foreign) and T is the tax burden. See Obstfeld and Rogoff (1996) for a more complete discussion.

5. Otherwise, a country could play "Ponzi games" indefinitely—that is, borrowing to repay interest on its outstanding debt, without violating solvency conditions, as long as total indebtedness rises at a rate below the economy's growth rate. This possibility, which can arise in a Samuelson-type overlapping-generations model (see Gale 1974), implies that the economy follows a dynamically inefficient growth path.

6. Equation (17.5) shows that the ratio of current-account imbalances to domestic GDP is not invariant to the world inflation rate, analogously to the measure of the domestic budget deficit (inclusive of interest payments) in the presence of domestic inflation. A more precise measure of the current account would need to account for the fact that with positive world inflation and foreign assets (liabilities) denominated in nominal terms part of the measured current-account imbalances reflect anticipated repayment of principal.

7. We ignore the term $\gamma\varepsilon$, which is a discrete time residual.

8. Cohen (1995) considers the Mexican resource transfers (as a fraction of GDP) after the 1982 debt crisis as an "upper bound" on the feasible resource transfers for heavily indebted countries. He then compares this magnitude with the equivalent of equation (17.6) for other highly indebted countries in order to assess their solvency prospects.

9. See the appendix C, chapter 7, for the analytical derivations. The coefficients α, β, and v, are assumed for simplicity to be equal across countries. Traded goods are typically industrial and agricultural products, as well as some services (e.g., travel), while nontraded goods comprise construction and other services, including government services. A terms of trade shock would affect the level of d.

10. As shown in Calvo (1995) and Calvo and Mendoza (1995), small "news" about the mean return of the investment project in the home country can have a large effect on the share of world portfolio allocated to the home country, provided that the portfolio is well diversified (J is large).

11. Equation (17.11) can be rearranged to yield a risk premium-adjusted interest rate parity condition as a function of the deviation of the portfolio share of the home country θ from the minimum variance portfolio share θ_{min}:

$$rp = i_H - \frac{\dot{s}}{s} - \rho = \gamma W \left(\sigma_H^2 + \frac{\sigma^2}{J} \right)(\theta - \theta_{min}),$$

$$\theta_{min} = \frac{\sigma^2/J}{\sigma^2/J + \sigma_H^2}.$$

(17.11)'

The risk premium is exogenous in this model, and the home country's share of the world portfolio adjusts so as to ensure that (17.11) holds. A more complete model would endogenize the domestic rate of return and its variance, the rate of depreciation and hence the risk premium.

12. In this case B represents gross external imbalances for the country as a whole. However, the virtual impossibility to tax foreign assets held abroad by domestic residents make this the relevant measure of debt.

13. The political and economic costs of default, and hence the risk premium, could be different for domestic and external debt.

14. This assumes that investment projects are growth enhancing. It is possible, however, that investment projects are not chosen efficiently, because of financial market distortions or because they are driven by political priorities.

15. In terms of equation (17.12), higher investment would be reflected in a higher present value of output (a higher Y), reducing default risk.

16. In terms of equation (17.12), higher costs of default would be equivalent to a higher C.

17. Ghosh and Ostry (1994) found support for the view that large current-account deficits are more likely to be unsustainable in countries with a less diversified export base in the context of a model based on precautionary savings. Mendoza (1995) presents evidence that the *volatility* of terms of trade is associated with lower economic growth in a wide sample of countries.

18. For some empirical evidence on the importance of international productivity spillovers, see Coe and Helpman (1995) and Coe, Helpman, and Hoffmaister (1995).

19. In terms of equation (17.12), a shift to equity financing could also improve lending terms for the same total amount of external liabilities, if Y is interpreted as the country's share in the resources generated by the project (B/Y would remain unchanged, but C/Y would rise, reducing default risk).

20. For evidence on Latin American countries, see Rojas-Suarez and Weisbrod (1995).

21. The link between inconsistent monetary and exchange rate policies and speculative attacks on a country's foreign exchange reserves was elegantly formalized by Krugman (1979). See also appendix A.

22. On problems posed by large capital inflows, see, for example, Fernandez-Arias and Montiel (1995).

23. This result can be understood by considering the effect of public-sector deficits (negative public savings) on private-sector savings. If the private sector fully internalizes the fact that higher deficits today will need to be covered by higher taxation in the future, private savings will rise, to fully offset the negative public savings, without any interest rate change (and therefore without any effect on investment). In that case government bonds issues associated with the deficit are not regarded as net wealth and do not influence current private consumption. The invariance of the domestic savings/investment balance implies that the current account is unaffected.

24. If the future tax obligations arising from the deficit are expected to be met by higher consumption taxes, present consumption would rise (and present savings would fall) as the increase in the relative price of future consumption induces intertemporal substitution of present for future consumption (see chapter 5 and Frenkel and Razin 1987). The same argument applies if future tax obligations are to be met with the inflation tax (e.g., after the abandonment of an exchange rate peg). Indeed, if consumers have to hold money balances for consumption purposes, future inflation increases the relative cost of future consumption purchases (e.g., see Calvo 1986), thereby encouraging a shift from future to present consumption. Differences between present and expected future tax burden can be the effect of political factors. Consider, for example, a model in the spirit of Alesina and Tabellini (1990) where there exists a politically motivated fiscal deficit bias, caused by the fact that the current government does not share the spending priorities of a possible successor and is therefore willing to commit future tax revenues to debt service rather than to spending. This will result in future tax rates being higher than current tax rates. If taxes fall on consumption, intertemporal substitution would push private agents toward higher consumption in the present than in the future, therefore implying a current-account deficit.

25. For an analytical presentation of this argument, see Sutherland (1995).

26. This is exemplified by the experience of several Latin American countries (such as Argentina, Mexico, Peru, and Venezuela) in the run-up to the debt crisis (see, for example, Diaz Alejandro (1985) and Sachs (1985)). For those countries, the level of "official" foreign debt at the time of the debt crisis was much higher

than the cumulative value of past current account imbalances, indicating that the accumulation of debt had financed not only excess of imports over exports, but also private capital outflows.

27. See, for example, Aizenman (1992), Alesina, Ozler, Roubini, and Swagel (1992) and Cukierman, Edwards, and Tabellini (1992).

28. This may reflect the possibility that financial markets react too late or too abruptly, or that they are plagued by misperceptions and expectational errors, making them less reliable in ascertaining sustainability.

29. Korea experienced a deep recession in 1980, but growth picked up rapidly thereafter. In Ireland and Israel the fiscal stabilization was accompanied by higher growth.

30. There is a widespread difference of views on how serious external problems are. For an "optimistic" view, see Pitchford (1989). For a pessimistic view, see the November 4, 1995, leader in the *Economist*.

31. In 1993 interest payments on external debt were around 2 percent of GDP.

32. As pointed out by Edwards and Cox Edwards (1987) among others, private foreign borrowing did not carry government guarantees. A large fraction of foreign borrowing was carried out by the so-called *grupos*—large conglomerates that included industrial firms as well as banks. They had been major buyers of privatized firms, and their banks extended most of their lending to firms of the same conglomerate, circumventing lax regulations.

33. The real appreciation of the peso was compounded by the fact that the dollar (to which the peso was pegged) was appreciating against other major currencies during the period 1979–82.

34. Clearly the latter simply reflects a shift from implicit to explicit government liabilities in the context of a move from a pay as-you-go system to funded system.

35. The intensity of these effects was compounded by the narrow commodity specialization of exports.

36. Since its entry in the European Community in 1973, Ireland has received large foreign direct investment.

37. The fraction of the external debt denominated in dollars was substantial in 1984.

38. The ratio of public external debt to GDP also declined. During this period, there was an increase in foreigners' holdings of punt-denominated securities, so the decline in foreign currency debt overstates the actual decline in public external debt.

39. OECD figures on the level of FDI in Ireland are somewhat misleading. See OECD (1991).

40. As a result the difference between GDP and GNP was over 11 percent in 1993 (OECD 1995).

41. There is a debate regarding the degree to which transfer pricing, encouraged by favorable tax treatment of capital, increases recorded exports. Even "correcting" exports for profit repatriation, however, their increase is remarkable.

42. For a discussion of the Israeli stabilization episode, see Bruno (1993) and Bufman and Leiderman (1995).

43. The expansionary effects of fiscal consolidation come from a decline in the present value of future taxes. This can occur for two reasons: permanent reductions in government spending and the reduction in the present value of the excess burden of taxation due to a restoration of tax smoothing (Giavazzi and Pagano 1990). Unemployment in Israel began to increase, however, two years after the stabilization program.

44. The cost of the increase in interest rates was lower for Korea than for Latin American countries because most of its outstanding debt was at fixed interest rates.

45. There is some controversy on the actual degree of policy adjustment in the period 1980–82: For example, Haggard and Collins (1994) argue that during these years "Korea's macroeconomic policy was characterized by a mix of conventional stabilization measures with a number of expansionist policies," such as expansionary fiscal policy in 1980–81. According to this view, strong stabilization measures and structural reform began in earnest in 1983–84.

46. Korea's current-account imbalances were mostly financed through foreign borrowing rather than through foreign direct investment or other forms of equity.

47. During the 1970s, faced with the situation that banks were poor saving mobilizers because most of the deposit rates have been held artificially low, and bad loan decisions were made by banks whereby large number of nonperforming assets were created, Korea begun to develop nonbank financial institutions and securities markets. If in 1970 the banking institutions accounted for 82 and 78 percent of the deposit market and loan market, respectively, by 1982 these deposit and lending shares fell to 64 and 62 percent, respectively (see Soon 1993). A law was enacted in 1972 to induce firms that received bank loans over a specific amount to go public and issue stocks, and various tax incentives were provided.

48. Some observers (Díaz-Alejandro 1984) attributed the debt crisis mainly to external factors, and underline that several distinguished commentators (and the

commercial banks themselves) argued that there was nothing to be worried about because the current-account deficits were financing higher public and private investment. Indeed the macroeconomic performance between 1978 and 1981 was very good, with high growth and rapid increases in public and private investment.

49. The investment slowdown was related to the decision of the authorities to raise interest rates in early 1993 in order to contain the expansion in aggregate demand; later in the year uncertainties about NAFTA may also have played a role.

50. See IMF (1995a) for an early assessment of these explanations.

51. The reluctance of the monetary authorities to raise domestic interest rates was allegedly driven by the fragile situation of the banking system, characterized by a large fraction of bad loans, and a mismatch between the maturity structure of assets and liabilities. However, a drastic increase in interest rates was later forced upon the authorities by the currency crisis.

52. The ratio of exports to GDP in Mexico is different depending on whether it is calculated using national income accounts or balance of payments statistics (as reported in International Financial Statistics).

53. It is interesting that Chile's successful recovery after the crisis was characterized by a rapid increase in the export ratio.

54. The term d_t can alternatively be interpreted as the primary deficit (surplus) plus debt service on long-maturity foreign debt (consols). In this case, b would represent short-term foreign indebtedness.

55. If the interest rate earned on foreign exchange reserves is below i^*, results would be analogous. Where reserves earn the same interest rate as short-term debt, a crisis will eventually occur if the present discounted value of the flow of primary deficits d/i^* exceeds initial reserves R_0, so the government is fundamentally insolvent.

56. In the Krugman case the analogue to the growth of debt is the constant decline in reserves driven by the expansion of domestic credit.

57. We are implicitly assuming that equation (17.7) has a unique solution for π; that is, the economy is on the left side of the Laffer curve.

Selected References

The following list of references also contains recent applications of the intertemporal approach to open-economy macroeconomics that are applicable to the problem sets.

Abel, Andrew B. 1979. *Investment and the Value of Time*. New York: Garland.

Abel, Andrew B., and Olivier Blanchard. 1983. The present value of profits and cyclical movements in investment. *Econometrica* 51:675–92.

Adams, Charles, and Jeremy Greenwood. 1985. Dual exchange rate systems and capital controls: An investigation. *Journal of International Economics* 18:43–63.

Aghion, P., and P. Bolton. 1990. Government debt and the risk of default: A political economic model of the strategic role of debt. In *Public Debt Management: Theory and Practice*, ed. by R. Dornbusch and M. Draghi. Cambridge: Cambridge University Press.

Aizenman, Joshua. 1992. Trade Reforms, Credibility, and Development. *Journal of Development Economics* 39:163–87.

Alesina, A., and A. Drazen. 1991. Why are stabilizations delayed? A political–economic model. *American Economic Review*: 1170–88.

Alesina, Alberto, Sule Ozler, Nouriel Roubini, and Phillip Swagel. 1996. Political instability and growth. *Journal of Economic Growth*, forthcoming.

Alesina, A., and R. Perotti. 1994. The political economy of budget deficits. NBER working paper 4637. February.

Alesina, A., and N. Roubini. 1992. Political cycles in OECD economies. *Review of Economic Studies*. October.

Alesina, Alberto, and Guido Tabellini. 1989. External debt, capital flight and political risk. *Journal of International Economics* 27:199–220.

Alesina, Alberto, and Guido Tabellini. 1990. A positive theory of fiscal deficits and government debt in a democracy. *Review of Economic Studies* 57:403–14.

Alexander, Sidney S. 1952. Effects of a devaluation on a trade balance, *IMF Staff Papers* 2:263–78.

Altonji, Joseph G. 1985. The intertemporal substitution model of labor market fluctuations: An empirical analysis. *Review of Economic Studies* 49 (special issue on unemployment): 783–824.

Arrow, Kenneth, J. 1963–64. The role of securities in the optimal allocation of risk bearing. *Review of Economic Studies* 31:91–96.

Aschauer, David A. 1985. Fiscal policy and aggregate demand. *American Economic Review* 75:117–27.

Aschauer, David A., and Jeremy Greenwood. 1985. Macroeconomic effects of fiscal policy. In *The New Monetary Economics: Fiscal Issues and Unemployment*, ed. by Karl Brunner and Allan H. Meltzer. Carnegie Rochester Conference Series on Public Policy 23, Autumn, pp. 91–138.

Atkeson, Andrew, and Jose-Victor Rios-Rull. 1995. How Mexico lost its foreign reserves. NBER working paper 5329. October.

Atkeson, Andrew, and Tamim Bayoumi, "Do Private Capital Markets Insure Regional Risk? Evidence from the United States and Europe," *Open Economies Review* 4 (1993): 303–24.

Auerbach, Alan J., and Laurence J. Kotlikoff. 1987. *Dynamic Fiscal Policy*. Cambridge: Cambridge University Press.

Azariadis, Costas. 1978. Escalator clauses and the allocation of cyclical risks. *Journal of Economic Theory* 18:119–55.

Azariadis, Costas, and Allan Drazen. 1990. Threshold externalities in economic development. *Quarterly Journal of Economics* 105:501–26.

Backus, David K., Patrick J. Kehoe, and Finn E. Kydland. 1992. International real business cycles. *Journal of Political Economy* 100:745–75.

Bailey, Martin J. 1962. *National Income and the Price Level*. New York: McGraw-Hill.

Balassa, Bela. 1964. The purchasing power parity doctrine: A reappraisal. *Journal of Political Economy* 72:584–96.

Barro, Robert J. 1974. Are government bonds net wealth? *Journal of Political Economy* 82:1095–1117.

Barro, Robert J. 1979. On the determination of public debt. *Journal of Political Economy* 87, part 1:940–71.

Barro, Robert J. 1981a. Output effects of government purchases. *Journal of Political Economy* 89:1086–1121.

Barro, Robert J. 1981b. *Money, Expectations, and Business Cycles: Essays in Macroeconomics*. New York: Academic Press.

Barro, Robert J., and David B. Gordon. 1983. A positive theory of monetary policy in a natural rate model. *Journal of Political Economy* 91:589–610.

Barro, Robert J., and Xavier Sala-i-Martin. 1991. Convergence across states and regions. *Brookings Papers on Economic Activities* 1:107–82.

Barro, Robert J., and Xavier Sala-i-Martin. 1992. Convergence. *Journal of Political Economy* 100:223–51.

Barro, Robert J., N. Mankiw, N. Gregory, and Xavier Sala-i-Martin. 1995. Capital mobility in neoclassical models of growth. *American Economic Review*, forthcoming.

Bartolini, Leonardo, and Allan Drazen. 1994. Capital controls as a signal. Mimeo. International Monetary Fund and University of Maryland.

Bartolini, Leonardo, Assaf Razin, and Steve Symansky. 1995. G-7 fiscal restructuring in the 1990s: Macroeconomic effects. *Economic Policy: A European Forum* 20: 111–46.

Baumol, William J. 1986. Productivity growth, convergence and welfare: What do the long-run data show? *American Economic Review* 76:1072–85.

Baumol, William J., and Edward N. Wolff. 1988. Productivity growth, convergence, and welfare: Reply. *American Economic Review* 78:1155–59.

Becker, Gary S., and Robert J. Barro. 1988. A reformulation of the economic theory of fertility. *Quarterly Journal of Economics* 103:1–25.

Becker, Gary S., Kevin M. Murphy, and Robert Tamura. 1990. Human capital, fertility, and economic growth. *Journal of Political Economy* 98:S12–S37.

Ben-David, Dan. 1994. Convergence clubs and diverging economies. Working paper. Ben Gurion University.

Benhabib, Jess, and Roberto Perli. 1994. Uniqueness and indeterminacy: Transitional dynamics in a model of endogenous growth. *Journal of Economic Theory* 63:113–42.

Bertola, Guiseppe, and Allan Drazen. 1993. Trigger points and budget cuts: Explaining the effects of fiscal austerity. *American Economic Review* 83:11–26.

Blanchard, Olivier J. 1984. Current and anticipated deficits, interest rates and economic activity. *European Economic Review* 25:7–27.

Blanchard, Olivier J. 1985. Debt, deficits, and finite horizons. *Journal of Political Economy* 93:223–47.

Blanchard, Olivier J., and Lawrence H. Summers. 1984. Perspectives on high world interest rates. *Brookings Papers on Economic Activity* 2:273–333.

Blinder, Alan S., and Robert M. Solow. 1973. Does fiscal policy matter? *Journal of Public Economics* 2:319–37.

Bovenberg, Lans A. 1989. The effects of capital income taxation on international competitiveness and trade flows. *American Economic Review* 79:70–89.

Bovenberg, Lans A., and Lawrence Goulder. 1989. Taxes on old and new capital under international capital mobility: An intertemporal general equilibrium assessment. Unpublished manuscript. International Monetary Fund. August.

Boyer, Russell S. 1977. Devaluation and portfolio balance. *American Economic Review* 67:54–63.

Branson, William H. 1970. Monetary policy and the new view of international capital movements. *Brookings Papers on Economic Activity* 2:235–62.

Branson, William H. 1986. Cases of appreciation and volatility of the dollar. In *The U.S. Dollar-Recent Developments, Outlook, and Policy Options*. Kansas City: Federal Reserve Bank of Kansas City, pp. 33–52.

Branson, William H., J. A. Frenkel, and M. Goldstein. eds. 1990. *International Policy Coordination and Exchange Rate Fluctuations*. Chicago: University of Chicago Press.

Brock, William, and Mirman Leonard. 1972. Optimal economic growth and uncertainty: The discounted case. *Journal of Economic Theory* 4:479–513.

Brock, William, and Stephen Turnovsky. 1981. The analysis of macroeconomic policies in perfect foresight equilibrium. *International Economic Review* 84:179–209.

Bruno, Michael. 1976. The two-sector open economy and the real exchange rate. *American Economic Review* 66:566–77.

Bruno, Michael. 1982. Adjustment and structural change under raw material price shocks. *Scandinavian Journal of Economics* 84:199–221.

Bruno, Michael. 1993. *Crisis, Stabilization and Economic Reform: Therapy by Consensus,* Oxford: Oxford University Press.

Bryant, R. C., D. W. Henderson, G. Holtham, P. Hooper, and S. A. Symansky. 1988. *Empirical Macroeconomics for Interdependent Economics*. Washington: Brookings Institution.

Buchanan, James M. 1958. *Public Principles of Public Debt*. Homewood: Irwin.

Buchanan, J. M., C. K. Rowley, and R. D. Tollison 1986. *Deficits*. New York: Basil Blackwell.

Buffie, Edward F. 1989. Economic policy and foreign debt in Mexico. In *Developing Country Debt and Economic Performance*, vol. 2, ed. by Jeffrey Sachs. Chicago: University of Chicago Press.

Bufman, Gil, and Leonardo Leiderman. 1995. Israel's stabilization: Some important policy lessons. In *Reform, Recovery and Growth*, ed. by Sebastian Edwards and Rudiger Dornbusch. Chicago: University of Chicago Press.

Buiter, Willem H. 1981. Time preference and international lending and borrowing in an overlapping-generations model. *Journal of Political Economy* 89:769–97.

Buiter, Willem H. 1987. Fiscal policy in open interdependent economies. In *Economic Policy in Theory and Practice*, ed. by Assaf Razin and Efraim Sadka. London: Macmillan, pp. 101–44.

Buiter, Willem H. 1988. Death, birth, productivity growth and debt neutrality. *The Economic Journal* 98:279–93.

Buiter, Willem H. 1988. Structural and stabilization aspects of fiscal and financial policy in the dependent economy. *Oxford Economic Papers* 40:220–45.

Bulow, Jeremy, and Kenneth Rogoff. 1988. The buyback boondoggle. *Brookings Papers in Economic Activity* 2:675–98.

Bulow, Jeremy, and Kenneth Rogoff. 1990. Cleaning up the debt crisis without getting taken to the cleaners. *Journal of Economic Perspectives* 4:31–42.

Caballero, Ricardo J. 1991 Earnings uncertainty and aggregate wealth accumulation. *American Economic Review* 81:859–71.

Calvo, Guillermo A. 1978. On the time consistency of optimal policy in a monetary economy. *Econometrica* 46:1411–28.

Calvo, Guillermo A. 1986. Temporary stabilization. *Journal of Political Economy* 94:1319–29.

Calvo, Guillermo A. 1987. On the costs of temporary policy. *Journal of Development Economics* 27:245–61.

Calvo, Guillermo A. 1988. Costly trade liberalizations: Durable goods and capital mobility. *IMF Staff Papers* 35:461–73.

Calvo, Guillermo A. 1995. Varieties of capital market crises. Mimeo. University of Maryland.

Calvo, Guillermo A., and Enrique G. Mendoza. 1995. Reflections on Mexico's balance-of-payments crisis: A chronicle of a death foretold. Mimeo. University of Maryland and Federal Reserve Board. August.

Calvo, Guillermo A., and Maurice Obstfeld. 1988. Optimal time-consistent fiscal policy with finite lifetimes. *Econometrica* 56:411–32.

Campbell, John Y. 1994. Inspecting the mechanism: An analytical approach to the stochastic growth model. *Journal of Monetary Economics* 33:463–506.

Campbell, John Y., and Richard H. Clarida. 1987. The term structure of Euromarket interest rates: An empirical investigation. *Journal of Monetary Economics* 19:25–44.

Canzoneri, M. B., and B. T. Diba. 1991. Fiscal deficits, financial integration, and a central bank for Europe. NBER-TCER-CEPR Conference on Fiscal Policy in Open Macroeconomies, Tokyo, January.

Canzoneri, Matthew, and Jo Anna Gray. 1985 Monetary policy games and the consequences of noncooperative behavior. *International Economic Review* 26:547–64.

Canzoneri, M. B., and D. Henderson. 1988. Is sovereign policymaking bad? *Carnegie Rochester Conference Series on Public Policy* 28:93–140.

Canzoneri, Matthew, and Dale Henderson. 1991. *Monetary Policy in Interdependent Economies*. Cambridge: MIT Press.

Cass, David. 1965. Optimal growth in an aggregative model of capital accumulation. *Review of Economic Studies* 32:233–40.

Chamley, C. P. 1986. Optimal taxation of capital income in general equilibrium with infinite lives. *Econometrica* 54:607–22.

Christiansen, V., K. Hagen, and A. Sandmo. 1994. The scope for taxation and public expenditure in an open economy. *Scandinavian Journal of Economics* 96:289–310.

Claessens, Stijn. 1995. The emergence of equity investment in developing countries: Overview. *World Bank Economic Review* 9:1–17.

Claessens, Stijn, Michael Dooley, and Andrew Warner. 1995. Portfolio flows: Hot or cold? *World Bank Economic Review* 9:153–74.

Clarida, Richard H., and Jodi Gali. 1994. Sources of exchange rate fluctuations. NBER working paper 4658.

Cline, William R. 1995. *International Debt Reexamined*. Washington: Institute for International Economics.

Clower, Robert W. 1967. A reconsideration of the microfoundations of monetary theory. *Western Economic Journal* 6:1–8.

Cnossen, Sijbren, and Carl S. Shoup. 1987. Coordination of value-added taxes. In *Tax Coordination in the European Community*, ed. by Cnossen Sijbren. Antwerp: Kluwer Law and Taxation Publishers.

Coe, David, and Elhanan Helpman. 1995. International R&D spillovers. *European Economic Review* 39:859–87.

Coe, David, Elhanan Helpman, and Alex Hoffmaister. 1994. North–South R&D spillovers. IMF working paper 94/144. December.

Cohen, Daniel. 1991. *Private Lending to Sovereign States: A Theoretical Autopsy*. Cambridge: MIT Press.

Cohen, Daniel. 1992. The debt crisis: A postmortem. *NBER Macroeconomics Annual*, ed. by Olivier Blanchard and Stanley Fischer. Cambridge: MIT Press.

Cohen, Daniel. 1995. The sustainability of African debt. Mimeo. CEPREMAP, September.

Cohen, Daniel, and Jeffrey Sachs. 1986. Growth and external debt under risk of debt repudiation. *European Economic Review* 30:529–58.

Collins, Susan M., and Won-Am Park. 1989. External debt and macroeconomic performance in South Korea. In *Developing Country Debt and Economic Performance* vol. 3, ed. by Jeffrey Sachs. Chicago: University of Chicago Press, pp. 153–369.

Collins, Susan. 1994. Savings, investment and external balance in South Korea. In *Macroeconomic Policy and Adjustment in Korea, 1970–1990*, by Stephen Haggard, Richard Cooper, Susan Collins, Choongsoo Kim, and Sung-Tael Ro. Cambridge: Harvard Institute for International Development.

Cooper, Richard N. 1968. *The Economics of Interdependence*. New York: McGraw-Hill.

Cooper, Richard N. 1985. Economic interdependence and coordination of economic policies. In *Handbook of International Economics*, vol. 2, ed. by Ronald W. Jones and Peter B. Kenen. Amsterdam: North Holland, pp. 1195–1234.

Corbo, Vittorio, and Stanley Fischer. 1994. Lessons from the Chilean stabilization and recovery. In *The Chilean Economy: Policy Lessons and Challenges*, ed. by Barry P. Bosworth, Rudiger Dornbusch, and Raúl Labán, Washington: Brookings Institution.

Corbo, Vittorio, and Leonardo Hernández. 1996. Macroeconomic adjustment to capital inflows: Lessons from recent Latin American and East Asian experience. *World Bank Research Observer*, forthcoming.

Corden W. Max, and Peter J. Neary. 1982. Booming sector and de-industrialization in a small open economy. *Economic Journal* 92:825–48.

Corsetti, Giancarlo, and Nouriel Roubini. 1991. Fiscal deficits, public debt and government solvency: Evidence from OECD countries. *Journal of the Japanese and International Economies* 5:354–80.

Cukierman, Alex, Sebastian Edwards, and Guido Tabellini. 1992. Seigniorage and political instability. *American Economic Review* 82:537–55.

Cukierman, A. and Meltzer. 1989. A political theory of government debt and deficits in a neo-Ricardian framework. *American Economic Review,* 4:713–32.

Dantas, Daniel V., and Rudiger Dornbusch. 1984. Anticipated budget deficits and the term structure of interest rates. NBER working paper 1518. December.

De la Cuadra, Sergio, and Salvador Valdes-Prieto. 1992. Myths and facts about financial liberalization in Chile: 1974–83. In *If Texas Were Chile: A Primer on Banking Reform,* ed. by Philip Brock. San Francisco: ICS Press.

DeLong, Bradford. 1988. Productivity growth, convergence, and welfare: Comment. *American Economic Review* 78:1138–54.

Devereux, Michael. 1987. Fiscal spending, the terms of trade, and real interest rates. *Journal of International Economics* 22:219–36.

Devereux, Michael. 1988. Non-traded goods and the international transmission of fiscal policy. *Canadian Journal of Economics* 21:265–78.

Diamond, Peter A. 1965. National debt in a neoclassical growth model. *American Economic Review* 55:1126–50.

Diamond, Peter A. 1967. The role of a stock market in a general equilibrium model with technological uncertainty. *American Economic Review* 57:759–76.

Diamond, Peter A., and Mirrlees. J. 1971. Optimal taxation and public production. *American Economic Review* (March): 8–17; (June): 261–78.

Díaz-Alejandro, Carlos F. 1984. Latin American debt: I don't think we are in Kansas anymore. *Brookings Papers on Economic Activity* 1:335–89.

Díaz-Alejandro, Carlos F. 1985. Goodbye financial repression, hello financial crash. *Journal of Development Economics* 19:1–24.

Dixit, Avinash. 1985. Tax policies in open economies. In *Handbook of Public Economics,* ed. by A. Auerbach and M. Feldstein. Amsterdam: North Holland, pp. 314–74.

Djajic, Slobodan. 1987a. Effects of budgetary policies in open economies: The role of intertemporal consumption substitution. *Journal of International Money and Finance* 6:373–83.

Djajic, Slobodan, 1987b. Temporary import quota and the current account. *Journal of International Economics* 22:349–62.

Dooley, Michael P. 1990. Market valuation of external debt. In *Analytical Issues in Debt*, ed. by Jacob A. Frenkel, Michael P. Dooley, and Peter Wickham. Washington: International Monetary Fund, pp. 75–82.

Dooley, Michael P. 1991. Market-based debt reduction schemes. In *Analytical Issues in Debt*, ed. by Jacob A. Frenkel, Michael P. Dooley, and Peter Wickham. Washington: International Monetary Fund, pp. 258–78.

Dornbusch, Rudiger. 1976. Expectations and exchange rate dynamics. *Journal of Political Economy* 84:1161–76.

Dornbusch, Rudiger. 1980. *Open Economy Macroeconomics*. New York: Basic Books.

Dornbusch, Rudiger. 1983. Real interest rates, home goods, and optimal external borrowing. *Journal of Political Economy* 91:141–53.

Dornbusch, Rudiger. 1985. Intergenerational and international trade. *Journal of International Economics* 18:123–39.

Dornbusch, Rudiger. 1986. Special exchange rates for capital account transactions. *World Bank Economic Review* 1:3–33.

Dornbusch, Rudiger. 1989. Credibility, debt and unemployment: Ireland's failed stabilization. *Economic Policy* 8:173–210.

Dornbusch, Rudiger, Ilan Goldfajn, and Rodrigo Valdes. 1995. Currency crises and collapses. *Brookings Papers on Economic Activity* 2:1–29.

Easterly, William, and Sergio T. Rebelo. 1995. Fiscal policy and economic growth: An empirical investigation. *Journal of Monetary Economics* 34.

Eaton, Jonathan, and Mark Gersovitz. 1981. Poor-country borrowing in private financial markets and the repudiation issue. *Princeton Studies in International Finance* 47 (June).

Edison, Hali J., and B. Dianne Pauls. 1993. A re-assessment of the relationship between real exchange rates and real interest rates: 1974–90. *Journal of Monetary Economics* 31:165–87.

Edwards, Sebastian. 1989. *Real Exchange Rates, Devaluation and Adjustment*. Cambridge: MIT Press.

Edwards, Sebastian, and Alejandra Cox-Edwards. 1987. *Monetarism and Liberalization: The Chilean Experiment.* Cambridge: MIT Press.

Emerson, Michael, Michel Aujean, Michel Catinat, Philippe Goybet, and Alexis Jacquemin. 1988. Fiscal barrier. *The European Economy* (March):45–107.

Engel, Charles, and Kenneth Kletzer. 1990. Tariffs and saving in a model with new generations. *Journal of International Economics* 28:71–91.

Faig, Miguel. 1991. A simple economy with human capital: Transitional dynamics, technology shocks, and fiscal policies. Working paper 9121. Institute for Policy Analysis, University of Toronto. May.

Feldstein, Martin. 1988. Distinguished lecture on economics in government: Thinking about international economic coordination. *Journal of Economic Perspectives* 2:3–13.

Feldstein, Martin S. 1974. Tax incidence in a growing economy with variable factor supply. *Quarterly Journal of Economics* 88:551–73.

Feldstein, Martin S. 1977. The surprising incidence of a tax on pure rent: A new answer to an old question. *Journal of Political Economy* 85:349–60.

Feldstein, Martin S. 1982. Government deficits and aggregate demand. *Journal of Monetary Economics* 9:1–20.

Feldstein, Martin S. 1986. The effects of fiscal policies when incomes are uncertain: A contradiction to Ricardian equivalence. NBER working paper 2062. November.

Feldstein, Martin, and C. Horioka. 1980. Domestic saving and international capital flows. *Economic Journal* 90:314–29.

Fernández-Arias, Eduardo, and Peter Montiel. 1995. The surge in capital inflows to developing countries: An analytical overview. Mimeo. The World Bank. August.

Fischer, Stanley. 1986. *Indexing, Inflation, and Economic Policy.* Cambridge: MIT Press.

Fisher, Irving. 1930. *Theory of Interest.* New York, Macmillan.

Fleming, J. Marcus. 1962. Domestic financial policies under fixed and under floating exchange rates. *IMF Staff Papers* 9:369–79.

Flood, Robert P. 1978. Exchange rate expectations in dual exchange markets. *Journal of International Economics* 8:65–78.

Flood, Robert P., and Nancy P. Marion. 1982. The transmission of disturbances under alternative exchange-rate regimes with optimal indexing, *Quarterly Journal of Economics* 67:43–66.

Floyd, John E. 1969. International capital movements and monetary equilibrium. *American Economic Review* 59, part 1:472–92.

Frenkel, Jacob A., and Harry G. Johnson, eds. 1976. *The Monetary Approach to the Balance of Payments.* London: Allen and Unwin.

Frenkel, Jacob A., and Michael L. Mussa. 1985. Asset markets, exchange rates and the balance of payments. In *Handbook of International Economics*, vol. 2, ed. by Ronald W. Jones and Peter B. Kenen. Amsterdam: North Holland, pp. 680–747.

Frenkel, Jacob A., and Assaf Razin. 1985a. Government spending, debt and international economic interdependence. *Economic Journal* 95:619–39.

Frenkel, Jacob A., and Assaf Razin 1985b. Fiscal expenditures and international economic interdependence. *International Economic Policy Coordination*, ed. by Willem H. Buiter and Richard C. Marston. Cambridge: Cambridge University Press, pp. 37–73.

Frenkel, Jacob A., and Assaf Razin. 1986a. The international transmission and effects of fiscal policies. *American Economic Review* 76:330–35.

Frenkel, Jacob A., and Assaf Razin. 1986b. The international transmission and effects of fiscal policies. *American Economic Review* 76:330–35.

Frenkel, Jacob A., and Assaf Razin. 1986c. Fiscal policies in the world economy. *Journal of Political Economy* 94, part 1: 564–94.

Frenkel, Jacob A., and Assaf Razin. 1986d. Real exchange rates, interest rates and fiscal policies. *Economic Studies Quarterly* 37:99–113.

Frenkel, Jacob A., and Assaf Razin. 1987a. The international transmission of fiscal expenditures and budget deficits in the world economy. In *Economic Policy in Theory and Practice*, ed. by Assaf Razin and Efraim Sadka. London: Macmillan, pp. 51–96.

Frenkel, Jacob A., and Assaf Razin. 1987b. The Mundell-Fleming model: A quarter century later. *IMF Staff Papers* 34:567–620.

Frenkel, Jacob A., and Assaf Razin. 1988a. Exchange rate management viewed as tax policies. *European Economic Review* 33:761–81.

Frenkel, Jacob A., and Assaf Razin. 1988b. *Spending, Taxes and Deficits; International-Intertemporal Approach.* Princeton Studies in International Finance 63. International Finance Section.

Frenkel, Jacob A., and Assaf Razin. 1989. International effects of tax reforms. *Economic Journal* 99:38–59.

Frenkel Jacob A., and Assaf Razin. 1992. Fiscal policies in open economies. In *The Now Pelgrave Dictionary of Money and Finance*, ed. by Peter Newman. London: Macmillan.

Frenkel, Jacob A., Assaf Razin, and Efraim Sadka. 1991. *International Taxation in an Integrated World*. Cambridge: MIT Press.

Frenkel, Jacob A., Assaf Razin, and Steve Symansky. 1990. International spillovers of taxation. In *International Aspects of Taxation*, ed. by A. Razin and J. Slemrod. Chicago: University of Chicago Press.

Frenkel, Jacob A., Assaf Razin, and Steve Symansky. 1991. The international macroeconomic effects of VAT harmonization. *IMF Staff Papers* 38.

Frenkel Jacob A., and Carlos A. Rodriguez. 1975. Portfolio equilibrium and the balance of payments: A monetary approach. *American Economy Review* 65:674–88.

Froot, Kenneth A. 1988. Credibility, real interest rates, and the optimal speed of trade liberalization. *Journal of International Economics* 25:712–93.

Fried, Joel. 1980. The intergenerational distribution of the gains from technical change and from international trade. *Canadian Journal of Economics* 13:65–81.

Friedman, Milton. 1957. *A Theory of the Consumption Function*. Princeton: Princeton University Press.

Friedman, Milton. 1992. Do old fallacies ever die? *Journal of Economic Literature* 21:29–32.

Gale, David. 1973. Pure exchange equilibrium of dynamic economic models. *Journal of Economic Theory* 6:12–36.

Ghez, Gilbert R., and Gary S. Becker. 1975. *The Allocation of Time and Goods over the Life Cycle*. New York: Columbia University Press.

Ghosh, Atish R., and Jonathan D. Ostry. 1994a. Export instability and the external balance in developing countries. *IMF Staff Papers* 41:214–35.

Ghosh, Atish R., and Jonathan D. Ostry. 1994b. Have external deficits in developing countries been excessive? Mimeo. International Monetary Fund.

Ghosh, Atish R., and Jonathan D. Ostry. 1995. The current account in developing countries: A perspective from the consumption smoothing approach. *World Bank Economic Review* 9:305–33.

Giavazzi, Francesco, and Macro Pagano. 1990. Can fiscal contractions be expansionary? Tales of two small European countries. *NBER Macroeconomics Annual*, ed. by Olivier Blanchard and Stanley Fischer. Cambridge: MIT Press.

Giovannini, Alberto. 1989. National tax systems vs. European capital market. *Economic Policy* 9:345–86.

Giovannini, A. 1990. Reforming capital income taxation in open economies: Theoretical issues. In *Reforming Capital Income Taxation*, ed. by H. Siebert. Tubingen: Mohr.

Glick, Reuven, and Kenneth S. Rogoff. 1992. Global versus country-specific productivity shocks and the current account. NBER working paper 4140. August. (Also issued as *International Finance Discussion Paper 443*. Washington: Board of Governors of the Federal Reserve System. April 1993.)

Glick, Reuven, and Kenneth Rogoff. 1995. Global versus country-specific productivity shocks and the current account. *Journal of Monetary Economics* 36:39–64.

Greenwood, Jeremy. 1983. Expectations, the exchange rate and the current account. *Journal of Monetary Economics* 12:543–69.

Greenwood, Jeremy, and Kent P. Kimbrough. 1985. Capital controls and fiscal policy in the world economy. *Canadian Journal of Economics* 18:743–65.

Greenwood, Jeremy, and Kent P. Kimbrough. 1986. An investigation in the theory of foreign exchange controls. Working paper 86 (13). Duke University.

Gregory, R. G. 1976. Some implications of the growth of the mineral sector. *Australian Journal of Agricultural Economics* 20:71–91.

Gordon, Roger H. 1986, Taxation of investment and savings in a world economy. *American Economic Review* 76:1087–1102.

Gordon, Roger H., and James Levinsohn. 1990. The linkage between domestic taxes and border taxes. In *Taxation in the Global Economy*, ed. by A. Razin and J. Slemrod. Chicago: University of Chicago Press.

Hall, Robert E. 1978. Stochastic implications of the life cycle–permanent income hypothesis: Theory and evidence. *Journal of Political Economy* 86:971–87.

Hamada, Koichi. 1976. Strategic analysis of monetary interdependence. *Journal of Political Economy* 84, part 1: 677–700.

Hamada, Koichi. 1985. *The Political Economy of International Monetary Interdependence*, Cambridge: MIT Press.

Harberger, Arnold C. 1950. Currency depreciation, income and the balance of trade. *Journal of Political Economy* 58:47–60.

Hayashi, Fumio. 1982. Tobin's marginal q and average q: A neoclassical interpretation. *Econometrica* 50:213–24.

Heckman, James J. 1974. Shadow prices, market wages and labor supply. *Econometrica* 42:679–94.

Helpman, Elhanan. 1981. An exploration in the theory of exchange rate regimes. *Journal of Political Economy* 89:865–90.

Helpman, Elhanan. 1991. The simple analytics of debt-equity swaps and debt forgiveness. *American Economic Review* 81:20–35.

Helpman, Elhanan, and Assaf Razin. 1978. *A Theory of International Trade under Uncertainty*. New York: Academic Press.

Helpman, Elhanan, and Assaf Razin. 1979. Towards a consistent comparison of alternative exchange rate regimes. *Canadian Journal of Economics* 12:394–409.

Helpman, Elhanan, and Assaf Razin. 1982. A comparison of exchange rate regimes in the presence of imperfect capital markets. *International Economic Review* 23:365–88.

Helpman, Elhanan, and Assaf Razin. 1984. The role of saving and investment in exchange rate determination under alternative monetary mechanisms. *Journal of Monetary Economics* 13:307–25.

Helpman, Elhanan, and Assaf Razin. 1987. Exchange rate management: Intertemporal tradeoffs. *American Economic Review* 77:107–23.

Hierro, Jorge, and Allen Sanginés. 1991. Public sector behavior in Mexico. In *The Public Sector and the Latin American Crisis*, ed. by Felipe Larraín and Marcelo Selowsky. San Francisco: International Center for Economic Growth.

Horne, Jocelyn. 1991. Criteria of external sustainability. *European Economic Review* 35:1559–74.

Hotelling, Harold. 1933. Review of *The Triumph of Mediocrity in Business*, by Horace Secrist. *Journal of the American Statistical Association*: 463–65.

Hubbard, R. Glenn, and Kenneth L. Judd. 1986. Liquidity constraints, fiscal policy, and consumption. *Brookings Paper on Economic Activity* 1:1–50.

Ingersoll, Jonathan E., Jr. 1987. *A Theory of Financial Decision Making*. New York: Rowman and Littlefield.

International Monetary Fund. *International Financial Statistics*. Washington: IMF, various issues.

International Monetary Fund. *World Economic Outlook*. Washington: IMF, various issues.

International Monetary Fund. 1991. Determinants and systemic consequences of international capital flows. *IMF Occasional Paper* 77 (March).

International Monetary Fund. 1995a. *World Economic Outlook*. Washington: IMF.

International Monetary Fund. 1995b. *International Capital Markets: Developments, Prospects and Policy Issues*. Washington: IMF.

Inversen, Carl. 1935. *Aspects of the Theory of International Capital Movements*. London: Oxford University Press.

Jappelli, Tullio, and Marco Pagano. 1994. Savings, growth, and liquidity constraints. *Quarterly Journal of Economics* 109:83–109.

Johnson, Harry G. 1956. The transfer problem and exchange stability. *Journal of Political Economy* 59:212–25.

Johnson, Harry G. 1958. *International Trade and Economic Growth*. London: Allen and Unwin.

Jones, Charles I. 1995. Time series tests of endogenous growth models. *Quarterly Journal of Economics* 110:495–525.

Jones, Larry E., and Rodolfo E. Manuelli. 1990. A convex model of equilibrium growth. *Journal of Political Economy* 98:1008–38.

Judd, Kenneth L. 1987. A dynamic theory of factor taxation. *American Economic Review* 77:42–48.

Judd, K. L. 1985. The welfare cost of factor taxation in a perfect foresight model. *Journal of Political Economy* 93:298–319.

Kaldor, Nicholas. 1963. Capital accumulation and economic growth. In *Proceedings of a Conference Held by the International Economics Association*, ed. by Friedrich A. Lutz and Douglas C. Hauge. London: MacMillan.

Kehoe, Patrick. 1989. Policy cooperation among benevolent governments may be undesirable. *Review of Economic Studies* 56:289–96.

Kenen, Peter B. 1985. Macroeconomic theory and policy: How the closed economy was opened. In *Handbook of International Economics*, vol. 2, ed. by Ronald W. Jones and Peter B. Kenen. Amsterdam: North Holland, pp. 625–77.

Keynes, John M. 1929. The German transfer problem. *Economic Journal* 39:1–7.

Kimbrough, Kent P. 1986. Foreign aid and optimal fiscal policy. *Canadian Journal of Economics* 17:35–61.

King, Mervin A. 1983. The economics of saving. NBER working paper 1247. October.

King, Robert G., Charles I. Plosser, and Sergio T. Rebelo. 1988. Production, growth, and business cycles I: The basic neoclassical model. *Journal of Monetary Economics* 21:195–232.

King, Robert G., and Sergio T. Rebelo. 1990. Public policy and economic growth: Developing neoclassical implications. *Journal of Political Economy* 98:S126–49.

Kletzer, Kenneth, M. 1984. Asymmetries of information and LDC borrowing with sovereign risk. *Economic Journal* 94:287–307.

Kochin, Levis. 1974. Are future taxes discounted by consumers? *Journal of Money, Credit, and Banking* 6:389–94.

Koopmans, Tjalling C. 1965. On the concept of optimal economic growth. In *The Econometric Approach to Development Planning*. Amsterdam: North Holland, pp. 225–87.

Kormendi, Roger. 1983. Government debt, governments spending, and private sector behavior. *American Economic Review* 73:994–1010.

Kotlikoff, Laurence J. 1992. *Generational Accounting: Knowing Who Pays, and When, for What We Spend*. New York: Free Press.

Kotlikoff, Lawrence, J., Assaf Razin, and Robert W. Rosenthal. 1990. A strategic altruism model in which Ricardian equivalence does not hold. *Economic Journal* 100:1261–69.

Krugman, Paul R. 1985a. International debt-strategies in an uncertain world. In *International Debt and the Developing Countries*, ed. by Gordon W. Smith and John T. Cuddington. Washington: World Bank.

Krugman, Paul. 1985b. Is the strong dollar sustainable. In *The US Dollar—Recent Developments, Outlook and Policy Options*. Kansas City: Federal Reserve Bank of Kansas City.

Krugman, Paul R. 1990. Market based debt-reduction schemes. In *Analytical Issues in Debt*, ed. by Jacob A. Frenkel, Michael P. Dooley, and Peter Wickham. Washington: IMF, pp. 258–78.

Kydland, Finn E., and Edward Prescott. 1980. A competitive theory of fluctuations and the feasibility and desirability of stabilization policy. In *Rational Expectations and Economic Policy*, ed. by Stanley Fischer. Chicago: University of Chicago Press, pp. 169–98.

Kydland, Finn E., and, Edward C. Prescott. 1992. Time to Build and Aggregate Fluctuations. *Econometrica* 50:1345–70.

Labán, Raúl, and Felipe Larraín. 1995. Continuity, change and the political economy of transition in Chile. In *Reform, Recovery and Growth*, ed. by Sebastian Edwards and Rudiger Dornbusch. Chicago: University of Chicago Press.

Larraín, Felipe. 1991. Public sector behavior in a highly indebted country: The contrasting Chilean experience. In *The Public Sector and the Latin American Crisis*, ed. by Felipe Larraín and Marcelo Selowsky. San Francisco: International Center for Economic Growth.

Larrañaga, O. 1989. *El Deficit del Sector Publico y la Politica Fiscal en Chile, 1978–87*. Santiago de Chile: ECLA.

Laursen, Svend, and Lloyd A. Metzler. 1950. Flexible exchange rates and the theory of employment. *Review of Economics and Statistics* 32:281–99.

Leiderman, Leonardo, and Mario I. Blejer. 1988. Modelling and testing Ricardian equivalence: A survey. *IMF Staff Papers* 35:1–35.

Leiderman, Leonardo, and Assaf Razin. 1988. Testing Ricardian neutrality with an intertemporal stochastic model. *Journal of Money Credit and Banking*. 20:1–21.

Leiderman, Leonardo, and Assaf Razin. 1991. Determinants of external imbalances: The role of taxes, government spending, and productivity. *Journal of the Japanese and International Economies* 5:421–50.

Lerner, Abba P. 1936. The symmetry between export and import taxes. *Economica* 3:306–13.

Levy, H., and H. Markowitz. 1979. Approximating expected utility by a function of mean and variance. *American Economic Review* 69:308–17.

Lopez Ramon, and Dani Rodrik. 1990. Trade restrictions with imported intermediate inputs: When does the trade balance improve? *Journal of Development Economics* 34:329–38.

Lucas, Robert E., Jr. 1967. Optimal investment policy and the flexible accelerator. *International Economic Review* 8:78–85.

Lucas, Robert E. Jr. 1978. Asset prices in an exchange economy. *Econometrica* 46:1429–45.

Lucas Robert E., Jr. 1980. Equilibrium in a pure currency economy. *Economic Inquiry* 18:203–20.

Lucas, Robert E. Jr. 1981. *Studies in Business Cycle Theory*. Cambridge: MIT Press.

Lucas, Robert E., Jr. 1982. Interest rates and currency prices in a two-country world. *Journal of Monetary Economics* 10:335–59.

Lucas, Robert E., Jr. 1988. On the mechanics of economic development. *Journal of Monetary Economics* 22:3–42.

Lucas, Robert E., Jr. 1990a. Supply side economics: An analytical review. *Oxford Economic Papers* 42:293–316.

Lucas, Robert E., Jr. 1990b. Why doesn't capital flow from rich to poor countries? *American Economic Review Papers and Proceedings* 80:92–96.

Lucas, Robert E., Jr., and Edward C. Prescott. 1971. Investment under uncertainty. *Econometrica* 39:659–81.

Lucas, Robert E., Jr., and Leonard A. Rapping. 1969. Real wages, employment and inflation. *Journal of Political Economy* 77:721–54.

Lucas, Robert E., Jr., and Nancy L. Stokey. 1983. Optimal fiscal and monetary policy in an economy without capital. *Journal of Monetary Economics* 12:55–93.

McAleese, Dermot, and F. Desmond McCarthy. 1989. Adjustment and external shocks in Ireland. PPS working paper 262. World Bank. August.

Machlup, Fritz. 1943. *International Trade and the National Income Multiplier*. Philadelphia: Blakiston.

MaCurdy, Thomas E. 1981. An empirical model of labor supply in a life cycle setting. *Journal of Political Economy* 89:1059–85.

McKinnon, Ronald I. 1969. Portfolio balance and international payments adjustment. In *Monetary Problems of the International Economy*, ed. by Alexander K. Swoboda and Robert A. Mundell. Chicago: University of Chicago Press, pp. 199–234.

Mankiw Gregory N. 1987. Government purchases and real interest rates. *Journal of Political Economy* 95:407–19.

Mankiw, Gregory N., Julio J. Rotemberg, and Lawrence H. Summers. 1985. Intertemporal substitution in macroeconomics. *Quarterly Journal of Economics* 100:225–51.

Marion, Nancy P. 1984. Nontraded goods, oil price increases, and the current account. *Journal of International Economics* 16:29–44.

Marston, Richard C. 1985. Stabilization policies in open economies. In *Handbook of International Economics*, vol. 2, ed. by Ronald W. Jones and Peter B. Kenen. Amsterdam: North Holland, pp. 859–916.

Masson, Paul R., Jeroen Kremers, and Jocelyn Horne. 1994. Net foreign assets and international adjustment: The United States, Japan and Germany. *Journal of International Money and Finance* 13:27–40.

Meade, James E. 1951. *The Theory of International Economic Policy: The Balance of Payments*, vol. 1. Oxford: Oxford University Press.

Meese, Richard A., and Kenneth Rogoff. 1988. Was it real? The exchange rate–interest differential relation over the modern floating rate period. *Journal of Finance* 43:933–48.

Mendoza, Enrique G. 1991a. Real business cycles in a small open economy. *American Economic Review* 81:797–810.

Mendoza Enrique G. 1991b. A quantitative examination of current account dynamics in equilibrium models of barter economies. IMF draft.

Mendoza, Enrique G. 1992. The terms of trade and economic fluctuations. IMF working paper 92/98, Washington. December.

Mendoza, Enrique G. 1995. The terms of trade and economic fluctuations. FRB discussion paper. February.

Merton, R. C. 1971. Optimum consumption and portfolio rules in a continuous-time model. *Journal of Economic Theory* 3:373–413.

Metzer, Allan H., Alex Cukierman, and Scott F. Richard. 1991. *Political Economy*. New York: Oxford Economic Press.

Metzler Lloyd A. 1942a. Underemployment equilibrium in international trade. *Econometrica* 10:97–112.

Metzler, Lloyd A. 1942b. The transfer problem reconsidered. *Journal of Political Economy* 50:397–414.

Milesi-Ferretti, Gian Maria, and Assaf Razin. 1996a. Persistent Current-Account Deficits: A Warning Signal?. International Journal of Finance and Economics 1:103–160.

Milesi-Ferretti, Gian Maria, and Assaf Razin. 1996b. *Current-Account Sustainability*. Princeton Essays in International Finance. Princeton University, International Finance Section, Princeton, NJ.

Modigliani, Franco. 1961. Long-run implications of alternative fiscal policies and the burden of the national debt. *Economic Journal* 71:730–55.

Modigliani, Franco. 1987. The economics of public deficits. In *Economic Policy in Theory and Practice*, ed. by Assaf Razin and Efraim Sadka. London: Macmillan, pp. 3–44.

Modigliani, Franco, and Richard Brumberg. 1954. Utility analysis and the consumption function: An interpretation of cross section data. In *Post-Keynesian Economics*, ed. by Kenneth K. Kurihara. New Brunswick: Rutgers University Press, pp. 383–436.

Mundell, Robert A. 1960. The pure theory of international trade. *American Economic Review* 50:67–110.

Mundell, Robert A. 1964. A reply: Capital mobility and size. *Canadian Journal of Economics and Political Science* 30:421–31.

Mundell, Robert A. 1968. *International Economics.* New York: Macmillan.

Mundell, Robert A. 1971. *Monetary Theory.* Pacific Palisades: Goodyear.

Murphy, Robert G. 1986. Tariffs, non-traded goods and fiscal policy. *The International Trade Journal* 1:193–211.

Musgrave, Peggy. 1987. International tax competition and gains from tax harmonization. NBER working paper 3152. October.

Mussa, Michael L. 1979. Macroeconomic interdependence and the exchange rate regime. In *International Economic Policy: Theory and Evidence*, ed. by Radiger Dornbusch and Jacob A. Frenkel. Baltimore: Johns Hopkins University Press, pp. 160–204.

Neary, J. Peter, and Douglas D. Purvis. 1982. Sectoral shocks in a dependent economy: Long-run adjustment and short-run accommodation. *Scandinavian Journal of Economics* 84:229–53.

Nerlove, Marc, Assaf Razin, and Efraim Sadka. 1988. A bequest-constrained economy: Welfare analysis. *Journal of Public Economics* 37:203–20.

Nordhaus, W. 1975. The political business cycle. *Review of Economic Studies* 42: 169–190.

Obstfeld, Maurice. 1982. Aggregate spending and the terms of trade: Is there a Laursen Metzler effect? *Quarterly Journal of Economics* 97:251–70.

Obstfeld, Maurice. 1986a. Capital controls, the dual exchange rate and devaluation. *Journal of International Economics* 20:1–20.

Obstfeld, Maurice. 1986b. Capital mobility in the world economy: Theory and measurement. *Carnegie-Rochester Conference Series on Public Policy* 24:55–103.

Obstfeld, Maurice. 1994. The logic of currency crises. *Cahiers Economiques et Monétaires* 3:1–19.

Obstfeld, Maurice. 1995. International capital mobility in the 1990s. In *Understanding Interdependence: The Macroeconomics of the Open Economy*, ed. by Peter B. Kenen. Princeton: Princeton University Press.

Obstfeld, Maurice. 1996. Models of currency crises with self-fulfilling features. *European Economic Review*, forthcoming.

Obstfeld, Maurice, and Kenneth Rogoff. 1996. Foundations of international macro-economics. Cambridge: MIT Press, forthcoming.

Obstfeld, Maurice, and Kenneth Rogoff. 1995. The intertemporal approach to the current account. In *Handbook of International Economics*, vol. 3, ed. by Gene Grossman and Kenneth Rogoff. New York: Elsevier Science Publishers.

Obstfeld, Maurice, and Alan C. Stockman. 1985. Exchange rate dynamics. In *Handbook of International Economics*, vol. 2, ed. by Ronald W. Jones and Peter B. Kenen. Amsterdam: North Holland, pp. 917–77.

O'Driscoll, Gerald P. 1977. The Ricardian nonequivalence theorem. *Journal of Political Economy* 85:207–10.

OECD. *Economic Surveys: Ireland*, various years.

OECD, *Economic Surveys: Australia*, various years.

Ohlin, Bertil. 1929. The reparation problem: A discussion. *Economic Journal* 39:172–78.

Ostry, Jonathan D. 1988. The balance of trade, terms of trade, and real exchange rate: An intertemporal optimizing framework. *IMF Staff Papers* 35:541–73.

Ostry, Jonathan D. 1989. Government purchases and relative prices in a two-country world. IMF working paper 89/28. April.

Ostry, Jonathan D. 1990. Tariffs and the current account: The role of initial distortions. *Canadian Journal of Economics* 23:348–56.

Ostry, Jonathan D. 1991a. Tariffs, real exchange rates, and the trade balance in a two-country world. *European Economic Review* 35:1127–42.

Ostry, Jonathan D. 1991b. Trade liberalization in developing countries: Initial trade distortions and imported intermediate inputs. *IMF Staff Papers* 38:447–79.

Ostry, Jonathan D. 1992a. Trade restrictions with imported intermediate inputs: A comment. *Journal of Development Economics* 38:23–32.

Oudiz, Gilles, and Jeffrey D. Sachs. 1985. International policy coordination in dynamic macroeconomic models. In *International Economic Policy Coordination*, ed. by Willem H. Buiter and Richard C. Marston. Cambridge: Cambridge University Press, pp. 274–319.

Pechman, Joseph, A., ed. 1988. *World Tax Reform: A Progress Report*. Washington: Brookings Institution.

Penati, Alessandro. 1987. Government spending and the real exchange rate. *Journal of International Economics* 22:237–56.

Perraudin, W. P. M., and T. Pujol. 1991. European fiscal harmonization and the French economy. *IMF Staff Papers*, October.

Persson, Torsten. 1984. Real transfers in fixed exchange rate systems and the international adjustment mechanism. *Journal of Monetary Economics* 13:349–69.

Persson, Torsten. 1985. Deficits and intergenerational welfare in open economies. *Journal of International Economics* 19:1–19.

Persson, Torsten, and Lars E. O. Svensson. 1985. Current account dynamics and the terms of trade: Harberger-Laursen-Metzler two generations later. *Journal of Political Economy* 93:43–65.

Persson, Torsten, and Guido Tabellini. 1990. *Macroeconomic Policy, Credibility and Politics*. New York: Harwood Academic Publishers.

Pitchford, John. 1989. *Australia's Foreign Debt: Myths and Realities*. London: Allen and Unwin.

Pitchford, John, and Stephen J. Turnovsky, eds. 1977. *Applications of Control Theory of Economic Analysis*. Amsterdam: North-Holland.

Polak, Jacques J. 1957. Monetary analysis of income formation and payments problems. *IMF Staff Papers* 6:1–50.

Poterba, James M., and Lawrence H. Summers. 1986. Finite lifetimes and the crowding-out effects of budget deficits. NBER working paper 1955.

Prais, S. J. 1961. Some mathematical notes on the quantity theory of money in an open economy. *IMF Staff Papers* 8: 212–26.

Purvis, Douglas D. 1985. Public sector deficits, international capital movements, and the domestic economy: The medium-term is the message. *Canadian Journal of Economics* 18:723–42.

Quah, Danny. 1993. Galton's fallacy and of the convergence hypothesis. *Scandinavian Journal of Economics* 95:42–63.

Ramsey, Frank P. 1928. A mathematical theory of saving. *Economic Journal* 38:543–59.

Razin, Assaf. 1972. Investment in human capital and economic growth. *Metroeconomica* 24:100–16.

Razin, Assaf. 1984. Capital movements, intersectoral resource shifts and the trade balance. *European Economic Review* 26:135–52.

Razin, Assaf. 1990. Fiscal policies and the integrated world stock market. *Journal of International Economics* 29:109–22.

Razin, Assaf. 1995. The dynamic-optimizing approach to the current account: Theory and evidence. In *Understanding Interdependence: The Macroeconomics of the Open Economy*, ed. by Peter B. Kenen. Princeton: Princeton University Press.

Razin, Assaf, and Uri Ben-Zion. 1975. An intergenerational model of population growth. *American Economic Review* 69:923–33.

Razin, Assaf, and Andrew K. Rose. 1994. Business cycle volatility and openness: An exploratory analysis. In *Capital Mobility: The Impact on Consumption, Investment and Growth*, ed. by Leonardo Leiderman and Assaf Razin. Cambridge: Cambridge University Press.

Razin, Assaf, and Efraim Sadka, eds. 1987. *Economic Policy in Theory and Practice: Essays in Memory of Abba P. Lerner*. London: Macmillan.

Razin, Assaf, and Efraim Sadka. 1991. Efficient investment incentives in the presence of capital flight. *Journal of International Economics* 31:171–81.

Razin, A., and E. Sadka. 1991. International tax competition and gains from tax harmonization. *Economics Letters* 37:69–76.

Razin, Assaf, and Efraim Sadka. 1996. Fiscal balance during inflation, disinflation and immigration: Policy lessons. In *Macroeconomic Dimensions of Public Finance: Essays in Honor of Vito Tanzi*, ed. by M. Blejer and T. Ter-Minassian. IMF.

Razin, Assaf, and Lars E. O. Svensson. 1983. The current account and the optimal government debt. *Journal of International Money and Finance* 2:215–24.

Razin, A., and L. E. O. Svensson. 1983. Trade taxes and the current account. *Economic Letters* 13:55–58.

Razin, Assaf, and Chi-Wa Yuen. 1995a. Utilitarian tradeoff between population growth and income growth. *Journal of Population Economics* 8:81–87.

Razin, Assaf, and Chi-Wa Yuen. 1995b. Factor mobility and economic growth: Tax-driven divergence. Working paper.

Razin, Assaf, and Chi-Wa Yuen. 1995c. Factor mobility and income growth: Two convergence hypotheses. NBER working paper 5135.

Razin, Assaf, and Chi-Wa Yuen. 1996. Capital income taxation and long run growth: New perspectives. *Journal of Public Economics* 59:239–63.

Rebelo, Sergio T. 1991. Long run policy analysis and long run growth. *Journal of Political Economy* 99:500–21.

Rebelo, Sergio T. 1992. Growth in open economies. *Carnegie-Rochester Conference Series on Public Policy* 36:5–46.

Robinson, R. 1952. A graphical analysis of the foreign trade multiplier. *Economic Journal* 62:546–64.

Rodriguez, Carlos A. 1979. Short- and long-run effects of monetary and fiscal policies under flexible exchange rates and perfect capital mobility. *American Economic Review* 69:176–82.

Rodrik, Dani. 1987. Trade and capital account liberalization in a Keynesian economy. *Journal of International Economics* 23:113–29.

Rodrik, Dani. 1989. Promises, promises: Credible policy reform via signalling. *Economic Journal* 99:756–72.

Rodrik, Dani. 1995. Getting interventions right: How South Korea and Taiwan grew rich. *Economic Policy* 20:55–107.

Rogoff, Kenneth. 1985. Can international policy coordination be counterproductive? *Journal of International Economics* 18:199–217.

Rogoff, Kenneth. 1986. Reputational constraints on monetary policy. NBER working paper 1986. July.

Rogoff, Kenneth S. 1992. Traded goods consumption smoothing and the random walk behavior of the real exchange rate. NBER working paper 4119. October.

Rojas-Suarez, Liliana, and Steven Weisbrod. 1995. Financial fragilities in Latin America: The 1980s and the 1990s. IMF occasional paper 132. October.

Rogoff, Ken. 1988. Equilibrium political budget cycles. *American Economic Review* 80:21–36.

Rogoff, Ken, and Ann Sibert. 1989. Elections and macroeconomic policy cycles. *Review of Economic Studies* 55:1–6.

Roubini, Nouriel. 1991. Economic and political determinants of budget deficits in developing countries. *Journal of International Money and Finance* 10:549–72.

Roubini, Nouriel, and Jeffrey Sachs. 1989a. Political and economic determinants of budget deficits in the industrial democracies. *European Economic Review* (May): 903–33.

Roubini, Nouriel, and Jeffrey Sachs. 1989b. Government spending and budget deficits in the industrial countries. *Economic Policy* 8:99–132.

Rueff, Jacques. 1929. Mr. Keynes' views on the transfer problem: A criticism. *Economic Journal* 39:388–99.

Sachs, Jeffrey D. 1981. The current account and macroeconomic adjustment in the 1970s. *Brookings Papers on Economic Activity* 1:201–68.

Sachs, Jeffrey. 1982. The current account in the macroeconomic adjustment process. *Scandinavian Journal of Economics* 84:147–60.

Sachs, Jeffrey D. 1984. Theoretical issues in international borrowing. *Princeton Studies in International Finance* 54 (July).

Sachs, Jeffrey D. 1985. External debt and macroeconomic performance in Latin America and East Asia. *Brookings Papers on Economic Activity* 2:523–74.

Sachs, Jeffrey, Aaron Tornell, and Andrés Velasco. 1995. The collapse of the Mexican Peso: What have we learned? NBER working paper 5142.

Sachs, Jeffrey, and Andrew Warner. 1995. Economic reform and the process of global integration. *Brookings Papers on Economic Activity* 1:1–95.

Samuelson, Paul A. 1952. The transfer problem and transport costs: The terms of trade when impediments are absent. *Economic Journal* 62:278–304.

Samuelson, Paul A. 1958. An exact consumption-loan model with or without the social contrivance of money. *Journal of Political Economy* 66:467–82.

Samuelson, Paul A. 1964. Theoretical notes on trade problems. *Review of Economics and Statistics* 46:145–54.

Sargent, Thomas J. 1978. Estimation of dynamic labor demand schedules under rational expectations. *Journal of Political Economy* 86:1009–44.

Sargent, Thomas J. 1987. *Macroeconomic Theory.* 2d ed. New York: Academic Press.

Sinn, Hans-Werner. 1990a. Tax harmonization and tax competition in Europe. NBER working paper 3263. February.

Sinn, Hans-Werner 1990b. Tax competition and tax harmonization in the European Community. *European Economic Review* 34:489–504.

Solow, Robert M. 1956. A contribution to theory of economic growth. *Quarterly Journal of Economics* 70:65–94.

Soon, Cho. 1993. The dynamics of Korean economic development. Washington: Institute for International Economics.

Stiglitz, Joseph, and Andrew Weiss. 1981. Credit rationing in models with imperfect information. *American Economic Review* 71:393–410.

Stockman, Alan C. 1980. A theory of exchange rate determination. *Journal of Political Economy* 88:673–98.

Stokey, Nancy L., and Sergio T. Rebelo. 1995. Growth effects of flat rate taxes. *Journal of Political Economy* 103:519–50.

Summers, Robert, and Alan Heston. 1991. The Penn World Tables (Mark 5): An expanded set of international comparisons, 1950–1988. *Quarterly Journal of Economics* 106:327–68.

Sutherland, Alan. 1995. Fiscal crises and demand: Can high public debt reverse the effects of fiscal policy? CEPR discussion paper 1246. September.

Svensson, Lars E. O. 1981. Oil prices, welfare and the trade balance. *Quarterly Journal of Economics* 94:649–72.

Svensson, Lars E. O. 1988. Trade in risky assets. *American Economic Review* 78:375–94.

Svensson, Lars E. O., and Assaf Razin. 1993. The terms of trade and the current account: The Harberger-Laursen-Metzler effect. *Journal of Political Economy* 91: 91–125.

Swoboda, Alexander K., and Rudiger Dornbusch. 1973. Adjustment, policy, and monetary equilibrium in a two-country model. In *International Trade and Money*, ed. by Michael G. Connolly and Alexander K. Swoboda. London: Allen and Unwin, 225–61.

Tabellini, G., and A. Alesina. 1990. Voting on the budget deficit. *American Economic Review* 80:37–52.

Tait, Alan A. 1988. *Value Added Tax: International Practice and Problems*. Washington: IMF.

Tanzi, Vito, and Bovenberg, Lans. 1989. Economic interdependence and the international implications of supply-side policies. In *A Supply-Side for Germany*, ed. by G. Fels, and George M. von Furstenberg. New York, pp. 153–80.

Tobin, James 1969. A general equilibrium approach to monetary theory. *Journal of Money, Credit, and Banking* 1:15–29.

Turnovsky, Stephen J. 1995. *Methods of Macroeconomic Dynamics*. Cambridge: MIT Press.

Uzawa, Hirofumi. 1965. Optimum technical change in an aggregative model of economic growth. *International Economic Review* 6:18–31.

Uzawa, Hirofumi. 1969. Time preference and the Penrose effect in a two-class model of economic growth. *Journal of Political Economy* 77, part 2: 628–52.

Van Wijnbergen, Sweder. 1986. On fiscal deficits, the real exchange rate and the world rate of interest. *European Economic Review* 30:1013–23.

Van Wijnbergen, Sweder. 1987. Tariffs, employment and the current account: Real wage resistance and the macroeconomics of protectionism. *International Economic Review* 28:691–706.

Velasco, Andrés. 1993. Liberalization, crisis, intervention: The Chilean financial system, 1975–85. In *Banking Crises: Cases and Issues*, ed. by Tomás J. T. Baliño and V. Sundararajan. Washington: IMF.

Velasco, Andrés. 1993. Are balance of payments crises rational? A dynamic game approach. Mimeo. New York University.

Weil, Philippe. 1987. Overlapping families of infinitely lived agents. *Quarterly Journal of Economics* 110:33–50.

Xie, Danyang. 1994. Divergence in economic performance: Transitional dynamics with multiple equilibria. *Journal of Economic Theory* 63:97–112.

Yaari, Menahem E. 1965. Uncertain lifetime, life insurance, and the theory of the consumer. *Review of Economic Studies* 32:137–50.

Yuen, Chi-Wa. 1991. Taxation, human capital accumulation, and economic growth. Ph.D. dissertation. University of Chicago.

Appendix

Computer Routines for Solving Stochastic Dynamic Models

The following GAUSS procedure entitled SOLVE.PRC, adapted from the MATLAB programs of King, Plosser, and Rebelo (1988), can be used to solve systems of linear stochastic dynamical equations. It requires as inputs the dimensions of the system, matrices that specify the relations among the control, state, costate, other observable flow, and exogenous forcing variables. It generates as outputs the eigenvalues of the dynamical system, the state transition matrix, and an matrix linking the costate, control, and flow variables to the state vector. Using these outputs, one can easily simulate solution paths, carry out impulse response exercises, and compute moments among the variables.

To begin, one has to compute the (detrended) steady state, around which the originally nonlinear dynamical system is to be linearized. After linearization, the control and state-costate equations have to be specified as follows:

$$[Mcc]\Delta \hat{Y}_t = [Mcs]\Delta \hat{S}_t + [Mce]\Delta \hat{F}_t$$

and

$$[Mss0]\Delta \hat{S}_{t+1} + [Mss1]\Delta \hat{S}_t = [Msc0]\Delta \hat{Y}_{t+1} + [Msc1]\Delta \hat{Y}_t$$
$$+ [Mse0]\Delta \hat{F}_{t+1} + [Mse1]\Delta \hat{F}_t,$$

where [M?*] are matrices that relate ? to * (c for control, s for state-costate, and e for exogenous; 0 means same period, and 1 means one-period lag). $\hat{Y}$ is the control vector, $\hat{S}$ is the state-costate vector (i.e., state vector stacked on top of the costate vector), $\hat{F}$ is the forcing vector, and Δ denotes proportionate deviation from the steady state. The dimensions of the matrices $[Mcc]$, $[Mcs]$, $[Mce]$, $[Mss]$, $[Msc]$, and $[Mse]$ are $nc * nc$, $nc * 2ns$, $nc * nex$, $2ns * 2ns$, $2ns * nc$, and $2ns * nex$, respectively, where nc is the number of control variables, ns the number of state (costate) variables, and nex the number of exogenous forcing variables. One can also relate other flow variables to the control, state-costate, and exogenous forcing variables through a set of F matrices: $[FVc0]$, $[FVc1]$, $[FVse0]$, $[FVse1]$, and $[FV1]$.

@ SOLVE.PRC @

```
proc (2) = solve(nc,ns,nex,Mcc,Mcs,Mce,Mss0,Mss1,Msc0,Msc1,Mse0,Mse1,
        FVc0,FVc1,FVse0,FVse1,FVl);
local
@ - Local variables in argument list - @
    nc, ns, nex, mcc, mcs, mce, mss0, mss1, msc0, msc1, mse0, mse1, fvc0,
    fvc1, fvse0, fvse1, fvl,
@ - Other local variables - @
    msss0, msss1, msse0, msse1, w, r, q, mu, vai, p, vei, amu, amu1,
    i, ps, mu1, mu2, p11, p12, p21, p22, ps11, ps12, ps21, ps22, rke,
    rle, qke, qle, sp1, sp2, klk, ktl, rhoaa, rhogg, rhoga, rhoag, rho,
    fl, lee, irho, mu2i, dsum, kec, ule, ulk, mke, mke1, lke, z, mock,
    mocl, moce, mocke, fke, mh;
/* Part 1: DYN.PRG */
/* FUNDAMENTAL STATE-COSTATE DIFFERENCE EQUATION
    Derive fundamental difference equation for states and co-states.
    The memnonic MS is used to indicate the M* matrices in the technical
    appendix of King, Plosser, and Rebelo (1988). */

MSss0 = Mss0 — Msc0*(inv(Mcc)*Mcs);
MSss1 = Mss1 — Msc1*(inv(Mcc)*Mcs);
MSse0 = Mse0 + Msc0*(inv(Mcc)*Mce);
MSse1 = Mse1 + Msc1*(inv(Mcc)*Mce);

/* Put the fundamental difference equation in normal form. */

W = — inv(MSss0)*MSss1;
R = inv(MSss0)*MSse0;
Q = inv(MSss0)*MSse1;
```

/* EIGENVECTOR-EIGENVALUE DECOMPOSITION OF STATE
TRANSITION MATRIX
    Compute the eigenvalues (MU) and eigenvectors (P) of the matrix W. */

{MU,vai,P,vei} = eigrg2(W);

/* Order the eigenvalues, in order of ascending absolute value
    Sort by the absolute value of the eigenvalues, then reorder the
    columns of the eigenvector matrix (P) by this sort.   */

```
amu = abs(MU) ~ P' ~ MU;
amu1 = sortc(amu,1);
MU = amu1[.,rows(W) + 2];
P = amu1[.,2:rows(W) + 1]';
i = 1;
do until i > rows(P);
P[.,i] = P[.,i]./P[1,i];
i = i + 1;
endo;
```

/* Next, we need to order the eigenvalue (diagonal) matrix in order of
    ascending absolute value. As it was unclear how to accomplish this,
    the matrix is simply computed from the standard diagonalization
    formula given the sorted eigenvalue matrix and its inverse, denoted PS
    (matches the technical appendix notation, where the inverse of P is
    denoted with a star).   */

```
PS = inv(P);
MU = PS*W*P;
" ";
"Computing Markovian Decision Rules";

"MU = ";;MU;
```

/* PARTITIONING MATRICES
    The P, PS, MU, R, and Q matrices must be partitioned, as discussed in
    the technical appendix section B.2, for the purpose of computing the
    different components of the solution.   */

```
MU1 = MU[1:ns,1:ns];
MU2 = MU[ns + 1:2*ns,ns + 1:2*ns];

P11 = P[1:ns,1:ns];
P12 = P[1:ns,ns + 1:2*ns];
P21 = P[ns + 1:2*ns,1:ns];
P22 = P[ns + 1:2*ns,ns + 1:2*ns];
```

```
PS11 = PS[1:ns,1:ns];
PS12 = PS[1:ns,ns + 1:2*ns];
PS21 = PS[ns + 1:2*ns,1:ns];
PS22 = PS[ns + 1:2*ns,ns + 1:2*ns];

Rke = R[1:ns,1:nex];
Rle = R[ns + 1:2*ns,1:nex];
Qke = Q[1:ns,1:nex];
Qle = Q[ns + 1:2*ns,1:nex];
```

/* COMPOSITE EXPRESSIONS */
/* The solution for the shadow price involves some composite expressions.
   These are: */

```
SP1 = − inv(MU2)*(PS21*Rke + PS22*Rle);
SP2 = − inv(MU2)*(PS21*Qke + PS22*Qle);
```

/* The solution for the capital stock involves some composite expressions.
   These are the following, where the memnonic is that the KLK gives the
   response of capital to lagged capital and the matrix KTL gives the
   response to the transformed shadow price.   */

```
KLK = P11*MU1*inv(P11);
KTL = (P11*MU1*PS12 + P12*MU2*PS22)*inv(PS22);
```

/* Part 2: MDR.PRG */
/* COMPUTATION OF DECISION RULES
   This program computes the Markovian decision rules (MDR) for the
   specified linear dynamic model. The structure of forcing variables
   can be altered without re-running part 1 of the program (DYN.EX).
   Let the exogenous variables be generated by an nex*nex VAR(1)
   process. Let the transition matrix be RHO.   */

```
rhoaa = .90;
rhogg = .70;
rhoga = 0;
rhoag = 0;
RHO = rhoaa ~ rhoag|
      rhoga ~ rhogg;
```

/* The shadow price solution requires the evaluation of a (matrix)
   discounted forward sum. The strategy employed in the following
   set of computations is to exploit the standard forecasting formulas
   for scalar discounted sums (generalizations along Hansen-Sargent
   lines for ARMA processes, if desirable, should be relatively direct.)

The composite expression that summarizes the exogenous influences
in (A48) is: */

FL = SP1*RHO + SP2;

/* This is an ns*nex matrix. Partibion this matrix into ns row vectors.
   Then, there is an individual difference equation for each of the
   transformed shadow prices equation, which can be solved in the forward
   direction, with a simple application of the forecasting formula for the
   relevant linear combination of the discounted sum of exogenous
   variables. This is accomplished in the following do-loop.   */

```
LEE = zeros(ns,nex);
IRHO = eye(rows(RHO));
i = 1;
do until i > ns;
   q = FL[i,1:nex];
   mu2i = 1/MU2[i,i];
   dsum = inv((IRHO-mu2i*RHO));
   LEE[i,1:nex] = q*dsum;
i = i + 1;
endo;
```

/* The matrix LEE links the transformed shadow price to the exogenous
   (forcing) state variables.   */

/* THE STATE DECISION RULE
   To derive the decision rule for the state (e.g., capital), we need
   to combine the influences of the transformed shadow price with
   the "direct" influence of exogenous variables, as in (A56). Call
   this KEC, where the memnonic is that this is the combined
   impact (deicison rule) of the exogenous variables on capital */

KEC = Rke*RHO + Qke + KTL*LEE;

/* Thus, the decision rule for capital is given by the coefficents KLK and
   KEC. The decision rule for the untransformed shadow price is given by
   the coefficients ULE and ULK, where from (A55b)   */

ULE = inv(PS22)*LEE;
ULK = inv(−PS22)*PS21;

/* SYSTEM DYNAMICS
   The system dynamics are then generated by the system comprised of states
   (ns elements) and exogenous variables (nex elements). In matrix form,
   these are governed by the matrix M built up as follows: */

Mke = KLK ~ KEC;
Mke1 = zeros(nex,ns);
Mke1 = Mke1 ~ RHO;
Mke = Mke|Mke1;
" ";
"State Transition Matrix Mke = ";;Mke;

/* Note that this matrix incorporates the restriction that some dynamics
   are exogenous, by means of zero restrictions in M.   */

/* INCORPORATION OF SHADOW PRICE, CONTROLS AND OTHER
   FLOWS
   The shadow price is linked to the state by the ns*(ns + ne) matrix */

Lke = ULK ~ ULE;

/* The solutions for the controls can be obtained by a simple application
   of the optimal control equations to the optimal state equations. The
   nc*(ns + nex) matrices linking the evolution of the controls to the state
   and exogenous forcing variables (uncontrolled states) are calculated as
   follows. The matrix linking optimal controls to states and costates is */

Z = inv(Mcc)*Mcs;
/* This can be partitioned to separate responses to states and co-states */

MOck = Z[1:nc,1:ns];
MOcl = Z[1:nc,ns + 1:2*ns];

/* The matrix linking optimal controls to forcing variables is */

MOce = inv(Mcc)*Mce;

/* These expressions can be combined with the structure for the optimal
   shadow price vector, given above, to obtain a link between optimal
   controls and the optimal state vector.   */

MOcke = MOck + MOcl*ULK ~ MOce + MOcl*ULE;

/* Matrix that links the nf flow variables to controls, states, costates,
   and exogenous forcing variables   */

Fse = FVcO*MOcke + FVc1*MOcke*inv(Mke) + FVseO + FVse1*inv(Mke)
   + FVl*Lke;

/* Thus the stacked vector of shadow prices, controls, other flows, and
   returns is linked to the state vector by the (ns + nc + nf + ns)*(ns + ne) matrix */

```
MH = Lke|MOcke|Fke;
" ";
"MH Matrix Linking Costate, Control & Flow to the State Vector = ";;MH;
" ";

retp(MU,Mke|MH);
endp;
```

Index